J.

# THE DEVELOPING CHILD

# THE DEVELOPING CHILD

SIXTH EDITION

## HELEN BEE

HarperCollinsCollegePublishers

Sponsoring Editor: Anne Harvey
Development Editor: Jenny DeBiase/Marian Wassner
Cover Photo: Michel Tcherevkoff/The Image Bank
Photo Researcher: Ferret Research, Inc./Mira Schachne
Director of Production: Kewal K. Sharma
Graphic Supervision: John Callahan/Rosanne Lufrano
Graphics: Rohit Sawhney
Production Manager: Willie Lane
Compositor: Black Dot Graphics
Printer and Binder: Arcata Graphics/Hawkins
Cover Printer: The Lehigh Press, Inc.

155.4
B44d
1992

For permission to use copyrighted material, grateful acknowledgment is made to the copyright holders on p. 635, which are hereby made part of this copyright page.

**The Developing Child, Sixth Edition**

Library of Congress Cataloging-in-Publication Data

Bee, Helen L.
    The developing child / Helen Bee. —6th ed.
        p.    cm.
    Includes bibliographical references and indexes.
    ISBN 0-06-040628-3 (student ed.)   ISBN 0-06-501252-6 (free copy)
1.  Child psychology.          2.  Child development.          I.  Title.
BF721. B336   1992                                            91-45073
155.4—dc20                                                    CIP

92   93   94   95     9   8   7   6   5   4   3   2   1

*To*
*my children, Rex and Arwen, now grown*
*and to the next generation, Samuel Charles, just born*

# CONTENTS IN BRIEF

# DETAILED CONTENTS

## 7 COGNITIVE DEVELOPMENT II: STRUCTURE AND PROCESS        245

# 8   THE DEVELOPMENT OF LANGUAGE        295

# PART FIVE   THE SOCIAL CHILD   337

## 9  PERSONALITY DEVELOPMENT: ALTERNATIVE VIEWS   339

# 11  THE DEVELOPMENT OF SOCIAL RELATIONSHIPS  411

# TO THE STUDENT

Hello and welcome. Let me invite you into the study of a fascinating subject—children and their development. This is a bit like inviting you into my own home, since I have lived in the world of the study of children for a great many years. Unfortunately, I cannot know each of you individually, but by writing this book as if it were a conversation between you and me, I hope I can make your reading of this book and your study of this subject very personal processes.

Because such personal involvement is one of my goals, you will find that I often write in the first person and that I have included a number of anecdotes about my own life. (One of the amusing side effects of this style of writing is that I often meet students from around the country who, having read this book, know all kinds of personal things about me and feel that they know me well, even though we have never met.)

Welcome, too, to the adventure of science. From the very first edition of this book, one of my goals has been to try to convey a sense of excitement about scientific inquiry. I want each of you to take away some feeling for the way psychologists think, the kinds of questions we ask, and the ways we go about trying to answer those questions. I also want you to take away with you some sense of the theoretical and intellectual ferment that is part of any science. Think of psychology as a kind of detective story. We discover clues after hard, often painstaking, work; we make new guesses or hypotheses; and then we search for new clues to check on those hypotheses.

Of course, I also want you to come away from reading this book with a firm grounding of knowledge in the field. There is much that we do not yet know or understand. But a great many facts and observations have accumulated. These facts and observations will be of help to you professionally if you are planning (or are already in) a career with children—such as teaching, nursing, social work, medicine, or psychology; the information will also be useful to you as parents, now or in the future. There is much to be learned. In the midst of all that learning, though, I hope you enjoy the reading as much as I have enjoyed the writing.

Helen Bee

# TO THE INSTRUCTOR

Writing this sixth edition of *The Developing Child* has been full of surprises, even some adventures. The most pleasant surprise was the opportunity to use photos from the excellent new PBS series, *Childhood,* produced by Geoff Haines-Stiles and Peter Montagnon in association with Thirteen/WNET, which many of you will have seen in the fall of 1991. Happily, this sixth edition will also be used for the telecourse to be based on the *Childhood* series. It was a real pleasure to be able to include pictures of children and families whose stories I knew. When photos have a context, they become more informative for students. And because families from all over the world were filmed for the series, these photos also show graphically just how universal the process of development is.

The only drawback to this otherwise-splendid connection with *Childhood* was that the final draft of this edition had to be written on a tighter deadline than usual. And as all of you know, tight deadlines are an invitation to disaster of one kind or another. My computer died during the final push, eating a half day's work. Then the new computer would not talk to my printer. To cap it all off, on the final day of work, a tornado came through town. When I submitted the manuscript to my editors, I wrote them of this particular adventure:

> Sunday, as I was slaving away, a huge thunderstorm rolls in, I'm in the middle of something and don't want to take the time to stop and turn off the machine; (my husband) Carl sticks his head in the door and tries to tell me there is a tornado warning. I tell him to go away; I'm in the middle of something. Then the power goes off, eliminating the work since the last save, and the tornado sirens go off all over town. So I finally take it seriously (besides, with the power off, how could I work?) and we run down to the basement which is the official safe place. Then I realize that if there really is a tornado, *the book will be lost.* So I rush upstairs with a laundry basket and madly gather up all the parts and pieces, tossing them into the laundry basket, including two sets of disks and the art manuscript and other crucial items, then rush back to the basement. I tell Carl that if there really is a tornado, his job is to fall on the laundry basket and save the book and I'll be right on top of him. Apparently there really was a tornado in a town about 4 miles from here, and the radio said it was headed our way. Lots of tree limbs down, but we didn't actually see a black funnel. Heck of a wind, though, and rain in buckets. Twenty minutes later all was clear.

Still, in the midst of all the adventure and the tearing out of hair over dead or dying computers, a new edition was indeed written—an edition with many of the same goals as before, but with updates and changes.

## Goals of the Sixth Edition

A major goal of a new edition of any text is to update theories and research information. In a field changing as fast as developmental psychology—with new journals proliferating and literally thousands of papers presented at professional meetings—that is no small task. Inevitably, the addition of new ideas and new research seems to make each edition longer than the one before. To balance the scales as much as possible, one must omit favorite old examples, theories that are no longer as influential as they once were, even delete whole topics to make room for new areas of inquiry. Inevitably, in this process, I will have left out some of your favorite material from earlier editions. I trust that what replaces it will be equally interesting.

But writing a revision is not just a process of updating. It is also necessary to continue to pursue the broader goals that have been a part of this book from the first edition:

1. To find that difficult but essential balance between theory, research, and practical application;
2. To make the study of child development relevant not just for psychologists but also for students in many other fields in which this information is needed—nursing, medicine, social work, education, home economics;
3. To keep all discussions as current as possible, so that students can encounter the very latest thinking, the most recent research;
4. To write in as direct a way as possible, so that the book is more like a conversation than a traditional text. Such a personal style is still possible along with theoretical clarity and research rigor—both of which I have worked hard to achieve.

## Changes in the Sixth Edition

The basic chapter organization remains the same as it has been since the fourth edition, with fifteen chapters. But I have made significant changes internally in several chapters, and I have updated content throughout.

*Major Chapter Revisions* Chapter 5, on perceptual development, has been extensively rewritten and reorganized so that much more of the fascinating new research and theory on infant pattern perception could be included. Chapter 13, on the ecology of development, is now organized around a more explicit systems perspective, using Bronfenbrenner's categories as an organizational rubric. This change makes much greater sense out of the wide variety of topics covered in that chapter. Chapter 14, on atypical development, now includes an extensive discussion of developmental psychopathology. The discussion of emotional/behavioral disturbances is now divided into two broad sections, one dealing with externalizing and one with internalizing disorders, an organization that considerably clarifies the subject matter.

*New Topics* There are many new topics in this edition, including:

- Neural development prenatally and in the first few years, including the fascinating new information on dendritic pruning and other changes at 12–24 months
- AIDS and its transmission to infants
- Perception/discrimination of language sounds in the first year of life
- Perception/discrimination of faces, including the very interesting new work on babies' preferences for attractive faces
- "Theory of mind" and other research on a possible cognitive change at age 4
- Cross-linguistic comparisons of early language
- Alternative definitions of temperament
- Patterson's research on highly aggressive children

- Secure and insecure attachments in adults, and their implications for child rearing
- Sex differences in patterns of peer relationships from early childhood
- Perception/understanding of others' emotions
- Systems theory
- Developmental psychopathology

*Significantly Updated Topics*  I can't possibly list all of the smaller (but significant) changes, but here are a few of the topics that will look quite different to you in this edition:

- Long-term effects of prenatal alcohol exposure
- Strategies for studying perception in young infants
- Changes in perceptual acuity in the early months
- Perception of faces
- Cross-modal transfer
- Heritability of IQ, including the new French cross-fostering studies
- The use of IQ tests in the schools
- Imitation in infancy
- Information processing—theory and research
- Current theories of language acquisition
- Long-term outcomes for securely and insecurely attached children
- Long-term outcomes for rejected or unpopular children
- Day care: the latest information on the Great Debate
- Impact of parental occupations and social support on the child
- Effects of divorce, particularly long-term effects
- Alternative views of moral development, including Gilligan's theory
- Depression in childhood and adolescence
- Attention-deficit hyperactivity disorder and its long-term consequences
- Autism, which I have treated in a distinctly new way in this edition

*New Pedagogical Aids*  Another change in this edition is the addition of **critical thinking** questions at the end of each chapter.  In most instances there is one question of each of three types: (1) a practical application ("How would you apply this information to X situation?"), (2) a methodological question ("How might we go about trying to answer X question?"), and (3) a theoretical question.

There are also nine new projects in this edition, including four of an entirely new variety that I call "investigative projects."  Each of these four is intended as a group project for a small set of students, perhaps three or four, and each involves some exploration of community resources: prenatal care services available for the poor; local school district policies on the uses of IQ and achievement tests; types of day care available in the community; programs for the gifted and retarded in the local schools.   Five new individual projects have been added to the following chapters:

Chapter 3—observation of mother-infant turn-taking during feeding
Chapter 7—conservation of mass, number, and weight
Chapter 7—the pendulum problem as a measure of formal operations
Chapter 11—observation of altruistic behavior in preschoolers
Chapter 13—comparative evaluation of a set of any three different day-care centers

## Supplements

The supplements for this edition have been greatly expanded.

*Instructor's Manual*  This is now a very hefty document indeed! My intention here is to lay out a whole course using the sixth edition, including the pre-planning, the syllabus, the organization of lectures, and lecture material for each chapter. For those of you who have taught this course many times, much of the planning detail will not be needed, though I hope you may still find the lecture suggestions helpful.  For those of you approaching the teaching of this course for the first time, the manual may be a timely form of assistance.

Included with the Instructor's Manual is a set of transparency masters—some of which duplicate figures that appear in the text—to make it easier to review some figures in class.  Many of the transparencies provide new data, designed to illustrate particular points you may cover in lecture.

Finally, there is a new film/video guide included in the manual, which includes a section on using the videos from the *Childhood* series with *The Developing Child.*

*Test Bank*  All multiple choice questions in the test bank are either new or revised from earlier editions.  I wrote some of them; the rest were written by Marite Rodriguez-Haynes of the Clarion University of Pennsylvania.  All are available either in book form or on disk using TestMaster, an excellent microcomputerized test generation system that allows instructors to create fully customized tests. TestMaster is available free to all adopters, in either Macintosh or IBM forms.

*Study Guide*  The Study Guide, prepared by Bill Cunningham, has been thoroughly rewritten to correspond with the sixth edition.  Each chapter includes chapter objectives, key terms and concepts, a multiple-choice self-quiz, open-ended study questions, and an end-of-chapter review unit.

## Acknowledgments

As always, my work has been greatly aided by the comments of excellent reviewers.  Some reviewed the fifth edition and suggested changes; others read and critiqued the revised draft.  The remarkable degree of care and effort they brought to the task have been of enormous value in helping me to improve the quality of this text.  They are listed alphabetically here:

Cathryn L. Booth
*University of Washington*

Maria G. Cisneros-Solis
*Austin Community College*

Meg Clark
*California State Polytechnic University*

Joan E. Coughlin
*Palo Alto College*

Ganie DeHart
*State University of New York-Geneseo*

Claire Etaugh
*Bradley University*

Hiram E. Fitzgerald
*Michigan State University*

Kathleen B. Fox
*Salisbury State University*

John Hensley
*Tulsa Junior College*

Laverne K. Jordan
*Olivet Nazarene University*

Daniel W. Kee
*California State University-Fullerton*

Billy J. Laney
*Central Texas College*

Special bouquets are also due to the HarperCollins staff. Anne Harvey has been a remarkable editor—supportive, responsive, and full of ideas. It was through her efforts, and those of Editor-in-Chief Susan Driscoll, that the link with *Childhood* was created. Jenny DiBiase and Marian Wassner served as developmental editors and persuaded this skeptical author that developmental editors are a wonderful breed. Both were astonishingly thorough in their analyses and always ready to check on possibilities or answer questions. My deep appreciation to them all, and to my production editor, Kathleen Ermitage, of Proof Positive/Farrowlyne Associates, Inc., whose voice on the phone has become a pleasurable part of my day for the past months.

Finally, thanks to my husband, Carl de Boor, whose personal support helps maintain my sanity. It also helps that he is a computer science professor. Not only did he have a spare computer when mine died at the crucial last moment, he was able to recover the contents of the one file with a flawed backup copy. He and I now both know more than we did before about a wonderful program called Norton Utilities. Ah, the joys of modern technology!

Helen Bee

Two of the most powerful resources in child development education have now joined forces to create an unprecedented multidimensional educational tool. *Childhood,* the highly acclaimed television portrait of the journey from infancy to adolescence, and *The Developing Child,* Sixth Edition, have come together to form a unified, mutually supportive learning package. The video series and the text work together to create a learning environment that reaches beyond the printed page, offering a unique opportunity to breathe life into your classroom.

As the presence of photographs taken from the *Childhood* series indicates, this revised edition of Helen Bee's text will also serve as the companion textbook to the *Childhood* telecourse, which will begin in the Fall of 1992. Whether you view the original seven one-hour programs, or the 24 half-hour telecourse programs, we hope you find the video and print components mutually illuminating. For instance, Chapter Six in *The Developing Child* discusses Urie Bronfenbrenner's "Ecology of Human Development," as the *Childhood* series shows the dramatic images of the contrasting first days of school in Russia, Japan, or America; and rites of passage, both formal and informal, in the rain forests of Cameroon, the suburbs of New York, and in the streets of Sao Paulo.

Thirteen·wnet

# INTRODUCTION

PART

1

1

# BASIC QUESTIONS, MAJOR THEORIES

When new acquaintances ask me what I do, I have to choose between several options. If I answer "I'm a psychologist," a common reaction is a slight recoil. The person may take a small step backwards, or laugh awkwardly, or say something like, "Well don't psychoanalyze me!" But if I say, "I'm a child psychologist," the reaction is very different. If the person I am talking to has children, or expects to have children, the typical reaction is immediately to ask some practical question:

"My husband is from Italy; should we be speaking both English and Italian to our children?"

"Our first child is a year old, and my wife is planning to go back to work. How on earth do we find a good day-care situation for the baby? Is there such a thing as 'good day care' anyway?"

"My wife and I are having an argument about how much TV we should let our kids watch. Is it really bad for them?"

"I thought my baby was going to be placid and easy going, but boy was I wrong! He's antsy, doesn't like to be held for very long, won't try anything new, screams if we leave him with a sitter. I'm at my wit's end. What do I do now?"

Legislators, too, ask questions like these when they are faced with writing laws or regulations designed to protect or promote the health and welfare of children—regulations about day care, programs to provide prenatal care for mothers living in poverty, possibly even laws regulating violence on television.

When psychologists are asked questions like these, they are often expected to answer in twenty-five words or less, saying "yes," or "no," or "Here's what you should do." Occasionally I can give an answer like that. The question about raising bilingual children, for example, can be answered quite briefly: "Yes, do speak both languages to your children, from the beginning" (though even this answer requires some elaboration, as you'll see in Chapter 8). Most often, I have to hedge a bit. Sometimes the difficulty is that we simply don't know anything, or not much. More often, we have a lot of research on a given subject, but the results don't add up to a simple answer. To give a really complete reply I would have to give a short course in theories and data about children's development, so that my answer can be embedded in the proper context. Few casual acquaintances will sit still for such a lecture!

I do not want to imply that developmental psychologists are only interested in questions about children that have some immediate practical application. On the contrary, most psychological research is aimed at expanding basic knowledge, at understanding fundamental developmental processes—although of course, answers to basic questions may ultimately contribute to practical solutions to child-rearing or educational problems. A quick look at current journals points to a few of the puzzles that are the focus of current study:

Should you let your kids watch as much TV as they want, or should you set some limits? What kind of limits make sense? What about cartoons or educational programs? Parents hope that psychologists will have answers to questions like these. In fact we do have some answers—although the answers are not always as simple or clear-cut as parents (or legislators) might like.

- Why do aggressive children perceive their interactions with others as more threatening and hostile than do less aggressive children? Where do such differences in social perception come from?
- During adolescence, we see the physical changes of puberty occurring about the same time as changes in the sophistication of children's thinking and in the quality of their social relationships. Are these changes causally connected?
- How early can an infant notice and respond to patterns of sound, such as different rhythms or melodies?
- What is the long-term effect of a secure or an insecure first attachment of a child to her mother or father? What other intervening experiences may mitigate that long-term effect?

Just as is true for the directly practical questions, providing answers for such theoretical and empirical questions requires a broader framework. It is precisely that framework that I want to give you in this book, not only to enable you to make more intelligent decisions about the myriad practical questions associated with raising your own children, but more importantly to give you some sense of developmental psychology as a *science.* I hope I can convey my own conviction that the study of children and their development is complex and fascinating in itself, whether it leads to clear practical applications or not.

To create the necessary framework, psychologists must accomplish at least two things: to *describe* development (*what* happens) and to *explain* development (*why* it happens the way it does.)

## Describing and Explaining

The first task in any scientific endeavor is to *describe,* to answer the "what" question. What do we observe about children and the ways they change (or stay the same) over the first 15 or 18 years of life? What is the "normal" or expected rate of growth? How wide a variation is there, for example, in the ages at which babies first crawl, or toddlers first use two-word sentences? Which children are faster, which slower, and what else can we find out about those children?

What we need, in a word, are *facts* about the way children are the same, how they change, and how they differ from one another. The vast majority of research on children that I will be talking about throughout the book is aiming for just such basic description.

Good description is much harder to achieve than you probably imagine, and in many areas we are still a long way from even minimally good description. Even so, describing is not enough. The second major task is to answer the question "why," to *explain* development. Why do children change in the ways that they do, and why do children differ from one another? Such explanation is the role of theory. A good theory not only ties together many bits of descriptive information; it proposes general principles. By using those principles, we may be able to predict patterns of behavior we have not observed before, or we may be able to devise ways to intervene effectively in the lives of children to change an unwanted outcome.

Theory and descriptive research are intimately linked. Researchers don't confine themselves to the realms of description for twenty or thirty years and then say one morning: "Well I guess it's time to try to figure out why." Theory is present from the very beginning, sometimes as a full-fledged model that a researcher is explicitly testing, more often as explicit or implicit assumptions about the nature of development and what is likely to affect it. The very questions that we ask and the methods that we use to try to find answers are affected by such assumptions or theories.

Theories differ from one another in myriad ways. I can make the diversity more understandable by focusing on three key questions that any researcher or theorist must answer:

1.  When we study children's development, should we focus on the ways children are the *same*, or the ways in which they *differ?*
2.  What are the major influences on development? In particular, do we look to internal, or to external, influences in trying to understand why children develop the way they do?
3.  What is the nature of developmental change? Are the changes qualitative or only quantitative; does change occur continuously and smoothly, or are there stages or steps?

 ## Similarities or Differences: Which Should We Study?

The first key question concerns what we should be studying. It may seem obvious that ultimately we will have to understand both the ways in which all children develop similarly, and the ways in which they differ from one another. But in fact most developmental psychologists, and most theorists, have focused on only one or the other. To a considerable degree, those who have studied children's social behavior and personality have focused almost entirely on questions of individual differences, while those who have studied physical changes, language, perception, and major aspects of cognitive development have searched primarily for shared regularities—ways in which children are the same, and ways in which all children change or develop in the same sequences (Maccoby, 1984).

This rather uncomfortable split in the basic questions being asked means that when we look at each aspect of development in subsequent chapters, we will not have the same kinds of descriptive information in each case. This split is not as deep as it once was; several current bodies of research or theories deal with both aspects, such as theories of attachment (see Chapter 11), or explorations of information processing approaches to cognition (see Chapter 7). Individual researchers, however, still clearly lean one way or the other on this question.

## What Are the Major Influences on Development?

The second key question is one of the oldest and most central theoretical issues within philosophy as well as psychology, the so-called **nature-nurture controversy**—a dichotomy that goes by other names as well: nativism versus empiricism, or heredity versus environment. Does a child develop as he does because the pattern is built in at birth, or because of the influence of experiences after birth? Historically, Plato and René Descartes (in the more modern era) represent the nativist/nature side of the controversy. They believed that at least some ideas are innate. On the other side of the philosophical argument are a group of British philosophers called "empiricists," such as John Locke, who insisted that at birth the mind is a blank slate, (in Latin) a *tabula rasa.* All knowledge, Locke argued, is created by experience.

I cannot think of a psychologist today who would cast this issue in such black-and-white terms. Virtually all would agree that a child's development is a product of some interaction between nature and nurture—a point I'll elaborate on in a moment. Still, there are important concepts on each side of this (artificial) dichotomy with which you need to be familiar.

### The Nature Side of the Equation

*Inborn Biases.* Descartes' notion of inborn ideas has not totally disappeared from our thinking. Today we see analogous concepts, particularly in the theories about perceptual and language development that emphasize built-in biases within the infant's system for dealing with incoming information. Dan Slobin (1985), for example, proposes that children are born with certain "operating principles" that govern the way they listen to and make sense out of the flow of sounds—paying attention to the beginnings and ends of strings of sounds. Similarly, in the study of infants' perceptual skills a number of researchers and theorists have emphasized built-in "rules babies look by" (Haith, 1980), such as paying attention to movement or to shifts between dark and light. Unlike Descartes, current theorists do not propose that these built-in response patterns are the end of the story; rather they are seen as the starting point. What then develops is a result of experience filtered through these initial biases.

*Maturation.* Another key modern "nature" concept goes beyond Descartes in another way, by emphasizing the role of genetic programming

**nature-nurture controversy**
A common label for the classic dispute about the relative roles of heredity versus environment.

on sequences of development that we observe long after birth. Arnold Gesell (1925) used the term **maturation** to describe such *genetically programmed sequential patterns of change*. This term is still uniformly used today. Changes in body size and shape, in hormones at puberty, in muscles and bones, and in the nervous system all may be programmed in this way. You can probably remember your own physical changes during adolescence. The timing of these pubertal changes differs from one teenager to the next, but the basic sequence is essentially the same for all children. Such sequences, which begin at conception and continue until death, are shared by all members of our species. Other species have equivalent sequences of shared changes. The instructions for these sequences are part of the specific hereditary information that is passed on at the moment of conception.

According to Gesell, maturationally determined development in its pure form occurs regardless of practice or training. You don't have to practice growing pubic hair; you don't have to be taught how to walk. In fact it would take almost herculean efforts to *prevent* such sequences from unfolding. But even confirmed maturational theorists would not argue that experience has no effect. Even these powerful, apparently automatic, maturational patterns require at least some minimal environmental support, such as adequate diet and opportunity for movement and experimentation.

I should point out that the term *maturation* does not mean the same thing as *growth*, although the two terms are sometimes used as if they were synonyms. Growth refers to some kind of step-by-step change in quantity, as in size. We speak of the growth of a child's vocabulary or the growth of her body. Such changes in quantity may be the result of maturation, but not necessarily. A child's body might grow because of a change in diet, which is an external effect, or because muscles and bones have grown, which is probably a maturational effect. To put it another way, the term *growth* is a *description* of change, while the concept of maturation is one *explanation* of change.

*Canalization.* A more recent variant of the concept of maturation is the notion of **canalization,** first suggested by Waddington (1957), an embryologist, and subsequently adapted by several current developmental theorists (e.g., Scarr-Salapatek, 1976; McCall, 1981). The metaphor Waddington proposed, depicted in Figure 1.1, is of development as a marble rolling down a hillside with gullies or canals. In any portion of the hillside in which the canal is narrow and deep, virtually all marbles will remain in that gully or canal. Waddington would say that such aspects of development are "highly canalized." In a flatter or wider area, or one in which there are many alternative shallow channels, the marble might roll out of the main channel into any one of a variety of smaller side channels, and there is weaker canalization. Both Robert McCall and Sandra Scarr argue that development is particularly highly canalized in the first year or two of life when the maturational program seems to be clear and dominant. During these years, the built-in program may be so powerful that almost any environment is sufficient to support it.

McCall and Scarr suggest that canalization is much weaker in later childhood. Optimum development at later ages seems to demand much more specific input, so that only a narrow range of environments provide sufficient support.

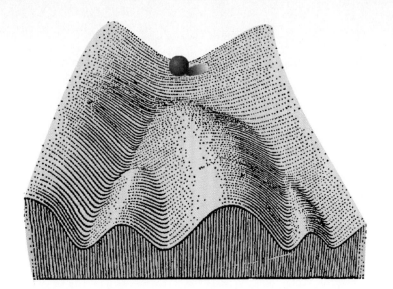

**FIGURE 1.1**

Waddington's "epigenetic landscape." A narrow and deep gully depicts strong canalization. Almost any environment will support or sustain that development (*Source:* Waddington, 1957).

Not all developmental psychologists would agree with McCall's or Scarr's conclusions about the degree of canalization at various ages. Indeed recent theorists have suggested that canalization may also be environmentally caused, or created by some complex interaction of genetic and experiential forces. For example, Greenough (1991) points to the fact that one of the proteins required for the development of the visual system is controlled by a gene whose action is only triggered by visual experience; so some visual experience is needed for the genetic program to operate. In normal development, of course, every (non-blind) child will have some such experience. So the commonness of early experience, as well as (or in interaction with) shared genetic patterning, may account for any strong canalization of development that we observe.

This debate about the concept of canalization illustrates not only the greater subtlety of current concepts about the nature half of the equation, but also the increasing emphasis on the complex interactions between experience and genetics.

### The Nurture Side of the Equation

Concepts on the nurture side of this ancient dispute have also become considerably more subtle and complex. One particularly helpful analysis of the potential impact of environment has been proposed by Aslin (1981a). He suggests five models of influence, shown schematically in Figure 1.2 on the next page. In each drawing the dashed line represents the path of development of some skill or behavior that would occur without a particular experience; the solid line represents the path of development if the experience were added.

The first of the five models actually shows a maturational pattern in which there is no environmental effect. The second model, which Aslin calls *maintenance*, describes a pattern in which some environmental input is necessary to sustain some skill or behavior that has already developed maturationally. For example, kittens are born with full binocular vision, but if you

**FIGURE 1.2**

Aslin proposes five different types of interaction between maturation and environmental influence: The top model shows a purely maturational effect; the bottom model (induction) shows a purely environmental effect. The other three show various other combinations: **Maintenance,** in which some experience prevents the deterioration of a maturationally developed skill; **facilitation,** in which some experience speeds up the development of some maturational process; and **attunement,** in which experience increases the ultimate level of some skill or behavior above the "normal" maturational level (*Source:* Aslin, 1981, p. 50).

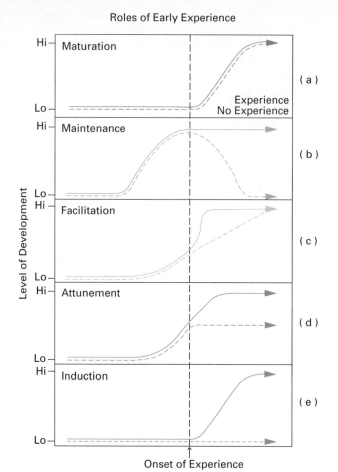

Roles of Early Experience

cover one of their eyes for a period of time, the kittens' binocular skill diminishes. Similarly, muscles will atrophy if not used.

The third model shows a *facilitation* effect of the environment in which a skill or behavior develops earlier than it normally would because of some experience. Grammatical development may follow such a model. As you'll see in Chapter 8, some research suggests that children whose parents talked to them more, and in more complex sentences, in the first 18–24 months of life may develop two-word sentences and other early grammatical forms somewhat earlier. But less talked-to children catch up shortly thereafter, so there is no permanent gain. When some particular experience does lead to a permanent gain or an eventually higher level of performance, Aslin calls it *attunement.* There is some indication, for example, that an enriched early language environment may lead not only to more rapid development of intellectual skills, but perhaps to a higher eventual level of such skills, such as what we measure with an IQ test.

Aslin's final model, *induction,* describes a pure environmental effect. Without some experience a particular behavior would not develop at all.

Giving a child tennis lessons or exposing him to a second language are examples of experiences that would fall into this category.

These five models illustrate the greater complexity of current thinking about nature/nurture issues. However, even this does not go far enough. At least three other aspects of the environmental side of the equation are also significant in current thinking about development: the timing of experience, the child's own interpretation of experience, and the total ecological system in which experiences occur.

*The Timing of Experience.*   Just as the importance of nature may vary from one period of development to another, so the timing of specific experiences may matter as well. The impact of day care on an infant may be quite different when the infant is 6 months old than when he is 16 months old. Moving from one school to another may be different if it coincides with puberty than if it does not. The opportunity to explore one's environment freely may be particularly important at the point when the baby can first locomote independently.

Our thinking about the importance of timing was stimulated, in part, by ethological research on other species that showed that specific experiences had quite different, or much stronger, effects at some points in development than at others. For example, baby ducks will become *imprinted* (become attached to and follow) any duck or any other quacking, moving object that happens to be around them 15 hours after they hatch. If nothing is moving or quacking at that critical point, they do not become imprinted at all (Hess, 1972). So the period just around 15 hours after hatching is a **critical period** for the duck's development of a proper following response.

We can see similar critical periods in the action of various teratogens in prenatal development. A **teratogen** is an outside agent, such as a disease organism or chemical, which if present during prenatal development, adversely affects the developmental process. While some teratogens have negative consequences at any time in gestation, many (if not most) have effects only during some critical period. For example, if a mother contracts rubella (commonly called German measles) during a narrow range of days in the first 3 months of pregnancy, some damage or deformity occurs in the fetus. Infection with the same virus after the third month of pregnancy has no such effect.

Equivalent examples of critical periods of this same very precise type are much harder to find in development after birth (Colombo, 1982), but the broader and somewhat looser concept of a **sensitive period** has been widely adopted. A sensitive period is some stretch of months or years during which a child may be particularly responsive to specific forms of experience, or particularly influenced by their absence. So, for example, the period from 6 to 12 months of age may be a sensitive period for the formation of a core attachment to the parents. Other periods may be particularly significant for intellectual development or language (Tamis-LeMonda & Bornstein, 1987).

In some respects the concept of a sensitive period is the opposite of the concept of canalization. Both suggest that nature and nurture may be differentially important at different points in development. The irony is that precisely the same stretch of months, from birth to about age 2, has been described as the time of greatest canalization *and* as the most sensitive period

**critical period**
A period of time during development when the organism is especially responsive to and learns from a specific type of stimulation. The same stimulation at other points in development has little or no effect.

**teratogen**
Any outside agent, such as a disease or a chemical, whose presence significantly increases the risk of deviations or abnormalities in prenatal development.

**sensitive period**
Similar to a critical period except broader and less specific. A time in development when a particular type of stimulation is particularly important or effective.

for the impact of experience on later developments such as attachment or intellectual development. Clearly we have not reached agreement either on the facts or on the explanation of those facts. Both concepts, however, are present in our current theoretical repertoire.

*Internal Models of Experience.* Another idea becoming more prominent in that repertoire is that a child's *interpretation* of some experience may be more important in the long run than are the objective properties of it. John Bowlby expresses such an idea when he talks about the child's "internal working model" of attachment (Bowlby, 1969, 1980). Often a child is described as "securely attached" or "insecurely attached," as if these were labels somehow printed on the forehead, external to the child. But Bowlby, who is one of the key theorists in this area, has emphasized that we should really think in terms of a "secure (or insecure) internal working model of attachment." The child's internal model is made up of certain expectations or assumptions—for example, that someone will come if he cries, or that affection and attention are reliably available, or that if you don't stay out of the way someone is likely to hit you, or that when someone frowns it usually means you're about to get yelled at. These expectations are based on actual experiences, to be sure, but once formed into an internal model they affect the way the child interprets future experiences.

A child's self-concept may operate in much the same way, as an internal working model of "who I am," a possibility I'll explore more in chapters 9 and 10. The self-concept is based on experience, but it is made up of a series of expectations and assumptions through which subsequent experiences are filtered.

Such a view of the pathway of environmental effects is not yet dominant in developmental psychology, but it has gained a good deal of currency in recent years.

Like Avery Gholston, whose family was filmed as part of the *Childhood* series, infants and young children all over the world are being cared for in group settings at least part of the time. Some theorists argue that this is a very risky trend since they see the first year of life as a "sensitive period" for the establishment of key attachments. Others think that children are resilient enough to handle the separations, especially if the care is good, as it appears to be in this case. This photo is a video still from the *Childhood* television series (*Source:* ©Thirteen/WNET).

*The Ecological Perspective.*    A third facet of current thinking about environmental effects is a growing emphasis on casting a much wider environmental net. Until quite recently, most research on environmental influences focused on a child's family (frequently only the child's mother), or on some proximate inanimate stimulation such as toys. If we studied a larger family context at all it was usually in terms of the general wealth or poverty of the family.

In the past ten or fifteen years, however, there has been a strong push to widen our scope. The key figure has been Urie Bronfenbrenner, whose book *The Ecology of Human Development* (1979) helped set a new agenda. He has since been joined by a chorus of other voices (Pence, 1988; Horowitz, 1987; Lerner, 1986; Sameroff, 1982). Bronfenbrenner emphasizes that each child grows up in a complex social environment with a distinct cast of characters: brothers, sisters, one or both parents, grandparents, baby-sitters, pets, schoolteachers, friends. And this cast is itself embedded within a larger social system; the parents have jobs which they may like or dislike; they may have close and supportive friends or they may be quite isolated; they may be living in a safe neighborhood or one full of dangers; the local school may be excellent or poor, and the parents may have good or poor relationships with the school. Bronfenbrenner's argument is that we must not only include descriptions of these more extended aspects of the environment in our research, but we must understand the ways in which all the components of this complex system interact with one another.

A particularly nice example of research that examines such a larger system of influences is Gerald Patterson's work on the origins of antisocial behavior in children (Patterson et al., 1989). His studies show that conduct problems, like aggressiveness, originate in parent-child interactions. Parents who use poor discipline techniques and poor monitoring of the child are more likely to have noncompliant or antisocial children. Once the child's antisocial behavior pattern has been established, however, it has repercussions in other areas of his life, such as rejection from peers and academic difficulty. These problems, in turn, are likely to push the young person toward a deviant peer group and still further delinquency (Dishion, Patterson, Stoolmiller, & Skinner, 1991). So a pattern that began in the family is maintained and exacerbated by interactions with peers and with the school system.

Patterson expands the net still further by exploring the factors that influence a parent's tendency to use poor discipline techniques in the first place. He finds that parents who were themselves raised using poor disciplinary practices are more likely to use those same poor strategies with their children. However, even parents who possess good basic child-management skills may fall into poor patterns when the stresses in their own lives increase. A recent divorce or unemployment increase the likelihood of poor disciplinary practices, and thus increase the probability that the child will develop a pattern of antisocial behavior. Figure 1.3 on the next page shows Patterson's conception of how these various components fit together. Clearly, by taking into account the larger social ecological system in which the family is embedded, our understanding of the process is greatly enhanced.

The ecological approach underlines the importance of understanding the interactions among many different environmental influences. Equally, we need to understand the interactions among various internal and external influences, between nature and nurture.

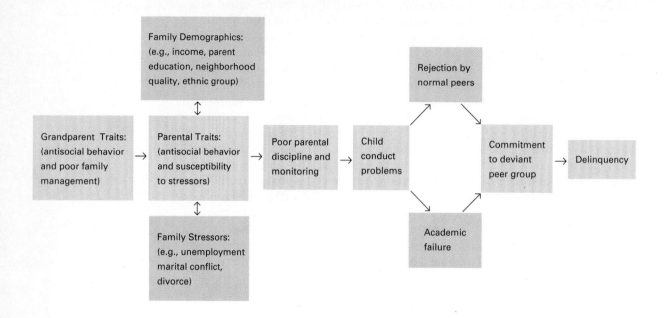

**FIGURE 1.3**

Patterson's model describes the many factors that influence the development of delinquency. The core of the process, in this model, is the interaction between the child and the parent. One might argue that the origin of delinquency lies in that relationship. But Patterson argues that there are larger ecological or contextual forces that are also "causes" of the delinquency (*Source:* Patterson, 1989, Figures 1 and 2, pp. 331, 333).

### *Interactionist Views of Nature and Nurture*

There are at least two ways we could look at the interactions between nature and nurture, paralleling the division between those who study common patterns and those who study individual differences. On the one hand, we could look for the common or normative patterns of interaction between nature and nurture. What skills is every child born with, how is the basic system "wired," and how does it mature? And how are those skills altered or shaped by specific experience? This basic approach is taken by researchers who study perceptual development, language development, and (to some extent) cognitive development. I'll describe the current conclusions drawn from this work in later chapters.

Alternatively, we could search for some individual variations in the ways nature and nurture interact. The basic idea is that the same environment may have quite different effects on children who are born with different characteristics. Two current approaches of this type are particularly interesting.

*Vulnerability and Resilience.* One such approach is the concept of vulnerability and resilience, proposed by theorists such as Norman Garmezy and Michael Rutter (Garmezy & Rutter, 1983; Rutter, 1987). They point out that some children appear to be far more vulnerable to the stresses of childhood than are others. For example, given a parental divorce, some children show serious depression or a major decline in school performance; others show little effect. Garmezy and Rutter argue that such differences in vulnerability have their origins primarily in the child's early social interactions, such as the adequacy of the child's relationship with parents. But vulnerability might also have inborn origins as well, resulting from premature birth or from a "difficult" temperament. Using such a definition of vulnerability, Frances Horowitz has proposed a particularly clear model of how nature and nurture might interact (1987, 1990).

As you can see in Figure 1.4 on the next page, Horowitz proposes that the degree of the child's inborn vulnerability interacts in a particular way with the "facilitativeness" of the environment. A highly facilitative environment is one in which the child has loving and responsive parents and is provided with a rich array of stimulation. If the relationship between these two dimensions were merely additive, we would find that the best outcomes occurred for resilient infants reared in optimum environments, the worst outcomes for vulnerable infants in poor environments, and the other combinations would lie somewhere in between. But that is not what Horowitz proposes. Instead she suggests that a resilient child in a poor environment may do quite well, since such a child can take advantage of all the stimulation and opportunities available. She also suggests that a vulnerable child may do quite well in a highly facilitative environment. According to this model it is only the double whammy—the vulnerable child in a poor environment—that leads to really poor outcomes for the child.

In fact, as you will see throughout the book, there is a growing body of research showing precisely this pattern. For example, very low IQ scores are most common among children who had low-birth-weights *and* were reared in poverty level families. However, low-birth-weight children reared in middle-class families develop essentially normal IQs, as do normal-weight infants reared in poverty-level families (Werner, 1986). We are beginning to understand that the same environment can have very different effects, depending on the qualities or capacities the child brings to the equation.

*Goodness-of-Fit.* Another variation on this same theme is the concept of **goodness-of-fit,** proposed chiefly by Richard and Jacqueline Lerner (Lerner & Lerner, 1983; Lerner, 1986; Lerner et al., 1990). According to this view, the degree of match between the child's characteristics and the demands or responses of the environment largely determines the child's eventual outcome. For instance, a poor fit would exist between a baby who is very slow to develop regular sleeping/waking patterns, and a mother or father who expect or need such regularity. The same infant growing up in a family that is accepting of his or her sleep/wake cycles would be experiencing a good fit. For example, among subjects in the New York Longitudinal Study, Puerto Rican families characteristically were very accepting of any sleeping/waking schedule the infant developed; babies were allowed to sleep whenever they wanted. However, most parents in the non-Puerto Rican middle-class families

**goodness-of-fit**
A hypothesis about the interaction of nature and nurture suggesting that negative outcomes occur when the child's characteristics do not fit with the demands of a particular family or school environment.

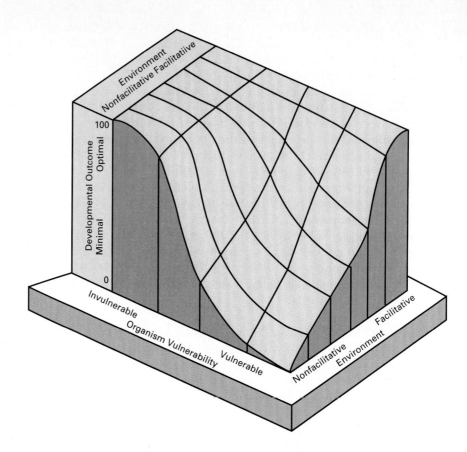

**FIGURE 1.4**

Horowitz's model describes one possible type of interaction between the vulnerability of the child and the quality of the environment. The height of the surface is the goodness of the developmental outcome (such as IQ or skill in social relationships). The higher the surface, the better the outcome. In this model, only the combination of a vulnerable infant and a nonfacilitative environment will result in really poor outcomes (*Source:* Horowitz, 1982, Figure 2.1, p. 28).

in this study had strong demands that the child develop a predictable sleeping schedule. When researchers looked at the incidence of later problem behavior in the children, they found that irregular sleeping patterns were *unrelated* to problems among the Puerto Rican children, but were strongly predictive of children's later problems among the caucasian middle class (Korn, 1978; Thomas et al., 1974). That is, a poor fit led to greater problems.

Support for the concept of goodness-of-fit also comes from a recent Swedish study (Stattin & Klackenberg-Larsson, 1991) that explored the effect of having a child whose gender was not what both parents had strongly desired. In a group of 113 subjects studied from birth to age 25, girls whose parents had wanted a boy experienced more conflicted relationships with their fathers beginning at about age 4 than was true for girls whose parents had wanted a girl or who had not had a strong preference. The effect was smaller for boys, but there were some suggestions that boys whose parents had wanted a girl had had more conflicted relationships with their mothers in early childhood.

Despite these confirmations, neither Horowitz's model, nor the goodness-of-fit model, have been uniformly supported. Part of the difficulty is the fuzziness of the definitions of the key terms. It is not always easy to measure "vulnerability," or to define a "good fit" or a "poor fit." Such fuzziness makes these models more difficult to test clearly, and thus more difficult to support or disconfirm. Both models, however, illustrate the kind of theorizing about the nature/nurture interaction that is entering our current debates about human development.

## What Is the Nature of Developmental Change?

The third key question on which researchers and theorists differ concerns the nature of developmental change itself: Is a child's expanded ability just "more of the same," or does it reflect a new kind of activity? For example, a 2-year-old is likely to have no individual friends among her playmates, while an 8-year-old is likely to have several. We could think of this as a *quantitative* change (a change in amount) from zero friends to some friends. Or we could think of it as a *qualitative* change (a change in kind or type) from disinterest in peers to interest, or from one sort of peer relationship to another. Where a given researcher or theorist stands on this question has a profound effect on the way he or she perceives children and their behavior. Does development consist simply of becoming more of x or y? Does a child simply get better and better at things, such as walking, running, or reading? That is, are the *processes* the same and only the efficiency or the speed different, or are there different processes at different ages? Do older children and young children learn things in the same way, following the same rules, or do older children approach new tasks in distinctly different ways?

*Stages and Sequences.* An important related question concerns the presence or absence of *stages* in the course of development. If development consists only of additions (quantitative change), then the concept of stages is not needed. But if development involves reorganization or the emergence of wholly new strategies or skills (qualitative change), then the concept of stages may become attractive. Certainly we hear a lot of "stagelike" language in everyday conversation about children: "He's just in the terrible twos," or, "It's only a stage she's going through."

Although researchers do not always agree on what qualifies as evidence of discrete stages, most agree that a stage shift involves not only a change in skills but some discontinuous change in underlying *structure* (McHale & Lerner, 1990). The child in a new stage approaches tasks differently, sees the world differently, is preoccupied with different issues.

As we move through the chapters, you will see that stage theories are common in studies of development; although the concept has come under considerable attack recently. As we have learned more, the idea of stages of development, which at first seemed to be a simple way to describe changes with age, has turned out to be slippery and difficult to sustain. You should keep that in mind as you encounter the various stage theories that are still part of our theoretical language. You should also keep in mind, however, that stages are not necessary for a theory of development that emphasizes qualitative as well as (or instead of) quantitative change. Qualitative change may be gradual as well as abrupt, sequential rather than stage-like.

## Theories of Development

Each of the many possible combinations of answers to the key questions I have been describing might form the basis of a theory of development. However, certain combinations of assumptions have been much more prominent than others. Of these, four families of theories have been most influential: biological theories, learning theories, psychoanalytic theories, and cognitive-developmental theories. Since you will meet members of these four theoretical families again and again through the book, let me describe them to you briefly here and point out the ways in which they differ in their answers to the key questions.

### Biological Theories

Biological theories of development essentially propose that common patterns of development and unique individual behavioral tendencies are partially or wholly programmed in the genes, or are influenced by physiological processes like hormone changes. Biologically oriented theorists do not deny the role of the environment; no one takes such an extreme position. Genetic programming, however, is regarded by many psychologists as a powerful framework, affecting both shared and individual patterns of development. Several subvarieties of biological theories have been important in the field.

*Maturational Theory.* Gesell's theory of maturation is obviously one such biologically based theory, in this case designed to explain shared patterns of development. Current research in this tradition, such as Esther Thelen's work (1984) on the development of crawling and walking in children, has involved detailed analysis of the maturational changes required for the emergence of some new skill.

*Behavior Genetics.* The second major variant of biological theory, which focuses on explanations of individual differences rather than on common patterns of development, is generally referred to as **behavior genetics.** It is not altogether clear that we ought to call behavior genetics a "theory." Rather it is a set of techniques for exploring the basic hypothesis: Individual differences are profoundly affected by heredity. This hypothesis, and the techniques for studying it, have undergone a remarkable resurgence of interest and acceptance in the past decade. Robert Plomin, one of the major researchers in this area, says "Increasing acceptance of hereditary influence on individual differences in development represents one of the most remarkable changes in the field of psychology that has occurred in the decade since. . . 1979" (1989, p. 105).

**behavior genetics**
The study of the genetic basis of behavior, such as intelligence or personality.

Behavior geneticists have studied a wide range of behaviors in adults as well as children, including IQ, academic achievement, psychopathology such as depression and schizophrenia, as well as personality and temperament. I'll be looking at two sets of research in this tradition in some detail, the work on the genetics of IQ in Chapter 6, and studies of the heritability of temperamental differences in Chapter 9, which will give you a more extensive look at this approach.

Considering the key questions, we can see that biological theorists are attempting to explain both common patterns of development and individual differences. Although they acknowledge the role of environment, they strongly emphasize the "nature" side of the nature/nurture dispute. And when they talk about developmental change, they generally talk about quantitative change. Gesell did address sequences of maturational change, but he did not

All over the world, babies shift from crawling to walking at essentially the same ages. Here Vitaly Popov, filmed in Russia as part of the *Childhood* series, passes through this transition. Gesell and others argue that such universal, sequential developmental changes must be based on underlying maturational sequences. This photo is a video still from the *Childhood* television series (*Source:* ©Thirteen/WNET).

assume that these sequences led to qualitatively different stages or outcomes.

### Learning Theories

Learning theorists have started from the other end of the nature/nurture argument. A leading theorist, Albert Bandura, put it this way: "Except for elementary reflexes, people are not equipped with inborn repertoires of behavior. They must learn them" (Bandura, 1977, p. 16). Learning theorists do not reject biology any more than biological theorists reject environment. Bandura goes on to point out that hormones or inherited propensities *can* affect behavior, but specific experiences are the stuff of which development is made.

This emphasis on the importance of the environment, and on the central processes of learning, is common to all the theorists in this group. Two basic processes of learning are also agreed upon: classical condition-

One of three major types of learning. An automatic unconditioned response such as an emotion or a reflex comes to be triggered by a new cue, called the conditioned stimulus (CS), after the CS has been paired several times with the original unconditioned stimulus.

**unconditioned stimulus**
In classical conditioning this is the cue or signal that automatically triggers (without learning) the unconditioned response.

**unconditioned responses**
In classical conditioning this is the basic unlearned response that is triggered by the unconditioned stimulus.

**conditioned stimuli**
In classical conditioning, the stimuli that, after being paired a number of times with an unconditioned stimulus, come to trigger the unconditioned response.

ing and operant conditioning. You have doubtless already encountered these concepts in earlier classes, but let me review them quickly.

*Classical Conditioning.* This type of learning, made famous by Pavlov's experiments with his salivating dog, involves the acquisition of new signals for existing responses. If you touch a baby on the cheek, he will turn toward the touch and begin to suck. In the technical terminology of **classical conditioning,** the touch on the cheek is the **unconditioned stimulus;** the turning and sucking are **unconditioned responses.** The baby is already programmed to behave this way; these are automatic reflexes. The learning occurs when some *new* stimulus is hooked into the system. Specifically, other stimuli that are present just before or at the same time as the unconditioned stimulus will eventually trigger the same responses. In the typical home situation, for example, a number of stimuli occur at about the same time as the touch on the baby's cheek before feeding. There is the sound of the mother's footsteps approaching, the kinesthetic cues of being picked up, the tactile cues of being held in the mother's arms. All of these stimuli may become **conditioned stimuli** and may trigger the infant's response of turning and sucking without any touch on the cheek at all. The steps in the process are shown in Figure 1.5.

Although the study of classical conditioning in children has not been a hot research topic, it continues to be of interest for several reasons. First, by identifying how early an infant or child can be classically conditioned, we can learn about what kind of neurological connections are possible early in life. A more interesting issue is the role of classical conditioning in the development of emotional responses. Objects or people present when you feel good will become conditioned stimuli for that same sense of goodwill, while those previously associated with some uncomfortable feeling may become conditioned stimuli for a sense of unease or anxiety. Since a child's mother or father is present so often when pleasing things happen—when the child feels warm, comfortable, and cuddled—mother or father usually come to be conditioned

**FIGURE 1.5**

The three steps in the development of a classically conditioned response. In the first step, the unconditioned stimulus automatically triggers the unconditioned response. In step 2, some additional stimulus occurs at the same time as the unconditioned stimulus. In the final step, the new stimulus—called the conditioned stimulus—acquires the capacity to trigger the original response.

| Step 1 | | Step 2 | | Step 3 | |
|---|---|---|---|---|---|
| Stimulus | Response | Stimulus | Response | Stimulus | Response |
| Touch on the → Head turn cheek (Unconditioned stimulus: UCS) (Unconditioned response: UCR) | | Touch on the → Head turn cheek (UCS) (UCR) Mother's voice (Conditioned stimulus: CS) | | Voice (CS) → Head turn (CR) | |

stimuli for pleasant feelings. This fact then gives the parent's presence the power to reinforce other behaviors as well. In contrast, a tormenting older sibling might become a conditioned stimulus for angry feelings, even long after the sibling has stopped tormenting.

These classically conditioned emotional responses are remarkably powerful. They begin to form early in life, continue to form throughout childhood and adulthood, and profoundly affect each individual's emotional experiences.

*Operant Conditioning.* The second major type of learning is most often called **operant conditioning,** although you will also see it referred to as instrumental conditioning. Unlike classical conditioning, which involves attaching an old response to a new stimulus, operant conditioning involves attaching a new response to an old stimulus, achieved by the application of appropriate principles of reinforcement.

Any behavior that is reinforced will be more likely to occur again in the same or in a similar situation. There are two types of reinforcements. A **positive reinforcement** is any event, which following some behavior, increases the chances of repeating that behavior in that situation. Note that the reinforcement is defined by its effect; we don't know something is reinforcing unless we see that its presence increases the probability of some behavior. Although, there are certain classes of pleasant consequences, such as praise, a smile, food, a hug, or attention that serve as reinforcers for most people most of the time.

The second major type is a **negative reinforcement.** This term has been used in a variety of ways over the years, so there is some confusion about the meaning (Maccoby, 1980a). The most widely used definition says that negative reinforcement occurs when something an individual finds *unpleasant* is *stopped.* Suppose your little boy is whining and begging you to pick him up. At first you ignore him, but finally you do pick him up. What happens? He stops whining. So your "picking-up" behavior has been *negatively reinforced* by the cessation of his whining, and you will be *more* likely to pick him up the next time he whines. At the same time, his whining has probably been *positively reinforced* by your attention and picking up, so he will be more likely to whine on similar occasions.

Both positive and negative reinforcements strengthen behavior. **Punishment,** in contrast, is intended to weaken some undesired behavior. Sometimes punishments involve eliminating pleasurable conditions (like "grounding" a child, or taking away TV privileges, or sending the child to his or her room). Punishments also involve administering unpleasant things such as a scolding or a spanking. This use of the word *punishment* fits with the common understanding of the term and shouldn't be too confusing. What *is* confusing is the fact that such punishments don't always do what they are intended to do; they do not always suppress the undesired behavior. If your child had thrown a milk glass at you to get your attention, a spanking may be a positive reinforcement instead of the punishment you had intended. Punishment—as you will see more fully in Chapter 13—is definitely a double-edged sword.

Reinforcements do not strengthen a behavior permanently. The reverse process is **extinction,** which is a decrease in the likelihood of some response after repeated nonreinforcements. If you simply stopped reinforcing whining

**operant conditioning**
One of the three major types of learning in which the probability of a person performing some behavior is affected by positive or negative reinforcements.

**positive reinforcement**
Strengthening of a behavior by the presentation of some pleasurable or positive stimulus.

**negative reinforcement**
The strengthening of a behavior that occurs because of the removal or cessation of an unpleasant stimulus.

**punishment**
Unpleasant consequences, administered after some undesired behavior by a child or adult, with the intent of extinguishing the behavior.

**extinction**
A decrease in the strength of some response after nonreinforcement.

behavior in your child, eventually the child would stop whining, not only on this occasion but on subsequent occasions.

In laboratory situations, experimenters can reinforce some behavior every time it occurs, or stop reinforcements completely so as to produce extinction of the response. In the real world, however, such consistency of reinforcement is the exception rather than the rule. Much more common is a pattern of **partial reinforcement,** in which some behavior is reinforced on some occasions but not others. Systematic studies of partial reinforcement show that children and adults take longer to learn some behavior under partial reinforcement conditions, but once established, such behaviors are much more resistant to extinction. If you smile at your daughter only every fifth or sixth time she brings a picture to show you (and if she finds your smile reinforcing), she'll keep on bringing pictures for a very long stretch, even if you were to stop smiling altogether.

These basic principles of operant conditioning not only help researchers understand the origins and maintenance of many patterns of behavior in children, such as the antisocial behavior Patterson has studied, they also have direct practical relevance for day-to-day child rearing as well as for therapeutic interventions with children with deviant behavior patterns. I've discussed some of the applications in the box on page 24.

*Subvarieties of Learning Theory.* All theorists who emphasize the central role of learning would agree on the importance of these basic processes. Beyond that basic agreement, however, there are significant theoretical variations.

On one end of the theoretical continuum are the *radical behaviorists.* These theorists, strongly influenced by the work of B. F. Skinner, take an extreme environmental position. Theorists of this persuasion assume that the basic principles of learning are the same no matter how old the learner may be. Children may appear to "develop" in similar ways, but this is only because they are likely to have similar learning experiences. If we could devise the right sequence of experiences, a 2-year- old should be able to learn tasks we normally think of as requiring a 10 -year-old's skills (Baer, 1970).

Few developmental psychologists today would take such an extreme position. Many trained in this tradition have broadened their theoretical scope and introduced interactive and ecological concepts, as has Gerald Patterson, whose model I showed in Figure 1.3. Yet this approach is still influential in some areas, particularly among those who devise educational interventions for children who display deviant patterns of behavior.

A second subvariety of learning theory is normally called *social-learning theory.* The key figure here is Albert Bandura (1977, 1982), a theorist whose views have undergone some interesting changes over the years. Bandura accepts the importance of classical and operant conditioning, but he makes several additional assertions.

Bandura argues that direct reinforcement is not always necessary for learning to occur. Learning may occur merely as a result of watching someone else perform some action. Learning of this type, called **observational learning** or **modeling,** is involved in a wide range of behaviors. Children learn ways of hitting from watching other people in real life and on TV. They learn generous behaviors by watching others donate money or goods. They learn

partial reinforcement
Reinforcement of behavior on some schedule less frequent than every occasion.

observational learning (modeling)
Learning of motor skills, attitudes, or other behaviors through observing someone else perform them.

physical skills such as bike riding or skiing partly from watching other people demonstrate them. They are also affected by the rewards or punishments they see someone else receive for some behavior, a process usually called *vicarious reinforcement.*

Bandura also calls attention to another class of reinforcements called **intrinsic reinforcements** or intrinsic rewards. These reinforcements are internal to the individual—for example, the pleasure a child feels after discovering how to draw a star, or the sense of satisfaction you may experience after strenuous exercise. Pride, discovery, that "aha" experience are all powerful intrinsic rewards, and all have the same power to strengthen some behavior as do extrinsic reinforcements such as praise or attention.

Bandura's theory has also helped to bridge the gap between learning theory and cognitive-developmental theory by emphasizing important *cognitive* elements in learning—indeed he now refers to his theory as "social cognitive theory" (Bandura, 1986). For example, observational learning is not automatic. What we learn from observing someone else is influenced by what we pay attention to, by our ability to make sense out of what we saw and to remember it, and by our actual capacity to repeat the observed action. I will never become an expert tennis player merely by watching Martina Navratilova play!

Bandura introduces other cognitive components as well. In learning situations, children and adults *set goals, create expectations* about what kinds of consequences are likely, and *judge* their own performances. The addition of such concepts introduces more developmental features into the theory. If we assume, for example, that children of different ages observe or notice different things and that they analyze or process those observations differently, then learning is going to vary systematically by age. As Bandura says, "Thought mediates reinforcement effects" (1982, p. 13); to the extent that thought differs at different ages, so will reinforcement processes.

Bandura is clearly correct that children learn an enormous amount by modeling themselves after the adults in their lives. Here Kouchiro Nouhata, in Japan, is not only learning to fold clothes by copying his mother, he is also demonstrating the helpful and altruistic behavior common to children this age. As this picture was taken, he was saying "Mother, when you are tired, let me fold for you." This photo is a video still from the *Childhood* television series (*Source:* © Thirteen/WNET).

## Some Applications of Learning Principles to Child Rearing

All parents, whether they are aware of it or not, reinforce some behaviors in their children by praising them or by giving them attention or treats. And all parents do their best to discourage unpleasant behavior through punishment. Often, however, parents (myself included) think they are rewarding behaviors they like and ignoring those they don't like, and yet the results do not seem to meet their expectations. When this happens, it may be because more than one learning principle is operating at once, or because we have misapplied those principles.

For example, suppose you have a favorite armchair in your living room that is being systematically ruined by the dirt and pressure of little feet climbing up the back of the chair. You want the children to *stop* climbing up the chair. So you scold them. After a while you may even stoop to nagging. If you are really conscientious and knowledgeable, you may carefully try to time your scolding so that it operates as a negative reinforcer, by stopping your scolding when they stop climbing. But nothing works. They keep on leaving those muddy footprints on your favorite chair. Why? It could be because the children *enjoy* climbing up the chair. So the climbing is intrinsically reinforcing to the children, and that effect is clearly stronger than your negative reinforcement or punishment. One way to deal with this might be to provide something *else* for them to climb on.

A second example of the complications of applying learning principles to everyday dealings with children is what happens when you inadvertently create a partial reinforcement schedule. Suppose your 3-year-old son repeatedly demands your attention while you are fixing dinner (a common state of affairs, as any parent of a 3-year-old can tell you). Because you don't want to reinforce this behavior, you ignore him the first six or eight times he says "Mommy" (or "Daddy") or tugs at your clothes. But after the ninth or tenth repetition, with his voice getting louder and whinier each time, you can't stand it any longer and finally say something like "All right! What do you want?" Since you have ignored most of his demands, you might well be convinced that you have not been reinforcing his demanding behavior. But what you have actually done is to create a partial reinforcement schedule; you have rewarded only every tenth demand or whine. And we know that this pattern of reinforcement helps to create behavior that is *very* hard to extinguish. So your son may continue to be demanding and whining for a very long time, even if you succeed in ignoring it completely.

Because many parents have difficulty with situations just like this and with seeing exactly what it is they are reinforcing, many family therapists ask families to keep detailed records of their child's behavior and their responses to it. Gerald Patterson, in his book *Families* (1975), lays out a plan for families to follow in doing this. He has used such strategies successfully in treating families with highly aggressive or noncompliant children, and you may find it helpful as well. When you see, through your own records and observations, just what it is you are doing to reinforce whining or noncompliance or destructive behavior (or whatever), it is much easier to change your pattern of response.

To summarize, and to return to the key questions I discussed earlier, learning theorists—particularly the more radical behaviorists—focus on environmental influences and individual differences. They see developmental change as primarily quantitative, without stages. Current forms of social-learning theory have softened many of these fairly extreme positions by emphasizing the child's own role in interpreting and organizing the information given by reinforcements.

### Psychoanalytic Theories

In contrast, psychoanalytic theorists emphasize sequential, often stage-like qualitative change, and they assume that internal processes are as important as external experience in shaping behavior. I'm not going to describe the theories in this group in much detail at this point since I'll be presenting them more fully in Chapter 9. But you should at least begin with some knowledge of the key individuals and the central assumptions.

The word *psyche*, in Greek, refers to the soul, spirit, or mind. So psychoanalysis is the analysis of the mind or spirit. All the theorists who share this general tradition have been interested in explaining human behavior by understanding the underlying processes of the mind and the personality. And nearly all psychoanalytic theorists have begun by studying and analyzing adults or children who are disturbed in some way. Many believed they could come to understand the normal processes by analyzing how certain functions and behaviors had gone wrong.

As with learning theories, there is a whole family of "psychoanalytic" theories, originating with Freud and continuing with Carl Jung (1916, 1939), Alfred Adler (1948), Erik Erikson (1963, 1964, 1974), and many others.

Sigmund Freud (1905, 1920) is usually credited with originating the psychoanalytic approach, and his terminology and many of his concepts have become part of our intellectual culture, even while his explicit influence upon developmental psychologists has waned. Among current theorists in this tradition, Erik Erikson (1950/1963, 1959/1980) is probably the most influential, although there are other important thinkers whose work has been strongly influenced by psychoanalytic theory, such as John Bowlby and Jane Loevinger.

The most distinctive and central assumption of the psychoanalytic approach is that behavior is governed not only by conscious but by *unconscious* processes. Some of these unconscious processes are present at birth, others develop over time. For example, Freud proposed the existence of a basic unconscious, instinctual sexual drive he called the **libido.** He argued that this energy is the motive force behind virtually all our behavior, and that the desire for gratification drives each child to learn to speak and reason in order to achieve gratification more effectively. Freud also proposed that unconscious material is created over time through the functioning of the various defense mechanisms—normal, automatic, unconscious strategies for reducing anxiety that we all use on a daily basis, such as repression, denial, or projection.

A second basic assumption is that personality has a structure, and that such a structure develops over time. Freud proposed three parts: the **id,** which is the center of the libido; the **ego,** a much more conscious element and the executive of the personality; and the **superego,** which is the center of conscience and morality, incorporating the norms and moral strictures of the family and society. In Freud's theory, these three parts are not all present at birth. The infant and toddler are all id, all instinct, all desire, without the restraining influence of the ego or the superego. The ego begins to develop from 2 to about 4 or 5 years of age as the child learns to adapt his instant-grat-

libido
The term used by Freud to describe the pool of sexual energy in each individual.

id
In Freudian theory, the first, primitive portion of the personality; the storehouse of basic energy, continually pushing for immediate gratification.

ego
In Freudian theory, that portion of the personality that organizes, plans, and keeps the person in touch with reality. Language and thought are both ego functions.

superego
In Freudian theory, the "conscience" part of personality, which develops as a result of the identification process. The superego contains the parental and societal values and attitudes incorporated by the child.

ification strategies. Finally the superego begins to develop just before school age, as the child starts to incorporate the parents' values and cultural mores.

Psychoanalytic theorists also see development as fundamentally stage-like, with each stage centered on a particular form of tension, or a particular task. The child moves through these stages, resolving each task, reducing each tension, as best as possible. So there is direction to this development, an ideal sequence.

I'll be describing both Freud's and Erikson's versions of these various stages in some detail in Chapter 9. For now, the key point is that theories in this tradition assume stages of some kind and that both theorists proposed that the degree of success a child experiences in meeting the demands of these various stages will depend heavily on the interactions with people and objects in the child's world. This *interactive* element in Freud's and all subsequent psychoanalytic theories is absolutely central. Further, any time one stage is not fully resolved, the old patterns or the unmet need are carried forward and affect the person's ability to handle later tasks or stages.

Returning to the key questions, you can see that while psychoanalytic theorists started out trying to explain individual differences, particularly individual differences in personality, the theories they devised to account for deviance are really descriptions of a shared, normative process of development. They take an intermediate position on the nature/nurture question, emphasizing the combined importance of inborn instincts, appropriate environmental supports, and the child's own processing of the experience. They see development itself as primarily qualitative change, in distinct stages.

### Cognitive-Developmental Theories

In psychoanalytic theories, the quality and character of a child's relationships with a few key people are seen as central to the child's whole development. The child's encounters with the inanimate world—with toys and objects, with sights and sounds—are rarely discussed. Cognitive-developmental theorists, whose interest has been primarily in cognitive development rather than personality, reverse this order of importance, emphasizing the centrality of the child's explorations of objects. But cognitive-developmental theorists share with their psychoanalytically inclined colleagues the assumption that the cause or source of change is internal as well as external. The child is engaged in the process of development and is an active participant.

The central figure in cognitive-developmental theory is Jean Piaget (1952, 1970, 1977; Piaget & Inhelder, 1969), a Swiss psychologist whose theories have shaped the thinking of several generations of developmental psychologists. Piaget, along with other early cognitive theorists such as Lev Vygotsky (1962) and Heinz Werner (1948), was struck by the great regularities in the development of children's thinking. He noticed that all children seemed to go through the same kinds of sequential discoveries about their world, making the same sorts of mistakes and arriving at the same solutions. For example, 3- and 4-year-olds all seem to think that if you pour water from a short, fat glass into a tall, thin one, there is now more water, since the water level is higher in the thin glass than it was in the fat glass. But most 7-year-olds realize that there is still the same amount of water in either case. A 2-year-old who loses a shoe may look for it briefly and haphazardly, but is unable to undertake a systematic search. A 10-year-old, in contrast, is likely to use good strategies like retracing previous steps or looking in one room after another.

Piaget's detailed observations of children's thinking led him to several assumptions. The most central assumption is that the nature of the human organism is to *adapt* to its environment. This is an active process, not a passive one. In contrast to many learning theorists, Piaget does not think that the environment *shapes* the child. Rather the child (like the adult) actively seeks to understand his environment. In the process, the child explores, manipulates, and examines the objects and people in his or her world.

The process of adaptation, in Piaget's view, is made up of several important subprocesses—*assimilation, accommodation,* and *equilibration*—all of which I will define fully in Chapter 7. For now, the key idea is that the child's exploration of the environment leads over a period of time to a series of fairly distinct "understandings" or "theories" about the way the world works, each of which comprises a specific stage. Since Piaget thought that virtually all infants begin with the same skills and built-in strategies, and since the environments children encounter are highly similar in important respects, their thinking moves through similar stages. Piaget proposes a fixed sequence of four major stages, each growing out of the one that preceded it, and each consisting of a more-or-less complete system or organization of concepts, strategies, and assumptions.

Returning to the key questions, cognitive-developmental theorists clearly are involved in explaining common patterns of development; neither Piaget nor most of his followers have had a great deal of interest in individual differences in development. On the nature/nurture question, cognitive theorists take neither side, emphasizing instead the child's own active processing of the environment. Finally, cognitive-developmental theorists clearly argue for qualitative rather than quantitative change, although many current proponents of this view no longer agree with Piaget about the existence of fixed stages.

### Contrasting the Theories

No doubt by now your head is swimming with theories. To help you sort out the similarities and differences, I have summarized the several positions on the key questions in Table 1.1 on p. 29. In this table, as in my descriptions of the theories, I have intentionally made the contrasts as great as possible to help you keep the alternatives clearly separate. As we continue, you will find that many current theories involve very interesting mixtures of these approaches. You have already seen the cognitive elements contained in Bandura's theories and the ecological concepts added to a basic learning theory approach in Patterson's work. But there are many more examples. The newer theories of attachment, for example, introduce clearly cognitive themes (such as the notion of an internal working model) into an otherwise psychoanalytically oriented approach. In virtually every area of study we see a return to an emphasis on biological roots.

Before we begin looking at newer theories and at the current descriptions of children's development in more detail, I need to give you one more tool—some basic knowledge about the way research in this field is done.

# Finding the Answers: Research on Development

How do we set about the task of describing or explaining the changes or continuities we see in children as they grow? How do we try to answer the "what" and the "why" questions?

## Describing Behavior

The most basic need for any research on development is to describe children's actual behavior accurately. How does a 2-year-old or a 4-year-old react to the presence of a strange adult? What are the physical skills of an 8-year-old? What is the vocabulary of a 10-year-old? The two time-honored ways of trying to answer questions like this are observing people and asking them questions. Because infants and young children are not particularly good at answering questions, observation has been an especially prominent research strategy among developmental psychologists.

*Observation.* Any researcher planning to use observation to collect information about children or their environments will have to make at least three decisions: What shall I observe? Where shall I observe? How shall I record the observations?

The decision about what to observe can be divided still further: Should you try to observe everything a child does, or focus only on selected behaviors? Should you observe only the child, or also the context, such as the quality of the environment? Clearly the decisions any given researcher makes are heavily dependent on the basic question he or she is trying to address. If I am interested in the child's first words I would not need to pay much attention to facial expressions, or how close the child was sitting to an adult. However, I might want to make note of what the child was playing with, whether there were other people there and what they said to the child. On the other hand, if I were interested in the development of attachment, I would make note of facial expressions and the nearness of key adults.

It is also no simple matter to decide *where* we will observe. We can observe in a natural setting, such as a child's home or school, in which case we are introducing an enormous amount of variability into the system and increasing the complexity of the observation immensely. Or we can choose a controlled setting, keeping it the same for each child observed. For example, the most widely used measure of the security of a child's attachment to an adult is based on a standardized laboratory observation in what is called the Strange Situation. The child is observed in a series of episodes in a laboratory including a period with the mother (or father), with the mother and a stranger, alone with the stranger, completely alone, and reunited with the mother. Such standardized procedures give us the enormous advantage of yielding comparable information for each child, but we may lose some ecological validity. We cannot be sure that what we observe in this unfamiliar laboratory is representative of the child's behavior in more accustomed settings.

Finally, a researcher must decide how to record the observations. On one end of the continuum is what Bakeman and Gottman (1987) call a narrative report—a running description of what is observed. (The project at the end of this chapter involves having you try just such a narrative report, so that

**TABLE 1.1**

*Comparison of Developmental Theories on Some of the Key Questions About Development*

| Issue | Biological Theory | Radical Learning Theory | Social Learning Theory | Psycho-analytic Theory | Cognitive-Developmental Theory |
|---|---|---|---|---|---|
| What should we study? shared patterns or individual differences? | Both | Individual differences | Individual differences | Both | Primarily shared patterns of development |
| What is the major influence on development: nature or nurture? | Primarily nature | Primarily nurture | Primarily nurture | Both | The child's own internal processing of experience |
| What is the nature of developmental change? qualitative or quantitative? | Both, although maturational theorists emphasize quantitative change | Primarily quantitative | Both; learning occurs, but child's interpretation and understanding change | Qualitative | Qualitative |
| Are there stages or sequences? | Sequences but not stages | Neither is emphasized | No stages, but perhaps sequences | Stages | Certainly sequences; some argue stages |
| Examples of research questions emerging from that theoretical tradition | Tempera-mental differences and their effects; role of heredity and environment in intelligence | Modification of deviant behavior using basic learning principles | Impact of TV on children's behavior; origins of social behaviors such as aggression | Children's fantasies and attachment | Moral development; gender concepts; development of logic |

you can see how difficult it is.) Language researchers often use a limited version of the narrative report when they record a child's utterances along with descriptions of what is happening in the environment at the time the child spoke.

The other end of the continuum might include various kinds of rating scales, in which an observer watches for some period of time and then summarizes everything with a rating on one or more dimensions, such as rating the overall quality of the environment, or the affectionateness of the parent's responses to the infant. In between lies an enormous number of specific coding schemes in which the researcher defines some set of behaviors and counts or measures the length of their occurrence. For example, a researcher could record each time a child shared a mutual gaze with an adult, or count episodes of aggression, and so on. The difficult task is to define each category clearly, and to train the observers carefully so that each observer is classifying behaviors in the same fashion.

No one of these is an easy decision; the usefulness of a given piece of research very often rests on the quality of the observation and the suitability

How might theorists from each of the four major theoretical traditions explain this child's angry or aggressive outburst?

of the method of recording that observation. If you choose to complete the projects suggested at the end of most of the chapters you will be exposed to several different observational and coding techniques, which should give you some feeling for the difficulties involved in doing really good observation.

*Questionnaires and Interviews.* Among researchers studying older children, especially those who are interested in children's thinking, questionnaires and interviews provide an excellent alternative to observation. For example, Lawrence Kohlberg's assessment of a child's stage of moral reasoning, which you'll read about in Chapter 12, is based on a structured interview in which the child is presented with a series of moral dilemmas and asked to say what he or she would do. As is true of observations, such interviews are time consuming and may be quite difficult to reduce to comparable scores. Kohlberg and his colleagues tried and discarded several different scoring schemes before they arrived at one that could be used reliably by trained raters and that accurately captured the dimensions of interest (Colby et al., 1983). A questionnaire may be used in place of an interview since it solves this scoring problem and takes less time. The down side, of course, is that it may be less valid.

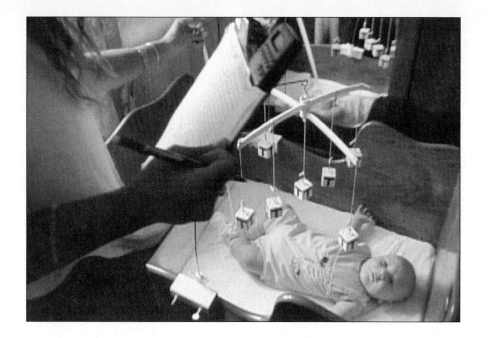

Careful observation of children in both natural and experimentally-created settings has formed the backbone of our knowledge about early development. In this particular case, Carolyn Rovee-Collier and her research assistant have tied a ribbon to a baby's foot, so that the baby can make a mobile jiggle if he moves his foot. The observer is counting the number of leg moves, and will compare that to the baseline level of leg moving she has already observed. This photo is a video still from the *Childhood* television series (*Source:* © Thirteen/WNET).

Questionnaires may also be used in place of observation. For example, researchers interested in parent-adolescent interactions have quite commonly measured those interactions with questionnaires rather than by direct observation of the parents and teenagers. Not only is this a much shorter strategy, it may have considerable validity as well, especially if the crucial element in the relationship equation is how each member of the pair *perceives* the relationship rather than the quality of the actual interactions. Still, just as an observation can be no better than the quality of the observers and of the coding scheme, a questionnaire can be no better than the quality of its questions.

### Describing Changes with Age

A special problem facing developmental psychologists is describing changes over age. Two basic research designs have been devised to solve this problem: cross-sectional and longitudinal research.

*Cross-Sectional Research.*   If we want to know whether 4-year-olds can learn some particular concept in the same way as 8-year-olds, or to answer any one of hundreds of equivalent descriptive questions about development, the simplest and least time-consuming strategy is to study separate groups that differ in age. Such comparisons of age groups are called **cross-sectional studies.** You will encounter dozens of examples as you read through the book: comparisons of the generosity of 4-year-olds and 8-year-olds, comparisons of the self-knowledge of 18-month-olds and 3-year-olds, and the like.

Cross-sectional research is often enormously useful. It is relatively quick to do, and by revealing age differences in some domain it often points the way to better understanding of the developmental process. But this design also has distinct limitations. First of all, it cannot tell us much about *sequences* of development, such as the sequence of concepts children have about their

**cross-sectional studies** Studies in which different groups of individuals of different ages are all studied at the same time.

own gender. A cross-sectional study might show that 2-year-olds have a different idea of gender than 4-year-olds, but that won't tell us whether there are steps in between or whether every child acquires this concept in the same sequence. Similarly, cross-sectional studies will not tell us anything about the consistency of individual behavior over time, such as whether a temperamentally difficult infant remains crankier than average at school age.

Finally, cross-sectional studies have the serious limitation that the subjects in each group may differ in more than just age. Each broad age group is typically called a **cohort**, roughly similar to a generation, though the term *cohort* is also used to describe a much smaller span of years. Each cohort lives through a specific set of experiences at a specific time in their lives. When we compare age groups, we also compare cohorts, and the differences we see in behavior or skill may be due to the different life experiences of these several cohorts and not just to age. When the age groups we are comparing are relatively close together this is not usually a major problem, since we can assume roughly similar life circumstances. However, comparing wider age groups can present significant difficulties. For example, children now in their teens were much less likely to have had an employed mother when they were of preschool age than is true for current preschoolers.

*Longitudinal Research.*   To answer questions about sequence or consistency, we have to study the *same* group of individuals over time—a strategy called **longitudinal study.** Short-term longitudinal studies, in which groups of children are studied for a period of several years, have become common in recent years. There are also a few long-term longitudinal studies in which groups of children have been followed from infancy through adolescence or even into adulthood (e.g., Werner, 1986; Block, 1971). These sets of observations have yielded very rich veins of information about development.

Longitudinal designs help to get around the "cohort problem" that is built into cross-sectional comparisons. But there are still real difficulties with this design. First, there is the problem of attrition. Families move, parents divorce, children get sick or get tired of participating in the study. So as a longitudinal study progresses, fewer and fewer subjects remain. Typically it is the least functional families or the most vulnerable children who drop out, which may leave a decidedly unrepresentative sample at the end. A second serious difficulty is that each longitudinal study follows only a *particular* group, born at a particular time in history. Many of the longitudinal studies of greatest duration have studied cohorts born in the 1930s, 1940s, and 1950s. Can we be sure that the developmental patterns we see in such studies would be replicated in a group of children born in 1980 or 1990?

One solution to this problem is to repeat a longitudinal study several times, each time with a new cohort. This particular strategy, called a *cohort sequential design*, is one of a family of research designs, referred to as **sequential designs,** which circumvent some of the difficulties inherent in more ordinary cross-sectional and longitudinal designs. For instance, a researcher could do one cross-sectional study and then repeat the same cross-sectional comparison five or ten years later. This strategy, called a *time-sequential design*, can begin to get around the cohort problem inherent in cross-sectional comparisons. Alternatively, you could begin with a cross-sectional comparison and

**cohort**
A group of persons of approximately the same age who have shared similar major life experiences, such as cultural training, economic conditions, or a type of education.

**longitudinal study**
A research design in which the same subjects are observed or assessed repeatedly over a period of months or years.

**sequential designs**
A family of research designs which involve multiple cross-sectional, or multiple longitudinal, studies, or a combination of the two.

then follow the children in *each* age group for some period of time, retesting them all at a later point. This is called a *cross-sequential design*, and it obviously combines some of the features of cross-sectional and longitudinal designs. These more sophisticated alternatives are also beginning to be used more frequently in studies of children.

### Describing Relationships Among Variables

Another central task for developmental psychologists is to describe the *relationships* between variables: What sorts of behaviors go together? Which features of the environment are associated with rapid or slow development or with one pattern of development or another? The most common way to describe relationships of this kind is with a statistic called a correlation.

A **correlation** is simply a number, which can range from -1.00 to +1.00, that describes the strength of a relationship between two variables. A zero correlation indicates that there is no relationship between two variables. For instance, you might expect to find a zero or near-zero correlation between the length of big toes and IQ. People with toes of all sizes have high IQs, and those with toes of all sizes have low IQs too. The closer a correlation comes to -1.00 or +1.00, the stronger the relationship being described. If the correlation is positive, it indicates that high scores on the two dimensions tend to go together, and low scores tend to go together, such as we would find if we correlated the length of big toes and shoe size. Height and weight are also strongly positively correlated, as are the weekly hours of exercise you engage in and your aerobic capacity.

A negative correlation describes a relationship in which high scores on one variable are associated with low scores on the other. There is a negative correlation between the amount you eat when you are on a diet and the number of pounds you lose, or between the amount of disorder and chaos in a family and the child's later IQ (high chaos is associated with lower IQ, low chaos with higher IQ).

Perfect correlations (-1.00 or +1.00) do not happen in the real world. However, correlations of .80 or .70 do occur and correlations of .50 are common in psychological research, and indicate a relationship of moderate strength.

Correlations are an enormously useful descriptive tool, but they do not tell us *why* some relationship exists. They do not tell us about *causal* relationships. For example, several researchers have found a moderate positive correlation between the "difficultness" of a child's temperament and the amount of punishment the child receives from his parents: the more difficult the temperament the more punishment the child experiences. But which way does the causality run? Do difficult children *elicit* more punishment? Or, does a greater rate of punishment lead to a more difficult temperament? Might there be a third factor that may cause both, such as some genetic contribution both to the child's difficultness and to the parent's personality? The correlation alone does not allow us to choose among these alternatives. Stating the point more generally, no correlation—standing alone—can prove causality. A correlation may point in a particular direction, or suggest possible causal links, but to answer the why question we must then explore such possibilities with other techniques.

correlation
A statistic used to describe the degree or strength of a relationship between two variables. It can range from +1.00 to -1.00. The closer it is to 1.00 the stronger the relationship being described.

The traditional way to approach the task of explanation is to shift from observing naturally occurring events to introducing some intentional variations or controlling the situation systematically. That is, we do experiments. An **experiment** is normally designed to test some specific hypothesis, some particular causal explanation. An absolutely critical feature is that subjects are assigned *randomly* to participate in one of several groups, with each group receiving different treatment. In the simplest designs there are only two groups: Subjects in the **experimental group** receive the treatment the experimenter thinks is going to produce some identified effect, while those in the **control group** receive either no special treatment or some neutral treatment. In more complex designs there may be more than one experimental treatment, or several different control or comparison groups, but the basic rationale is the same in either case. The presumed causal element in the experiment is called the **independent variable,** and any behavior on which the independent variable is expected to show its impact is called a **dependent variable.**

Suppose, for example, that you were interested in the effects of a special massage treatment for infants born before the full gestation period (called preterm infants). You think that such a massage treatment will increase weight gain and reduce the incidence of neurological difficulties in the infants. In this example, the independent variable is massage treatment, and the dependent variables are weight and neurological status. To test your hypothesis you assign infants randomly to the experimental group, which will receive the massage, and the control group, which will not. You weigh all the infants before you begin and then weigh them again after some specified number of days or weeks of massage treatment, and you compare the two groups on neurological status as well.

You could make the design more complex (and probably more informative) by creating more than one experimental group, such as by varying the amount of massage, or by comparing massage to some other form of extra stimulation, like rocking. You could also include more than one control group. For instance, to see if the massage itself or merely the physical contact is crucial, you might include a control group in which infants were held in an adult's arms for the same amount of time as the massage normally occurred. Each of these variations allows the experimenter to test some specific hypothesis, some particular explanation of the phenomenon under study.

Random assignment of subjects is absolutely crucial in any experiment, a point that is clear if you think about just one example: If we put only the sickest preterm infants in the massage group, how could you interpret the results of the experiment?

*Problems with Experiments in Studying Development.*   It may seem from my description that experiments are absolutely the only way to go, the only way to reach real understanding of causal links. And of course they are essential for our understanding of many aspects of development. There are, however, two special problems in studying children and their development that limit the use of experimental designs.

First, many of the questions we want to answer involve the effects of un-

---

**experiment**
A research strategy in which subjects are assigned randomly to groups which are then provided with experiences that vary along some key dimension.

**experimental group**
The group (or groups) of subjects in an experiment that is given some special treatment intended to produce some specific consequence.

**control group**
The group of subjects in an experiment that receives either no special treatment or some neutral treatment.

**independent variable**
A condition or event that an experimenter varies in some systematic way in order to observe the impact of that variation on the subjects' behavior.

**dependent variable**
The variable in an experiment that is expected to show the impact of manipulations of the independent variable.

pleasant or stressful experiences on children—abuse, prenatal influences such as the mother's drinking or smoking, low birth weight, poverty, rejection by peers. For obvious ethical reasons, we simply cannot manipulate those variables. We cannot ask some pregnant women to have two alcoholic drinks a day and others to have none; we cannot assign some children to poverty environments and some to middle-class families. To study the effects of such negative experiences, we must rely on various forms of correlational designs, including longitudinal and sequential studies.

Second, the independent variable in which we are often most interested is age itself, and we cannot assign subjects randomly to age groups. If we want to compare the ways in which 4-year-olds and 6-year-olds approach some particular task—such as searching for a lost object—we can compare the two groups. But the children differ in a host of ways in addition to their ages. Older children have had more and different experiences. Thus, unlike psychologists studying other aspects of behavior, developmental psychologists *cannot* systematically manipulate many of the variables we are most interested in, such as age or many environmental features.

To get around this problem, we can use any one of a series of strategies that are sometimes called *quasi experiments*, in which we compare groups without assigning the subjects randomly. Cross-sectional comparisons are a form of quasi experiment. So are studies in which we select naturally occurring groups that differ in some dimension of interest, such as children with prenatal malnutrition compared to those with normal nutrition, or children whose parents choose to place them in day-care programs compared to children whose parents rear them at home.

Such comparisons have built-in problems, since groups that differ in one way are likely to be different in other ways as well. Families who place their children in day care, compared to those who rear them at home, are also likely to be poorer, may more often be single-parent families, and may have different values or even different religious backgrounds. If we find that the children differ on some dependent variable, is it because they have spent their daytime hours in different places or because of these other differences in their families? We can make such comparisons a bit clearer if we select our comparison groups initially so that they are matched on other variables we think might matter, such as income or marital status or religion. Quasi experiments, however, by their very nature, will always be more complicated to interpret and understand than completely controlled experiments.

I do not expect you to become experts in research design. But I do hope that the issues and questions I have raised here, and will continue to raise throughout the book, will help you develop some skill in judging the quality of research you may encounter. Table 1.2 on the next page gives you a checklist you might use as a starting point in research.

You should be particularly careful, even skeptical, when you come across accounts of research in magazines and newspapers. For example, you should be cautious about reports based on "reader surveys," such as when readers of the *Ladies' Home Journal* or *Psychology Today* are invited to respond to a questionnaire printed in the magazine. The group of people who respond to such a survey is not at all a representative sample of adults, so you simply cannot know whether their answers tell us anything about general trends. You should also be skeptical about statements like "Research shows that pregnant women who drink coffee have smaller babies." Ask yourself what kind of research would have to have been done to support that particular point and whether the evidence given really is good enough. Remember that not everything you read is true!

TABLE 1.2

*A Checklist of Things to Look for in Evaluating Research*

| | |
|---|---|
| Clarity | Can you understand what was done and what was found? |
| Importance of Findings | Does the study have some obvious practical relevance? Does it help to untangle a theoretical puzzle? Does it advance our understanding of some problem? |
| Promotion of New Ideas | Good research should lead to new ideas, new theoretical insights, and new questions as well as answer old questions. Does this study do that? |
| Consistency | Are the findings from this study consistent with the results of other research? Are they consistent with your own experience? This may be hard for you to judge, since you don't know all the other research on a given question, but it is important to keep it in mind if you can. Don't throw out inconsistent results, but look carefully at any study that doesn't fit with other evidence. |
| Replicability | If the same research were done again, would the same result occur? Exact replications aren't often done in social science research, but they probably ought to be done more often. |
| Choice of Subjects | Were all the children or families studied middle-class? Or were they all from poverty environments? Did all the subjects volunteer? Can we generalize the results to apply to other groups? |
| Appropriateness of Method | Was the method chosen for the study consistent with the questions being asked? For example, is the researcher using a cross-sectional design to study consistency of behavior? If so, it's the wrong design for that question. |

# S U M M A R Y

1. The study of child development may lead to answers to important practical questions, but the scientific study of development is also fascinating in and of itself.

2. In understanding development we must both describe developmental sequences and processes and explain the patterns we see.

3. Differing answers to several key questions lie behind many of the differences in research strategy and theorizing we see among developmental psychologists.

4. The first key question is whether we should be focusing our attention on describing and explaining common patterns of development or on individual differences.

5. A second key question centers on an ancient philosophical issue: the relative roles of nature and nurture (heredity and environment) in promoting development.

6. Current thinking about the nature side of the equation emphasizes not only the role of maturation but also points to potential inborn strategies of perceiving or responding to the environment, and to the possibility that nature may be differentially important at different periods in development (canalization).

7. Current thinking about the nurture side of the equation emphasizes not only the potential importance of the timing of some experience and the significance of a child's interpretation of some experience, but also the importance of examining the entire ecological system in which development occurs.

8. Current interactionist views of the nature/nurture question focus on the interactions between the child's inborn qualities (vulnerability or resilience) and the supportiveness of the environment, or on the goodness-of-fit between the child's characteristics and the demands of her environment.

9. A third key question concerns the nature of developmental change, whether it is qualitative or quantitative, continuous, or stage-like.

10. Four families of theories represent different combinations of answers to these key questions: biological, learning, psychoanalytic, and cognitive-developmental.

11. Biological theorists, such as Gesell or behavior geneticists, generally assume that the most significant influences on development are internal and that developmental change is primarily quantitative.

12. Learning theorists generally place strongest emphasis on environmental influences, thought to produce largely quantitative change. Radical behaviorists take the most extreme position, arguing that the basic laws of learning can account for all of what we think of as development. More

cognitively oriented social-learning theorists, such as Bandura, argue that the child's understanding of a learning situation also has some effect.

13. All learning theorists emphasize the importance of such basic processes as classical and operant conditioning; social-learning theorists also emphasize the role of observational learning.

14. Psychoanalytic theorists such as Freud and Erikson have primarily studied the development of personality, emphasizing the interaction of internal instincts and environmental influences in producing shared stages of development as well as individual differences in personality.

15. Cognitive-development theorists, such as Piaget and his many followers, emphasize the child's own active exploration of the environment as a critical ingredient leading to shared stages of development. They strongly emphasize qualitative change.

16. Newer theories have combined many of the features of these four positions.

17. Research designed to describe and explain development requires accurate and detailed observation of children's behavior in various settings. Choosing a method of observation requires deciding what shall be observed, where to observe, and how to convert the observations into some kind of descriptive information.

18. Both cross-sectional studies (of different people at different ages) and longitudinal studies (of the same people at several ages) can be used to study age changes; only longitudinal studies can tell us about sequences or individual consistencies. Each method has flaws, some of which can be circumvented with more complex sequential designs.

19. To describe the relationships among variables, the statistic called a correlation is normally used. It can range from +1.00 to -1.00, and describes the strength of a relationship.

20. Explaining development ordinarily requires an experiment or a quasi experiment. In an experiment, the researcher controls (manipulates) one or more relevant variables and assigns subjects randomly to different treatment and control groups.

21. In a quasi experiment, subjects are not randomly assigned to separate groups, but existing groups are used for comparison. Quasi experiments are needed in developmental research because subjects cannot be randomly assigned either to age groups or to experience such negative treatments as poverty or abuse or poor attachment.

22. Because research on development is difficult, readers should be properly skeptical of claims made both by researchers and in the popular press.

## CRITICAL THINKING QUESTIONS

1. After observing at a day-care center, you note that some of the 18-month-old children are very friendly with strangers, smile readily, and play easily with other children. Other toddlers seem more fearful, appear to cry more easily, and are less likely to approach another child. How would such differences be explained by theorists from each of the four theoretical traditions described in this chapter?

2. Suppose you are a researcher interested in understanding the origin of differences in temperament in babies and young children. Are such differences the product of differing upbringing, or are they the result of genetic differences, or both? What kind of research would you need to do to try to settle this question?

3. A friend with a 5-year-old comes to you in despair because the child is consistently defiant, aggressive, angry, and noncompliant. What advice could you give your friend?

## KEY TERMS

**behavior genetics** The study of the genetic basis of behavior, such as intelligence or personality.

**canalization** Term used to describe the degree to which development may be shaped by underlying maturational forces (as opposed to environment) during some period in the lifespan.

**classical conditioning** One of three major types of learning. An automatic unconditioned response such as an emotion or a reflex comes to be triggered by a new cue, called the conditioned stimulus (CS), after the CS has been paired several times with the original unconditioned stimulus.

**cohort** A group of persons of approximately the same age who have shared similar major life experiences, such as cultural training, economic conditions, or a type of education.

**conditioned stimuli** In classical conditioning, the stimuli that, after being paired a number of times with an unconditioned stimulus, come to trigger the unconditioned response.

**control group** The group of subjects in an experiment that receives either no special treatment or some neutral treatment.

**correlation** A statistic used to describe the degree or strength of a relationship between two variables. It can range from +1.00 to -1.00. The closer it is to 1.00 the stronger the relationship being described.

**critical period** A period of time during development when the organism is especially responsive to and learns from a specific type of stimulation. The same stimulation at other points in development has little or no effect.

**cross-sectional studies** Studies in which different groups of individuals of different ages are all studied at the same time.

**dependent variable** The variable in an experiment which is expected to show the impact of manipulations of the independent variable.

**ego** In Freudian theory, that portion of the personality that organizes, plans, and keeps the person in touch with reality. Language and thought are both ego functions.

**experiment** A research strategy in which subjects are assigned randomly to groups which are then provided with experiences that vary along some key dimension.

**experimental group** The group (or groups) of subjects in an experiment that is given some special treatment intended to produce some specific consequence.

**extinction** A decrease in the strength of some response after nonreinforcement.

**goodness-of-fit** A hypothesis about the interaction of nature and nurture suggesting that negative outcomes occur when the child's characteristics do not fit with the demands of a particular family or school environment.

**id** In Freudian theory, the first, primitive portion of the personality; the storehouse of basic energy, continually pushing for immediate gratification.

**independent variable** A condition or event that an experimenter varies in some systematic way in order to observe the impact of that variation on the subjects' behavior.

**intrinsic reinforcements** Those inner sources of pleasure, pride, or satisfaction that serve to increase the likelihood that an individual will repeat the behavior that led to the feeling.

**libido** The term used by Freud to describe the pool of sexual energy in each individual.

**longitudinal study** A research design in which the same subjects are observed or assessed repeatedly over a period of months or years.

**maturation** The sequential unfolding of physical characteristics, governed by instructions contained in the genetic code and shared by all members of the species.

**nature/nurture controversy** A common label for the classic dispute about the relative roles of heredity versus environment.

**negative reinforcement** The strengthening of a behavior that occurs because of the removal or cessation of an unpleasant stimulus.

**observational learning (modeling)** Learning of motor skills, attitudes, or other behaviors through observing someone else perform them.

**operant conditioning**   One of the three major types of learning in which the probability of a person performing some behavior is affected by positive or negative reinforcements.

**partial reinforcement**   Reinforcement of behavior on some schedule less frequent than every occasion.

**positive reinforcement**   Strengthening of a behavior by the presentation of some pleasurable or positive stimulus.

**punishment**   Unpleasant consequences, administered after some undesired behavior by a child or adult, with the intent of extinguishing the behavior.

**sensitive period**   Similar to a critical period except broader and less specific. A time in development when a particular type of stimulation is particularly important or effective.

**sequential designs**   A family of research designs which involve multiple cross-sectional, or multiple longitudinal, studies, or a combination of the two.

**superego**   In Freudian theory, the "conscience" part of personality, which develops as a result of the identification process. The superego contains the parental and societal values and attitudes incorporated by the child.

**teratogen**   Any outside agent, such as a disease or a chemical, whose presence significantly increases the risk of deviations or abnormalities in prenatal development.

**unconditioned responses**   In classical conditioning this is the basic unlearned response that is triggered by the unconditioned stimulus.

**unconditioned stimulus**   In classical conditioning this is the cue or signal that automatically triggers (without learning) the unconditioned response.

## SUGGESTED READINGS

Bornstein, M. H. (Ed.) (1987). *Sensitive periods in development: Interdisciplinary perspectives.* Hillsdale, NJ: Lawrence Erlbaum Associates.

Bornstein's own paper in this collection of reports is an excellent introduction to the concept of sensitive periods, but the book also contains a number of reports of research exploring potential sensitive periods both in humans and in other animals.

Seitz, V. (1988). Methodology. In M. H. Bornstein & M. E. Lamb (Eds.) *Developmental psychology: An advanced textbook* (2nd ed.). Hillsdale, NJ: Lawrence Erlbaum Associates.

Another very good source for a further exploration of various methods of research. Well organized and clearly written.

Thomas, R. M. (Ed.) (1990a). *The encyclopedia of human development and education: Theory, research, and studies.* Oxford: Pergamon Press.

This is a very useful volume. It includes brief descriptions of virtually all the theories I have described in this chapter as well as a helpful chapter on the concept of stages. Each chapter is quite brief but covers many of the critical issues.

# PROJECT 1

## Observation of a Child

I have several purposes in suggesting this project. First, many of you will have had relatively little contact with young children and need to spend some time simply observing a child to make other sections of the book more meaningful. Second, I think it is important for you to begin to get some sense of the difficulties involved in observing and studying children. Later projects involve other types of observation, but I think it is helpful to start with the least structured (but perhaps the most difficult) form, namely a narrative report in which you will attempt to write down everything a child does or says for about one hour.

- *Step 1*   Locate a child between 18 months and 6 years of age; age 2, 3, or 4 would be best.
- *Step 2*   Obtain permission from the child's parents for observation. You will need to check with your instructor to find out what the proper method for obtaining permissions may be at your institution. When you speak to the parents, be sure to tell them that the purpose of your observation is for a course assignment, that you will not be testing the child in any way but merely want to observe a normal child in a normal situation.
- *Step 3*   Arrange a time when you can observe the child in a "natural habitat" for about one hour. If the child is in nursery school, you can observe there as long as you get permission from the teachers. If you cannot observe there, the observation should be done in the home or in some situation familiar to the child. You must not babysit during the observation. You must be free to be in the background and cannot be responsible for the child during the observation.
- *Step 4*   When the time for the observation arrives, place yourself in as unobtrusive a place as possible. Take a small stool with you if you can so that you can move around as the

child moves. If you are in the child's home, she will probably ask what you are doing. Say that you are doing something for school and will be writing things down for a while. Do not invite any kind of contact with the child; don't meet her eyes; don't smile; and don't talk except when the child talks directly to you, in which case you should say that you are busy and will play a little later.

- *Step 5*   For one hour, try to write down everything the child does. Write down the child's speech word for word. If the child is talking to someone else, write down the other person's replies, too, if you can. Describe the child's movements. Throughout, keep your description as free of evaluation and words of intent as you can. Do not write "Sarah went into the kitchen to get a cookie." You don't know why she went. What you saw was that she stopped what she had been doing, got up, and walked into the kitchen. There you see her getting a cookie. Describe the behavior that way rather than making assumptions about what is happening in the child's head. Avoid words like *try, angrily, pleaded, wanted,* and the like. Describe only what you see and hear.
- *Step 6*   When you have completed the observation, reread what you wrote and consider the following questions: Did you manage to keep all description of intent out of your record? Were you able to remain objective? Since you obviously could not write down *everything* that the child did, think about what you left out. Did you find that you paid more attention to some aspects of behavior than others, such as listening to language rather than noting physical movements? What would such a bias do to the kind of information you could obtain from your narrative? Would it be possible for

you or some other rater to obtain systematic information about the child from your record, such as a measure of the child's level of activity or a score reflecting the number of times the child asked for attention? What changes in this method of observation would you have to introduce to obtain other sorts of information? What do you think was the effect on the child of your presence?

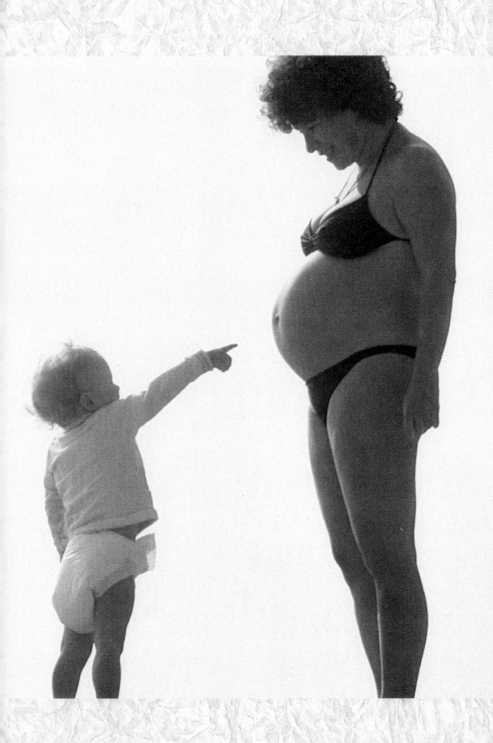

# THE BEGINNINGS OF LIFE

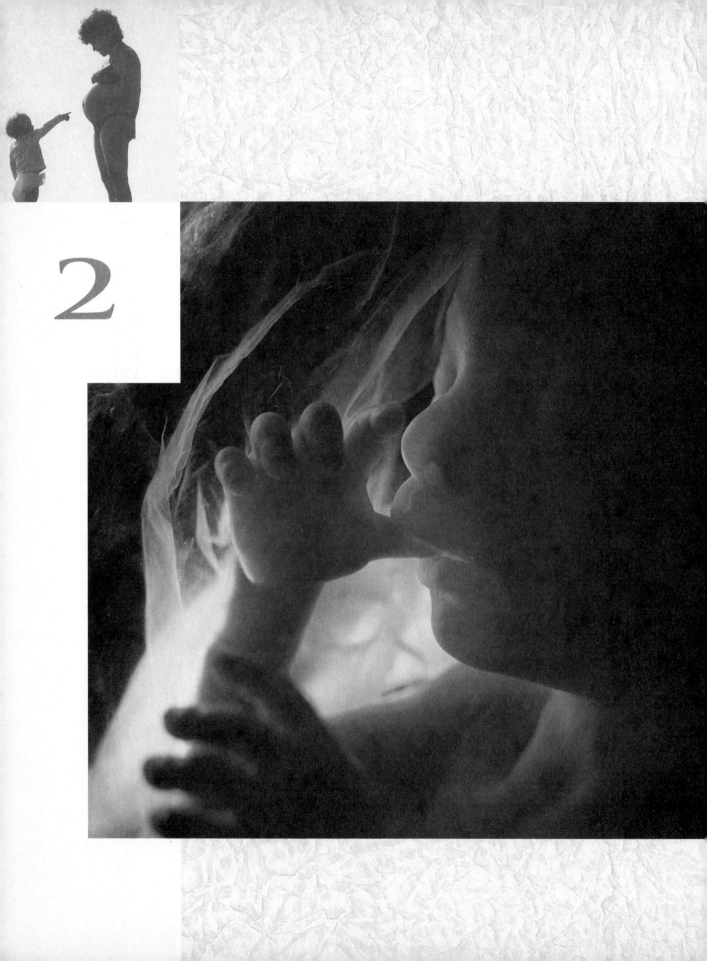

2

# PRENATAL DEVELOPMENT

everal years ago, while my large extended family was gathered for our traditional Christmas celebration, my four-months-pregnant sister-in-law Nancy complained of a headache. Having heard warnings about the possible ill effects of various kinds of drugs during pregnancy, she was reluctant to take aspirin or any other pain relief medication. We tried all the usual home remedies (shoulder rubs, warm baths, herb tea) but the headache persisted. Finally she took a non-aspirin pain medicine, which did the trick.

This incident brought home to me just how much more sensitized most women are today than they were ten or fifteen years ago to the various hazards (teratogens) during pregnancy. I was impressed by Nancy's knowledge and by her determination to avoid anything potentially harmful. I was also struck by how long the list of "don'ts" had become and by how difficult it is for a conscientious woman to be sure of what is okay and what is not. At that time I was not able to give her unequivocal information about the possible effects of aspirin. As our knowledge increases, however, we are better able to give specific advice.

In this chapter I want to explore what physicians, psychologists, and biologists have discovered about the basic processes of development from conception to birth. What does normal prenatal development look like? What are the forces that shape that development? Equally important are questions about what can influence or alter those normal patterns. How much can the mother's health practices, such as drugs or diet or exercise, help or hinder the process? Do other characteristics of the mother, such as age, level of anxiety, or general health, make a difference? These questions have great practical importance for those of you who expect to bear (or father) children in the future. They are also important basic issues as we begin the study of the developing child.

**ovum**
The gamete produced by a woman, which, if fertilized by a sperm from the male, forms the basis for the developing organism.

**fallopian tube**
The tube down which the ovum travels to the uterus and in which conception usually occurs.

**uterus**
The female organ in which the blastocyst implants itself and within which the embryo/fetus develops. (Commonly referred to as the womb.)

## Conception

The first step in the development of a single human being is the moment of conception when a single sperm cell from the male pierces the wall of the ovum of the female. That sounds so simple when it is put into one sentence, but since the sperm and the ovum both have to be in the right place at the same time, it is far more complicated than it sounds.

Ordinarily, a woman produces one **ovum** (egg cell) per month from one of her two ovaries. This occurs roughly midway between two menstrual periods. If it is not fertilized, the ovum travels from the ovary down the **fallopian tube** toward the **uterus,** where it gradually disintegrates and is expelled as part of the next menstruation.

Most parents, like these, find the nine months of a pregnancy to be a time of delighted anticipation. It is also a time in which the genetic patterning for the child (the genotype) is established, and in which complex maturational sequences unfold.

When a couple has intercourse, millions of sperm are deposited in the woman's vagina. They travel through the cervix and the uterus, and several thousand of them survive to make their way up the fallopian tubes. If there is an ovum in the fallopian tube (which typically happens only during a few days each menstrual cycle), then one of the sperm may manage to penetrate the ovum, and a child will be conceived.

Once conception has occurred, the ovum continues down the fallopian tube. Then, instead of disintegrating, it implants itself in the wall of the uterus. Figure 2.1 on the next page shows the sequence of events up to conception in schematic form; Figure 2.2 (p. 49) shows an actual photo of an ovum just after it has been fertilized.

This description may leave you with the impression that virtually all fertilized ova eventually progress through the full sequence of prenatal development. In fact, that is far from true. Experts now estimate that only about one-half to two-thirds of fertilized ova eventually result in a live baby. One current study (Wilcox et al., 1988) suggests that about one-fourth of the loss occurs within the first few days; typically these women do not even know that they are pregnant. Of those pregnancies that continue for 3–4 weeks, including implantation, perhaps one-third are subsequently spontaneously aborted—an event usually called a *miscarriage* in everyday language.

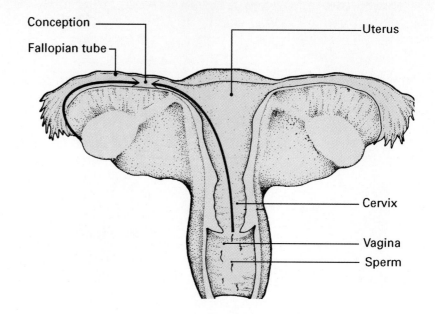

## FIGURE 2.1

This schematic diagram of the female reproductive system shows how conception occurs. The ovum has traveled from the ovary partway down the fallopian tube. There it is met by one or more sperm, which have traveled from the vagina through the cervix and the uterus.

Conception — Uterus
Fallopian tube —
Cervix
Vagina
Sperm

# The Basic Genetics of Conception

**chromosomes**
Structures in the cells in the body that contain genetic information. Each chromosome is made up of many genes.

As most of you know from biology courses, the nucleus of each cell of our bodies contains a set of 46 **chromosomes**, arranged in 23 pairs. These chromosomes include all the genetic information for that individual. They control the development of unique physical characteristics; shared growth patterns; and possibly temperament, intelligence, and other individual qualities.

Whenever a new cell is needed for growth or tissue replacement, an existing cell divides in a process called **mitosis**. Just before the division, the chromosomes are duplicated so that when the division is complete, both the old cell and the new cell have the full set of 23 pairs of chromosomes.

**mitosis**
The process of cell division common for all cells other than gametes, in which both new cells contain 23 pairs of chromosomes.

### Gametes

**gametes**
Sperm and ova. These cells, unlike all other cells of the body, contain only 23 chromosomes rather than 23 pairs.

The process differs only in the case of the sperm and the ovum, which are called **gametes** (also often called germ cells). In the early stages of development, gametes divide by mitosis, just as other cells do. But the final step, called **meiosis,** is different. In meiosis, after the chromosomes have duplicated themselves, each of the four sets of 23 chromosomes that now exist forms a new gamete. In men, all four of these gametes survive, helping to replace the millions of spermatozoa used up in a single ejaculation. In women, however, the final stages of meiosis occur only at ovulation each month, and only one of the four new gametes survives in the form of an egg cell. The remaining three disintegrate.

**meiosis**
The process of cell division that produces gametes in which only one member of each chromosome pair is passed on to the new cell.

The end result of meiosis is obviously that each gamete will have only 23 chromosomes, instead of 23 *pairs*. When a child is conceived, the 23 chromosomes in the ova and the 23 in the sperm combine to form the 23 *pairs* that will be part of each cell in the newly developing body. This process allows for

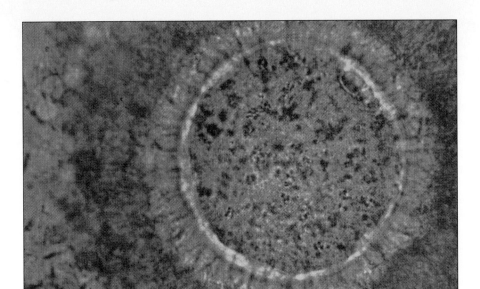

FIGURE 2.2

An ovum just after being fertilized, before the first cell division.

a vast number of possible combinations of chromosomes in the fertilized ovum —about 70 *trillion.*

This immense variability is further augmented by a process called **crossing over.** At one point in meiosis, before the cell divides, the two chromosomes that make up each pair line up directly opposite one another, and some portions of each chromosome may be exchanged from one member of the pair to the other. Only after the process of crossing over is complete does the cell divide. In this way the chromosomes themselves are altered, thus increasing still further the number of possible different combinations of chromosomes in the gametes.

**crossing over**
The process that occurs during meiosis in which genetic material from pairs of chromosomes may be exchanged.

### Genes

The 23 pairs of chromosomes are themselves made up of thousands of **genes,** which are even tinier particles. A gene controls a specific aspect of an individual characteristic or developmental process. At a still finer level, we find that the genes are composed of molecules of a chemical called **deoxyribonucleic acid** (DNA). James Watson and Francis Crick (1953) deduced that DNA is in the shape of a *double helix,* a kind of twisted ladder. The remarkable feature of this ladder is that the rungs can "unzip" and then each half can guide the duplication of the missing part. This characteristic of DNA makes it possible for the chromosomes contained in the fertilized ovum to duplicate during mitosis so that each cell in the developing embryo will then contain a full set.

Each chromosome is linear—made up of a long string of genes. A gene that controls some specific feature or developmental pattern is located in the same place in every individual of the same species, not only on the same chromosome, but in a specific spot on the chromosome (called a *locus*). The locus of the gene that determines whether you have type A, B, or O blood is on chromosome 9; the locus of the gene that determines whether the Rh factor in your blood is on chromosome 1, and so forth (Scarr & Kidd, 1983). Geneti-

**genes**
Uniquely coded segments of DNA in chromosomes that affect one or more specific body processes or developments.

**deoxyribonucleic acid**
Called DNA for short, this is the chemical of which genes are composed.

cists have made remarkable strides in recent years in mapping the loci for a great many features or characteristics—a scientific achievement that has allowed similarly giant strides in our ability to diagnose various genetic defects or inherited diseases prenatally.

Since each individual inherits *two* of each chromosome (one from the mother and one from the father), the genetic instructions at any given locus may be contradictory. For example, if you get a gene for blond hair from your mother and one for black hair from your father, or a blue-eye gene from one parent and a brown-eye gene from the other, what happens? What are the possibilities?

Sometimes the end result is some intermediate blending of the two characteristics, which seems to be what happens in the case of height: one tall parent and one short parent generally have children whose height is in between. Another, less common, possibility is that the child may express *both* characteristics. For example, type AB blood results from the inheritance of a type A gene from one parent and a type B gene from the other. Yet a third possibility is that one of the two genes is *dominant* over the other, and only the dominant gene is expressed. The "weaker" gene, called a *recessive* gene, is not expressed at all although it continues to exist and can be passed on to offspring through meiosis.

Eye color usually serves as an example of the operation of such dominant and recessive genes—although in fact geneticists have recently found that even eye color is controlled by more than one gene. For simplicity, though, let's assume there are only two eye colors, blue and brown, and that brown is dominant over blue. Table 2.1 shows the possible combinations. You can see that whenever a child inherits the dominant gene from either parent, he or she will invariably express that dominant gene, in this case brown eyes. Only if the child inherits the recessive gene from both parents will the child show the recessive characteristic, in this case blue eyes. If a child inherits one dominant and one recessive gene, the dominant gene will be expressed, but the child will carry the recessive gene as well, and will pass on that gene in half of the gametes later formed. Thus two brown-eyed parents can have a blue-eyed child if both of them carry the blue recessive.

In most cases the process is far more complex than this simple example suggests. Inheritance of most characteristics—such as intelligence, temperament, or rate of physical development—appears to be controlled not by a single gene but by many genes interacting in ways that are as yet poorly understood. Nonetheless, it is useful to understand the operation of dominant and recessive genes, if only because they play an important role in the inheritance of many diseases—as I'll describe shortly.

### Males and Females

Still greater complexity comes from the fact that there are actually two types of chromosomes. In 22 of the pairs, called **autosomes,** the members of the pair look alike and contain exactly matching genetic loci. But one pair, called the **sex chromosomes,** is unique. These two quite different-looking sex chromosomes are referred to as the X and the Y chromosomes. A normal human female has two X chromosomes on the 23rd pair (an XX pattern), while the normal human male has one X and one Y (an XY pattern). There

**autosomes**
The 22 pairs of chromosomes in which both members of the pair are the same shape and carry parallel information.

**sex chromosomes**
The X and Y chromosomes, which determine the sex of the child. In humans, XX is the female pattern, XY the male pattern.

**TABLE 2.1**

*Example of the Operation of a Single Dominant/Recessive Gene Pair*

| Parents' Genetic Pattern | | Offspring's Genetic Patterns | | |
|---|---|---|---|---|
| Mother | Father | From Mother | From Father | Eye Color |
| 1. BL BL | BL BL | BL | BL | All have blue eyes |
| 2. BR BR | BR BR | BR | BR | All have brown eyes |
| 3. BR BR | BL BL | BR | BL | All have brown eyes, but carry blue recessive |
| 4. BR BL | BR BL | BR | BR | Brown |
| | | BR | BL | Brown, with blue recessive |
| | | BL | BR | Brown, with blue recessive |
| | | BL | BL | Blue |
| 5. BR BL | BL BL | BR | BL | Brown, with blue recessive |
| | | BR | BL | Brown, with blue recessive |
| | | BL | BL | Blue |
| | | BL | BL | Blue |

are genetic loci on each sex chromosome that are not matched on the other, and the large X chromosome carries many more genes than the much smaller Y.

Two implications of this difference are particularly important and intriguing. First, you can see that the sex of the child is determined by the X or Y chromosome from the sperm. Since the mother has *only* X chromosomes, every ovum carries an X. But the father has X and Y chromosomes. When the father's gametes divide, half the sperm will carry an X, half a Y. If the sperm that fertilizes the ovum carries an X, then the child inherits an XX pattern and will be a girl. If the fertilizing sperm carries a Y, then the combination is XY, and the infant will be a boy.

Geneticists have recently pushed this understanding a step further. They have discovered that only one very small section of the Y chromosome actually determines maleness—a segment referred to as *TDF*, or *testis-determining factor* (Page et al., 1987). Fertilized ova that are genetically XY, but lack the TDF, develop physically as female.

Since the Y chromosome and its TDF can come only from the sperm, it seems clear that contrary to common historical belief the father, and not the mother, determines the sex of the child. But even that is too simple a statement for this splendidly complicated process. It turns out that the mother really does have an effect, since the relative acidity or alkalinity of the mucus in the vagina affects the survival rate of X-carrying or Y-carrying sperm. This chemical balance varies from one woman to the next, and in all women over the course of their monthly cycle. So the timing of intercourse, or a woman's typical chemical balance, can sharply alter the probability of conceiving a child of a particular gender, even though it is still true that the X or Y in the sperm is the final determining factor.

A second important consequence of the difference between X and Y chromosomes is that because the X chromosome contains more genetic material than the Y, a boy inherits many genes from his mother on his X chromosome that are not matched by, or counteracted by, equivalent genetic material on the Y chromosome. Since the X chromosome contains the loci for genes that, when abnormal, cause specific diseases, such as hemophilia and muscular dystrophy, a boy may inherit these if his mother carries the (recessive) gene for the disease, since there is no equivalent gene from the Y chromosome to counteract the effect. A girl, in contrast, could not inherit such a disease unless she received the gene signaling that disease on both of her X chromosomes, one from her mother and one from her father. Such *sex-linked* inheritance patterns occur for other characteristics besides diseases. Furthermore, the difference in the amount of genetic material in the X and Y chromosome may help to account for the greater general physical vulnerability of males—a point I will be returning to later.

### Twins and Siblings

Given what I have said so far, I am sure it is clear to you why brothers and sisters are not exactly like one another. Each has inherited a unique combination of genes from mother and father.

The exception to this rule is in the case of identical twins, who come from the *same* fertilized ovum. In such cases the ovum divides into two distinct identities *after* it has been fertilized by the sperm. Each of the two developing organisms has the same genetic material in the same combination, and the two children should turn out to be alike in all those areas affected by heredity.

Fraternal twins, on the other hand, develop out of separately fertilized ova. This can happen if the woman ovulates more than once in a given month (fairly common in women taking fertility drugs). Because two separate combinations of chromosomes are involved, fraternal twins don't even need to be of the same sex while identical twins are always same-sex pairs.

### Genotypes and Phenotypes

With all the emphasis on genes as causes of physical patterns, disease, or other characteristics, I may have given you a false impression about the unchangeability of genetic effects. In fact, no geneticist today would assert that the inherited combination of genes *determines* the outcome for any given individual. Geneticists (and psychologists) make an important distinction between the **genotype,** which is the specific set of "instructions" contained in a given individual's genes, and the **phenotype,** which is the actual observed characteristics of the individual. The phenotype is a product of three things: the genotype, all the environmental influences from the time of conception onward, and the interaction between the environment and the genotype.

Let me give you an example. A well-known disorder called phenylketonuria (PKU) is caused by a defective gene that prevents normal processing of a particular amino acid (phenylalanine). Toxins accumulate that damage the central nervous system and cause quite severe mental retardation. This disease is clearly inherited; geneticists have even located the specific gene involved. An individual who inherits that gene from both parents "has" the disease. However, the worst effects of the disease can be prevented by initially

**genotype**
The pattern of characteristics and developmental sequences mapped in the genes of any specific individual. Will be modified by individual experience into the phenotype.

**phenotype**
The expression of a particular set of genetic information in a specific environment; the observable result of the joint operation of genetic and environmental influences.

Identical twins, like the ones in the upper photo, come from the same fertilized ovum and have exactly the same heredity. They look alike and frequently act alike, too. Fraternal twins, like the ones in the lower photo, come from two separately fertilized ova and are no more like each other than are any other pair of brothers or sisters.

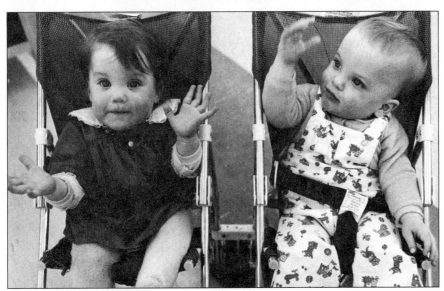

identifying PKU from an infant's blood test and then placing the child on a diet with low levels of phenylalanine. There is a critical period involved here; unless treatment begins in the first few months of life, retardation is permanent. Those who are treated early show normal or only slightly subnormal IQs. Thus while such a child still *has* the disease in the sense that the genotype still contains the defective gene, the disease is not *expressed* in the phenotype.

This distinction between the genotype and the phenotype is important. Genetic codes are not irrevocable signals for this or that pattern of development, or this or that disease. They are all affected by the specific experiences the individual may have from conception onward.

# Development from Conception to Birth

The period of gestation for the human infant is usually stated as 280 days, or 40 weeks, counting from the first day of the last menstrual period. But since actual conception normally takes place about 2 weeks after the last menstrual period the actual length of gestation from conception to delivery is about 265 days, or 38 weeks. In the discussion that follows, I will be counting from the presumed time of conception, rather than from the final menstrual period.

These 38 weeks have been subdivided in several different ways. Physicians typically talk in terms of three equal periods, called *trimesters*, of roughly three months each. Biologists and embryologists also typically divide the weeks of gestation into three sub-periods: the germinal, the embryonic, and the fetal. Unlike the trimesters, these stages are of unequal length and are linked to specific changes within the developing organism.

### The Germinal Stage: From Conception to Implantation

**zygote**
Term used to describe the developing organism from conception until implantation is complete.

This first stage lasts roughly two weeks, from the moment of conception until implantation in the wall of the uterus is complete. The term **zygote** is used to refer to the organism throughout this period, although there are additional terms used for various subperiods. You can see the various developments of this period in Figure 2.3.

Sometime during the first 24 to 36 hours after conception, mitosis begins. The DNA ladders making up the chromosomes "unzip" so that each chromosome can duplicate. Then the single cell splits in two. The two new cells each contain a set of the full 23 pairs of chromosomes. The process continues, and within two to three days there are several dozen cells with the whole mass about the size of a pinhead.

**blastocyst**
The name used for the small mass of cells, about two weeks after conception, that implants itself into the wall of the uterus.

In the early stages, the mass of cells is undifferentiated. However, about four days after conception some differentiation begins, at which point the organism is called a **blastocyst.** At this point a cavity appears within the ball of cells, and the mass divides into two parts. The outer cells will form the placen-

**FIGURE 2.3**

This schematic shows the normal progression of development for the first 10 days of gestation, from conception to implantation (*Source:* Smith & Stenchever, 1978, p. 43).

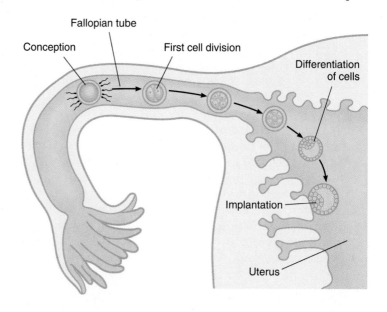

ta, the amniotic sac, the amniotic fluid, and the other related structures that will support the developing organism, while the inner mass will form the embryo. When it touches the wall of the uterus, the outer shell of cells in the blastocyst breaks down at the point of contact. Small tendrils develop and attach the cell mass to the uterine wall, a process called *implantation*. When implantation occurs, normally 10 days to 2 weeks after conception, there are perhaps 150 cells in the blastocyst (Tanner, 1978).

## The Embryonic Stage

The second major phase of prenatal development begins with completion of implantation, and continues for another six weeks until the various support structures are fully formed and all the major organ systems have been laid down in at least rudimentary form.

*Development of Support Structures.* Three main support structures develop out of the outer layer of cells. The *amnion*, which is the sac or bag, fills with liquid (amniotic fluid) in which the baby floats; the **placenta,** a plate-like mass of cells that lies against the wall of the uterus and serves as liver, lungs, and kidneys for the embryo and fetus. The placenta is fully developed by about four weeks after conception, and makes up perhaps one-fifth of the uterine volume.

The embryo's circulatory system is connected to the placenta through the *umbilical cord*. The placenta is connected to both the mother's and the embryo's (fetus's) blood systems, but the two systems are not directly connected. Small molecules pass back and forth through this large filtering system, but large ones cannot. So nutrients such as oxygen, proteins, sugars, and vitamins from the maternal blood pass through to the **embryo** or **fetus,** while digestive wastes and carbon dioxide from the infant's blood pass back through to the mother, whose own body can eliminate them (Rosenblith & Sims-Knight, 1989). At the same time, many (but not all) harmful substances, such as viruses, are too large to pass through the various placental membranes and are filtered out, as are most of the mother's hormones. Most drugs and anesthetics, however, do pass through the placental barrier (Smith, 1978), as do some disease organisms—as we'll see in more detail shortly. You can see all of these separate organs in Figure 2.4 on the next page.

*Development of the Embryo.* At the same time, the mass of cells that will form the embryo is also differentiating further into three types or layers of cells: the *ectodermal* cells, which will become the skin, sense receptors, and nerve cells; *mesodermal* cells, which eventually form the muscles, connective tissue, and circulatory system; and *endodermal* cells, which form many of the internal organs. Differentiation of all three types of cells occurs swiftly during the embryonic period, so that by the end of this stage every organ system, including sense organs, is present in at least rudimentary form. By eight weeks gestation, the embryo is roughly 1 1/2 inches long, has a heart that beats, a primitive circulatory system, the beginnings of eyes and ears, a mouth that opens and closes, legs, arms, and a primitive spinal cord. When this "organogenesis" is complete, a new stage, that of the fetus, begins.

placenta
An organ that develops during gestation between the fetus and the wall of the uterus. The placenta filters nutrients from the mother's blood, acting as liver, lungs, and kidneys for the fetus.

embryo
The name given to the organism during the period of prenatal development from about two to eight weeks after conception, beginning with implantation of the blastocyst into the uterine wall.

fetus
The name given to the developing organism from about eight weeks after conception until birth.

**FIGURE 2.4**

You can see here how the various structures are organized during the fetal period. Note especially the placenta and the umbilical cord, and the fact that the fetus floats in the amniotic fluid.

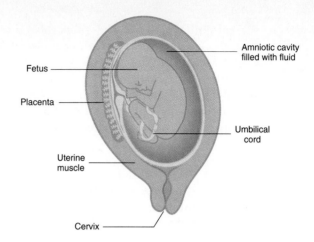

Amniotic cavity filled with fluid

Fetus

Placenta

Umbilical cord

Uterine muscle

Cervix

## The Fetal Stage

The seven months of the fetal stage involve primarily a process of refining all the primitive organ systems already in place. It's a bit like the process of building a house. You first construct the floor and then the framework for the walls and roof. The plumber and the electrician do their work early, too, while the framework is still open. This skeleton of the house has its full and final shape; you can see where the windows and doors will go, what the shape of the rooms will be, and how the roof will look. This stage is reached quickly, but after that there is a long process of filling in around the skeleton. The embryo and the fetus develop much the same way. At the end of the embryonic period, the main parts exist in some basic form; the next seven months are for the finishing process. Table 2.2 lists some of the milestones of fetal development; you can see the changes even more vividly in the series of photos in Figure 2.5 on p. 58.

Analogies like this can be very useful, but I want to be careful about pushing this particular one too far. When you build a house the full final size is present as soon as the framing is completed; and when the electrician is finished, all the wiring for the final house is in place. Neither of these things is true at the end of the embryonic period.

*Development of the Nervous System.*   To understand the development of the nervous system you'll need a few more technical terms. The nervous system is composed of two basic types of cells, neurons and glial cells. The **glial cells** are the glue that holds the whole system together, providing firmness and structure to the brain, helping to remove debris after neuronal death or injury, and segregating neurons from one another (Kandel, 1985). **Neurons** receive and send messages from one part of the brain to another, or from one part of the body to another.

Neurons have four main parts, which you can see in the drawing in Figure 2.6 on p. 59: (1) A cell body, (2) branch-like extensions of the cell body called **dendrites,** which are the major *receptors* of nerve impulses; (3) a tubular extension of the cell body called the **axon,** which can extend as far as 1 meter in length in humans (about 3 feet); and (4) branch-like terminal fibers at the end of the axon, which form the primary *transmitting* apparatus of the nervous system. Because of the branch-like appearance of dendrites, physiologists

**glial cells**
One of two major classes of cells making up the nervous system, glial cells provide the firmness and structure, the "glue" to hold the system together.

**neurons**
The second major class of cells in the nervous system, neurons are responsible for transmission and reception of nerve impulses.

**dendrites**
The branch-like parts of a neuron that serve as the receptors in synaptic connections with the axons of other neurons.

**axon**
The long appendage-like part of a neuron; the terminal fibers of the axon serve as transmitters in the synaptic connection with the dendrites of other neurons.

**TABLE 2.2**

*Milestones of Fetal Development*

| Gestational Age | Major Developments |
|---|---|
| 12 weeks | Sex of child can be determined; muscles are developed more extensively; eyelids and lips are present; feet have toes and hands have fingers. |
| 16 weeks | First fetal movement is usually felt by the mother at about this time; bones begin to develop; fairly complete ear is formed. |
| 20 weeks | Hair growth begins; child is very human-looking at this age and "thumbsucking" may be seen. |
| 24 weeks | Eyes are completely formed (but closed); fingernails, sweat glands, and taste buds are all formed; some fat deposit beneath skin. The infant is capable of breathing if born prematurely at this stage but survival rate is still low for infants born this early. |
| 28 weeks | Nervous system, blood, and breathing systems are all well enough developed to support life; prematures born at this stage have poor sleep/wake cycles and irregular breathing, however. |
| 29–40 weeks | Interconnections between individual nerve cells (neurons) develop rapidly; weight is added; general "finishing" of body systems takes place. |

describe these structures in a language intriguingly reminiscent of botany, speaking of the "dendritic arbor" or of "pruning" of the arbor.

The point at which two neurons connect, where the axon's transmitting fibers come into close contact with another neuron's dendrites, is called a **synapse.** Synapses can also be formed between neurons and other kinds of cells, such as muscle cells. The number of such synapses is vast. A single cell in the part of the brain that controls vision, for instance, may have as many as 10,000 to 30,000 synaptic inputs to its dendrites (Greenough, Black, & Wallace, 1987).

Glial cells begin to develop about 13 weeks after conception and continue to multiply for two years following birth. Neurons begin to appear at about 12 weeks gestation, and are virtually all present by 28 weeks. At this early stage, however, the neurons consist largely of the cell body. Axons are short and show little dendritic development. It is in the last two months before birth and the first few years after birth that the axons lengthen and the "dendritic arbor" grows rapidly, which creates the vast numbers of synapses necessary for all aspects of human functioning (Parmelee & Sigman, 1983).

*Development of Length and Weight.* The major growth in fetal size also occurs late in the fetal period, with the gain in length occurring earlier than the major gain in weight. The fetus is about half her birth length by about 20 weeks gestation, but does not reach half her birth weight until nearly 3 months later, at about 32 weeks.

**synapse**
The point of communication between the axon of one neuron and the dendrites of another, where nerve impulses are passed from one neuron to another, or from a neuron to some other type of cell, such as a muscle cell.

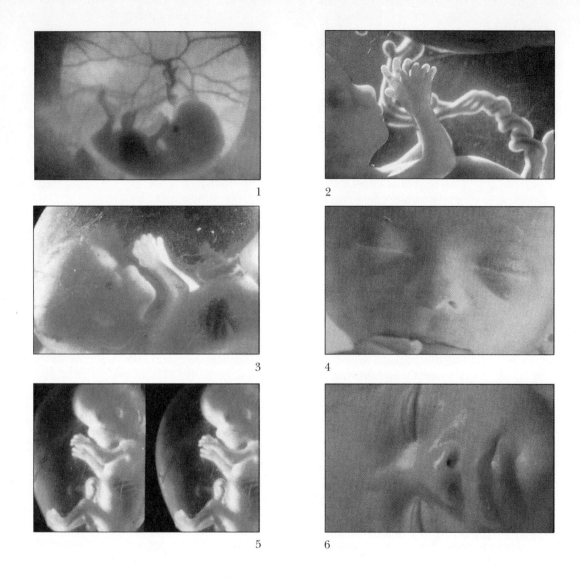

This sequence of photos shows the changes in the fetal period much more graphically. Photo 1 shows a fetus at 9–10 weeks; Photo 2 a fetus 14–16 weeks. Fingers and toes are clearly present, as are many facial features. In the middle of the fetal period changes are gradual. Photo 3 is of a fetus at about 16–18 weeks; photo 4 was taken only slightly later, at perhaps 18–20 weeks, and photo 5 was taken at about 22 weeks. Infants as small as the one shown in photo 5 are now sometimes saved if born prematurely, although the rate of survival is extremely low. Photo 6 shows a fetus at about 32 weeks gestation, an age at which most infants now survive if born prematurely, although lungs and nervous system are still quite immature at this stage.

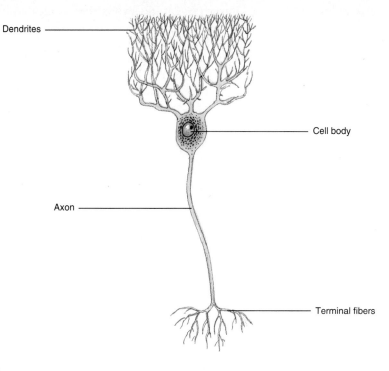

Dendrites

Cell body

Axon

Terminal fibers

**FIGURE 2.6**

The structure of a single developed neuron. The cell bodies are the first to be developed, primarily during the second trimester of prenatal development. Axons and dendrites develop later and continue to increase in size and complexity for several years after birth.

 ## Prenatal Sexual Differentiation

Earlier in the chapter, I said that the child's sex is determined at the moment of conception by the XX or XY combination of chromosomes. You'd think that was the end of the story, but it is not. As I pointed out in the discussion of genotypes and phenotypes, the basic genetic patterning does not *guarantee* a particular outcome. In this case it does not guarantee that the newborn infant will have the appropriate sexual characteristics, or that he or she will have the behaviors and sexual preferences typical for his or her genetic pattern.

Prenatal gender differentiation is also significantly influenced by the actions of a series of hormones (Hines, 1982). Simplifying a bit, for the development of a male child, both the genetic programming (XY) *and* a particular pattern of hormone action are required for normal gender development. Sometime between 4 and 8 weeks after conception, the male hormone *testosterone* begins to be secreted by the rudimentary testes in the male embryo. If this hormone is not secreted or is secreted in inadequate amounts, the embryo will be "demasculinized" (Money, 1987), even to the extent of developing female genitalia. Normal development of a girl does not require any additional hormonal input, but the accidental presence of testosterone (because of heightened levels in the mother, for example, perhaps from some drug she has taken) at the critical time acts to "defeminize" or masculinize the female fetus, possibly resulting in male-like genitalia.

Even more interesting is the recent evidence, particularly from studies of other animals, that suggests such prenatal hormones affect not just the development of genitalia but also the pattern of brain development (Hines, 1982; Meyer-Bahlburg, Ehrhardt, & Feldman, 1986), influencing such functions as the pattern of growth-hormone secretions in adolescence and the relative dominance of the right and left hemispheres of the brain. Most speculatively, John Money (1987) has suggested that the sexual orientation of the developing child and adolescent may also be partially influenced by the prenatal hormonal environment. In lower species, prenatal hormones appear to permanently affect later male or female sexual behavior. In humans, prenatal hormones are only part of the picture; the child's experiences in the early years of life are also critical influences. However, growing evidence suggests that the pattern of prenatal hormones may help to create a propensity toward heterosexual, bisexual, or homosexual orientations at later ages (Money, 1987).

## Explanations of the Normal Sequence of Development

One of the most important points about the child's prenatal development is how remarkably regular and predictable it is. If the embryo has survived the early, risky period, development usually proceeds smoothly, with the various changes occurring in a fixed order, at fixed time intervals. To be sure, things can go wrong. But in perhaps 90 percent of recognized pregnancies the entire process occurs in a predictable, fixed pattern.

We don't have to look far for an explanation. Whenever there is that much regularity in a fixed sequence, maturation seems the obvious answer. The fetus doesn't learn to grow fingernails and it doesn't have to be stimulated from the outside to grow them. The fingernails, along with all the other parts of the complex system, are controlled by the developmental codes contained in the genes. This sequence of development is not immune to modification or outside influence. Indeed, as psychologists and biologists have looked more carefully at various kinds of teratogens, it has become clear that the sequence is more vulnerable than had earlier appeared. Still, it takes a fairly sizable intervention to make a large difference in the outcome.

A second important point is that the effect of any teratogen depends heavily on the *timing* of the intervention or interference (Vorhees & Mollnow, 1987)—an example of *critical periods*, or *sensitive periods*, as I described in Chapter 1. The general rule is that each organ system—the nervous system, heart, ears, reproductive system, and so on—is most vulnerable to disruption at the time when it is developing most rapidly (Kopp & Parmelee, 1979). At that point the system is maximally sensitive to outside interference, whether from a disease organism that passed through the placental barrier or from inappropriate hormones or drugs or whatever. Since the most rapid development of most organ systems occurs during the first 12 weeks of gestation, this period holds the greatest risk. Figure 2.7 on p. 62 shows the maximum times of vulnerability for different parts of the body.

Before discussing the things that can go wrong, I want to reemphasize that the maturational system is really quite robust. Normal prenatal development requires an adequate environment, but "adequate" seems to be a fairly broad range. *Most* fetuses are quite normal. The list of things that *can* go wrong is long (and getting longer as our knowledge expands), but many of these possibilities are quite rare. More important, a very great number of them are partially or wholly preventable, and many of the remaining problems need not have permanent consequences for the child. As I go along, I will try to point out the preventive actions that are possible in each instance. I'll return to the question of long-term consequences of prenatal difficulties at the end of the chapter.

## Genetic Errors

The first point at which something can go wrong is in the genetic material itself. Either the chromosomes can divide improperly during meiosis, or a gene that causes a specific disease or physical problem can be passed on to the child.

### Chromosomal Problems

Chromosomal anomalies can take the form either of too many chromosomes or too few. The creation of gametes by meiosis actually involves two chromosomal divisions in sequence. At either point, any one chromosome may fail to divide properly, so a very large number of deviant patterns is possible. Gametes with too few chromosomes usually fail to survive, but many gametes with too many chromosomes do survive. Such anomalies in chromosome number appear to occur in 3–8 percent of all fertilized ova (Kopp, 1983), but as many as 90 percent of these abnormal conceptuses are spontaneously aborted. Only about 1 percent of live newborns have such abnormalities.

Over 50 different types of chromosomal anomalies have been identified, many of them very rare. The most common is **Down syndrome** (also called *mongolism* and *trisomy 21*), which occurs in approximately 1 out of every 600 or 700 live births (Cicchetti & Beeghly, 1990). Down syndrome is caused when the two copies of chromosome 21 fail to separate during meiosis. When the gamete (either ovum or sperm) with the extra copy of chromosome 21 combines with a normal gamete at conception, the fertilized egg contains three instead of two copies of chromosome 21 (hence the label *trisomy 21*). Children with Down syndrome have distinctive facial features (as you can see in Figure 2.8 on p. 63) and are typically retarded. They often have congenital heart or intestinal deformities and have a considerably higher than normal risk of developing leukemia. Using these patterns of deformities as clues, geneticists have been able to identify the loci of genes affecting these various disorders on chromosome 21.

The risk of bearing a child with this deviant pattern is greatest for mothers over 35 (although there is also a heightened risk for teenage mothers). Among women 35–39, the incidence of Down syndrome is about one in 280 births; among those over 45 it is as high as 1 in 50 births (Kopp, 1983; Mikkelsen & Stone, 1970).

*The Father's Role in Chromosomal Anomalies.* Until quite recently, most physicians and physiologists assumed that the source of such chromo-

**Down syndrome**
A genetic anomaly in which every cell contains three copies of chromosome 21 rather than two. Children born with this genetic pattern are usually mentally retarded and have characteristic physical features.

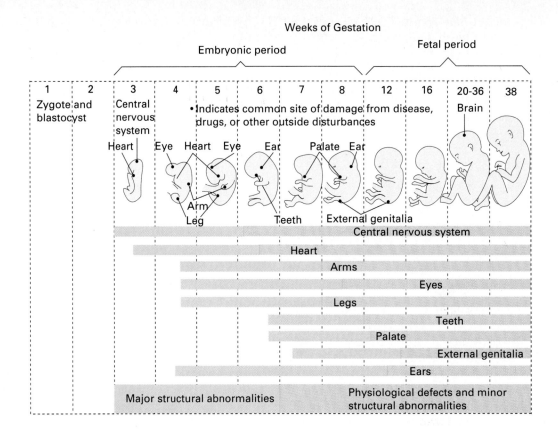

Weeks of Gestation

Embryonic period

Fetal period

| 1 | 2 | 3 | 4 | 5 | 6 | 7 | 8 | 12 | 16 | 20-36 | 38 |

Zygote and blastocyst

Central nervous system

•Indicates common site of damage from disease, drugs, or other outside disturbances

Brain

Heart    Eye    Heart    Eye    Ear    Palate    Ear

Arm
Leg    Teeth    External genitalia

Central nervous system

Heart

Arms

Eyes

Legs

Teeth

Palate

External genitalia

Ears

Major structural abnormalities

Physiological defects and minor structural abnormalities

**FIGURE 2.7**

The figure shows some critical periods in the prenatal development of various body parts. The red portion of each line signifies the period during which any teratogen (drugs, disease in the mother, chemicals in the environment, or the like) is likely to produce a major structural deformity in that particular body part. The gray part of each line shows the period in which more minor problems may result. You can see that the embryonic period is generally the time of greatest vulnerability (*Source:* Moore, 1988, Figure 8-14, page 136; Moore, 1988).

somal anomalies was in the ovum. Recent research, however, is revealing what should (perhaps) have been obvious from the beginning: The anomalies can as readily be caused by some problem with meiosis in the father. We know, for example, that in about one-third of the cases of Down syndrome, the improper cell division occurs in the sperm and not the ovum (Magenis, 1977). More interesting is current work linking fathers' exposure to environmental toxins of various kinds to the risk of chromosomal anomalies or other birth defects in offspring. In particular, men who are regularly exposed to certain chemicals—such as solvents, oils, lead, and pesticides used by farmers, mechanics, or sawmill workers—are at higher risk for fathering Down syndrome children than are men who work in cleaner environments (e.g., Olshan, Baird, & Teschke, 1989). This new body of research not only begins to explore the im-

FIGURE 2.8

Note the distinctive eye characteristics and the flattened face of this Down syndrome girl.

portant connections between environmental exposures and chromosomal anomalies, it helps to redress the imbalance of blame for anomalies or defects which has been borne by mothers.

*Sex Chromosome Anomalies.*    Other types of genetic anomalies are caused by an incomplete or incorrect division of the sex chromosome, which also may occur in either mother or father. Such sex chromosomal anomalies occur in roughly 1 in 400 births (Berch & Bender, 1987). Perhaps the most common is an XXY pattern, called Klinefelter's syndrome, which may occur as often as once in 500 births. This pattern results in boys who often have very long legs, poor coordination, poorly developed testes, sterility, and sometimes mild mental retardation. Not quite as common is the XYY pattern. These children also develop as boys, are typically unusually tall, with mild retardation. A single-X pattern (XO) called Turner's syndrome, and a triple-X pattern (XXX) may also occur, and in both cases the child develops as a girl. Girls with Turner's syndrome are among the infrequent examples of embryos who survive with too few chromosomes. These girls show stunted growth, are usually sterile, and are often particularly poor on tests that measure spatial ability. On tests of verbal skill, however, Turner's syndrome girls are at or above normal levels (Scarr & Kidd, 1983). Girls with an XXX pattern are of normal size but are slower than normal in physical development. They also have markedly poor verbal abilities (Rovet & Netley, 1983).

Overall, children with sex chromosome anomalies are not typically as severely affected as what we see in Down syndrome, but there are nonetheless measurable consequences.

*Fragile X Syndrome.*   A quite different type of genetic anomaly that recently has received a good deal of attention involves not an improper amount of chromosomal material, but a weakness or fragility in an X chromosome. Both boys and girls may have a fragile X, but boys, lacking the potentially overriding influence of a normal X, are much more susceptible to the negative intellectual or behavioral consequences. The affected child appears to have a considerably heightened risk of mental retardation. Experts currently estimate that 5–7 percent of all retardation among males is caused by this syndrome (Zigler & Hodapp, 1991).

## Single Gene Defects

A second type of genetic problem can occur if a child inherits a gene for a specific disease. When the gene is dominant, the disease occurs if the child inherits the gene from *either* parent. (In such instances, of course, the parent who passes along the problem *also* has the same disorder.) A particularly distressing example of this type is Huntington's disease; symptoms do not appear until midlife, and the victim then suffers a rapid loss of both mental and physical functioning.

Fortunately, dominant-gene defects, although varied, are not all that common, in part because many people who inherit serious dominant gene defects do not have children and so do not pass the problem to the next generation. Thus over time these genes disappear from the gene pool. Huntington's disease has been an exception to this general rule, precisely because the symptoms appear so late, after the childbearing years are largely completed.

The situation is quite different for *recessive-gene* diseases like PKU or cystic fibrosis, which are remarkably numerous. Geneticists estimate that the average adult carries genes for four different recessive diseases or abnormalities (e.g., Scarr & Kidd, 1983). But since these are recessive gene disorders, the inheritance pattern is like the example for blue eyes I gave in Table 2.1. Like a brown-eyed person with a blue-eyed recessive gene, a normal, healthy person normally does not even know that he carries these recessive disease genes. Only if both parents in any given pair carry the same recessive gene will they have a child with the particular disorder and then only one-fourth of their children (on average) will inherit the disease itself—just as two brown-eyed parents can have a blue-eyed child only if they both have blue recessive genes.

When a recessive gene signaling some disease is carried on the X chromosome—a pattern referred to as *sex-linked*—the risks are somewhat different, as I explained earlier. In this case, a girl will have the disease only if she inherits the gene from both parents, but a boy will show the disease if he inherits the gene only from his mother.

Table 2.3 lists a few of the better known recessive gene diseases, but such a brief list cannot convey the diversity of such disorders. For example, among known causes of mental retardation, there are 73 diseases or disorders with known genetic loci on the X chromosome, another 69 located on other chromosomes, and 361 more whose locus has not yet been identified (Wahlstrom, 1990).

**TABLE 2.3**

*Some Major Inherited Diseases*

| | |
|---|---|
| Phenylketonuria | A metabolic disorder that prevents metabolism of a common amino acid (phenylalanine). Treatment consists of a special phenylalanine-free diet. The child is not allowed many types of food, including milk. If not placed on the special diet shortly after birth, the child usually becomes very retarded (IQs of 30 and below are not uncommon). Affects only 1 in 8000 children. Diagnostic tests for this disorder are now routinely given at birth; cannot be diagnosed prenatally. |
| Tay-Sachs disease | An invariably fatal degenerative disease of the nervous system; virtually all victims die within the first 3–4 years. This gene is most common among Jews of eastern European origin, among whom it occurs in approximately one in 3500 births. Can be diagnosed prenatally. |
| Sickle-cell anemia | A sometimes fatal blood disease, with joint pain, increased susceptibility to infection, and other symptoms. The gene for this disease is carried by about 2 million Americans, most often blacks. Can now be diagnosed prenatally. |
| Cystic fibrosis | A fatal disease affecting the lungs and intestinal tract. Many children with CF now live into their twenties. The gene is carried by over 10 million Americans, most often whites. Carriers cannot be identified before pregnancy, and affected children cannot be diagnosed prenatally. If a couple has had one CF child, however, they know that their chances of having another are one in four. |
| Muscular dystrophy | A fatal muscle-wasting disease, carried on the X chromosome, found almost exclusively among boys. The gene for the most common type of MD, Duchenne's, has just been located, so prenatal diagnosis may soon be available. |

### Diagnosing Chromosomal Anomalies and Single Gene Defects

Because of the enormous recent advances in genetic research, it is now possible to diagnose many of these anomalies and diseases very early in a pregnancy. Such early diagnosis has made it possible to reduce the number of children born with crippling problems, but the new technology also forces couples—and the rest of society—to deal with a wide range of extremely difficult personal and moral issues, some of which I have discussed on pages 66–67.

## Environmental Influences: Disease, Drugs, and Diet

So far I have discussed only the genetically caused deviations from normal development that begin at the moment of conception. However, the environment in which the embryo fetus grows for the rest of prenatal life also has an impact. The list of teratogens is long, but the critical ones can be classified as the "three Ds": disease, drugs, and diet.

### Diseases of the Mother

Although many diseases the mother may contract do not affect the fetus because the disease organisms cannot pass through the placental barrier,

## Genetic Counseling: Better Information Brings Difficult Decisions

Not too long ago, when a child was conceived, that child was born with whatever good or bad qualities happened to come along. The parents had no choices. That is no longer true. New scientific advances now give parents many options, some of which may require extremely difficult decisions. There are basically two sources of information: prepregnancy genetic testing of the parents and several forms of tests available during pregnancy to diagnose abnormalities in the fetus directly.

### Prepregnancy Genetic Testing

Before conceiving, you and your spouse could have blood tests done that will tell you whether you are carriers of genes for those specific diseases for which the loci are known, such as Tay-Sachs, sickle cell anemia, or Huntington's disease. This is a fairly expensive process, and is not normally indicated unless there is some known genetic disorder in one or both families, or if one or both partners come from an ethnic group known to have high rates of carriers of some recessive-gene disorder.

Such advance testing is no cure-all. The locations of genes for all genetic diseases have not yet been identified, so carriers of many diseases (such as cystic fibrosis) cannot yet be identified in this way. Geneticists, however discover the locations of additional diseases yearly. The locus of the gene for Duchenne's muscular dystrophy, for example, was recently identified (Kunkel et al., 1986).

For an individual couple the ethical dilemmas involved in prepregnancy testing may be less agonizing than with prenatal diagnosis, but the decisions can nonetheless be extremely difficult. Suppose that you discover that both you and your spouse carry recessive genes for some disease, such as Tay-Sachs. You could decide not to have any children at all or to adopt children. Or you could count on the fact that you have a three out of four probability of having a normal child and take a

chance (since the child would have a recessive-gene disease only if he received the gene from both parents, and that would happen, on average, only 25 percent of the time). Or you could conceive and then use any one of several new techniques for diagnosing disease or abnormality prenatally. If such techniques revealed a problem, you could choose to abort the fetus. The options are clear, but the choices are immensely difficult.

### Prenatal Diagnosis of the Fetus

Several prenatal diagnostic strategies are now available. Probably the most commonly used is *ultrasound*, which involves the use of sound waves to provide an actual "moving picture" of the fetus. Some kinds of spinal cord abnormalities can be diagnosed with ultrasound, as can other major physical defects. The procedure is not painful, and gives parents an often delightful chance to see their unborn child moving, but it cannot provide information about the presence of chromosomal anomalies or inherited diseases.

Such information can be obtained from either of two tests that involve taking samples of cells from the developing embryo. In **chorionic villus sampling** (CVS) a needle is inserted and cells are taken from what will become the placenta. In **amniocentesis,** the sample is from the amniotic fluid.

Both CVS and amniocentesis will provide information about any of the chromosomal anomalies, and about the presence of genes for many of the major genetic diseases. Amniocentesis was developed earlier and is the more widely used of the two. Its major drawback is that, because the amniotic sac must be large enough to allow a sample of fluid to be taken with very little danger to the fetus, the test cannot be done until the sixteenth week of gestation and the results are not typically available for several more weeks. If the test reveals an abnormality, and the parents decide to abort, it is quite late for an abortion to be

**chorionic villus sampling**
A technique for prenatal genetic diagnosis involving taking a sample of cells from the placenta. Can be performed earlier in the pregnancy than amniocentesis.

**amniocentesis**
A medical test for genetic abnormalities in the embryo/fetus that may be done at about 15 weeks of gestation.

performed. CVS, in contrast, is done between the ninth and eleventh weeks of gestation. The major drawback is that CVS is riskier than amniocentesis. In 3–5% of cases, CVS causes a miscarriage; the equivalent risk for amniocentesis is about .5%.

It will not be long before the range of choices for prenatal diagnosis will be far greater than it is even now. New methods for prenatal diagnosis based only on analysis of maternal blood are in the experimental stage. For example, some chromosomal anomalies, including Down syndrome, can be detected with a blood test called an *alphafetoprotein* (AFP) test (e.g., Wald et al., 1988). At the moment this diagnostic technique has a very high rate of false positives, and is best used as a preliminary screen. But more sophisticated uses of blood tests are bound to come. As just one example: Y. D. Lo and his colleagues (1989) have been able to predict the sex of the fetus from blood tests in a small sample of cases. There seems little doubt that procedures that will allow very early diagnosis will be developed and become widely available within the next decade or two.

## Choices and Dilemmas

The very existence of such techniques for prenatal diagnosis creates a whole nest of remarkably complex personal and societal ethical decisions. Suppose you have used one of these diagnostic techniques, and an abnormality or chromosomal anomaly or recessive-gene disease is revealed. What do you do? Are you prepared to abort? Many people have very strong moral feelings about abortion. Others have equally strong feelings about the morality of bringing handicapped individuals into the world, especially those who require long-term care.

Even setting aside the moral dilemma of abortion, the choices are often enormously difficult. In one case, some friends of mine had an amniocentesis done that showed a chromosomal anomaly, but it was a type so rare that the physicians could

not provide any information about likely abnormalities. What choice would you make?

Or what about the case of diseases that can occur in mild or moderate as well as severe forms—such as sickle-cell anemia. Prenatal tests can tell you if the child will inherit the disease, but they cannot tell you how severely the child will be affected. John Lauerman (1990) comments on this particular dilemma:

> If a fetus tests positive for sickle cell disease, does that mean it is irresponsible to allow the pregnancy to go to term? Many laboratories across the world . . . are seeking and developing therapies for sickle cell disease that can make the patient's life more comfortable than in the past. The severity of sickle cell disease is highly variable. Are parents self-serving if they decide not to take on the responsibility of a child that may be either almost completely healthy or close to morbid? (Lauerman, 1990, p. 44)

Prenatal tests may also eventually be available to determine if an unborn child has a high risk of developing such emotional disturbances as depression or schizophrenia, or of having early heart disease. By making such tests widely known and available are we risking conveying a cultural message that only "perfect" children should be born?

Perhaps most troubling of all (to me at least) is the question of whether it is proper for prenatal testing to be used solely to diagnose the sex of the fetus. Is it morally legitimate to choose to abort a fetus because it is not of the desired gender?

Many of us are used to thinking of scientific knowledge as morally neutral. But these few examples show clearly that it is not. As genetic counseling becomes more common, and as diagnostic techniques become still more sophisticated, these will become compelling questions for future couples—including many of you.

many other diseases may have an impact on the child. There are at least three pathways of influence or transmission. Some diseases, particularly viruses, can attack the placenta, reducing the nutrients available to the embryo. Other diseases can pass through the placenta and attack the embryo or fetus directly. The organisms that cause rubella and rubeola (both forms of measles), syphilis, diphtheria, influenza, typhoid, serum hepatitis, and chicken pox all may be passed to the child in this way. A third form of transmission can occur during birth, when disease organisms present in the mucus membranes of the birth canal may infect the infant. Genital herpes, for example, is transmitted this way. In the case of AIDS, we do not yet know which form of transmission occurs, although it begins to look as if both direct transmission through the placental barrier and infection during delivery can occur.

In the first two types of transmission, as I indicated earlier, the timing of the infection is critical in determining the degree of effect. If infection occurs during the first months of gestation when organ systems are first being formed, there may be major malformations. If it occurs later, there may be some growth retardation but the effects seem to be less pervasive.

Of the diseases on this list, probably the riskiest for the child are rubella, AIDS, and CMV, although recent evidence suggests that genital herpes may also have serious side effects.

*Rubella.* **Rubella** (also called German measles) is most dangerous if transmitted during the first month of gestation. One-half of the infants exposed in this period show abnormality, while only one-fourth show effects if they are exposed in the second month (Berg, 1974; Kopp, 1983). The particular organ systems most affected by rubella are the ears, eyes, and heart, with deafness a common outcome.

Fortunately, rubella is preventable. Vaccination is available and should be given to all children as part of a regular immunization program. Adult women who were not vaccinated as children can be vaccinated later, but it must be done at least three months before a pregnancy to ensure complete immunity. Those women among you who wish to have children and who have not been vaccinated for rubella should be checked for immunity. If you are not immune, you should be vaccinated, but only if you are sure you are not pregnant at the time of vaccination. Rubella vaccine uses a live virus that can cross the placenta, so vaccination during the first three months of a pregnancy might have the same effect on the embryo as does the disease itself—although this is now in dispute among epidemiologists.

*AIDS.* Although not as common as some other diseases that may be transmitted to the fetus, neonatal AIDS is a growing problem. Current estimates are that there will be 3000 cases of pediatric AIDS by the end of 1991. In some areas, such as New York City, where there are many intravenous (IV) drug users, 1 in every 80 births involves an HIV-infected woman (Novick et al., 1989). As the incidence of HIV infection increases among childbearing women, the numbers of affected infants will continue to rise. Fortunately, only a fraction of infants born to HIV infected mothers themselves become infected.

The best current information comes from the European Collaborative Study (1991) in which 600 children born to HIV-positive mothers were followed for a period of years. Only 13 percent of these children were infected, and the majority of these (83 percent) showed symptoms of the disease within 6 months of birth. Studies in the United States generally have shown higher rates of infection for infants (30 percent or more) (e.g., Ryder et al., 1989; Blanche et al., 1989), but these studies have typically included more mothers diagnosed with AIDS itself rather than those who were HIV positive but symptom free. Whatever the eventual resolution of the question of infection rate, the more enduring puzzle is to explain why some fetuses are infected and others are not.

*CMV.* Cytomegalovirus (CMV), a virus in the herpes group, is remarkably widespread. This disease may affect the genitalia, urinary tract, or breasts, although it is usually "silent" in adults, with no observable symptoms. As many as 60 percent of women have antibodies to CMV, but most have no recognized symptoms. But when the mother passes this disease to the fetus or newborn, the baby may have severe problems.

This virus can be passed to the fetus in utero if the mother has been newly infected or if her disease is in the active phase, or the baby can be infected during delivery, or through breast milk after delivery. One to two percent of babies whose mothers have CMV antibodies become infected prenatally. Among those mothers with an active infection the transmission rate is more like 40–50 percent (Blackman, 1990). Fortunately, given the commonness of the disease, only about 5–10 percent of babies infected prenatally show clear symptoms of the disease at birth—roughly 2500 babies each year in the United States. These babies have a variety of serious problems, including deafness along with widespread damage to the central nervous system. Most are mentally retarded (Blackman, 1990). In fact, CMV is now considered the single most important known infectious cause of both congenital mental retardation and deafness.

*Herpes Simplex.* This form of herpes, also known as *genital herpes,* has received a great deal of public attention. Most of you know that once it is contracted, this disease is not presently curable. Like CMV, the virus may be transmitted to the fetus during delivery if the mother's disease is in the active phase at that time. Not only will the child experience the genital sores periodically, but other complications are also possible—most notably a potentially serious inflammation of the brain and spinal cord called *meningoencephalitis.* Because of this increased risk, many physicians recommend surgical delivery (cesarean section) of infants of mothers with herpes, although vaginal delivery is possible if the disease is inactive. I should point out that *oral* herpes (often shown by cold sores on or around the mouth) has no such known detrimental effect on the developing fetus.

### Drugs Taken by the Mother

Try sitting down and making a list of all the drugs you have taken in the past month or the past year. If you include not only everyday legal drugs like aspirin, decongestants, vitamins, sleeping pills, or tranquilizers, but also alcohol, tobacco, and caffeine, and any illegal drugs you may have chosen to take, you are likely to discover that the list is quite long. Ours is a drug-taking culture, and this is no less true of pregnant women. Ten or fifteen years ago, the average pregnant woman took six to seven prescribed drugs and another three or four over-the-counter drugs (such as aspirin) during the course of her pregnancy (Stewart, Cluff, & Philp, 1977). Today that number is doubtless lower, but it is not zero. What are the effects of any of these drugs on the embryo or fetus?

This turns out to be a harder question to answer than you might suppose. Because many women take several different drugs the effects of any one specific drug are often difficult to identify. And the effects may be subtle. Long-term learning problems, for example, may not show up for many years. There may also be many different effects from the same drug, which makes the risk analysis even harder. Thus a child exposed to a drug may be at increased risk for *some* problem, but not necessarily for a *particular* problem (Jacobson et al., 1984).

Studies of drug effects during pregnancy also suffer from all the problems typical of *quasi experiments* that I described in Chapter 1. For obvious ethical reasons, it is not possible to assign some pregnant women randomly to a drug-taking experimental group. So we must rely on studies of women who *choose* to take some drug (including alcohol or nicotine) compared to those who choose not to. Such groups are likely to differ in a great many other ways as well, so it is difficult to demonstrate conclusively that a given drug causes a particular negative outcome. Careful researchers have mitigated this problem by collecting information from their subjects about a very wide variety of other characteristics and then matching the drinking and non-drinking, or smoking and non-smoking, groups on as many of these other factors as possible. But the interpretive problem remains substantial.

*Drugs Prescribed for Pregnant Women.*  Some drugs prescribed specifically for pregnant women have later been found to have significant negative effects. Thalidomide, for example, was a tranquilizer prescribed fairly often during the early 1960s. Later it was found that this drug, if taken during the first 52 days of pregnancy, greatly increased the risk of a physical deformity in which the infant was born with foreshortened or missing limbs.

Another drug, *diethylstilbestrol* (DES), was prescribed during the 1940s and 1950s to help prevent miscarriages, although it was later found to be ineffective for this purpose. No obvious deformity was detected at first in the offspring of women who received DES during their pregnancies, but a number of subtle long-term effects have appeared, including increased risk of vaginal cancer among women and increased risk of sterility in men (Henley & Altman, 1978).

Current findings suggest that antibiotics such as tetracycline, anticoagulants, insulin, amphetamines, and tranquilizers may also have negative effects on the developing embryo or fetus, as may lithium carbonate, a drug often prescribed for serious depression (Kopp, 1983). Caffeine and aspirin have also come under suspicion, although the findings are mixed in both cases (Vorhees & Mollnow, 1987; Streissguth et al., 1991a). Given this list, any pregnant woman would obviously be well advised to consult her physician before taking *any* medication, particularly over-the-counter drugs.

*Drugs a Mother Chooses for Herself: Smoking.* The most consistent finding is that the birth weights of infants of mothers who smoke are lower than those of infants of nonsmoking mothers (Jacobson et al., 1984; Vorhees & Mollnow, 1987; Werler, Pober, & Holmes, 1985). On average, the difference is about 200 grams (a bit less than half a pound). This may not seem like a very sizable difference, but this reduced size seems to result from a reduction of placental blood flow. Nicotine constricts the blood vessels, so the fetus appears to suffer from a loss of nutrition. In addition, women who smoke also roughly double their risk of delivering a preterm infant. In one very large study involving over 30,000 women, Patricia Shiono and her colleagues (Shiono, Klebanoff, & Rhoads, 1986) found that women who smoked a pack a day or more while pregnant had a 20 percent greater chance of delivering their baby at 37 weeks gestation or earlier, and a 60 percent increased chance of delivering at 33 weeks or earlier, compared to women who did not smoke at all.

We have less information about possible long-term consequences of prenatal nicotine, but several large longitudinal studies have now shown increased risk of learning problems or poor attention span in school-age children whose mothers smoked during the pregnancy. As one example, Naeye and Peters (1984) traced the outcomes of the pregnancies of over 9000 women who had given birth in Boston between 1959 and 1966. Included in this large sample was a subgroup of women who had given birth twice in this period, and who had smoked during one pregnancy and not during the other—an extremely clever solution to the usual methodological dilemma. Both the comparisons between smokers and nonsmokers in the total sample and between the two sets of pregnancies in the subsample show higher rates of learning problems in children whose mothers smoked during the pregnancy. The differences are about 2–5 percent, so the effect is not enormous. But it is detectable even years later.

Despite the inherent difficulty of assigning causality from such research, the moral to be drawn from this research seems clear: do not smoke during pregnancy. If you cannot quit entirely then at least cut back, since all these studies show a relationship between the "dose" (the amount of nicotine you are taking in) and the severity of consequences for the child.

*Drinking.* An equally clear moral emerges from a look at the recent work on the effects of maternal alcohol ingestion on prenatal and postnatal development. In the early 1970s, Kenneth Jones and his colleagues (Jones et al., 1973) identified a syndrome characteristic of children born to alcoholic mothers, which they labeled **fetal alcohol syndrome (FAS).** Infants with FAS are generally smaller than normal, with smaller brains. They frequently have heart defects, and their faces are distinctively different (as you can see in Figure 2.9 on the next page). As children, adolescents, and adults, they continue to be shorter than normal, with smaller heads, and with IQ scores averaging between 60 and 70, scores classed as "mild" mental retardation. Indeed, FAS is the leading known cause of retardation in the United States, exceeding even Down syndrome (Streissguth et al., 1991b).

**fetal alcohol syndrome (FAS)**
A pattern of physical and mental abnormalities, including mental retardation and minor physical anomalies, found often in children born to alcoholic mothers.

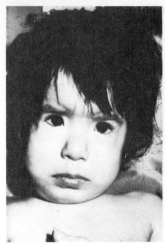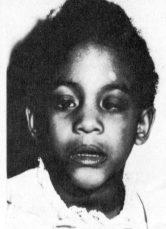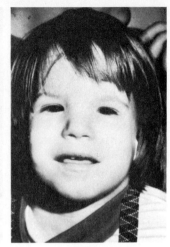

**FIGURE 2.9**

These three children, from three racial backgrounds (from left: American Indian, black, and white) have all been diagnosed as having fetal alcohol syndrome (FAS). All are mentally retarded and have relatively small heads. Note also the short nose and low nasal bridge typical of FAS children (*Source:* Streissguth et al., Science 209 [July 18, 1980]: 355, Figure 2; copyright 1980 by the American Association for the Advancement of Science).

The extensive research on prenatal alcohol makes it clear that children of women who are alcoholics or who drink heavily during pregnancy are at significantly higher risk for not only full-scale FAS, but for milder deformities or retardation. New studies also show that even moderate levels of "social drinking" are associated with increased risks of a broader array of problems now often called "fetal alcohol effects." The best single study has been done by Ann Streissguth and her colleagues (1980a, 1981, 1984, 1989, 1990, 1991a), who have followed a group of over 500 women from pregnancy until their children were 11 years of age. Since the study began before there were widespread warnings about the possible impact of alcohol during pregnancy, the sample includes otherwise low-risk women—well-educated, middle-class women with good diets who did not take many other recreational drugs and varied widely in the amount of alcohol they drank while pregnant. In this sample, alcohol consumption was associated with sluggishness and weaker sucking in infancy; lower scores on a test of infant intelligence at 8 months; lower IQ at 4 and 7 years; problems with attention and vigilance at 4, 7, and 11; and overall lower ratings of performance and higher ratings of problems by teachers at age 11. All these relationships persist even when smoking, other drug use, diet, education, and other variations in life-style and habits are controlled statistically.

The effects of moderate levels of alcohol use during pregnancy are not great, especially in comparison to the long-term consequences of the full FAS. For example, Streissguth and her colleagues find an IQ difference at age 7 of about 6 points between children of abstainers and children of women who drank 1 ounce or more of alcohol per day during their pregnancy (Streissguth, Barr, & Sampson, 1990). However, this relatively small absolute difference actually triples the risk of a subnormal IQ (one below 85) among children of mothers who drank. Children born to such pregnancies are thus markedly over-represented among those in special classes in schools and probably also appear in over-large numbers among high-school dropouts and the underemployed in adulthood. Those links, however, remain for longer-term longitudinal studies to confirm.

Whether there is any safe level of alcohol consumption during pregnancy we do not yet know. Those who work in this field (*behavioral teratology*) are generally convinced that there is a linear relationship between the amount of alcohol ingested and the risk for the infant. Thus even at low dosage there is some increased risk. Other important factors include when the drinking occurs in the pregnancy, and how many drinks the mother drinks on any one occasion. Binge drinking has been shown to be significantly riskier than regular smaller doses (e.g., Streissguth, Sampson, & Barr, 1990). The *safest* course is not to drink at all.

*Cocaine.* Various illegal drugs, most notably cocaine (in its various forms, including crack) are also taken by significant numbers of pregnant women. In one recent survey of 1776 consecutive births in a Chicago hospital, Mark Neerhoff and his colleagues (Neerhof et al., 1989) found that 8 percent of the mothers tested positive for cocaine use. Infants born to such mothers appear to be at considerably higher risk for a variety of problems, including premature birth, stillbirth, low birth weight, crib death in the first year of life, retarded growth prenatally, and neurological abnormalities that may show up years later as significant learning disabilities (Keith et al., 1989; Kaye et al., 1989; Neerhof et al., 1989).

Cocaine-affected newborns display a variety of symptoms, including jerky movements, flushed skin, grating cry, grimaces, and averted or closed eyes. These babies are easily agitated and hard to soothe, which makes the mother's task even more difficult. Thus a cycle of poor mother-infant interaction may also develop as a secondary effect of the cocaine.

As with many of the drugs I have described, the most dangerous effects of cocaine for the infant's development occur in the first two to three months of the pregnancy. However, even a single hit of cocaine can have a devastating effect at any time in the pregnancy, since in some cases the drug appears to cause a stroke in the fetus, resulting in partial paralysis. As with all the other "recreational" drugs I have described, clearly the best policy for the developing embryo or fetus is for the pregnant woman to abstain completely.

## The Mother's Diet

Just as drugs matter, so does a mother's diet, although no one knows *exactly* what is the best diet or what are the precise effects of too much or too little of each particular nutrient. I have explored some of what we know about a good diet in the box on pages 74–75. The other half of the question concerns what we know about the effects of malnutrition.

It is important here to distinguish between chronic *subnutrition*, and acute *malnutrition*. When a woman experiences severe malnutrition during pregnancy—such as has happened during wartime in many countries—she has a greatly increased risk of stillbirth, low birth weight, and infant death

## Diet and Exercise During Pregnancy

Life-styles have been changing. Slimness and fitness in women are perhaps more highly valued now than ever before, especially among younger women of childbearing age. And all women want to give their unborn child the best possible start in the world. So questions about weight gain, diet, and exercise during pregnancy are of vital concern to many women. The quality of the evidence does not quite match the concern in every case, but at least there are a few facts and a few suggestions that I can pass on to you.

### Weight Gain

For many years, physicians thought that the fetus acted as a sort of "parasite" on the mother's body, taking whatever nourishment it needed even at the expense of the mother. Recent evidence has challenged this assumption, as well as other customs about nutritional needs in pregnancy. We now know that even among obese women, the amount of weight the mother gains is directly related to the infant's birthweight. Among women who are underweight at the beginning of their pregnancies, the relationship is even stronger (e.g., Seidman, Ever-Hadani, & Gale, 1989). Low weight gain is also associated with higher risk of preterm birth (Abrams et al., 1989).

The old rule of thumb was that a woman should gain 2 pounds per month during the pregnancy. The newer research indicates that this is not nearly enough. Current advice stresses a gain of approximately 25–30 pounds for a woman who is at her normal weight before pregnancy, and a slightly greater gain for a woman who is underweight before pregnancy. Women who gain less than this may have infants who suffer from some fetal malnutrition and who are thus born underweight for their gestational age.

Furthermore, it matters *when* the weight is gained. During the first 3 months, the woman needs to gain only a minimal amount (2 to 5 pounds). But during the last 6 months of the pregnancy the woman should be gaining at the rate of about 14 ounces (350 to 400 grams) per week in order to support fetal growth (Pitkin, 1977; Winick, 1980). One practical consequence of this is that a woman who has gained 20 pounds or so during the first 4 or 5 months should *not* cut back in order to hold her weight gain to some magic total number. Restricting caloric intake during those final months is exactly the wrong thing to do.

### A Good Diet

Pure poundage is not enough to ensure optimal development for the child. It also matters *what* the mother eats. Caloric requirements increase 10–20% (perhaps 300 calories a day beyond your maintenance level), but protein needs go up much more markedly. The current recommendation is that a pregnant woman of 19 or older needs to take in 1.3 grams of protein per kilogram (2.2 pounds) of her weight. As an example, this would mean that a

during the first year of life (e.g., Stein et al., 1975). The effects seem to be worse when malnutrition occurs during the last half of the pregnancy, particularly in the final three months. Babies whose mothers suffer severe malnutrition during the final trimester are lighter at birth and have a greatly increased risk of dying during the first year. When you think back to the general rule I gave earlier—that interference with prenatal development has the greatest effect during the time of maximum growth of any system—this pattern makes sense. The major gain in weight occurs during the final three months, so you would expect these babies to be small, as they are, and perhaps therefore more vulnerable to disease.

woman weighing 125 pounds would require about 75 grams of protein per day. For teenagers, the protein requirement is still higher because they are still growing. (Since one egg has about 7 grams of protein and 1 cup of cottage cheese has 33 grams, this heightened requirement is not difficult to meet.) Requirements for most vitamins and minerals also increase during pregnancy. Calcium needs rise 50% (from 800 mg to 1200 mg daily), and iron requirements also rise, to perhaps 75 mg daily (Winick, 1980).

## Exercise

Two questions about exercise during pregnancy are relevant: Is it safe for the fetus, and does it make labor and delivery easier? The tentative answer to both questions seems to be "yes," although there are a few red flags.

Since blood oxygen levels appear to remain fairly constant in exercising pregnant women, the fetus does not appear likely to suffer from any oxygen deprivation. Furthermore, the few existing studies comparing babies born to mothers who exercised and those who did not show generally no differences in birth weight, length, or healthiness at birth (Leaf, 1982; Clapp, 1989). Still, caution is in order because there are a few studies that show that women who maintain very high rates of exercise (such as long distance running) during the final 2 to 3 months of the pregnancy may be at greater risk of delivering a low birth weight infant.

Another caution comes from the observation that the fetal heart rate may show deceleration for brief periods during or after a woman has exercised (Sady & Carpenter, 1989). Such an effect is only noted when the pregnant woman's own heart rate has risen above 150 beats per minute; below that level there appears to be little effect on the fetus.

Evidence on the impact of exercise on labor duration or severity is scarcer, and the findings are even less clear-cut. Some studies show that women who have exercised regularly before and during pregnancy have shorter labors and lower rates of complications during pregnancy, while other studies show no effect (Sady & Carpenter, 1989).

It is heartening to have increasing amounts of research on questions like these. However, the answers are still tentative, and the findings are not always easy to convert into clear advice. Researchers and physicians like Stanley Sady and Marshall Carpenter (1989) suggest that the most appropriate forms of exercise are rhythmic, large muscle group activities such as walking, swimming, cycling, or cross-country skiing. Such activities as water-skiing or scuba diving are universally thought to be inappropriate for a pregnant woman. But the experts disagree about many other forms of exercise, including stretching, jogging, weightlifting, racquetball, hockey, or soccer. So you will have to make your own judgment, based on your previous levels of exercise and the advice of your physician or midwife.

The final three months of gestation is also a time of rapid growth of dendrites (those branch-like parts of neurons), so we might expect that malnutrition then would have some impact here as well. This is exactly what has been found, most clearly in research with animals. Malnutrition seems to result in less fully branched dendrites, and it slows development of the sheathing around the nerves in the developing fetus (Lewin, 1975).

The effects of chronic subnutrition—experienced by large numbers of women throughout the world and by at least some women in the United States—have been more difficult to document. The effects of subnutrition are more subtle and many children born to such mothers are themselves chronically subnourished throughout childhood, which complicates attempts to identify the separate effects of the prenatal and postnatal malnutrition. The available evidence suggests that such children are smaller at birth, and continue to have somewhat stunted growth patterns throughout childhood. Girls with such growth histories are also more likely, as adults, to bear low birth weight infants, even if their nutrition during their own pregnancy is entirely adequate (Werner, 1979). It seems plausible that there are also effects of chronic subnutrition on the development of the fetal nervous system, and thus eventually on the child's intellectual development, but such effects have not been clearly documented.

### Other Teratogens

The list of other potential environmental hazards is very long, including some chemicals such as pesticides. One chemical about which we have relatively good information is lead. In most industrialized countries, adults are exposed to fairly high dosages of lead, although the introduction of unleaded gasoline has had a significant impact on dosages, as has the elimination of lead based paint. Still, researchers are beginning to find that even quite low levels of lead in the blood of the newborn—levels classified as "safe" by current federal guidelines—are associated with slightly lower IQ scores at later ages compared to children with still lower lead levels (Bellinger, 1987; Dietrich et al., 1987).

## Other Characteristics Affecting the Normal Sequence

Beyond the potential teratogens in diet, drugs, and diseases, there are three characteristics of mothers that seem to make a difference in prenatal development: the mother's age, the number of children she has already had, and her overall emotional state during the pregnancy.

### The Mother's Age

One of the particularly intriguing trends in modern family life in the United States is the increasing likelihood that women will postpone their first pregnancy until their late 20s or early 30s. In 1989, roughly 20 percent of all first births were to women over 30, double the rate in 1970 (Berkowitz et al., 1990; U.S. Bureau of the Census, 1990). There are many reasons for such decisions, including the increased need for second incomes in families and the desire of young women to complete job training and early career steps before bearing children—the more education a young woman has completed, the more likely she is to delay childbearing into her thirties. For my purposes in this chapter, the key question is not why a mother may delay but what the impact of maternal age may be on the mother and on the developing child.

Research suggests that the optimum time for childbearing is in a woman's early twenties. Mothers in their teens, and those over 30 (particularly those over 35), are at increased risk for several kinds of problems.

*Older Mothers.*  Let me get the most depressing news over with first. Maternal mortality during pregnancy or delivery is very low for any woman, but it is slightly higher for those over 30 or 35 (Buehler et al., 1986; National Center for Health Statistics, 1989). However, this risk has been dropping rapidly: The mortality rate for pregnant women over 35 has more than halved in the past decade and now stands at about 25 deaths per 100,000 births. Women over 35 are also more likely to miscarry (McFalls, 1990) and experience higher rates of various other kinds of complications of pregnancy. In one large recent study of nearly 4000 women in New York, all of whom had received adequate prenatal care, Gertrud Berkowitz and her colleagues (1990) found that women 35 and older during their first pregnancies were almost twice as likely as those 20 to 29 years old to suffer some pregnancy complication, such as gestational diabetes, pregnancy-induced high blood pressure, or bleeding.

In addition, older mothers are also at higher risk of conceiving an infant with Down syndrome—a pattern I have already discussed. The link between maternal age and this particular anomaly is so well established that women over 35 are now quite routinely urged to undergo some type of prenatal diagnostic procedure to check for the presence of an extra chromosome 21.

The good news is that Down syndrome is the exception. Despite the greater risks for older mothers, the infants born to such mothers are *not* more likely to have other types of birth defects or poor outcomes of pregnancy. For example, Berkowitz and her associates found that their older mothers were only slightly more likely to have low birth weight infants and no more likely to have premature deliveries than were mothers in their twenties. Other epidemiologists (Baird, Sadovnic, & Yee, 1991) have found no increased risk of birth defects for older mothers.

Although Berkowitz's study points to increased risks even among older mothers with good prenatal care, other evidence suggests that the effect of age on pregnancy is even greater among women living in poverty or among those with poor prenatal care (e.g., Roosa, 1984). Such findings suggest that age may interact with other factors, such as the overall health of the mother. For example, the negative effect of maternal smoking on birth weight is considerably *greater* among women over 35 than among young women (Wen et al., 1990). Similarly, inadequate prenatal care may be even more detrimental among older mothers, who are at risk for more pregnancy complications in any case. All in all, although robust and healthy infants are the most likely outcome of later pregnancies, the message seems to be that basic good health, fitness, diet, and prenatal care are even more vital for older mothers than for young ones.

*Young Mothers.*  In 1987, 12.4 percent of births in the United States were to teenage mothers (U.S. Bureau of the Census, 1990), with roughly 10,000 births to girls under 15. Simple comparisons of the pregnancies of such teenage mothers and those of mothers over 20 typically show that the teenagers are at higher risk for all kinds of problems. But as is true for pregnancies in older women, teenage pregnancies appear to be risky in large part because teenagers who get pregnant are more likely to be poor (and thus probably have poor nutrition) and because teenagers are less likely to get decent prenatal care. Except for those teenagers who are under 15 when they give birth, among whom the risks are slightly higher regardless of prenatal

Teenage mothers are more likely to have low birth weight infants or experience other complications of pregnancy and delivery than are mothers in their 20s, but that higher risk seems to be caused not by age itself but by the lower rate of prenatal care and the higher rate of poverty among teenage moms.

care, those teenagers who have decent diets and adequate prenatal care are no more likely to have problems with the pregnancy or delivery than are women in their twenties (Robertson, 1981; Strobino, 1987).

So while the mother's age can help us to predict problems in a pregnancy, age itself is probably not the most critical factor in most difficulties; rather it is the general physical and nutritional condition of the mother that matters the most.

### Number of Pregnancies

As a general rule, women who have had more than four pregnancies are at greater risk than women who have had fewer. Their babies are more likely to be stillborn or smaller at birth (Kessner, 1973). Eleanor Maccoby and her colleagues (Maccoby et al., 1979) have also found that any child after the first, especially if the pregnancies are closely spaced, has lower levels of hormones at birth. In particular, firstborn boys in this study had much higher levels of testosterone (the male hormone) at birth than did later-born boys. We don't know the implications of such a difference for development, but this study points to the possibility of some kinds of physical "depletion" in the mother as a result of pregnancy that could affect the physical development of later-born children.

Finally, the mother's state of mind during the pregnancy may be significant, although the research findings are decidedly mixed (Istvan, 1986). Results from infrahuman studies are clear: Exposure of the pregnant female to stressors such as heat, light, noise, shock, or crowding significantly increases the risk of low birth weight. Studies of humans, however, have not pointed to such a clear conclusion, in part because researchers have not agreed on how to measure such potentially relevant maternal states as anxiety or stress, nor even how to measure the outcome for the child. Many investigators have failed to find a link between measures of the mother's overall life stress and either complications of her pregnancy or problems in the infant. Other investigators have found such links for some groups and not others. Current research suggests that long-term, chronic stressors have only a small impact on a specific pregnancy, while increases in anxiety or stress during a pregnancy may have more deleterious effects.

Folklore in virtually all cultures certainly points to a causal link between the mother's emotional experiences during her pregnancy and the outcome for the child. But at the moment this hypothesis must be considered plausible but not proven. Better epidemiological studies are needed if we are to be able to go further.

## Risks and Long-Term Consequences of Prenatal Problems

Every time I write this chapter I am aware that the list of things that can go wrong seems to get longer and longer and scarier and scarier. Physicians, biologists, and psychologists continue to learn more about both the major and subtle effects of prenatal environmental variations, so the number of warnings to pregnant women seems to increase yearly, if not monthly. One of the ironies is that too much worry about such potential consequences can make a woman more anxious, and anxiety is on the list of warnings! So before you begin worrying too much, let me try to put this information into perspective.

First, let me say again that *most* pregnancies are normal and largely uneventful, and most babies are healthy and normal at birth. Second, there are specific preventive steps that any woman can take to reduce the risks for herself and her unborn child. She can be properly immunized; she can quit smoking and drinking; she can watch her diet and make sure her weight gain is sufficient; and she and the child's father can have genetic counseling. In addition, she can get early and regular prenatal care. It is *very* clear from many studies that mothers who received adequate prenatal care are at less risk to themselves and their infants. Jann Murray and Merton Bernfield (1988), in a study of over 30,000 births, found that the risk of giving birth to a low birth weight infant was more than three times as great among women who had received inadequate prenatal care as among those receiving adequate care, and this pattern held among both blacks and whites. Unfortunately, inadequate care remains common in the United States. In 1988, 21 percent of white mothers and 39 percent of black mothers had no prenatal care in the first trimester; 4.9 percent of whites and 10.5 percent of blacks had either no care at all or first saw a physician in the seventh month or later (Wegman, 1990).

Given such statistics, it is perhaps not surprising that the United States continues to have a relatively high rate of infant mortality. These rates have declined steadily in recent years, but in 1988 the rate stood at 10.0 infant deaths per 1000 live births, a rate that placed the United States twenty-first in the world. Virtually all European countries, in which prenatal care is free or low-cost and universally available, have lower infant mortality rates, as does Japan (with the lowest rate in the world), Hong Kong, and Singapore.

A third point to be made about prenatal problems is that if something does go wrong, chances are good that the negative consequences to the child will be short-term rather than permanent. And many physical defects can be treated successfully after birth.

Of course some negative outcomes *are* permanent and have long-term consequences for the child. Chromosomal anomalies, including Down syndrome or deviations in sex chromosome patterns, are permanent and nearly always associated with lasting mental retardation or school difficulties (Pennington et al., 1982). Some teratogens also have permanent effects, such as fetal alcohol syndrome, deafness resulting from rubella, or limb defects from thalidomide. In Chapter 3 you will see that *very* low birth weight infants (those under 1500 g, about 3 1/2 pounds) have an increased risk of persistent long-term learning problems or low IQ, regardless of the richness of the environment in which they are reared.

But many of the effects discussed in this chapter may be detectable only for the first few years of the child's life, and then only in certain families. The relationship between prenatal problems and long-term outcomes, in fact, is a perfect example of the kind of interaction effect Horowitz proposes, which I described in Chapter 1 (Figure 1.4). Low birth weight infants, or those with poor prenatal nutrition, higher lead exposures, or other difficulties, are likely to show persisting problems if they are reared in unstimulating or unsupportive environments (Kopp, 1990; Werner, 1986). The same children reared in richer and more varied environments typically catch up to their healthier peers by school age, if not before. The prenatal problem by itself is not the cause of the later problem; it is the combination of a prenatal problem and a relatively poor early environment that seems to produce long-term negative effects.

Let me give you a specific example to clarify this point. Philip Zeskind and Craig Ramey (1981) have studied a small group of 10 infants, born to poverty-level mothers, who were extremely thin at birth—usually a sign of prenatal malnutrition. Half of these babies happened to have been assigned randomly to a special enriched day-care program beginning when they were 3 months old. The other 5 malnourished babies received nutritional supplements but were reared at home in much less stimulating circumstances. Other children in the day-care center had been of normal weight at birth, as were other home-reared children included in the study. Table 2.4 gives the IQ scores of these four groups of children when they were 3 years old. Despite the very small sample, the differences are statistically significant and match Horowitz's model very well. Malnourished infants did well in the stimulating environment of the day-care center but extremely poorly in a less-supportive

TABLE 2.4

*IQ Scores of 3-year-old Children*

| | Prenatal Nutritional Status | |
| Experience After Birth | *Malnourished* | *Well-Nourished* |
|---|---|---|
| Enriched day care | 96.4 | 98.1 |
| Home-reared | 70.6 | 84.7 |

*Source:* Zeskind & Ramey, 1981, p. 215.

environment. Well-nourished infants also did better in the day-care environment than at home, but the difference is not nearly so large.

Studies like these—and there are many—suggest that problems experienced by the embryo or fetus may make an infant more vulnerable to later stresses or problems, or may mean that the child requires a better family environment to develop normally. But in many cases such normal development *is* possible. So don't despair when you read the long list of cautions and potential problems. The story isn't as gloomy as it first seems.

## Sex Differences in Prenatal Development

Since nearly all prenatal development is controlled by maturational codes that are the same for all members of our species—male and female alike—there are few sex differences in prenatal development. These few, however, set the stage for some of the physical differences we'll see at later ages.

- As I've already pointed out, boys secrete testosterone during the early months of gestation, which leads to "programming" of the brain so that the proper male hormones are secreted at the right moment later in life. Girls do not secrete any equivalent hormone prenatally.
- Girls are a bit faster in some aspects of prenatal development, particularly skeletal development. They are about 1–2 weeks ahead in bone development at birth (Tanner, 1978).
- Despite the more rapid development of girls, boys are heavier and longer at birth (Tanner, 1978).
- Boys are considerably more vulnerable to all kinds of prenatal problems. Many more boys than girls are conceived—about 120 to 150 male embryos to every 100 females—but more of the males are spontaneously aborted. At birth, there are about 105 boys for every 100 girls. Boys are also more likely to experience injuries at birth (perhaps because they are larger), and they have more congenital malformations (Zaslow & Hayes, 1986). Among those infants who experience severe complications during delivery, boys are more likely to die. Emmy Werner, in the Kauai longitudinal study, for instance, finds that more than 50 percent of the boy infants experiencing such severe complications died in infancy, compared to less than 20 percent among the girl infants (Werner, 1986).

The striking sex difference in vulnerability is particularly intriguing, especially since it seems to persist. Older boys are more prone to problems as well—a pattern I'll discuss more thoroughly in Chapter 14. One possible explanation for this, as I suggested earlier, may lie in the basic genetic difference. The XX combination affords the girl more protection against the fragile-X syndrome and against "bad" genes that may be carried on the X chromosome. For instance, geneticists have recently found that a gene affecting susceptibility to infectious disease is carried on the X chromosome (Brooks-Gunn & Matthews, 1979). Because boys have only one X chromosome, such a gene is much more likely to be expressed phenotypically in a boy.

## Social Class Differences in Prenatal Development

I will be talking much more fully about social class differences in development in Chapter 13, but I cannot leave this chapter without saying a word about the impact of social class on the risks of pregnancy and birth.

The basic sequence of fetal development is clearly no different for children born to poor mothers than children born to middle-class mothers. But many of the problems that can affect prenatal development negatively are more common among the poor. For example, mothers who have not graduated from high school are about twice as likely as mothers with a college education to have a low birth weight infant or to have an infant stillborn (Kessner, 1973). Among the poor, women are also likely to have their first pregnancy earlier, have more pregnancies overall, and are less likely to be immunized against such diseases as rubella. Perhaps most critically, poor women are less likely to seek prenatal care or to seek it much later in their pregnancies.

We know that the lack of prenatal care is a key factor because when low cost or free prenatal care is made easily available to the poor, the infant mortality rate has dropped sharply (Kessner, 1973). If we were willing to devote the resources needed for such an effort, we could significantly reduce not only the rate of infant death but also the rate of physical abnormalities and perhaps even mental retardation. To my mind, this is a goal worth striving for.

## S  U  M  M  A  R  Y

1. Conception occurs when the man's sperm penetrates the woman's ovum, ordinarily in the fallopian tube.
2. At conception, the 23 chromosomes from the sperm join with the 23 from the ovum to make up the set of 46 that will be reproduced in each cell of the new child's body.

3. Chromosomes, which are made up of deoxyribonucleic acid (DNA), carry genes in a particularly linear sequence.

4. The child's sex is determined by one of the 23 pairs of chromosomes, XX for a girl and XY for a boy.

5. Geneticists distinguish between the genotype, which is the pattern of inherited characteristics, and the phenotype, which is the set of characteristics of an individual that emerges when the genotype interacts with a specific experience.

6. During the first days after conception, the initial cell divides (mitosis), travels down the fallopian tube, and is implanted in the wall of the uterus.

7. Over the next several weeks, cell differentiation takes place and the placenta, umbilical cord, and amniotic cavity all form.

8. The developing organism is first called the ovum; then the blastocyst; then (beginning at about 2 weeks after gestation) the embryo. After 8 weeks it is called the fetus.

9. Most organ systems are developed in rudimentary form during the embryonic period; enlargement and refinements take place during the fetal period.

10. During the embryonic period, the XY embryo secretes the hormone testosterone, which stimulates the growth of male genitalia and shifts the brain into a "male" pattern. Without that hormone, the embryo develops as a girl, as do normal XX embryos.

11. Normal prenatal development seems heavily determined by maturation—a "road map" contained in the genes. Disruptions in this sequence can occur. The timing of the disruption determines the nature and severity of the effect.

12. Problems in prenatal development can begin at conception if a genetic abnormality, such as Down syndrome, occurs or if the child receives genes for specific diseases.

13. Prior to conception, it is possible to test for the presence of genes for many inherited diseases. After conception, several diagnostic techniques may be used to determine the presence of genetic signals for diseases or anomalies.

14. Some diseases contracted by the mother may affect the child, including rubella, AIDS, CMV, and genital herpes. These may result in disease or physical abnormalities in the child.

15. Alcohol, nicotine, and cocaine all appear to have significantly harmful effects on the developing fetus; the greater the dose, the greater the potential effect appears to be.

16. The mother's diet is also important. If she is severely malnourished there are increased risks of stillbirth, low birth weight, and infant death during the first year of life.

17. Older mothers and very young mothers, along with those who have borne four or more children, also run increased risks, but these risks are greatly reduced if the mother is in good health and receives adequate prenatal care.

18. Among other teratogens, prenatal lead exposure has been shown to be associated with lower IQs in infancy and early childhood.

19. High levels of anxiety or stress in the mother may also increase the risk of complications of pregnancy or difficulties in the infant, although the research findings here are mixed.

20. Some difficulties in prenatal development can produce permanent disabilities or deformities, such as Down syndrome or deafness from rubella. Other lasting problems, such as learning disabilities, may also be caused by teratogens. But many disorders associated with prenatal problems can be overcome if the child is reared in a supportive and stimulating environment.

21. Sex differences in prenatal development are few in number. Boys are slower to develop, bigger at birth, and more vulnerable to most forms of prenatal stress.

22. Nearly all potential problems of prenatal development are more common among poor women, but these increased risks can be greatly reduced with good diet and adequate prenatal care.

## CRITICAL THINKING QUESTIONS

1. Based on the information in this chapter, what *specific* advice would you give to a pregnant woman? Which of these items of advice seems to be most critical and why?

2. Many women who have been physically active before pregnancy continue with their exercise programs during pregnancy. Others stop exercising, fearing it will harm the infant. Design a study to test the effects of exercise on the mother, the delivery, and the infant.

3. The concept of a critical period has figured prominently in discussions of prenatal development. Why is this concept of interest to theorists? What are its practical ramifications?

## KEY TERMS

**amniocentesis**   A medical test for genetic abnormalities in the embryo or fetus that may be done at about 15 weeks of gestation.

**autosomes**   The 22 pairs of chromosomes in which both members of the pair are the same shape and carry parallel information.

**axon**   The long appendage-like part of a neuron; the terminal fibers of the axon serve as transmitters in the synaptic connection with the dendrites of other neurons.

**blastocyst**   The name used for the small mass of cells, about two weeks after conception, that implants itself into the wall of the uterus.

**chorionic villus sampling (CVS)**   A technique for prenatal genetic diagnosis involving taking a sample of cells from the placenta. Can be performed earlier in the pregnancy than amniocentesis.

**chromosomes**   Structures in the cells in the body that contain genetic information. Each chromosome is made up of many genes.

**crossing over**   The process that occurs during meiosis in which genetic material from pairs of chromosomes may be exchanged.

**dendrites**   The branch-like parts of a neuron that serve as the receptors in synaptic connections with the axons of other neurons.

**deoxyribonucleic acid**   Called DNA for short, this is the chemical of which genes are composed.

**Down syndrome**   A genetic anomaly in which every cell contains three copies of chromosome 21 rather than two. Children born with this genetic pattern are usually mentally retarded and have characteristic physical features.

**embryo**   The name given to the organism during the period of prenatal development from about two to eight weeks after conception, beginning with implantation of the blastocyst into the uterine wall.

**fallopian tube**   The tube down which the ovum travels to the uterus and in which conception usually occurs.

**fetal alcohol syndrome (FAS)**   A pattern of physical and mental abnormalities, including mental retardation and minor physical anomalies, found often in children born to alcoholic mothers.

**fetus**   The name given to the developing organism from about eight weeks after conception until birth.

**gametes**   Sperm and ova. These cells, unlike all other cells of the body, contain only 23 chromosomes rather than 23 pairs.

**genes**   Uniquely coded segments of DNA in chromosomes that affect one or more specific body processes or developments.

**genotype**   The pattern of characteristics and developmental sequences mapped in the genes of any specific individual. Will be modified by individual experience into the phenotype.

**glial cells**   One of two major classes of cells making up the nervous system, glial cells provide the firmness and structure, the "glue" to hold the system together.

**meiosis**   The process of cell division that produces gametes in which only one member of each chromosome pair is passed on to the new cell.

**mitosis**   The process of cell division common for all cells other than gametes, in which both new cells contain 23 pairs of chromosomes.

**neurons**   The second major class of cells in the nervous system, neurons are responsible for transmission and reception of nerve impulses.

**ovum**   The gamete produced by a woman, which, if fertilized by a sperm from the male, forms the basis for the developing organism.

**phenotype**   The expression of a particular set of genetic information in a specific environment; the observable result of the joint operation of genetic and environmental influences.

**placenta**   An organ that develops during gestation between the fetus and the wall of the uterus. The placenta filters nutrients from the mother's blood, acting as liver, lungs, and kidneys for the fetus.

**rubella**   A form of measles that, if contracted during the first three months of a pregnancy, may have severe effects on the developing baby.

**sex chromosomes**   The X and Y chromosomes, which determine the sex of the child. In humans, XX is the female pattern, XY the male pattern.

**synapse**   The point of communication between the axon of one neuron and the dendrites of another, where nerve impulses are passed from one neuron to another, or from a neuron to some other type of cell, such as a muscle cell.

**uterus**   The female organ in which the blastocyst implants itself and within which the embryo or fetus develops. (Commonly referred to as the womb.)

**zygote**   Term used to describe the developing organism from conception until implantation is complete.

The Boston Women's Health Collective. (1984). *The new our bodies, ourselves: A book by and for women* (2nd ed.). New York: Simon & Schuster.

This relatively recent revision of a popular book is really focused on the adult female's body, rather than on prenatal development, but it has an excellent discussion of health during pregnancy and good descriptions and diagrams showing stages of prenatal development. You may not be entirely in sympathy with all of the political views included, but it is nonetheless a very good compact source of information on all facets of pregnancy, including prenatal diagnosis of anomalies or diseases.

Nilsson, L. A. (1977). *A child is born*. New York: Delacorte Press, Seymour Lawrence.

This book is full of marvelous photographs of the embryo and fetus. It also has a good basic text describing prenatal development and problems of pregnancy.

Vorhees, C. V., & Mollnow, E. (1987). Behavioral teratogenesis: long-term influences on behavior from early exposure to environmental agents. In J. D. Osofsky (Ed.), *Handbook of infant development* (2nd ed.) (pp. 913–971). New York: Wiley.

A thorough review of the literature on the effects of various commonly discussed teratogens such as alcohol and smoking, this article also covers many other teratogens, such as lead, anticonvulsants, PCBs, hormones, radiation, and aspirin. If you are interested in this topic, this is an excellent next source, especially in view of the extensive bibliography.

# PROJECT 2

## Investigation of Available Prenatal Services

This project, like the other investigative projects I have suggested later in the book, should be undertaken either by a *single* student in a class, or by one small group of students working collaboratively. It is neither reasonable nor fair to flood local agencies with calls from dozens of students about services or programs.

### Basic Questions to Answer

The basic purpose of the project is to discover what kinds of prenatal services are available to poor mothers in your area.

- What programs are available through the public health service, through local hospitals, or other clinics?

- What funds are available to support those services from local, state, and federal sources?

- How many women take advantage of such services? Are there waiting lists? Is there any information available about the number or percentage of local women who receive no prenatal care at all or receive such care only in the final trimester?

- Has there been any change in the availability of such services in your area in the past decade or two? (This may be difficult to determine, but it is worth a try.)

- What is the infant mortality rate for your state, and for your community? How does this compare to national statistics?

Some of the statistics may be available through the federal document center at your university library. The annual volume, *Statistical Abstract of the United States* normally has state-by-state figures on infant mortality; more detail may be available through data from the Centers for Disease Control. The December issue of the journal *Pediatrics* also has a summary paper each year (authored in recent years by M. E. Wegman). Most states also have departments of vital statistics that may helpful.

For local information, try the city, county, or state public health departments. The yellow pages of your local phone book is a good place to start. A visit to the offices of the local public health department is likely to be fruitful. You should of course explain that this is part of a class project, and that you wish to be able to report back to your class.

3

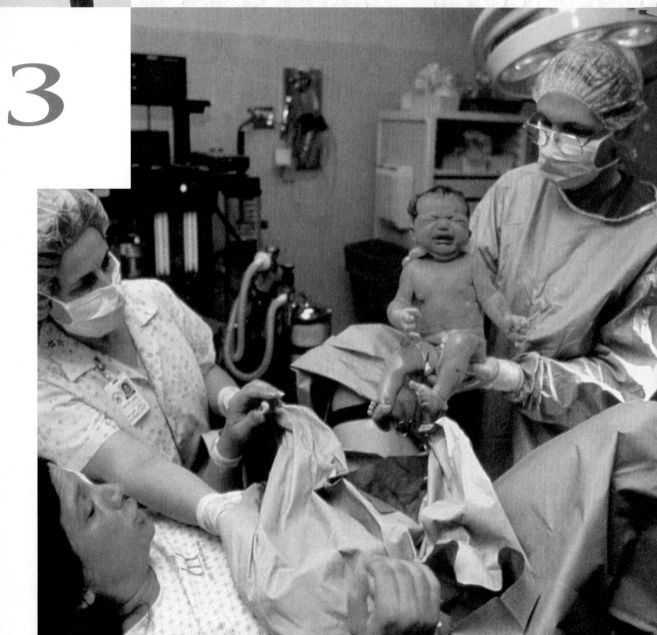

# BIRTH AND THE NEWBORN CHILD

Try to imagine that you are a woman 9-months pregnant with your first child. The long months of prenatal life are over and the baby is about to be born. If you are like many of today's mothers, you and your partner have explored the options for the location and conditions for your delivery. You may have taken prenatal classes and you have tried to prepare yourselves for what the baby will be like and how the advent of this new member of the family will change your life. You are a little apprehensive about the process of delivery, and a bit uncertain about what to expect from the baby and about your own abilities to cope, but you are eager for the whole adventure to begin.

In this chapter, I want to try to answer some of the questions that new parents ask about birth and newborn babies. Does it make a difference whether the baby is born in a hospital or at home? Does it matter if the father is present or not? What happens if the birth is too early or if something else goes wrong? I also want to describe the beginning of the child's independent life so that you can have a clear picture of the starting point for the long developmental journey. In the past few decades, researchers have discovered a great many things about newborns, and we now realize that these apparently helpless creatures have a wide range of remarkable abilities. This knowledge has not only changed the information given to new parents, it has also changed our theories of development.

## Birth

### *The Normal Process*

Labor progresses through three stages of unequal length.

*The First Stage of Labor.*    Stage 1 covers the period during which two important processes occur: dilation and effacement. The cervix (the opening at the bottom of the uterus) must open like the lens of a camera (**dilation**) and also flatten and thin out (**effacement**). At the time of actual delivery, the cervix must normally be dilated 10 centimeters (about 4 inches), as you can see in Figure 3.1. This part of labor has been likened to putting on a sweater with a neck that is too tight. You have to pull and stretch the neck of the sweater with your head in order to get it on. Eventually the neck is stretched wide enough so that the widest part of your head can pass through.

A good deal of the effacement may occur in the last weeks of the pregnancy, as may some dilation. It is not uncommon for women to begin labor 80 percent effaced and one or two centimeters dilated. The contractions of the

**dilation**
The first stage of childbirth when the cervix opens sufficiently to allow the infant's head to pass into the birth canal.

**effacement**
The flattening of the cervix which, along with dilation, allows the delivery of the infant.

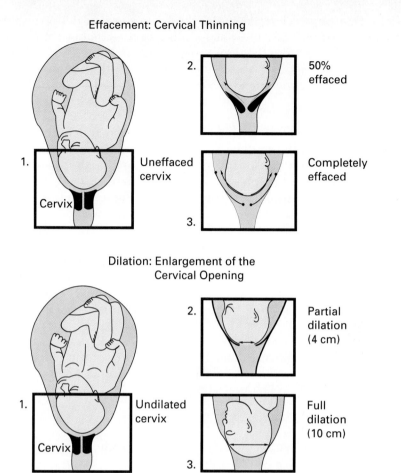

Effacement: Cervical Thinning

1. Uneffaced cervix

Cervix

2. 50% effaced

3. Completely effaced

Dilation: Enlargement of the Cervical Opening

1. Undilated cervix

Cervix

2. Partial dilation (4 cm)

3. Full dilation (10 cm)

**FIGURE 3.1**

The process of effacement and dilation during labor (*Source:* Stenchever, 1978, Figure 5–4, p. 84).

first stage of labor, which are at first widely spaced and later more frequent and rhythmical, serve to complete both processes.

Customarily, stage 1 is itself divided into phases. In the *early* phase (also sometimes called the *latent* phase) contractions are relatively far apart and typically not too uncomfortable. In the *late* phase, which begins when the cervix is about halfway dilated (5 cm) and continues until dilation reaches 8 cm, contractions are closer together and more intense. The last two centimeters of dilation are achieved during a period usually called the *transition* phase. It is this period, when contractions are closely spaced and strong, that women typically find the most painful. Fortunately, transition is also ordinarily the shortest phase. Following this comes the urge to help the infant out by "pushing." When the birth attendant (physician or midwife) is sure the cervix is fully dilated, she or he will encourage this pushing and the second stage of labor begins.

The length of the first stage varies widely, but you can get some sense of the average duration from the results of a recent study of 6991 vaginal deliveries in a hospital in San Francisco (Kilpatrick and Laros, 1989). In this sample, as you can see in Figure 3.2 on the next page, the average length of Stage 1 was roughly 8 hours for women delivering a first infant without anesthesia.

The longest first stage recorded in this study among first deliveries was 19 hours, with the vast majority of women falling in a range between 3 and 12 hours. You can also see from the figure that women delivering second or later children typically had shorter labors, and that those with some form of anesthesia typically had slightly longer labors—both patterns reported for other samples as well.

*Second Stage of Labor.* The second stage is the actual delivery, when the baby's head moves past the stretched cervix, into the birth canal, and finally out of the mother's body. Most women find this part of labor markedly less distressing than the transition phase because it is here that they can now assist the delivery process by pushing. As you can see in Figure 3.2, this stage typically lasts less than an hour and rarely takes longer than two hours.

Most infants are delivered head first, facing toward the mother's spine. Perhaps 3 percent, however, are oriented differently, either feet first or bottom first (called *breech* presentations). Several decades ago most breech deliveries were accomplished with the aid of medical instruments such as forceps. Today nearly four-fifths of breech presentations are delivered by cesarean section (Taffel, Placek, & Liss, 1987)—a procedure I'll discuss more fully in a moment.

*The Third Stage of Labor.* Stage 3 is the delivery of the placenta (also called the "afterbirth") and other material from the uterus. You can see all of these steps schematically in Figure 3.3 on p. 94.

### The First Greeting: Parents and Newborns

The brief description I've just given does not begin to convey the emotional impact of the experience of childbirth for the mother or for the father if he is present. Many women experience intense joy as they greet the infant for the first time: laughter, exclamations of delight at the baby's features, first

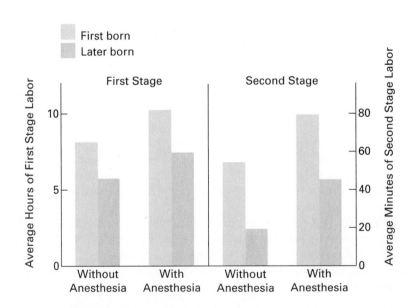

**FIGURE 3.2**

These findings from a large study of normal births show that both first and second stage labor are longer among women bearing their first child, and among those given anesthesia (*Source:* Kilpatrick & Laros, 1989, from Table 2, p. 86).

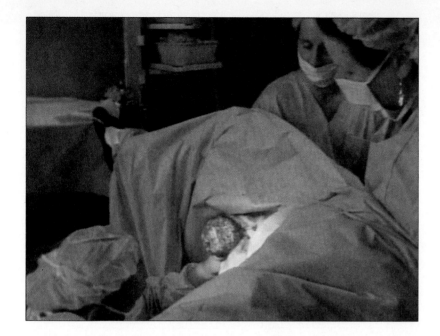

Michele Kaufman, beginning to emerge into the outside world. Note that she is positioned normally, facing downward or slightly to the side. This photo is a video still from the *Childhood* television series (*Source:* ©Thirteen/WNET).

tentative and tender touching. Here's an excerpt from one mother's greeting (Macfarlane, 1977, p. 64–65).

> She's big, isn't she? What do you reckon? (Doctor makes a comment.)  Oh look, she's got hair. It's a girl—you're supposed to be all little. Gosh. Oh, she's lovely. Oh, she's opened her eyes (laughs). Oh, lovely (kisses baby).

Most parents are intensely interested in having the baby look at them right away. They are delighted if the baby opens her eyes, and they will try to entice her to open them.

I need to be careful not to leave you with the impression that such an immediate greeting is essential for the healthy development of either the child or the parent-child relationship. I'll explore the research on such immediate "bonding" in detail in Chapter 11, but as a brief preview let me simply say that there is little indication that such early contact is necessary (or sufficient) for the establishment of a strong attachment or affectional bond of parent to child. But we do not need to demonstrate any long-term effect of such early greetings to justify encouraging hospital practices that allow time for immediate contact between parents and newborn. The joy, the amazement, the delight are reason enough.

### Birth Choices

In 75 to 80 percent of all births the delivery occurs with few or no complications. The whole process is normal and satisfying to the mother, and the infant emerges from the process looking quite healthy. Still, many decisions about the delivery can affect the child's health or the mother's satisfaction with the delivery—whether to receive pain killing drugs during delivery,

*FIGURE 3.3*

The sequence of steps during delivery are shown clearly in these drawings. You can see the dilation stage, transition, the delivery itself, and the delivery of the placenta.

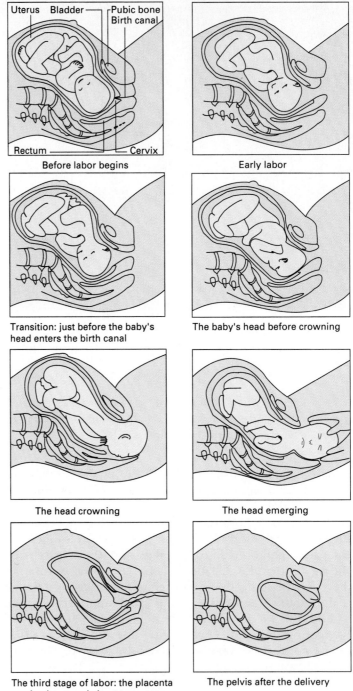

Before labor begins

Early labor

Transition: just before the baby's head enters the birth canal

The baby's head before crowning

The head crowning

The head emerging

The third stage of labor: the placenta coming loose and about to emerge

The pelvis after the delivery

whether to deliver in a hospital or at home, or whether the father should be present during the birth. These choices are made by a variety of people in the system—the parents, the birth attendant, and the hospital staff. Since many

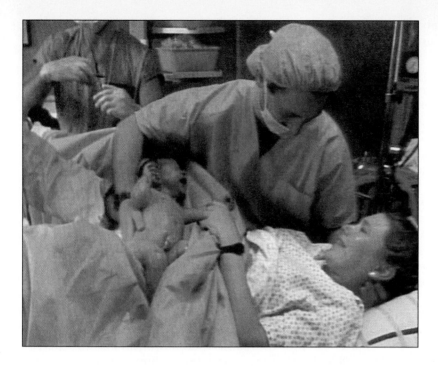

Hello Michele! This photo was taken only minutes after the one shown on p. 93. This photo is a video still from the *Childhood* television series (*Source:* ©Thirteen/WNET).

of you will face these choices at some point in the future, I want to give you the best current information I have.

*Drugs During Delivery.* One key decision concerns the use of drugs during delivery. Three types of drugs are commonly used: *analgesics, sedatives* (or *tranquilizers*), and *anesthesia.* Analgesics (such as the common drug Demerol) are all forms of opium and are given during the first stage of labor to reduce pain. Sedatives or tranquilizers (such as Nembutol, Valium, or Thorazine) may be given during Stage 1 labor to reduce anxiety. Anesthesia may be given during transition or the second stage of labor to block pain either totally (general anesthesia) or in portions of the body (local anesthesia). Some women receive all three types of drugs; others may receive only one or two of them; others none of them.

Brackbill (1979; Brackbill, McManus & Woodward, 1985) estimated that in the late 1970s and early 1980s approximately 95 percent of deliveries in the United States involved some drug administration. Because "natural" (drug-free) childbirth has received a great deal of emphasis in the past decade this number has declined. The use of anesthesia in particular appears to have dropped significantly. In the Kilpatrick and Laros study from which I drew the data in Figure 3.2, for example, only 15 percent of the women delivering their first child and 11.5 percent of those delivering subsequent children received any anesthesia. Nonetheless, it is still true that the great majority of women receive at least *some* medication during delivery.

Just what are the effects of such drugs on the infant? Despite the obvious practical relevance of this question, it has been next to impossible to answer clearly. Controlled experiments are not possible, since women cannot be randomly assigned to specific drug regimens. And naturally occurring drug administration occurs in myriad different combinations of specific drugs, timing, and dosages. A few clear conclusions have emerged from this messy body of research, but most of what we can say is still highly tentative.

The clearest conclusion is that nearly all drugs given to the mother during labor pass through the placenta and enter the fetal bloodstream. And because the newborn lacks the enzymes necessary to break the drug down quickly, the effect of any drug lasts longer in the baby than it does in the mother. We can see the effects of such drugs in the infant during the first days and weeks after delivery: Infants whose mothers have received any type of drug are ordinarily found to be more sluggish, to suck less vigorously, to gain less weight, and to spend more time sleeping (Brackbill, 1979; Maurer & Maurer, 1988). The size of this drug effect is quite small—much smaller than the effect of such other variations as birth weight, for example.

What is less clear is whether these initial effects on the infants persist past the first few days. The best current hypothosis about long-term consequences is that analgesics and tranquilizers probably have no lasting consequences; where there are hints of long-term effects it is in cases in which anesthesia has been used (e.g., Rosenblith & Sims-Knight, 1989). For example, Ann Murray and her colleagues (1981) found that mothers who had received anesthesia thought their 1-month- olds were harder to care for and less sociable than did mothers who had received no anesthesia. In another study, Carol Sepkoski (1987) compared children of 20 women who had received one specific anesthesia with children of a matched group of 20 women who had received no drugs at all during delivery. Sepkoski found that at age 5, the unmedicated children had significantly higher scores on a measure of intellectual and motor skills than did the medicated children. At the same time, other researchers have *not* found such lasting effects, and a few have found that infants whose mothers were given drugs during delivery actually perform *better* on various tests than do non-drugged infants.

This confusing set of findings makes it difficult to arrive at meaningful advice for the individual mother, but let me try anyway. The most cautious choice is to have as little medication as possible during delivery—consistent with your level of tolerance. Perhaps a more important point is that if you have received medication, you need to bear in mind that the child is also drugged, and his behavior will be affected for the first few days. If you allow for this effect, and realize that it will wear off, your long-term relationship with your child is likely to be unaffected.

*The Location of Birth: Four Alternatives.* A second choice parents must make is *where* the baby is to be born. Today there are typically four alternatives: (1) a traditional hospital maternity unit; (2) a birth center or birthing room located within a hospital but with a more homelike setting, with labor and delivery both completed in the same room and family members often present throughout; (3) a freestanding birth center, like a hospital birth center except located away from the hospital, with delivery typically attended by a midwife rather than (or in addition to) a physician; and (4) home delivery.

At the turn of the century, only about 5 percent of babies in the United States were born in hospitals; today the figure is close to 99 percent (U.S. Bureau of the Census, 1990). In these statistics, birthing centers are included among the hospital deliveries, so it is impossible to know how much the availability of this intermediate alternative has increased, although it would appear to be more common today than it was a decade ago.

Because home deliveries are so uncommon in the United States, most of the research comes from Europe, where this type of delivery continues to be a widely chosen alternative. There is also a limited amount of research focused directly on birthing centers or hospital-based birthing rooms.

The arguments made for home or birth center deliveries are primarily that they are more natural, that they treat pregnancy and delivery as normal processes rather than as illnesses, and that they are likely to provide a less traumatic birth because the mother is in a comfortable or familiar setting. The counterargument, made particularly against home deliveries, is that such alternative birth practices are less safe. If anything should go wrong, full hospital facilities may not be available quickly enough.

European evidence, and limited U.S. research, largely refutes the safety argument, although with an important qualification. In *uncomplicated pregnancies* in which the woman has received good prenatal care, and in which a trained birth attendant is present at delivery, the rate of delivery complications or infant problems is no higher in home or birth center deliveries than in hospital deliveries (Kitzinger & Davis, 1978; Schramm, Barnes, & Bakewell, 1987; Rooks et al., 1989; Tew, 1985). In contrast, infant mortality rates *are* significantly higher in *unplanned* home deliveries, in those without trained attendants, or in those in which the mother had experienced some complication of pregnancy.

Another argument sometimes made for home or birth center delivery is that babies born in such settings may be better off psychologically as well as physically. If the parents' birth experience is more positive then their bond to the infant may be stronger, and their initial and long-term interactions with the child may be more positive.

This assertion is difficult to test because women who choose home or birth center delivery are different in other ways from women who opt for more traditional hospital procedures. They may have used fewer drugs during pregnancy, have eaten differently, or have different attitudes about delivery and motherhood. If we find later that nonhospital-delivered infants have different types of interactions with their parents, or score higher on tests of development, we cannot be sure that it was the delivery location, and not one of these other differences, that was the cause.

Given all this ignorance, and barring any signs of trouble in the pregnancy, the decision about the location of the delivery seems to be very much a matter of personal choice. However, if there are any indicators of increased risk in your pregnancy, some variant of hospital delivery is clearly the safer alternative.

*The Presence of Fathers at Delivery.*    A third important decision has to do with who should be present at the delivery. In particular, how important is it that the father should be present?

Participation by fathers in the delivery room—as "coach," observer, or emotional supporter of the mother—is clearly on the increase. While as recently as 1972 only about one-fourth of U.S. hospitals permitted the father to be present in the delivery room, by 1980, four-fifths of them did (Parke & Tinsley, 1984), and today it is clearly the norm for fathers to be present.

Three arguments are typically given in support of the father's presence: (1) he can provide psychological support for the mother; (2) through coaching or other assistance he can help her control the pain she experiences; and (3) he will become more strongly attached to the infant by being present at the birth. There is at least some evidence in support of the first two of these arguments, but highly mixed findings regarding the third.

When fathers are present during labor and delivery, mothers report lower levels of pain and receive less medication (Henneborn & Cogan, 1975). When the mother has a coach (the father or someone else), the incidence of labor and delivery problems goes down, as does the duration of labor (Sosa et al., 1980). Furthermore, at least one study shows that women are more likely to report that the birth was a "peak" experience if the father was present (Entwisle & Doering, 1981).

What we do not know is whether the father's relationship with his infant is affected positively by being present at delivery or by having an opportunity for early contact with the infant. Assertions about such positive benefits were made quite widely by both psychologists and pediatricians in the 1970s (e.g., Macfarlane, 1977; Greenberg & Morris, 1974), and seem to have been accepted by many parents. (It is now very difficult, for example, to find fathers who are willing to be assigned randomly to a nonparticipation group in such an experiment.) On the plus side there is some evidence that those fathers

David Kaufman was able to be with his wife Barbara during her entire labor and for the delivery of their baby Michele. Here he is coaching her during a contraction. Such participation by Dads is now the norm in the U.S. and many Western countries. This photo is a video still from the *Childhood* television series (*Source:* ©Thirteen/WNET).

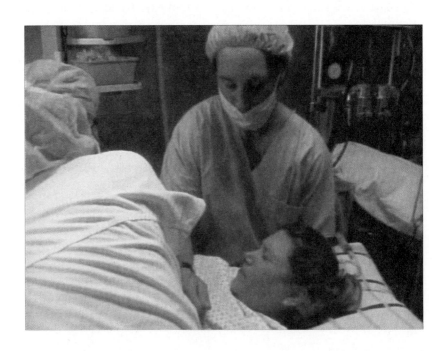

whose birth experience has been particularly positive show signs of greater attachment to their infant throughout the first year (Peterson, Mehl, & Leiderman, 1979). But there is no indication that actual presence at the birth is required for a "positive experience" or for later attachment to the baby. Palkovitz (1985), who has reviewed all the evidence, concludes that the father's presence at delivery may enhance the marital relationship, but is neither necessary nor sufficient for the father's emerging attachment to his infant.

All of this is not intended as an argument against fathers' participation in the delivery process. Aside from fathers' own reported delight at being present at the birth of their children, the fact that the father's presence seems to help the mother control pain, reduce medication and labor duration, and may enhance the husband-wife relationship all seem to me to be compelling reasons for continuing the move toward greater paternal participation.

### Problems at Birth

So far I have been discussing the process of normal, uncomplicated vaginal delivery. However, as with prenatal development, there are some things that can alter the normal pattern. The delivery itself may not proceed normally, leading to a surgical delivery through an abdominal incision, called a **cesarean section,** (or **C-section**). The infant may not breathe immediately after birth, or may be born too early, or even too late.

*Cesarean-Section Delivery.* The goal of any delivery is to have a healthy child. So whenever the health of the fetus seems at risk in a vaginal delivery —such as when the mother's pelvis is not wide enough to accommodate the infant's head, even when fully dilated, or when the fetus shows signs of significant distress during labor—a C-section may be the better alternative. There is no doubt that C-section deliveries have saved many infants and prevented many cases of birth damage.

There is also no doubt that the rate of C-section deliveries has risen to rather startling levels, having more than quadrupled in the United States in the past 25 years, as you can see in Figure 3.4. In 1987, the rate was a remarkable 24.4 percent (U.S. Bureau of the Census, 1990), and the rate has continued to rise despite general agreement among physicians that the rate is far

cesarean section
(C-section)
Delivery of the child
through an incision in
the mother's abdomen.

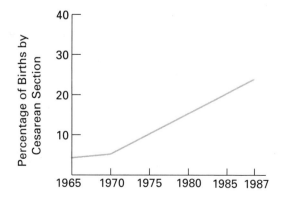

**FIGURE 3.4**

The rate of cesarean section deliveries in the United States has been rising steadily over the past few decades, despite efforts by many obstetricians to reverse the trend (*Source:* U.S. Bureau of the Census, 1990, Table 89, p. 66).

higher than necessary (e.g., Berkowitz et al., 1989; de Regt et al., 1986; Taffel, Placek, & Liss, 1987).

The reasons for the increasing use of C-sections appear to be myriad. Fear of malpractice suits may be one element, but changes in standard medical practices appear to be the main cause. C-sections are now routinely used for breech presentations, for women with active herpes infections, and for women who have had a previous cesarean delivery. The use of fetal monitors during delivery is also a factor, since signs of fetal distress— such as a drop in the fetal heart rate—are now much easier to detect and may lead the physician to choose cesarean delivery to reduce the apparent risk to the infant. However, physicians disagree about the necessity or advisability of C-section deliveries in all such circumstances. For example, only about 7 percent of women who have had one C-section deliver later children vaginally, although there is now research to suggest that such subsequent vaginal delivery is quite safe in at least half the cases. Similarly, some physicians (e.g., Leveno et al., 1986) argue that fetal monitoring has led to many unnecessary C-sections, particularly in otherwise low-risk pregnancies.

All of this has been the subject of quite heated discussion among physicians for at least the past decade. Nonetheless, the rate of cesarean delivery continues to rise.

*Anoxia: Lack of Oxygen.* Another complication that can occur during delivery—and that may in fact be detected by a fetal monitor—is an insufficiency of oxygen for the infant. Such reduced oxygen supply is called **anoxia.** During the period immediately surrounding birth, anoxia may occur because the umbilical circulation system fails to continue the supply of blood oxygen until the baby breathes, or because the umbilical cord has been squeezed in some way during labor or delivery. Perhaps as many as 20 percent of newborns experience some degree of anoxia.

Long-term consequences of anoxia are difficult to check and the research has suffered from serious problems of definition and measurement. *Prolonged* anoxia is often (but not at all invariably) associated with such major consequences as cerebral palsy or mental retardation. Briefer periods of oxygen deprivation appear to have little long-term effect, but that is still a very tentative conclusion.

*Low Birth Weight.* Another potentially serious complication is to have an infant born weighing less than the normal or optimum amount, a condition generally labeled **low birth weight** (LBW). The cut-off point for this designation is generally 2500 grams (about 5.5 pounds). Those babies below 1500 grams (about 3.3 pounds) are usually described as **very low birth weight**. The incidence of low birth weight has declined in the past decade, but it is still high: In 1987, 6.9 percent of all newborns were below 2500 grams, with 1.2 percent below 1500 grams (U.S. Bureau of the Census, 1990).

All low-birth-weight infants used to be lumped into a single group, often called *premature*. It is now clear, though, that it is very important to distinguish between several subgroups or types of low-birth-weight infants. Some infants have low birth weight because they are born too soon; these infants are usually called **preterm** infants. Any birth before 36 weeks of gestation is usually la-

**anoxia**
A shortage of oxygen. If it is prolonged, it can result in brain damage. This is one of the potential risks at birth.

**low birth weight (LBW)**
The phrase now used (in place of the word premature) to describe infants whose weight is below the optimum range at birth. Includes infants born too early (preterm or short gestation infants) and those who are "small-for-date."

**very low birth weight**
The phrase now commonly used to describe infants who weigh 1500 grams (3 1/3 lbs) or less at birth.

**preterm**
Descriptive phrase now widely used to label infants born before 37 weeks gestational age.

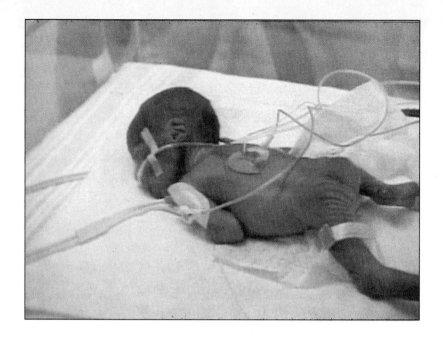

The mother of this low birth weight baby, filmed as part of the *Childhood* series, had had no prenatal care and may have been using cocaine. Like all LBW babies he is amazingly small, skinny, and wrinkly because he lacks most of the layer of fat under the skin that you see in a full-term newborn. Remarkably enough, though, many infants this small do survive—although those who have been exposed to cocaine have a much higher risk of later problems. This photo is a video still from the *Childhood* television series (*Source:* ©Thirteen/WNET).

beled in this way. A second subtype is the **small-for-date** baby. These are infants who are unusually light, given the number of weeks of gestation they have completed. They may even have completed the full 38 weeks of gestation but be under 2500 grams. Infants in this group appear to have suffered from some kind of prenatal malnutrition, or from constriction of blood flow, such as from the mother's smoking, or from other significant problems prenatally. The preterm infant, in contrast, may be merely early and may be developing normally in other respects (Tanner, 1978).

small-for-date
A term used to describe an infant who weighs less than is normal for the number of weeks of gestation completed.

All low-birth-weight infants share some characteristics, including markedly lower levels of responsiveness at birth and in the early months of life (DiVitto & Goldberg, 1979; Barnard, Bee, & Hammond, 1984a). They are also all at higher risk of experiencing respiratory distress in the early weeks, and may be slower in motor development than their normal weight peers.

Low-birth-weight infants are also at considerably greater risk of death in the days and weeks immediately after birth. The lower the birth weight the greater the risk of neonatal death. Still, with recent improvements in medical knowledge and technology, some astonishingly small infants do survive. As many as one-half of infants as small as 500 to 1000 grams at birth (1-2 lbs) now survive in some hospitals (e.g., Astbury et al., 1990), with survival rates as high as 80 percent for those born weighing 1000 grams or more (Resnick et al., 1989). (You can get some sense of what such tiny babies look like from the photo above.)

What becomes of these extremely small survivors? Are they likely to have long-term impairments of some kind? Do they have lower IQs or motor difficulties? The answers to such questions depend in part on how much the infant weighed at birth and when the infant was born. Preterm infants above 1500 grams who are normal sized for their length of gestation generally catch up to their normal peers within the first few years of life. However, very low-birth-weight and small-for-date infants show higher rates of long-term problems, including lower IQs, smaller size, and greater problems in school (Kopp, 1983; McCormick, Gortmaker, & Sobol, 1990).

Among these smaller or riskier infants, those born in the 1980s—as the quality of care in neonatal intensive care units improved dramatically—are much more likely to be unimpaired than are those who were born in the 1970s or before. Among those born in the late 1970s or 1980s, only about 5–10 percent appear to have major long-term impairment, such as IQ below 70 (e.g. Hoy, Bill, & Sykes, 1988; Kitchen et al., 1987) although higher impairment rates are generally found for infants born below 750 grams (Ehrenhaft, Wagner, & Herdman, 1989; Sostek et al., 1987).

Unfortunately, some of the negative outcomes become detectable only after infancy or at school age. A child may seem unimpaired at age 1 or 2, but show problems at 3, or seem to have caught up by 4, but still show some kind of learning disability later. The good news is that even among very low birth weight infants, most show no long-term disability at all. Regrettably (and perhaps surprisingly), we are not yet proficient at predicting the outcomes of different infants. We can say that those with very low birth weight and those who are sicker at birth—such as those who require more help with breathing or those who suffer brain hemorrhage—have poorer outcomes.

The pattern of long-term outcomes also appears to follow the general interaction pattern that Horowitz suggests, and that I described earlier in Figure 1.4: The worst outcomes are for those vulnerable children who are also reared in unstimulating or unfavorable environments (e.g., Pederson et al., 1987). However, even among these children there are some who develop normally. We simply do not know all the risk factors yet.

One other piece of good news is that we do now know something about treatments that seem to improve the long-term chances of good functioning for low-birth-weight infants. Babies provided with special kinds of rhythmic stimulation while still in the hospital—such as water beds, rocking beds, heartbeat sounds, or body massage—are more alert, gain weight faster, and may even have higher IQs than preterm babies receiving more typical hospital care (e.g., Barnard & Bee, 1983; Scafadi et al., 1990).

## Assessing the Newborn

In most hospitals it is customary to evaluate an infant's status immediately after birth and then again five minutes later to detect any problems that may require special care. An **Apgar score,** developed by Virginia Apgar (1953), is the most widely used assessment system. The newborn is rated on five criteria, listed in Table 3.1, and given a score of 0, 1, or 2 on each criterion, with a maximum score of 10. A score of 10 is fairly unusual immediately after birth, since most infants are still somewhat blue in the fingers and toes at that stage. At the five-minute assessment, however, scores of 10 become much more common: 85 to 90 percent of infants are scored as 9 or 10 at that time, indicating that they are getting off to a good start (National Center for Health Statistics, 1984). Low scores can occur for any number of reasons, but most often they are due to reduced oxygen supply or low birth weight.

Extremely low Apgar scores are associated with very high rates of infant death. However, scores in the range of 5–8, like low birth weight and most

**Apgar score**
An assessment of the newborn completed by the physician or midwife at one minute and again at five minutes after birth, assessing five characteristics: heart rate, respiratory rate, muscle tone, response to stimulation, and color.

TABLE 3.1

*Evaluation Method for Apgar Scoring*

| Aspect of Infant Observed | Score Assigned | | |
|---|---|---|---|
| | 0 | 1 | 2 |
| Heart rate | Absent | <100/min. | >100/min. |
| Respiratory rate | No breathing | Weak cry and shallow breathing | Good strong cry and regular breathing |
| Muscle tone | Flaccid | Some flexion of extremities | Well flexed |
| Response to stimulation of feet | None | Some motion | Crying |
| Color | Blue; pale | Body pink, extremities blue | Completely pink |

*Source:* Francis, Self, & Horowitz, 1987, p. 731–732.

other types of initial vulnerability, are associated with long-term risk primarily when the infant grows up in less favorable circumstances. In stimulating and supportive environments, most children with low Apgar scores appear to develop normally (Breitmayer & Ramey, 1986).

## Adapting to the Newborn

The baby is born and Mom, Dad, and infant return home and must now adapt to one another and to the massive changes in their lives. One of the common features of that adaptation is **postpartum depression**—an experience I have explored in the box on page 104. The arrival of an infant also changes the family interaction patterns in significant ways.

Sociologists have shown for years that marital satisfaction typically declines in the first months and years after the first child is born (e.g., Rollins & Feldman, 1970). Individuals and couples report a sense of strain made up partly of fatigue, partly of a sense that there is too much to cope with, a sense of ignorance about caring for the child, and a strong sense of loss of time and intimacy in the marriage relationship itself (e.g., Belsky, Lang, & Rovine, 1985; Feldman, 1987; Roosa, 1988). In longitudinal studies in which couples have been observed or interviewed during pregnancy and then again in the months after the first child's birth, spouses typically report fewer expressions of love, fewer positive actions designed to maintain or support the relationship, and more expressions of ambivalence (Belsky et al., 1985). Such strains and reduced satisfaction are less noticeable when the child was planned rather than unplanned and among those couples whose marriage was strong and stable before the birth of the child. But virtually all couples experience some strain.

This strain on the family system is even greater if the infant is impaired in some way, like a low birth weight infant. Such babies are quite unresponsive and are therefore remarkably hard to read; they do not enter well into the

**postpartum depression** A severe form of the common experience of postpartum blues. Affecting perhaps 20 percent of women, this form of clinical depression typically lasts six to eight weeks.

## Postpartum Depression

In the first few days after the birth of a child, the majority of women experience some depressed mood, often called the "maternity blues" or "postpartum blues." Estimates vary, but studies in Western cultures suggest that about 50–75 percent of all women go through a brief period in which they find themselves crying often and feeling unexpectedly low in mood (Hopkins, Marcus, & Campbell, 1984). Most women pass through this mild depressed state in a few days and then return to a more positive and more stable mood state. But as many as 20 percent of women experience a longer-lasting and more severe postpartum mood disturbance, commonly called a *postpartum depression*.

Clinicians use the term *depression* or the phrase *clinical depression* to describe more than just the blues, although sadness or persisting low mood is one of the critical ingredients. To be diagnosed as suffering from a clinical depression, including postpartum depression, a person must also show some other symptoms, such as poor appetite, sleep disturbances (inability to sleep, or excessive sleep), loss of pleasure in everyday activities, feelings of worthlessness, complaints of diminished ability to think or concentrate, or recurrent thoughts of death or suicide. An individual need not show all of these symptoms to be diagnosed as clinically depressed, but must show at least half of them.

You can see from this description that such a depressive episode is not a trivial experience. So the fact that as many as one-fifth of women may experience such feelings after the birth of a child is striking. Fortunately, postpartum depression normally lasts for shorter periods than is common for other forms of clinical depression. A duration of six to eight weeks seems to be typical, after which the woman gradually recovers her normal mood (Hopkins et al., 1984), although for perhaps 1 or 2 percent of women the depression persists for a year or longer.

Such depressions seem to be more common in women who did not plan their pregnancy, who were high in anxiety during the pregnancy, or whose partner is not supportive of them or is displeased with the arrival of the child (Field et al., 1985; Hopkins et al., 1984). They are also more likely to occur in any woman who has experienced high levels of life changes during the pregnancy and immediately after the birth—changes such as moving, death of someone close, loss of a job, or the like. Interestingly, though, postpartum depression does not seem to be more common after a first child than after later children, although a woman who experienced such a depression after her first child is more likely to have a repeat episode after later births (Hopkins et al., 1984).

Understandably, mothers who are in the midst of a significant postpartum depression interact differently with their infants than do mothers whose mood is more normal. Alison Fleming and her colleagues (1988), for example, found that depressed mothers stroked and touched their infants with affection less frequently in the first three months after delivery than did nondepressed mothers. However, these differences did *not* persist after the mother's depression lifted. At 16 months, Fleming could find no differences in mother-child interaction between the mothers who had been depressed and those who had not.

I think it is quite common in our society to pass off a woman's postpartum depression as if it were a minor event, "just the blues." And of course for many women, it is. For a substantial minority, however, the arrival of a child ushers in a much more significant depressive episode, requiring at the very least a sympathetic and supportive environment, if not clinical intervention.

"dance" of interaction. As a result, parents have to struggle to keep attending, to keep trying, and to keep maintaining their emotional involvement with the child. Several observers (including my colleagues and I) have noted that mothers of LBW infants, in the first few months after the baby has come home from the hospital, show *higher* rates of interaction with their infants than do mothers of full-term infants, as if they were trying extra hard to stimulate and relate to the baby. However, if you check again 10 or 12 months later, you find that the mothers of the low-birth-weight infants show lower levels of interaction with their babies, as if the infant's unresponsiveness was so unreinforcing that the mother had backed away slightly (e.g., Barnard, Bee, & Hammond, 1984a).

The pattern of interaction that develops within the family is clearly a product of the qualities and skills the parents bring to the system, including the quality of their relationship with each other. However, the individual characteristics of the infant also have a clear impact—a point I'll return to shortly when I talk about temperamental differences among infants.

## What Can the Newborn Do?

What are the qualities and skills the newborn brings to the interactive process? He cries, breathes, looks around a bit. But what else can he do in the early hours and days? On what skills does the infant build?

### Reflexes

Infants are born with a large collection of **reflexes,** which are automatic physical responses triggered involuntarily by a specific stimulus. Many of these reflexes are still present in adults and are familiar to you, such as the knee jerk the doctor tests for, your automatic eyeblink when a puff of air hits your eye, or the involuntary narrowing of your pupil when you are in a bright light.

In addition to these lifelong reflexes, the newborn has a set of "primitive" reflexes, so called because they are controlled by the more primitive parts of the brain, the medulla and the midbrain, both of which are almost fully developed at birth. By about 6 months, when the portion of the brain governing such complex activities as perception, body movement, thinking, and language has developed more fully, these primitive reflexes begin to disappear, as if superceded by the higher level brain functions.

Some primitive reflexes are essential for survival, such as the breathing reflex and the various reflexes involved in eating. If an infant is touched on the cheek, she will automatically turn toward the touch and search for something to suck on (the rooting reflex). Then when she gets her mouth around something suckable, she automatically begins to suck (the sucking reflex), and then swallows.

Other primitive reflexes have less obvious usefulness. You can see one of these, the *Moro* or *startle reflex,* in Figure 3.5 on the next page. When an infant is confronted with a loud noise or some kind of physical shock, she will throw her arms outward and arch her back. If you touch an infant on the bottom of her foot, she will show what is called the *Babinsky reflex* by first splaying out her

reflexes
Automatic body reactions to specific stimulation, such as the knee jerk or the Moro reflex. Many reflexes remain among adults, but the newborn also has some "primitive" reflexes that disappear as the cortex is fully developed.

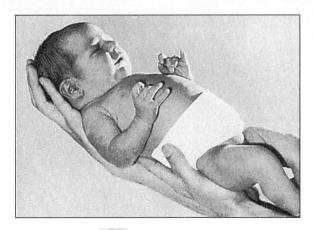

**FIGURE 3.5**

You can see the first part of the Moro reflex very well in this sequence. In the left photo the baby is fairly relaxed, but when the adult suddenly drops the baby (and catches him again), the baby throws his arms out. The part of the reflex you don't see here is the closing of the fingers. This reflex may be left over from our ape ancestry; young monkeys do this when their mother lets go briefly. The result is that the baby grabs hold of a bunch of fur and thus clings. Although this reflex has little usefulness in human babies, it can be seen for the first six months or so.

toes and then curling them in. And if you touch an infant on her palm, she will curl her fingers around your hand, or around any graspable object and hold tightly, a pattern called the grasp reflex. These patterns are interesting not only because they may be remnants from our evolutionary past, but because their presence past the age of roughly 6 months may signal the existence of some kind of neurological problem. The Babinsky reflex, in particular, is used as a diagnostic tool by neurologists who may suspect the existence of some dysfunction.

### Perceptual Skills: What the Newborn Sees, Hears, and Feels

I'll be describing the infant's perceptual skills in detail in Chapter 5, and do not want to steal all that thunder. So let me merely summarize very briefly. The newborn can:

- focus both eyes on the same spot, with 8 inches being roughly the best focal distance. Within a few weeks the baby can at least roughly follow a moving object with his eyes, and by one or two months he can discriminate Mom's face from other faces.
- easily hear sounds within the pitch and loudness ranges of the human voice; he can roughly locate objects by their sounds, and can discriminate some individual voices, particularly the mother's voice.
- discriminate the four basic tastes (sweet, sour, bitter, and salty) and can identify familiar body odors.

Brief as this summary is, several points nonetheless stand out. First of all, newborns are remarkably proficient at many perceptual skills, contrary to the beliefs of most parents and many psychologists until a few years ago. The better our research techniques have become, the more we have discovered that newborns and young infants have complex perceptual skills. Even more striking is how well adapted the baby's perceptual skills are for the interactions he will have with the people in his world. He hears best in the range of the human voice; he can discriminate mother (or other regular caregiver) from others on the basis of smell or sound almost immediately, and can discriminate by sight within a few weeks. He can focus his eyes best at a distance of about 8 inches, which is approximately the distance between the infant's eyes and the mother's face during nursing.

This is not to say that there is not a long way to go in the development of sophisticated perceptual abilities. There is, as you'll see in Chapter 5. But the newborn begins life able to make key discriminations and to locate objects through various perceptual cues.

### Motor Skills: Moving Around

In contrast, the motor skills of newborns are not very impressive. They cannot hold up their heads, coordinate their looking and their reaching yet, and they cannot roll over or sit up. Some of these skills emerge fairly rapidly in the early weeks. By one month, for example, infants can hold up their chins from the floor or mattress. By two months, they are beginning to swipe at nearby objects with their hands.

Young infants also show a lot of what Esther Thelen (1981) has called *rhythmical stereotypies*—those patterns of kicking, rocking, waving, bouncing, banging, rubbing, scratching, and swaying which the infant repeats over and over and in which he seems to take such delight. Thelen (1981) has observed that these repeated, rhythmical patterns peak at about 6 or 7 months of age, although you can see some such behavior even in the first weeks, particularly in finger movements and leg kicking. While this type of movement does not seem to be totally voluntary or coordinated, it also does not appear to be random. For instance, Thelan has observed that kicking movements peak just before the baby begins to crawl, as if the rhythmic kicking were a part of the preparation for crawling. Thelan's work has helped us see patterns and order in the apparently random movements of the young infant. However, even this understanding does not alter the fact that, by contrast with perceptual abilities, the baby's initial motor abilities are quite limited.

### Learning and Habituation

Both the presence of perceptual abilities and the relative lack of motor skills at birth seem to be heavily influenced by the processes of maturation. Those body systems and those parts of the nervous system that are required for many perceptual skills are largely complete at birth, while those needed for motor control are not developed sufficiently.

But is maturation the only process involved here? Can a newborn also learn from his or her experiences? This question has intrigued researchers for decades, for both theoretical and practical reasons: From a theoretical perspective this question is obviously crucial for understanding the relative influences of nature and nurture. Those who argue that a child's behaviors and characteristics are a product of experience, rather than being genetically pat-

Newborn infants have very poor motor control. Their heads must be supported when they are held; they cannot even raise their heads off a mattress. But progress comes rapidly. Vera Kalugin was just 3 months old when the *Childhood* filmmakers captured this moment. She can already hold her head and shoulders up off the mat. This photo is a video still from the *Childhood* television series (*Source:* ©Thirteen/WNET).

terned, must be able to demonstrate that an infant can indeed learn from such experience. For example, might a child's temperament be a product not of heredity, but of classically conditioned emotional responses in the earliest weeks of life? Might a child's growing preference for Mom or Dad be the result of operant conditioning, rather than any type of more built-in attachment processes? Questions of this sort require, at least, that we know how early an infant learns through classical or operant conditioning.

The same question is also important from a practical point of view if only because the answer affects the sort of advice parents may be given about suitable stimulation for their child. For example, if a child's perceptual abilities develop largely through maturation rather than through learning, then buying expensive mobiles to hang above the baby's crib does not make much sense. But if learning is possible from the earliest days of life, then various kinds of enrichment make much more sense.

What does the evidence tell us?

*Classical Conditioning.* The bulk of research suggests that the newborn can be classically conditioned, although it is difficult to do. By three or four weeks, classical conditioning is quite easy to demonstrate in an infant. This means that the conditioned emotional responses I talked about in Chapter 1 may begin to develop as early as the first weeks of life. Thus the mere presence of Mom or Dad, or another favored person may trigger the sense of "feeling good," a pattern that may contribute to what we see as the child's attachment to the parent. Similarly, a child might develop various classically conditioned negative emotional responses that may be part of what we see as temperament.

*Operant Conditioning.* Newborns also clearly learn by operant conditioning. Both the sucking and head turning have been successfully increased

In the very natural process of nursing, babies like Vera Kalugin are learning a whole new set of stimulus-response connections through classical conditioning. For example, the mother's smell may come to be a conditioned stimulus for the baby's sucking reflex; the sight of the mother's face may become a conditioned stimulus for the baby's emotional response of contentment or satisfaction. This photo is a video still from the *Childhood* television series (*Source:* ©Thirteen/WNET).

by the use of such reinforcements as sweet liquids (Sameroff & Cavanaugh, 1979) or the sound of the mother's voice or heartbeat (DeCasper & Sigafoos, 1983; Moon & Fifer, 1990). At the least, the fact that conditioning of this kind can occur means that whatever neurological "wiring" is needed for learning is present at birth. Results like this also tell us something about the sorts of reinforcements that are effective with very young children. The fact that the mother's voice is an effective reinforcer as early as the first weeks of life is clearly significant for the whole process of mother-infant interaction.

*Schematic Learning.* The fact that babies can recognize voices and heartbeats in the first days of life is also important because it suggests that another kind of learning is occurring as well. This third type of learning, sometimes referred to as *schematic learning*, draws its name and many of its conceptual roots from Piaget's theory. The basic idea is that from the beginning infants organize their experiences into expectancies or "known" combinations. These expectancies, often called *schemas*, build up with many exposures to particular experiences, but thereafter help babies distinguish between the familiar and the unfamiliar. Carolyn Rovee-Collier (1986) recently suggested that we might think of classical conditioning in infants as a variety of schematic learning. When a baby begins to move her head as if to search for the mother's nipple when she hears her Mom's footsteps coming into the room, this is not just some kind of automatic classical conditioning, but the beginning of the development of expectancies. From the earliest weeks, babies seem to begin to map links between events in their world—between the sound of their mother's footsteps and the feeling of being picked up, between the touch of the breast and the feeling of a full stomach. Thus what researchers have previously identified as early classical conditioning may be more correctly thought of as the beginnings of the process of cognitive development.

habituation
An automatic decrease
in the intensity of a re-
sponse to a repeated
stimulus, which enables
the child or adult to ig-
nore the familiar and
focus attention on the
novel.

*Habituation.* A related concept is **habituation**. Habituation is the auto-matic reduction in the strength or vigor of a response to a repeated stimulus. An example would probably help: Suppose you live on a fairly noisy street. The sound of cars going by is repeated over and over during each day. But after a while, you not only don't react to the sound, you quite literally *do not perceive it as being as loud.* This ability to dampen the intensity of a physical re-sponse to some repeated stimulus is obviously vital in our everyday lives. If we reacted constantly to every sight, sound, and smell that came along, we'd spend all our time responding to these repeated events and would not have energy or attention for things that are new and deserve attention.

The ability to *dishabituate* is equally important. When there is a change in a habituated stimulus, such as a sudden screech of tires on the busy street by your house, you again respond fully. Thus the reemergence of the original response strength is a sign that the perceiver—infant, child, or adult—notices some significant change.

The capacity both to habituate and to dishabituate are present in the newborn (Lipsitt, 1982). She will stop looking at something you keep putting in front of her face; she will stop showing a startle reaction (Moro reflex) to loud sounds after the first few presentations, but will again show a startle re-sponse if the sound is changed. Such habituation itself is not a voluntary pro-cess; it is entirely automatic. However, for this ability to function, the newborn must be able to "recognize" familiar experiences. That is, he or she must develop schemas of some kind.

The existence of these processes in the newborn has an added benefit for researchers: It has enabled them to figure out just which things an infant responds to as if they were "the same" and which things she responds to as "different." If a baby is habituated to some stimulus, such as a sound or a par-ticular picture, the experimenter can then present slight variations on the original stimulus to see the point at which dishabituation occurs. In this way, researchers have begun to map the normal pattern of schemas of the new-born or very young infant.

## Social Skills

All of the skills of the newborn I have described so far are important for the baby's comfort and survival. But unlike newborns in many other species, human newborns are a long way from being independent. If they are to sur-vive, someone must provide consistent care over an extended period. So the infant's capacity to entice others into the caregiving role is critical. It is here that the "social" skills of infants come into play.

When you think about newborn babies, you probably do not think of them as particularly social. They don't talk and don't flirt. They smile but not often during the first weeks. Normal newborns, nonetheless, have a collection of behaviors that are remarkably effective for attracting and keeping the at-tention (and attachment) of adults. Furthermore, as I just pointed out about the baby's perceptual skills, the social interaction process is very much a two-way street: Adult faces and voices are remarkably effective for attracting and keeping the baby's attention too. It is as if the adult and the baby are pro-grammed from the beginning to join in a crucial social "dance," one which

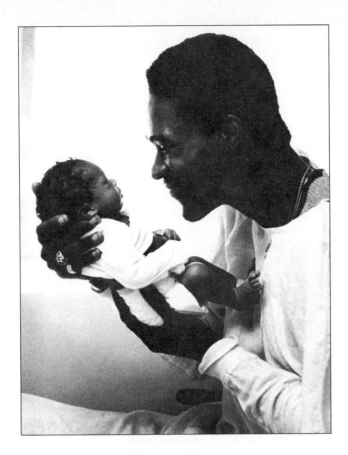

Newborn babies are very skilled at attracting and keeping the attention of adults (this Dad seems clearly captured!)—a useful trait, since they need to be cared for so continuously. They can meet your gaze after the first few weeks, smile, "take turns" during feeding, snuggle, be consoled, cry.

forms the root of the developing relationship between parent and child and that is critical for the formation of the parent's attachment to the child.

Babies' repertoire of social behaviors are quite limited, but these few behaviors appear to be very effective in eliciting care. They cry when they need something, which ordinarily brings someone to them to provide care. And infants then respond to that care by being soothed, which is reinforcing to the caregivers. Babies adjust their bodies to yours when you pick them up. After the first few weeks, they get quite good at meeting your eyes in a mutual gaze or smiling quite easily—both of which are very powerful "hooks" for the adult's continued attention.

One other thing the baby does from the beginning, which seems to be critical for any social interaction, is to take turns. As adults, we take turns in a range of situations, including conversations and eye contacts. In fact, it's very difficult to have any kind of social encounter with someone who does *not* take turns. Kenneth Kaye (1982) argues that the beginning of this "turn-taking" can be seen in very young infants in their eating patterns. As early as the first days of life, the baby sucks in a "burst-pause" pattern. He sucks for a while, pauses, sucks for a while, pauses, and so on. Mothers enter this "conversation" too, often by jiggling the baby during the pauses. The eventual sequence looks something like this: suck, pause, jiggle, pause, suck, pause, jiggle, pause. The rhythm of the interaction is very much like a conversation and seems to underlie many of the social encounters among people of all ages. To be sure, we cannot be certain whether this conversational quality of very early interaction occurs because the adult figures out the baby's natural rhythm and adapts her own responses to the baby's timing, or whether there is some mutual adaptation occurring. Nonetheless, it is extremely intriguing that we can see this apparent turn-taking in an infant 1 day old.

 ## The Daily Life of Infants

Parents are obviously interested in the various skills and capacities of the newborn infant. They are also vitally concerned with a more prosaic set of questions: What does the baby do with her time? How is the infant's day organized? What sort of natural rhythms occur in the daily cycles? What can you expect from the baby, as you struggle to adapt to and care for this new person in your life?

Researchers such as Heinz Prechtl and his colleagues (Prechtl & Beintema, 1964), who have studied newborns, have described five different states of sleep and wakefulness in infants, referred to as **states of consciousness,** which I've summarized in Table 3.2. You can see that the baby spends more time sleeping than doing anything else. Of the time awake, only about two to three hours is either quiet or active awake rather than fussing.

The five main states tend to occur in cycles, just as your own states occur in a daily rhythm. In the newborn, the basic period in the cycle is about 1 1/2 or 2 hours. Most infants move through the states from deep sleep, to lighter sleep, to fussing, to hunger, and then to alert wakefulness, after which they become drowsy and drop back into deep sleep. This sequence repeats itself about every two hours. By about 6 weeks of age most infants begin to string two or three of these periods together without coming to full wakefulness, at which point we say that the baby can "sleep through the night" (Bamford et al., 1990). One of the implications of this rhythm is that the best time for really satisfying social encounters with a young infant is likely to be just after she is fed, when she is most likely to be in a quiet awake state. Let me take a somewhat more detailed look at the major states.

### Sleeping

Sleeping may seem like a fairly uninteresting part of the infant's day, except that parents find the child's sleep periods quite helpful, particularly as the infant develops a pattern with a long nighttime sleep. But there are two other aspects of an infant's sleep that are intriguing to psychologists.

First, irregularity in a child's sleep patterns may be a symptom of some disorder or problem. In Chapter 2, I mentioned that one of the characteristics of babies born to drug-addicted mothers is that they seem unable to establish a pattern of sleeping and waking. Brain-damaged infants often have the same kind of difficulties, so any time an infant fails to develop clear sleep-waking regularity, it *may* be a sign of trouble.

Second, sleeping newborns show the external signs that signify dreaming in older children or adults, a fluttering of the eyeballs under the closed lids, called **rapid eye movement (REM) sleep.** REMs are not seen in very

**states of consciousness**
Five main sleep/awake states have been identified in infants, from deep sleep to active awake states.

**rapid eye movement (REM) sleep**
One of the characteristics of sleep during dreaming, which occurs during the sleep of newborns, too.

TABLE 3.2

*Basic States of Infant Sleep and Wakefulness*

| State of Consciousness | Characteristics | Average Number of Hours Spent in State | |
|---|---|---|---|
| | | At Birth | At 1 Month |
| Deep sleep | Eyes closed, regular breathing, no movement except occasional startles | | |
| | | 16–18 hrs | 14–16 hrs |
| Active sleep | Eyes closed, irregular breathing, small twitches, no gross body movement. | | |
| Quiet awake | Eyes open, no major body movement, regular breathing | | |
| Active awake | Eyes open, with movements of the head, limbs, and trunk; irregular breathing. | | |
| | | 6–8 hrs | 8–10 hrs |
| Crying and fussing | Eyes may be partly or entirely closed, vigorous diffuse movement, with crying or fussing sounds. | | |

*Sources:* Based on the work of Prechtl & Beintema, 1964; Hutt, Lenard, & Prechtl, 1969; Parmelee, Wenner, & Schulz, 1964.

young preterm infants, so there is clearly some neurological maturity required for this pattern of activity. Among normal-term newborns, though, REM sleep makes up a larger portion of sleep time than is true in adults. In adults, REMs typically occur in brief bursts periodically over the sleep period; in newborns they occur more frequently but in a less burst-like pattern (Berg & Berg, 1987). Just what these differences in pattern may mean—either about the development of the nervous system or about dreaming in very young infants—is not yet clear. But some sort of internal activity is evident during the baby's sleep time.

### Crying

For many parents, the infant's crying may be mainly a disturbing or irritating element, especially if it continues for long periods and the infant is not easily consoled. However, crying is a crucial signal from the infant, telling the caregiver that the baby needs care. Infants have a whole repertoire of cry sounds, with different cries for pain, anger, or hunger. The basic cry, which often signals hunger, is usually a rhythmical pattern: cry, silence, breath, cry, silence, breath, with a kind of whistling sound often accompanying the in-breathing. An anger cry is typically louder, more intense, and the pain cry normally has a very abrupt onset—unlike the more basic kinds of cries, which usually begin with whimpering or moaning. However, not all infants cry in precisely the same way, so the parents must learn the appropriate discriminations. For example, Alan Wiesenfeld and his colleagues (Wiesenfeld, Malatesta, & DeLoach, 1981) found that mothers (but not fathers) of 5-month-olds could discriminate between taped episodes of anger and pain cries in their own babies, while neither parent could reliably make the same discrimination with the taped cries of another baby.

Newborns actually cry less than you might think. When Anneliese Korner (Korner et al., 1981) monitored the crying and non-crying activity of a group of normal newborns in the first three days of life she found that they cried only 2 to 11 percent of the time. Crying seems to increase over the first six weeks of life, and then decreases. Initially infants cry most in the evening, and then shift their crying more toward times just before feedings.

In all of this, as with the nature of the cries themselves, there are wide individual differences. Fifteen to twenty percent of infants develop a pattern called *colic*, which involves daily, intense bouts of crying, totaling three or more hours a day. The crying is generally worst in late afternoon or early evening (a particularly inopportune time, of course, since it is usually when the parents are tired and needing time with one another, too). Colic typically appears at about 2 weeks of age and then disappears spontaneously at 3 or 4 months of age. Neither psychologists nor physicians know why colic begins or why it stops without any intervention. It is a difficult pattern to live with, but the good news is that it *does* go away.

The gratingness of a child's cry also varies from one child to the next and may even be predictive of the child's later intellectual functioning. A number of very intriguing recent studies have shown that babies with some kind of physical problem—small-for-date babies, preterm infants, babies who experienced complications at delivery—have more piercing, grating, unpleasant cries than do physically normal infants (Lester, 1987; Zeskind & Lester, 1978). Among such babies, the quality of the cry is significantly correlated with IQ and other cognitive measures at age 2 (Huntington, Hans, & Zeskind, 1990). Eventually, it may be possible for physicians to use the presence of such a grating or piercing cry as a signal that there may be some underlying physical problem with the infant.

The most important function of the baby's cry, though, is as a signal of distress. For caregivers, it is absolutely vital to know when the child is in need, and most babies are very good at passing on this information in the form of a cry. Most parents quite naturally respond quickly to these signals, feeding the baby, changing diapers, holding and cuddling the infant. But there is a dilemma, too, for many parents. If you pick up your baby immediately every time she cries, will you be reinforcing crying? Or is such quick responding essential if the child is to learn, in some way, that his needs will be met? (See Figure 3.6.)

There has been a long, verbose, and inconclusive theoretical and empirical dispute about this question in the child development literature (e.g., Ainsworth, Bell, & Stayton, 1972; Gewirtz and Boyd, 1977; Hubbard & van IJzendoorn, 1987). Five or ten years ago, both theorists and researchers seemed to agree that infants who are picked up or cared for quickly when they cry, cry *less* than do infants whose caregivers delay in responding. Now even this conclusion is in dispute. It does seem clear that responding quickly to those intense infant cries that signal real distress or pain leads to less crying overall. However, immediate responding to milder crying or whimpering—the sort of crying a baby may do when she is put down for a nap, for

FIGURE 3.6

What to do?

example—may actually increase the overall rate of crying. And in children over 18 months or 2 years, rapid response to any kind of crying may reinforce the crying behavior and thus lead to increased levels of crying. What I am reduced to is a much vaguer statement than I would like: Parents who are *sensitive* to and responsive to their child's signals have children who cry less than do parents who are less sensitive or responsive. But just how we should define sensitivity and responsivity at each age is not so clear.

### Eating

Eating is not a "state," but it is certainly something that newborn babies do frequently! Given the approximately two-hour state-change cycle, newborn babies may eat as many as ten times a day. By 1 month the average number is down to about five-and-a-half feedings each day, and this drops further to about five per day by 4 months (Barnard & Eyres, 1979). From the parents' perspective, one of the critical decisions about feeding is whether to breast-feed or bottle-feed. I have summarized the arguments on both sides in the box on pages 116–117.

## Individual Differences Among Babies

Most of my emphasis in the past few pages has been on the ways in which infants are alike. Barring some kind of physical damage, all babies have similar sensory equipment at birth and can experience the same kinds of happenings around them. But babies differ, too, in important ways.

### Temperament

One of the key ways babies differ is in those aspects of behavior and responsiveness psychologists call *temperament,* which I mentioned briefly in

Several decades ago there were rather heated arguments about the relative merits of breast-feeding versus bottle-feeding. Although in developing countries breast-feeding has been widely practiced, in the United States bottle-feeding became the norm. Only about one-fourth of infants in the United States in 1970 were breast-fed at all, and only about 10 percent were breast-fed for as long as 3 months. In the past 20 years this has changed dramatically. In 1987 over half of mothers reported breast-feeding for at least a short time (Ryan & Martinez, 1989) and the number has been steadily rising. Breast-feeding today is more common among whites than among blacks, more among older than younger mothers, and more among the middle class than among the poor or working class. But for most groups it is recognized as the preferred option.

The argument today, then, is not whether breast-feeding is to be preferred, but whether it is practically feasible. Since the majority of women are employed outside the home, with short maternity leaves and often inflexible work schedules, breast-feeding becomes logistically very difficult to sustain. Because of this, mothers who are employed full-time are much less likely to continue breast-feeding past the first few months than are women who are not employed. Other groups may choose bottle-feeding too, such as those women who are physically unable to breast-feed successfully, or those who wish to have the child's father much more actively involved in the child's care. For any of these groups of women the central question becomes one of potential effects of breast- versus bottle-feeding. Is the infant's health likely to be affected adversely by bottle-feeding? Might the interaction of the mother and infant be altered in any significant ways?

### Effects on the Baby

The nutritional and physical evidence provides a strong case for breast-feeding. Breast milk provides important protection for the infant against many kinds of diseases. The baby receives antibodies from the mother that he can't produce himself but that help to protect him against infec-

Chapter 1. Babies range from placid to vigorous in their response to any kind of stimulation. They also differ in their rate of activity, their emotional dispositions (irritable or sunny), in their preference for social interactions or solitude, in the regularity of their daily rhythms, and in many other ways. I'll be talking about temperament at greater length in Chapter 9, but at this point it is important to introduce a few more concepts and some particularly common terminology.

Psychologists who have been interested in these differences have proposed several different ways of describing the key dimensions of temperament. Buss and Plomin (1984, 1986), whose approach I talked about in Chapter 1 because they have most clearly argued for the genetic basis of temperament, propose three dimensions, Rothbart and Derryberry propose two dimensions, while Thomas and Chess (1977) describe nine dimensions, which they organize into three types, the easy child, the difficult child, and the slow-to-warm-up child.

It is not yet clear which of these views, or some other, will eventually carry the theoretical day. What is clear is that the Thomas and Chess formulation, particularly their description of the difficult child, has been the most

tions and allergies. Human breast milk also includes high levels of enzymes that promote the growth of nerves and intestinal tract (Carter, 1988). Breast milk is also easier for the baby to digest than is cow's milk or formula based on cow's milk. In particular, the fat in breast milk is almost entirely absorbed by the baby, while only about 80 percent of the fat in formula is absorbed. This is especially relevant for low-birth-weight infants, who have difficulty digesting fats. The high-cholesterol fats in breast milk may also have a long-lasting benefit. Isabelle Valadian (cited in Marano, 1979) has found that adults who were exclusively breast-fed for at least two months have lower cholesterol levels than those who were given formula.

Clearly infants can survive and even thrive on formula or on combinations of formula and breast milk. While the comparisons in most studies favor the breast-fed infant, the differences are not huge. Still, if it is feasible, breast-feeding seems clearly to be the optimal choice for the child's physical development.

## Mother-Infant Interaction

No such advantage for breast-feeding is found, however, when we look at patterns of mother-infant interaction. Bottle-fed babies are held and cuddled in the same ways as are breast-fed babies, and their mothers appear to be just as sensitive and responsive to their babies as are the breast-fed infants' mothers. Tiffany Field (1977), for example, looked at the kind of "turn-taking" that Kenneth Kaye describes. She found that both breast-feeders and bottle-feeders entered into the dialogue equally well.

Thus if your circumstances make it difficult or impossible for you to breast-feed, you should be reassured about the potential impact this choice will have on your interaction with your infant. For the emerging attachment of mother to child, or child to mother, there is nothing either necessary or sufficient about breast-feeding. As with so many of the decisions surrounding pregnancy, childbirth, and early infant care, the choice is an individual one.

heuristic and influential so far. Because their system has been used in many studies I'll mention in later chapters, I need to describe their three basic types for you.

*The Easy Child.*    Easy children approach new events positively. They try new foods without much fuss, for example. They are also regular in biological functioning, with good sleeping and eating cycles, are usually happy, and adjust easily to change.

*The Difficult Child.*    By contrast, the difficult child is less regular in body functioning and is slow to develop regular sleeping and eating cycles. These children react vigorously and negatively to new things, are more irritable, and cry more. Their cries also have a more "spoiled," grating sound than do the cries of "easy" babies (Boukydis & Burgess, 1982). Thomas and Chess point out, however, that once the difficult baby has adapted to something new, he is often quite happy about it, even though the adaptation process itself is very difficult.

*The Slow-to-Warm-Up Child.*   Children in this group do not respond as negatively to new things or new people as does the difficult child. They show instead a kind of passive resistance. Instead of spitting out new food violently and crying, the slow-to-warm-up child may let the food drool out and may resist mildly any attempt to feed her more of the same. These infants show few intense reactions, either positive or negative, although once they have adapted to something new, their reaction is usually fairly positive.

Interestingly, there is some evidence that these temperamental features occur in differing frequency in different cultures—a set of findings I've explored in the box on page 119. And in every culture some kind of temperamental variation can be seen in very young infants, and are at least somewhat persistent throughout childhood.

Neither Thomas and Chess nor other psychologists studying temperament are suggesting that such individual differences are absolutely fixed at birth. Any inborn temperamental differences are shaped, strengthened, bent, or counteracted by the child's relationships and experiences. What we do know is that infants enter the world with somewhat different repertoires or patterns of behavior, and that those differences affect not only the experiences the infant may choose, but also help shape the emerging pattern of interaction that develops between infant and parents. For example, toddlers and preschoolers with difficult temperaments are more often criticized or physically punished by their parents than are easy children, presumably because the child's behavior *is* more troublesome (Bates, 1989; Rutter, 1978a). Once established, however, such a pattern of criticism and punishment itself is likely to have additional consequences for the child.

Nonetheless, not all parents of difficult children respond in this way. A skilled parent, especially a parent who correctly perceives that the child's "difficultness" is a temperamental quality and not a result of the child's willfulness or the parent's ineptness, can avoid some of the pitfalls, and can handle the difficult child more adeptly.

## Sex and Social Class Differences in Infants

Two other kinds of individual differences among infants deserve at least a brief mention at this early stage: sex differences and differences associated with social class. A newborn child's sex is the very first thing we ask about when we inquire about a new baby, as if gender were the single most important thing: "Is it a boy or a girl?" Given that preoccupation with gender, it may surprise you to know that there are remarkably few sex differences among young infants. As was true at birth, girls continue to be a bit ahead in some aspects of physical maturity, and boys continue to be more vulnerable. For example, more boys die during the first year of life. Male infants also have more muscle tissue than do girls, and they seem to be slightly more physically active (Eaton & Enns, 1986). But boys and girls do not seem to differ on the temperamental dimensions Thomas and Chess have described: Boys are not more often "difficult" in temperament, and girls are not more often "easy," even though that is what our stereotypes might lead us to expect.

When we compare infants born to middle-class and poor families, we again find fewer differences than you might expect. You already know from

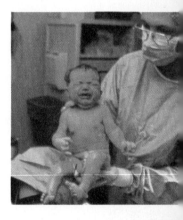

Daniel Freedman (1979) has observed newborn babies from four different cultures: caucasian, Chinese, Navaho, and Japanese. Of the four, he found that the caucasian babies were the most active and irritable and the hardest to console (the most "difficult" in Chess and Thomas's terms). Both the Chinese and the Navaho infants were relatively placid, while the Japanese infants responded vigorously but were easier to quiet than the caucasian infants.

For example, when Freedman tested each baby for the Moro reflex he found that the caucasian babies showed the typical pattern in which they reflexively extended both arms, cried vigorously and persistently, and moved their bodies in an agitated way. Navaho babies, on the other hand, showed quite a different pattern. Instead of thrusting their limbs outward they retracted their arms and legs, rarely cried, and showed little or very brief agitation.

Since such differences are visible in newborns they cannot be the result of systematic shaping by the parents. The par-ents, however, also bring their temperament and their cultural training to the interaction, which may tend to strengthen or perpetuate such temperamental differences. For instance, Freedman and other researchers have observed that both Japanese and Chinese mothers talk much less to their infants than do caucasian mothers. These differences in mothers' behavior were present from their first encounters with their infants after delivery, so the pattern is not a response to the baby's quieter behavior. But such similarity of temperamental pattern between mother and child is likely to strengthen the pattern in the child, which would tend to make the cultural differences larger over time.

One of the key points from this research is that our notions of what is "normal" behavior for an infant may be strongly influenced by our own cultural patterns and assumptions. More research like Freedman's is needed for us to describe and understand the range of variations that exist among babies.

## Cross-Cultural Differences in Temperament

Chapter 2 that the infant mortality rate is roughly twice as high among babies born to poor families. Such infants are also more likely to be born with low birth weights or to experience other complications of pregnancy or delivery. However, if we compare only healthy babies from the two social class groups, there are no differences between poor and middle-class babies in perceptual skills, motor development, or learning in the early months of life.

## S U M M A R Y

1. The normal birth process has three parts: dilation, delivery, and placental delivery.
2. The first "acquaintance" process after delivery may be an especially important one for parents. Most parents show an intense interest in the baby's features, especially the eyes.
3. Most drugs given to the mother during delivery pass through to the infant's

bloodstream. They have short-term effects on infant responsiveness and on feeding patterns. They may have some long-term effects as well.

4. The location of the delivery (hospital, birth center, or home) *may* make some difference, but we know little yet about the effects of location on the baby or on the parent-infant bond.

5. The presence of the father during delivery appears to help reduce the mother's discomfort, but it is not clear whether it also enhances the father's attachment to the infant.

6. Perhaps one-fifth of all deliveries in the United States today are by abdominal incision, called cesarean section, because of indications of fetal distress or other specific problems.

7. Several types of problems may occur at birth, including reduced oxygen supply (anoxia) to the infant, or low birth weight.

8. Low-birth-weight infants have higher risk of death during the first year of life, but if they survive, most catch up to full-size peers by school age. Those with birth weights below 1500 grams, or who are very small-for-date, are more likely to show lasting problems but the rate of problems has declined as neonatal intensive care has improved.

9. The birth, and the presence of the infant in the family system, have an effect not only on the mother, but on the marriage relationship. The majority of mothers have at least a brief period of "blues"; as many as one-fifth experience a more serious, longer depression. Marital satisfaction typically also declines.

10. The newborn has far more skills than most physicians and psychologists had thought, including excellent reflexes, good perceptual skills, and effective social skills.

11. The important infant reflexes include feeding reflexes, such as rooting and sucking, and the Moro reflex.

12. Perceptual skills include focusing both eyes, tracking slowly moving objects, discrimination of some sounds and some faces, and responsiveness to smells, tastes, and touch.

13. Motor skills, in contrast, are only rudimentary at birth.

14. Social skills, while rudimentary, are sufficient to bring people close for care and to keep them close for social interactions. The baby can meet a gaze and smile within the first month of life.

15. Newborns can learn from the first days of life, most easily by operant conditioning, but also through classical conditioning.

16. Newborns also habituate to repeated stimulation.

17. Young infants spend the majority of their days sleeping and are in an awake and alert state only a fraction of the time. Rhythms and daily cycles of sleeping, waking, crying, and eating are established early.

18. Babies differ from one another on several dimensions, including vigor of response, general activity rate, restlessness, irritability, and cuddliness. These temperamental dimensions, which Thomas and Chess have grouped into "difficult," "easy," and "slow-to-warm-up" types, appear to be at least somewhat stable.

19. Male and female babies differ at birth on a few dimensions. Girls are more mature physically. Boys are more active, have more muscle tissue, and are more vulnerable to stress. No sex differences are found, however, on temperamental dimensions such as cuddliness or sootheability.

20. No consistent differences between middle-class and poor infants are found on the usual measures of infant development.

# CRITICAL THINKING QUESTIONS

1. Assume for the moment that you (or your partner) is newly pregnant. You are trying to decide where and under what conditions you would like to deliver your infant. What decisions would you make, based on the information in this chapter? Why?
2. I've pointed out in this chapter that we have relatively little information about the possible impact of the location of delivery on the mother or the child. What kind of study or studies could you design that would give us better information?
3. Researchers and theorists interested in newborns and infants have been arguing for some decades about how early a baby can learn via classical or operant conditioning, and how early a baby shows habituation. To many students these seem like pretty uninteresting questions. But put yourself in the shoes of the theorists: Why might these questions be important, both theoretically or practically?

# KEY TERMS

**Apgar score**   An assessment of the newborn completed by the physician or midwife at one minute and again at five minutes after birth, assessing five characteristics: heart rate, respiratory rate, muscle tone, response to stimulation, and color.

**anoxia**   A shortage of oxygen. If it is prolonged, it can result in brain damage. This is one of the potential risks at birth.

**cesarean section (C-section)**   Delivery of the child through an incision in the mother's abdomen.

**dilation**   The first stage of childbirth when the cervix opens sufficiently to allow the infant's head to pass into the birth canal.

**effacement**   The flattening of the cervix which, along with dilation, allows the delivery of the infant.

**habituation**   An automatic decrease in the intensity of a response to a repeated stimulus, which enables the child or adult to ignore the familiar and focus attention on the novel.

**low birth weight (LBW)**   The phrase now used (in place of the word premature) to describe infants whose weight is below the optimum range at birth. Includes infants born too early (preterm or short gestation infants) and those who are "small-for-date."

**preterm**   Descriptive phrase now widely used to label infants born before 37 weeks gestational age.

**postpartum depression**   A severe form of the common experience of postpartum blues. Affecting perhaps 20 percent of women, this form of clinical depression typically lasts six to eight weeks.

**rapid eye movement (REM) sleep**   One of the characteristics of sleep during dreaming, which occurs during the sleep of newborns, too.

**reflexes**   Automatic body reactions to specific stimulation, such as the knee jerk or the Moro reflex. Many reflexes remain among adults, but the newborn also has some "primitive" reflexes that disappear as the cortex is fully developed.

**small-for-date**   A term used to describe an infant who weighs less than is normal for the number of weeks of gestation completed.

**states of consciousness**   Five main sleep/awake states have been identified in infants, from deep sleep to active awake states.

**very low birth weight**   The phrase now commonly used to describe infants who weigh 1500 grams (3 1/3 lbs) or less at birth.

# SUGGESTED READINGS

Brazelton, T. B. (1983) *Infants and mothers: differences in development.* (rev. ed.) New York: Delta/Seymour Lawrence.

An update of an excellent book, written by a remarkably observant and sensitive physician. It describes the first year of life in some detail and also chronicles the progress of several infants who differ in basic temperament.

Leach, P. (1983). *Babyhood.* (2nd ed.) New York: Knopf.

A detailed look at the first two years of life, written for a lay audience, but based very thoroughly on research. Very readable and practical.

Lipsitt, L. P. (1990). Learning and memory in infants. *Merrill-Palmer Quarterly,* 36, 53–66.

A review of 25 years of research on infant learning and memory by one of the leading theorists and researchers in the field.

Maurer, D., & Maurer, C. (1988). *The world of the newborn.* New York: Basic Books.

An excellent description of the newborn, written for the lay reader but based very clearly and strongly on research.

Osofsky, J. D. (Ed.) (1987). *Handbook of infant development.* (2nd ed.) New York: Wiley-Interscience.

The material in this splendid collection of papers is considerably more technical than what you will find in either the Maurer and Maurer or Slater and Bremner books listed here. But if you are interested in some specific aspect of infant development there is no better source for a comprehensive review.

Rosenblith, J. F., & Sims-Knight, J. E. (1989). *In the beginning. Development in the first two years of life.* Newbury Park, CA: Sage.

An excellent basic text on infant development.

Slater, A. M., & Bremner, J. G. (Eds.) (1989). *Infant development.* Hillsdale, NJ: Lawrence Erlbaum Associates.

Like the Maurer and Maurer book, this one was written by scientists, based on research, but aimed at the lay reader. In this case each chapter was written by a separate expert.

# PROJECT 3

## Observation in a Newborn Nursery

Despite the changes in birth practices, most hospitals still have newborn nurseries, and you can go and look through the window at the infants. However, you *must* obtain permission before you do so. Newborn nurseries are complex, busy places, and they cannot tolerate additional, unknown people crowding around the window. If your instructor has arranged for a number of students from your class to complete this assignment, he or she will need to obtain permission and make arrangements through the hospital, *and you should not contact the hospital invidually.* If your instructor has not made such group arrangements, you should check with the hospital office first, to determine if they have any standard procedure for obtaining permission to observe. If they do, then follow their procedure. If they have no procedure, you must at the least contact the head nurse in the obstetrics and newborn section of the hospital.

Once you have obtained the required permission and arranged a time that will be least disruptive of the hospital schedule (or signed up for a specific time among those arranged by your instructor), I would like you to observe the infants (through the window) for approximately half an hour. Proceed in the following way:

| 30-second Intervals | Baby's State | | | | |
|---|---|---|---|---|---|
| | Deep Sleep | Active Sleep | Quiet Awake | Active Awake | Crying Fussing |
| 1 | | | | | |
| 2 | | | | | |
| 3 | | | | | |

1. Set up a score sheet that should look something like the one shown, continuing the list for sixty 30-second intervals.
2. Reread the material in Table 3.4 until you know the main features of the five states as well as possible. You will need to focus on the eyes (open versus closed, and rapid eye movement), the regularity of the baby's breathing, and the amount of body movement.
3. Select one infant in the nursery and observe that infant's state every 30 seconds for a half hour. For each 30-second interval, note on your score sheet the state that best describes the infant over the preceding 30 seconds. Do *not* select an infant to observe who is in deep sleep at the beginning. Pick an infant who seems to be in an in-between state (active sleep or quiet awake), so that you can see some variation over the half-hour observation.
4. If you can arrange it, you might observe with a partner, each of you scoring the same infant's state independently. When the half hour is over, compare notes. How often did you agree on the infant's state? What might have been producing the disagreements?
5. When you discuss or write about the project, consider at least the following issues: Did the infant appear to have cycles of states? What were they? What effect, if any, do you think the nursery environment might have had on the baby's state? If you worked with a partner, how much agreement or disagreement did you have? Why?

You may find yourself approached by family members of babies in the nursery, asking what you are doing and why you have a clipboard and a stop watch. Be sure to reassure the parents or grandparents that your presence does not in any way suggest that there is anything wrong with any of the babies—you are doing a school project on observation. You may even want to show them the text describing the various states.

### Alternate Project

If it is not possible for you to observe in a newborn nursery—because local hospitals will not permit it, or your class is too large to be accommodated at local hospitals—the same project can be completed in a home setting with any infant under one or two months of age. The younger the better. You should observe the infant when he or she is lying in a crib or another sleeping location where it is possible for the child to move fairly freely (thus an infant seat won't do, nor will a baby carrier of any kind).

# PROJECT 4

## Observation of Turn-Taking During Feeding

If you know someone with a newborn infant, you might also want to try a somewhat more difficult type of observation—an observation of a feeding. For this project you will need an infant younger than 1 month. Ask the parents if you could simply watch one feeding, either a breast-feeding or a bottle feeding by either mother or father. Tell them that the purpose of your observation is simply for you to develop better observational skills. You will not be interfering in any way and there are no "right" or "wrong" ways to go about the task. If your instructor so specifies, or if your college or university requires it, you may need to obtain written permission from the parents to do this observation. If so, follow whatever written format your instructor indicates.

This observation is designed to examine "turn-taking" in the feeding interaction. I want you to observe for a total of about 10 minutes, keeping a running record of behaviors by the child and by the parent. To make the task manageable, I want you to focus on only three behaviors for each member of the pair:

1. *Infant behaviors:* sucking (S), fussing or crying (C), and other vocalizing (grunts, any other non-crying sounds) (V).
2. *Parent behaviors:* jiggling (J), vocalizing (any talking to the infant, or other sounds such as singing or cooing) (V), and stroking or touching (T).

To record these behaviors you will need a sheet with two columns, one column for the infant and one for the parent, as follows:

| Infant | Parent |
|--------|--------|
|        |        |
|        |        |
|        |        |
|        |        |
|        |        |

Begin your observation a few minutes after the feeding has begun, so that the infant and parent can adapt a bit to your presence and settle into some kind of pattern of interaction. Then start recording whatever behavior is occurring. If the infant is doing nothing but the parent is jiggling or talking or touching, then put the relevant letter in the parent box for the first row. If the infant is doing something and the parent is simultaneously doing something, record each in the adjacent boxes in a single row. And if the infant is doing something but the parent is not, then put the relevant letter in the infant box for that row and leave the parent box blank. When either member of the pair *changes* behavior, move to the next row in your record sheet. So if the baby sucks and then stops, the mother then jiggles, then says something, and then the baby sucks again, it would look like this:

| Infant | Parent |
|--------|--------|
| S      |        |
|        | J      |
|        | V      |
| S      |        |
|        |        |

If the baby sucks and the mother talks to him at the same time, and then the infant stops sucking and the mother talks to the baby, it would look like this:

| Infant | Parent |
|--------|--------|
| S      | V      |
|        | V      |
|        |        |
|        |        |

For this observation you should pay no attention to the duration of an activity. For the purposes of this exercise, it doesn't matter if the child sucks for 3 seconds or for 30 seconds before some change occurs.

When you have completed 10 minutes of observation, or when the feeding is completed—whichever comes first—stop recording. You will need to remain seated and quiet until the feeding is over so as not to distract the parent and infant. Be sure to thank the parent, and feel free to show the parent your observational record if he or she asks.

In examining your observational record, see if you can detect any signs of "turn taking" in the patterns of interaction. Does the parent jiggle or talk primarily in the pauses of the infant's sucking? Or does the parent talk and jiggle at the same time as the sucking? Can you devise some way of scoring the sequence of interactions that would yield a measure of "turn-taking"? What are the difficulties involved in devising such a score?

# THE PHYSICAL CHILD

4

# PHYSICAL DEVELOPMENT

In the last two chapters I talked about the earliest months of the child's life, from conception through the first few months after birth. Many texts at this point continue to organize the material around the child's age, with chapters describing the toddler, the preschooler, the school-age child, and the adolescent. From my perspective, the difficulty with this strategy is that the underlying sequences of development—in language, physical change, thinking, and personal relationships—tend to get lost. So I have chosen another tack: In each of the chapters that follow I will examine the development of a single facet of the child's functioning—perceptual skills, language, thinking, and relationships with others. Then in the final chapters I will try to weave all these facets together to form a single whole. Let me begin with perhaps the most basic facet of all, the development of the child's physical body from birth through adolescence.

Some years ago, when my daughter was about 8 1/2, a lot of well-rehearsed family routines seemed to unravel. She was crankier than usual, both more assertive and more needful of affection, and alternately compliant and defiant. What on earth was happening? Had I done something dreadfully wrong? Was there something going on at school? I mentioned my problems to several colleagues and began to hear tales from other parents about the special difficulties they had had with their daughters between ages 8 and 9.

Nothing in any of the developmental research or theory I had ever read suggested this ought to be a particularly stressful time. But slowly I began to put some faith in my observations and to search for an explanation. Having been trained with a heavy emphasis on environmental influences on development, I looked at those factors first. But that didn't offer me much in the way of answers. The 8- or 9-year-old has been in school for two or three years, and there didn't seem to be any major new adaptation being demanded. Belatedly, I began to think about physical changes and an explanation occurred to me: Girls of 8 or 9 are actually beginning puberty! The first hormone changes begin around this age, and many of the inconsistent and uncomfortable behaviors I was seeing could easily be a response to the changing hormones in the system.

It may amuse you to think of the clever psychologist being stumped by something so obvious. But in fact developmental psychologists have often placed too little emphasis on physical growth. We describe it briefly and then take it for granted. But I am convinced both by the research literature on the effects of physiological change and by my observations as a parent that an understanding of physical development is an absolutely critical first step in understanding children's progress, for at least four reasons.

## Four Reasons for Studying Physical Development

### The Child's Growth Makes New Behaviors Possible

Specific physical changes are needed before the infant can crawl or walk. Other changes are needed for an older child's growing skill at running, kicking a ball, or jumping rope. At adolescence, the development of full reproductive capacity is based on a complex sequence of physical changes. All of these important skills or capacities are made possible by specific physical changes.

The flip side of this is that the *lack* of a particular physical development may set limits on the behaviors a child is capable of performing. An infant of 10 months cannot be toilet trained, no matter how hard parents may try, because the anal sphincter muscle is not yet fully mature. Toddlers cannot easily pick up raisins or Cheerios from their high chair trays until the muscles and nerves required for thumb-forefinger opposition have developed.

It seems to me that such limits deserve far more attention than they normally receive. For example, think about children who participate in Pee Wee League football or Little League baseball. I have several times watched coaches reduce their young charges to tears by demanding levels of coordination and skill that 5- and 6-year-olds or even 10- and 11-year-olds can rarely achieve. Parents can easily do the same.

### The Child's Growth Determines Experience

Children's range of physical capacities or skills can also have a major indirect effect on cognitive and social development and on the variety of experiences they can have. For example, an infant who cannot crawl can only explore things that are brought to her or are within easy reach. When she begins to crawl, her experiences are greatly expanded. Similarly, children who learn to ride a bike widen their horizons still further, as they explore the neighborhood on their own, perhaps for the first time.

### The Child's Growth Affects Others' Responses

The effect of these changes in the child's skills works both ways: They alter the child's experiences, and they change the way the people around the child respond to her. For example, parents react quite differently to an infant who can crawl than to one who cannot. They begin to say "no" more often, put things out of reach, or put the baby in a playpen more of the time. Such changes in the pattern of interaction between parent and child may have both immediate and long-term consequences for the child's emotional or mental development.

Adults' expectations for children are also affected by the child's size and shape, attractiveness, or physical skills. Children who are pretty, tall, or well coordinated are treated differently from those who are homely, petite, or

Benji Gholston, at age five, has not quite mastered the art of bike riding. But it will not be long before he does, and that new physical skill will make a very large difference in his independence and therefore in the kinds of experiences he can have. This photo is a video still from the *Childhood* television series (*Source:* ©Thirteen/WNET).

clumsy (Brackbill & Nevill, 1981; Lerner, 1985). A Little League baseball coach may be more supportive of a child with advanced large-muscle coordination (useful for home runs), while a classroom teacher may be especially appreciative of children whose small-muscle coordination (necessary for writing and drawing) is superior. As a general rule, the larger or more developed a child, the more "adult" his behavior is expected to be.

Adults and children are also biased in favor of some specific body types. In the terminology introduced by Sheldon some years ago (Sheldon, 1940), the most favored type is one that is well muscled and square in build, which Sheldon called **mesomorphic. Endomorphic** (rounded) and **ectomorphic** (skinny, tall, bony) body types are less preferred by both children and adults (Lerner, 1985, 1987). Thus individual differences in physical patterns, or speed of growth, can have profound effects on children's early experiences.

### The Child's Growth Affects Self-Concept

The final reason for us to pay close attention to physical development is that physical characteristics and physical skills (or lack of them) have a significant influence on a child's self-concept. I'll be talking about this topic more fully in Chapters 9 and 10, but let me point out here that this is another example of the importance of internal models, a concept I introduced in Chapter 1. A child's body image, which is part of her self-concept, is not an accurate match to some observable reality, but is an internal model shaped not only by direct experience, but by what the child overhears from others, and by the

**mesomorphic**
Body type characterized by amount of muscle mass; a mesomorphic male is square-chested, broad-shouldered, and muscular.

**endomorphic**
Body type defined by amount of body fat; an endomorphic individual is soft and round in shape.

**ectomorphic**
Body type defined by bone length; an ectomorphic individual is tall and slender, usually with stooped shoulders.

These children are the same age, but you'd never guess it by looking at them. Most adults will automatically assign the larger child more complex tasks, expect more, and perhaps even talk in a more adult way to this child.

child's ideas about the current cultural image of an ideal body (Thomas, 1990b). Like all internal models, the body image, once created, becomes relatively difficult to change. A child's choice of activities, her behavior in social situations, and her sense of self-worth are all likely to be affected throughout childhood and adolescence, perhaps even into adulthood by the body image formed early in childhood. My own body image, for example, includes a strong element of "gawkiness," since I was always taller than everyone else and saw myself as uncoordinated. Whether that is *objectively* true is less important than the fact that it forms a key part of my internal model of myself.

For all of these reasons, I think it is important to begin our exploration of development with a fairly detailed look at physical growth and change.

 ## Basic Sequences and Common Patterns

### Height and Weight

Obviously children get bigger as they get older. But even this simple statement may conceal some surprises. The biggest surprise for most people is the fact that at birth an infant is already one-third of his final height. By age two he is one-half as tall as full adult height. Another possible surprise is the fact that growth from birth to maturity is neither continuous nor smooth. Figure 4.1 on the next page shows the growth patterns for height for boys and girls and the four different phases in this process.

During the first phase, which lasts for about two years, the baby gains in height very rapidly, adding 10 to 12 inches in length in the first year and tripling his body weight in the same span. After this rapid growth, the second phase begins: The child settles into a slower but steady addition of 2 to 3 inches and about 6 pounds per year until adolescence.

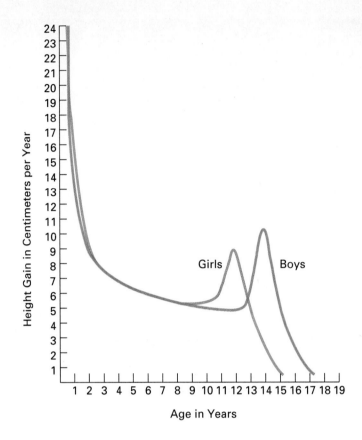

**FIGURE 4.1**

These curves show the gain in height for each year from birth through adolescence. You can see the several clear phases: very rapid growth in infancy, slower growth in the preschool and elementary school years, the growth spurt at adolescence, and the cessation of growth at adulthood (*Sources:* Tanner, 1978, p. 14; Malina, 1990).

The third phase begins with the dramatic adolescent "growth spurt," (shown clearly in Figure 4.1) when the child may add 3 to 6 inches a year for several years. After the growth spurt, in the fourth phase, the child again adds height and weight slowly until his or her final adult size is reached.

### Shape

At the same time, the shape and proportions of the child's body are changing. In an adult, the head is about one-eighth or one-tenth of the total height. But the toddler isn't built like that. In the 2-year-old, the head is about one-fourth of the total body length.

Individual body parts do not all grow at the same rate either. This is particularly striking at adolescence. During those years, a teenager's hands and feet grow to full adult size earliest, followed by the arms and legs, with the trunk usually the slowest part to grow. (In fact, a good signal for a parent that puberty is beginning in a child is a rapid increase in shoe size.) Because of this asymmetry in the body parts we often think of an adolescent as awkward or uncoordinated. Interestingly, research does not support that perception. Robert Malina, who has done extensive research on physical development, has found no point in the adolescent growth process at which teenagers become consistently less coordinated or less skillful on physical tasks (Malina, 1990).

Children's heads and faces also change from infancy through adolescence. During the elementary school years, the size and shape of a child's jaw change when the permanent teeth come in. And in adolescence both jaws grow forward and the forehead becomes more prominent. This set of changes often gives teenagers' faces (especially boys') an angular, bony appearance, quite unlike their earlier look—as you can see in the set of photographs of one boy in Figure 4.2.

### Bones

The observable outside changes in size and shape are the result of changes on the inside in bones, muscles, and fat. Bones change in three ways with development: They increase in number, become longer, and grow harder.

*Number of bones.* Bones increase in number in the hand, wrist, ankle, and foot. For example, in an adult's wrist there are nine separate bones. In the 1-year-old, there are only three. The remaining six develop over the period of childhood, with complete growth by adolescence.

In one part of the body, though, the bones fuse rather than differentiate. The skull of an infant is made up of several bones separated by spaces called **fontanels.** Fontanels allow the head to be compressed without injury during the birth process, and they also give the brain room to grow. In most children, the fontanels are filled in by bone by 12 to 18 months (Kataria et al., 1988) creating a single connected skull bone (although the originally separate parts of the skull retain distinctive names).

*Hardening of bones.* All of the infants' bones are softer and have a higher water content than adults' bones. The process of bone hardening, called **ossification,** occurs steadily from birth through puberty. Bones in different parts of the body harden in a sequence that follows a general plan that is characteristic of many (but not all) physical developments, moving from the head downward (**cephalocaudal**) and from the trunk outward (**proximodistal**). For example, bones of the hand and wrist harden before those in the feet. Clearly, though, not all physical development follows these two patterns. Growth to final adult size follows largely an opposite pattern, since hands and feet, legs and arms, all grow to final height before the trunk does.

You may well be thinking that bone hardening is pretty boring and irrelevant stuff. However, if you think about it you'll realize that a high degree of

**fontanels**
The "soft spots" in the skull present at birth. These disappear when the several bones of the skull grow together.

**ossification**
The process of hardening by which soft tissue becomes bone.

**cephalocaudal**
From the head downward. Describes one recurrent pattern of physical development in infancy.

**proximodistal**
From the center outward. With cephalocaudal, describes the pattern of physical changes in infancy.

**FIGURE 4.2**

In these photos of the same boy before, during, and after puberty, you can see the striking changes in jaw and forehead shape that dramatically alter the appearance of many teenagers (*Source:* Tanner, 1962, Plate 1, p. 17).

body flexibility is necessary if the fetus is going to fit into the cramped space of the uterus. But that very flexibility is also one of the factors that contributes to a newborn human's relative helplessness. Newborns are remarkably floppy; they cannot even hold their heads up, let alone sit up or walk. As the bones stiffen, the baby is able to manipulate his body more surely, which increases the range of exploration he can enjoy and makes him much more independent.

### Muscles

Although the bones are not all formed at birth, the newborn baby has virtually all the muscle fibers she will ever have (Tanner, 1978). Like the infant's bones, muscle fibers are initially small and watery, becoming longer, thicker, and less watery at a fairly steady rate until adolescence, when there is a growth spurt in muscles as well as in height. One of the clear results of this rapid adolescent increase in muscle tissue is that adolescents become quite a lot stronger in just a few years. Both boys and girls show this increase in muscle tissue and strength, but as you can see in Figure 4.3, the increase is much greater in boys. Among adult men, about 40 percent of total body mass is muscle, compared to only about 24 percent in adult women.

Some of you may be asking yourselves at this point whether this sex difference in strength is an inevitable physiological difference, or whether higher levels of physical exercise among teenage boys (from sports as well as simply greater body movement) may not be contributing to their greater

**FIGURE 4.3**

Both boys and girls get stronger over the years of childhood and adolescence, but boys gain much more strength, particularly at puberty. Some of this might be caused by boys' greater amount of exercise, but a good portion of this difference seems to be the effect of increases in male hormone at adolescence in boys (*Source:* Adapted from Montpetit, Montoye, & Laeding, 1967, from Tables 1 and 2, p. 233).

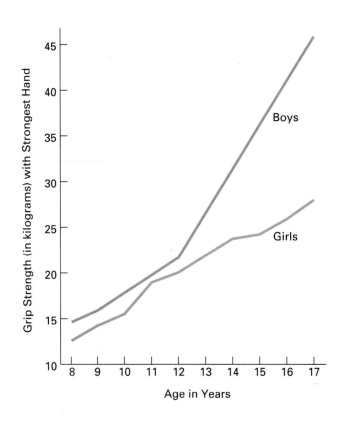

growth of muscle tissue and hence greater strength. As is often the case, the answer is probably both. Differences in hormone patterns at adolescence appear to be major contributors to the sex differences in muscle growth. However, there are also some hints that sex differences in muscle use may be involved. For example, Tanner and his colleagues (Tanner, Hughes, & Whitehouse, 1981) found much larger sex differences in arm muscle than in calf muscle strength gains at adolescence. These findings make sense if we assume that arm muscle use varies more as a function of sports or other exercise than is true of leg muscles, which everyone uses for locomotion. What is needed now is a set of longitudinal comparisons of equally fit boys and girls, both involved in the same physical activities at similar levels of intensity, such as comparisons of competitive swimmers or gymnasts.

### Fat

Another major component of the body is fat, most of which is stored immediately under the skin. This *subcutaneous fat* begins to develop at about 34 weeks prenatally and has an early peak at about 9 months after birth. The thickness of this layer of fat then declines until about age 6 or 7, after which it rises until adolescence.

Once again there is a very large sex difference in these patterns. From birth, girls have slightly more fat tissue than boys do, and this difference becomes gradually more marked during childhood. At adolescence, the difference becomes particularly striking. One current study of a large group of Canadian teenagers (Smoll & Schutz, 1990) shows that among girls in the seventh grade, 21.8 percent of body weight was made up of fat, while among eleventh grade girls fat represented 24 percent. Among groups of boys the equivalent figures were 16.1 percent and 14.0 percent. So during and after puberty, proportions of fat rise among girls and decline among boys, a pattern found consistently by other researchers as well (e.g., Chumlea, 1982).

Of course, as with muscle tissue, this sex difference in fat may be partially a lifestyle or activity level effect. Girls and women who are extremely athletic, such as long-distance runners or ballet dancers, typically have body fat levels that approximate those of the average boy. But if we compare equally fit boys and girls, boys have lower fat levels.

### Development of the Nervous System

Growth in height and weight involve changes you can see. Even the changes in muscles, bones, and fat can be detected fairly easily in the child's longer legs, greater strength, or softness or leanness of body. However, there are two enormously important types of developmental changes in the body that are not so easy to perceive. The first of these is change in the nervous system.

*Composition of the Nervous System.* Figure 4.4 on the next page shows the main structures of the central nervous system. As I mentioned briefly in Chapter 3, the **midbrain** and the **medulla** are most fully developed at birth. These two parts, both in the lower part of the skull and connecting to the spinal cord, regulate such basic tasks as attention and habituation, sleeping, waking, elimination, and movement of the head and neck (but not move-

**midbrain**
A section of the brain lying above the medulla and below the cortex that regulates attention, sleeping, waking, and other "automatic" functions. Largely developed at birth.

**medulla**
A portion of the brain that lies immediately above the spinal cord; largely developed at birth.

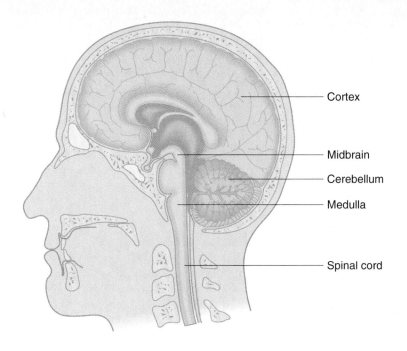

**FIGURE 4.4**

The medulla and the midbrain are largely developed at birth. In the first two years after birth it is primarily the cortex that develops, although increases in the dendritic arbor and in synapses occur throughout the nervous system.

Cortex

Midbrain

Cerebellum

Medulla

Spinal cord

**cortex**
The convoluted gray portion of the brain which governs most complex thought, language, and memory, among other functions.

ment of the trunk or limbs). As you saw in the last chapter, these are all tasks a newborn can perform at least moderately well.

The least developed part of the brain at birth is the **cortex,** the convoluted gray matter that wraps around the midbrain and is involved in perception, body movement, and all complex thinking and language.

As I described in Chapter 2 (Figure 2.6) the nervous system is composed of two basic types of cells, *neurons* and *glial cells*. Since virtually all of both types of cells are already present at birth, the developmental process after birth is primarily the creation of synapses, which involves enormous growth of the dendritic arbor, axons, and axonal terminal fibers. Most of that dendritic growth occurs in the cortex, primarily during the first year or two after birth, resulting in a tripling of the overall weight of the brain during those years (Nowakowski, 1987). But even this development is not smooth and continuous. Neurophysiologists have found an initial burst of synapse formation, followed by a "pruning" of synapses, at about age 2, which eliminates the redundant ones and cleans up the " wiring diagram" (Greenough et al., 1987). Taken together, these two developmental patterns (which you can see illustrated in Figure 4.5) mean that the 1-year- old actually has a *denser* set of dendrites and synapses than an adult does.

The pruning process, which is only now beginning to be understood by physiologists, is especially fascinating. An example: Early in development each skeletal muscle cell seems to develop synaptic connections with several motor neurons in the spinal cord. After the pruning process has occurred, each muscle fiber is connected to only one neuron. In an argument reminiscent of the concept of "inborn biases" I introduced in Chapter 1, some neurophysiologists, such as Greenough, Black, & Wallace (1987), have suggested that the initial surge of development of the dendrite arbor and synaptic formation follows a built-in pattern. They assert that the organism is programmed to create certain kinds of neural connections and does so in abundance, creating re-

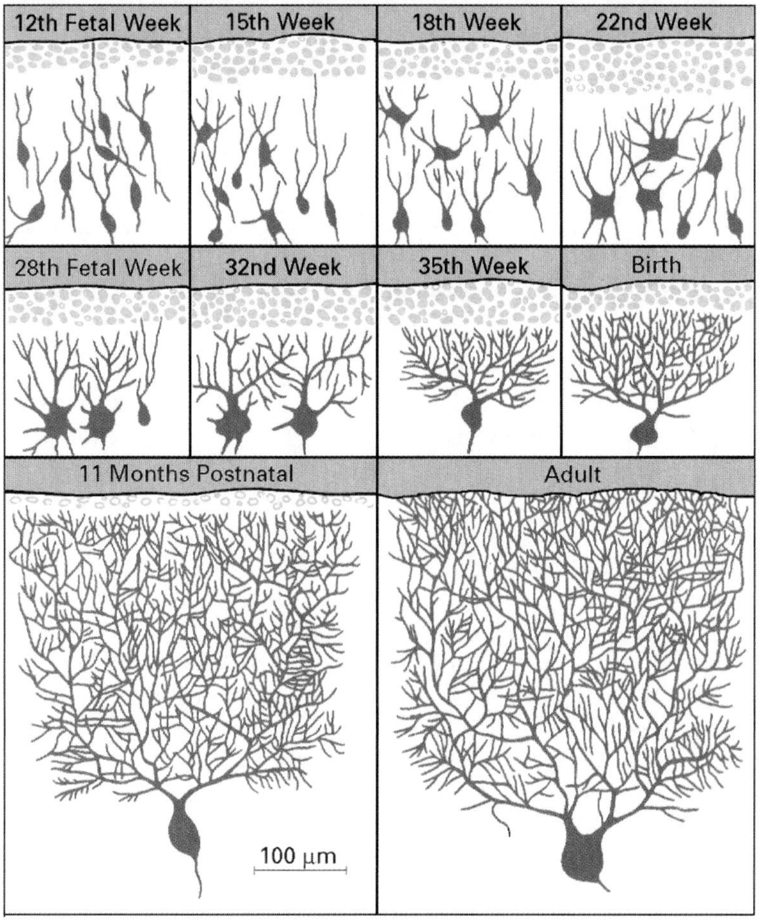

| 12th Fetal Week | 15th Week | 18th Week | 22nd Week |
| 28th Fetal Week | 32nd Week | 35th Week | Birth |

| 11 Months Postnatal | Adult |

100 μm

FIGURE 4.5

Nerve cells are almost all present at birth; what changes after birth is an immense growth of the "dendritic arbor" of each neuron, peaking at about 12 months, after which there is a "pruning" of the dendrites and synapses.

dundant pathways. According to this argument, the pruning that occurs at about age 2 is a response to a specific experience, resulting in selective retention of the used or the most efficient pathways. Putting it briefly, "experience does not create tracings on a blank tablet; rather experience erases some of them" (Bertenthal & Campos, 1987). Interestingly, there appears to be another pruning of synapses at adolescence, suggesting that there may be a further reorganization of pathways at that time.

Greenough and his colleagues do not think that all synaptic development is governed by such built-in programming. He suggests that other synapses are formed entirely as a result of specific experience and continue to form throughout our lives. However, the emergence of neuronal control of the basic motor and sensory processes may initially follow built-in patterns, with pruning then based on experience.

*Myelinization.* Another crucial process in neuronal development is the development of sheaths around individual axons, which insulate them from one another and improve the conductivity of the nerve. This sheath is made up of a substance called **myelin**; the process of developing the sheath is called **myelinization.**

myelin
Material making up a sheath that develops around most axons. This sheath is not completely developed at birth.

myelinization
The process by which myelin is added.

The sequence with which nerves are myelinized follows roughly the same cephalocaudal and proximodistal patterns I described for muscular development. Thus nerves serving muscle cells in the arms and hands are myelinized earlier than are those serving the lower trunk and the legs. Most myelinization is complete by age 2, although some continues at a slower rate in the brain well into adolescence.

To understand the importance of myelin, it may help you to know that *multiple sclerosis* is a disease in which the myelin begins to break down. An individual with this disease gradually loses motor control, with the specific symptoms depending on the portion of the nervous system affected by the disease.

### Hormones

**endocrine glands**
These glands, including the adrenals, the thyroid, the pituitary, the testes, and the ovaries, secrete hormones governing overall physical growth and sexual maturing.

**pituitary gland**
One of the endocrine glands that plays a central role in controlling the rate of physical maturation and sexual maturing.

A second less visible set of changes we need to look at is in *hormones*— secretions of the various **endocrine glands** in the body. Hormones govern growth and physical changes in several ways, which I've summarized in Table 4.1.

Of all the endocrine glands, the most critical is the **pituitary gland,** since it provides the trigger for release of hormones from other glands. For example, the thyroid gland only secretes thyroxine when it has received a signal to do so in the form of a specific thyroid-stimulating hormone secreted by the pituitary.

Hormones play a role at every stage of physical development, perhaps most strikingly at adolescence, but significantly at earlier stages as well.

*Prenatal Hormones.*   Thyroid hormone (thyroxine) is present from about the fourth month of gestation, and appears to be involved in stimulating nor-

***TABLE 4.1***

*Major Hormones of Physical Growth and Development*

| Gland | Hormone(s) Secreted | Aspects of Growth Influenced |
| --- | --- | --- |
| Thyroid | Thyroxine | Affects normal brain development and overall rate of growth. |
| Adrenal | Adrenal androgen | Involved in some changes at puberty, particularly the development of secondary sex characteristics in girls. |
| Testes (in boys) | Testosterone | Crucial in the formation of male genitals prenatally; also triggers the sequence of primary and secondary sex characteristic changes at puberty in the male. |
| Ovaries (in girls) | Estradiol | Affects development of the menstrual cycle and breasts in girls but has less to do with other secondary sex characteristics than testosterone does for boys. |
| Pituitary | Growth hormone; activating hormones | Affects rate of physical maturation. Signals other glands to secrete. |

mal brain development. Growth hormone is also produced by the pituitary beginning as early as 10 weeks after conception. Presumably it helps to stimulate the very rapid growth of cells and organs of the body. As I mentioned in Chapter 2, testosterone is produced prenatally in the testes of the developing male and influences both the development of male genitals and some aspects of brain development.

*Hormones Between Birth and Adolescence.* The rate of growth between birth and adolescence is governed largely by thyroid hormone and pituitary growth hormone. Thyroid hormone is secreted in greater quantities for the first two years of life and then falls to a lower level and remains steady until adolescence (Tanner, 1978). This pattern of rapid early development followed by slower and steadier secretions obviously matches the pattern of change in height and weight already shown in Figure 4.1.

Secretions from the testes and ovaries, as well as adrenal androgen, remain at extremely low levels until about age 7 or 8. At this time, adrenal androgen begins to be secreted, which is the first sign of the changes of adolescence, and no doubt one of the sources of the changes I observed in my 8-year-old daughter (Shonkoff, 1984).

*Hormones in Adolescence.* The early rise in adrenal androgen is only the first step in a complex sequence of hormone changes at adolescence, which you can see laid out briefly in Figure 4.6 on the next page.

The timing of these changes varies a lot from one child to the next, but the sequence remains the same. A signal from the hypothalamus gland prompts the pituitary gland to secrete increased levels of **gonadotrophic hormones** (two in males, three in females). These in turn stimulate the development of the glands in the testes and ovaries which then begin to secrete more hormones: testosterone in boys and a form of **estrogen** called *estradiol* in girls. Over the course of puberty, the levels of testosterone increase eighteenfold in boys, while levels of estradiol increase eightfold in girls (Nottelmann, et al., 1987).

At the same time, the pituitary also secretes three other hormones that affect growth and that interact with the specific sex hormones. As you can see in Figure 4.6, the interaction is a little different for boys and girls. In particular, the growth spurt and pubic hair development in girls are more influenced by adrenal androgen than is true for boys. Adrenal androgen is chemically similar to testosterone, so it takes a "male" hormone to produce the growth spurt in girls. For boys, adrenal androgen is less significant, presumably because they already have male hormone in the form of testosterone floating about in their bloodstream.

It is somewhat misleading, by the way, to talk about "male" and "female" hormones. In fact both males and females have at least some of each (estrogen or estradiol and testosterone or androgen). The difference is essentially in the relative proportion of the two. Within any one gender, these proportions differ as well, so some males have relatively more testosterone or less androgen, while in others the two may be more balanced. Similarly, some girls may have a pattern of hormones that includes relatively more testosterone, while others may have relatively little.

Just how this hormonal process is turned off (or toned down) at the end of puberty is much less clear (Dreyer, 1982). In some fashion, the levels of

**gonadotropic hormone**
Hormones produced in the pituitary gland which stimulate the sex organs to develop.

**estrogen**
The female sex hormone secreted by the ovaries.

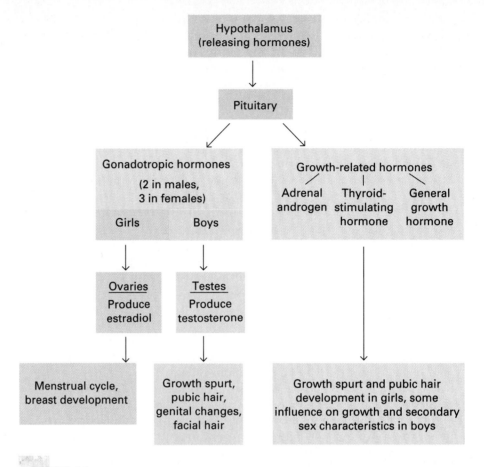

**FIGURE 4.6**

The action of the various hormones at puberty is exceedingly complex. This figure over-simplifies the process but gives you some sense of the sequence and the differences between the patterns for boys and girls.

growth hormones and gonadotrophic hormones produced in the pituitary drop to a lower level and the rate of body change gradually tapers off at the adult levels.

 ## Development of Sexual Maturity

**puberty**
The collection of hormonal and physical changes at adolescence that brings about sexual maturity.

The physical results of the hormonal changes in **puberty** are not only a spurt in height but, more importantly, a set of physical changes that bring about full sexual maturity. There are changes not only in primary sex characteristics, which involve changes in the reproductive systems themselves (testes and penis in the male, and ovaries, uterus, and vagina in the female), but also in secondary sex characteristics, such as breast development, body and facial hair, and lowered voice pitch in boys.

Each of these physical developments occurs in a defined sequence. Fol-

**140**    **Part Three**    The Physical Child

lowing the work of J. M. Tanner (1978), each sequence is customarily divided into five stages. Stage 1 represents the preadolescent stage, Stage 2 the first signs of pubertal change, Stages 3 and 4 the intermediate steps, and Stage 5 the final adult characteristic. Table 4.2 provides two examples of these sequences, one for a secondary sex characteristic (breast development) and one for a primary characteristic (genital development in boys). These stages have proven to be extremely helpful not only for describing the normal progress through puberty but for assessing the rate of development of individual youngsters.

### Sexual Development in Girls

Studies of preteens and teens in both Europe and North America (summarized by Robert Malina, 1990) show that in girls the sets of sequences are interlocked in a particular pattern. The early steps include both Stages 2 and 3 of breast and pubic hair development, which are followed by the peak of the growth spurt and then by Stage 4 of both breast and pubic hair development. Only then does first menstruation occur, an event more properly called **menarche** (pronounced men-ar-kee). Menarche typically occurs two years after the beginning of other visible changes and is succeeded only by the final stages of breast and pubic hair development, a pattern you can see in Figure 4.7 on the next page. In Malina's analysis, the average ages for menarche ranged from 12.8 to 13.5 in various studies, with 95 percent of all girls experiencing this event between the ages of 11 and 15.

menarche
Onset of menstruation in girls.

*TABLE 4.2*

*Tanner's Stages of Pubertal Development: Breast and Male Genital Development*

| Breast Development | Stage | Male Genital Development |
|---|---|---|
| No change except for some elevation of the nipple. | 1 | Testes, scrotum, and penis are all about the same size and shape as in early childhood. |
| Breast bud stage: elevation of the breast and the nipple as a small mound. Areolar diameter is enlarged over Stage 1. | 2 | Scrotum and testes slightly enlarged. Skin of the scrotum is reddened and changed in texture but little or no enlargement of the penis. |
| Breast and areola both enlarged and elevated more than in Stage 2 but no separation of their contours. | 3 | Penis slightly enlarged, at first mainly in length. Testes and scrotum are further enlarged. |
| Areola and nipple form a secondary mound projecting above the contour of the breast. | 4 | Penis further enlarged, with growth in breadth and development of glans. Testes and scrotum further enlarged and scrotum skin still darker. |
| Mature stage: Nipple only projects with the areola recessed to the general contour of the breast. | 5 | Genitalia are adult in size and shape. |

*Source:* Petersen & Taylor, 1980, p. 127

**FIGURE 4.7**

The figure shows the normal sequence and timing of pubertal changes for girls. The box on each line represents the average attainment of that change, while the line indicates the range of normal times. Note the *wide* range of normality for all of these changes. Also note how relatively late in the sequence the growth spurt and menarche occur (*Sources:* Chumlea, 1982; Garn, 1980; Malina, 1990; Tanner, 1978).

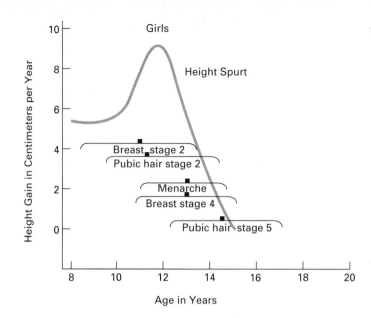

Menarche is a clear single event that is often taken as a measure of sexual maturity. And it is possible to conceive shortly after menarche. However, irregularity is actually the norm for some time. In as many as three-fourths of the cycles in the first year, and one-half the cycles in the second and third years after menarche, no ovum is produced (Vihko & Apter, 1980). Full adult fertility thus develops over a period of years.

The initial irregularity of both ovulation and of the timing of menstrual cycles has some significant practical consequences for sexually active teenagers. For example, such irregularity no doubt contributes to the widespread (but false) assumption among early-teenage girls that they cannot get pregnant because they are "too young." At the same time the irregularity makes any form of rhythm contraception unreliable, even among teenagers who have enough basic reproductive knowledge to realize that the time of ovulation is normally the time of greatest fertility—knowledge that is not widespread.

### Sexual Development in Boys

In boys, as in girls, the point of peak growth typically comes fairly late in the sequence. Malina's data suggest that on average a boy completes Stages 2, 3, and 4 of genital development and Stages 2 and 3 of pubic hair development before the growth peak is reached (Malina, 1990). Facial hair and deeper voice levels appear only near the end of the sequence. You can see the basic features of the pattern in Figure 4.8 and compare it to the pattern for girls.

Precisely when in this sequence the boy achieves reproductive maturity is very difficult to determine. Unlike menarche, which normally occasions both discussion and assistance, the first nocturnal emission is a private event and it is hard to tell just when the seminal fluid begins to contain viable sperm. For most boys, real fertility seems to occur sometime between 12 and 16.

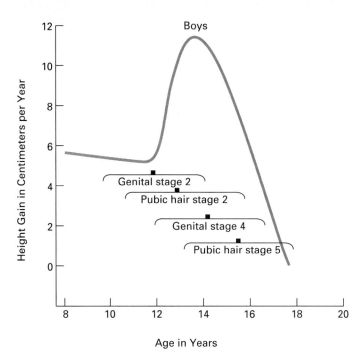

**FIGURE 4.8**

The sequence of pubertal changes for boys begins about two years later than does the girls' sequence, but as with pubertal change in girls, the height spurt occurs relatively late in the sequence for boys (*Sources:* Chumlea, 1978; Malina, 1990; Tanner, 1978).

Two facts are particularly interesting about these sequences. First, if you compare Figures 4.7 and 4.8, you will see that girls are about two years ahead of boys in their pubertal development. Most of you remember that period in late elementary school or junior high when all the girls were suddenly taller than the boys, and began to show secondary sex characteristics while the 11- and 12-year-old boys were still pre-pubertal. (A painful time for a lot of us.) A second intriguing point is that while the order of development seems to be highly consistent *within* each sequence (such as breast development, or pubic hair development), there is quite a lot of variability *across* sequences. I have given you the normative or average pattern, but individual teenagers often do not follow that normative pattern. For instance, a boy may be in Stage 2 of genital development but already in Stage 5 of pubic hair development. A girl might move through several stages of pubic hair development before the first clear breast changes, or she might experience menarche much earlier in the sequence than normal. So far physiologists have not figured out why this occurs but it is an important point to keep in mind if you are trying to make a prediction about an individual teenager.

### Other Changes in Puberty

Aside from the changes in primary and secondary sex characteristics, in height, musculature, and fat, there are some important changes in the body organs that seem to be triggered by the same hormones that produce pubertal changes. In particular, the heart and lungs increase considerably in size and the heart rate drops. Both of these changes are more marked for boys than for girls—another of the factors that increases the capacity for sustained effort for boys relative to girls. Before about age 12, boys and girls have similar physical strength, speed, and endurance (although even at these earlier ages, any difference favors the boys because of their lower levels of body fat). After puberty, boys have a clear advantage in all three categories (Smoll & Schutz, 1990).

## Using the Body: The Effects of Physical Changes on Behavior

Obviously, children's bodies change enormously over the first 15 years of life. The brief picture I have provided of these changes should give you some sense of the alterations in muscles, fat, internal organs, and nervous system. However, this description does not convey the impact of all those changes on the child's behavior, particularly the remarkable emergence of the child's ability to move around in his world. Esther Thelen (Thelen, Kelso, & Fogel, 1987), one of the leading researchers and theorists in the area of physical development, explains this change in abilities as follows:

> The passage from the limited motor repertoire of the newborn to the complex loco-motor and manipulatory skills of the toddler stands among the most visible and dramatic transformations in the human life cycle. (p. 39)

The generic name for this collection of manipulative and locomotor skills is *motor behavior;* the emergence of these skills is **motor development**.

**motor development** Growth and change in ability to do physical activities, such as walking, running, or riding a bike.

### Motor Development

Robert Malina (1982) suggests that we can divide the wide range of motor skills into three groups: *locomotor* patterns (such as walking, running, jumping, hopping and skipping), *non-locomotor* patterns (such as pushing, pulling, bending), and *manipulative* skills (such as grasping, throwing, catching, kicking, and other actions involving receiving and moving objects). Nearly all the *basic* skills in all three areas are complete by about 6 or 7 years of age. Afterward, change is mostly improvement in performance as the child refines the basic skills and integrates them into more and more complex movement sequences. So 6- and 7-year-olds can run, and they can probably dribble a basketball, but they can't yet do both at the same time.

To get some sense of the sequence of developments in each of these three areas, take a look at Table 4.3. You might start by looking down each column, and then look across the rows to see what skills are emerging at roughly the same times.

You can see part of the sequence of locomotor skills more graphically in Figure 4.9 on page 148, and I have explored some of the practical ramifications of these developments in the box on pages 150–151.

*Theories of Motor Development.* After the seminal work on motor development by Arnold Gesell and Myrtle McGraw in the 1930s, most developmental psychologists assumed that the emergence of these skills was fundamentally governed by some maturational process, by an unfolding of instructions contained in the genetic code. As the brain and muscles developed the child became able to perform new behaviors and simply did so.

These developments were thought of as being supported by the environment but caused internally.

In the past decade, however, a number of psychologists have found such a simple maturational explanation of motor development to be insufficient and misleading. Esther Thelen (1987; 1989; Thelen, Kelso & Fogel, 1987), one of the central proponents of this new view, argues that

> movement is the "final common pathway" for many sub-systems working together to accomplish a task or goal. For a child to move, perception, motivation, plans, physiological status, and affect must all interact with a mechanical system that is composed of muscles, bones, and joints. Although we may not choose to study all these contributing elements at the same time, it is conceptually impossible (and empirically foolish) to encapsulate the movement outcome from the motives that inspired it, the information that guided it, and the body parts that produced it. (1989, p. 946)

Using a spoon to feed yourself requires development of muscles in the hand and wrist, bone development in the wrist, eye-hand coordination skills that allow you to readjust the aim of the spoon as you move it toward your

**TABLE 4.3**

*Sequences of Development of Locomotor, Non-locomotor, and Manipulative Motor Skills*

| Age | Locomotor Skills | Non-locomotor Skills | Manipulative Skills |
| --- | --- | --- | --- |
| 1 Month | Stepping reflex | Lifts head; visually follows slowly moving objects | Holds object if placed in hand |
| 2–3 Months | | Briefly keeps head up if held in sitting position | Begins to swipe at objects within visual range |
| 4–6 Months | Sits up with some support | Holds head erect in sitting position | Reaches for and grasps objects |
| 7–9 Months | Sits without support; rolls over in prone position; moves on hands and knees ("creeping") | | Transfers objects from one hand to the other |
| 10–12 Months | Crawls; walks grasping furniture, then without help | Squats and stoops | Some signs of hand preference; grasps a spoon across palm but poor aim of food to mouth |
| 13–18 Months | Walks backward and sideways | Rolls ball to adult | Stacks two blocks; puts objects into small containers and dumps them |

**TABLE 4.3—Continued**

*Sequences of Development of Locomotor, Non-locomotor, and Manipulative Motor Skills*

| Age | Locomotor Skills | Non-locomotor Skills | Manipulative Skills |
|---|---|---|---|
| 18–24 Months | Runs (20 mo); walks well (24 mo); climbs stairs both feet on each step | Pushes and pulls boxes or wheeled toys; unscrews a lid on a jar | Shows clear hand preference; stacks 4–6 blocks; turns pages one at a time; picks things up without overbalancing |
| 2–3 Years | Runs easily; climbs up and down from furniture unaided | Hauls and shoves big toys around obstacles | Picks up small objects (e.g., cereal); throws small ball forward while standing |
| 3–4 Years | Walks upstairs one foot per step; skips on both feet; walks on tiptoe | Pedals and steers a tricycle; walks in any direction pulling a big toy | Catches large ball between outstretched arms; cuts paper with scissors; holds pencil between thumb and first two fingers |
| 4–5 Years | Walks up *and* down stairs one foot per step; stands, runs, and walks well on tiptoe | | Strikes ball with bat; kicks and catches ball; threads bead but not needle; grasps pencil maturely |
| 5–6 Years | Skips on alternate feet; walks a thin line; slides and swings | | Plays ball games quite well; threads needle and sews stich |
| 7–8 Years | Skips 12 or more times | Rides 2-wheel bike, but not very far | Writes individual letters |
| 8+ | Skips freely | Rides bike easily | |

*Sources:* Connolly & Dalgliesh, 1989; Capute et al., 1984; The Diagram Group, 1977; Fagard & Jaquet, 1989; Mathew & Cook, 1990; Thomas, 1990a.

mouth, and coordination of all of these with a properly timed mouth opening (Connolly & Dalgleish, 1989).

Obviously Thelen and her followers are not denying the fundamental significance of the maturation of nerves and muscles. But they are saying that the concept of maturation alone does not *explain* the development of motor skills. There is no specific unfolding genetic code for crawling, walking, or holding a spoon. Each of these complex skills is instead built out of many much smaller components that are cognitive, perceptual, and motivational as well as neural and muscular.

### Adolescent Sexuality

We can also look at the impact of physical changes on behavior in another part of the age spectrum—in adolescence—when body changes bring about sexual fertility. What effect do these changes have on teenagers' actual sexual behavior? Do all teenagers become sexually active at the same time?

Obviously some do. Adolescent sexual activity increased fairly dramatically in the 1960s and 1970s and then leveled off or even declined slightly in the 1980s. The best current estimates (Hayes, 1987) are that in the United States today, about 50 percent of boys and about 25 percent of girls aged 15–17 are sexually active. Among 18- and 19-year-olds, the equivalent rates are 77 and 63 percent, and at every age the rates among black teenagers are considerably higher. In boys, the likelihood of sexual activity is correlated with the amount of testosterone in the blood. Among girls, sexual interests but not sexual behavior are associated with testosterone levels, which suggests that social influences are more involved in girls' than boys' sexual behavior (Brooks-Gunn & Furstenberg, 1989).

Given these trends, and the ignorance about reproduction and physiology in most teens, we shouldn't be surprised that the rate of teenage pregnancy is high. Approximately one million teenage girls become pregnant every year (roughly one in ten girls) and about 50 percent of these pregnancies are carried to term. Perhaps 10,000 of these babies are born every year to girls under 15. The most striking version of these statistics is an estimate by Sandra Hofferth that fully 44 percent of all girls will be pregnant at least once before the age of 20 (Hofferth, 1987a). Those who choose to deliver their babies have a very different adult life pattern than do teenagers who do not give birth. Teenage mothers finish fewer years of school, have poorer paying jobs later on, have more children, and higher likelihood of divorce (e.g., Moore et al., 1981; Hofferth, 1987b). To avoid some of these unpleasant consequences, we may need to rethink our attitudes about the timing and importance of sex education in the schools.

## Big or Fast Versus Slow or Small: Some Individual Differences in Physical Development

So far I have been concentrating on patterns of physical development that are common to virtually all children. But I have pointed out at least briefly as I have gone along that there are wide individual differences in the *rate* and *timing* of these common physical developments, as well as in children's physical shape or skills. Not only are these differences interesting in their own right, but they may affect a child's self-image, her relationships with peers, or general contacts with the world.

### Differences in Rate

Children vary *widely* in the speed with which they go through all the body and motor changes I have described. Some children walk at 7 or 8 months; others walk at 18 months. Some are skillful soccer players at 5 or 6; others do not develop this skill until much later (if at all). These differences are most striking at puberty, when young people of the same age may range from Stage 1 to Stage 5 in the steps of sexual maturation—as you can see very vividly in Figure 4.10 on page 152.

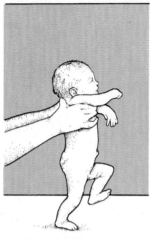
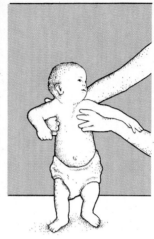
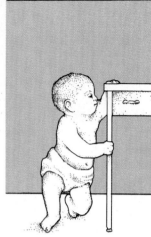

A newborn baby held with the sole of the foot on a table moves his legs in a reflex walking action.

At 8 weeks the baby briefly keeps his head up if he is held in a standing posture.

By 36 weeks he can pull himself up and remains standing by grasping hold of furniture.

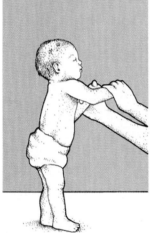
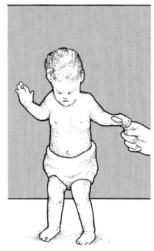
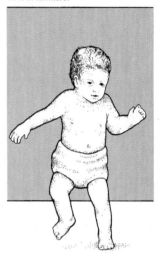

By 48 weeks he can walk forward if both hands are held (or sideways, gripping furniture).

At 1 year the child walks forward if someone holds one of his hands.

By 13 months the child has become capable of walking without help.

**FIGURE 4.9**

These drawings show one of the key locomotor skill sequences, from standing to walking, and then to more complex skills (*Source:* The Diagram Group, *Child's body: An owner's manual.* New York: Paddington Press, 1977, section D-13).

As a general rule, a child tends to be consistently early, average, or late in most aspects of physical development. The child who shows slower bone development is also likely to walk later and to have later puberty (Tanner, 1978). Similarly, tall infants tend to be taller teenagers and taller adults. There are exceptions to both of these generalizations, but what Tanner calls the *tempo of growth* is a powerful element in development.

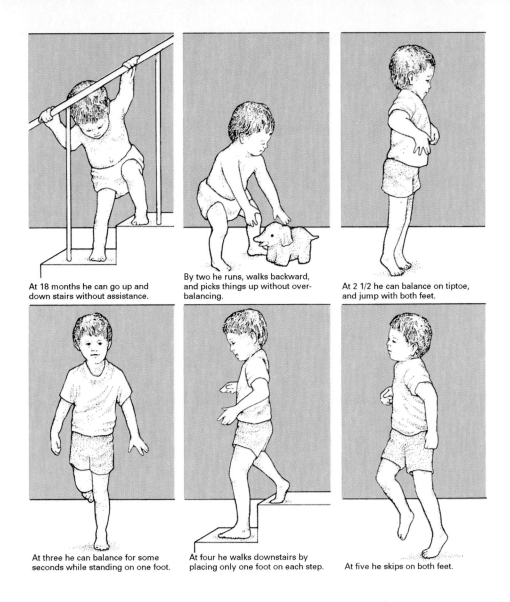

At 18 months he can go up and down stairs without assistance.

By two he runs, walks backward, and picks things up without over-balancing.

At 2 1/2 he can balance on tiptoe, and jump with both feet.

At three he can balance for some seconds while standing on one foot.

At four he walks downstairs by placing only one foot on each step.

At five he skips on both feet.

*Effects of Differing Rates on Mental Development.* These differences in rates of development appear to have at least some small link to a child's mental development, so that children who are more rapid in physical development are also slightly ahead in mental development (e.g., Tanner, 1978; Newcombe & Baenninger, 1989). It is also true that taller children of any given age tend to score higher on IQ tests than do shorter children of the same age (Humphreys, Davey, & Park, 1985; Dornbusch et al., 1987a). None of these differences is terribly large. Most of the correlations are in the range of .20 to .30 (modest at best), and in actual IQ points, the difference between the tallest and the shortest is probably no more than 5–10 points (Tanner, 1978). Still, the relationship is found consistently.

## Motor Development and Toys

If you have ever tried to buy a toy for a child, you know how bewildering it can be to walk into a store and see aisles and aisles of bright, attractive items. You want to find something that is right for your child's skills, but how do you know what makes a good toy, and what toys are good at what ages? The answers to these questions can come partly from what we know about a child's motor development.

### Birth to 6 Months

Little babies use their hands and their eyes to play, so a good choice is something that is bright, safe to hold, and hooked to the crib so it won't fall. Mobiles and "cradle gyms" fit the category, and so do soft toys tied to the sides of the crib.

### 6 to 12 Months

Older babies are more mobile and are interested in toys that let them try out their new large-muscle skills. Sling seats that hang from doorways and let babies jump are good and so are "walkers," similar seats set on frames with wheels. Probably the best thing to do for a child this age is to "childproof" your house, (removing hazards like sharp objects and poisons) so the child can explore freely. Playpens (now usually called "play yards") are probably not as good, although they may sometimes be necessary for safety reasons.

Infants of this age also enjoy stacking and nesting toys. Measuring cups, pots, and pans are often better for this than are expensive baby toys.

### Second Year

Give a toddler an expensive toy and chances are she will show at least as much interest in the box it came in as the toy itself. (Big boxes that can be crawled into are a particularly big hit.) At the other end of the size scale, since he can now pick things up with his thumb and forefinger, smaller objects (but not so small that they can be swallowed) are often favorites.

Toddlers like toys with wheels, but *push toys* are better than *pull toys* because the child can see the object while it moves. Near the end of the year, toward the second birthday, the child can sometimes handle a big crayon or pencil and may enjoy "drawing." For obvious reasons, washable colors are preferred!

### Third Year

When in doubt, get something with wheels. Kiddie cars, tricycles, and other riding toys are favorites among large toys, and cars and trucks (for both sexes) are favorites among small ones. Building toys also start to be interesting, especially those with many possibilities, like wooden blocks (and again, homemade are just as satisfactory as expensive kits from a store). But for children this age the construction pieces have to be fairly large. Tiny beads or very small blocks are too small for the grasping skills of most children in this age range. They need objects that can be picked up in the whole hand.

Coloring and drawing are also great favorites, as are those messy classics, paint-

---

What might be the cause of such a correlation? There are many possibilities. It could arise directly from differences in brain development that affect both rate of maturation and intellectual skill. The correlation could also reflect differences in diet or differences in confidence or self-esteem between larger, fast-developing children and the slower developers. Differences in the responsibilities or opportunities offered by the people around the child or the expectancies of the adults or the child might also affect the correlation.

Whatever the cause, it is interesting that these differences persist into adulthood. That is, adults who were early developers as children still have a

ing and playdough. As with younger children, "washable" is an important label to look for.

## Ages 3–7

Small-muscle coordination develops rapidly during this period, and the child can manage toys like beads (to be strung on a string), and more accurate cutting (although typical children's scissors are too dull for much accuracy; a sharp pair of scissors is a great gift for a child old enough to use them safely). Jacks, marbles, and checkers are also good choices among older children in this age group, since these toys require the kind of small motor skill the child now has. These objects also provide stimulating interactions with other children and challenge the child's intellectual skills.

Large-muscle skills are improving too, and smaller balls (baseball or tennis size) can be used as well as large ones. By the end of this period, the child can often manage a bicycle, or at least start on one with training wheels.

Toys that stimulate fantasy are also greatly enjoyed by children in this age range, including dolls or other figures that represent some well-known fantasy, dress-up clothes or costumes, toy doctor kits, and puppets.

## Elementary School

Coordination is well developed by this age. Seven- and eight-year-old children can usually ride a bicycle easily, skip rope, and play most games that require hitting, kicking, or throwing a ball. I should emphasize that children as young as 3 can do most of these things too, *if* a large enough ball, a wide enough hockey stick, or a light enough racket is used. From age 3 through at least age 10, the development of play and athletic skills is more one of degree than of kind. So if you are interested in having your child develop specific abilities needed for later organized sports, you can begin quite early, as long as the materials are sized properly for the child's ability and you do not press for perfect coordination too early.

Practice in small-muscle coordination over the earlier years also makes the elementary school-age child much more skillful with model building, arts and crafts, sewing, and more complex kinds of construction systems such as Legos or the equivalent—all of which may make excellent toys, games, and gifts for children this age. Puzzles, too, at this time make good gift choices. Children this age certainly have the manual dexterity to deal with jigsaw puzzles with quite small pieces, and they have the cognitive skill to work on puzzles with 100 or more pieces.

As a general rule, at every age steer clear of expensive, complex toys that do only one or two things (especially all those wretched toys that require batteries!), such as robots that only whir and walk. Children are intrigued the first time, but rapidly lose interest, and such toys are not adaptable to other forms of play.

slight intellectual advantage over their slower-developing peers, even though the latter group has caught up in height, brain growth, and physical skill. Presumably this carryover into adulthood is a consequence of the psychological effects of earliness or lateness rather than of the physiological effects.

*Effects of Differences in Rate on Personality.* When we look directly at the psychological effects of fast or slow tempo of growth, some interesting information emerges. Most of the relevant research has focused on the impact of early versus late puberty on teenagers' mental health or self-image. What hap-

**FIGURE 4.10**

Teenagers vary enormously in the timing and speed of pubertal changes, as you can see very graphically from these photographs. Each of these boys is the same age, as is each of the three girls, but they range from Stage 2 to Stage 5 of pubertal development (*Source:* J. M. Tanner, Growth and endocrinology of the adolescent. In L. J. Gardner [Ed.], *Endocrine and genetic diseases of childhood and adolescence*, 2nd ed. ©1975 by W. B. Saunders Co., Philadelphia, Penn., p. 28).

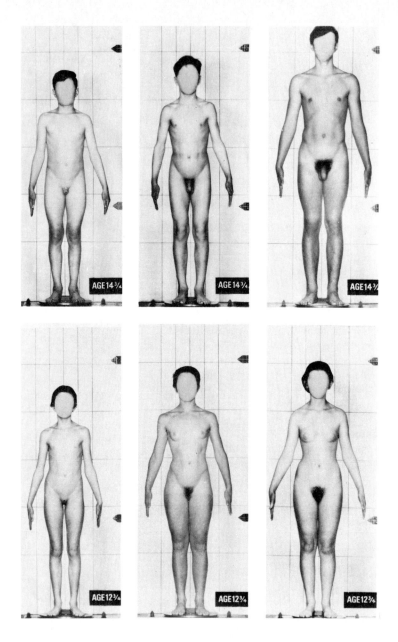

pens to a girl who begins to menstruate at 10, or a boy who does not go through a growth spurt until age 16? Do they turn out differently from kids who are more "on time"?

A whole burst of recent research on this question has led to an interesting, complex hypothesis that once again points to the importance of internal models. The general idea, proposed by a number of psychologists—including Mary Faust (1983), Richard Lerner (1985, 1987), and Anne Petersen (1987)—is that each young child or teenager has an internal model about what is "normal" or "right" about puberty. Each girl has an internal model about the "right age" to develop breasts or begin menstruation; each boy has an internal model or image about when it is right to begin growing a beard or for his voice to get lower. According to this hypothesis, it is the discrepancy between an adolescent's expectation and what actually happens that determines the psychological effect. Those whose development occurs outside the desired or expected range are likely to think less well of themselves, perhaps have fewer friends, or experience other signs of distress.

In our culture today, most young people seem to share the expectation that pubertal changes will happen sometime between age 12 and 14; anything earlier is judged as "too soon" and anything later is thought of as late. If you compare these expectations to the actual average timing of pubertal changes, you'll see that such a norm includes girls who are average in development and boys who are *early*. So we should expect that these two groups—normal developing girls and early developing boys—should have the best psychological functioning. Early maturing boys may have an added advantage because they are also more likely to be of the *mesomorphic* body type (broad shouldered and well muscled). Since this body type is consistently preferred at all ages, and since boys with this body type tend to be good at sports, the early developing boy should be particularly advantaged.

Figure 4.11 on the next page shows the specific predictions graphically. Early boys should be best off, followed by average boys and girls. The least well off should be late developing boys and early developing girls. And in fact, that is generally what the current research shows. Girls who are early developers (before 11 or 12 for major body changes) show consistently more negative body images, such as thinking themselves too fat (Tobin-Richards et al., 1983; Petersen, 1987; Simmons, Blyth, & McKinney, 1983). Such girls are also more likely to have trouble in school and at home (Magnusson, Stattin, & Allen, 1986). There is also evidence that very late development for girls is also somewhat negative, but the effect of lateness is not so striking for girls as for boys.

Among boys, as Figure 4.11 predicts, the relationship is essentially linear. The earlier the boy's development, the more positive his body image, the better he does in school, the less trouble he gets into, and the more friends he has (e.g., Duke et al., 1982).

In nearly all of these studies, earliness or lateness has been defined in terms of the actual physical changes. However, when researchers have asked teenagers about their internal model of earliness or lateness, the results are even clearer. For example, Rierdan, Koff, and Stubbs (1989) have found that the negativeness of a girl's menarchal experience was predicted by her *subjective* sense of earliness; those who perceived themselves as early reported a more negative experience. But such a negative experience was *unrelated* to the actual age of her menarche.

This link between the internal model and the outcome is even clearer in an interesting study of ballet dancers by Jeanne Brooks-Gunn (Brooks-Gunn & Warren, 1985; Brooks-Gunn, 1987). She studied 14- to 18-year-old girls, some of whom were highly serious ballet dancers studying at a national ballet company school. In this group, a very lean, almost prepubescent body is highly desirable. We would expect that among dancers, those who were very late in pubertal development would actually have a better image of themselves than those who were "on time." And that is exactly what they found as you can see in Figure 4.12 on page 155. Among nondancers of the same age, normal menarche was associated with a better body image than late menarche, but exactly the reverse was true for the dancers.

**FIGURE 4.11**

According to this model of the effects of early and late puberty, the best position for girls is to be "on time," while for boys the best position is to be "early." For both sexes, however, it is the *perception* of earliness or lateness, and not the actual timing, that is thought to be critical (*Source:* adapted from Tobin-Richards et al., 1983, p. 137).

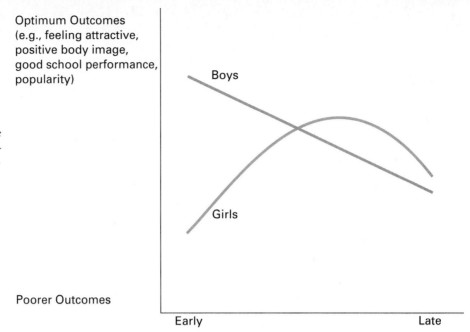

Optimum Outcomes
(e.g., feeling attractive,
positive body image,
good school performance,
popularity)

Boys

Girls

Poorer Outcomes

Early                                    Late

Teenager's Perception of Her or His Pubertal Timing

It seems that the discrepancy or mismatch between the desired pattern and any given child's actual pattern is critical, while the absolute age of pubertal development is not as important. Because the majority of young people share similar expectations, we can see common effects of early or late development. However, to predict the effect of early or late development in any individual teenager, we would need to know more about her or his internal model.

### Sex Differences in Physical Growth

I have mentioned a number of sex differences in physical growth in this chapter, but let me pull together all the bits and pieces for you here. Table 4.4 on page 156 summarizes the major findings.

You can see from the table that most physical differences between males and females become more pronounced after puberty. Preadolescent girls and boys are about equal in strength and speed. After adolescence, boys become stronger and faster, as well as larger. One of the implications of this is that some, perhaps many, 12-year-old girls should be able to compete effectively in sports against boys their own age, such as in Little League baseball. A few years later, though, it will be the unusual girl who is able to compete successfully with boys in sports that call for considerable strength or speed. This is not an argument against athletics for girls. On the contrary, everything I know about the effect of maintaining fitness for adult health and longevity points to the importance of encouraging both boys and girls to develop athletic interests and skills that will carry forward into adult life. But this *is* an argument against mixed-sex competitive teams in high school.

**FIGURE 4.12**

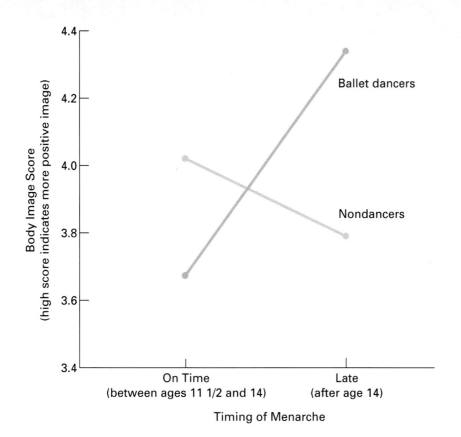

Body Image Score
(high score indicates more positive image)

4.4

4.2

4.0

3.8

3.6

3.4

Ballet dancers

Nondancers

On Time
(between ages 11 1/2 and 14)

Late
(after age 14)

Timing of Menarche

Serious ballet dancers, for whom a very lean, pre-pubescent shape is highly valued, clearly prefer to have a very late puberty. Those dancers whose menarche was "on time" by ordinary standards actually had poorer body images than did those who were objectively quite late, while the reverse was true for nondancers. This shows nicely that the critical variable is not the actual earliness or lateness of puberty, but the adolescent's perception of what is normal or desirable (*Source:* Brooks-Gunn & Warren, 1985, From Table 1, p. 291).

## Social Class and Racial Differences

As a group, poor children grow a bit slower and are a bit shorter than middle-class children, probably because of dietary differences. Menarchal age is also about six months later in girls growing up in less affluent homes than in girls in middle-class homes (Garn, 1980).

Different racial groups, too, show somewhat different rates or patterns of development. Of course in the United States, in which minority racial status and poverty so often coexist, some of the racial differences may well be caused by the underlying economic differences. But there appear to be some genuine racial differences as well.

Black infants and children are slightly ahead of white children in some aspects of physical development. In fact, the gestational period for the black fetus seems to be slightly shorter than for the white fetus (Smith & Stenchever, 1978). Black babies also show somewhat faster development of motor skills, such as walking, and are slightly taller than their white counterparts, with longer legs, more muscle, and heavier bones (Tanner, 1978). At puberty, black girls have slightly earlier menarche as well (3 months on average). Thus the tempo of growth appears to be slightly faster in black children than in white.

Asian children also have a relatively rapid tempo of growth but are smaller, with long upper bodies and shorter final height.

TABLE 4.4

*Sex Differences in Physical Growth*

| Characteristic | Nature of Difference |
|---|---|
| Rate of maturation | Girls are on a faster timetable throughout development; this difference is about 2–4 weeks at birth and about two years at adolescence. |
| Predictability or regularity | Girls' physical growth is more regular and predictable, with fewer uneven spurts. It is easier to predict the final height of a girl, for example, than of a boy. |
| Strength and speed | There is little difference until adolescence, although on measures of arm and upper body strength boys are higher even in elementary school; after puberty, boys are stronger and faster. |
| Heart and circulation | At adolescence, boys develop larger hearts and lungs and a greater capacity for carrying oxygen in the blood than do girls. |
| Fat tissue | Girls from birth on have a thicker layer of fat tissue just below the surface of the skin; this difference in proportion of fat increases after puberty. |
| Motor skills | In the preschool years, girls are better at tasks requiring jumping, hopping, rhythmic movement, and balance. In elementary school and later, boys are better at activities requiring running, jumping, and throwing, while girls are better at hopping. |

*Sources:* Tanner, 1978; Archer, 1981; Malina, 1982

## Health and Illness in Childhood and Adolescence

The study of both the common patterns and individual differences in normal physical growth forms the core of research on physical development. For parents, as well as for physicians and society as a whole, a child's health is another key aspect of physical status.

Physicians distinguish between *acute* and *chronic* illnesses. The former are all those illnesses lasting less than three months, usually much less time, such as colds and flu. The latter are illnesses lasting longer than three months, often for years or even permanently, such as diabetes, muscular dystrophy, or asthma.

Acute illnesses are common among young children. In the United States, children between ages 1 and 3 get sick eight or nine times a year, mostly with colds or other upper respiratory illnesses, ear infections, and the like. Preschoolers and elementary school children have fewer acute illnesses, but still get sick perhaps six times each year (Parmelee, 1986). In contrast, chronic illnesses are found in only approximately one in ten children at some time during their childhood (Starfield & Pless, 1980).

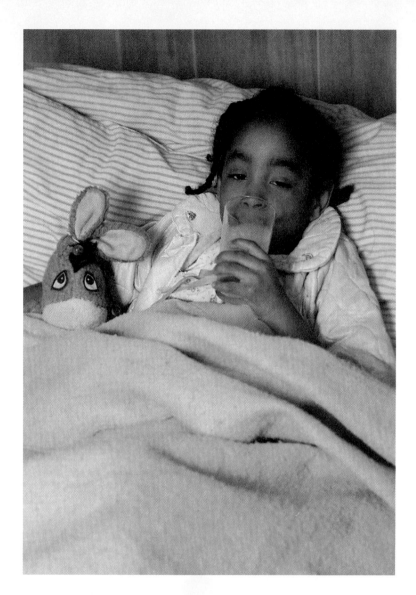

Acute illnesses like colds or flu are common in early childhood. Most kids this age are sick in bed like this about six times a year.

One of the most interesting findings on childhood illness is that a pattern of repeated illness in childhood—even just unusually frequent colds—is correlated with higher rates of illness in adolescence and poorer health in adulthood (e.g., Power & Peckham, 1990). The correlation is by no means perfect. Many "sickly" children are quite healthy as adults. And since we are dealing here with correlational evidence we must be careful about making causal statements. But we can make a *risk* statement: A pattern of frequent or chronic early illness increases the probability of health problems later.

Another danger for children is accidents. In fact, because of improvements in health care that have enormously reduced the risk of death from infectious diseases, accidents are the major cause of death in the United States for children over the age of 1. Automobile accidents are the most common fatal accident, accounting for 36 percent of deaths among teenagers and young adults and 20 percent of deaths among children between 1 and 14 years (National Center for Health Statistics, 1984). Happily, the rate of such fatalities has dropped noticeably since the advent of laws mandating the use of restraint devices for infants and toddlers traveling in cars (Christophersen, 1989).

Among teenagers, one increasing risk is suicide. Rates have tripled since 1960, and now represent about 12 percent of teen deaths, which is about 15 deaths per 100,000 teenage males per year (Hawton, 1986)—a pattern I'll have more to say about in Chapter 14.

Still a third potential problem among children and adolescents is poor health habits, including too little exercise and poor food. Perhaps the most troubling of these are the various *eating disorders*—obesity, bulimia, and anorexia nervosa—which I have discussed in the box on pages 160–161. More generally, researchers are finding that the sedentary, high-calorie life-style of American youngsters is contributing not only to current physical problems, but may also create significantly higher risk of later disease. By some reports 40 percent of adolescents already have at least one risk factor associated with heart disease—high cholesterol, overweight, or high blood pressure (The Harvard Education Letter, March 1987). It is clear that regular exercise can help to counteract all of these effects, as well as improve school performance, but such exercise has become less common rather than more so in recent years.

Overall, it is clear that all children get sick at least some of the time; a minority are sick fairly regularly. Such regular or persistent sickness may have long-term implications for a child's physical and emotional development, as can poor health or exercise habits.

 ## Determinants of Growth: Explanations of Physical Development

So far, I have mostly been dealing with description, with answering "what" questions. But "why" questions are equally important. Why does physical development occur as it does, and what can affect it?

### Maturation

Maturational sequences certainly are part of the explanation, especially for such central patterns as neuronal changes and changes in muscles, bones, and fat. In all these areas, while the *rate* of development varies from one child to the next, the *sequence* is virtually the same for all children, even those with marked physical or mental handicaps. Whenever we find such robust sequences, maturation of some kind seems an obvious explanation.

Thelen and others, however, have pointed out that this is an overly simplistic view of the process. As yet, we do not know the precise genetic mechanisms by which these sequences are triggered or controlled. Nor do we understand the ways in which several sets of sequences interact with one another and with the child's developing thinking and motivation to produce what we see as emerging motor skills. We also should not forget that there are other elements in the explanatory equation as well.

## Heredity

Our genetic heritage is individual as well as species-specific. In addition to being programmed for many basic sequences of physical development, each of us also receives instructions for unique growth tendencies. Both size and body shape seem to be heavily influenced by such specific inheritance. Tall parents tend to have tall children; short parents tend to have short children (Garn, 1980). And there are similarities between parents and children in such characteristics as hip width, arm length (some ancestor certainly passed on a gene for long arms to me!), and sitting height (long or short trunk).

Rate or tempo of growth, as well as final shape or size, seems to be an inherited pattern as well. Parents who were themselves early developers, as measured by such things as bone ossification or age of menarche, tend to have children who are faster developers too (Garn, 1980).

## Environmental Effects

As usual, though, nothing is completely one-sided. There are potent external influences on physical growth as well.

*Secular Trends.*   One of the kinds of evidence that points most clearly to environmental influences is the observation that children in different cohorts show different timing of physical changes, or grow at different rates, a pattern of findings referred to as **secular trends.** For example, the age of menarche has decreased at the rate of about 4 months per decade over the past 100 years among European populations, shifting from an average age of roughly 17 in 1840 to roughly 12 1/2 or 13 today (Roche, 1979). Over the same decades, average final height and weight have increased, not only among European populations but among the Japanese as well.

**secular trends**
Patterns of change over several cohorts in such things as the timing of menarche or height or weight.

What could account for such changes over time? The most obvious possibility is that there have been changes in life-style and diet.

*Diet.*   Differences in diet may not only help to explain secular trends; they also contribute to the individual differences we see in rate of physical development in any one cohort. In general terms, we know that poorly nourished children grow more slowly and then don't end up as large. More specifically, malnutrition in the early years may have a permanent effect on some parts of the brain and nervous system.

As I pointed out earlier, the period of maximum dendritic and synaptic growth is in the final three to five months of pregnancy and the first two to three years after birth. Severe malnutrition during that time, even if the child later has an adequate diet, may produce a lasting slow rate of physical and motor development (Malina, 1982). Research with animals (and some parallel studies of the brains and nervous systems of malnourished children who have died) shows that the main physical effects of malnutrition are a reduction in the size of the dendritic arbor and in the number of synapses, and a slowing of the rate of myelinization (Dickerson, 1981; Ricciuti, 1981). As a consequence, the cortex does not become as heavy. If the child's diet continues to be poor for the first two or three years, the effects appear to be permanent.

# Eating Disorders: Obesity, Bulimia, and Anorexia

Among the many health hazards for children and adolescents, some of the most common are the several *eating disorders*. The most frequent of these is obesity. If we define obesity as more than 20 percent heavier than the normal weight for a given height, then 15 to 20 percent of children and teenagers are obese. Both boys and girls are counted in the ranks of the obese. In contrast, two other eating disorders, bulimia and anorexia nervosa, are found predominantly in girls.

Bulimia (sometimes called *bulimia nervosa*) is a pattern of "intense concern about weight, recurrent episodes of excessive overeating accompanied by a subjective sense of loss of control, and the use of vomiting, exercise, and/or purgative abuse to counteract the effects of binge eating" (Attie, Brooks-Gunn, & Petersen, 1990, p. 410). Binge eating, alternating with periods of restrained eating, is common among individuals in all weight groups. Only when such binge eating is combined with some kind of purging is the syndrome properly called *bulimia*.

Incidence of bulimia appears to have been increasing rather rapidly in recent decades, particularly among white teenage and young adult women, among whom as many as 1 in 20 may show the syndrome. In contrast, less than 1 percent of college age men are bulimic (Attie et al., 1990; Howat & Saxton, 1988; Johnson et al., 1984; Pyle et al., 1983).

Anorexia nervosa is less common but potentially more deadly. It is characterized by "behavior directed toward weight loss, intense fear of gaining weight, body image disturbance, amenorrhea (cessation of menstruation), and an implacable refusal to maintain body weight" (Attie et al., 1990, p. 410). Some girls literally starve themselves to death. The incidence of anorexia has been hard to establish; the best current estimate is that it affects roughly 1 in 200 girls or young women, but is considerably more common among subgroups who are under pressure to maintain extreme thinness, such as ballet dancers.

Let me look a bit further at what we know about the causes of each of these three problems.

## Obesity

Obesity is a significant long-term health problem. Among adults, the obese have shorter life expectancies and higher risk of heart disease and high blood pressure. We also know that there is a correlation between fatness in childhood and obesity in adulthood. Obese *infants* have only a slightly higher risk of obesity in adulthood compared to leaner babies. However, obesity in older children—beginning perhaps at age 4 or 6 —is quite strongly predictive of adult fatness (Roche, 1981; Grinker, 1981).

Three basic classes of causes have been identified: heredity, exercise or activity level, and diet. Children clearly seem to inherit a tendency toward fatness or leanness. Studies of adult twins, for example, show that identical twins—even those reared completely apart from each other—have extremely similar adult weights, while fraternal twins differ much more in weight (Stunkard et al., 1990). A very different research strategy was used by Bouchard and his colleagues (Bouchard et al., 1990), who deliberately fed sets of twins 1000 extra calories a day for 84 days. He found that the amount of weight gain varied a great deal from one pair of twins to the next, but was quite similar within each twin pair. We also know that adopted children reared by obese parents are less likely to be obese than are the natural children of obese parents (Mayer, 1975). All this evidence clearly points to a strong genetic propensity toward leanness or fatness, probably operating through differences in metabolic efficiency.

But environment does matter. Both exercise and diet affect a child's (or adult's) weight at any particular time, as is clear from the effects of Bouchard's overfeeding experiment. All the subjects in this experiment gained weight when they ate excessive calories, even though the amount of weight gain differed markedly from one pair of twins to the next. When low levels of exercise are combined with high fat diets, the highest level of obesity is found. One group of researchers, studying a national sample of over 6000 children, estimates that the prevalence of obesity increases roughly 2 percent for each additional hour of television a child or teenager watches per day, even when prior weight, family influences, and other background variables were taken into account (Dietz & Gortmaker, 1985). These investigators are not arguing that watching TV makes you fat; they are suggesting that the more TV a child watches, the less exercise he or she is getting and the greater the likelihood that the youngster will eat high-fat-content junk food.

## Bulimia and Anorexia

We know much less about the causes of bulimia and anorexia, in part because recognition of these disorders is much more recent. Researchers and theorists now consider them to be variations on a basic theme rather than distinctly different disorders. Both seem to be centrally a response by some girls and women to a currently intense cultural emphasis on thinness. From very early in life, girls (much more than boys) are taught both explicitly and implicitly that it matters if they are pretty or attractive, and that thinness is one of the critical variables in attractiveness. Current research, for example, shows that roughly 75 percent of teenage girls have dieted or are dieting, while boys rarely do so (Leon et al., 1989). (Speculatively, among boys the recent increase in steroid use may reflect some of the same

kinds of processes.) If a socially desirable body type requires big muscles, then boys may be drawn to the "magical forumla" of steroids, just as girls are drawn to the "quick fix" of a diet or bulimic patterns.

Those girls who most fully accept and internalize this model of beauty are most prone to develop bulimia or anorexia. So, for example, both syndromes are more common among girls and women in the middle and upper class, in which the ideals of fitness and thinness are particularly emphasized. Ruth Striegel-Moore and her colleagues (Striegel-Moore, Silberstein, & Rodin, 1986) have also found that bulimic girls and women are more likely than are non-bulimics to agree with statements like "attractiveness increases the likelihood of professional success."

Bulimia and anorexia seem to develop in adolescence, and not before that, precisely because one of the effects of puberty is an increase in the amount of fat in the girl's body. This is particularly true of early developing girls, who characteristically acquire and retain higher fat levels than do later maturing girls. Thus an early developing girl who deeply believes that thinness is essential for beauty, and that beauty is essential for happiness—especially if she sees her own body as failing to meet her internalized standard—seems at particularly high risk for developing bulimia or anorexia (Attie & Brooks-Gunn, 1989; Striegel-Moore et al., 1986).

Of course, this research does not tell us why some girls (or more rarely, young men) develop the bulimic pattern while others become anorexic. We also do not know whether one tends to lead to the other or whether one or both are preceded by patterns of disordered eating such as chronic dieting. However, the emphasis on the significance of the young person's internalized standard of an ideal body underscores once again the centrality of such internal models for understanding many facets of development.

The effects of more mild malnutrition, typically referred to as "subnutrition" or "undernutrition," are harder to detect. We don't yet know how poorly the child must be nourished before we see the effects in growth rate or motor coordination. It does appear, however, that chronic subnutrition affects the child's level of energy, which in turn can affect the nature of the interactions the child has with both the objects and the people around him (Barrett, Radke-Yarrow, & Klein, 1982; Lozoff, 1989). Just how this might affect social or intellectual development is a question I'll return to in later chapters.

*Prenatal Environmental Influences.*    Some of the other teratogens I talked about in Chapter 2 may also have lasting effects on a child's physical development. For example, Streissguth and her colleagues have found that 4-year-olds whose mothers drank while pregnant, compared to those whose mothers did not drink or drank less, had poorer balance and poorer fine motor skills, such as hand steadiness or the ability to tap rapidly with a finger (Barr, Streissguth, Darby, & Sampson, 1990). In the same study, caffeine ingestion and high use of aspirin during the pregnancy were also related to poorer fine motor skills among the 4-year-olds.

*Practice.*    Another variation in experience that could affect a child's physical development is simply the amount of practice a child has with various kinds of physical activities. Does a child who climbs stairs a lot learn to climb stairs sooner or more efficiently than a child who has little practice? Does a child who is kept in a playpen many hours each day, who therefore has little chance to run around, learn to walk or run at a later age?

There has been a good deal of dispute about the answers to such questions. What is clearest is that even in an area such as motor development, where maturation appears so strong, there is no such thing as a purely maturational effect. Practice is also necessary. For example, we know that when opportunities to practice certain motions are greatly restricted, children's motor development is retarded.

Wayne Dennis's (1960) classic study of children raised in Iranian orphanages provides an example of such a finding. The babies in one of the institutions Dennis observed were routinely placed on their backs in cribs with very lumpy mattresses. They had little or no experience of lying or moving on their stomachs as a normal baby would, and even had difficulty rolling over because of the hollows in the mattresses. These babies almost never went through the normal sequence of learning to walk—presumably because they didn't have enough opportunity to practice all the "on-the-stomach" parts of the skill. They did learn to walk eventually, but they were about a year late.

It would appear from this and equivalent research (e.g., Razel, 1985), that for the development of such universal, basic skills as crawling or walking, some minimum amount of practice is needed just to keep the system working as it should (maintenance). For more complex combinations of basic actions, such as those required for kicking or throwing objects, practice is essential for specific skill development. It is also likely that in infancy and childhood, opportunities to move and practice individual movements are necessary to stimulate the development of the brain, particularly the myelinization of the nerves. That is, the effects work both ways—from the brain development to better motor skill and from practicing movements to faster brain development.

Overall, we can find examples of all of Aslin's models (recall Figure 1.2) of experiential effects *except* a pure maturational pattern. That exception does not deny the fundamental importance of the underlying maturational influences at work in physical growth, but it does point up the importance of practice of various kinds.

## The Shape of Physical Development: A Last Look

Of all the facets of development I'll describe in this book, physical development is probably least influenced by specific experience and most governed by underlying maturational patterns. However, it is a mistake to conclude that environment has only minor effects. The strength and coordination required to throw a basketball high enough to reach the basket undoubtedly does develop in predictable ways over the early years, providing that the environment is sufficiently rich to provide needed maintenance. To develop the skill needed to get the ball through the hoop with regularity, from different angles and distances, requires endless practice. The development of really smooth, coordinated skill in virtually all complex motor tasks requires practice. This development also requires an adequate enough diet to maintain the system and decent health. More importantly, the rate and pattern of the child's physical development also affect his self-image, personality, and interactions with the world. So physical development influences experience as much as the reverse.

## S U M M A R Y

1.  It is important to know something about physical growth and development because specific new behaviors are triggered by physical changes, because physical skills affect the kinds of experiences the child can have, and because a child's feelings about her body can affect self-concept and personality.
2.  Changes in height and weight are rapid during the first year, then level off to a steady pace until adolescence, when there is a sharp "growth spurt."
3.  Bones develop in a similar pattern, with rapid early growth, and another rapid growth at adolescence. Bones increase in number, and harden slowly.
4.  Muscle tissue increases primarily in density and length of fibers, with a much larger increase at adolescence for boys than for girls.
5.  Fat cells are added in the early years, and then again rapidly at adolescence, in this case more for girls than for boys.
6.  At birth the medulla and midbrain are most developed; the cortex develops primarily over the first two years. Major neural changes after birth are the growth of dendrites and of synapses, as well as myelinization of axons.

7.  Hormones are vital influences throughout growth, particularly during adolescence. The pituitary gland secretes triggering hormones at the beginning of puberty, which stimulate the development of sex hormones, which in turn trigger the development of primary and secondary sex characteristics.

8.  Pubertal changes begin as early as 8 or 9 in girls, and continue until the mid-teens. In boys, the changes begin about two years later. In both sexes, the physical changes occur in reliable sequences, starting with changes in secondary sex characteristics, followed by the growth spurt, with reproductive maturity late in the sequence.

9.  Development of locomotor and manipulative skills are based on all the more fundamental physiological changes, but each involves a complex combination of more basic skills or responses. Most basic motor skills are present by about age 6.

10. Physical changes are also reflected in adolescent sexual behavior, which has increased in recent decades. Perhaps 50 percent of teenage boys and 25 percent of teenage girls are sexually active, and one in ten teenage girls becomes pregnant each year.

11. Illness is a normal part of children's early lives; some kind of illness occurs six to nine times each year on average. Chronic illness is less common. Repeated or frequent illness in childhood is associated with poorer health later in life.

12. Children differ markedly in the rate with which all these changes take place. In general, rapidly developing children have advantages over slower developing children in intellectual skill. Personality effects are more complex. In general, children whose physical development is markedly earlier or later than they expect or desire show more negative effects than do those whose development is "on time."

13. Males and females also differ in both rate and pattern of physical development. Girls are accelerated in physical growth, but at adolescence, boys develop more muscle tissue and larger hearts and circulatory systems than girls.

14. Some social class and racial differences can also be detected, with children from poverty-level environments developing more slowly. Both black and Asian children show more rapid tempo of development than do white children.

15. Maturation is a key process underlying physical growth and development, but maturation alone cannot account for the patterns that we see. Some environmental support is required, and specific heredity, prenatal teratogens, and prenatal and postnatal diet affect both the rate and pattern of development in individual children.


## CRITICAL THINKING QUESTIONS

1.  One of the body changes we see at adolescence is that boys develop relatively higher muscle mass and relatively lower proportions of body fat than is true for girls. What

are the alternative explanations of this observation? What kind of study might you do to check on the role of exercise in causing such a sex difference? What naturalistic observations might you do? What kind of experiment could you design?

2. If you could be monarch (or god) and have the power to change our culture in such a way that the rate of bulimia and anorexia would go way down, what changes would you want to make? Why?

3. Suppose you needed to buy a toy for a baby between the ages of 1 and 2. Given the information in this chapter, what three toys would you buy, and why?

## KEY TERMS

**cephalocaudal**   From the head downward. Describes one recurrent pattern of physical development in infancy.

**cortex**   The convoluted gray portion of the brain which governs most complex thought, language, and memory, among other functions.

**ectomorphic**   Body type defined by bone length; an ectomorphic individual is tall and slender, usually with stooped shoulders.

**endocrine glands**   These glands, including the adrenals, the thyroid, the pituitary, the testes, and the ovaries, secrete hormones governing overall physical growth and sexual maturing.

**endomorphic**   Body type defined by amount of body fat; an endomorphic individual is soft and round in shape.

**estrogen**   The female sex hormone secreted by the ovaries.

**fontanels**   The "soft spots" in the skull present at birth. These disappear when the several bones of the skull grow together.

**gonadotropic hormones**   Hormones produced in the pituitary gland which stimulate the sex organs to develop.

**medulla**   A portion of the brain that lies immediately above the spinal cord; largely developed at birth.

**menarche**   Onset of menstruation in girls.

**mesomorphic**   Body type characterized by amount of muscle mass; a mesomorphic male is square-chested, broad-shouldered, and muscular.

**midbrain**   A section of the brain lying above the medulla and below the cortex that regulates attention, sleeping, waking, and other "automatic" functions. Largely developed at birth.

**motor development**   Growth and change in ability to do physical activities, such as walking, running, or riding a bike.

**myelin**   A material making up a sheath that develops around most axons. This sheath is not completely developed at birth.

**myelinization**   The process by which myelin is added.

**ossification**   The process of hardening by which soft tissue becomes bone.

**pituitary gland**   One of the endocrine glands that plays a central role in controlling the rate of physical maturation and sexual maturing.

**proximodistal**   From the center outward. With cephalocaudal, describes the pattern of physical changes in infancy.

**puberty**   The collection of hormonal and physical changes at adolescence that brings about sexual maturity.

**secular trends**   Patterns of change over several cohorts in such things as the timing of menarche or height or weight.

The Diagram Group. (1977). *Child's Body*. New York: Paddington Press.

> Although not new, this is a nifty book, designed as a parents' manual and full of helpful information about physical development, health, and nutrition.

Hayes, C. D. (1987). *Risking the future. Vol. 1. Adolescent sexuality, pregnancy, and childbearing.* Washington, D. C.: National Academy Press.

> This book summarizes the results of an extensive study done for the Committee on Child Development Research and Public Policy of the National Research Council. The chapter on "trends in adolescent sexuality and fertility" is especially thorough and informative.

Malina, R. M. (1990). Physical growth and performance during the transitional years (9–16). In R. Montemayor, G. R. Adams, & T. P. Gullotta (Eds.), *From childhood to adolescence: A transitional period?* Newbury Park, CA: Sage.

> To some extent Malina has picked up where Tanner left off, providing us with updated information on normal physical growth. This particular paper focuses on puberty, but it contains references to much of Malina's work on other ages as well.

Tanner, J. M. (1978). *Fetus into man. Physical growth from conception to maturity.* Cambridge, MA: Harvard University Press.

> A detailed but very thorough and remarkably understandable small book that covers all but the most current information about physical growth.

# PROJECT 5

## Plotting Your Own Growth

This project will work best if your parents are among those who routinely stood you up against a convenient doorjamb and measured you—and if you still live in the house with the marked-up doorjamb. Alternatively, you may have a friend or acquaintance who has access to doorjamb data you could use. Assuming you can locate such a set of measurements, you should plot your own (or your friend's) rate of growth over the years of childhood. Calculate the inches you grew each year (estimating when needed), and draw a curve similar to the one in Figure 4.3.

How does your curve compare to the averaged data in the figure? When was your maximum height spurt (the year in which you grew the most inches)? During elementary school, did you grow about the same number of inches per year? If you are female, add to the graph a point that represents your first menstruation (to the best of your recollection). Where did menarche fall on the curve? Does it match the pattern shown in Figure 4.9? That is, did menarche occur *after* your major growth spurt?

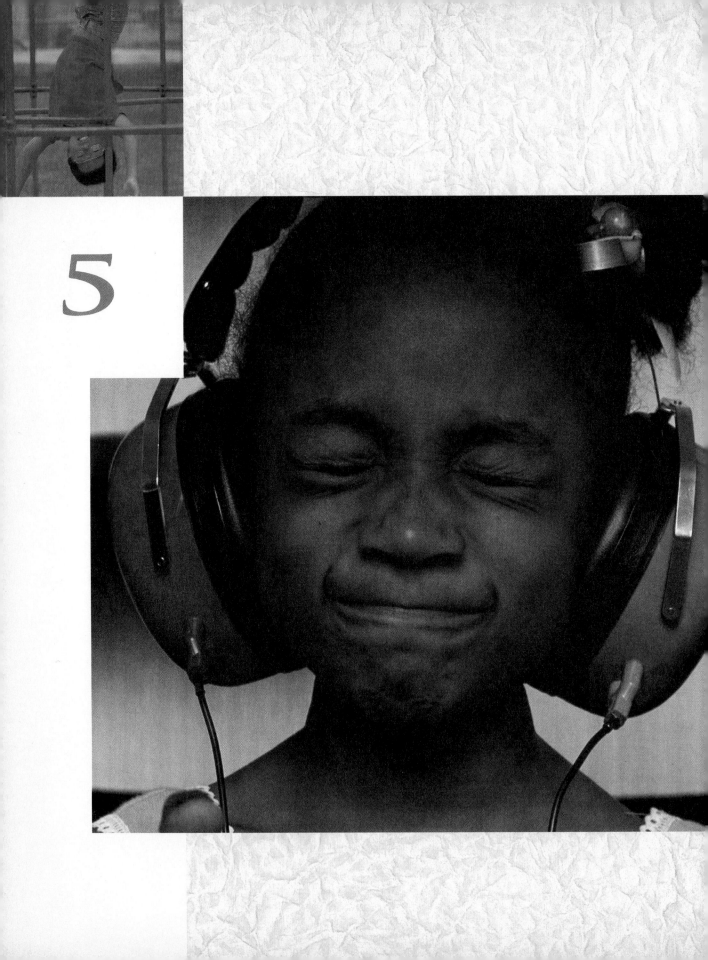

5

# PERCEPTUAL DEVELOPMENT

P erceptual processes form a part of virtually every task a child must perform—every motor or cognitive skill that is developed. To reach for an object dangling in front of her the child must be able to put together cues for depth perception so that she will know just how to aim her hands. To distinguish Mom or Dad from other adults she has to discriminate among smells, voices, or faces. To learn to talk she must make myriad discriminations among sounds, focusing eventually on the repertoire of sounds used in the language spoken around her.

To understand a child's development, then, we have to understand what kinds of sense impressions are possible for the child, both at birth and over the years of development. We also have to understand how the child comes to interpret those sense impressions—to discriminate among them and to recognize or understand patterns. In this sense the study of perceptual development forms a kind of bridge between the study of physiological changes, such as changes in the nervous system I described in the last chapter, and the study of thinking, which I'll be turning to in Chapter 6.

The study of perceptual development has also been a key ground on which the basic theoretical battle about nature versus nurture, **nativism** versus **empiricism,** has been fought. How much of our basic perceptual understanding of the world is built in? How much is the product of experience? All psychologists today would argue that both nature and nurture are required, but

**nativism**
See "empiricism." The view that perceptual skills are inborn and do not require experience to develop.

**empiricism**
Opposite of "nativism." The theoretical point of view that all perceptual skill arises from experience.

For Vera Kalugin (age 4 months) to be able to do something so apparently simple as reaching for this dangling toy she has to have developed a whole range of perceptual skills: she must be able to see the toy, to focus both eyes on it so that it is not blurry, to judge how far away it is, and to follow its movements with her eyes. This photo is a video still from the *Childhood* television series (*Source:* ©Thirteen/WNET).

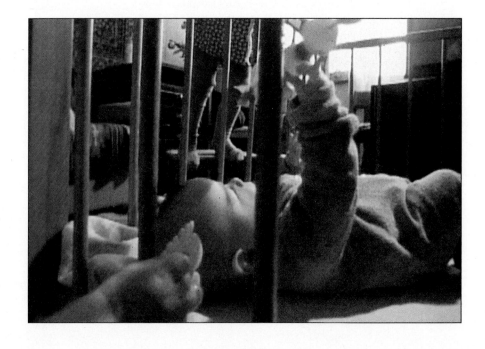

the fundamental philosophical question continues to be the basis for many of the theoretical arguments in the study of perceptual development.

The centrality of this issue has also meant that the vast majority of the research on perceptual development has focused on the early months and years of life in order to observe the organism when it is relatively uninfluenced by specific experience. The early months and years are also the time of most rapid change in perceptual skills, and hence a time of greater interest to psychologists trying to understand the processes of development. For both these reasons, most of the information in this chapter describes perceptual processes in very young infants. But that age limitation makes the issues no less fascinating.

Despite the philosophical and empirical importance of the questions involved, until roughly 25 or 30 years ago, we knew virtually nothing about infants' perceptual skills or their development. As T. G. R. Bower put it, "Infancy was like the dark side of the moon" (1977a, p. 5). Researchers couldn't figure out how to discover what the infant could see, hear, or feel, since the baby seemed to have so few ways of communicating with a researcher. However, with the development of several crucial methodologies in the 1960s and 1970s came an explosion of research in this area—much of it clever and provocative—leading to a considerable theoretical and empirical ferment. In the words of one leading developmental psychologist, John Flavell, "Infant perception is one of the headiest, most exhilarating areas in all of developmental psychology today" (1985, p. 198).

## Methods for Studying Early Perception

To understand this heady and exhilarating research, you need to know something about the basic research techniques that have been devised to allow infants to reveal what they can do. Three main techniques have been developed, with many variations.

*Robert Fantz's Preference Technique.*   The first breakthrough was Robert Fantz's suggestion (1956) that we could discover what babies could discriminate and what they preferred to look at by simply recording how long babies looked at various pictures. Most typically, the infant, propped in an infant seat, is shown two pictures. The baby's eye movements are then watched carefully to see which of the two pictures or objects the baby looks at the most. If many infants shown the same pair of pictures consistently prefer (look longer at) one picture rather than the other, not only do we know that the infant can tell the difference between them, we may gain some hints about just what captures babies' attention.

*Habituation Techniques.*   Another strategy takes advantage of the processes of habituation and dishabituation. You present an infant with a particular sight or sound over and over until he gets bored with it and stops looking at it or turning toward it (habituates). Then you present another sight or sound or object that varies in some fashion from the original to see if the baby shows renewed interest (dishabituation). If the baby does show such renewed interest, you know he perceives it as "different" in some way.

*Operant Conditioning Techniques.*   The third major group of research strategies relies on the principles of operant conditioning, most often involving the use of sucking or head turning responses in the infant. For example, an infant might be trained to turn her head when she hears a particular sound, with the sight of an interesting moving toy as the reinforcement. After this response is well established, the experimenter can vary the sound to see what class of sounds will still trigger the conditioned head turn and which will not.

Research using such techniques has now yielded a rich array of information about young infants' perceptual capacities. To simplify the descriptive task, let me divide the array into two rough groups, which we might call "basic" and "more complex" skills. The distinction here is similar to the distinction between sensation and perception given in most psychology texts. When we study *sensation,* we are identifying the information the sensory organs receive. Does the structure of the eye permit infants to see color? Is the structure of the ear and of the cortex such that a very young infant can discriminate among different pitches? When we study *perception* we are asking what the individual does with the sensory information and how it is interpreted or combined. So let me begin with the basic sensory capacities present in the newborn or developing over the first years of life.

## Basic Sensory Skills

As I mentioned in Chapter 3, there is a common theme that runs through all of what I will say about basic sensory skills: Newborns and young infants have far more sensory capacity than physicians or psychologists once believed. Perhaps because babies' motor skills are so obviously poor, we assumed that their sensory skills were equally poor. But we were wrong. A newborn does not have all the sensory capacities of a 2-month-old, a 1-year-old, or an adult. However, most of the basic skills are in place in at least rudimentary form.

### Seeing

There are many basic visual skills, but let me focus on just three that seem especially important: acuity, tracking moving objects, and color vision.

**acuity**
Sharpness of perceptual ability—how well or clearly one can see, hear, or use other senses.

*Acuity.*   **Acuity** refers to how well or how clearly you can perceive something. When you apply for a driver's license and take the eye test that involves reading the letters on a large chart, you're being tested for visual acuity. The usual standard for visual acuity in adults is 20/20 vision. This means that you can see and identify properly something that is 20 feet away that the average person can also see at 20 feet. A person with 20/100 vision, in contrast, has to be as close as  20 feet to see something that the ordinary person can see at 100 feet. In other words, the higher the second number, the poorer the person's visual acuity.

Until 25 or 30 years ago, when the current burst of research began, many medical texts stated that newborn infants were blind. Now we know that newborns have quite poor visual acuity but are definitely not blind. At birth ba-

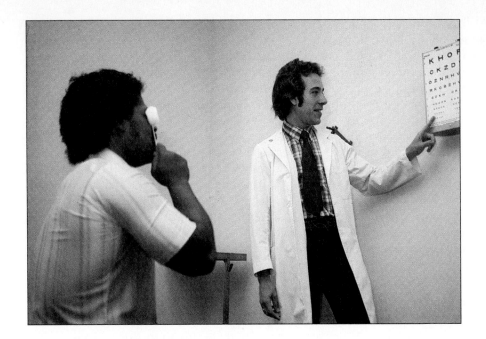

Eye tests like this one, which you may have been given when you applied for a driver's license, are measures of visual acuity.

bies' acuity is in the range of 20/200 to 20/400 and reaches roughly adult levels (20/20) by about one year of life (Haith, 1990). Even with such poor initial acuity, however, infants see quite well close up, which is all that is necessary for most encounters with the people who care for them or with objects immediately at hand, such as blankets or toys in a crib.

*Locating Objects in the Visual Field.*   When some new object comes into view, some object moves across your field of vision, or you are examining some object carefully, you locate it, follow it, or scan it using a series of eye movements. The quick shifts of the eyes that you use when you scan, or when you move your eyes quickly to identify some new object, are called **saccadic movements.** The slower, smoother movement you use when you are following a moving object with your eyes is called **tracking** or smooth pursuit. It is obviously important to know whether infants can do this, since such skills are clearly vital for children's ability to explore the visual world around them. Studies by Richard Aslin (1987a) and others show that both tracking and saccadic movements are initially fairly inefficient but that they improve quite rapidly. By 2 weeks of age infants can reliably get their eyes shifted toward some new object on the periphery, but it takes more small separate saccadic movements to do so than is true of older infants or adults. Similarly, when newborn infants scan some object, their eye movements are less well aimed. They swing past the target and then have to move their eyes further back for the next scan.

Smooth pursuit seems to develop at roughly 2 months of age, although younger infants can track for very brief periods if the target is moving very slowly. You can see the change that occurs between 6 weeks and 10 weeks in Figure 5.1 on the next page, taken from a study by Aslin. He argues that this shift results from changes in the physiology of the eyeball in these early weeks.

**saccadic movements**
The rapid adjustments of the aim of the eye toward some object, such as when you scan an object to identify it or to learn its properties, or to locate some new object in your visual field.

**tracking**
Also called smooth pursuit. The smooth movements of the eye used to follow the track of some moving object.

*Color Vision.*   The story on color vision is similar. Researchers in this field, such as Marc Bornstein and Davida Teller (Teller & Bornstein, 1987; Bornstein, 1988) have established that the cells in the eye necessary for perceiving red and green are clearly present by one month or perhaps at birth. Those required for perceiving blue are probably present by then as well, although this point is still in some dispute (Haith, 1990). Thus infants do see and discriminate among various colors.

Taken together, these findings certainly do not support the notion that an infant is blind at birth! While the infant's acuity is initially poor, it improves rapidly, and other visual capacities are remarkably well developed at an early stage. Some of the evidence also suggests that there may be a change of some kind at roughly 2 months, since a number of skills (such as smooth pursuit) improve incrementally at about that age. Whether such a change is the result of neurological changes—such as the rapid proliferation of synapses and the growth of dendrites—or of changes in the eye itself, or the child's experience, we don't yet know.

## Hearing

*Acuity.*   Although children's hearing continues to improve until adolescence, newborns' auditory acuity is actually better than their visual acuity. Current research suggests that within the general range of pitch and loudness of the human voice, newborns hear nearly as well as adults do. Adults are

**FIGURE 5.1**

The darker line in each figure shows the trajectory of the moving line that each baby tried to follow with its eyes in Aslin's experiment. As you can see, 6-week-old babies more or less followed the line, but they used a series of saccadic adjustments to do so; by 10 weeks, babies were able to use smooth pursuit movements (*Source:* Aslin, 1987a, p. 87; redrawn from Aslin, 1981b).

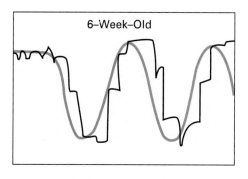

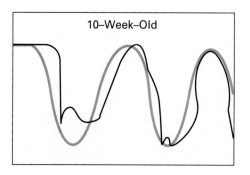

clearly better only with high pitched sounds, which they can detect at lower levels of loudness than can an infant (Werner & Gillenwater, 1990).

*Detecting Locations.*    Another basic auditory skill that exists at birth but improves with age is the ability to determine the location of a sound. You can tell roughly where a sound is coming from because your two ears are separated from one another, so that the sound arrives at one ear slightly before the other. If the sound comes from a source equidistant from the two ears (the "midline") then the sound arrives at the same time to the two ears. We know that newborns can judge at least the general direction from which a sound has come because they will turn their heads in roughly the right direction. But finer grained location of sounds is not well developed at birth. For example, Barbara Morrongiello has observed babies' reactions to sounds played at the midline, and then sounds coming from varying degrees away from the midline. Among infants 2 months old it takes a shift of about 27 degrees off the midline before the baby shows a changed response. Among 6-month-olds only a 12 degree shift is needed, while by 18 months discrimination of a 4 degree shift is possible—nearly at the skill level seen in adults (Morrongiello, 1988a; Morrongiello, Fenwick, & Chance, 1990). Morrongiello suggests that this rather gradual improvement is based on the systematic changes in the portion of the cortex responsible for processing sound information. Thus while the structures in the ear needed for basic acuity are present at birth, as are the neural structures needed to identify general location, finer auditory analysis may depend on further neuronal development.

### Other Senses

*Smelling and Tasting.*    The senses of smell and taste have been studied much less, but we do have some basic knowledge. As with adults, the two senses are intricately related—that is, if you cannot smell for some reason (like when you have a cold), your taste sensitivity is also significantly reduced. Taste is detected by the taste buds on the tongue, which register four basic tastes: sweet, sour, bitter, and salty. Smell is registered in the mucous membranes of the nose and has nearly unlimited variations.

Newborns appear to respond differentially to all four of the basic flavors (Crook, 1987), as is clear from an elegantly simple set of studies by Jacob Steiner (1979; Ganchrow, Steiner, & Daher, 1983). Newborn infants who had not yet been fed were photographed before and after flavored water was put into their mouths. By varying the flavor, Steiner could determine whether the babies reacted differently. As you can see in Figure 5.2 on the next page, babies respond to the sweet liquid with a relaxed face and an expression that looks a lot like a smile. The response to the sour liquid is pursed lips, while to the bitter liquid the baby responds with an arched mouth with sides turned down and an expression resembling disgust. Such distinctive expressions tell us that the different flavors do taste different to the infant.

Babies as young as a week old can also tell the difference between such complex smells as personal body odors. Specifically, they can discriminate between their mother's and other women's smells, although this seems to be true only for babies who are being breast-fed and who thus spend quite a lot

**FIGURE 5.2**

These are three of the babies Steiner observed in his experiments on taste responses of newborns. The left hand column shows each baby's normal expression. You can see that their expressions changed in very similar ways when they were given a sweet taste, a sour taste, and a bitter taste. [*Source:* J. E. Steiner, Human facial expressions in response to taste and smell stimulation. In H. W. Reese & L. P. Lipsett (Eds.), *Advances in child development and behavior*, Vol. 13. New York: Academic Press, 1979, Figure 1, p. 269.]

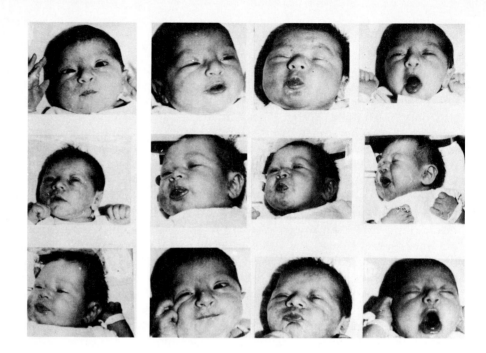

of time with their noses against the mother's bare skin (Cernoch & Porter, 1985).

*Senses of Touch and Motion.* If anything, the infant's sense of touch and motion are the best developed of all. Certainly they are sufficiently well- developed to get the baby fed. If you think back to the list of reflexes in the newborn I gave you in Chapter 3, you'll realize that the rooting reflex relies on a touch stimulus to the cheek and the sucking reflex relies on touch in the mouth. Babies appear to be especially sensitive to touches on the mouth, the face, the hands, the soles of the feet, and the abdomen, with less sensitivity in other parts of the body. Probably the sense of touch becomes more finely tuned over the early years of life, with the child able to detect and respond to more subtle differences in the form or location of stimulation. However, this is merely supposition since there has been relatively little research on touch perception in infants or children (Reisman, 1987).

Given all the basic skills present at birth or very soon after, you would probably agree with Reisman that "we think of infants as helpless but they are born with some exquisitely tuned sensory abilities" (1987, p 265). When we turn to studies of more complex perceptual skills—preferences, discriminations, and pattern perception—the abilities of very young infants seem even more remarkable.

## Complex Perceptual Skills: Preferences, Discriminations, and Patterns

Let's begin, as we did before, with vision.

*Looking*

*Depth Perception.* Arguably I could include depth perception as a basic skill. I have included it here instead because it is not based on some single process but appears to result from any of a number of different kinds of input or the combination of many kinds of input. Thus it requires some kind of analysis of basic information.

It is possible to judge depth using any (or all) of three rather different kinds of information: (1) *binocular cues* arise because each of your two eyes receives a slightly different visual image of an object. These are combined in the brain so that you do not see everything as blurry, but the brain can still use the varying information to judge depth since the closer something is the more the views from the two eyes differ. (2) *pictorial* information, also sometimes called *monocular* cues, can tell you about depth even with data from only one eye. Included here are cues such as interposition of one object in front of another, which tells you that the partially occluded object is further away; linear perspective (like railroad lines that seem to get closer together as they are further away); and relative size of two similar objects. (3) *kinetic* information allows depth to be judged from motion, either your own motion or motion of some object. If you move your head, objects near you seem to move more than objects further away. Similarly, if objects in your visual field are moving, those that are closer appear to move over larger distances in the same space of time than is true of further away objects.

How early can an infant judge depth, and which of these cues does he use? This is still a hot area of research, so the answer I can give you is not definitive. The best conclusion at the moment seems to be that kinetic information is used first, perhaps by about 3 months of age; binocular cues are used beginning at roughly 4 months; and pictorial cues are used last, perhaps at 5-7 months (Aslin, 1987b; 1988).

Although there is abundant research on each of these three types of cues, let me concentrate on the most extensive, most fascinating, and most controversial line of research, which has involved the use of kinetic cues. In a remarkably clever early study, Eleanor Gibson and Richard Walk (1960) devised an apparatus called a *visual cliff,* shown in Figure 5.3 on the next page. It consists of a large glass table with a sort of runway in the middle. On one side of the runway there is a checkerboard pattern immediately below the glass; on the other side—the "cliff" side—the checkerboard is several feet below the glass. The baby could judge depth here by several means, but it is primarily kinetic information that is useful, since the baby in motion would see the nearer surface move more than the further surface. If a baby has no depth perception, she should be equally willing to crawl on either side of the runway, but if she can judge depth by this method, she should be reluctant to crawl out on the "cliff" side. From the baby's perspective, the cliff side would indeed look like a cliff and she should stay away.

Since an infant had to be able to crawl in order to be tested in the Gibson and Walk procedure, the original subjects were all 6 months old or older. By and large these infants did *not* crawl out on the cliff side, but were quite willing to crawl out on the shallow side. In other words, 6-month-old babies have depth perception.

But what about younger infants? The traditional visual cliff procedure

FIGURE 5.3

The "visual cliff" apparatus used by Gibson and Walk in their studies of depth perception in infants. In the original procedure, as in this photo, the mother tried to coax the baby out onto the "cliff" side (*Source:* Gibson & Walk, 1960, p. 65).

can't give us the answer, since the babies must be able to crawl in order to "tell us" whether they can judge depth. Two other lines of evidence, however, including a modified visual cliff study, suggest that some depth perception is present as early as 2–3 months of age.

Joseph Campos and his colleagues (Campos, Langer, & Krowitz, 1970), used equipment attached to the infants that recorded their heart rates while they were on the visual cliff apparatus. He observed that babies' heart rates went down slightly when they were on the cliff side, but did not do so when they were on the non-cliff side. This difference in response, which suggests that some discrimination took place, occurred in infants as young as 2 months, but *not* in younger babies.

Another procedure for studying kinetic cues for depth perception in very young infants has involved seeing how they react to looming objects. Most often the baby observes a film of an object moving toward him, apparently on a collision course. If the infant has some depth perception, he should flinch, move to one side, or blink, as the object appears to come very close. Albert Yonas has established that such an avoidance response is consistently found in 3-month-olds (e.g., Yonas & Owsley, 1987), indicating at least some depth perception at that age. Thus two separate lines of evidence converge on a conclusion that babies have at least some depth perception by 2 or 3 months of age.

*What Babies Look At.* Even though babies cannot judge depth right away, their behavior is governed by visual information from the first minutes of life. We know that from the beginning, babies look at the world around them in a non-random way. In Marshall Haith's phrase (1980), there are "rules babies look by." Furthermore, those rules seem to change with age.

In the first two months, a babies' visual attention is focused on *where* objects are in their world (Bronson, 1974, 1991). They scan the world around them—not very smoothly or skillfully, to be sure, but nonetheless regularly (Haith, 1980). This general scanning continues until they come to a sharp light/dark contrast, which typically signals the edge of some object. Once they find such an edge, babies stop searching and move their eyes back and forth across and around the edge. Thus the initial rules seem to be: Scan until you find an edge and then examine the edge. Motion also captures infants' attention at this same age, so they will look at things that move as well as things with large light/dark contrast.

These rules seem to change at about 2 months, perhaps because the cortex has then developed more fully, or perhaps because of experience, or because of both factors. At about this time the baby's attention seems to shift from *where* an object is to *what* an object is. Put another way, the baby seems to move from a strategy designed primarily to *find things* to a strategy designed primarily to *identify* things. Babies this age begin to scan rapidly across an entire figure, rather than getting stuck on edges. As a result, they spend more time looking at the internal features of some object or array of objects, and are thus better able to identify the objects.

What is amazing about this shift is the degree of detail infants now seem able to take in and respond to. They notice whether two pictures are placed horizontally or vertically and can tell the difference between pictures with two things in them and pictures with three things in them. They also clearly notice patterns, even apparently abstract patterns such as "big-thing-over-small-thing."

An example would probably help. In one experiment using a habituation procedure, Albert and Rose Caron (1981) chose stimuli like those in Figure 5.4 on the next page. The babies were first shown a series of pictures, like the ones on the left in Figure 5.4, each of which depicted some particular relationship. The two examples I've shown in the figure are "small over big" and "two pictures alternating." After the baby got bored and stopped looking at pictures in this set (that is, habituated), the "test stimulus" was slipped into the series. This test picture was either another of the same original pattern or one showing a different pattern, as those shown on the right-hand side of Figure 5.4. If the baby had really habituated to the *pattern* of the original pictures (e.g., small over large) he should show little interest in test stimuli like those in Column A, but should show renewed interest to test stimuli like the ones in Column B. Caron and Caron found that 3- and 4-month-old children did precisely that, indicating that even at this early age, babies are finding and paying attention to patterns and not just to specific stimuli.

*Faces: An Example of Responding to a Complex Pattern.* One particular pattern that has especially interested researchers studying babies is the face pattern. How early can a baby discriminate one face from another? Is there something special about the configuration of faces that is uniquely or especially interesting to babies? These questions have obvious relevance not only

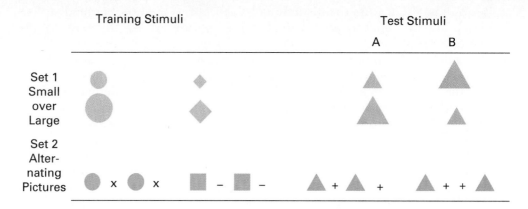

**Training Stimuli**

**Test Stimuli**

A      B

Set 1
Small
over
Large

Set 2
Alter-
nating
Pictures

**FIGURE 5.4**

Albert and Rose Caron used stimuli like these in their study of infants' responses to visual patterns. In the habituation (training) phase, they showed each baby a series of figures all of which represented a particular pattern. Some babies were habituated to a whole series with a small figure on top of a larger one, as in Set 1; other babies saw alternating figures like the ones in Set 2. After habituation, each baby was then shown each of two test stimuli: another set that displayed the same pattern as had the training stimuli (like those in Column A), and one that showed a different pattern, like those in Column B. Caron & Caron found that 4-month-old babies showed renewed interest in Column B patterns but not in Column A patterns (*Source:* Caron & Caron, 1981, p. 227).

for parent-child interaction, but for the nativism/empiricism issue. Thirty years of research has now yielded some well-supported conclusions (Nelson, 1989).

First, there is little evidence that faces are uniquely interesting to infants, which fails to support one of the early assumptions of many nativists. The nativists have gained a point in the argument, though, from some remarkably interesting recent research on children's preferences for *attractive* faces. Infants as young as 2–3 months of age seem to prefer to look at faces that have been judged attractive by adult raters rather than at less attractive faces (Langlois et al., 1987, 1991; Langlois, Roggman, & Rieser-Danner, 1990). Langlois has found that both black and white babies show such preferences, and that the preferences occur with male as well as female faces and black as well as white faces. We do not know whether infants reared in cultures with different standards of attractiveness might respond in the same way to the same pairs of faces, but it is difficult to imagine how infants as young as 2 months could have learned culture-specific standards of attractiveness. So there may be some built-in preferences for face patterns of particular kinds, and those built-in patterns may form the basis of our adult judgments of attractiveness. Speculative stuff, but interesting.

Second, when babies look at faces they seem to begin by looking mostly at the edges—the hairline and the chin. This pattern prevails for about the first two months of life, after which they seem to look more at the internal features, especially the eyes. This pattern makes sense given what I've already said about early scanning patterns.

Third, babies can discriminate between Mom's face and other female faces by at least 4 to 6 weeks of age—perhaps even earlier. Not surprisingly, these early discriminations seem to be based mostly on differences in the shapes of edges, such as hairlines. When researchers disguised the hairlines by having the mother and the stranger wear bathing caps, then 2-month-olds could no longer discriminate between a picture of Mom and a picture of another woman. In the same vein, other research shows that 1-month-old infants can discriminate full-face photos or three-quarter views, but not profiles. By 3 months of age, however, infants seem to be able to discriminate mother from stranger in almost any guise.

Infants are also able to discriminate among emotional expressions on the faces around them. By 6 or 7 months, babies can discriminate between happy, surprised, and fearful faces (Nelson, 1987). By roughly 10 months, infants use such emotional cues in Mom's or Dad's face to judge the fearfulness or safety of some new situation or toy—a process referred to as *social referencing* (e.g., Hirshberg & Svejda, 1990).

## Listening

When we turn from looking to listening we find similarly intriguing indications that very young infants pay attention to auditory patterns, and make remarkably fine discriminations among individual sounds.

A baby this age can already discriminate her Mom's face from the face of another woman; she can also recognize her Mom by her voice and her smell.

*Discriminating Speech Sounds.* Just how early can a baby make discriminations among different speech sounds? This question has relevance for the beginnings of language, since babies cannot learn language until they can hear the individual sounds as distinct. Perception researchers have also been interested in this question because the answers may reveal some very interesting things about what may be built into the neurological system. And those answers have turned out to be remarkable.

For starters, researchers established that as early as one month, babies can discriminate between speech sounds like *pa* and *ba* (Trehub & Rabinovitch, 1972). Studies using conditioned head turning responses have shown that by perhaps 6 months of age they can discriminate between two syllable "words" like *bada* and *baga* and can even respond to a syllable which is hidden inside a string of other syllables, like *tibati* or *kobako* (Morse & Cowan, 1982; Goodsitt et al., 1984; Kuhl, 1983). The voice quality of the sound doesn't even seem to make any difference. By 6 months, babies respond equivalently to individual sounds whether they are spoken by male or female voices or a child's voice (Kuhl, 1983).

That's already pretty impressive evidence that infants can listen to quite fine variations in speech sounds, not just at the beginnings of words but in other vocal positions as well. Even more striking is the evidence that infants can accurately discriminate all sound contrasts that appear in *any* language, including contrasts from languages they are not exposed to. Babies in an English-speaking environment can discriminate pairs of sounds that occur in Hindi (a language of India) but not in English. Babies in Spanish-speaking environments can discriminate pairs of sounds that are relevant in English but not in Spanish. However, by one year of life, the ability to discriminate among sound contrasts not used in the language the child is hearing have largely disappeared.

You can see both these types of findings in the results of a complex and impressive study by Werker & Tees (1984). They have both cross-sectional and longitudinal data on sound discrimination ability of English-environment babies presented with two sound distinctions not present in English—one from Hindi and one from Salish (a North American Indian language). In the cross-sectional study, they tested separate groups of 6–8 month-old, 8–10 month-old, and 10–12 month-old babies. In the longitudinal portion of the study they then retested some of the 6–8 month olds three more times. Both cross-sectional and longitudinal comparisons, which you can see in Figure 5.5, show that the infants could make these discriminations at 6 months but could not do so at 12 months. In a separate set of tests, Werker and Tees found that 1-year-old Salish-environment babies and 1-year-old Hindi-environment babies could continue to make the discriminations salient for their own language. So young infants actually make *more* speech discriminations than is true at any later age.

Fascinating stuff, isn't it? It seems to me that results like those in Figure 5.5 are consistent with what we now know about the pattern of rapid, apparently preprogrammed, growth of synapses in the early months of life, followed by synaptic pruning. Many connections are initially created, permitting discriminations along all possible sound continua. But only those pathways that are actually used in the language the child hears are retained.

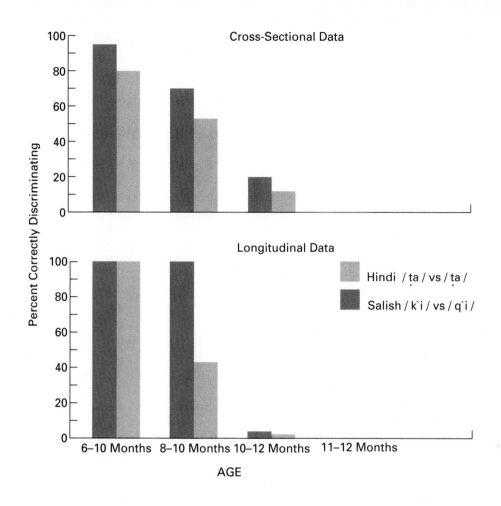

Cross-Sectional Data

Longitudinal Data

Hindi / ṭa / vs / ta /
Salish / k`i / vs / q`i /

6–10 Months   8–10 Months  10–12 Months   11–12 Months

AGE

Percent Correctly Discriminating

**FIGURE 5.5**

In these studies, babies growing up in English-speaking environments were tested for
their ability to make two discriminations: between two speech sounds that are used differently in Hindi but that are treated the same in English, and between a pair of sounds
used differently in Salish but treated as the same in English. The upper part of the figure
shows a cross-sectional comparison, with 12 babies tested at each age. The lower part of
the figure shows what happened to the discrimination ability of six babies longitudinally.
You can see that virtually all the babies could make these discriminations at 6 months,
but that this ability rapidly disappeared (*Source:* Werker & Tees, 1985, p. 61, Figure 4).

*Discriminating Individual Voices.*  Newborns also seem to be able to discriminate between individual voices. DeCasper and Fifer (1980) have
found that newborns can tell their mother's voice from another female
voice (but not their father's voice from another male voice) and prefer the

mother's, possibly because the baby has become familiar with the mother's voice while still in utero. By 6 months, babies even know which voice is supposed to go with which face. If you put infants of this age in a situation where they can see their father and mother and can hear a tape recorded voice of one of them, they will look toward the parent whose voice they hear (Spelke & Owsley, 1979).

*Other Sound Patterns.* As was true with studies of looking, there is also evidence that infants pay attention to *patterns* of sounds from the very beginning. One particularly striking demonstration of this comes from another study by DeCasper (DeCasper & Spence, 1986). He instructed pregnant women to read a children's story, such as Dr. Seuss's *The Cat in the Hat,* out loud each day for the final six weeks of the pregnancy. After the infants were born, he played recordings of the mother reading this same story, or another previously unheard story, to see which the infant preferred. The newborns clearly preferred the sound of the story they had heard in utero. Not only does this study demonstrate that key features of the auditory system are well-developed some weeks before birth, but it shows that even before birth, infants are paying attention to and discriminating among complex patterns of sounds. Whether such pattern perception skills are built into the neurological system as it develops, or whether they are the result of the child's learning after birth, is still a matter of theoretical and empirical debate (e.g., Morrongiello, 1988b). But the fact that such skills are present very early in life is not in dispute.

The ability of the young infant to make such fine auditory discriminations and pattern judgments also has some unexpected practical applications. Thomas Bower studied blind infants (1977b) with the use of a special ultrasonic device (see Figure 5.6) that provided sound information that replaced the typical visual information available to a sighted infant. I've described Bower's study on the box on pages 186–187.

### Cross-Modal Transfer: Combining Information from Several Senses

I have been talking about each sense separately, as if we experience the world through only one sense at a time. But if you think about the way you receive and use perceptual information, you'll realize quickly that you rarely have information from only one sense at one time. Ordinarily you have *both* sound and sight, or touch and sight, or still more complex combinations of smell, sight, touch, and sound. Psychologists have been interested in knowing how early an infant can combine such information. For example, can infants recognize simultaneously changing visual and auditory patterns like the mouth movements that go with speech sounds or learn something through one sense and then use that knowledge with another sense?. The latter skill is normally called **cross-modal** (or intermodal) **transfer.** For example, if you have seen an object but not touched it you could probably still pick it out in the dark, since you know what it *ought* to feel like, based on what you saw.

Piaget believed that integration or transfer of cross-modal information was simply not possible until quite late in the first year of life, after the infant had many experiences with specific objects and how they simultaneously

**cross-modal transfer**
The ability to coordinate information from two senses, such as matching the shape of the mouth with the sound being spoken, or to transfer information gained through one sense to another sense at a later time, such as identifying visually something you had previously explored only tactually.

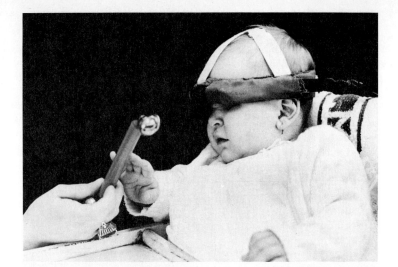

**FIGURE 5.6**

A blind baby using the special sonic guide Bower has studied. Notice how she reaches accurately for the object, much as a sighted infant does using visual cues (*Source:* T. G. R. Bower, Blind babies see with their ears. *New Scientist,* 1977, *73,* p. 255, photographs by Ric Gemmel).

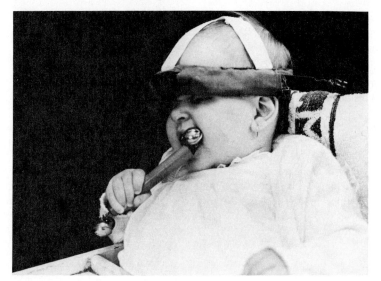

looked, sounded, and felt. Other theorists, including James and Eleanor Gibson, have argued that some intermodal coordination of perceptual information is built-in from birth. The baby then builds on that in-born set of skills with specific experience with objects. In this case the research favors the Gibsonian view: The empirical findings show that cross-modal transfer is possible as early as 1 month and becomes common by 6 months (Rose & Ruff, 1987).

For example, if you attach a nubby or a smooth sphere to a pacifier and give one or the other to each of several babies to suck, you can test for cross-modal transfer using Fantz's preference technique: You show the babies pictures of the two spheres to see if infants look longer at one than at the other. When Meltzoff and Borton (1979) used this technique, they found that 1-month-old babies preferred to look at the picture of the object they had sucked on earlier. Other investigators have not always found such transfer in infants as young as 1 month, so the phenomenon is not robust at this age. However, the fact that this behavior can be demonstrated at all is significant.

## Blind Babies Can "See" with Their Ears

Of the many fascinating studies of infant perception I have seen in recent years, one of the most practically relevant is a series of observations by T. G. R. Bower. He studied blind infants equipped with a special ultrasonic device that allows them to perceive the world around them. Figure 5.6 shows what the apparatus looks like.

The system works in a way that is similar to the echolocation system of dolphins or bats. The transmitter continuously irradiates the environment with ultrasonic waves, which bounce off of the objects—toys, walls, and people—around the baby. The bounced-back sound is received by the headset and transmitted to the infant's ears through the speakers. The whole thing is remarkably sensitive to variations in the shape, distance, and size of objects.

- The pitch of the sound the baby hears tells her how far away the object may be. Low pitches signal a nearby object, while high pitches signal faraway objects.
- The loudness of the sound tells the baby how big the object is. Loud sounds signal large objects, softer sounds signal smaller objects.
- The clarity of the sound tells the baby something about the texture of the surface. Very clear sounds indicate a hard surface; fuzzy sounds indicate soft surfaces.
- The right/left location of the sound tells the baby where the object is located in space, since the two ears receive signals at different times, depending on the object's location. Objects on the right make sounds that arrive at the right ear fractionally sooner than at the left ear, while objects on the left do the reverse.

Bower has tested this apparatus on six blind babies, ranging in age from 5 to 16 months, with remarkable results. First of all, the babies were able to learn to use this device very quickly—within hours or days. The babies quickly begin to reach accurately for objects, to crawl or walk through doorways, even to hold out their hands and move them around (which changes the sound). These actions are accompanied by signs of great joy and delight.

All of these behaviors are strikingly similar to what we see in sighted infants, who begin reaching for objects within the first 2–3 months, and show visual regard of the moving hand in the early months as well.

---

In older infants intersensory integration or transfer is more consistently found. For instance, in several delightfully clever experiments, Elizabeth Spelke has shown that 4-month-old infants can connect sound rhythms with movement (1979). She showed babies two films simultaneously. One film showed a toy kangaroo bouncing up and down and the other showed a donkey bouncing up and down, with one of the animals bouncing at a faster rate. Out of a speaker located between the two films, the infant heard a tape recording of a rhythmic bouncing sound that matched one of the two rates. In this situation, babies spent more time watching the film that had the rhythm matching the sound they were hearing—a result I find remarkable.

All of this burgeoning (and I think fascinating) research on combining information from several senses has raised some interesting theoretical issues. It is now perfectly clear that one does not need language to transfer information from one mode to another. And the fact that at least some transfer is possible within the first few weeks of life, before the infant has had much direct

What Bower's experiments show is that blind infants can glean essentially the same information about the environment from auditory cues as sighted infants do with visual cues.

A second finding, which you may not find so surprising in view of the data on speech discriminations I've been describing in the past few pages, is that the younger babies actually have an *easier* time learning to use this apparatus than the older babies do. And adults have a very difficult time with it—taking weeks or months to learn what an infant learns within a few hours or days.

Bower explains this finding by suggesting that the very young infant is really not treating the stimulus input as "sound." Rather he is treating it as a description of the world around him, much as sighted people perceive light. Light is a background variable that gives us information, but it is not usually a property of objects. Blind infants treat the sounds the same way—as if they told about the world "out there." This suggests that for the infant, auditory and visual information are essentially interchangeable.

But the older infant (and the adult)—starting as early as about 12 months of age—perceives the sounds as *part of* the objects in some way. So the 13-month-old Bower tested with the apparatus kept putting the toys and objects up to her ear, as if the sound were being made by the object, rather than telling her where the object was. This older infant, and the adults who have been tested, appear to treat sound and sight as distinct sources of information, rather than as interchangeable sources as the younger infant does.

On the basis of evidence like this, Bower argues that babies are operating on very abstract perceptual principles. Over time, however, perceptual information becomes more and more specific, more and more differentiated. Obviously we need to use perceptual information in such differentiated ways in order to make discriminations, to recognize objects or people and the like. But one of the prices of that developmental "advance" is that we lose the baby's rapid ability to use the information interchangeably. The practical implication of this finding is that blind babies should begin training with the ultrasonic device as early as possible.

In view of these findings, it is surprising to me that there has not been more widespread use of such devices for blind infants.

experience with either mode, supports the naturist view that *some* connections may be built-in. So this body of information enriches but does not settle the nativism/empiricism debate.

## Ignoring Perceptual Information: The Perceptual Constancies

All of what I have said so far has been aimed at persuading you that babies are remarkably skillful, from early in life, in making perceptual discriminations of various kinds. At the same time, there is another, very different, kind of perceptual skill the infant must also acquire—the ability to *ignore* some kinds of perceptual data. Specifically, the child must acquire a set of rules we call **perceptual constancies.**

**perceptual constancies**
A collection of constancies, including shape, size, and color constancy.

If you've spent any time around babies, you know that infants this age put almost everything they can pick up into their mouths. While the baby is also still holding on to the object, like this interestingly shaped toy, he will get several types of perceptual information at the same time—the feel in the mouth, the shape in the hand, and the sight of the object. Cross-modal transfer may be based on such experience. This photo is a video still from the *Childhood* television series (*Source:* © Thirteen/ WNET).

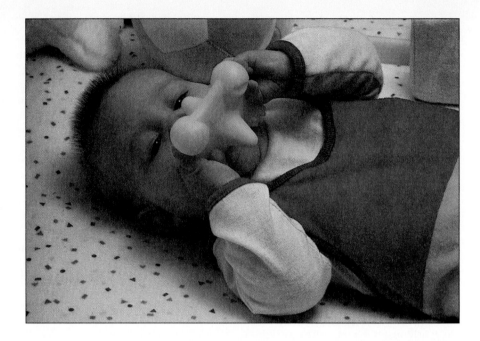

**size constancy**
The ability to see an object's size as remaining the same despite changes in size of the retinal image. A key element in this constancy is the ability to judge depth.

**shape constancy**
The ability to see an object's shape as remaining the same despite changes in the shape of the retinal image. A basic perceptual constancy.

**color constancy**
The ability to see the color of an object as remaining the same despite changes in illumination or shadow. One of the basic perceptual constancies that make up "object constancy."

**object constancy**
The general phrase describing the ability to see objects as remaining the same despite changes in retinal image.

When you see someone walking away from you, the image of the person on your retina actually becomes smaller, but you don't see the person getting smaller. You see him as the same size but moving farther away. When you do this, you are demonstrating **size constancy;** you are able to see the size as constant even though the retinal image has become smaller or larger.

Other constancies include the ability to recognize that shapes of objects are the same even though you are looking at them from different angles, which we call **shape constancy. Color constancy** is the ability to recognize that colors are constant even though the amount of light or shadow on them changes.

Taken together, the several specific constancies add up to the larger concept of **object constancy,** which is the recognition that objects remain the same even when they appear to change in certain ways. The evidence suggests that babies may be born with rudimentary forms of several constancies, but the constancies become more fully established over the first several years.

*Size Constancy.*   Size constancy is obviously intimately related to depth perception, since maintaining a sense of the size of an object typically requires judgments about how far away the object may be. In fact, we do not see size constancy in infants until roughly 4 months of age, which is approximately the age at which infants first seem to use kinetic cues for depth perception. Granrud (1986) tested size constancy in infants this age using a habituation technique. The babies were first habituated to the sight of a cube of a particular size as it moved through various distances, thus creating many different sizes of the retinal images. The babies were then shown a new cube of a different size, also moving through various distances but arranged in such a way that the range of retinal images was the same for the test cube as for the cube on which the babies had been originally habituated. Babies of 4 months showed renewed interest in this new-sized cube, clearly indicating that they had size constancy; that is, they "knew" that the new cube was different, even though the retinal images were the same.

*Color Constancy.*    Color constancy appears at approximately the same age. James Dannemiller (1989) has used a habituation technique to demonstrate that 20-week-old but *not* 9-week- old babies showed some color constancy. The older infants showed no renewed interest in the familiarized color when it was shown in different illumination, but did show recovery of interest when shown a new color at the old level of illumination or a new color at a new level of illumination.

*Shape Constancy.*    Shape constancy perhaps has the most obvious day-to-day relevance for babies. They need to understand that the bottle is still the bottle even though it is turned slightly and presents a different shape; their toys are the same when they are in different positions. Current research indicates that at least rudimentary shape constancy is present by 2 or 3 months of age (e.g., Cook & Birch, 1984; Bower, 1966). In Thomas Bower's classic study (1966) using a conditioned head-turning strategy, 2-month-old infants responded to tilted or turned rectangles as if they were the same as the original rectangle, even though the retinal images cast by these tilted rectangles were actually trapezoids.

One of the ironies about perceptual development is that at a later age, when learning to read, a child has to *unlearn* some of these shape constancies. For the first four to five years of life, the basic rule is that an object is the same whether you see it right side up, upside down, or turned around to the left or to the right. When a child learns to read, that old rule has to be modified. Letters like b and d are the same shape except with the direction reversed. The letters p and q are the same kind of pair, and p and b are the same except that one is upside down. So in order to learn to read children must now learn to pay attention to something they'd learned to ignore— namely the rotation of a shape in space.

Of course there is a good deal more to learning to read than simply ignoring shape constancy. However, we do know that among 5-year-olds, those who have difficulty discriminating between mirror images of shapes also have more difficulty learning to read (Casey, 1986).

Taken together, the evidence indicates that certainly by 4 months of age infants have acquired some of the basic elements of object constancy. All of the separate constancies improve over the first year of life, but it is significant that we find such complex responses present as early as 3 or 4 months of age.

## The Object Concept

A related development is the extension of the various constancies to a broader understanding of the invariance of objects themselves. First of all, an infant must somehow learn to treat some combinations of stimuli as "objects" and others not, a process usually referred to now as *object perception*. If a baby sees a heap of blocks on a carpet, does she "know" that each block is a separate object? Does she treat the carpet as an object as well? What makes one set of sense information signal an "object"?

A still more sophisticated aspect of the infant's emerging concept of objects is the understanding that objects continue to exist even when they are
out of view. For example, even when the mother goes out of the room, she
still exists. That understanding is usually referred to as **object permanence.** Finally, for a full object concept the baby must come to understand that individual objects retain a unique identity from one occasion to another. That is,
mother is the same mother no matter when she is seen; the rattle that is seen
today is the same rattle from yesterday. This understanding is referred to as
**object identity.**

### Object Perception

The most thorough and clever work on object perception in infants has
been done by Elizabeth Spelke and her colleagues (e.g., Spelke, 1982, 1985;
Spelke, von Hofsten, & Kestenbaum, 1989). Spelke suggests that there are two
unlearned principles that govern a baby's conclusions about what is a separate
object and what is not. Babies judge that surfaces that move together belong
to the same object (*the common movement principle*), and they judge that when
two surfaces are connected to one another they belong to the same object (*the
connected surface principle*).

In one study, Spelke (1982) first habituated some 3-month-old babies to
a series of displays of two objects and other babies to one-object displays. As
usual in studies of this type, a "test object" was then introduced after the babies were no longer interested in the original set. In this case, the test object
was two objects touching each other. If babies consider such joined surfaces
to be a single object, then the babies habituated on the single objects should
still be bored, while those who had originally been looking at two-object displays should become interested again—which is precisely what happened.
Other Spelke research shows, similarly, that babies treat objects that move together as if they were a single object, while those that move separately are
treated as distinct objects (Spelke et al., 1989).

Spelke is not suggesting that all of the child's knowledge of objects is
built-in; she is suggesting that *some* rules are built-in and that others are
learned through experience. Whether she is correct in this theoretical position remains to be seen, but for now her research results are impressive and
provocative.

### Object Permanence

The study of object perception is a rather new area of research. In contrast, object permanence has been extensively explored, in large part because
this particular understanding was strongly emphasized in Piaget's theory of
infant development. According to his observations, replicated frequently by
later researchers, there are a series of steps in the child's emerging understanding of object permanence.

The first sign that the baby is developing object permanence comes at
about 2 months of age. Suppose you show a toy to a child of this age, put a
screen in front of the toy, and then remove the toy. When you remove the
screen, the baby shows some indication of surprise, as if she knew that something should still be there (Piaget, 1954; Gratch, 1979). The child thus seems
to have a rudimentary schema or expectation about the permanence of an

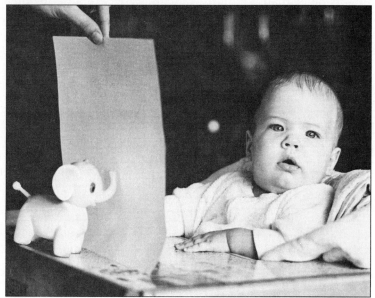

**FIGURE 5.7**

These photos show very graphically the response of a 6- or 7-month-old infant in an object permanence test. The baby stops reaching for or searching for the toy when it is hidden from him. An older baby would keep searching or push the screen aside to reach for the toy.

object. However, infants of this age show no signs of searching for a toy they may have dropped over the edge of the crib or that has disappeared beneath a blanket or behind a screen.

Six- or eight-month-old babies, however, *will* look over the edge of the crib for the dropped toys or for food that was spilled. (In fact babies of this age may drive their parents nuts playing "dropsy" in the high chair.) Infants this age will also search for partially hidden objects. If you put a favorite toy under a cloth but leave part of it sticking out, the infant will reach for the toy, which suggests that in some sense the infant "recognizes" that the whole object is there even though she can see only part of it. But if you cover the toy completely with the cloth or put it behind a screen, the infant will stop looking at it and will not reach for it, even if she has seen you put the cloth over it. You can see an example of this stage in Figure 5.7.

This behavior changes again somewhere between 8 and 12 months; infants this age will reach for or search for a toy that has been covered completely by a cloth or hidden by a screen (Dunst, Brooks, & Doxsey, 1982). There are further refinements of object permanence which appear during the second year of life, but by 12 months, most infants appear to grasp the basic fact that objects continue to exist even when they are no longer visible.

### Object Identity

Object identity, in contrast, does not seem to be part of the child's understanding even in rudimentary form until perhaps 5 months of age. One approach to studying this, developed by Thomas Bower (1975), is to violate the principle of object identity and see if the infant shows surprise. Bower used mirrors to give the impression that several mothers were standing in front of the infant. Infants younger than about 5 months showed no surprise at this—in fact they seemed to view the idea of multiple mothers with some pleasure. Infants older than 5 months, though, were very upset by the multiple mothers, suggesting that they realized that there should be only one mother—evidence for object identity.

I have discussed object constancy and the object concept in some detail because they form one bridge between perception and early cognitive development. These phenomena have also intrigued theorists because of what seems like an obvious link with social development. It seems reasonable to assume that some kind of object permanence is required before the baby can become attached to an individual person, such as his mother or father. Since we know that clear single attachments don't appear much before 5 months, right about the time that the baby is showing signs of object permanence, the basic hypothesis seems very sensible. Interestingly, and surprisingly to a lot of us, most direct tests of this hypothesis have not shown much sign of such a causal link. Still, the problem may be with our research techniques rather than the hypothesis. As John Flavell says:

Ten-month-old Kenzaburo Nouhata, in Japan, shows the same delight with the game of Peek-A-Boo as do children all over the world. The pleasure appears to come from knowing that the face or person still exists when it is covered up. When the face reappears, this confirms the baby's expectancy and he is delighted. This photo is a video still from the *Childhood* television series (*Source:* ©Thirteen/ WNET).

How ever could a child persistently yearn and search for a specific other person if the child were still cognitively incapable of mentally representing that person in the person's absence? (1985, p. 135).

I find Flavell's logic persuasive, but as usual we will have to wait for further research evidence to be sure.

## Individual Differences in Perception

I pointed out in the last chapter that the shared patterns of physical development are extremely robust. Virtually the same sequences are seen in all children. Clearly the same is true for many of the patterns of perceptual development I've been describing here. Yet as with physical development, there are nonetheless some individual variations in the process.

### Differences in Rate

Babies do not develop muscles and bones at precisely the same rates; we should not expect them to develop the sensory and neural structures necessary for perceptual skills at the same rate either. For the kinds of sensory and perceptual skills I have discussed in this chapter the range of variation does not seem to be terribly large—a matter of weeks rather than months in most cases. Such variations seem to be primarily a result of differing rates of maturation of whatever basic neural mechanisms underlie perceptual processes.

### Differences in Speed or Efficiency

More interesting are the indications that babies may differ in the efficiency with which they are able to deal with perceptual information. The most extensive body of research has focused on reasonably consistent variations among infants in what has most often been called "recognition memory"—the ability to recognize that one has seen or experienced some object or person before. Standard habituation paradigms are one way to measure this, since we can count how many repeated exposures it takes before a baby stops responding with interest to some stimulus. The speed with which such habituation takes place may tell us something about the efficiency of the perceptual system and its neurological underpinnings. If such efficiency lies behind the characteristic we normally call intelligence, then it is possible that individual differences in rate of habituation in the early months of life may predict later intelligence test scores.

That is exactly what researchers have found in studies over the past 15 years. The speed of habituation that babies show at 4 or 6 months of age is correlated positively with IQ and language development at 3 or 4 years of age or older; slower habituation is associated with lower IQ and poorer language (Colombo & Mitchell, 1990; Fagan, 1984). The average correlation is in the range of .45 to .50, which is quite remarkably high, given the difficulties involved in measuring habituation rates in babies.

Certainly these correlations do not prove that intelligence, as we measure it on an IQ test, is only a reflection of some kind of "speed of basic processing." Results like these nonetheless underline the potential importance of individual differences in perceptual skills in early infancy.

### Differences in Style

A very different way to look at individual differences is in terms of variations in the *style* with which infants and adults examine the world around them.

*Reflection versus Impulsivity.* The most often studied dimension of perceptual style has been the speed or care with which an individual examines objects or situations, a dimension Jerome Kagan calls **conceptual tempo** (Kagan, et al., 1964; Kagan, 1971). In Kagan's original formulation, the two ends of this dimension were called **reflection** and **impulsivity.** In a more recent reconceptualization, Holly Ruff (1990) has described this dimension in terms of the degree or length of *sustained attention* a child gives to some object or situation.

Evidence of conceptual tempo can be seen in quite young infants (Kagan, 1971). Babies with slower tempo will remain still and look at something new with fixed concentration, while the faster tempo baby will thrash around, become excited, gurgle, and look away after only a short period of examination. The task Kagan and his colleagues devised to measure tempo in preschool and school-age children is a picture matching game, like the pictures in Figure 5.8. The child's job is to find which of the six pictures at the bottom *exactly* matches the picture at the top. A *reflective* child looks carefully at all the alternatives before making a choice. Not surprisingly, he makes few errors. An *impulsive* child, on the other hand, looks over the options quickly and chooses one—a frequently inaccurate method.

Not all children fit neatly into this category system. Some, often called "fast accurates," work quickly but still make few errors. Others, called "slow inaccurates," take a lot of time but still end up making mistakes. Very little research has been addressed to these groups of children. In most cases, only the slow-accurate (reflective) and fast-inaccurate (impulsive) children have been contrasted.

This dimension of style is at least somewhat stable during childhood. In one longitudinal study, Kagan and his colleagues Deborah Lapidus and Michael Moore (1978) compared measures of tempo when children were 8 months old with measures at age 10 and found a significant (though not very large) correlation. Reflective infants were somewhat more likely to become reflective children, and impulsive infants were more likely to become impulsive children. Kagan has also found that reflective children have a somewhat easier time learning to read, presumably because the early stages of reading require careful examination of letter forms (Kagan, 1965). Other school tasks may also demand reflective skill, so reflectives are often found to do slightly better in school (e.g., Haskins & McKinney, 1976). Similarly, in her studies of sustained attention Ruff has found that longer sustained attention in infancy, such as while examining some new toy, is moderately correlated with both IQ and later school performance (Ruff, 1990). According to Ruff, this relationship occurs because the infant or toddler who examines new objects more intently and fully thereby establishes a more complete foundation for knowledge of the environment and for cognitive development in general.

**conceptual tempo**
A dimension of individual differences in perceptual/conceptual style suggested by Kagan, describing the general pace with which objects (or people) are examined or explored.

**reflection**
The other end of the "tempo" dimension of perceptual style. Reflective individuals examine objects or arrays very carefully and slowly. When fine discriminations are required, they normally perform better than impulsive individuals.

**impulsivity**
One end of the continuum of conceptual tempo described by Kagan. Impulsive individuals examine objects or arrays quickly, with rapid scans, and may make more errors if fine discriminations are required.

**FIGURE 5.8**

A sample item from Kagan's test of "reflection versus impulsivity." The child taking the test must try to select the picture from among the bottom six that exactly matches the figure at the top. (*Source:* J. Kagan, B. L. Rosman, D. Day, J. Albert, & W. Phillips. Information processing in the child: Significance of analytic and reflective attitudes. *Psychological monographs,* 1964, *78* [1, Whole No. 578], p. 23. Copyright 1964 by the American Psychological Association. Reprinted with permission.)

Despite this research, we shouldn't jump to the conclusion that reflectiveness (or sustained attention) is always best. Many tasks in everyday life do not require careful examination or search. A quick look is often enough, and someone with a reflective style may take far longer than the task requires. If you're driving down a street looking for a sign that says "Connecticut Avenue," you don't need to stop at every corner and carefully examine the street sign. You can tell just by the length of the name whether it could be Connecticut or not. In other words, any time a simple glance is enough, the impulsive person will be more efficient. It is only when a detailed examination is needed to make a discrimination or a judgment that the reflective style is helpful.

The research on reflection/impulsivity has been full of contradictions and confusions. The variations in style are not as consistent or as pervasive as theorists at first proposed. However, all of this work points to the possibility that there may be underlying differences in the ways in which infants and children examine and understand their worlds that may cut across our traditional categories of analysis. Ruff's research on sustained attention begins to point toward just such a cross-cutting type of individual difference. For instance, as you can see in Figure 5.9 on the next page, she finds (1990) that the tendency for a child to be inattentive is often combined with other characteristics, in-

**FIGURE 5.9**

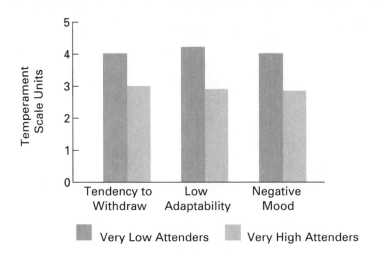

In this study Ruff contrasted the temperamental characteristics of two groups of one-year-olds who were at extreme ends of the continuum of sustained attention. Those who had shown low levels of sustained attention in play situations were rated as more likely to withdraw, as lower in adaptability, and as more negative in mood (*Source:* Ruff, 1990, p. 258, Figure 10.2).

cluding lower adaptability to new situations, more negative mood, and less soothability—all qualities which sound like the definition of temperamental "difficultness" I described in Chapter 3.

Correlational results like these obviously don't tell us what is causing what. However, Ruff's point seems well-taken: We should think of attention as "part of a style of coping with the environment" rather than merely as a more-or-less-automatic perceptual process.

### *Sex and Social Class Differences*

There are fewer sex differences in perceptual skills than in any other area of development. Boy babies and girl babies do not seem to have different levels of acuity or discrimination ability. They also do not appear to differ in the rate of acquisition of such basic concepts as object identity or object permanence, nor on measures of conceptual tempo.

Similarly, there are no consistent social class differences in the basic maturation of perceptual skills. Middle-class children do not shift from looking at contours to looking at the middle of pictures any sooner than do poor children, for example. In older children, however, researchers have found differences in conceptual tempo, with poor children more often being impulsive and middle-class children being more reflective, which may be one of many factors explaining why poor children have more difficulty learning to read.

## Explanations of Perceptual Development

At the beginning of this chapter, I pointed out that this subject, more than perhaps any other in developmental psychology (with the possible exception of studies of intelligence), has been dominated by questions of nature versus nurture, nativism versus empiricism. Certainly other theoretical approaches or issues have emerged, but given the importance of the historical argument between the nativists and the empiricists, it's worthwhile to take a look at where we stand on this question in our current understanding of perceptual development.

## Nativism Versus Empiricism

*Arguments for Nativism.*   It is certainly not hard to find strong arguments for a nativist position on perceptual development. As researchers have become more and more clever in devising ways to test infants' perceptual skills, they have found more and more skills already present in newborns or very young infants. Newborns show good auditory acuity, poor but adequate visual acuity, and excellent tactual and taste perception. They have some color vision and at least rudimentary ability to locate the source of sounds around them.

More important, babies do not have to be taught what to pay attention to. There are "rules" for looking, listening, and touching that can be detected at birth. As Kagan explains, "Nature has apparently equipped the newborn with an initial bias in the processing of experience. He does not, as the nineteenth-century empiricists believed, have to learn what he should examine" (Kagan, 1971, p. 60).

The fact that the "rules" seem to change with age can also be explained in nativist terms, since we know that the nervous system is undergoing rapid maturation during the early months of life. The evidence that synapses are first formed in abundance, apparently following some built-in plan, and then later pruned, is entirely consistent with what we see in children's perceptual skills and strategies.

Furthermore, the fact that there seem to be age periods in which a series of perceptual skill changes all occur further supports the possibility of some underlying maturational process. One such set of changes seems to occur at about 2 months when infants appear to shift away from fixation on contours or edges and toward more detailed analysis of objects or figures. At about the same age the baby can track objects smoothly, and significant changes in the visual cortex are apparent. Another shift seems to occur at about 3 or 4 months, when we see a whole host of discrimination skills for the first time, including depth perception based on kinetic cues, size and color constancy, identification of "objectness" based on motion or shared boundaries, and consistent evidence of cross-modal transfer, especially coordination of auditory and visual information.

Of course this apparent pileup of changes at 4 months may reflect the accidental fact that many researchers have chosen to study babies of this age rather than younger babies, so we simply know a great deal more about 4-month-olds. But why do researchers choose to study this age? Perhaps because some underlying maturational shift makes them more attentive, more able to focus, and more stable in state.

*Arguments for Empiricism.*   On the other side of the ledger, however, is a great deal of evidence from research with other species that some *minimum level* of experience is necessary to support the development of the perceptual systems—the pattern of environmental effect Aslin calls *maintenance*. Animals deprived of light show deterioration of the whole visual system and a consequent decrease in perceptual abilities (e.g., Hubel and Weisel, 1963).

It is also possible to find support for a negative version of Aslin's facilitation effect: Infants lacking sufficient perceptual stimulation may develop more slowly. Wayne Dennis's study of orphanage babies in Iran, which I described in Chapter 4, illustrates this possibility. The infants who didn't have a chance to look at things, to explore objects with hands and eyes and tongue, or to move around freely, were retarded in the development of both perceptual and motor skills.

Attunement, too, may occur. Evidence from studies of other species suggests that those who are deprived of visual experiences in the early months of life never develop the same degree of depth perception as do those with full visual experience (e.g., Gottlieb, 1976).

The relationship between the built-in process and the role of the environment is somewhat like the difference between computer hardware and software. The perceptual hardware—specific neural pathways, rules for examining the world, and a bias toward searching for patterns—may be preprogrammed. The software—the specific program that governs the child's response to a particular real environment—depends on specific experience. Children are *able* to make visual discriminations between people or objects within the first few months of life; that is built into the hardware. However, the specific discriminations children learn and the number of separate objects they recognize will depend on their experience. They initially are able to discriminate all the sound contrasts that exist in any spoken language, but the specific sound contrasts that they eventually focus on and the actual language they learn is dependent on the language they hear. The basic system is thus adapted to the specific environment in which each child finds herself.

Thus as is true of virtually all dichotomous theoretical disputes, both sides are correct. Both nature and nurture are involved. No doubt this particular dichotomy will continue to be part of the theoretical vocabulary in studies of perception for a long time. But in the past decade or so, theorists have been moving away from the either/or, yes/no approach to studying perception in young infants and are asking a different set of questions: What are the dimensions of *change* in perceptual skills or preferences with age? What are the roles of context and specific experience in those changes? How are the basic sensory skills and the basic perceptual discrimination abilities combined into higher order perceptual skills, such as judging "objectness" or patterns of sounds or sights? Eleanor Gibson has been one of the key figures in this newer view, so let me sample some of her ideas very briefly, to give you some of the flavor.

### An Alternative Theoretical Approach: Eleanor Gibson's Views

Setting aside the nativism/empiricism issue, Gibson turns instead to a search for systematic patterns or dimensions of change in perceptual skills or strategies. She identifies a number of such dimensions (Gibson, 1969; Gibson & Spelke, 1983), four of which are particularly interesting for this discussion.

*Purposefulness of Perceptual Activity.* As recently as a decade ago, many psychologists thought that young infants were "captured" by stimulation; babies were thought to be relatively passive recipients of stimulation. As

William James put it, babies are surrounded by a "blooming, buzzing confusion." Now we know that even newborns explore the world in an apparently nonrandom way, using some rules and some strategies. Nonetheless, as children get older, their rules become more flexibly applied, more intentional, and more adaptive to the setting. We can see a change in this dimension at 2 months, when the infants seem to shift into a higher gear, exploring visually and with other senses in a more systematic way. But we can also see the operation of this same dimension of change among much older children.

For example, Brian Vandenberg (1984) gave children aged 4 through 12 years a series of toys to play with, including many novel toys. The younger children tended to fix attention right away on one particular toy and to stay with that toy for most of the session. The older children typically looked at and explored all the toys first and then went back to the ones of special interest. Thus as children get older, they not only explore more systematically, they do so more intentionally, less controlled by some dominant stimulus.

*Awareness of the Meaning of Perceptual Information.*   If you see a ball that reflects light, you would guess that the ball would feel smooth. You also recognize that round things can be held easily in the hand and easily thrown. Gibson calls these qualities of objects *affordances:* An object affords the opportunity for certain actions. With development, the child gradually learns the links between how objects appear and what those objects can do or be used for.

It is striking that what the infant seems to pay attention to, almost from the first day of life, is not just the specific properties of a given stimulus, but the underlying pattern of *information* given in that stimulus (Pick, 1986). Yet while this ability seems to be present very early in life, it clearly increases over the months of infancy. By 4 months of age babies can connect sound and sight patterns and can recognize melodies and many other patterns. Beyond the first year of life, the child of course continues to show development in this domain, particularly as he is able to move more freely in the world and can thus explore on his own in new ways. Over the years of early childhood he discovers more subtle, more complex, or more superordinate meanings or affordances.

*Degree of Differentiation.*   Gibson suggests that initially the baby focuses on fairly big chunks or prominent features. With development, the child focuses on more and more detail, on finer gradations, on more difficult discriminations. Newborns pay attention to only a few features, such as the edges of things or movement. Older babies attend to many more properties of objects, including texture, color, shape, density, and flexibility. In each of these areas, the child's discriminations become still more subtle in preschool and later years. However, there are some interesting exceptions here, such as the *loss* of discriminability of speech sounds not heard in the child's language environment.

*Ignoring the Irrelevant.*   The fourth dimension Gibson suggests is a gradually improving ability to ignore the irrelevant. This ability is obviously needed for the child to acquire the various perceptual constancies. More generally, the child slowly becomes more efficient at focusing only on those critical things that are essential in some situation and ignoring the rest.

Children in a noisy classroom, for example, must learn to focus their attention on the teacher's voice and ignore the voices of the children around them. Children become steadily better at identifying what is irrelevant and then ignoring it. We see this trend in the fact that children become less and less distractible with age. In one study, for example, Higgins and Turnure (1984) gave preschoolers, second graders, and sixth graders easy and difficult learning tasks, with music playing in the background at either a low or very high sound level. Preschoolers were much more disrupted by the sound than were older children. In fact the sixth graders actually performed better when there was music playing, as if the distractor forced them to focus their attention more fully on the task. (Parents take note: Maybe your teenager is right when he says he can study better with the music playing!)

This sample of Gibson's ideas does not begin to convey the richness of her thinking or the extent of her influence on current researchers, such as Elizabeth Spelke. Whether Gibson's views will form the framework for a dominant future theory of perceptual development is not yet clear. However, she has at least helped to turn the field away from a preoccupation with answering questions about whether newborns can do X or Y toward what may be a much more fruitful search for underlying patterns of change or continuity.

 ## Perceptual Development: A Summing Up

Overall, the research on perceptual development in the early years of life has called into question a whole series of previously cherished beliefs about infants and their abilities. Despite their many limitations, infants seem to approach and respond to the world around them in a much more organized and sophisticated way than most psychologists had thought 20 or 30 years ago. The fact that babies respond to patterns of stimulation and under-

This toddler's attention seems to have been "captured" by the stuffed toy and he seems to be ignoring the rest. Of course we can't tell from this picture whether he explored all the toys before homing in on this one. In older children, such an initial exploration of all the options would be the norm, while toddlers are more likely to sieze on the first toy that catches their interest. This photo is a video still from the *Childhood* television series (*Source:* ©Thirteen/WNET).

lying information, and not just to the surface sensory input, means that infants are capable of far more complex cognitive processes than we had thought—a point that takes us directly to the next subject for study: cognitive development.

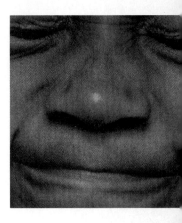

# S U M M A R Y

1. A central issue in the study of perceptual development continues to be the nativism/empiricism controversy: Are sensory and perceptual skills built-in at birth? If not, how early do they develop?

2. Studies of perceptual development were greatly aided by methodological advances, such as Fantz's preference technique or the adaptation of habituation or operant conditioning paradigms for use with the young infant.

3. Most basic sensory capacities are present in at least rudimentary form at birth or develop soon thereafter.

4. Color vision is present at birth, but visual acuity, visual tracking skill, and the ability to converge both eyes on a single visual stimulus are relatively poor at birth and then develop rapidly during the first few months.

5. Auditory perceptual skills are more fully developed at birth. Acuity is good within the range of the human voice and the newborn can locate at least the approximate direction of sounds. The sensory capacities for smelling, tasting, and the senses of touch and motion are also well-developed at birth.

6. Depth perception is not present at birth; it is present in at least rudimentary form by 3 months, initially using kinetic cues, then binocular cues, then finally pictorial cues by about 5–7 months.

7. Visual attention appears to follow definite rules, even in the first hours of life. Newborns search for objects and focus on the edges, on points of dark/light contrast, or on movement. At about 2 months, babies' focus shifts toward examining the middle as well as the edges and attending to more complex relationships and patterns.

8. Babies can discriminate the mother's face from other faces by 1 or 2 months, initially relying on variations in the "edges" such as hairline or chinline. Auditory discrimination of the mother's voice from other voices appears even earlier, at birth.

9. Infants appear to attend to and discriminate among speech contrasts present in all possible languages. By 1 year, infants make fine discriminations only among speech sounds salient in the language they actually hear.

10. From early in life, certainly by 4 months, babies also appear to discriminate among different patterns of sounds, such as melodies or speech inflections.

11. Touch/sight and sound/sight cross-modal transfer has been demonstrated as early as 1 month and is consistently found by 4 months.

12. The ability to ignore some distracting information is also present fairly early. Perceptual constancies such as size constancy, brightness constancy, and shape constancy are all present in at least rudimentary form by 4 months, perhaps earlier.

13. By 4 months the baby also identifies "objects" based on movement and shared-surface cues. At roughly the same age the baby begins to understand both object permanence (the realization that objects exist even when they are out of sight) and object identity (the realization that an object is the same from one encounter to the next).

14. Babies differ somewhat in the rate with which the various underlying maturational processes occur. They also differ in the apparent speed or efficiency of perceptual processes, such as habituation to a repeated stimulus. Such variations in speed are correlated with later measures of IQ and language.

15. There are no consistently found sex differences in basic perceptual skills. Social class differences in perceptual abilities are also rare, although poor children tend to have a faster conceptual tempo (be more "impulsive" in style) than do middle-class children.

16. Both the empiricists and the nativists are correct to some extent about the origin of perceptual skills. Many basic perceptual abilities, including strategies for examining objects, appear to be built into the system at birth or develop as the brain develops over the early years. Specific experience, however, is required both to maintain the underlying system and to learn fundamental discriminations and patterns.

17. Gibson's theoretical approach focuses more on dimensions of change than on the either/or approach common to earlier studies of perceptual skills in infancy. She identifies four dimensions of increase from early infancy through childhood: purposefulness of activity, awareness of meaning, degree of differentiation of features of a stimulus, and ability to ignore the irrelevant.

## CRITICAL THINKING QUESTIONS

1. The theoretical controversy cast in terms of nativism versus empiricism in perceptual development is one of the very oldest in psychology. Why is this issue important?

2. If you believed that newborn infants could not see, could hear only a little, and could not learn—as many pediatricians did believe until fairly recently—you'd be likely to behave quite differently with a newborn or young infant than if you knew the findings I've talked about in this chapter. In what specific ways might your behavior as a parent be guided by this new research on perceptual skills in young infants?

3. Several recent studies suggest that babies prefer looking at "attractive" rather than less attractive faces. This raises the interesting question of whether there are universal properties of "attractiveness" that all babies respond to and prefer, or whether there are cultural or ethnic differences. How would you design a study to explore this question?

# KEY TERMS

**acuity** Sharpness of perceptual ability—how well or clearly one can see, hear, or use other senses.

**color constancy** The ability to see the color of an object as remaining the same despite changes in illumination or shadow. One of the basic perceptual constancies that make up "object constancy."

**conceptual tempo** A dimension of individual differences in perceptual/conceptual style suggested by Kagan, describing the general pace with which objects (or people) are examined or explored.

**cross-modal transfer** The ability to coordinate information from two senses, such as matching the shape of the mouth with the sound being spoken, or to transfer information gained through one sense to another sense at a later time, such as identifying visually something you had previously explored only tactually.

**empiricism** Opposite of *nativism.* The theoretical point of view that all perceptual skill arises from experience.

**impulsivity** One end of the continuum of conceptual tempo described by Kagan. Impulsive individuals examine objects or arrays quickly, with rapid scans, and may make more errors if fine discriminations are required.

**nativism** See *empiricism* above. The view that perceptual skills are inborn and do not require experience to develop.

**object constancy** The general phrase describing the ability to see objects as remaining the same despite changes in retinal image.

**object identity** Part of the object concept. The recognition that objects remain the same from one encounter to the next.

**object permanence** Part of the object concept. The recognition that an object continues to exist even when it is temporarily out of sight.

**perceptual constancies** A collection of constancies, including shape, size, and color constancy.

**reflection** The other end of the "tempo" dimension of perceptual style. Reflective individuals examine objects or arrays very carefully and slowly. When fine discriminations are required, they normally perform better than impulsive individuals.

**saccadic movements** The rapid adjustments of the aim of the eye toward some object, such as when you scan an object to identify it or to learn its properties, or to locate some new object in your visual field.

**shape constancy** The ability to see an object's shape as remaining the same despite changes in the shape of the retinal image. A basic perceptual constancy.

**size constancy** The ability to see an object's size as remaining the same despite changes in size of the retinal image. A key element in this constancy is the ability to judge depth.

**tracking** Also called smooth pursuit. The smooth movements of the eye used to follow the track of some moving object.

# SUGGESTED READINGS

Aslin, R. N. (1987b). Visual and auditory development in infancy. In J. D. Osofsky (Ed.), *Handbook of infant development* (2nd ed.). New York: Wiley-Interscience.

Aslin has written a number of relatively recent summaries and reviews of the research on early perceptual development, of which this is perhaps the easiest to understand.

Bower, T. G. R. (1977). *The perceptual world of the child.* Cambridge, MA: Harvard University Press.

This is the most readable book I know of on perceptual development. Unfortunately it is also out of date; a great deal of the most fascinating research in this field has been done since 1975. But Bower's book can at least give you some sense of the issues as they were understood at that time.

Haith, M. M. (1990). Progress in the understanding of sensory and perceptual processes in early infancy. *Merrill-Palmer Quarterly, 36,* 1–26.

In this relatively brief paper Haith looks back on the last 25 years of research on perceptual development. He comments not only on the knowledge gained but on the processes by which scientific progress has been made and the tasks still facing the field. Very interesting reading.

# PROJECT 6

## Development of the Object Concept

For this project, you will need to locate an infant between 6 and 12 months of age. Obtain permission from the baby's parents, assure them that there is nothing harmful or difficult in the tasks you will be using, and inform them that you would like one of them to be there while you're presenting the materials to the baby.

Obtain from the parents one of the baby's favorite toys. Place the baby in a sitting position or on his stomach in such a way that he can reach for the toy easily (similar to the photos in Figure 5.7). Then perform the following steps:

Step 1: While the baby is watching, place the toy in full view and easy reach. See if the infant reaches for the toy.

Step 2: In full view of the infant, cover part of the toy with a handkerchief, so that only part is visible. Does the baby reach for the toy?

Step 3: While the infant is reaching for the toy (you'll have to pick your moment), cover it completely with the handkerchief. Does the baby continue reaching?

Step 4: In full view of the child, while the child is still interested in the toy, cover the whole toy with the cloth. Does the baby try to pull the cloth away or search for the toy in some way?

You may need to use more than one toy to keep the baby's interest and/or spread the tests over a period of time.

Jackson, Campos, and Fischer (1978) report that Step 2 (continuing to reach for the partly covered toy) is typically "passed" at about 26 weeks, Step 3 at about 28 or 29 weeks, and the final step (reaching for the toy that was fully covered before the child began to reach) at about 30 or 31 weeks. The closer to these ages your infant is, the more interesting your results are likely to be.

Did your subject's performance conform to those expectations? If not, why do you think it might be different? You might read the Jackson, Campos, and Fischer paper to see some of the reasons they give for differences in results from several studies. Do you think it mattered, for example, that a familiar toy was used? Did it matter that the mother or father was present?

# THE THINKING CHILD

## 4

PART

6

# COGNITIVE DEVELOPMENT I: COGNITIVE POWER

For the past several years I have been rather halfheartedly trying to teach myself German. At times this feels like a hopeless task, since languages have never been my strong suit. But I have persisted in an on-again, off-again way since, having married a man whose native language is German, it seems only reasonable that I learn his language—vocabulary, complex grammar, pronunciation, and all.

In our everyday lives, each of us faces myriad tasks that call for the same kinds of skills I have had to use to learn a new language. We study for exams, try to remember what to buy at the grocery store, balance the checkbook, remember phone numbers, use a map, and so forth. Not all of us do these things equally well or equally quickly. But all of us perform such activities every day of our lives.

These activities are all part of what we normally describe as *cognitive functioning* or "intelligence." What I will be exploring in this and the next chapter is how we have all acquired the ability to do all these things. One-year-olds cannot use maps or balance a checkbook. How do they come to be able to do so? And how do we explain the fact that not all children learn these things at the same rate or become equally skilled?

Answering questions like these has been complicated by the fact that there are three distinctly different views of cognition or intelligence, each of which has led to a distinct and huge body of research and commentary. Blending the three views turns out to be a tricky task—one that I don't want to attempt until I have first presented each view separately.

## Three Views of Intelligence

Historically, the first approach to studying cognitive development or intelligence focused on individual differences. The incontrovertible fact is that people differ in their intellectual skill, their ability to remember lists for the grocery store, the speed with which they solve problems, the number of words they can define, and their ability to analyze complex situations. When we say someone is "bright" or "very intelligent," it is just such skills we mean, and our label is based on the assumption that we can rank order people in their degree of "brightness." It was precisely this assumption that led to the development of intelligence tests, which were designed simply to give us a way of measuring such individual differences in intellectual **power.**

This "power" definition of intelligence, also referred to as a *psychometric* approach, held sway for many years. But it has one great weakness. It does not deal with the equally incontrovertible fact that "intelligence develops: Behavior becomes increasingly complex and abstractly organized with age" (Butterfield, Siladi, & Belmont, 1980). If you give a 5-year-old a mental list of things to remember to buy at the grocery store she will have trouble remembering more than a few of them and she will not use many good strategies to aid her memory, such as rehearsing the list or organizing the items into groups. An 8-

**power**
That aspect of intellectual skill that has to do with how well or how quickly a child can perform cognitive tasks. A dimension of individual difference in intellectual skill.

year-old would remember more things and probably would rehearse the list under his breath, or in his head, as he was walking to the store.

The fact that intelligence develops in this way forms the foundation of the second great tradition in the study of cognitive development, the *cognitive developmental* approach of Jean Piaget and his many followers. Piaget's focus was on the development of cognitive **structures** rather than on intellectual power, on patterns of development that are *common* to all children rather than on individual differences.

These two traditions have lived side by side for some years now, rather like not-very-friendly neighbors who smile vaguely at one another when they meet but never get together for coffee. In the past few years, though, the two have developed a mutual friend—a third view, called the *information processing* approach, that at least partially integrates the first two. Proponents of this third view—such as Robert Sternberg (1985), Earl Butterfield (Butterfield, Siladi, & Belmont, 1980), and Robert Siegler (1986; Siegler & Richards, 1982)—stress the importance of the *underlying processes* or strategies that make up all cognitive activity. What are the building blocks or basic elements, such as memory processes or planning strategies? Once we have identified such basic processes, we can then ask both developmental and individual difference questions: Do these basic processes change with age, and do people dif-

**structures**
Aspects of intellectual skill that change with age and are shared by all children. Focus on *how* the child arrives at a particular answer, rather than on the correctness of the answer.

Tests of intellectual performance, like the achievement test these children are taking, have become an inescapable part of the lives of youngsters today. Such tests reflect an "intellectual power" view of cognitive development.

fer in their speed or skill in using them? This third approach is very much the new (and biggest) kid on the block.

Each of these three views tells us something useful and different about intelligence, so we need to look at all three. In other chapters I usually begin by talking about developmental changes and then turn to a discussion of individual differences. But in this case, I will follow the historical pattern and begin by describing the oldest of these three traditions—the measurement of individual differences in intellectual skill. In the next chapter I'll talk about Piaget's views of developmental changes in intellectual structure and about information processing.

## Measuring Intellectual Power: IQ Tests

Intelligence tests have a certain mystique about them, and most of us have a greatly inflated notion of the permanence or importance of an IQ score. If you are going to acquire a more realistic view, it's important for you to know something about what such tests were designed to do, and something about the beliefs and values of the men and women who devised them.

### The First IQ Tests

The first modern intelligence test was published in 1905 by two Frenchmen—Alfred Binet and Theodore Simon. It was written at the request of the French government, which sought a way to identify children who would be likely to have trouble in school. From the beginning, the test was based on the assumption that individuals differed in mental ability. Equally important, from the beginning the test had a practical purpose, which was to predict school success. For this reason—and because Binet and Simon defined intelligence as including judgment, comprehension, and reasoning—the tests were very much like some school tasks, including measures of vocabulary, comprehension of facts and relationships, and mathematical and verbal reasoning. Can the child describe the difference between wood and glass? Can the child tell which of two weights is heavier?

Lewis Terman and his associates at Stanford University (Terman, 1916; Terman & Merrill, 1937) modified and extended many of Binet's original tests when they translated and revised the test for use in the United States. The several Terman revisions, called the **Stanford-Binet,** consist of a series of individual tests for children of each age group. There are six tests for 4-year-olds, six tests for 5-year-olds, and so on. A child taking the test is given the age tests for children below his actual age, and then is tested with items for his own age and those for older children until a level is reached at which he fails them all.

Terman initially described a child's performance in terms of a score called an **intelligence quotient,** later shortened to **IQ.** This score was computed by comparing the child's chronological age (in years and months) with his *mental age* (the level of questions he could answer correctly). A child who could solve the problems for a 6-year-old but not those for a 7-year-old would have a mental age of 6. The formula used to calculate the IQ was

**Stanford-Binet**
The best-known American intelligence test. It was written by Louis Terman and his associates based upon the first tests by Binet and Simon.

**intelligence quotient (IQ)**
Originally defined in terms of a child's mental age and chronological age, IQs are now computed by comparing a child's performance with that of other children of the same chronological age.

$$\frac{\text{Mental Age}}{\text{Chronological Age}} \times 100 = \text{IQ}$$

This formula results in an IQ above 100 for children whose mental age is higher than their chronological age and an IQ below 100 for children whose mental age is below their chronological age.

This old system for calculating the IQ is not used any longer. Nowadays IQs from any type of test are calculated by a direct comparison of a child's performance with those of a large group of other children his own age. But an IQ of 100 is still average, and higher and lower scores still mean above and below average performance. The majority of children achieve scores that are right around the average of 100, with a smaller number scoring very high or very low. Figure 6.1 shows the distribution of IQ scores that we would see if we gave the test to thousands of children. You can see that two-thirds of all children will achieve scores between 85 and 115. The groups we refer to as *gifted* or *retarded*, both of which I'll discuss in some detail in Chapter 14, clearly represent only small fractions of the distribution.

## Modern IQ Tests

The tests used most frequently by psychologists today are the Revised Stanford-Binet and the Wechsler Intelligence Scales for Children (Revised), usually called the **WISC-R**, which was developed by David Wechsler (1974). To give you some idea of the sort of items included in tests like these, I've described the WISC-R in some detail in the box on page 212.

*Infant Tests.*    Neither the Binet nor the WISC-R can be used with infants much younger than about 3. Infants and toddlers don't talk well, if at

**WISC-R**
The Wechsler Intelligence Scale for Children, Revised. Another well-known American IQ test which includes both verbal and performance (nonverbal) subtests.

**FIGURE 6.1**

The approximate distribution of scores on most modern IQ tests. The tests are designed so that the average score is 100 and two-thirds of the scores fall between about 85 and 115. Because of brain damage and genetic anomalies, there are slightly more low-IQ children than there are very high-IQ children.

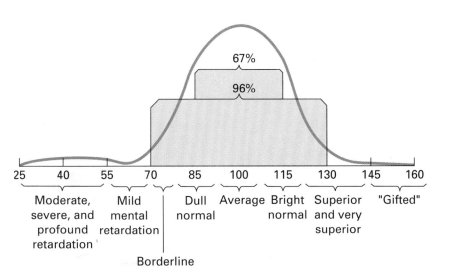

## The Wechsler Intelligence Scale for Children-Revised (WISC-R)

Unlike the Binet—which has separate tests for children of each age— on the WISC-R, all children are given the same ten types of problems, with each type running from very easy to very difficult items. The ten subtests are divided into two groups, those that rely heavily on verbal abilities and a group called performance tests, which involve less language ability and test the child's perceptual skills and nonverbal logic. The ten tests, with examples of items similar to those on the actual tests, are as follows:

### Verbal Tests

- *General Information:* "How many eyes have you?"
- *General Comprehension:* "What is the thing to do when you scrape your knee?"
- *Arithmetic:* "James had ten marbles and he bought four more. How many marbles did he have altogether?"
- *Similarities:* "In what way are a pear and an orange alike?"
- *Vocabulary:* "What is an emerald?"

### Performance Tests

- *Picture Completion:* The child is shown pictures of familiar objects in which a part has been left out. He has to identify the missing part, such as a comb with a tooth missing.
- *Picture Arrangement:* Pictures like the frames of a comic strip are laid out in the wrong order in front of the child. The child has to figure out the right order to make a story.
- *Block Design:* Sets of blocks that are red and white on different sides, and half red/half white on the other sides, are given to the child. Using these blocks, he has to copy designs. The first problems involve only four blocks; harder problems include nine blocks.
- *Object Assembly:* Large pictures of familiar objects like a horse or a face have been cut up into pieces — rather like a jigsaw puzzle, except bigger pieces. The child has to put them together in the correct configuration as rapidly as possible.
- *Coding:* A series of abstract symbols like balls and stars are each shown with a paired symbol, such as a single line. The child then has several rows of the first set of symbols and must fill in the paired symbol next to each one.

### Uses of Scores on the WISC-R

One of the reasons many educators prefer the WISC-R to the Stanford-Binet is that it allows you to look at the variation in a child's performance. Gifted children typically do well on all the tests. Very retarded children typically do poorly on all the tests, although they may do a little better on the performance tests than on the verbal ones. But children with some kind of learning disability or brain damage may show a lot of variability. For example, children who have difficulty learning to read nearly always do better on the performance tests. But they may often do quite well on the vocabulary subtest and very poorly on the coding subtest (Sattler, 1974). So it isn't just words that are the problem.

The key point is that significant *unevenness* in a child's performance on the WISC-R (or on any other IQ test) may alert the teacher to a specific learning problem. Two children with the same total IQ scores may have very different patterns of test performance and may need very different kinds of special help.

all, and the usual childhood tests rely heavily on language. So how do we measure "intelligence" in an infant? This becomes an important question if we want to identify infants who are not developing normally or if we want to predict later intelligence or school performance.

Early tests designed to meet this need were constructed rather like IQ tests for older children in that they included a series of items of increasing difficulty. But the items measured primarily sensory and motor skills, such as reaching for a dangling ring (an item for a typical 3-month-old), putting cubes in a cup on request (9 months), or building a tower of three cubes (17 months). Some more clearly cognitive items were also included, such as uncovering a toy hidden by a cloth (an item designed for an 8-month-old and used to measure an aspect of object permanence). In the most widely used modern version of such a test, the **Bayley Scales of Infant Development** (Bayley, 1969), the score is subdivided into two parts, one reflecting mental development and the other motor development.

Many of the creators of such infancy tests assumed that the tests were measuring the same basic intellectual processes as the tests for older children. But the empirical results do not support that assumption. Scores on infant tests do not predict later IQ scores very well—a point I will return to shortly. As a result, today scores on tests like the Bayley are primarily used to identify children who may have significant developmental problems; the scores are not used as a prediction of later IQ.

### Achievement Tests

Another kind of test of intellectual skill with which you are probably more personally familiar is the **achievement test,** which nearly all of you have taken in elementary and high school. Such tests are designed to assess *specific* information learned in school, using items like the ones in Table 6.1 on the next page. The child taking an achievement test doesn't end up with an IQ score, but his performance is still compared to that of other children in the same grade across the country.

How are these tests different from an IQ test? The original idea was that an IQ test was measuring the child's basic capacity, her underlying **competence,** while an achievement test was supposed to measure what the child had actually learned, her **performance.** This is an important distinction. Each of us presumably has some upper limit of ability—what we could do under ideal conditions, when we are maximally motivated, well, and rested. But since everyday conditions are rarely ideal we typically perform below our hypothetical ability.

In fact, it is not possible to measure competence. We can never be sure that we are assessing any ability under the best of all possible circumstances. We *always* measure performance. The authors of the IQ tests believed that by standardizing the procedures for administering and scoring the tests they could come close to measuring competence. But no test really measures "underlying" competence, only today's performance.

If you follow this logic to the end, you realize that all IQ tests are achievement tests to some degree. The difference between tests called IQ tests and those called achievement tests is really a matter of degree. IQ tests include items that are designed to tap fairly fundamental intellectual processes like comparison or analysis. The achievement tests call for specific infor-

TABLE 6.1

*Some Sample Items from a Fourth-Grade Achievement Test*

| Vocabulary | Reference skills |
|---|---|
| *jolly* old man | Which of these words would be first in ABC order? |
| 1. angry | 1. pair |
| 2. fat | 2. point |
| 3. merry | 3. paint |
| 4. sorry | 4. polish |

| Language expression | Spelling |
|---|---|
| Who wants _____ books? | Jason took the *cleanest* glass. |
| 1. that | right _____ wrong _____ |
| 2. these | |
| 3. them | |
| 4. this | |

| Mathematics | Mathematics computation |
|---|---|
| What does the "3" in 13 stand for? | 79    149    62 |
| 1. 3 ones | + 14    −87    x 3 |
| 2. 13 ones | |
| 3. 3 tens | |
| 4. 13 tens | |

*Source:* From Comprehensive Tests of Basic Skills, Form S. Reprinted by permission of the publisher, CTB/McGraw-Hill, Del Monte Research Park, Monterey, CA 93940. Copyright © 1973 by McGraw-Hill, Inc. All rights reserved. Printed in the USA.

mation the child has learned in school or elsewhere. College entrance tests, like the Scholastic Aptitude Tests (SATs, which some of you may have taken recently) fall somewhere in between. They are designed to measure fairly basic "developed abilities," such as the ability to reason with words, rather than just specific knowledge. All three types of tests, though, measure aspects of a child or young person's performance and not competence.

If that's so, why bother with IQ tests at all in the schools? Educators and psychologists are still arguing about this question. I've explored some of the uses of IQ tests in the schools in the box on pages 216–217, along with some of the reservations.

## What IQ Tests Predict

The fact that IQ tests do not fully measure basic ability or competence, as they were originally intended to do, does not mean that they are useless. For most psychologists, the critical question is what the tests predict. If IQ test scores can help us make predictions about future problems or successes, then such tests may still be useful tools.

### School Performance

In the case of IQ tests, following in Binet's footsteps, psychologists have most often looked at predictions of school performance. The research findings on this point are quite consistent: The correlation between a child's test score and her grades in school or performance on other school tests is about .60 (Carver, 1990; Sattler, 1988). This is a strong but by no means perfect correlation. It tells us that on the whole, children with top IQ scores will also be among the high achievers in school, and those with low scores will be among the low achievers. Still, some children with high IQ scores don't shine in school while some lower IQ children do.

IQ scores also predict future grades as well as current grades. Preschool children with high IQ scores tend to do better when they enter school than those with lower scores; children in fourth or fifth grade who test well are likely to be performing well in high school.

There is also a consistent finding that the higher a child's IQ, the more years of school she's likely to complete (Brody & Brody, 1976). Children with lower scores are more likely to drop out of high school or to complete high school but not go on to college. And of those kids who *do* decide to try college, those with lower IQ scores have more trouble finishing. So the test scores do predict school performance reasonably well.

I am *not* saying that IQ *causes* good or poor performance in school—although that is one possibility and one that has been widely believed. All we are sure of is that the two events—high or low IQ scores and high or low school performance—tend to go together so that we can use one to predict the other.

### Later Job Success

Once a person gets out of school, does his IQ still predict anything important? Do people with higher IQs get better jobs, or do they do better in the jobs they hold? The answer is mostly yes, although there are some caveats.

Job *choice* or job *access* are clearly related to IQ, primarily through the mechanism of "entrance requirements" for many higher-paying and higher prestige jobs. A college degree or some other specified number of years of education is required for a great many jobs, and since years of education is correlated with IQ, lower IQ adults are likely to have far fewer job choices. Entrance to many occupations is further restricted to those who can pass a special IQ-like test, such as exams for entrance to medical or law school or for acceptance as apprentice firefighters or police officers. Because most higher-prestige and higher-paying jobs have entrance requirements, we should not be surprised that IQ scores correlate with the prestige of occupations. As one example, Dorothy Eichorn (Eichorn, Hunt, & Honzik, 1981) found that for one group of 117 men studied longitudinally, IQ scores at age 17–18 were correlated .46 with the status of the men's occupations when they were in their 40s. The relationship is clearly not perfect; there are a lot of people with high IQs who don't end up in high-level jobs and quite a few with low IQs who do. But job choice or access is clearly linked to whatever it is an IQ test measures.

The existence of entrance requirements also affects the relationship between IQ and job success. Among those in occupations with such requirements, such as medicine or law, IQ is *not* related to job success or performance. Doctors with IQs of 150 don't make more money or have more satisfied patients than doctors with IQs of 120. In part this is true because the entrance requirement has restricted the range of IQs within the group being

# Testing in
# the Schools

Two major functions are served by the use IQ tests or achievement tests in the schools: Diagnosis and sorting, and accountability or assessment of program quality.

## The Functions of Testing in the Schools

**Diagnosis and Sorting.** The dominant use of IQ tests in the schools today is the same as what Binet envisioned nearly 100 years ago: to diagnose children who lack intellectual skills, or those with unusual abilities, so that such children can be placed in special programs. Children whose speed of learning seems to be much faster or slower than normal may be given an IQ test to see if they might be retarded or gifted. Similarly, a child who is having difficulty learning to read but is otherwise doing okay may be given a test like the WISC-R or other special tests designed to diagnose specific learning disabilities or brain damage. In each case, the test score is then used along with other data to decide if the child should be in a special class.

**Accountability and Assessment.** School systems and their constituents, including parents and elected officials, also need some way to tell how successful the schools are in teaching children basic skills. Achievement tests are routinely used for this purpose. Scores on nationally administered achievement tests are used to compare schools, school districts, or state educational systems with one another. The results can also be used to pinpoint those skills children are or are not learning so that curriculum content or teaching strategies can be altered.

An IQ test may be used in a very similar way to evaluate any program that is expected to have some effect on more basic skills rather than just on specific knowledge. For example, Head Start was initially evaluated by measuring the extent of IQ gains among children who had attended such programs.

## Arguments Against Testing in the Schools

Over the years, many voices have been raised against using tests in schools for either of these purposes.

**Arguments Against the Sorting Function.** No one that I know argues that schools should never diagnose or sort children; clearly some children do require additional assistance; many benefit from special programs. The arguments center around whether IQ tests ought to be used as the central basis for such sorting. Several strong reasons are given that they should not.

First, IQ tests do not measure all the facets of a child's functioning that may be relevant. For example, by using IQ test scores to identify a child as "retarded," we may ignore important compensatory skills, such as social knowledge. Second, there is the problem of the self-fulfilling prophecy of an IQ test score. Since many parents and teachers still believe that IQ scores are fixed, once a child is labeled as "having" a particular IQ, that label tends to be difficult to remove later.

Third and most important is the argument that tests may simply be biased in such a way that some sub-groups of children are more likely to score high or low. It is a fact that when IQ tests are used to identify children for placement in special classes, proportionately many more black children end up being classified as slow or retarded than is true for whites. Many parents, educators, and psychologists have argued that such a pattern of results occurs because the tests are biased: The tests may contain items that are not equally accessible to blacks and whites; taking such tests and doing well may also require certain test-taking skills, motivations, or attitudes less common among black children.

Assertions of such bias have led to careful reexamination of individual test items, and all obvious types of bias have been eliminated from recent revisions. Despite this, proportionately more black than white children continue to be diagnosed as retarded or slow. This fact has led to a number of lawsuits, including *Larry P. v. Riles*, in which a group of parents of black children sued the California school system for bias in labeling a disproportionately large number of black children as retarded and assigning them to special classes. The parents argued that there was no underlying difference in *competence* between black and white children, so if the tests showed a difference the tests must clearly be biased. The school system argued that IQ tests don't measure underlying capacity or competence but only a child's existing repertoire of basic intellectual skills. By school age, that repertoire has already been affected by such environmental factors as prenatal care, diet, health, and family stability—all of which tend to be poorer among blacks. Thus the test may accurately reflect a child's current abilities and be a proper basis for assigning the child to a special program, even though that child might have far greater underlying capacity or competence which could have been expressed under more ideal life circumstances. The judge in this case, Judge Peckham, ruled in favor of the parents and prohibited the use of standardized IQ test scores for placement in special classes in California.

Other legal decisions have gone the other way (Elliott, 1988), so the legal question is not settled, although there are now many places in the United States in which the use of IQ tests for diagnosis and placement of black or other minority children is forbidden. One unintended consequence of this is that since placement decisions must still be made, they are now being made based on evidence that is probably considerably less reliable or valid, including less standardized tests and teacher evaluations.

***Accountability and Assessment.*** The use of IQ or achievement tests for accountability or program assessment similarly has its critics. For one thing, such usage may encourage "teaching to the test." To the extent that this occurs, the validity of the test as a measure of the overall quality of some program is greatly reduced.

More generally, by using any standardized test to judge the quality of some program we limit ourselves to judging on the basis of whatever skills the test measures. For example, to measure the success of Head Start by assessing changes in IQ carries the clear message that we will define success only in terms of a change in skills measured on such a test. A change in self-concept or an increase in confidence would not count as success (Weinberg, 1989). In general, IQ tests and achievement tests simply do not tap a whole host of skills which may be as important for success outside of school as are specific intellectual abilities.

My own conclusion from all of this is that part of the difficulty arises from widespread confusion about what IQ and achievement tests are and are not. Because most adults believe that "intelligence is innate" and that IQ tests are meant to measure such innate ability, the score given to a child carries a heavy freight of excess meaning. But I hate to throw the baby out with the bathwater. Despite the difficulties, I still think that IQ test scores (or achievement test scores) can be used to aid in the process of diagnosis and placement, but I am mindful of the strong counterarguments.

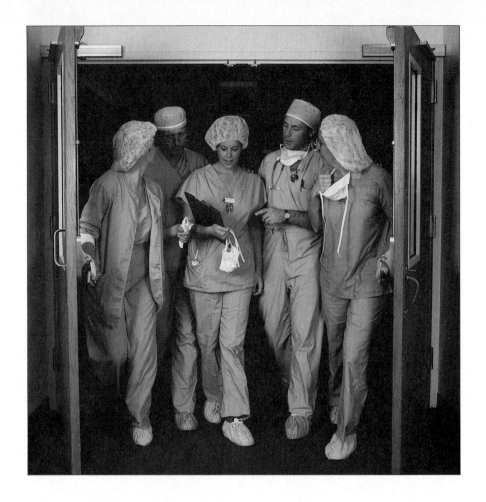

These doctors undoubtedly have higher IQs than average because the entrance requirements for the profession demand such skill. But once into the profession, IQ doesn't help explain relative success. Doctors with higher IQs are not richer or more famous or more admired than are doctors with lower IQs.

studied. We simply don't have doctors with IQs of 80 or 90. If we did, they might indeed be less successful. But among those who meet the entrance requirements, further variation in IQ is not the critical variable for job success.

In jobs without such entrance requirements, however, job success and IQ *are* correlated. This is especially clear in results from hundreds of studies of jobs performed by military personnel, whose job performance is regularly rated by their superiors. When such job ratings are correlated with separate measures of IQ, significant correlations are consistently found, even for electronic and mechanical jobs where IQ-test-like skills are less obviously involved (Hunter, 1986). Results like these tell us that IQ scores have some validity beyond the narrow confines of the school system.

## Stability of IQ Test Scores

One bit of folklore about IQ tests is that a particular IQ score is something you "have," like blue eyes or red hair. This notion is based on the assumption that IQ scores remain stable over time—that a child who achieves a score of, say, 115 at three years of age will continue to score in about the same range at age 6, 12, or 20. The fact that IQ scores can predict future school performance certainly tells us that there is *some* stability, but scores on IQ tests are less stable than you probably think.

First of all, as I pointed out earlier, scores on infant IQ tests like the Bayley are not strongly related to later IQs. The typical correlation between a Bayley mental test score of a 12-month-old and the Binet IQ of the same child at age 4 is only about .20 to .30 (e.g., Bee et al., 1982)—significant, but not robust.

Of course this fact could mean that our existing standardized measures of infant cognitive performance, such as the Bayley, are simply not assessing the same basic cognitive skills that later IQ tests reflect. This possibility has gained considerable credence from the research I mentioned in the last chapter, which shows remarkably strong correlations between measures of infant habituation or recognition memory and later IQ (Colombo & Mitchell, 1990; Bornstein, 1989). This evidence certainly suggests that it may be possible to devise a standardized infant test that will show greater consistency across age than is true of current infant tests (e.g., Fagan & Shepherd, 1986).

In contrast, cross-age consistency of scores on tests like the Binet or the WISC-R are reasonably strong, beginning at about age 3. If two tests are given a few months or a few years apart, the scores are likely to be very similar. The correlations between adjacent-year IQ scores in middle childhood, for example, are typically in the range of .80 (Honzik, 1986). This high level of predictability, however, masks an interesting fact: Most children show quite wide fluctuations in their scores. Robert McCall and his colleagues (McCall, Appelbaum, & Hogarty, 1973), for example, looked at the test scores of a group of 80 children who had been given IQ tests at regular intervals from age 2 1/2 until they were 17. The *average* difference between the highest and the lowest score achieved by each child in this group was 28 points, and 1 child in 7 showed a shift of more than 40 points. You can see several examples in Figure 6.2 on the next page.

Such wide fluctuations are more common in young children. The general rule of thumb is that the older the child the more stable the IQ score becomes. In older children scores may nonetheless still fluctuate in response to major stresses such as parental divorce, changing schools, or the birth of a sibling.

## Limitations of Traditional IQ Tests

I have pointed out some of the limitations of the traditional tests as I have gone along. But let me reemphasize a few key points about what IQ tests do *not* do.

They do not measure underlying competence. An IQ score cannot tell you (or a teacher, or anyone else) that your child has some specific, fixed, underlying capacity.

The scores are not etched on a child's forehead at birth, never to change. IQ scores become quite stable in late childhood, but individual children can and do shift, particularly in response to any stress in their lives.

Perhaps most importantly, traditional IQ tests simply do not measure a whole host of skills that are likely to be highly significant for getting along in the world. IQ tests were originally designed to measure only the specific range of skills that are needed for success in school; this they do reasonably

**FIGURE 6.2**

These four cases, all children who participated in the Fels longitudinal study and had been given IQ tests repeatedly from early childhood through adolescence, illustrate some of the kinds of changes in IQ scores that can occur over time. Case 4 showed an unusually large increase in IQ; case 22 did not vary as much but showed a rapid rise during the preschool years (a fairly common pattern); case 119 showed a more variable pattern; and case 128 showed a slight overall decline (*Source:* Sontag, Baker, & Nelson, 1958, Appendix, pp. 58, 61, 77, 79. © The Society for Research in Child Development, Inc.).

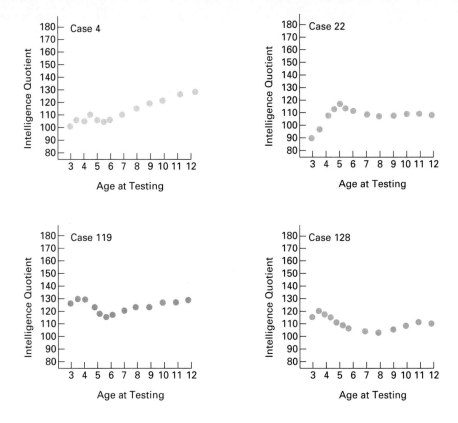

**triarchic theory of intelligence**
A theory introduced by Sternberg, proposing the existence of three types of intelligence, the componential, the contextual, and the experiential.

**componential intelligence**
One of three types of intelligence in Sternberg's triarchic theory of intelligence; that type of intelligence typically measured on IQ tests, including analytic thinking, remembering facts, and organizing information.

**experiential intelligence**
One of three types of intelligence described by Sternberg in his triarchic theory of intelligence; includes creativity, insight, and seeing new relationships among experiences.

well. What they do not tell us is how good a particular person may be at other cognitive tasks requiring skills such as creativity, insight, "street-smarts," reading social cues, or understanding spatial relationships.

In the past decade, a number of psychologists have been particularly struck by these limitations of traditional tests and ways of thinking about intelligence. Howard Gardner (1983), for example, suggests that there are six separate types of intelligence (linguistic, musical, logical-mathematical, spatial, bodily-kinesthetic, and personal), only two of which are actually measured on traditional IQ tests. Another current view, which I find even more intriguing, is Robert Sternberg's **triarchic theory of intelligence.**

## An Alternate View: Sternberg's Triarchic Theory of Intelligence

Sternberg argues that there are three aspects or types of intelligence. The first, which he calls **componential intelligence,** includes what we normally measure on IQ and achievement tests. Planning, organizing, remembering facts and applying them to new situations—all of these are part of componential intelligence.

The second aspect he calls **experiential intelligence.** A person with well-developed experiential intelligence is creative, can see new connections be-

*TABLE 6.2*

*Insight Questions from Sternberg's Tests of Experiential Intelligence*

1. Aeronautical engineers have made it possible for a supersonic jet fighter to catch up with the bullets fired from its own guns with sufficient speed to shoot itself down. If a plane, flying at 1000 miles an hour, fires a burst, the rounds leave the plane with an initial velocity of about 3000 miles an hour. Why won't a plane that continues to fly straight ahead overtake and fly into its own bullets?
2. If you have black socks and brown socks in your drawer, mixed in a ratio of 4 to 5, how many socks will you have to take out to make sure of having a pair of the same color?
3. In the Thompson family, there are five brothers, and each brother has one sister. If you count Mrs. Thompson, how many females are there in the Thompson family?

*In solving the following analogies, assume that the statement given before the analogy is true, whether it actually is true or not, and use that assumption to solve the analogy.*

4. LAKES are dry.
   TRAIL is to HIKE as LAKE is to:
   a. swim
   b. dust
   c. water
   d. walk
5. DEER attack tigers.
   LION is to COURAGEOUS as DEER is to:
   a. timid
   b. aggressive
   c. cougar
   d. elk

*The following problems require detecting the relationship between the first two items and finding a parallel relationship between the second two. In answering, explain what those relationships are.*

6. VANILLA is to BEAN as TEA is to LEAF.
7. ATOM is to MOLECULE as CELL is to ORGANISM.
8. NOON is to EVE as 12:21 is to 10:01.

*Answers:* 1. Gravity pulls the bullets down. If the plane continues to fly a level course, it cannot shoot itself. 2. Three (the proportion of black and brown socks is irrelevant). 3. Two, the mother and her daughter, who is sister to each brother. 4. d. 5. b. 6. Vanilla comes from a bean, tea from a leaf. 7. Atoms combine to form molecules, cells combine to form an organism. 8. Each of the terms is the same forward as backward.

*Source:* From *Intelligence Applied* by R. J. Sternberg, copyright © 1986 by Harcourt Brace Jovanovich, Inc. Reprinted by permission of the publisher.

tween things, and can relate to experiences in insightful ways. A graduate student who can come up with good ideas for experiments or who can synthesize a great many facts into a new organization would be high in experiential intelligence. In Table 6.2, you might like to try your hand at some of the kinds of tests Sternberg has devised to measure this kind of ability. The answers are at the bottom in case you are stumped—as many people are.

The third aspect Sternberg calls **contextual intelligence,** sometimes also called "street-smarts." People who are skilled in this area are able to manipulate their environments, see how they can fit in best, know which people to cultivate and how to cultivate them, adapt themselves to their setting, or adapt the setting to themselves. In college you would see this form of intelligence in a student who was particularly good at figuring out what the professor wanted in any given course, went regularly to office hours to talk to the professor, and chose paper topics he knew the professor preferred. But this is not just manipulation. It requires being attuned to a variety of fairly subtle signals and then acting on the information. Good salespeople, for example, need to have a high level of contextual intelligence.

Sternberg's point is not just that standard IQ tests have omitted many of these kinds of items, but that in the world beyond the school walls, experiential or contextual intelligence may be required as much or more than is the type of intelligence measured on an IQ test.

Thus while the standard IQ tests do measure a significant aspect of intellectual ability, they do not measure *all* significant aspects of intellectual skill. It is important to keep this limitation in mind as we move on to questions about the origins of individual differences in IQ. In focusing on IQ, I will be talking about the origins of only one aspect of intelligence, componential intelligence—the kind of intelligence demanded in school.

## Explaining the Differences: Factors Influencing IQ Test Scores

Just as was true of explanations of perceptual development, the arguments about the causes of differences in IQ have been cast almost exclusively as a question of nature versus nurture. When Binet and Simon wrote the first IQ test, they did not assume that intelligence as measured on an IQ was fixed or inborn. However, many of the American psychologists who revised and promoted the use of the tests *did* believe that intellectual capacity is inherited and largely fixed at birth. To the extent that IQ tests measure such a basic capacity, IQ test scores are going to be largely genetically determined. Those psychologists who promote this view, and those who disagree, have been arguing for at least 60 years. Let me walk you through some of the major points.

## Influence of Heredity on IQ: A Journey into Some Classic Research

There are two basic ways of searching for a genetic influence on IQ (or on any other trait, for that matter). You can study identical and fraternal twins or adopted children. As I explained in Chapter 2, identical twins share exactly the same genetic patterning, while fraternal twins do not. If identical

What skills does this plant salesman need to have in order to persuade customers to buy from him, or to buy more than they meant to buy? If we want to predict who is likely to do well at such a job, chances are that we wouldn't learn much that would be helpful from a score on a standard IQ test. A measure of what Sternberg calls contextual intelligence might be much more predictive.

twins turn out to be more like one another in IQ or any other trait than do fraternal twins, that would be evidence for the influence of heredity on that trait.

In the case of adopted children, the strategy is to compare the child's IQ with that of her *birth* parents (with whom she shares genes but not environment) and with that of her *adoptive* parents (with whom she shares environment but not genes). If the child's IQ turns out to be more similar to, or better predicted by her *birth* parents' IQs, that would again be a point for the influence of heredity.

*Twin Studies.*    The results of many studies of identical twins over the past 50 years show consistently that the IQ scores of identical twins are more alike than the scores of fraternal twins. Bouchard and McGue (1981), in the most comprehensive recent synthesis of the research, estimate that the correlation between the IQ scores of identical twins who have grown up together is .85 (a *very high* correlation). The correlation between scores of same-sex fraternal twins reared together is about .58 (lower, but still fairly substantial). Score one point for heredity.

But can we be sure this is all a genetic effect? We also know that identical twins are *treated* more alike and spend more time together than fraternal twins (e.g., Lytton, 1977). The logical way out of this dilemma is to look at the

IQ scores of identical twins who were not reared together, perhaps because they were separated by adoption at an early age. If such twins are *still* like each other in IQ, even though they have not been reared together, that would surely show a hereditary effect.

As you might imagine, there aren't many pairs of identical twins who have been reared in different families. But there are a few, and when psychologists have studied them they have found that the correlations between the twins' IQ scores are in the range of .60 to .70 (Bouchard & McGue, 1981)— lower than what is found for identical twins reared together, but higher than what we see in fraternal twins. At the same time, more detailed analyses of these cases also show that the less similar the environments in which the twins were reared, the less alike are their IQ scores (Bronfenbrenner, 1975; Kamin, 1974; Farber, 1981). Thus, the twin data, which appear to show an extremely strong hereditary influence on IQ, are not quite as clear-cut as they seem.

*Adoption Studies.* Results from adoption studies are also two-sided. The most common finding is that adopted children's IQs can be predicted better from knowing the IQs or the level of education of their birth parents than from knowing the IQs or education of their adoptive parents (Horn, 1983; Scarr & Weinberg, 1983; Plomin & DeFries, 1983, 1985a; Skodak & Skeels, 1945). Again, this evidence sounds like a clear point for a genetic influence, but again there are some signs of environmental influences.

First of all, there is typically *some* correlation (in the range of .20) between the IQs of the adoptive parents and those of the adopted child. Second, the IQs of pairs of unrelated children adopted into the same families are also significantly correlated (about .30) even though they have *no* shared inheritance at all (Bouchard & McGue, 1981). Interestingly, this seems to be true only for young children. By adolescence, two adopted children reared in the same family have IQs that are uncorrelated (Scarr & Weinberg, 1983; Willerman, 1987), a finding that has led a number of behavior geneticists to conclude that the genotype becomes *more* powerful with increasing age.

Finally and most persuasively, the actual level of IQ scores of adopted children seems clearly to be influenced by the environment in which they have grown up. Early studies of adopted children typically involved children born to poverty-level parents who were adopted into middle-class families. Such children typically have IQs that are 10–15 points higher than their birth mothers' (Scarr & Kidd, 1983). But this doesn't tell us whether the opposite combination would have the opposite effect. That piece of information is now available from a remarkable recent study done in France by Christiane Capron and Michel Duyme (1989), who have managed to locate adopted children born to both high and low social class parents who were then reared from early infancy by high- and low-class adoptive parents. Table 6.3 shows the IQ scores in adolescence of the 38 children studied. It's plain that both heredity and environment play a part here. Clearly the social class of the birth parents makes a difference since children born to high social class parents have higher average IQs than those born to low social class parents. Equally clearly, the social class of the adoptive parents has a significant impact, since those children reared in low social class families have lower average scores than do those reared by middle-class families.

TABLE 6.3

*IQ Scores at Adolescence of Subjects in Capron and Duyme's Study of Adopted Children*

| | | Social Class of Adoptive Parents | |
| | | High | Low |
|---|---|---|---|
| Social Class of Biological Parents | High | 119.60 | 107.50 |
| | Low | 103.60 | 92.40 |

*Source:* Capron & Duyme, 1989, Table 2, p. 553.

*Summing Up the Journey.*   One cannot dispute Robert Plomin's statement that it is "difficult to escape the conclusion that heredity importantly influences individual differences in IQ scores" (1989, p. 106). Studies around the world consistently yield estimates that roughly half of the variation in IQ within the population is due to heredity (Plomin & Rende, 1991). The remaining half is clearly due to environment or to interactions between environment and heredity. But just what is it about the child's environment that makes a difference?

## The Influence of the Environment on IQ

As you might imagine, there has been an enormous amount of research addressed to this question, all of which has begun to converge on several common findings.

### Differences in Environments Between Families

*Social Class Differences.*   One of the most consistent findings is that children from poor or working-class families, or from families in which the parents are relatively uneducated, have lower average IQs than do children from middle-class families. You've already seen one demonstration of this effect in the Capron and Duyme data I gave in Table 6.3. You can see it even more vividly in Figure 6.3 on the next page, which is based on data from a national study of over 50,000 children born in 12 different hospitals around the United States between 1959 and 1966 (Broman, Nichols, & Kennedy, 1975). In this figure I have given only the results for white children who were tested with the Stanford-Binet at age 4, a total sample of over 11,800 children. As you can see in the figure, the average IQ of the children rises as the social class rises and as the mothers' education rises.

These differences are *not* found on standardized tests of *infant* IQ such as the Bayley (Golden & Birns, 1983). But after age 2 1/2 or 3, social class differences appear to widen steadily with age (Farran, Haskins, & Gallagher, 1980), producing what is sometimes called a **cumulative deficit.**

**cumulative deficit**
Any difference between groups in IQ (or achievement test) scores that becomes larger over time.

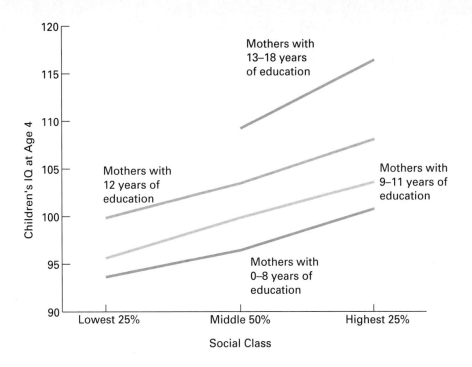

**FIGURE 6.3**

These results from a very large national study of test scores of 4-year-old children show very clearly that IQ is related to the social class of the child's family (measured by the family income and the occupations of the adults) and to the education of the child's mother. Each line represents the scores for children of mothers at a particular education level, living in three different social class environments. (There were too few low-social-class mothers with 13–18 years of education in this sample, so there are no data for this point.) Higher social class and higher education in the mother are each related to higher IQ in the child (*Source:* Broman, Nichols, & Kennedy, 1975, p. 47).

Genetic differences could obviously be contributing to the pattern in Figure 6.3, since brighter parents presumably have more education, earn more money, and pass on their "bright" genes to their children. The results could also be due to differences in prenatal risks, in diet, or general health. In addition, there are also real differences in the ways infants and children are treated in these two groups of families that are independently important in cognitive development. It is these differences in early experiences that have been the focus of most of the research on environmental effects on IQ.

*Specific Family Characteristics and IQ.* When we look at individual families, watch the ways in which they interact with their infants or young children, and then follow the children over time to see which ones later have high or low IQs, we can begin to get some sense of the kinds of specific family interactions that foster higher scores. My reading of the rich array of research of this type has led me to the following list of five general characteristics of families whose children achieve higher IQ scores:

1.  They provide an *interesting and complex physical environment* for the child, including play materials that are appropriate for the child's age and developmental level (e.g., Bradley et al., 1989).

2.  They are *emotionally responsive* to and *involved* with their child. This dimension of behavior includes more than the warmth of the parent toward the child, although that is important. What is more critical is the *contingency* of the parent's responses. In the optimum environment the parents smile when the child smiles, answer the child's questions, adjust their body to the child's when they hold the child, and in myriad ways respond to the child's cues (e.g., Barnard et al., 1989).

3.  *They talk to their child,* using language that is descriptively rich and accurate (e.g., Sigman et al., 1988).

4.  They *avoid excessive restrictiveness*, punitiveness, or control, instead giving the child room to explore, even opportunities to make mistakes (e.g., Yeates et al., 1983).

5.  They *expect* their child to do well and to develop rapidly. They emphasize and press for school achievement (e.g., Entwisle & Alexander, 1990).

Of all the studies I have drawn on in reaching these conclusions, the most influential and interesting are probably those of Bettye Caldwell and her colleague Robert Bradley (Elardo, Bradley, & Caldwell, 1975; Bradley & Caldwell, 1976, 1984; Bradley, 1989). Caldwell has devised a measure of the environment she calls the HOME Inventory (Home Observation for Measurement of the Environment). An observer visits a home, talks with the parent about a typical day in the family, and observes the kinds of materials available to the child and the kind of interactions the parent has with the child. The observer then scores yes or no for each of a series of specific items about that family. Some examples of items from this scale are in Table 6.4.

The HOME inventory has been used in a wide variety of studies of early environments, including a whole series of longitudinal studies that have recently been combined by Robert Bradley (Bradley et al., 1989) into a single analysis with a sample of nearly 1000 families. Table 6.5 on the next page gives

**TABLE 6.4**

*Sample Items from the HOME Inventory*

| | | |
|---|---|---|
| The mother spontaneously vocalizes to the child at least twice during the visit (excluding scolding). | Yes ____ | No ____ |
| When speaking of or to child, mother's voice conveys positive feeling. | Yes ____ | No ____ |
| Mother does not shout at child during visit. | Yes ____ | No ____ |
| Child gets out of house at least four times a week. | Yes ____ | No ____ |
| Child has push or pull toy. | Yes ____ | No ____ |
| Family provides learning equipment appropriate to age— mobile, table and chairs, high chair, playpen. | Yes ____ | No ____ |
| Mother structures child's play periods. | Yes ____ | No ____ |
| Mother reads stories at least three times weekly. | Yes ____ | No ____ |

*Source:* Caldwell & Bradley, 1978.

This child in England, filmed as part of the *Childhood* series, appears to be growing up in a physically rich environment. If her parents are also responsive to her, involved with her, talk often to her, and allow her to experiment, she is likely to have a higher IQ than if she had been reared in a less stimulating or more restrictive home. This photo is a video still from the *Childhood* television series (*Source:* ©Thirteen/WNET).

the correlations between the HOME score at 12 months and at 24 months and the child's IQ at age 3. You can also see the separate correlations for each of the six sub-scales of the HOME, which reflect many of the qualities of a good environment I listed earlier.

The correlations are obviously not perfect. Some mothers who do these things have children with moderate IQ scores, and some mothers who do not do these things have children who test well. But the relationship is remarkably strong considering how little time was spent observing each family. However,

**TABLE 6.5**

*Correlations of the Caldwell HOME Inventory and the Child's IQ Scores at Age 3*

|  | Correlations with IQ at age 3 and: | |
|---|---|---|
|  | HOME Inventory at 12 months | HOME Inventory at 24 months |
| **Subscales of the HOME:** | | |
| Mother's responsivity | .33 | .47 |
| Mother's acceptance | .20 | .39 |
| Organization of the environment | .22 | .31 |
| Appropriateness of play materials | .48 | .52 |
| Maternal involvement with child | .47 | .54 |
| Variety of daily experience | .36 | .45 |
| TOTAL SCORE | .53 | .62 |

*Source:* Bradley et al., 1989, from Table 3, p. 222. All correlations are statistically significant, with an N of 928.

before I leap to the conclusion that this scale captures all the crucial features of a stimulating environment, I should point out two things.

First, the strength of the relationships seems to vary as a function of ethnic group. For example, the 1000 families in Bradley's combined analysis included Mexican-Americans, blacks, and whites. Bradley found strong relationships between HOME scores and the child's IQ among the blacks and whites, but *not* among the Mexican-Americans. This lack of complete consistency in the results for all three ethnic groups forces us to be cautious about drawing broad conclusions about "ideal" environments (and reminds us that cross-cultural research ought to be done more often).

Second, because this is correlational evidence, we also have to be cautious about making (or implying) causal statements. Of course a causal link between family environments and the child's IQ is both possible and plausible. But there are other possible interpretations of these findings. For example, bright children may bring out more stimulating environments. Or, more obviously, the set of correlations in Table 6.5 may reflect genetic differences in the families since brighter parents are likely to provide a richer, more responsive, and more verbal environment for their child as well as passing on "good IQ genes" to the child. The fact that HOME scores are consistently correlated with the parents' IQ is evidence for this basic point.

Studies of adoptive families can help us get around this difficulty. The results of Capron and Duyme's adoption study in Table 6.3 obviously show that family environments make a considerable difference. Better still, in the Colorado Adoption Project (e.g., Plomin, Loehlin, & DeFries, 1985), Plomin and his colleagues looked at the relationship between specific environmental features and later IQ among adopted children; they found the same key environmental variables, although the correlations were weaker. Based on this study, Robert Plomin estimates that roughly half of the correlation between IQ and scores on the HOME inventory (or equivalent) is a direct causal effect of environment, while the rest is an indirect effect of heredity.

### Differences in Environments Within Families

Within families, there are also differences in the experiences of individual children that affect IQ. Being the oldest of a large family, for example, is a very different experience from being the youngest or being in the middle; being the only girl in a family of boys is different from being a girl with only sisters. Psychologists are just beginning to study these within-family variables. Thus far, we have been looking mostly at fairly obvious differences, like how many children there are in a family and a particular child's position within the family. Both of these variables seem to be at least slightly related to the child's IQ. On average, the more children there are in the family, the lower the average IQ of the children. And again on average, first-born children have the highest IQs, with average IQs declining steadily as you go down the birth order (e.g., Zajonc & Marcus, 1975; Zajonc, 1983; Storfer, 1990). One fairly typical example of birth order data is in Figure 6.4 on the next page, which is based on scores of nearly 800,000 students who took the National Merit Scholarship examination in 1965 (Breland, 1974).

How can we explain such a pattern? The best known and most controversial explanation, called the **confluence model,** has been proposed by

**confluence model** Zajonc's term for his explanation of family size and ordinal position effects on IQ. Assumes that a child's IQ is partially determined by the average intellectual level of the family members with whom the child has contact.

**FIGURE 6.4**

These data from the 1965 National Merit Scholarship Qualifying Test, including roughly 800,000 high-school juniors, show the commonly-found relationship between test scores and family size and birth order. Within each family size, the average score is highest for the first-born and declines with each position in the birth order sequence. And at each birth order position, the larger the family the lower the score (*Sources:* Data from Breland, 1974, recalculated by Storfer, 1990, Table 7, p. 32).

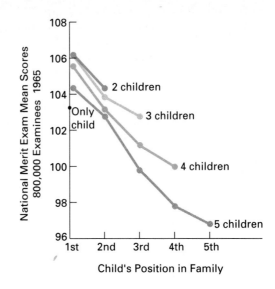

Robert Zajonc. He argues that the birth of each succeeding child "dilutes" the intellectual climate of the home. The oldest child initially interacts only with his parents and thus has a maximally complex and enriching environment. After siblings are born, the older child may also have the opportunity to "tutor" a younger sibling—a form of interaction that has been shown to be intellectually stimulating for the tutor. Second- or later-born children, in contrast, experience a lower average intellectual level in the family simply because they interact with both other children and adults. A later-born child *may* have an advantage if the children are very widely spaced, since then he is interacting entirely with others who are intellectually advanced, including both parents and much older siblings.

The confluence model has prompted a good deal of debate and criticism (e.g., Rogers, 1984). The predictions of the model work best for differences in family size; birth order seems to follow a less clear pattern, in part because the spacing of children seems to affect the outcome fairly strongly: Children born close together tend to have lower IQs than do those spaced further apart (Storfer, 1990). We also have hints that the oldest child doesn't have all the benefits either. Robert McCall (1984), for example, has found that among children in the Fels longitudinal study—children whose IQs had been assessed repeatedly in their early years—IQs dropped an average of about 4 points in the two years after the birth of a younger brother or sister. This decline was made up within three years of the sibling's birth, so the effect was not permanent. Findings like these make it clear that there is a lot more to learn about the impact of family configuration on children's intellectual development before we can explain the pattern of results in Figure 6.4.

*School Experiences and Special Interventions*

Home environments and family interactions are not the only source of environmental influence. Children also spend a large amount of time in group care settings, including day care, preschool, and elementary school. How do these environments affect the child's intellectual growth? Psychologists have been especially interested in one variant of this question: What is the impact of *early* school or group-care experience on children's IQ or other facets of intellectual development?

On a theoretical level, this question is of interest because it may tell us something about early experience in general and about the resilience of children. Are the effects of an initially impoverished environment permanent or can they be offset by some enriched experience, such as a special preschool? But our interest is clearly not entirely theoretical. Programs like Head Start are based squarely on the assumption that it *is* possible to modify the trajectory of a child's intellectual development, especially if you intervene early.

*Preschool Interventions.* Attempts to test the assumption on which Head Start is based have led to a messy body of research—messy in no small part because children are rarely assigned randomly to Head Start or non-Head Start groups (Lee et al., 1990). Typically the Head Start or other preschool group includes the most poverty-stricken children who are then compared to children who are from similar but not-quite-so-poor environments who are not enrolled in Head Start. Only in a few special, experimental preschool programs have researchers actually assigned children randomly, and these special programs are typically considerably more intensive than a garden variety Head Start program. These factors make interpretation very difficult, and researchers do not yet agree on how to read this set of tracks, but let me summarize.

1. Children enrolled in Head Start or in another enriched preschool program, compared to similar children without such preschool, typically show a gain of about 10 IQ points during the year of the Head Start experience.
2. This IQ gain typically fades and then disappears within the first few years of school, so that by second grade neither IQ nor achievement test scores normally reveal any difference in performance between those children who had been in Head Start and those who had not been in Head Start (McKey et al., 1985).
3. There *may*, however, be a sleeper effect of special preschool experiences. Several studies show that although the effects seem to wash out when children reach school, discernable effects may reappear at some later point (Lazar & Darlington, 1982). Figure 6.5 on the next page shows just such a sleeper effect in the achievement test results from one of 12 long-term projects analyzed by Lazar and Darlington.
4. The most lasting effects have been found not on IQ or achievement test scores but on measures of school behavior. Children with Head Start or other enriched preschool experience are less likely to be placed in special education classes, somewhat less likely to be held back to repeat a grade, and somewhat more likely to graduate from high school (Haskins, 1989). So although the children with preschool experience do not typically *test* a whole lot higher (and do *not* differ in IQ), they *function* better in school.
5. In general, the biggest effects are found in the best designed studies and among children who attended the most intensive preschool programs, such as the Weikart program shown in Figure 6.5.

**FIGURE 6.5**

A preschool enrichment program sometimes produces a "sleeper effect" on children's performance in grade school, as shown here. These results are from one of the best designed experimental preschool programs, including random assignment of children to the preschool or control groups. In the early elementary school grades the two groups were essentially equivalent, but in the 7th and 8th grades the experimental group forged ahead (*Source:* Bulletin of the High/Scope Foundation, 1977, p. 5. Reprinted with permission of High/Scope Educational Research Foundation, 600 N. River St., Ypsilanti, MI 48197).

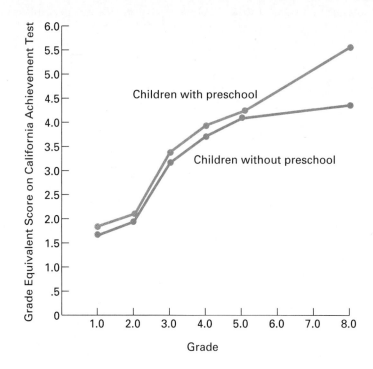

These results suggest that educational interventions can indeed have an effect, but that they work more like vitamins than one-time inoculations. If the effects are sustained, it appears to be more because the family interaction changed, or the child's attitude or motivation was changed, rather than that the intellectual gains from one year of a special program somehow permanently altered the child's intellectual trajectory. If we want to have a lasting effect, perhaps we need to start earlier, before an impoverished environment has established a pattern.

*Infancy Interventions.*　Just such an argument lay behind the development of several major intervention programs for infants born into poverty environments. By beginning early and continuing an enriched program over a period of years, experimenters thought it might be possible to overcome the effects of an unstimulating environment.

The best designed and most meticulously reported of the infancy interventions has been carried out by Craig Ramey and his colleagues at North Carolina (Ramey & Haskins, 1981a, 1981b; Ramey, Yeates, & Short, 1984; Ramey & Campbell, 1987; Ramey, Lee, & Burchinal, 1989)—a study I have mentioned in passing in earlier chapters. Infants from poverty-level families, whose mothers had low IQs, were randomly assigned either to a special daycare program (8 hours a day, 5 days a week) or to a comparison group which received nutritional supplements and medical treatment but no special preschool. The special program, which began when the infants were 6 to 12 weeks of age and lasted until they began kindergarten, involved exactly the kinds of "optimum" stimulation for children that I described in the last section.

This day-care center, attended by Avery Gholston—one of the children followed in the *Childhood* series—is a cognitively rich environment. Research on day care and preschools such as this one shows that such an environment has a beneficial effect on a child's intellectual performance. The beneficial effect is especially clear for those children (unlike Avery who comes from a middle-class family) growing up in poverty-level families, since they are less likely to receive this kind of enrichment at home. This photo is a video still from the *Childhood* television series (*Source:* © Thirteen/WNET).

The IQ scores of the children at various ages are shown in Figure 6.6 on the next page. You can see that the children who had been enrolled in the special program had significantly higher IQ scores than the control children, even a year and a half after the end of the enrichment program. They also performed better on achievement tests in first grade and were less likely to be held back for a second year in kindergarten. Without intervention, many of the children from the "control" families were performing at a level that would be considered subnormal or retarded; over 30 percent repeated kindergarten.

Even more striking results emerged when Ramey looked at the experiences of the children in the comparison group. Some of them had been placed by their parents in other types of day-care or preschool programs, most commonly during the second year of life, while some had been reared entirely at home. When he compared the IQ scores of these two groups with those in the special intervention program he found a consistent rank order: Children in the special program were highest, followed by those who had some kind of day-care experience, with those reared wholly at home the lowest. The IQs at age 4 for these three groups were 101.1, 94.0, and 84.2, respectively (Burchinal, Lee, & Ramey, 1989). So the length and quality of the intervention appeared to be directly related to the size of the effect.

Similar results have come from another major infant intervention study by Howard Garber (Garber, 1988), who found a 17-point IQ difference favor-

**FIGURE 6.6**

In the Ramey study, children had been randomly assigned to an experimental group or a comparison (control) group. The experimental group children attended a special enriched day-care program from about 1 month of life to age 5; the control group children had various rearing experiences; some were reared mostly at home, some spent some time in other kinds of day care. You can see that the difference in IQ between experimental and control groups remained statistically significant even after 18 months of regular school (*Source:* Ramey & Campbell, 1987, Figure 3, p. 135).

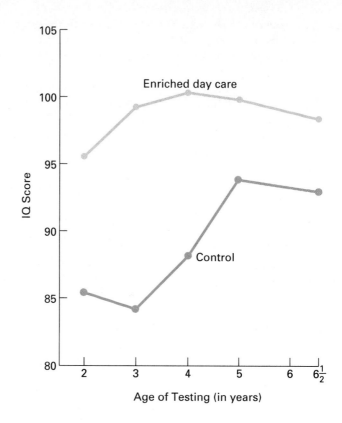

ing his enriched-experience experimental group when the children were age 10, five years after the end of the special program.

These results do *not* mean that all mental retardation could be "cured" by providing children with heavy doses of special education in infancy. What they do show is that the intellectual power of those children who begin life with few advanatages can be significantly increased if richer stimulation is provided.

## Interaction of Heredity and Environment: Reaction Range

Clearly, both heredity and environment influence IQ scores. But how do they interact? One helpful way to conceptualize this interaction is with the idea of *reaction range.* As Richard Weinberg puts it:

> Genes do not fix behavior. Rather, they establish a range of possible reactions to the range of possible experiences that environments can provide. (1989, p. 101)

Using the results of adoption and intervention studies, Weinberg estimates that the reaction range for IQ is about 20 to 25 points. That is, given some specific genetic heritage, each child's actual intellectual performance, as measured by an IQ test, may vary as much as 20 or 25 points, depending on the richness or poverty of the environment in which he grows up. When we change the child's environment for the better, as Ramey and Garber have done, we can move a child closer to the upper end of his reaction range. When we change the environment for the worse, as was the case with some of the children in the French adoption study I showed in Table 6.3, the child's effective intellectual performance falls to the lower end of his reaction range. Thus even though intelligence as measured on an IQ test is highly heritable, the absolute score within the reaction range is determined by environment.

We could also think about the interaction between heredity and environment in terms rather like Horowitz's model (recall Figure 1.4), or using Aslin's concept of maintenance. Some theorists (e.g., Turkheimer & Gottesman, 1991) have argued that within the normal range of environments, IQ scores may be largely a function of heredity, not because environment is unimportant, but simply because most environments are sufficiently rich to support or maintain normal intellectual development. It is only when environmental quality falls below some crucial threshold that it has a major effect on the level of measured IQ, such as might be true for children reared in an orphanage or in a severely impoverished environment. This view does not necessarily contradict the concept of reaction range. Rather the argument is that the lower end of any given child's reaction range is likely to be manifested only if the child is reared in an environment that falls below the critical threshold. If we think about it this way, then it makes sense that special education programs like Ramey's would be effective for children from poverty-level environments, since the program brings the child's experience up into the sufficiently supportive range and thus adequately supports normal intellectual development. The same program provided to a child from a more supportive family environment, however, should have little or no effect on IQ—which is essentially what researchers have found.

 ## Group Differences in IQ: Race and Sex Differences

So far in talking about individual differences in intellectual power, I have sidestepped two "hot" issues—namely, racial and sex differences in IQ or cognitive power. The truth is that I would rather sidestep them completely (some things are nearly too hot to handle). But that is not fair to you. You need to see what we know, what we don't know, and how we are trying to explain both kinds of differences. But since I do not want to place too much emphasis on this topic, I will be brief.

### Racial Differences in IQ

A number of racial differences in intellectual performance have been found, including consistently higher performance on achievement tests—particularly math tests—by Chinese and Japanese children (Stevenson et al., 1990; Sue & Okazaki, 1990). The basic finding that has given researchers and theorists the most difficulty, however, is that black children consistently score lower than white children on measures of IQ. The difference, which we begin to see when children are about 2 or 3 years old, is on the order of 15 IQ points.

Some scientists have argued that these findings reflect basic genetic differences between the races (e.g., Jensen, 1980). Other scientists, granting that IQ is highly heritable, point out that the 15 point difference falls well within the presumed reaction range of IQ. They emphasize that there are sufficiently large differences in the environments in which black and white children are reared to account for the average difference in score. Some of the most convincing research comes from Sandra Scarr and her colleagues (Scarr & Kidd, 1983).

For example, Scarr has found that black children adopted as infants into white middle-class families, and thus reared in the environment for which the tests are most valid, score as well as do white children adopted into the same families. In another study of adopted black children, Moore (1986) found that those who had been reared from infancy in white families not only had higher IQ scores than those adopted into black families (117 versus 103), they also approached the IQ testing situation quite differently. They stayed more focused on the task and were more likely to try some task even if they didn't think they could do it. Black children adopted into middle-class black families did not show this pattern of persistence and effort. They asked for help more often and gave up more easily when faced with a difficult task. When Moore observed each adoptive mother teaching her child several tasks he could see parallel differences. The white mothers were more positive, more encouraging, and were less likely to give the child the answer than were the black mothers.

Findings like these persuade me that the IQ difference we see is primarily a reflection of the fact that the tests, and the school, are designed by the majority culture to promote a particular form of intellectual activity (Sternberg's componential intelligence), and that many black or other minority families rear their children in ways that do not maximize or emphasize this particular set of skills. Sternberg has recently argued, in fact, (Sternberg &

In Japanese families like the Nakayamas, shown here studying English together, academic excellence is strongly stressed and parents not only expect their children to work hard and succeed, they supervise their efforts or work with them. This pattern is also common among many groups of Asian-Americans, but is less common among Caucasian Americans or African-Americans. Such differences in family values and style may help to explain the advantage Asian children often have on achievement tests. This photo is a video still from the *Childhood* television series (*Source:* ©Thirteen/WNET).

**Part Four**   The Thinking Child

Suben, 1986) that in some black subcultures, it is contextual and not componential intelligence that is particularly emphasized and trained.

In a similar vein, Harold Stevenson has argued that the differences between Asian and American children in performance on mathematics achievement tests result not from genetic differences in capacity, but from differences in cultural emphasis on the importance of academic achievement, number of hours spent on homework, and differences in the quality of the math instruction in the schools (Stigler, Lee, & Stevenson, 1987; Stevenson & Lee, 1990).

The fact that we may be able to account for such racial differences in IQ or achievement test performance by appealing to the concept of reaction range and to cultural or subcultural variations does not make the differences disappear, nor does it make them trivial. But perhaps it puts such findings into a less explosive framework.

### Sex Differences in IQ

In contrast, comparisons of total IQ test scores for boys and girls do *not* reveal consistent differences. It is only when we break down the total score into several separate skills that some patterns of sex differences emerge. As you can see in the summary in Table 6.6 on the next page, on average boys are better at spatial visualization tasks and numerical reasoning; girls are better at some verbal abilities and at arithmetic computation, although the differences in verbal skills have not been found in many recent studies (Jacklin, 1989).

Two crucial points need to be made about these differences. First, on *every* measure, there is a great deal of overlap between the scores of males and females. There are many girls good at spatial visualization and many boys good at verbal reasoning.

Second, the absolute size of the differences is mostly very small and has been decreasing over recent decades (Feingold, 1988). For example, even though it is true that girls typically do better on measures of verbal skill, sex accounts for only about *1 percent* of the variation in scores. So knowing a child's gender tells you very little about her likely performance on a test of verbal skill. Only in one area, spatial visualization—which I've illustrated in Figure 6.7 on p. 239—is the size of the gender effect really substantial. Overall, perhaps 5 percent of the variation in scores on spatial tests can be attributed to gender; if we look only at measures of mental rotation the difference is even larger. On such tests, as much as 15 percent of the variation in performance among high-school or college students' performance can be accounted for by gender (Halpern, 1986; Sanders, Soares, & D'Aquila, 1982).

The large overlap in the distributions and the small absolute size of the differences mean that most gender differences have (or should have) little practical importance for such real-life situations as job qualifications. The exception again is spatial visualization, particularly tests of mental rotation (like those shown in Figure 6.7), which are quite often included in entrance examinations for fields such as dentistry, pilot training, and some types of engineering. The fact that girls score lower on such tests does not mean that no women are qualified for such occupations; it does mean that fewer girls or young women will be able to pass the entrance requirements.

TABLE 6.6

*Sex Differences and Intellectual Abilities*

| Type of Ability | Nature of the Difference |
| --- | --- |
| **Spatial Visualization** (ability to manipulate abstract shapes, to visualize three-dimensional spaces from two-dimensional drawings, and so forth. Some items that measure this ability are in Figure 6.10.) | Boys are quite consistently better at this, beginning as early as age 10 and continuing in adolescence and adulthood. |
| **Arithmetic Computation** (basic adding, subtracting, and counting) | Young girls (up to about age 8) are slightly better at this. |
| **Mathematics** (more complex problems; high-school math) | Boys score higher on standard measures of math achievement given in high school or college; more boys are identified as highly gifted in mathematics too. |
| **Numerical Reasoning** (word problems involving numbers) | Boys again have a slight advantage. |
| **Verbal Abilities** | Before age 2, girls develop vocabulary more rapidly; at later ages girls are a bit more talkative and use slightly longer sentences. |
| **Verbal Reasoning** (e.g., anagrams) | Girls are a bit better, beginning at or just before adolescence, although more recent studies do not consistently find this difference. |

*Source:* Maccoby & Jacklin, 1974; Linn & Petersen, 1985; Halpern, 1986; Jacklin, 1989; Johnson & Meade, 1987; Huttenlocher et al., 1991; Hyde & Linn, 1988; Hyde, Fennema, & Lamon, 1990.

As with total IQ scores, there are probably both environmental and biological forces at work in creating these patterns. Biological influences have been most often argued in the case of sex differences in spatial abilities (e.g., Waber, 1977). In particular, there is now a growing body of research on the links between the biological changes of puberty and sex differences in spatial ability. At the moment, interest is being focused primarily on the processes of brain lateralization and its role in the development of spatial abilities (e.g., Newcombe & Baenninger, 1989), but the jury is still out on whether differences in lateralization can explain sex differences in spatial ability.

In contrast, there appear to be no reasonable biological hypotheses to explain the small sex differences in mathematical or verbal reasoning. Especially in the case of mathematics there is considerable evidence that girls' and boys' skills are systematically shaped by a series of environmental factors:

- Boys take more math courses than girls do. When the amount of math exposure is held constant, the sex difference becomes much smaller.
- Parental attitudes about mathematics are markedly different for boys and

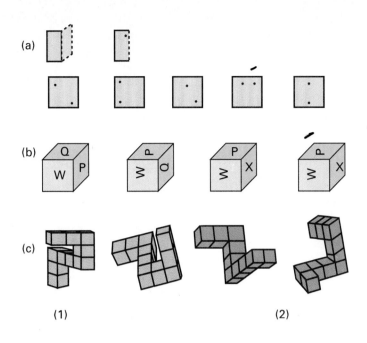

FIGURE 6.7

(a)

(b)

(c)

(1)                                                                (2)

Three illustrations of spatial ability: (a) *Spatial visualization.* The figure at the top represents a square piece of paper being folded. A hole is punched through all the thicknesses of the folded paper. Which figure shows what the paper looks like when it is unfolded? (b) *Spatial orientation.* Compare the three cubes on the right with the one on the left. No letter appears on more than one face of a given cube. Which of the three cubes on the right could be a different view of the cube on the left? (c) *Mental rotation.* In each pair, can the three-dimensional objects be made congruent by rotation? (*Source:* Halpern, 1986, Fig. 3.1, p. 50, & Fig. 3.2, p. 52).

girls. Parents are more likely to attribute a daughter's success in mathematics to effort or good teaching; poor performance by a girl is attributed to lack of ability. In contrast, parents attribute a boy's success to ability and his failure to lack of application (Parsons, Adler, & Kaczala, 1982; Holloway & Hess, 1985).

- Girls and boys have different experiences in math classes. In elementary school, teachers pay more attention to boys during math instruction (and more attention to girls during reading instruction), and in high school, math teachers direct more of their questions and comments to boys, even when girls are outspoken in class.

The cumulative effect of these differences in expectation and treatment show up in high school, when sex differences on standardized math tests become evident. In part, then, the small sex differences in test scores appear to be perpetuated by subtle family and school influences on children's attitudes. Whether these differences can explain the greater percentage of boys than girls who show real giftedness in mathematics is not so clear. But environmental factors appear to be the best explanation of the sex difference in average test scores.

## The Measurement of Intelligence: A Last Look

One of the questions that students often ask at about this point is whether, given all the factors that can affect a test score, it is worth bothering with IQ tests at all. I think that these tests do assess some important aspects of children's intellectual performance and that they can be helpful in identifying children who may have difficulties in school. But it is worth emphasizing again that they do *not* measure a lot of other things we may be interested in, including all the facets of intelligence Sternberg describes. An IQ test is a specialized tool, and like many such tools, it has a fairly narrow range of appropriate use. I don't want to throw out this tool, but you have to keep its limitations very firmly in mind when you use it.

## S U M M A R Y

1. When we study the development of "intelligence," we need to distinguish between measures of intellectual "power" and measures of intellectual "structure." The IQ taps individual differences in intellectual power.

2. The most commonly used individually administered tests are the Stanford-Binet and the Wechsler Intelligence Scales for Children (WISC-R).

3. All current IQ tests compare a child's performance to that of others her or his age. Scores above 100 represent better-than-average performance; scores below 100 represent poorer-than-average performance.

4. Both IQ tests and school achievement tests measure a child's performance, not capacity or underlying competence. Achievement tests, however, test much more specific school-related information than do IQ tests.

5. IQ test scores are quite good predictors of school performance and are moderately good predictors of later job choice and job success.

6. IQ scores are quite stable from one testing to the next, and this becomes more and more true the older the child gets. But individual children's scores still may fluctuate 20 or 30 points or more over the course of childhood.

7. IQ tests do not measure many other facets of intellectual functioning in which we might be interested, including what Sternberg calls experiential and contextual intelligence.

8. Studies of identical twins and of adopted children show clearly that there is at least some genetic influence on measured IQ. Most psychologists agree that approximately half of the variation in individual IQs may be attributed to heredity.

9. The remaining half is attributed to environmental variation: Poor children consistently test lower than do children from middle-class families; children whose families provide appropriate play materials and encourage the child's intellectual development test higher on IQ tests.

10. Environmental influence is also shown by increases in test performance among children who have been in special enriched preschool or infant day-care programs.

11. The interaction of heredity and environment can be understood with the concept of reaction range; heredity determines some range of potential; environment determines the level of performance within that range.

12. A consistent difference of about 15 points on IQ tests is found between white and black children. It seems most likely that this difference is due to environmental and cultural differences between the two groups, such as

differences in health and prenatal care, and in the type of intellectual skills trained and emphasized at home.

13. Males and females do not differ on total IQ test scores, but do differ in sub-skills. Males are better at spatial visualization and mathematical reasoning, females are better at verbal reasoning and some other verbal tasks.

## CRITICAL THINKING QUESTIONS

1. If you were in charge of deciding whether to continue to fund Head Start, what would you decide, based on the evidence presented in the text? Why?
2. Sandra Scarr, a major theorist and researcher in the area of intelligence, asserts that variations in IQ among white children are heavily dependent on genetic differences, but that average IQ differences between blacks and whites are largely cultural in origin. How could both of those be true?
3. What are the arguments for and against the use of IQ tests in the schools?

## KEY TERMS

**achievement test**   A test usually given in schools, designed to assess a child's learning of specific material taught in school, such as spelling or arithmetic computation.

**Bayley Scales of Infant Development**   The best known and most widely used test of infant "intelligence."

**competence**   The behavior of a person as it would be under ideal or perfect circumstances. It is not possible to measure competence directly.

**componential intelligence**   One of three types of intelligence in Sternberg's triarchic theory of intelligence; that type of intelligence typically measured on IQ tests, including analytic thinking, remembering facts, and organizing information.

**confluence model**   Zajonc's term for his explanation of family size and ordinal position effects on IQ. Assumes that a child's IQ is partially determined by the average intellectual level of the family members with whom the child has contact.

**contextual intelligence**   One of three types of intelligence in Sternberg's triarchic theory of intelligence; often also called "street smarts," this type of intelligence includes skills in adapting to an environment, and in adapting an environment to one's own needs.

**cumulative deficit**   Any difference between groups in IQ (or achievement test) scores that becomes larger over time.

**experiential intelligence**   One of three types of intelligence described by Sternberg in his triarchic theory

of intelligence; includes creativity, insight, seeing new relationships among experiences.

**Intelligence quotient (IQ)**   Originally defined in terms of a child's mental age and chronological age, IQs are now computed by comparing a child's performance with that of other children of the same chronological age.

**performance**   The behavior shown by a person under actual circumstances. Even when we are interested in competence, all we can ever measure is performance.

**power**   That aspect of intellectual skill that has to do with how well or how quickly a child can perform cognitive tasks. A dimension of individual difference in intellectual skill.

**Stanford-Binet**   The best-known American intelligence test. It was written by Louis Terman and his associates based upon the first tests by Binet and Simon.

**structures**   Aspects of intellectual skill that change with age and are shared by all children. Focus on *how* the child arrives at a particular answer, rather than on the correctness of the answer.

**triarchic theory of intelligence**   A theory proposed by Sternberg, proposing the existence of three types of intelligence, the componential, the contextual, and the experiential.

**WISC-R**   The Wechsler Intelligence Scale for Children, Revised. Another well-known American IQ test which includes both verbal and performance (nonverbal) subtests.

Elliott, R. (1988). Tests, abilities, race, and conflict. *Intelligence, 12,* 333–350.

   An especially clear and fascinating discussion of the several lawsuits about the use of IQ tests in the school.

Gallagher, J. J., & Ramey, C. T. (1987). *The malleability of children.* Baltimore: Paul H. Brookes Publishing Co.

   If you are interested in the subject of the impact of special programs on IQ, this is a recent and readable source. Included are papers by several of the researchers involved in major intervention studies (including Ramey), as well as reviews of this research by other key figures such as Bettye Caldwell.

Jensen, A. R. (1980). *Bias in mental testing.* New York: The Free Press.

   Jensen has been the most consistent spokesman for a "hereditary" position on IQ differences. This is a massive and fairly difficult book, but is the very best source for understanding this viewpoint.

Storfer, M. D. (1990). *Intelligence and giftedness. The contributions of heredity and early environment.* San Francisco: Jossey-Bass.

   Up-to-date coverage of the literature on every facet of the study of intelligence. Excellent source of current references.

# PROJECT 7

## Investigation of IQ Testing in Local Schools

As a follow-up to the information given in the box on page 212, one student, or a small group of students, may wish to investigate the policies on the uses of IQ and achievement tests in the local school districts.

### Basic Questions to Answer

- Is there a statewide policy on the use of IQ tests in public schools? Is there a local district policy instead of, or in addition to, a state policy?
- Is there a state or local policy on the use of achievement tests? Are they routinely given in specific grades? How are the scores used?
- If individual IQ tests are used in the district, who administers them? Are the scores used as part of

placement of children in special programs? What other types of information are also used as part of any placement process?

### Sources

The best sources will be the state department of education and local school district administrative offices. At the state level there is likely to be a public information office; large school districts may also have such a service. In smaller districts, you will have to use some ingenuity to figure out which person is the best one to talk to. Naturally you should identify yourself as a student and make it clear that this information is for a report for your class.

7

# COGNITIVE DEVELOPMENT II: STRUCTURE AND PROCESS

I imagine the following scene. Your 5-year-old, John, and your 8-year-old, Anne, come into the kitchen after playing outside, both asking for juice. With both children watching, you take two identical small cans of juice from the refrigerator and pour each into a glass. Since one of the glasses is narrower than the other, the juice rises higher in that glass. The 5-year-old, having been given the fatter glass, complains, "Anne got more than I did!" To which Anne replies (with the wonderful grace of the 8-year-old to her sibling), "I did not, you dummy. We both got the same amount. The two cans were just alike." To restore family harmony, you get out another glass identical to Anne's, and pour John's juice into this new glass. The level of the liquid is now the same and John is satisfied.

If this were an item on an IQ test, we'd say that Anne was "right" and John was "wrong." But such emphasis on rightness or wrongness misses an essential point about this interchange: There seems also to be a *developmental* change, a shift in the way the child sees or understands the world and the relationships of objects. John is not being pigheaded or "dumb." He is merely operating with a different kind of reasoning than Anne's. A year or two from now, John will sound like Anne does now.

If we are to understand children's thinking, we need to understand these changes in the *form* or *structure* of children's thinking as well as differences in *power*. How do children come to understand the world around them? What assumptions do they make? What kind of logic do they use, and how does it change over time?

These were precisely the kinds of questions that Jean Piaget asked throughout many years of research on children's thinking. By now his work has influenced so many generations of psychologists that it would be more accurate to say that he is the intellectual "grandfather" or "great-grandfather" of many current researchers, rather than their intellectual parent. The family resemblance is still visible, but a whole lot of other influences have entered the picture. To do justice to both Piaget's theory and the current variations, I will use Piaget's ideas as a basic framework, but I will also describe the current work and the criticisms of the theory that have emerged in recent years.

 ## Piaget's Basic Ideas

Piaget's early training was in biology, but as a student he worked briefly for Alfred Binet on the development of some of the early IQ tests. His job was to give the same items to a whole series of children and to score the correctness of each child's answer. Piaget soon found he was much more interested in the children's wrong answers than their right ones. It seemed to him that children of similar ages made very similar mistakes. Where could such shared mistakes come from? How did children arrive at them? How did children's knowledge of the world develop? Piaget spent the next 60 years of his life devising a model to try to answer such questions.

His most central assumption was that the child is an active participant in the development of knowledge, *constructing* his own understanding. As Kuhn puts it: "The child is engaged in an extended intellectual 'meaning-making' endeavor. . . the child is attempting to construct an understanding of self, other, and the world of objects" (1988, p. 214).

In constructing such an understanding, Piaget thought that the child is consistently trying to *adapt* to the world around him in ever more satisfactory ways. In Piaget's theory, this process of adaptation is in turn made up of several vital subprocesses.

### The Processes of Adaptation

*Schemes.*  The concept of a **scheme** (sometimes written as *schema*) is one of the most central concepts of this theory. In Piaget's view, knowledge itself is a repertoire of *actions,* either physical or mental, such as looking at something, or holding it a particular way, or categorizing it mentally as "a ball," or labeling it with the word "ball," or comparing it to something else. Piaget used the word "scheme" to refer to such actions. The baby begins life with a small repertoire of sensory or motor schemes, such as looking, tasting, touching, hearing, reaching. For the baby, an object *is* a thing that tastes a certain way, feels a certain way, or has a particular color. Later the baby clearly has mental schemes as well, creating categories, comparing one object to another, learning words for specific categories. By adolescence, we see such complex schemes as deductive analysis or systematic reasoning. But how does the child get from those simple, built-in, sensorimotor schemes to the more internalized, increasingly complex mental schemes we see in later childhood? Piaget proposed three basic processes to account for the change: **assimilation, accommodation,** and **equilibration.**

*Assimilation.*  Assimilation is the process of *taking in,* of absorbing some event or experience into some scheme. When a baby looks at and then reaches for a mobile above his crib, Piaget would say that the baby had assimilated the mobile to the looking and reaching schemes. When an older child sees a dog and labels it "dog," she is assimilating that animal to her dog category or scheme. When you read this paragraph you are assimilating the information, hooking the concept onto whatever other concept (scheme) you have that may be similar.

Assimilation obviously cannot occur unless there is some scheme to which an experience can be assimilated. If there is no scheme, or if our schemes are a poor match for the information, we simply don't take it in—either not noticing it at all or saying something like "That's over my head." To take just one example, if you are a novice tennis player, you assimilate your instructor's demonstrations as well as you can, but you simply don't notice many of the finer points, and your early attempts to imitate the actions will be poor.

**scheme**
Piaget's word for the basic actions of knowing, including both physical actions (sensorimotor schemes, such as looking or reaching) and mental actions, such as classifying, comparing, or reversing. An experience is assimilated to a scheme, and the scheme is modified or created through accommodation.

**assimilation**
That part of the adaptation process that involves the "taking in" of new experiences or information into existing schemes. Experience is not taken in "as is," however, but is modified (or interpreted) somewhat so as to fit the preexisting schemes.

**accommodation**
That part of the adaptation process by which a person modifies existing schemes to fit new experiences or creates new schemes when old ones no longer handle the data.

**equilibration**
The third part of the adaptation process, as proposed by Piaget, involving a periodic restructuring of schemes into new structures.

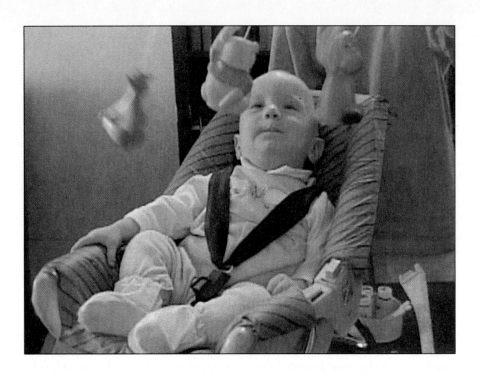

In Piaget's language, Robbie is "assimilating the mobile to his looking scheme." This photo is a video still from the *Childhood* television series (*Source:* ©Thirteen/WNET).

The key here is that assimilation is an *active*, not a passive process. There is selectivity in the information we assimilate, and the very act of assimilating changes the information that is assimilated. For example, if I see a friend wearing a new dress in an unusual color of orangish red, I may label the color "red" in my mind (assimilate it to my "red" scheme) even though it is not precisely red. Later, when I remember the dress, I will remember it redder than it really is because that's the scheme I assimilated it to. The process of assimilation has changed the perception. As you read this material, you assimilate these ideas to the closest ones in your repertoire, and your understanding of these concepts and your memory of them will be affected by the schemes to which you assimilate them.

*Accommodation.* The complementary process is accommodation, which involves *changing the scheme* as a result of the new information you have taken in by assimilation. After seeing my friend's dress, my "red" scheme may be expanded somewhat to include this unusual new variation. If I now learn a new word for this special shade of red, I will accommodate still further, perhaps by creating a new subcategory (a new scheme) altogether. The baby who sees and grasps a square object for the first time will accommodate her grasping scheme; so the next time she reaches for an object of that shape, her hand will be more appropriately bent to grasp it. Thus in Piaget's theory, the process of accommodation is the key to developmental change. Through accommodation, we reorganize our thoughts, improve our skills, and change our strategies.

*Equilibration.* Using these basic concepts, Piaget could have proposed a steady and gradual change in the child's understanding. But he added one further assumption, which led to what is probably the most famous feature of his theory—the notion of *stages*. Piaget assumed that in the process of adaptation the child is always striving for coherence, to stay "in balance," to have an understanding of the world that makes overall sense.

This is not unlike what scientists do when they develop a theory. Their goal is to create an internally coherent theory that will make sense out of every observation. When new research findings come along, the scientist assimilates them to the existing theory. If they don't fit perfectly, either the deviant data are simply set aside, or the scientist may make minor modifications in the theory. However, if enough non-confirmatory research findings are reported, the scientist may have to throw out his theory altogether and start over or may need to change some basic assumptions of his theory.

Piaget thought a child operated in a similar way, creating coherent, more or less internally consistent models or theories. But since the infant starts with a very limited repertoire of schemes, the early "theories" or structures the child creates are simply not going to hold up. So Piaget thought the child then made a series of more substantial changes in the internal structure—a process he called *equilibration.*

Piaget saw three particularly significant points of equilibration, each ushering in a new stage of development. One change occurs at roughly 18 months and involves an enormous shift from primary sensory and motor schemes to the first truly mental schemes; Piaget called these *internal representations.* Another major shift, at roughly ages 5 to 7, occurs when the child adds a whole new set of powerful schemes Piaget calls **operations,** which are far more abstract and general mental actions, such as mental addition or subtraction. The third major equilibration occurs at adolescence, when the child is able to "operate on" ideas as well as events or objects. These three major equilibrations create four stages:

1. **Sensorimotor stage**—from birth to 18 months
2. **Preoperational stage**—from 18 months to about age 6
3. **Concrete operational stage**—from 6 to about 12
4. **Formal operational stage**—from age 12 onward

To make all of this much more concrete, let me describe each of these four stages in considerably more detail, giving you not only Piaget's own ideas about that stage, but also some of the conclusions from more recent research. In some cases, as you'll see, Piaget's theory itself requires significant equilibration. But you'll understand the current work better if I start with Piaget's original observations and let you assimilate the newer material to that structure.

**operations**
Term used by Piaget for complex, internal, abstract, reversible schemes, first seen at about age 6.

**sensorimotor stage**
Piaget's term for the first major stage of cognitive development, from birth to about 18 months, when the child moves from reflexive to voluntary action.

**preoperational stage**
Piaget's term for the second major stage of cognitive development, from age 2 to 6, marked at the beginning by the ability to use symbols and by the development of basic classification and logical abilities.

**concrete operational stage**
The stage of development proposed by Piaget between ages 6 and 12, in which mental operations such as subtraction, reversibility, and multiple classification are acquired.

**formal operational stage**
Piaget's name for the fourth and final major stage of cognitive development, occurring during adolescence, when the child becomes able to manipulate and organize ideas as well as objects.

## Piaget's View of the Sensorimotor Period

The key features of this stage, according to Piaget, are: (1) the infant's response to the world is almost entirely sensory and motor; (2) the infant functions in the immediate present, responding to whatever stimuli present themselves; (3) the infant does not plan or intend; (4) the infant has no internal representation of objects—mental pictures, or words, that stand for objects and can be manipulated mentally. Piaget thought that such internal representations did not develop until about 18–24 months.

John Flavell (1985) summarizes all this very nicely:

> [The infant] exhibits a wholly practical, perceiving-and-doing, action-bound kind of intellectual functioning; she does not exhibit the more contemplative, reflective, symbol-manipulating kind we usually think of in connection with cognition. The infant "knows" in the sense of recognizing or anticipating familiar, recurring objects and happenings, and "thinks" in the sense of behaving toward them with mouth, hand, eye, and other sensory-motor instruments in predictable, organized, and often adaptive ways. . . . It is the kind of noncontemplative intelligence that your dog relies on to make its way in the world. (p. 13)

Piaget thought that sensorimotor intelligence developed through a series of six substages, which I've sketched in Table 7.1. As you look at the table, you may find that you can assimilate some of the information to concepts you've already encountered, particularly in Chapter 5. For example, the shift from Substage 1 to Substage 2 sounds a good deal like the transition in perceptual processes at about 2 months of age, when the infant shifts from examining edges and movement (*where* an object is) and focuses more on the internal features of objects (*what* an object is). Also note that Piaget placed the development of the object concept, including object permanence and object identity, in substage 3.

In Piaget's view, all these substages gradually build toward internal representation, which develops at about 18 months. Only then, he thought, can the child both form and manipulate mental images.

*TABLE 7.1  Substages of Piaget's Sensorimotor Period*

| Substage | Age | Piaget's Label | Characteristics of the Stage |
| --- | --- | --- | --- |
| 1 | 0–1 month | Reflexes | Almost entirely the practice of built-in schemes (reflexes) such as sucking and looking. But accommodation of these primitive schemes begins immediately. |
| 2 | 1–4 months | Primary circular reactions | The infant tries to make interesting things happen again with her body, such as getting her thumb in her mouth. Visual and tactual explorations are more |

TABLE 7.1—*Continued*

| Substage | Age | Piaget's Label | Characteristics of the Stage |
|---|---|---|---|
| | | | systematic. But infants in this period (so Piaget thought) do not distinguish between body and outside objects or events. They do not link their own actions to results outside themselves. |
| 3 | 4–8 months | Secondary circular reactions | The infant tries to make external interesting things happen again, such as moving a mobile by hitting it intentionally. He also begins to coordinate information from two senses and develops the object concept. He understands at some level that his own actions can have external results. |
| 4 | 8–12 months | Coordination of secondary schemes | The infant begins to combine actions to get what she wants, such as knocking a pillow away in order to reach for a toy. She uses familiar strategies in combination and in new situations. Piaget thought that cross-modal transfer was not possible until this stage; thus imitation of facial expressions should not be possible until this stage either. |
| 5 | 12–18 months | Tertiary circular reactions | "Experimentation" begins; the infant tries out *new* ways of playing with or manipulating objects. Improved motor skills make wider exploration possible as well. Piaget thought deferred imitation did not begin until this stage. |
| 6 | 18–24 months | Beginning of thought | Internal representation is now readily apparent; the child uses images, perhaps words or actions, to stand for objects. This substage is really the beginning of the next major stage, preoperational thought. |

One of Piaget's observations of his daughter, Lucienne, illustrates this transition. At the time of this observation, Piaget was playing with Lucienne and had hidden his watch chain inside an empty box. He describes what happened then:

Like Robbie on p. 248, Katrina is assimilating the mobile to her looking scheme. But she is also reaching toward the mobile, as if to make it jiggle or move—a behavior Piaget would call *secondary circular reactions*. Katrina is trying to make something interesting happen using objects outside her own body. This photo is a video still from the *Childhood* television series (*Source:* ©Thirteen/WNET).

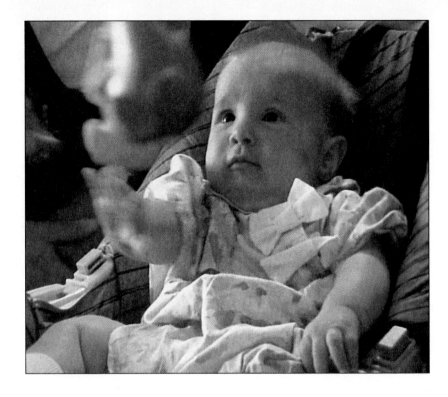

I put the chain back into the box and reduce the opening to 3 mm. It is understood that Lucienne is not aware of the functioning of the opening and closing of the match box and has not seen me prepare the experiment. She only possesses two preceding schemes: turning the box over in order to empty it of its contents, and sliding her fingers into the slit to make the chain come out. It is of course this last procedure that she tries first: she puts her finger inside and gropes to reach the chain, but fails completely. A pause follows during which Lucienne manifests a very curious reaction. . . . She looks at the slit with great attention; then, several times in succession, she opens and shuts her mouth, at first slightly, then wider and wider! [Then]. . . Lucienne unhesitatingly puts her finger in the slit, and instead of trying as before to reach the chain, she pulls so as to enlarge the opening. She succeeds and grasps the chain (Piaget, 1952, pp. 337–338).

What an enormous discovery this child seems to have made! Faced with a new situation, instead of going immediately to trial and error, she paused and appeared to discover the solution through some kind of analysis. Piaget saw this behavior as a sign of the very beginning of the child's ability to manipulate and combine, to experiment and explore, with *mental* images instead of with external objects or actions.

*Current Work on the Sensorimotor Stage*

Many of Piaget's observations about the young infant were made before the advent of the more sophisticated research techniques for studying babies. You know from what I said in Chapter 5 that research using these newer techniques has consistently shown that newborn and very young infants are far more cognitively skillful than Piaget had supposed. Let's look at a couple of additional examples.

*Imitation.*   Piaget thought infants could imitate actions they could see themselves make, such as hand gestures, as early as the first few months of life. Imitation of facial gestures, however, seems to require some kind of cross-modal transfer, combining the visual cues from seeing the other's face with the kinesthetic cues from one's own facial movements. Since Piaget did not think that cross-modal transfer was possible until the fourth substage, between 8 and 12 months, he didn't think this form of imitation could occur until then either. He further argued that imitation of any action that wasn't already in the child's repertoire did not occur until the fifth substage. In addition, he claimed that *deferred* imitation, in which a child sees some action and then imitates it at a later point, was possible only in Substage 6, since deferred imitation requires some kind of internal representation.

In broad terms Piaget's proposed sequence has been supported by research. Imitation of someone else's hand movements seems to improve steadily during the months of infancy starting at 1 or 2 months of age. Imitation of two-part actions (such as opening a box and then taking something out of it) develops much later, perhaps at 15–18 months (Poulson et al., 1989). The two exceptions to this general confirmation of Piaget's theory have been in studies of imitation in newborns and deferred imitation.

Several early studies showed that newborn babies would imitate certain facial gestures, particularly tongue protrusion (e.g., Meltzoff & Moore, 1983; Field et al., 1982). These findings are consistent with the observations I reported in Chapter 5 that quite young babies are capable of tactual/visual cross-modal transfer. But this key finding has not always been replicated (Poulson, Nunes, & Warren, 1989). It now appears that the critical factor is how long the model demonstrates the action. When the model demonstrates the tongue protrusion for at least 60 seconds, newborns will imitate it, but shorter demonstrations are not copied (Anisfeld, 1991).

There is also a dispute about how early a baby may show deferred imitation. Meltzoff (1988) has found some ability to defer imitation over a 24-hour period in babies as young as 9 months; the more typical finding is that it occurs at 14-18 months, which is closer to what Piaget proposed.

*Internal Representation.*   Meltzoff's study is among many that have raised the more general question of whether infants may be capable of some forms of internal representation at an earlier age than Piaget's estimated. The same point arises from several bodies of research I talked about in Chapter 5, including the findings that cross-modal transfer occurs as early as 1 month, and the research on children's responses to patterns like "big over little." All of these accomplishments seem to require that the baby create a fairly complex and abstract mental image. But such findings need not totally refute Piaget. What may develop at 18 or 24 months may be the ability to *manipulate* these images in his head, in the way that Lucienne seemed to do with opening the box to retrieve the chain.

### Overview of the Sensorimotor Period

In a number of important respects, Piaget seems to have underestimated the ability of infants to store, remember, and organize sensory and motor information. Babies pay much more attention to patterns, sequences, and prototypical features than Piaget thought, and they can apparently remember them over at least short intervals. At the same time, many of the sequences Piaget described, such as sequence of development of the object concept, have held up well to close research scrutiny. Furthermore, his image of the infant as a "little scientist" building theories about the world is very much in keeping with the recent evidence. The infant assimilates information to his existing schemes and modifies (accommodates) the schemes as he goes along. By the time the infant has reached the age of 18 or 24 months, his perceptions and actions are already quite well-organized.

 ## Preoperational Thought: From 18 Months to 6 Years

In Piaget's view, at about age 2 a radical change occurs in which the child can now not only manipulate images in his head, but can use *symbols*—images or words or actions that stand for something else. We can see this shift clearly in children's pretend play, which I have talked about in the box on pages 256–258. At ages 2, 3, or 4 a broom may become a horsey or a block may become a train. We can also see such symbol use in the emergence of language at about the same time (which I'll describe in the next chapter). And we see the child's improving ability to manipulate these symbols internally reflected in her improving memory and in her ability to search more systematically for lost or hidden objects.

Because we have come to see the young infant as so much more skilled than we had originally thought, it would be easy to dismiss this transition, either by assuming that the baby already has all these skills, or by suggesting that this is not really much of a change. But I am in agreement with John Flavell, one of the most thoughtful theorists and clever researchers in the area of cognitive development, who argues that:

> A cognitive system that uses symbols just seems . . . to be radically, drastically, qualitatively different from one that does not. So great is the difference that the transformation of one system into the other during the first 2 years of life still seems nothing short of miraculous to me, no matter how much we learn about it. (1985, p. 82)

Piaget did describe this remarkable achievement in some detail, but most of what he had to say about the preoperational period was oddly negative in tone. Beyond the accomplishment of symbol use, Piaget focused mostly on all the things the preschool age child still *cannot* do. More recent research has given us a much more positive view. I can contrast the two views most clearly by describing several key dimensions of the toddler's thinking, first through Piaget's eyes and then through the eyes of recent researchers.

### Piaget's View of the Preoperational Period

*Perspective Taking: Egocentrism.*   Piaget pointed out that children in this preoperational stage look at things entirely from their own perspective, from their own frame of reference, a quality Piaget called **egocentrism** (Piaget, 1954). The child is not being selfish; rather she simply thinks (assumes) that everyone sees the world her way.

Figure 7.1 shows a photo of a classic experiment illustrating this kind of egocentrism. The child is shown a three-dimensional scene with mountains of different sizes and colors. From a set of drawings, he picks out the one that shows the scene the way he sees it. Most preschoolers can do this without much difficulty. Then the examiner asks the child to pick out the drawing that shows how someone *else* sees the scene, such as the little doll figure, or the examiner. At this point preschool children have difficulty. Most often they pick the drawing that shows their *own* view of the mountains (e.g., Gzesh & Surber, 1985; Flavell et al., 1981). In Piaget's view, for the child to be able to succeed at this task she must "decenter"—she must shift from using herself as the only frame of reference.

**egocentrism**
A cognitive state in which the individual (typically a child) sees the world only from his own perspective, without awareness that there are other perspectives.

**FIGURE 7.1**

This kind of experimental situation has been used to study egocentrism in children. The child is asked first to pick out the picture that shows how the two mountains look to him, and then to pick out the picture that shows how the mountains look to the little clay man. Preschool children typically pick the same picture both times—the one that shows how it looks from their perspective.

# Young Children's Play

Go to a preschool or day-care center and watch the children during an unstructured time—when they are not eating, napping, or being "organized" by the adults. What are the kids doing? They are building towers out of blocks, moving dolls around in the doll house, making "tea" with the tea set, racing toy trucks across the floor, dressing up in grown-up clothes, and putting puzzles together. They are, in a word, *playing*. This is not trivial or empty activity; it is the stuff on which much of cognitive development seems to be built.

Any parent who has watched the development of his child during the preschool years knows that play changes in very visible ways during the years from 1 to 7. When psychologists have attempted to describe these changes, a series of "steps" or "stages" emerges (Rubin, Fein, & Vandenberg, 1983). These changes flow together; children show several of these kinds of play at any one time. But we can still see at least the following seven different kinds of play, in something like this order.

*Sensorimotor Play.* The child of 12 months or so spends most of her play time exploring and manipulating objects using all the sensorimotor schemes in her repertoire. She puts things in her mouth, shakes them, stacks them, and moves them along the floor. In this way she comes to understand what objects can do.

*Constructive Play.* Such exploratory play with objects does continue past 12 months, especially with some totally new object. But by age two or so, as their schemes become more elaborate and complex, children begin to use objects to build or construct things—creating a block tower, putting together a puzzle, or making something out of clay or with tinkertoys. Such "constructive" play makes up nearly half of the play of children aged 3 to 6 (Rubin, Fein, & Vandenberg, 1983).

*First Pretend Play.* The other new form of play that begins at about 12 or 14 months is the beginning of pretend play.

Sensorimotor Play

Early Pretend Play

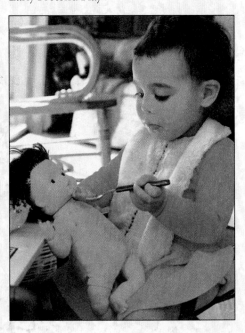

The first sign of such pretending is usually something like a child using a toy spoon to "feed" himself or a toy comb to comb his hair. The toys are still used for their actual or typical purposes (spoon for feeding), and the actions are still oriented to the *self*, but there is pretend involved. Between 15 and 21 months, there is a shift: The recipient of the pretend action now becomes another person or a toy. The child is still using objects for their usual purposes (such as drinking from a cup), but now she is using the toy cup with a doll instead of herself. Dolls are especially good toys for this kind of pretend, since it is not a very large leap from doing things to yourself to doing things with a doll. So children dress and undress dolls, feed them imaginary food, and comb their hair.

*Substitute Pretend Play.* Between 2 and 3 years of age children make another big change in their play and begin to use objects to stand for something altogether different. They may comb the doll's hair with a baby bottle while saying that it is a comb, or use a broom to be a horsey, or make "trucks" out of blocks. Constructive play, in which toys are used for their "real" purposes, does not disappear. But by age 4 or 5, children spend as much as 20 percent of their play time in this new, complicated kind of pretending (Field, De Stefano, & Koewler, 1982).

*Sociodramatic Play.* Somewhere in the preschool years children also begin to play parts or take roles. They play "daddy and mommy," "cowboys and indians," "doctor and patient," "train conductor and passengers," and many equivalent stories. You can see this among children as young as 2 or 3 when they are playing with their brothers or sisters; it appears a bit later in the play of non-sibling pairs or groups,

perhaps at age 3 or 4. Children clearly get great delight out of these often elaborate fantasies. Equally important, by playing roles, pretending to be someone else, they also become more and more aware of how things may look or feel to someone else, and their egocentric approach to the world declines.

*Awareness of the Roles.* Six-year-olds not only create elaborate "dramas," they will also describe or label the roles they are playing. They plan the play ahead of time, or assign people to different roles, rather than merely drifting into a new set of roles in the process of play. This change seems to reflect a cognitive advance, and is not usually seen until about age 6 or later—at about the time that we see the transition to concrete operations.

*Games with Rules.* At elementary school-age, pretend play begins to wane and is replaced by complex games with specific rules—jacks, marbles, baseball, or kick the can or equivalent. Earlier forms of play may involve spontaneously created rules, but in elementary school, children more and more play games that have persisting, agreed upon rules.

As adults, most of us associate the word "play" with "goofing off" or nonproductive activities. But in some very real ways, play is children's "work." Opportunities to manipulate and experiment with objects, pretend with them, play parts and roles, all seem to be important ingredients in the child's cognitive and social development (Rubin, Fein, & Vandenberg, 1983; Piaget, 1962). The key point is that children need to have *time* for play—time when they are not watching TV, not organized, not required to do anything "constructive."

*Understanding Identities.*    In a similar way, Piaget thought that the preschool child needed to acquire another whole level or layer of understanding of the identity of objects. The sensorimotor infant eventually understands that objects continue to exist even when they are out of sight. But there are other aspects of objects that also remain constant or are *conserved*, in Piaget's terms. These new constancies baffle the preschool child.

It was just such a problem of **conservation** that confronted Anne and John and their juice glasses. To understand that the amount was the same, John would have to realize that the amount of juice is not altered by pouring it into a differently shaped container. This is an example of conservation of quantity, one of six different conservations Piaget studied, which are listed in Table 7.2 (p. 261). In every case, his measurement technique involved first showing the child two equal sets or objects, getting the child to agree they were equal in some key respect such as weight or quantity or length or number, and then shifting or deforming one of the objects and asking the child if they were still equal. (If you are interested, one of the projects for this chapter uses Piaget's techniques for studying conservation.)  Children rarely show any of these forms of conservation before age 5, which Piaget took to be a sign that they were still captured by the appearance of change and did not focus on the underlying unchanging aspect.

*Classification.*    A third area Piaget describes is the child's ability to classify objects—to put things in sets or types and to use abstract or formal properties such as color, shape, or even verbal labels as a basis for such classification. Piaget studied this by giving young children sets of objects or picture cutouts of people, animals, or toys, and asking the children to put together the things that "go together" or "are similar" (Piaget & Inhelder, 1959). Two- and three-year-old children, faced with such an array, will usually make designs or pictures. At perhaps 4, children begin showing more systematic sorting and grouping of objects, using first one dimension (e.g., shape, such as round things versus square things) and later two or more dimensions at once (e.g., size *and* shape: small round things versus small square things and large round things versus large square things).

Despite this big advance, there is still some distance to go. In particular, the preoperational child still does not grasp the principle of **class inclusion.** He does not understand that some classes are fully contained within other classes; dogs are part of the larger class of animals, roses are part of the class of flowers, and so forth.

For a child to show that she understands class inclusion it is not enough for her simply to use words like *animal* to refer to more than one kind of creature. She must also understand the logical relationships. Piaget usually studied this by having children first create their own classes and subclasses and then asking them questions about them. He questioned one 5 1/2-year-old child, for example, who had a set of flowers made up of a large group of primroses and a smaller group of other mixed flowers.

**Piaget:**    "If I make a bouquet of all the primroses and you make one of all the flowers, which will be bigger?"

**Child:**    "Yours."

---

**conservation**
The concept that objects remain the same in fundamental ways, such as weight or number, even when there are external changes in shape or arrangement. Typically understood by children after age 5.

**class inclusion**
The relationship between classes of objects, such that a subordinate class is included in a superordinate class, as bananas are part of the class "fruit."

This girl may know that several different words can be used to label her dog—*basset, dog, animal,* and the dog's name. She may even use all these words herself at different times. But she may still not fully grasp the concept of class inclusion—that all individual critters like her family basset are included in the category of dog, and that all dogs are included in the category of animal.

**Piaget:**  "If I gather all the primroses in a meadow will any flowers remain?"
**Child:**  "Yes" (Piaget & Inhelder, 1959, p. 108).

The child understood that there are other flowers than primroses, but did *not* yet understand that all primroses are flowers—that the smaller, subordinate class is included in the larger class. Piaget thought this understanding did not come until about age 7.

*Reasoning.*  Piaget's daughter Lucienne announced one afternoon when she had not taken her nap, "I haven't had my nap so it isn't afternoon." This is a very good example of the kind of reasoning you'll hear in the preschool-age child. Lucienne knew that afternoon and nap usually go together, but she had the relationship between them wrong. She thought that the nap "caused" the afternoon. The basic characteristic of this type of reasoning, which Piaget called **transductive reasoning,** is that the child sees that two things happen at the same time and assumes that one is the cause of the other. (A lot of superstitious behavior in adults is based on the same type of logic. The baseball manager who always wears his "lucky" green socks because he had had them on the day his team won the pennant is showing a kind of transductive reasoning.)

**transductive reasoning** Reasoning from the specific to the specific; assuming that when two things happen together, one is the cause of the other.

### Current Work on the Preoperational Period

As was true for the sensorimotor period, the current work on the preoperational period shows us that children in the 2–6 age range are probably a good deal more cognitively skillful than Piaget supposed.

*Perspective Taking.*  There is now a great deal of evidence that children as young as 2 and 3 have at least some ability to understand that other people

**TABLE 7.2** *Subvarieties of Conservation Studied by Piaget*

| Conservation | Typical Measure |
|---|---|
| Number | Two rows with equal numbers of pennies or buttons, laid out parallel to one another with the items matching. Then one row is stretched out longer or squeezed together, or rearranged in some other way and the child is asked "Are there the same number?" |
| Length | Two pencils of identical length are laid one above the other so that they match perfectly; then one is displaced to the right or left so that one pencil's point sticks out further than the other and the child is asked if they are now the same length. |
| Quantity | Two equal beakers, with equal amounts of water; one is then poured into another shaped glass (tall and thin or short and squat) and the child is asked if there is still the same amount to drink in each. |
| Substance or Mass | Two equal balls of clay, one then squished into another shape, such as a sausage or a pancake. Child is asked if there is now the same amount of clay in each. |
| Weight | Two equal balls of clay, as for conservation of substance. They are weighed on a balance scale so that the child sees that they weigh the same, and then one is deformed into another shape. Child is then asked if they still weigh the same or "have the same amount of weight." |
| Volume | Again two balls of clay, placed in two equal beakers of water so that the child sees they each displace the same amount of water. Then one ball is deformed, and the child is asked if they will still "take up the same amount of space." |

see things or experience things differently than they themselves do. For example, children this age will adapt their speech or their play to the demands of their companion. They play differently with older or younger playmates and talk differently to a younger or a handicapped child (Brownell, 1990; Guralnick & Paul-Brown, 1984). But such understanding is clearly not perfect. John Flavell has proposed that there are two levels of such perspective taking ability. At Level 1, the child knows that some other person experiences something differently. At Level 2, the child develops a whole series of complex rules for figuring out precisely *what* the other person sees or experiences (Flavell, 1985; Flavell, Green, & Flavell, 1990). Two-and three-year-olds have Level 1 knowledge but not Level 2. We begin to see some Level 2 knowledge in 4- and 5-year-olds.

This clear shift in perspective taking ability is but one aspect of what begins to look like a broader change at about age 4:

- John Flavell has shown that before about age 4, children confuse appearance and reality. If you show them a sponge that has been painted to look like a rock, they will either say that the object looks like a sponge and is a sponge or that it looks like a rock and is a rock. But 4- and 5-year-olds can distinguish the two; they realize that it looks like a rock but *is* a sponge (Flavell, 1986; Flavell, Green, & Flavell, 1989; Flavell et al., 1987; Taylor & Hort, 1990). Thus the older child now understands that the same object can be represented differently, depending on one's point of view.

- Using the same type of materials, investigators have also asked if a child can grasp the principle of a *false belief.* After the child has felt the sponge/rock and has answered questions about what it looks like and what it "really" is, you can ask something like this: "John [a playmate of the subject's] hasn't touched this, he hasn't squeezed it. If John just sees it over here like this, what will he think it is? Will he think it's a rock or will he think that it's a sponge?" (Gopnik & Astington, 1988, p. 35). By and large, 3-year-olds think that John will believe it is a sponge, while 4-and 5-year-olds realize that because John hasn't felt the sponge, he will have a false belief that it is a rock. Thus the child of 4 or 5 understands that someone else can believe something that isn't true.

Evidence like this has led to the proposal by a number of theorists (e.g., Astington, Harris, & Olson, 1988; Gopnik & Slaughter, 1991; Moses & Flavell, 1990) that sometime around age 4 or 5, the child develops a **theory of mind.** The child of this age begins to understand that someone's thinking affects their actions, that what they know affects what they do. Furthermore, he understands that our beliefs do not always reflect reality accurately. A 3-year-old assumes that there is a single "real world" out there to be known and that everyone knows it in the same way. The 4-year-old knows better. He knows that others may experience the world in different ways and may know different things about it. What is more, he understands that someone else may believe something that is not true and act on that false belief. If he sees me search for my cat under the sofa, the 4-year-old understands that I am acting that way not because the cat is necessarily really there, but because I *believe* that the cat is there.

The 4-year-old also understands, at least in some preliminary way, that beliefs change. He can remember that he used to think something different; he used to think that the sponge was a rock, but he no longer believes that.

Collectively, this evidence suggests that what seems to change at about age 4 is that the child grasps the *representational* aspect of mental processes— that what we have in our minds is a representation of reality, not reality itself. This is no small feat for a 4- or 5-year-old.

*Understanding Identities.*    As has been so true in other areas, early research on conservation was mostly designed to determine whether Piaget was really correct that children younger than 5 or 6 simply didn't understand conservation. And as in other areas, the answer was that Piaget had probably underestimated the preschool-age child, although the basic sequence was confirmed. For example, in one widely quoted study, Rochel Gelman (1972) demonstrated that children as young as 3 could display a form of number conservation. She showed 3-year-olds two plates, one with a row of three toys (two mice and a truck), and one with a row of two toys. On each trial, the plates were shuffled, and the child had to pick one plate as "the winner." The child had to learn that the plate with three toys was always "the winner."

After the child had learned this, the experimenter rearranged the three

**theory of mind**
Phrase used to describe one aspect of the thinking of 4- and 5-year-olds when they show signs of understanding not only that other people think differently, but something about the way others' minds work.

toys so that they were pushed together and presented the two plates again. Gelman found that the 3-year-olds still picked the three-toy plate as "the winner," showing that they realized the rearrangement of the toys on the plate did not change the number. But children of the same age cannot do Piaget's typical conservation of number experiment, which involves larger numbers of candy pieces or poker chips in rows. Why the difference?

The answer seems to be that when the number of items is very small, the children solve the problem by counting, not by applying the principle of conservation (Wellman, 1982). But when the number of objects is increased to the point where they can no longer count easily or reliably, they are distracted by the rearrangement of the pieces. Only at about age 5 or 6 does the child appear to solve the problem by applying the concept or principle of conservation.

More recent work in this area has come at the problem from a different direction, bringing together the work on conservation with the work on perspective taking, especially Flavell's work on the appearance/reality distinction. A conservation problem can be thought of as a special case of an appearance/reality task. The child has to understand that the water in a tall thin glass *appears* higher but is *really* the same. It turns out, in fact, that if you present 5-year-olds with conservation problems but ask the questions as if it were an appearance/reality task, many of them can solve the problem. That is, if you say something like, "Which glass, according to you, *looks* like it has the most juice?" and then "Does that glass *really* have more juice?" some 5-year-olds can answer both questions correctly, even though they cannot yet answer the standard conservation question accurately (Bijstra, van Geert, & Jackson, 1989).

Conservation problems appear to require a deeper level of understanding than is true of the simpler appearance/reality tasks—an understanding of a principle that some properties of objects remain the same unless altered in specific ways. But this deeper understanding appears to be built on the cognitive changes that we see at about age 4 or 5.

*Classification Skills.* This ought to sound like a familiar refrain by now: Young children classify better than Piaget thought, particularly if you simplify the task or if you make it clear that you want them to use some kind of superordinate category for classifying. For example, Sandra Waxman and Rochel Gelman (1986) told 3- and 4-year-olds that a puppet really liked pictures of food (or animals, or furniture). The children were then given 12 pictures and asked to put the ones the puppet would like in one bin and the ones the puppet would not like in another bin. When they were given the category label in this way, these young children could quite easily classify the pictures into food and non-food or furniture and non-furniture categories.

Even 2-year-olds may be capable of such classification. In one study, Sugerman (1979, cited in Gelman & Baillargeon, 1983) gave toddlers sets of toys that included two groups, such as four dolls and four rings. She found that they tended to move the toys in these two groups into different piles or sets during play, which suggests that they already treated them as categories or classes to some extent.

All in all, this research shows that the basic understanding that things go together in groups is present by at least age 2 (and perhaps earlier). But whether the child can display this understanding will depend on the way you set up the task. Piaget happened to pick a relatively difficult version of the task, so he ended up underestimating the child's understanding.

Class inclusion, however, is another matter. Research by Ann McCabe and her colleagues (1982) shows that real understanding of class inclusion does not appear until age 7 or 8, just as Piaget originally suggested.

*Reasoning.* In this area, too, we hear the same song: Two- to 6-year-olds are not consistently as primitive in their logic as Piaget thought. For example, Merry Bullock and Rochel Gelman (1979) have shown that children as young as 3 understand that a cause has to come *before* an effect rather than after it—a remarkably sophisticated level of logical understanding at so early an age. Still, Piaget was quite correct in saying that 4-year-olds are less skillful in their logic than 7-year-olds.

### Overview of the Preoperational Child

If we add up the different bits of information I've just given you, two points seem clear. First, it is obvious that Piaget underestimated the preoperational child. Preschool children are capable of forms of logic that Piaget thought impossible at this stage. They show considerable awareness of others' perspectives, classify objects by form or function, and understand the beginnings of causal relationships.

However, while such performances can be *elicited,* 2-, 3-, and 4-year-old children do not necessarily show such understandings spontaneously. In order for the preschool child to demonstrate these relatively advanced forms of thinking, you have to make the task quite simple, eliminate distractions, or give special clues. The fact that children this age can solve these problems at all is striking, but it is still true that preschool children think differently from

Even children as young as this toddler show some signs of classification in their play with toys—such as putting similar blocks together. Piaget thought that systematic classification did not appear until late in the preoperational period, so these earlier forms of classification are not entirely consistent with his theory. This photo is a video still from the *Childhood* television series (*Source:* © Thirteen/WNET).

older children. In general, their attention is more likely to be captured by appearance. They simply do not seem to experience the world or think about it with as general a set of rules or principles as we see in older children and thus they do not easily generalize something they have learned in one context to a similar but not identical situation. It is precisely such a switch to general rules that Piaget thought characterized the transition to the next stage, concrete operations.

## Concrete Operational Thought: From 6 to 12 Years

### Piaget's View of Concrete Operations

The new skills we see at age 5, 6, or 7 build on all the small changes we have already seen in the preschooler, but from Piaget's perspective there is a great leap forward that occurs when the child "discovers" or "develops" a set of immensely powerful, abstract, general "rules" or "strategies" for examining and interacting with the world. Piaget calls this new set of skills *concrete operations,* with the term "operation" used specifically to refer to powerful, *internal* schemes such as reversibility, addition, subtraction, multiplication, division, and serial ordering. The child now understands the rule that adding something makes it more and subtracting makes it less. She understands that objects can belong to more than one category at once and that categories have logical relationships.

Of all the operations, Piaget thought the most critical was *reversibility*—the understanding that both physical actions and mental operations can be reversed. The ball of clay can be made back into a ball and the water can be poured back into the shorter, fatter glass. This understanding of the basic reversibility of actions lies behind many of the gains made during this period. For example, the ability to understand hierarchies of classes, such as Fido, spaniel, dog, and animal, rests on this ability to go backward as well as forward in thinking about relationships.

Somewhere between ages 5 and 7, children seem to develop an understanding of not only reversibility but also other operations. Signs of this shift in "mental gears" can be seen in the same lines of development I described in the last section: identities, classification, and logic.

*Identities in the Concrete Operations Period.* It is in this period that the child grasps the principle of conservation, by using any one of a number of different operations. Using reversibility, the child might say that "If I changed the clay back into a ball it would be the same." Or the child could use the operations of addition and subtraction, saying something like "You didn't add clay or take any away so it has to be the same." By using compensation the child can pay attention to more than one thing at a time and say "It (the hotdog shaped clay) is bigger around, but it's thinner, so it's the same."

*Classification.* Here the big change is one I have already described: the understanding of the principle of class inclusion. A good way to illustrate this is with the game of 20 Questions (which you can try out in one of the projects for this chapter). In one of my favorite older studies, Frederic Mosher and

Joan Hornsby (1966) showed 6- to 11-year-old children a set of 42 pictures of animals, people, toys, machines, and the like. The experimenter said he was thinking of one of the pictures, and the child was to figure out which one by asking questions that could be answered "yes" or "no."

There are several ways to figure out which questions to ask. You could simply start at one end of a row of pictures and ask "Is it this one?" about each one in turn until you hit on the right one, or you could point to them in some random order. Mosher and Hornsby called such strategies "hypothesis scanning." A second way is to classify the pictures mentally into a hierarchy of groups, and then ask first about the highest level in your hierarchy—a strategy that requires understanding class inclusion. You might start, for example, by asking "Is it a toy?" If the answer is yes, you might then ask about the subcategories: "Is it a red toy?" Mosher and Hornsby called this second strategy "constraint seeking."

You can see in Figure 7.2 on the next page, which shows the main results of this study, that 6-year-olds almost never used a constraint (classification) strategy. They relied essentially on guessing. By age 8, however, the majority of children's questions reflected a constraint strategy; by age 11, that strategy strongly dominated.

*Logic in the Concrete Operations Period.* Piaget argued that during these years the child develops the ability to use **inductive logic.** He can go from his own experience to a general principle. For example, he can go from the observation that when you add another toy to a set and then count it, that set always has one more, to a general principle that adding always makes it more. In science, we use inductive reasoning a lot. We make systematic observations and then try to figure out why things turned out the way they did.

**inductive logic**
Reasoning from the particular to the general, from experience to broad rules. Characteristic of concrete operational thinking.

Elementary school children are pretty good observational scientists, and will enjoy cataloging, counting species of trees or birds, or figuring out the nesting habits of guinea pigs. What they are not yet good at is **deductive logic,** which requires starting with a general principle and then predicting some outcome or observation, like going from a theory to a hypothesis. This is harder than inductive logic because it requires imagining things that you may never have experienced—something the concrete operations child typically does not do. Piaget thought that deductive reasoning did not develop until the period of formal operations in junior high or high school.

**deductive logic**
Reasoning from the general to the particular, from a rule to an expected instance, or from a theory to a hypothesis. Characteristic of formal operational thought.

An important practical application of this difference in the child's logic is that elementary school children ought to be able to learn science (and other subjects) more easily if the material is presented "concretely," with plenty of opportunity for hands-on experience and inductive experimentation. They ought to learn less well when scientific concepts or theories are presented in a deductive fashion, which is precisely what research on science instruction has shown (e.g., Saunders & Shepardson, 1987).

### Post-Piagetian Work on Concrete Operations

Unlike researchers who have studied Piaget's first two stages, those who have followed up on his descriptions of the concrete operational period have generally supported Piaget's observations on the timing of various

*FIGURE 7.2*

When six-year-olds play 20 Questions with sets of pictures, their questions are nearly all in the form of a specific hypothesis or guess ("Is it this one?"); 8-year-olds, who are in the period of concrete operations, use a constraint strategy that involves organizing the pictures into classes and hierarchies and then asking about a whole group of pictures (e.g.,"Is it a toy?") (*Source:* Mosher & Hornsby, 1966, p. 91).

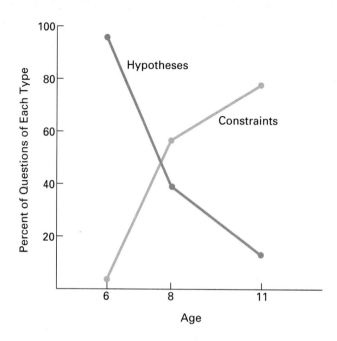

developments. They have found, as had Piaget, that conservation of quantity and mass developed early in this period, followed by conservation of weight and then conservation of volume. They have found that children in this age range do indeed show inductive logic, but that they typically fail on tasks that demand deductive logic (e.g., Markovitz, Schleifer, & Fortier, 1989). And as you have already seen in the 20-Questions research, researchers found that over the years of concrete operations children develop the ability to create hierarchical classification systems and use them to solve problems.

A good illustrative example of the research on this period is a longitudinal study of concrete operations tasks by Carol Tomlinson-Keasey and her colleagues (Tomlinson-Keasey et al., 1978). They followed a group of 38 children from kindergarten through third grade, testing them with five traditional concrete operations tasks each year: conservation of mass, weight, and volume; class inclusion; and hierarchical classification. You can see from Figure 7.3 that the children got better at all five tasks over the three-year period, with two spurts: one between the end of kindergarten and the start of first grade (about the age that Piaget thought that concrete operations really began) and another during second grade. More important, the different tasks were not equally easy. Conservation of mass was easier than conservation of weight, with conservation of volume the hardest of the three. Class inclusion was also generally harder than conservation of mass. In fact, they found that conservation of mass seemed to be a necessary precursor for the development of class inclusion.

Tomlinson-Keasey also found that a child's skill on these tasks, relative to the other children, stayed approximately the same throughout the three years of testing. A 6-year-old who had developed conservation of mass early continued to be ahead of other children later on; a late-developing child went through the same sequence about two years later.

*Overview of the Concrete Operational Child*

My own sense about this period is that Piaget was at least roughly correct about the general character and significance of the shift in children's thinking that takes place between about ages 5 and 7. Children do seem to be able to step back a bit from compelling, immediate sensations or experiences and work out the beginnings of general rules or general strategies. We see the ramifications of this change in an enormous number of ways. For example, kids of about this age get a lot more systematic at searching for lost toys, and their understanding of classes helps them learn beginning mathematics.

Where there have been serious questions raised about Piaget's version of this period of development—and there have been many—they have dealt with the issue of generality versus specificity of the child's understanding or use of the various concrete operations. The very fact that Tomlinson-Keasey found that not all concrete operations tasks were equally easy raises questions about Piaget's basic assumption that each stage represents a cohesive whole, a structure that affects all aspects of thinking. Investigators who have looked specifically at the consistency of children's performance across sets of supposedly equivalent tasks have found not only that children do better on some tasks than others, but that rather small variations in the tasks seem to produce rather different levels of performance. I'll be coming back to this set of issues

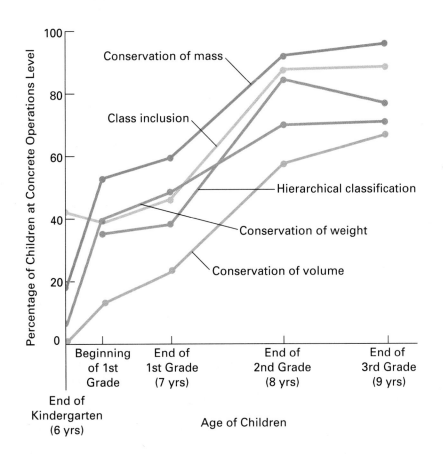

**FIGURE 7.3**

These results are from a longitudinal study in which the same children were given a set of concrete operations tasks five different times, beginning in kindergarten and ending in the third grade. As you can see, the percentage of children "solving" each type of problem increased, with spurts at similar ages for each task. Nonetheless, some tasks were clearly more difficult than others (*Source:* Tomlinson-Keasy et al., 1979, adapted from Table 2, p. 1158).

when I talk more generally about criticisms of Piaget's theory. For now I merely want to point out that many of the early doubts about consistency of performance arose directly from research on the concrete operations period, a period in which such consistency seems conspicuously absent.

## Formal Operational Thought: From Age 12 On

### Piaget's View of Formal Operational Thought

Piaget thought that the final step of cognitive development begins at about age 12 and continues to emerge through the teenage years. The major task of this period, according to Piaget, is to develop a new, more powerful set of cognitive skills called *formal operations*. Whereas the concrete operational child can use the various operations to think about objects or facts (things that can be seen or touched), the formal operational child is able to apply complex operations to ideas and thoughts. In addition, some even more powerful operations are also developed at this stage.

Piaget does *not* say that this new level of abstraction is achieved all at once one morning on a child's twelfth birthday. Fully consolidated formal operations is probably not completed until about age 15 or later. But he did believe that there was a fairly rapid spurt of development over a period of several years, when the major elements of this new level of abstract thinking were acquired. Let me describe some of those elements.

*From the Actual to the Possible.*   One of the first steps in this process is for the child to extend her reasoning abilities to objects and situations which she has not seen or experienced firsthand, or that she cannot see or manipulate directly. Instead of thinking only about real things and actual occurrences, she must start to think about possible occurrences. Such a skill is obviously essential for the teenager to think about the future systematically, such as about the jobs she might have or the roles she might fill as an adult. The preschool child plays "dress up" by putting on real clothes. The teenager *thinks* about options and possibilities, imagining herself in different roles, going to college or not going to college, marrying or not marrying, having children or not. She can imagine future consequences of actions she might take now, so that some kind of long-term planning becomes possible (Lewis, 1981).

*Systematic Problem Solving.*   Another important feature of formal operations is the ability to search systematically and methodically for the answer to a problem. To study this, Piaget and his colleague Barbel Inhelder (Inhelder & Piaget, 1958) presented adolescents with complex tasks, mostly drawn from the physical sciences. In one of these tasks, the youngsters are given varying lengths of string and a set of objects of various weights that can be tied to the strings to make a swinging pendulum. They are shown how to start the pendulum by pushing the weight with differing amounts of force and by holding the weight at different heights. The subject must figure out which one or combination of these four factors (length of string, weight of object, force of push, or height of push) determines the "period" of the pendulum (the amount of time for one swing). (In case you have forgotten your high-school physics, the answer is that only the length of the string affects the period of the pendulum. You can check this yourself, and with a teenage subject, if you select the third project for this chapter.)

If you give this task to a concrete operational child, she will usually try out many different combinations of length and weight and force and height in an inefficient way. She might try a heavy weight on a long string, and then a light weight on a short string. Since both string length and weight have changed, there is no way to draw a clear conclusion about either factor.

An adolescent, in contrast, is likely to try a much more organized approach, attempting to vary just one of the four factors at a time. She may try a heavy object with a short string, then with a medium string, and then with a long one. After that, she might try a light object with the three lengths of string. Of course not all adolescents (or all adults, for that matter) are quite this methodical in their approach. But there is a very dramatic difference in the overall strategy used by 10-year-olds and 15-year-olds that marks the shift from concrete to formal operations.

*Logic.* Piaget argued that another facet of this shift is the appearance of deductive logic in the child's repertoire of skills. This more difficult kind of reasoning involves "if, then" relationships: "If all people are equal, then you and I must be equal." Children as young as 4 or 5 can understand some such relationships, but only if the premises given are factually true. Only at adolescence are young people able to understand and use the basic logical relationship (e.g., Ward & Overton, 1990).

A great deal of the logic of science is of this deductive type. We begin with a theory and propose, "If this theory is correct, then I should observe such and such." In doing this, we are going well beyond our observations. We are conceiving things that we have never seen that *ought* to be true or observable. We can think of this process as being part of a general decentering process that began much earlier in cognitive development. The preoperational child gradually moves away from his egocentrism and comes to be able to take the physical perspective of others. During formal operations, the child takes another step by freeing himself even from his reliance upon specific experiences.

### Current Work on Formal Operations

Most of the current work on formal operations has centered around two questions: (1) Is there really a change in the child's thinking at adolescence, and if so, when does it happen? (2) Why can't we see this change in every youngster?

*Is There Really a Change?* All the recent research tells us that the answer to this question is clearly "yes." As Edith Neimark says (1982, p. 493), "An enormous amount of evidence from an assortment of tasks shows that adolescents and adults are capable of feats of reasoning not attained under normal circumstances by [younger] children, and that these abilities develop fairly rapidly during the ages of about 11 to 15."

A cross-sectional study by Susan Martorano (1977), while not recent, is still a good illustration. She tested 20 girls at each of four grades (sixth,

High school science classes, like this one, are more likely than are earlier science classes to require students to use deductive logic, a skill Piaget did not think was present until the period of formal operations.

eighth, tenth, and twelfth) on 10 different tasks that require one or more of the formal operations skills. Some of her results are in Figure 7.4. You can see that older students generally did better, with the biggest improvement in scores between eighth and tenth grades (between ages 13 and 15). This is somewhat later than Piaget originally proposed, but consistent with other recent findings. You can also see that—as with the tasks used to assess concrete operations—the problems are not equally difficult. Problems that required the child to consider two or more separate factors simultaneously were harder than problems that simply required the child to search for the logical possibilities. For example, the easiest problem, called "colored tokens," asks the child how many different pairs of colors can be made using tokens of six different colors. This requires only thinking up and organizing possible solutions.

The two hardest problems require understanding multiple, simultaneous causation. For example, in the "chemicals" problem, the young person is shown that when a drop of a special liquid (called $g$) was put into a glass of colorless liquid, the liquid turned yellow. The youngster was then given four beakers of different liquids, and a small supply of the $g$ liquid, and asked to figure out how to reproduce the effect. In fact the solution requires combining two of the colorless liquids plus $g$. So to get the answer the subject must test all possible combinations in some systematic way.

*Does Everybody Reach Formal Operations?*   The answer to this question seems to be "no." In Piaget's original studies there were signs that, unlike concrete operations, formal operations was not a universal achievement. Those early hints have been repeatedly confirmed in more recent research. Keating (1980) estimates that only about 50–60 percent of 18- to 20-year-olds in Western countries seem to use formal operations at all, let alone consistently. For example, Martorano found that only 2 of her 20 twelfth grade subjects showed formal operations on all the problems, and none of the younger students did. In non-Western countries the rates are even lower.

Why? One reason may be that the usual methods of measuring formal operations are simply extremely difficult or unclear. When the instructions are made clearer, or the subjects are given hints or rules, they can demonstrate some aspects of formal operations (e.g., Danner & Day, 1977). A related possibility is that most of us have some formal operational ability, but that we can only apply it to topics or tasks with which we are familiar. For example, I use formal operations reasoning about psychology because it is an area I know well. But I am a lot less skillful at applying the same kind of reasoning to fixing my car—about which I know next to nothing. Willis Overton and his colleagues (Overton et al., 1987) have found considerable support for this possibility in their research. They found that as many as 90 percent of adolescents could solve quite complex logic problems if they were stated using familiar content, while only half could solve the identical logical problem when it was stated in abstract language.

Still a third possibility is that most of our everyday experiences and tasks do not require formal operations. Concrete operations is quite sufficient most of the time. So we get into a cognitive rut, applying our most usual mode of thinking to new problems as well. We can kick our thinking up a notch under some circumstances, especially if someone reminds us that it would be useful

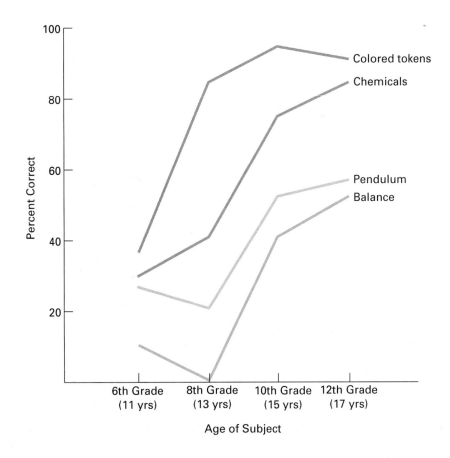

*FIGURE 7.4*

In this cross-sectional study, 20 girls of each age were tested on four different formal operations tasks. As was true for the set of concrete operations tasks shown in Figure 7.3, you can see that there was one age period (between 13 and 15) during which there seemed to be a big improvement in performance. But once again the problems also differ consistently in difficulty (*Source:* Martorano, 1977, p. 670. Copyright by the American Psychological Association).

to do so, but we simply don't rehearse formal operations very much. The fact that formal operations is found more often among young people or adults in Western cultures may be interpreted in the same way. Because of the high technology and the complexity of our lives, there is simply more demand for formal operational thought in Western culture. By this argument, all non-retarded teenagers and adults have the *capacity* for formal logic, but only those of us whose lives demand its development will actually acquire it.

## Overview of the Stages of Cognitive Development

The child comes a long way in only 15 years. He moves from very rudimentary abilities to represent things to himself with images and words, to classifications, to conservation, to abstract, deductive logic. As Piaget sees it, the progress along this chain is continuous but marked off into stages, with each stage characterized by particular kinds of logic. In broad outline, Piaget's observations have been frequently confirmed. But there are some distinct problems with Piaget's theory, many of which have been evident in what I have already said. Since these problems are part of what has led to the new information processing approach, let me be explicit about several of the key difficulties.

## Criticisms of Piaget's Theory

### The Timing of Developments

The most obvious criticism is that Piaget seems to have been wrong about just how early many cognitive skills develop. Not only do infants appear to pay attention to far more abstract properties of their environments than Piaget had thought, it is also clear that virtually all the achievements of the concrete operational period are present in at least rudimentary or fragmentary form in the preschool years. This might simply mean that Piaget just had the ages wrong—that concrete operations really begins at 3 or 4. But I think by now there is agreement even among modern Piaget enthusiasts that the problem goes far deeper than that. Piaget was really saying that each stage was a coherent structural whole. If that is true, then until a child reached a particular stage, she should be *unable* to use particular forms of logic, even if presented in simplified form. The fact that younger children can demonstrate parts or beginning phases of complex logic if the problems are made simple calls this whole assumption into serious doubt.

### Are There Stages?

Given such findings, does it still make sense to hold on to a notion of stages of development at all? Aside from the data on timing, the biggest doubts about the usefulness or validity of a stage concept have been raised by two somewhat related bodies of research: studies of expertise and studies of consistency of performance across sets of tasks thought to tap the same cognitive structures.

*Studies of Expertise.*    If Piaget was right in his original formulations—if children are applying broad forms of logic to all their experiences—then the amount of specific experience a child has had with some set of material shouldn't make a lot of difference. A child who understands hierarchical classification but who has never seen a picture of a dinosaur ought to be able to create classifications of dinosaurs about as well as a child who had played a lot with dinosaur models. But in fact that seems not to be the case. There is now a great deal of research that shows that specific knowledge makes a huge difference. Children and adults who know a lot about some subject or some set of materials (dinosaurs, baseball cards, mathematics, or whatever) not only categorize information in that topic area in more complex and hierarchical ways, they are also better at remembering new information on that topic and better at applying more advanced forms of logic to material in that area. Expertise not only fosters greater speed in performing some well-practiced task, it also changes the way we think about that material. Furthermore, such expertise seems to generalize very little to other tasks (Ericsson & Crutcher, 1990).

Much of the most interesting work has been done by Michelene Chi and her various colleagues (e.g., Chi, Hutchinson, & Robin, 1989; Chi & Ceci, 1987). In her most famous study (1978) she showed that expert chess players can remember the placement of chess pieces on a board much more quickly and accurately than can novice chess players, *even when the expert chess players are children and the novices are adults.* To paraphrase Flavell, the expert looks very smart, very cognitively mature, no matter what her age, while the novice looks cognitively very immature, no matter her age (1985, p. 83).

Since young children are novices at almost everything, while older children are more expert at many things, perhaps the difference in apparent cognitive strategies or functioning between younger and older children is just the effect of more specific knowledge, more experience, and *not* the result of stage-like changes in fundamental cognitive structures.

*Consistency Across Tasks.*    Consistency studies are conceptually rather similar to studies of expertise, although the two bodies of research have developed somewhat independently. Expertise studies ask whether the same individual can apply the same level of cognitive strategies to familiar and unfamiliar material. Studies of task consistency ask whether an individual performs at the same cognitive level on all tasks that are thought to tap the same basic cognitive structure. If there really are internally consistent structures emerging in sequence, then we ought to find that a "concrete operational child" applies very similar logic to a whole range of problems; we ought to find *horizontal* consistency. But researchers have generally not found such consistency from one task to another.

You've already seen two examples of such inconsistency, in the data from the Tomlinson-Keasey study of concrete operations (Figure 7.3) and in the results of Martorano's study of formal operations (Figure 7.4). Other researchers have generally found the same thing: A child may perform at one stage on one task, at another stage on a second task, even though the two tasks appear to tap the same basic cognitive structure in Piaget's model (e.g., Uzgiris, 1973; Martorano, 1977; Keating & Clark, 1980; Flavell, 1982, 1982b). The news is not all bad for Piaget's stage concept. Recent studies of toddlers, for example, have begun to show a whole set of apparently parallel developments in language, thinking, and social behavior, all of which seem to reflect the child's emerging understanding that things can be strung together into sequences—research I'll talk more about in Chapter 8. But studies of children supposedly "in" the stages of concrete and formal operations have consistently shown very little cross-task consistency.

*Some Neo-Piagetian Replies.* Those who advocate the usefulness of stage concepts have not given up without a fight. Some have argued that we should not expect cross-task consistency at the beginning of a new stage, but only at the end when the new structure is fully realized. Others have argued that the failure to find cross-task consistency arises because we have really not used tasks of equal difficulty; we have compared apples and oranges and then been surprised when they turned out to be different. When tasks are matched carefully for the types of underlying structures required, much better consistency seems to be found (e.g., Marini & Case, 1989; Kreitler & Kreitler, 1989).

Other replies to the critics have been in the form of slightly modified versions of stage theories. Robbie Case (1985, 1986; Case et al., 1988), for example, has offered his own "neo-Piagetian" theory, which includes stages very similar to Piaget's. The key difference is that Case does *not* assume that each new stage involves totally new types or forms of thinking, but only that each stage requires more complex *levels* or integrations of the same basic processes. Case is not surprised that young children can do simple versions of some of Piaget's tasks. That is precisely what he would expect and predict.

Kurt Fischer (1980; Fischer & Pipp, 1984; Fischer & Canfield, 1986), another modern developmental theorist, gets around the problem another way. He proposes a series of "developmental levels," but sees them as representing the *optimal level*—the upper limit of performance of which the child is then capable under maximally supportive conditions like clear instructions, familiar content, high levels of motivation, and so forth. In Fischer's theory, the

When children become expert at something, such as chess, their use of information strategies becomes much more complex and flexible than is true for novices at that task. So when Chi compared children who were expert chess players with adults who were novices, she found that the *children* showed the more mature and complex types of thinking—a finding that calls Piaget's stage theory into question.

optimal level rises discontinuously with age in a series of spurts. Each spurt is the result of the emergence of new strategies or the integration of old strategies. At any given moment, however, a child's actual performance on different kinds of tasks will vary a great deal, depending on the child's expertise, the clarity or simplicity of the instructions, or other situational factors. Thus Fischer proposes stage-like changes at the underlying level of competence but more variability at the level of performance.

Whether Case's or Fischer's proposals will ultimately provide the framework for a persuasive stage theory I simply can't tell at this point. What is clear now is that Piaget's version of structurally distinct stages of cognitive development does *not* work.

It is also clear that cognitive development is made up of a large number of apparently universal *vertical* sequences. That is, in any given concept area, such as number concepts, or concepts of gender, or ideas about appearance and reality, or in hundreds of other areas, children seem to learn the basic rules or strategies in the same order. To quote John Flavell, "Sequences are the very wire and glue of development. Later cognitive acquisitions build on or are otherwise linked to earlier ones, and in their turn similarly prepare the ground for still later ones" (1982b, p. 18).

Thus while Piaget appears to have been at least partially off-target in talking about stages, he was very much on-target in talking about sequences. Further, I am convinced that Piaget was right in arguing that the changes in cognitive skill from preschooler to adolescent are more than merely quantitative increases in specific task knowledge and experience—although Piaget himself acknowledged that such experience was a critical ingredient in the developmental process. There seem to be real differences in the way 2-year-olds and 10-year-olds approach problems that are not merely differences in experience. But if those differences are not in the basic structures, as Piaget thought, just what might those differences consist of? It is here that the third approach, information processing, may offer some answers.

 ## Information Processing in Children

The **information processing** approach is not really a theory of cognitive development; it is an approach to studying thinking and remembering—a set of questions and some methods of analysis. Theorists who study cognitive power ask *how well* a child does intellectual tasks compared to others. Those who study structure ask *what type* or structure of logic the child uses in solving problems and how those structures change with age. The information processing theorists ask what the child is *doing* intellectually when faced with a task, what intellectual processes she brings to bear, and how those *processes* might change with age.

This third approach has a whole series of theoretical fathers and grandfathers. The direct line of inheritance is from studies of adult intelligence, particularly computer simulations of adult intelligence. In fact the basic metaphor underlying the entire information processing approach has been that of the human mind as computer. Like a computer, we can think of the "hardware" of cognition (the physiology of the brain, the nerves and connective tissues) and the "software" of cognition (the program that uses the basic

**information processing** A way of looking at cognition and cognitive development that emphasizes both fundamental processes built into the "hardware" and the "software" of thinking, such as memory strategies, problem solving strategies, and planning.

hardware). To understand thinking in general, we need to understand the processing capacity of the hardware and just what programs have to be "run" to perform any given task. What inputs (facts or data) are needed, what coding, decoding, remembering, or analyzing are required? To understand cognitive *development,* we need to discover whether there are any changes with age in the basic processing capacity of the system and/or in the nature of the programs used. Do children develop new types of processing (new programs)? Or do they simply learn to use basic programs on new material?

In studies of children's thinking, there are at least two branches to the information processing family tree. On one side is a group of researchers and theorists with a somewhat Piagetian flavor who have given up the notion of stages but are still committed to the notion of qualitatively changing sequences of development (e.g., Siegler, 1981). On the other side are researchers with a strong intellectual-power flavor, who have been looking for those basic information processing capacities or strategies that may help to explain or underlie differences in IQ. What is it that "brighter" people really do that is different when confronted with a problem? These two approaches to the study of information processing are not divorced from one another, but for the moment let me talk about them somewhat separately.

### Developmental Approaches to Information Processing

*Changes in Processing Capacity.* One obvious place to look for an explanation of developmental changes in cognitive skills is in the hardware itself. Any computer has physical limits to the number of different operations it can perform simultaneously or in a given space of time. As the brain and nervous system develop in the early years of life, with synapses formed and then pruned to remove the redundant ones, perhaps the capacity, the speed, or the efficiency of the system increases. In fact, several neo-Piagetian theorists, including Case, have proposed just such an increase in processing capacity or efficiency as a basic component of their theories.

One type of evidence that is often mentioned to support the possibility that there is some age change in processing capacity is the finding that young children are able to remember fewer items in lists of numbers, letters, or words than are older children. You can see the results of one typical study in Figure 7.5.

Such results are consistent with the hypothesis that there is an increase in basic memory capacity with age, but there are a number of plausible competing explanations. For example, younger children clearly have less *experience* with numbers, letters, and words. Perhaps their poorer performance on tests that measure memory span is simply another example of the fact that experts can do things better than novices. In fact, when the degree of experience is better matched, such as by having older children try to remember new letter-like figures, much of the age difference in memory span disappears. The current conclusion by most experts in this area of research is that there is probably no basic increase in underlying capacity, but that there may well be improvements in efficiency, which in turn frees up more "memory space" for storage (Schneider & Pressley, 1989).

But just what does it mean to say that an older child's cognitive processing is "more efficient"? It could mean simply that the synaptic connections

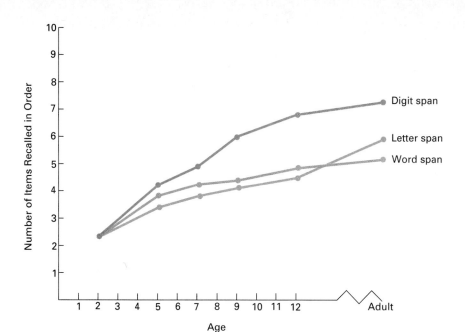

FIGURE 7.5

Psychologists have tried to measure basic memory capacity by asking subjects to listen to a list of numbers, letters, or words, and then to repeat back the list in order. This figure shows the number of such items that children of various ages are able to remember and report accurately. Memory on such tasks clearly improves with age, but whether this must mean that basic capacity increases is much more debatable (*Source:* Dempster, 1981, from Figures 1, 2, and 3, p. 66, 67, 68).

are more complete or more selective. It could also mean that cognitive processing gets faster as the child gets older. For example, Robert Kail (1991a, 1991b) has shown that virtually the same exponential pattern of increase in processing speed with age is found for a wide variety of tasks, including such perceptual-motor tasks as tapping, simple response time to a stimulus, and cognitive tasks such as mental addition or subtests from the WISC. The most plausible explanation for this common pattern is that there is some fundamental change in the physical system itself that allows greater and greater speed of both response and mental processing.

Another way in which processing could become more efficient with age is by increasing use of a variety of cognitive *strategies*—all those techniques we use to simplify or subdivide the cognitive tasks we face. A great deal of research within the information processing approach is aimed at understanding the emergence of just such strategies. The literature is vast, so I can only sample it, starting with a look at memory strategies.

*Strategies for Remembering.* You're about to go out the door to run some errands. You need to stop at the cleaners; buy some stamps; copy your IRS forms; and buy milk, bread, orange juice, carrots, lettuce, spaghetti and spaghetti sauce at the grocery store. How do you remember all those things? There are many possible strategies, some of which I have listed (with examples) in Table 7.3 on the next page. You could rehearse the list, you could organize the route in your mind, you could remember your menu for dinner when you get to the grocery store.

Do children do these things when they try to remember? Until fairly recently, the conventional wisdom was that toddlers and even 5-year-olds rarely used such strategies. For example, in one classic early study of the strategy of rehearsal, Keeney and his colleagues (Keeney, Cannizzo, & Flavell, 1967) showed children a row of seven cards with pictures on them and told them to

**TABLE 7.3**

*Some Information Processing Strategies Involved in Remembering*

- **Rehearsal.** Perhaps the most common strategy, which involves either mental or vocal repetition, or repetition of movement (as in learning to dance). May occur in children as young as 2 years under some conditions.
- **Clustering.** Grouping ideas or objects or words into clusters to help you remember them, such as "all animals," or "all the ingredients in the lasagna recipe," or "the chess pieces involved in the move called castling." This is one strategy that clearly benefits from experience with a particular subject or activity, since possible categories are learned, or are discovered in the process of exploring or manipulating a set of material. Primitive chunking occurs in 2-year-olds.
- **Elaboration.** Finding shared meaning or a common referent for two or more things that need to be remembered. The helpful mnemonic for recalling the names of the lines on the musical staff ("Every Good Boy Does Fine") is a kind of elaboration, as is associating the name of a person you have just met with some object or other word. This form of memory aid is not used spontaneously by all individuals, and is not used skillfully until fairly late in development, if then.
- **Systematic searching.** When you try to remember something, you can "scan" the memory for the whole domain in which it might be found. Three- and four-year-old children can begin to do this to search for actual objects in the real world, but are not good at doing this in memory. So search strategies may be first learned in the external world and then applied to inner searches.

*Source:* Flavell, 1985.

try to remember all the pictures in the same order they were laid out. Then a space helmet was placed over the child's head that kept the child from seeing the cards but allowed the experimenter to see if the child seemed to be rehearsing the list by muttering under his breath. Children under 5 almost never showed any rehearsal, while 8- to 10-year-old children usually did. Interestingly, when 5-year-olds were taught to rehearse, they were able to do so and as a result improved their memory scores. But when these same 5-year-olds were then given a new problem without being reminded to rehearse, they stopped rehearsing. That is, they could use the strategy if they were reminded, but they did not produce it spontaneously—a pattern described as a *production deficiency.*

Yet here is that familiar tune again: A series of studies by Judy DeLoache and her coworkers (DeLoache, 1989) demonstrate clearly that children as young as 2 and 3 show strategies if the task is not too complex, such as the game of hide-and-seek. In one of DeLoache's research techniques, the child watches the experimenter hide an attractive toy in some obvious place (e.g., behind a couch), and is then told that when a buzzer goes off, she can go and find the toy. While playing with other toys during the 4-minute delay interval, 2-year-olds often talked about the toy's hiding place, or pointed to or looked at the hiding place—all of which seem clearly to be early forms of mnemonic strategies.

These results tell us that a child does not magically shift at age 5, 6, or 7 from non-strategic to strategic behavior. Primitive strategies are used by children as young as 2, perhaps younger. But such findings do not tell us that strategies like rehearsal are equally well-established or as flexibly used throughout the age span. For example, we know that younger children do not rehearse in the same way that older ones do. When learning a list of words, for instance, 8-year-olds are more likely to practice the words one at a time ("cat, cat, cat") while older children practice them in groups ("desk, lawn, sky, shirt, cat"). When the younger children are followed longitudinally for as short a time as a year, researchers find that they show signs of a shift toward the more efficient strategy (Guttentag, Ornstein, & Siemens, 1987).

Other strategies that help improve memory involve putting the items to be learned or remembered into some meaningful organization. When you organize your grocery shopping list in your mind so that all the fruits and vegetables are in one group, and all the canned food in another, you are using this principle—usually called clustering or chunking. George Miller showed years ago (1956) that in active short-term memory, most of us can deal with only seven bits of information at a time, such as a seven-digit phone number. But if each "bit" contains not a single piece of information but a "chunk," such as "vegetables" or "things I need for the macaroni and cheese recipe," then the amount of information you can deal with will increase considerably.

Studies of such clustering or organizing strategies often involve having children or adults learn lists of words that have potential categories built into them. For example, I might ask you to remember a list of words that includes a mixture of names for furniture, animals, and foods. I let you learn the list any way you wish, but when you then name off the items later, I can check for the kind of organization you used by seeing whether you name the same-category words together.

Children do show this kind of internal organization when they recall things, but as we would expect, younger children do this less consistently and less efficiently than older ones (e.g., Bjorklund & Arce, 1987; Bjorklund & Muir, 1988). Among other things, they tend to use a greater number of small categories rather than a few larger ones.

Summing up the research on memory strategies: First, we can see some primitive signs of memory strategies under optimum conditions as early as age 2 or 3 (DeLoache et al., 1985) but with increasing age children use more and more powerful ways of helping themselves remember things. Second, in the use of each strategy children shift from a period in which they don't use it at all, to a period in which they will use it if reminded or taught, to one in which they use it spontaneously. Third, they use these strategies more and more skillfully, and generalize them to more and more situations. These are obviously changes in the *quality* of the child's strategies as well as the quantity.

*Rules for Problem Solving.*   Another area in which information processing researchers have found qualitative progressions is in problem solving. Some of the best known work in this area have been Robert Siegler's studies of the development of *rules* (Siegler, 1976, 1978, 1981). Siegler's approach is a kind of cross between Piagetian theory and information processing. He argues that cognitive development consists of acquiring a set of basic rules, which are then applied to a broader and broader range of problems on the basis of experience. There are no stages, only sequences.

Unless she has a written list, there is little hope that this shopper is going to remember all 25 or 30 things she needs at the store—*unless* she organizes those items in her memory in some way that reduces the memory load. Maybe she has a mental category of "vegetables" that includes six or seven items, and other mental categories of "snack food" (which she's searching for in this aisle) or "dairy stuff" or "frozen food." This type of memory strategy is often called *chunking*, and is one of the most useful ways of stretching memory capacity.

In one test of this approach, Siegler uses a balance scale with a series of pegs on either side of the center, like the one in Figure 7.6. Discs can be placed on these pegs, and the child is asked to predict which way the balance will fall, depending on the location and number of discs. A complete solution requires the child to take into account both the number of discs on each side, and the specific location of the discs. But children do not develop such a complete solution immediately. Instead, Siegler predicts that four rules will develop in a specific order. Rule I, which is basically a "preoperational" rule, takes into account only one dimension, the number of weights. Children using this rule will predict that the side with more discs will go down, no matter which peg they are placed on. Rule II is a transitional rule. The child still judges on the basis of number, except when there are the same number of weights on both sides. In that case, the child takes distance from the fulcrum into account. Rule III is basically a concrete operational rule, since the child tries to take both distance and weight into account simultaneously, except that when the information is conflicting (such as when the side with weights closer to the fulcrum has more weights), the child simply guesses. Rule IV is basically a formal operational rule. At this point the child/youth figures out the actual formula (distance **x** weight for each side).

Siegler has found that virtually all children perform on this and similar tasks as if they were following one or another of these rules, and that the rules seem to develop in the given order. Very young children behave as if they don't have a rule (they guess or behave randomly so far as Siegler can determine); when a rule develops, it is always Rule I that comes first. But progression from one rule to the next is heavily dependent on experience. If children are given practice with the balance scale so that they can make predictions and then check which way the balance actually falls, many show rapid shifts upward in the sequence of rules.

Thus Siegler is attempting to describe a logical sequence children follow, not unlike the basic sequence of stages that Piaget describes, but Siegler shows that the specific step in this sequence that we see in a particular child is dependent not so much on age as on the child's specific experience with that particular material. In Piaget's terminology, this is like saying that when accommodation of some scheme occurs, it always occurs in a particular sequence, but the rate with which the child moves through that sequence depends on experience.

*Metacognition and Executive Processes.* A third area in which information processing researchers have been active is in studying how children come to know what they know. If I gave you a list of things to remember and then asked you later how you had gone about trying to remember it, you could tell me what you had done. You may even have consciously considered the various alternative strategies and then selected the best one. You could also tell me good ways to study, or which kinds of tasks will be hardest, and why. These are all examples of **metamemory,** or **metacognition**—knowing about remembering or knowing about knowing. Information processing theorists sometimes refer to these skills as **executive processes,** since they involve planning and organizing in some central way, just as an executive may do.

These skills are of particular interest because there is some suggestion that it may be precisely such metacognitive or executive skills that emerge with age. Performance on a whole range of tasks will be better if the child can monitor her own performance or recognize when a particular strategy is called for and when it is not. While 4- and 5-year-old children do show some such monitoring (Schneider & Pressley, 1989), it is rarely found earlier than that and it clearly improves fairly rapidly after school-age. Such executive skills may well form the foundation of some of the other age changes I have been describing.

*A Summary of Developmental Changes in Information Processing.* I can summarize all of this evidence with a series of reasonable (albeit still tentative) generalizations:

1. There is probably *not* any increase in the basic processing capacity of the system, but there does seem to be an increase both in the speed and in the efficiency with which the "hardware" is used.

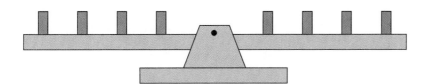

**FIGURE 7.6**

This balance scale is similar to what Siegler used in his experiments. The scale was held even by a lever while the experimenter placed weights on one or more of the pegs on either side. For each combination of weights, the child was asked to predict which way the balance would fall when the lever was released (*Source:* Siegler, 1981, p. 7).

**metamemory**
A subcategory of metacognition; knowledge about your own memory processes.

**metacognition**
General and rather loosely used term describing an individual's knowledge of his own thinking processes. Knowing what you know and how you go about learning or remembering.

**executive processes**
Proposed subset of information processes involving organizing and planning strategies. Similar in meaning to metacognition.

2. The sheer amount of specific knowledge the child has about any given task increases as the child experiments, explores, and studies things in school. This leads to more and more "expert" approaches to remembering and solving problems.

3. Genuinely new strategies are acquired, probably in some kind of order. In particular, the child seems to develop in middle childhood some "executive" or "metacognitive" abilities—she knows that she knows and can *plan* a strategy for the first time.

4. Existing strategies are applied to more and more different domains and more and more flexibly. If a child learned to rehearse on one kind of memory problem, the older child is more likely to try it on a new memory strategy; the younger child (particularly younger than 5 or 6) is not likely to generalize the strategy to the new task. Although once again it is true that some transfer is seen in children as young as 2 when the conditions are carefully constructed (Crisafi & Brown, 1986).

5. With increasing age, a wider range of different strategies can be applied to the same problem, so that if the first doesn't work, a backup or alternative strategy can be used. If you can't find your misplaced keys by retracing your steps, you try a backup, such as looking in your other purse or the pocket of your jacket, or searching each room of the house in turn. Young children do not do this; school-age children and adolescents do.

Thus some of the changes that Piaget observed and chronicled with such detail and richness seem to be the result simply of increased experience with tasks and problems (a quantitative change, if you will). But there also seems to be a qualitative change in the complexity, generalizability, and flexibility of strategies used by the child.

### Individual Differences in Information Processing

While some researchers in the information processing tradition have been asking about developmental changes or sequences, others have been trying to understand individual differences. IQ tests are intended to measure such underlying ability differences by giving people fairly complex cognitive tasks, each of which may require a whole series of more fundamental information processing strategies. Perhaps we could come closer to understanding individual differences in intelligence or intellectual performance if we shifted our attention to those more fundamental processes. Generally the strategy has been to look at the relationship between IQ scores on standard tests and measures of specific information processing. This strategy has yielded a few preliminary connections.

*Speed of Information Processing.* One of the possible sources of individual differences in IQ may simply be the speed with which an individual can perform basic information processing tasks, such as recognizing whether two letters or numbers are the same or different or bringing some piece of information out of long-term memory. A number of different investigators have found just such a link: Subjects who are able to do basic recognition and memory tasks more quickly also have higher IQ scores on standard tests (e.g.,

Vernon, 1987). Most of this research has been done with adults, but the same link has also been found in a few studies with children (e.g., Keating, List, & Merriman, 1985).

Furthermore, there are some pretty clear suggestions that such speed-of-processing differences may be built-in at birth. The fact that measures of infant habituation and recognition memory are correlated so strongly with later IQ—a set of research I described in Chapter 5—certainly points to such a conclusion, since it is difficult to imagine a set of experiences in the first four or five months of life that could have contributed to such differences.

*Other IQ-Processing Links.* Another research strategy has been to compare the information processing strategies used by normal-IQ and retarded children. Two examples illustrate this approach.

Judy DeLoache (DeLoache & Brown, 1987) has compared the searching strategies of groups of 2-year-olds who were either developing normally or showed delayed development. When the search task was very simple, such as searching for a toy hidden in some distinctive location in a room, the two groups did not differ in search strategies or skill. But when the experimenter surreptitiously moved the toy before the child was allowed to search, normally developing children were able to search in alternative, plausible places, such as in nearby locations. Delayed children simply persisted in looking in the place where they had seen the toy hidden. They either could not change strategies or did not have alternative, more complex strategies in their repertoires.

In several studies of older children, Joseph Campione and Ann Brown (1984; Campione et al., 1985) have found that both retarded and normal-IQ children could learn to solve problems like those in items (a), (b), and (c) in Figure 7.7. However, the retarded children could not transfer this learning to slightly differing problems of the same general type, like item (d) in Figure 7.7, while normal-IQ children could. Both sets of studies suggest that flexibility of use of any given strategy may be another key dimension of individual differences in intelligence.

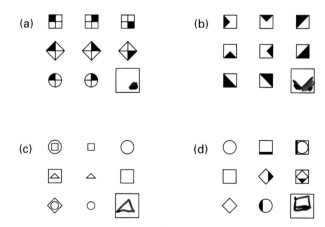

**FIGURE 7.7**

In problems (a), (b), and (c) the subject must figure out the "system" in each set and then describe what pattern should go in the empty box in the bottom right-hand corner. Problem (d) is a test problem requiring application of two rules simultaneously (*Source:* Campione et al., 1985, Figure 1, p. 302, Figure 4, p. 306).

## Putting the Three Approaches Together

I hope it is clear by now that the information processing approach offers us some important bridges between the power and structure theories of intelligence in children. It now looks as if there are some basic, inborn strategies, such as noting differences and sameness. These strategies also seem to change over the course of the early years of life, with more complex strategies or rules emerging and old strategies used more flexibly. Plain old experience is also part of the process. The more a child plays with blocks, the better she will be at organizing and classifying blocks; the more a person plays chess, the better he will be at seeing and remembering relationships among pieces on the board. So some of the changes that Piaget thought of as changes in underlying structure are, instead, specific task learning. But there seems to be some structural change as well, such as the emergence of new strategies, particularly metacognitive strategies.

Individual differences in what we normally think of as intelligence can then be conceived of as resulting both from inborn differences in the speed or efficiency of the basic processes (differences in the hardware, perhaps), and from differences in experiences. The child with a slower or less efficient processing system is going to move through all the various steps and stages more slowly; he will *use* the experience he has less efficiently or effectively, and may never develop as complete a range of strategies as does the initially quicker child.

The information processing approach may also have some real practical applications. The studies of recognition memory in infancy, for example, may give us a way to identify retarded children very early in life, or to sort out from among low birth weight infants those that seem at particular risk for later problems. By identifying the key differences between retarded and non-retarded children (or between brighter and less bright children), we may also be able to point to specific kinds of training that would be useful for a retarded child, or for a child with a "specific learning disability."

I do not want to wax too rhapsodic about the information processing approach. We need to remember that we do not yet have any tests of information processing ability that could replace the careful use of IQ tests in schools and clinics. Nor are the sequential theories of information processing development far enough along yet to explain all the differences we see between infants, preschoolers, and older children in performance on various Piagetian tasks. In short, information processing is an important, integrative addition to our understanding of cognitive development, but it does not explain away all the other approaches.

# SUMMARY

1.  The study of cognitive "power" does not tell us what we need to know about the shared changes in the *way* children think about the world around them. Piaget's studies of cognitive structure fill that gap.

2.  Piaget assumed that the child was an active agent in his own development, adapting to the environment by changing his basic schemes.

3.  Schemes and their relationships to one another are changed through the processes of assimilation, accommodation, and equilibration, beginning with primitive schemes at birth and progressing sequentially through several stages.

4.  The first stage Piaget calls the sensorimotor period, which lasts from birth to 18 months. In this period, the child moves from reflexive to intentional behavior. Current work places the development of internal representation earlier in this period than Piaget thought.

5.  The second Piagetian stage is the preoperational period, from 18 months to 6 years, when the child develops beginning forms of reasoning and classification and shows some primitive ability to see things from others' perspectives. Current work on children in this age range shows earlier signs of complex thought than Piaget had proposed.

6.  The third Piagetian stage is concrete operations, from age 6 to 12, when the child acquires powerful new mental tools, called operations, such as reversibility, addition, subtraction, multiplication, and serial ordering. Current work on this age period shows that these operations are applied less broadly by children than Piaget thought.

7.  The final stage Piaget proposed is formal operations, from age 12 onward, when the young person becomes able to manipulate *ideas* as well as objects, approaches problems systematically, and develops the ability to use deductive logic. Unlike earlier stages, which virtually all children achieve, formal operations are achieved by perhaps only half of adolescents.

8.  Piaget's concept of structurally consistent stages has been largely discarded because of substantive data showing that children develop at least beginning forms of complex thinking much sooner than Piaget thought. Children show much more complex levels of thinking in areas in which they are extremely knowledgeable than in less familiar areas, making developmental change look more like accumulating experience than structural change. And children do not show consistent levels of performance on tasks that appear to demand the same levels of cognitive skill.

9.  The apparent validity of *sequences* of development, but the relative failure of the *stage* concept, has been one force pushing psychologists toward a broader, "information processing" approach to cognitive development.

10. Information processing theorists ask not about structure, but about the basic processes that make up any cognitive activity, such as decoding, encoding, remembering, planning, and analyzing.

11. Information processing specialists interested in development have asked what ways the basic processes change with age among children. Some argue that there is an increase with age in basic processing capacity or efficiency in the hardware of the brain.

12. Others focus on changes in strategies. In memory, a series of mnemonic strategies such as rehearsal and clustering appear to develop and to be used more and more consistently, beginning at age 4 or 5.

13. Metacognitive skills or executive skills (knowing what you know, being able to plan good strategies) also appear to develop at about the same time.

14. Other information processing specialists focus on individual differences in efficiency of basic processes. Higher IQ individuals, for example, appear to process information more quickly and apply strategies or knowledge more broadly.

## CRITICAL THINKING QUESTIONS

1. Given all that you have read in the last two chapters about intelligence—power, structure, and process—how might you now explain the fact that children reared in poverty environments typically develop more slowly through the sequence of cognitive development described by Piaget? What are the alternative explanations? Which one or ones do you think have the most merit?

2. There have been some reasonably systematic attempts to apply some of Piaget's ideas to classroom education, but as yet there has been little application of information processing approaches. Can you think of any ways in which an information processing view of intelligence would affect the way school subjects were taught or the way individual children might be taught?

3. One of the hot theoretical arguments among cognitive developmental theorists in the past decade is whether Piaget is right about the existence of broad stages of development. Setting aside for the moment which side might be correct, why is the issue itself important? Why would it matter, either theoretically or practically, whether children develop in stages or not?

## KEY TERMS

**accommodation**   That part of the adaptation process by which a person modifies existing schemes to fit new experiences or creates new schemes when old ones no longer handle the data.

**assimilation**   That part of the adaptation process that involves the "taking in" of new experiences or information into existing schemes. Experience is not taken in "as is," however, but is modified (or interpreted) somewhat so as to fit the preexisting schemes.

**class inclusion**   The relationship between classes of objects, such that a subordinate class is included in a superordinate class, as bananas are part of the class "fruit."

**concrete operational stage**   The stage of development proposed by Piaget between ages 6 and 12, in which mental operations such as subtraction, reversibility, and multiple classification are acquired.

**conservation**   The concept that objects remain the same in fundamental ways, such as weight or number, even when there are external changes in shape or arrangement. Typically understood by children after age 5.

**deductive logic**    Reasoning from the general to the particular, from a rule to an expected instance, or from a theory to a hypothesis. Characteristic of formal operational thought.

**egocentrism**    A cognitive state in which the individual (typically a child) sees the world only from his own perspective, without awareness that there are other perspectives.

**equilibration**    The third part of the adaptation process, as proposed by Piaget, involving a periodic restructuring of schemes into new structures.

**executive processes**    Proposed subset of information processes involving organizing and planning strategies. Similar in meaning to metacognition.

**formal operational stage**    Piaget's name for the fourth and final major stage of cognitive development, occurring during adolescence, when the child becomes able to manipulate and organize ideas as well as objects.

**inductive logic**    Reasoning from the particular to the general, from experience to broad rules. Characteristic of concrete operational thinking.

**information processing**    A way of looking at cognition and cognitive development that emphasizes both fundamental processes built into the "hardware" and the "software" of thinking, such as memory strategies, problem solving strategies, and planning.

**metacognition**    General and rather loosely used term describing an individual's knowledge of his own thinking processes. Knowing what you know and how you go about learning or remembering.

**metamemory**    A subcategory of metacognition; knowledge about your own memory processes.

**operations**    Term used by Piaget for complex, internal, abstract, reversible schemes, first seen at about age 6.

**preoperational stage**    Piaget's term for the second major stage of cognitive development, from age 2 to 6, marked at the beginning by the ability to use symbols and by the development of basic classification and logical abilities.

**sensorimotor stage**    Piaget's term for the first major stage of cognitive development, from birth to about 18 months, when the child moves from reflexive to voluntary action.

**scheme**    Piaget's word for the basic actions of knowing, including both physical actions (sensorimotor schemes, such as looking or reaching) and mental actions, such as classifying, comparing, or reversing. An experience is assimilated to a scheme, and the scheme is modified or created through accommodation.

**theory of mind**    Phrase used to describe one aspect of the thinking of 4 - and 5 -year- olds when they show signs of understanding not only that other people think differently, but something about the way others' minds work.

**transductive reasoning**    Reasoning from the specific to the specific; assuming that when two things happen together, one is the cause of the other.

## SUGGESTED READINGS

Flavell, J. H. (1985). *Cognitive development.* (2nd ed.) Englewood Cliffs, NJ: Prentice-Hall.

  This is a first-rate basic text in the field, written by one of the major current figures in cognitive developmental theory. Some of the material is quite theoretical or technical, but Flavell has a fairly easy, anecdotal style, and the book is well worth the effort.

Ginsburg, H. P. (1981). Piaget and education: The contributions and limits of genetic epistemology. In I. E. Sigel, D. M. Brodzinsky, & R. M. Golinkoff (Eds.), *New directions in Piagetian theory and practice.* Hillsdale, NJ: Lawrence Erlbaum Associates.

  A good, brief discussion of some of the applications of Piaget's theory to education, along with a consideration of the limits of such an application.

This paper has also been reprinted in an excellent collection of papers, *Cognitive develoment to adolescence,* edited by K. Richardson & S. Sheldon. Erlbaum, 1988.

Kuhn, D. (1988). Cognitive development. In M. H. Bornstein & M. E. Lamb (Eds.), *Developmental psychology: An advanced textbook.* (2nd ed.). Hillsdale, NJ: Lawrence Erlbaum Associates.

  A first-rate discussion of the strengths and limitations of both Piagetian and information processing approaches.

Schneider, W., & Pressley, M. (1989). *Memory development between 2 and 20.* New York: Springer-Verlag.

  An excellent, thorough, up-to-date discussion of all the research on memory in children, including the current work within the information processing tradition.

Thomas, R. M. (1990c). Basic concepts and applications of Piagetian cognitive development theory. In R. M. Thomas (Ed.), *The encyclopedia of human development and education.* Oxford: Pergamon Press.

This is one of the very best short descriptions of Piaget's theory I have ever read. If you simply need another run at the basic ideas, expressed in someone else's language, this is the place to look.

# PROJECT 8

## The Game of 20 Questions

### General Instructions

The first step is to locate a child between the ages of 5 and 10. Tell the parents that you want to play some simple games with the child as part of a school project, reassuring them that you are not "testing" the child. Obtain their permission, describing the games and tasks if you are asked to do so.

Arrange a time to be alone with the child if at all possible. Having the mother, father, or siblings there can be extremely distracting, both for the child and for you.

Come prepared with the equipment you will need. Tell the child that you have some games you would like to play. Play with the child for a while to establish some kind of rapport before you begin your experimenting. At the appropriate moment, introduce your "game."

### The Task

"I am thinking of something in this room, and your job is to figure out what I am thinking of. To do this, you can ask any question at all that I can answer by saying yes or no, but I can't give you any other answer but yes or no. You can ask as many questions as you need to, but try to find out in as few questions as you can."

Choose the door to the room as the answer to your first game. (If there is more than one door, select one particular door as correct; if there is no door, use a particular window.) If the child asks questions that cannot be answered yes or no, remind her (or him) that you can't answer that kind of question, and restate the kind of question that can be asked. Allow the child as many questions as needed (more than 20, if necessary). Write down each question verbatim. When the child has reached the correct answer, praise her and then say, "Let's try another one. I'll try to make it harder this time. I'm thinking of something in the room again. Remember, you ask me questions that I can answer yes or no. You can ask as many questions as you need, but try to find out in as few questions as possible."

Use your pencil or pen as the correct answer this time. After the child has solved the problem, praise her or him. If the child has not been successful, find something to praise. ("You asked some good questions, but it's a really hard problem, isn't it?") When you are satisfied that the child's motivation is still reasonably high, continue. "Now we're going to play another question asking game. In this game, I will tell you something that happened, and your job will be to find out how it happened by asking me questions I can answer yes or no. Here's what happened: A man is driving down the road in his car; the car goes off the road and hits a tree. You have to find out how it happened by the way I answer questions you ask me about it. But I can only answer yes or no. The object of the game is to find out the answer in as few questions as possible. Remember, here's what happened: A man is driving down the road in his car; the car goes off the road and hits a tree. Find out what happened."

If the child asks questions that cannot be answered yes or no, remind him or her that you cannot answer that kind of question and that you can only answer yes or no. If the child can't figure out the answer, urge her or him to try until you are persuaded that you are creating frustration, at which point you should quit with lots of positive statements. The answer to the problem is that it had been raining, the car skidded on a curve, went off the road, and hit the tree.

## Scoring

Score each question asked by the child on each of the three problems as belonging to one of two categories:

1. *Hypothesis*. A hypothesis is essentially a guess that applies to only one alternative. A yes answer to a hypothesis solves the problem; with a no answer, all that has been accomplished is to eliminate one possibility. In the first two problems, a hypothesis would be any question that applied to only one alternative, only one object in the room, for example, "Is it your hair?" or "Is it the picture?" In the third problem, a hypothesis would be any question that covers only one alternative: "Did the man get stung in the eye by a bee?" "Did he have a heart attack?" "Was there a big snowbank in the middle of the road that the car ran into and then skidded?"
2. *Constraint*. A constraint question covers at least two possibilities, often many more. A yes answer to a constraint question must be followed up ("Is it a

toy?" "Yes." "Is it the truck?"). A no answer to a constraint question allows the questioner to eliminate a whole class of possibilities. On the first two problems, any of the following would be constraints: "Is it in that half of the room?" "Is it something big?" "Is it a toy?" "Is it something red?" (assuming there is more than one red thing in the room). For the third problem, any of the following (or equivalent) would be constraints: "Was there something wrong with the car?" "Was the weather bad?" "Did something happen to the man?"

## Data and Analysis

For your own analysis or for an assignment to be turned in to a course instructor, you should examine at least the following aspects.

1. How many questions did the child ask for each problem?
2. On each problem, how many were hypotheses and how many were constraints?
3. Did the child do better (ask more constraints) on the "concrete operations" problems (the first two) than on the "formal operations" problem (the story)? Or was the performance the same on both?
4. Is the child's overall performance on this task generally consistent with the findings from Mosher and Hornsby's (1966) study (Figure 7.6)? Does your subject behave in a way that would be expected on the basis of his or her age? If not, what explanation can you offer?

# PROJECT 9

## Conservation of Number, Mass, and Weight

### General Instructions

In this project you will be testing a child between ages 5 and 10 for three kinds of conservation: number, mass, and weight. Recall that the concept of conservation involves the understanding that some features of objects remain invariant despite changes in other features. The weight of an object remains the same regardless of how its shape is changed; the number of objects in a row remains the same regardless of how widely spaced the objects are. Typically, number and mass conservation are learned (or discovered) at about age 5 or 6, while conservation of weight is learned later, at perhaps age 8 or 9. So if you are able to find a child between 5 and 8 you may find that he/she can manage the first two conservation tasks but not the last.

The testing can ordinarily be done most easily in the child's home although other settings are okay if they can be arranged. In any case, you must of course obtain the parents' permission, following whatever procedure your instructor specifies. Present the child with the three tasks in the order given here, following instructions precisely.

### Conservation of Mass

You will need two equal balls of clay or play dough, each a size that can readily be handled by a child's palm. Handle them yourself, rounding them into a ball, and then hand them to the child, asking:

*Is there the same amount of clay in each of these balls? Are they the same?*

If the child agrees that they are the same, proceed. If not, say to the child: *make them the same.* The child may want to squish them a little or may actually shift some clay from one ball to the other. That's quite all right. When he's done, ask him again:

*Is there the same amount of clay in each of these balls? Are they the same?*

Once he has agreed that they are the same, say to the child:

*Now I'm going to squash this one into a pancake.*

Squash one of the two balls into a pancake and place the two objects—the remaining ball and the pancake—in front of the child. Read the following questions exactly as written and record precisely what the child says:

1.  *Is there the same amount of clay in this one* (pointing to the ball) *as there is in this one* (pointing to the pancake), *or is there more here* (pointing to the ball) *or more here* (pointing to the pancake)?
2.  Depending on the child's answer to the first question, follow up by asking, *Why is there more here?* or *Why are they the same?*

Mold the pancake back into a ball and set the two balls aside for the moment.

### Conservation of Number

For this part of the process you will need 14 pennies or identical buttons. Start with 10 items and place them between yourself and the child (preferably on a table, but the floor will do), spaced equally in two rows of five, as follows:

$$X \quad X \quad X \quad X \quad X$$
$$X \quad X \quad X \quad X \quad X$$

Ask the child:

*Are there the same number of pennies (buttons) in this row as there are in this row, or are there more here* (pointing to the child's row) *or more here* (pointing to your row)?

The child may want to move the objects around a bit before he agrees the two rows are the same, which is fine. Once the child has agreed they are the same, spread the objects in your row so that it is now noticeably longer than the child's row but still contains only 5 objects, like the following:

X       X       X       X       X

   X    X    X    X    X

Now ask the following questions, and record the child's exact answers:

3. *Are there the same number of pennies in this row as there are in this row, or are there more here, or more here?*
4. Depending on the child's answer to question 3, ask either *Why are they the same?* or *Why are there more here?*

Now spread out the child's row and add two objects to each row, so that your row and the child's row are again exactly matched, with seven items equally spaced in each. Ask questions three and four as previously listed and record the child's answer precisely.

Now move the objects in your row closer together so that the child's row is now longer. Ask questions three and four again, and record the answers.

## Conservation of Weight

Put away the pennies (or give them to the child), and bring out the two balls of clay again, saying *Now we're going to play with the clay again*. Hand the balls to the child and ask:

*Do these two balls weigh the same? Do they have the same amount of weight?*

If the child agrees that they weigh the same, proceed. If not, say *make them the same* and let him manipulate the balls till he agrees. Once he has agreed, say,

*Now I am going to make this ball into a hot dog.*

Roll one of the two balls into a hot dog shape. When you have completed the transformation, put the two pieces of clay in front of the child and ask:

5. *Does this one* (pointing to the hot dog) *weigh the same as this one* (pointing to the ball) *or does this one weigh more, or does this one weigh more?*
6. Depending on the child's answer to question five, ask either *Why do they weigh the same?* or *Why does this one weigh more?*

Record the answer carefully.

This ends the procedure, so you should praise and thank the child. You might also want to play a bit with the child with some other toy of the child's choosing, to make sure that the whole process is pleasant to the child.

## Scoring

For each of the crucial questions, decide whether or not the child "conserved." To be judged as having conserved, the child must not only have said the two objects or sets were the same after transformation, he must also give a valid reason, such as the following:

You haven't added any or taken any away so they have to be the same.

*or*

One is longer but it is also skinnier so it is still the same.

*or*

If I made it back into a ball it would be the same.

## Analysis

Compare the child's performance on the three types of conservation. Did the child conserve on all three? If not, was the child's performance consistent with the typically observed sequence of acquisition? (If the child conserved weight but not mass or number, that would be contrary to research data). What else, other than the child's basic comprehension of conservation, might affect the child's answers in a test of this kind? Was the child interested or bored? Were there distractions in the environment? Might the sequence in which the items were given have any effect? Do you think it would have mattered, for example, if conservation of weight had been tested before conservation of mass? If one were designing a study to examine the acquisition of these conservations, would one want to have all children given the items in the same order or should the order be randomized?

If several students have completed this project you may want to combine your data and analyze children's success on these three conservations as a function of age. Do your collective findings match the results of existing research?

# PROJECT 10

## The Pendulum

This is a simplified version of the Inhelder and Piaget pendulum problem. To complete this project you should locate a child between roughly age 8 and 16, obtaining the parents' permission for the testing in the usual way.

### Equipment

Because the physical objects are so important for this problem you need to collect your equipment carefully and test it before you start. You will need three pieces of strong, flexible string (one about 25 cm, one about 37 cm, and one 50 cm long). You will also need three similar objects of varying weights. Fishing sinkers work well, as do keys, but the lightest one should be heavy enough so that it will weigh down the string and allow it to swing.

If you can complete the testing in some location in which you have a chance to tie all three strings to some overhead rod or other object, that would be best, since it leaves you free to write down what your subject does. Otherwise you will have to hold the top of each string when your subject wishes to use that string in a test.

### Procedure

Tell your subject:

*I am doing a class project about how different people go about solving a problem. The problem I would like you to solve is to find out what makes a pendulum swing faster or slower.*

Pause at this point and demonstrate how you can attach a weight to the string, and push the weight to start the pendulum swinging. Demonstrate this with more than one weight/string combination so that it is clear that there is variability in the speed of the pendulum swing. Then say:

*You need to figure out what makes the pendulum swing faster or slower. You can use any of these three strings and these three weights to help you figure this out. I'll be taking notes about what you do and say while you are working on the problem.*

Record each combination the subject tries, in the order of the attempts. If you can, you should also record any comments the subject makes in the process. Allow the subject to continue until he or she gives you an answer; if no answer is forthcoming, you may ask after a period of time, some question like, *Can you figure out what makes the pendulum move fast or slow?* If that does not promote an answer, or the subject seems very frustrated or bored, you may terminate the procedure and thank the subject for his or her help. If the subject has not solved the problem, you'll want to reassure him or her by pointing out that this is a really hard problem and that lots of kids his or her age have a hard time figuring it out.

### Analysis and Report

Did your subject solve the problem? (That is, did he or she figure out that it is the length of string and not the weight that determines the speed of the pendulum?)

How many separate string/weight combination tests did it take to reach some conclusion, whether the conclusion was correct or not?

Did the subject try various string/weight combinations in any systematic order? Or were the various attempts more random?

Did the subject talk to himself/herself while working on the problem? Was this self-talk directed at keeping track of things he or she had tried, or at thinking through the problem?

Did your subject's performance fit the findings from Piaget's and others' studies on the age at which formal operations develops?

**8**

# THE DEVELOPMENT OF LANGUAGE

A friend of mine listened one morning at breakfast while her 6-year-old and 3-year-old had the following conversation about the relative dangers of forgetting to feed the goldfish versus overfeeding the goldfish:

**6-year-old:** It's worse to forget to feed them.
**3-year-old:** No, it's badder to feed them too much.
**6-year-old:** You don't say badder, you say worser.
**3-year-old:** But it's baddest to give them too much food.
**6-year-old:** No it's not. It's worstest to forget to feed them.

We are all amused by "mistakes" like *baddest* or *worst,* and linguists have learned an enormous amount about children's language by studying such errors—just as Piaget learned an enormous amount about the child's thinking by studying "mistakes." But one of the really remarkable things about language is that children make so few errors of this kind. Out of the enormously complex set of sounds they hear in the language of those around them, children somehow come to be able to speak their native tongue with fluency and accuracy within only a few years. At 6 or 8 months we hear a baby babbling a few sounds; by 18 months the child will probably be using 30 or 40 separate words; and by 3 years children construct long and complex sentences, like those of the 3-year-old in the conversation about the goldfish. Parents usually find this whole sequence charming, sometimes amusing, but most of us don't spend a lot of time worrying about just how a child manages all this.

For psychologists and linguists, though, the child's rapid and skillful acquisition of language has remained an enduring puzzle. Is some kind of language-learning faculty built into the organism? Is the child "taught" language in some direct way? Does the child "figure it out" based on what he hears?

In attempting to answer such questions, the vast majority of linguists have focused on describing and explaining changes in both grammar (which the linguists call **syntax**) and word meaning (called **semantics**). Lately there have also been some attempts to explain differences in the rate of language development from one child to the next, and differences in individual children's style of language learning. In the terms I used in chapters 6 and 7, then, most of the research I want to talk about deals with questions of changes in structure, although there is at least some data on differences in power as well. But before I can explore either, I need to go back a step.

**syntax**
The rules for forming sentences; also called grammar.

**semantics**
The rules for conveying meaning in language.

## What Is Language Anyway?

What do we mean by language? What are we trying to explain? Linguists use the term *language* to include several key features:

1.  It is an "arbitrary system of *symbols*" (Brown, 1965, p. 246). Words *stand for* things. The particular combination of sounds (or gestures, in language among the deaf) used to stand for some object or event or relationship varies from one language to another, so the symbols are arbitrary.

2. It is *rule governed*. Every language has certain rules for stringing together individual symbols, or creating new words—like the rules for creating superlatives, or for past tenses, or for the order of words in sentences.

3. Within those rules, language is *creative*. Speakers of a language combine symbols in new ways to create new meanings. You are not restricted to some repertoire of sentences you have heard and learned; you create sentences according to your need at the moment.

Thus language is not just a collection of sounds. Very young babies make several different sounds but we do not consider that they are using language since they do not appear to use those sounds to *refer* to things or events (that is, they do not use the sounds as symbols), and they do not combine individual sounds into different orders to create varying meaning. So far as we know, for example, it does not matter whether a 6-month-old says *kikiki bababa* or *bababa kikiki*.

Some other animals, most notably primates like chimps and possibly other mammals like dolphins, can also learn to use sound or gestural systems in the symbolic and creative way that we define as language. Chimps, for example, can learn to use sign language or point to sequences of symbols, even creating new combinations of such symbols (e.g., Savage-Rumbaugh, 1990). But in most cases it takes a long time to teach them, and they have to be given a steady dose of delicious goodies as reinforcers in order to maintain the language. In contrast, as Flavell puts it, "Draconian measures would be needed to *prevent* most children from learning to talk" (1985, p. 248). And as

Linguists who have worked with chimps like this one, who has been taught sign language, agree that the animals can fairly easily learn signs for individual objects or actions. But they do not agree about whether the chimps use these symbols creatively, to make new meanings, as children do from the beginning.

any parent can tell you, once they learn, it is virtually impossible to shut them up!

The developmental process in infants and young children, from prelanguage sounds and gestures to language, follows a remarkably common set of steps.

## The Early Steps of Language Development

### *Before the First Word: The Prelinguistic Phase*

**prelinguistic phase**
The period before the child speaks his first words.

Given the definition I've just offered, you may well think that there is little reason for language researchers to study the sounds or gestures of infants since the baby's early sounds are not yet language. Why not start by studying the first obvious words? But investigators have recently discovered that the sounds and gestures that infants make in this **prelinguistic phase** are intimately linked to the emergence of the first words. So let's go back to the beginning.

*Early Perception of Language.* Recall from Chapter 5 that babies are born with or very soon develop remarkably good ability to discriminate speech sounds. By 1 or 2 months they pay attention to and can tell the difference between many individual letter sounds and intonation patterns; within a few more months they clearly can discriminate among syllables or words. They also have figured out that these speech sounds are matched by the speaker's mouth movements. Thus from very early—perhaps from birth—the baby is tuned quite acutely to the language she hears around her.

**cooing**
An early stage during the prelinguistic period, from about 1–4 months of age, when vowel sounds are repeated, particularly the *uuu* sound.

*Early Sounds.* This early perceptual skill is not matched right away by much skill in producing sounds. From birth to about 1 month of age, the most common sound an infant makes is a cry, although there are other fussing, gurgling, and satisfied sounds. This sound repertoire expands at about 1 or 2 months, when we begin to hear some laughing and **cooing** vowel sounds, like *uuuuu*. Sounds like these are usually signals of pleasure in babies, and may show quite a lot of variation in tone, running up and down in volume or pitch.

**babbling**
The vocalizing, often repetitively, of consonant-vowel combinations by an infant, typically beginning at about 6 months of age.

Consonant sounds appear only at about 6 or 7 months, frequently combined with vowel sounds to make a kind of syllable. Babies this age seem to begin to play with these sounds, often repeating the same sound over and over (such as *babababababa,* or *dahdahdah*). This new sound pattern is called **babbling,** and it makes up about half of babies' non-crying sounds from about 6 to 12 months of age (Mitchell & Kent, 1990).

Any parent can tell you that babbling is a delight to listen to. The issue for researchers has been whether it is linked in any way to later language. Until perhaps 10 years ago, most psychologists thought that it wasn't. Babbling seemed to be only a sort of vocal play. But now there are several sets of evidence that suggest a much closer connection to language. For one thing, we know that infants' babbling gradually acquires some of what linguists call the *intonational pattern* of the language they are hearing—a process Elizabeth Bates refers to as "learning the tune before the words" (Bates et al., 1987). At the very least, infants do seem to develop at least two such "tunes" in their babbling. When they babble with a rising intonation at the end of a string of sounds it seems to signal a desire for a response; a falling intonation requires no response.

The other hint of a connection between babbling and language parallels some findings I talked about in Chapter 5. You'll remember that very young babies are able to make discriminations between many pairs of sounds, including some that do not appear in the language they are hearing. This broad range of auditory discrimination is largely lost by 12 months, as the baby begins to focus more and more on the sound distinctions that carry meaning in the language she is listening to. Similarly, babies' babbling initially includes sounds that are not present in the language they hear. Six-month-old babies hearing English may babble vowel sounds characteristic of German or French; babies hearing Japanese may use an l sound (as in *la la la*) that does not occur in Japanese. But by 9 or 10 months, the baby's babbling begins to drift more and more toward the sample of sounds she is hearing as the non-heard sounds drop out (e.g., Oller, 1981). Findings like these do not tell us that babbling is *necessary* for language development, but they certainly make it look as if babbling is part of a connected developmental process that begins at birth.

*Gestures in the First Year.*   Another part of that connected developmental process may be a kind of gestural language that develops in these same months. Babies will begin to play those wonderful gestural games, like patty-cake and bye-bye, at about 8 or 9 months; shortly afterward they begin to "demand" or "ask" for things using gestures or combinations of gestures and sound. A 10-month-old baby who apparently wants you to hand her a favorite toy may stretch and reach for it, opening and closing her hand, accompanied by whining sounds or other heartrending noises. There is no mistaking the meaning (Bates, Camaioni, & Volterra, 1975; Bates et al., 1987).

Interestingly, the infant's ability to *understand* the meaning of individual words, which linguists call **receptive language,** also seems to begin at about 9 or 10 months. In one recent study, Elizabeth Bates and her colleagues asked mothers about their 10-month-old babies' understanding of various words (Bates, Bretherton, & Snyder, 1988). On average, the mothers listed 17.9 words understood. By 13 months, that number was up to nearly 50 words. Since infants of 9 to 13 months typically do not speak any individual words, findings like these make it clear that receptive language comes before **expressive language;** children understand before they can speak.

Adding up these bits of information, we can see that a whole series of changes seem to come together at 9 or 10 months—the beginning of meaningful gestures, the "drift" of babbling toward the heard language sounds, imitative gestural games, and the first comprehension of individual words. It is as if the child now understands something about the process of communication and is intending to communicate to the adult.

### The First Words

Shortly afterward, the first words can be heard. A *word,* as linguists usually define it, is any sound or set of sounds that is used consistently to refer to

**receptive language**
Term used to describe the child's ability to understand (receive) language, as contrasted to his ability to express language.

**expressive language**
The term used to describe the child's skill in speaking and communicating orally.

Before they speak their first words, babies successfully use gestures and body language in consistent ways to communicate meaning. Even deaf children, like 10-month-old Kevin Berrigan whose family was filmed as part of the *Childhood* series, spontaneously use such gestures—pointing, reaching, and signaling meanings such as "come here" or "give me that." This photo is a video still from the *Childhood* television series (*Source:* ©Thirteen/WNET).

some thing, action, or quality. But it can be *any* sound. It doesn't have to be a sound that matches words the adults are using. Brenda, a little girl studied by Ronald Scollon (1976), used the sound *nene* as one of her first words. It seemed to mean primarily liquid food, since she used it for milk, juice, and bottle. But she also used it to refer to mother and sleep. (You can see some of Brenda's other early words in the left-hand column of Table 8.1.)

Parents may miss some of the more idiosyncratic of these early words, but they are nonetheless quite reliable reporters if you ask them carefully. You can get some sense of the timing of the first word from just such a source from Figure 8.1, which shows the average and typical range of timing for a group of 381 infants whose language milestones were reported by parents to their pediatricians during regular first-year office visits (Capute et al., 1986). The average baby spoke her first word at 11.1 months, and 95 percent of all the children used their first word between 6.5 and 15.2 months.

Often, a child's earliest words are used only in one or two specific situations and in the presence of many cues. The child may say doggie or bow-wow only to such promptings as "How does the doggie go?" or "What's that?" Later the child may use a word spontaneously and in a wider variety of contexts. Some linguists see this shift as a signal that the child has now grasped the basic *symbolic* characteristic of language—that things have names. There is some suggestive evidence of this in research by Elizabeth Bates and her

TABLE 8.1

*Brenda's Vocabulary at 14 and 19 Months*

| 14 months | 19 months[a] | | |
|---|---|---|---|
| aw u (I want, I don't want) | baby | nice | boat |
| nau (no) | bear | orange | bone |
| d di (daddy, baby) | bed | pencil | checkers |
| d yu (down, doll) | big | write | corder |
| nene (liquid food) | blue | paper | cut |
| e (yes) | Brenda | pen | I do |
| maem (solid food) | cookie | see | met |
| ada (another, other) | daddy | shoe | Pogo |
| | eat | sick | Ralph |
| | at | swim | you too |
| | (hor)sie | tape | climb |
| | mama | walk | jump |
| | mommy | wowow | |

[a]Brenda did not actually pronounce all these words the way an adult would. I have given the adult version since that is easier to read.
*Source:* R. Scollon, *Conversations with a one year old.* Honolulu: The University Press of Hawaii, 1976, pp. 47, 57–58.

coworkers (e.g., Bates, Bretherton, & Snyder, 1988). They have found, for example, that toddlers who show such broad and apparently symbolic use of words very early also show more rapid development at later stages of language than do those children whose early words are more "context bound." Whether this broader hypothesis is valid or not, we know that virtually all children begin to use individual words in symbolic ways by about 13 months of age.

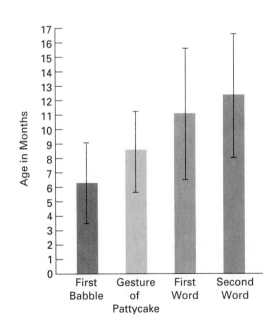

**FIGURE 8.1**

Average age and range of ages at which babies in the Capute study were reported to reach various early language milestones (*Source:* Capute et al., 1986, from Figure 1, p. 765).

*Adding New Words.*　Once the milestone of the first word is reached, toddlers typically go through a period of slow growth until they reach a vocabulary of perhaps 30 words. After that, it is common for children to spurt ahead, adding 10, 20, or 30 words in a period of weeks. You can see just such a pattern of slow and then rapid growth in Figure 8.2, which shows the vocabulary growth curves of six of the subjects studied longitudinally by Goldfield and Reznick (1990). You can also see the change in Table 8.1, which lists another child's vocabulary at 14 and at 19 months.

The rapid growth of vocabulary doesn't stop there. The typical 6-year-old English speaking child knows about *14,000* words (Templin, 1957), which translates to an addition of about nine words a day for the next four years. Amazing.

*Kinds of New Words.*　The early words in children's vocabularies are most likely to be what Katherine Nelson (1973) calls *general nominals*—names for classes of objects or people, like ball, car, milk, doggie, he, or that. Over half the first 50 words of the eight children she studied were of this type while only 13 percent were action words. Dedre Gentner (1982) has observed the same thing in her study of a little boy named Tad, whose early words are listed in Table 8.2, and the same pattern has been seen in studies of children learning other languages (including Japanese, Mandarin Chinese, German, English, and Turkish).

However, this noun-before-verb pattern does not hold for all children. Katherine Nelson (1973) first noticed that some toddlers use what she called an **expressive style.** For them, most early words are linked not to objects but to social relationships. They often learn pronouns (*you, me*) early, and use many more of what Nelson calls "personal-social" words, such as *no, yes, want,* or *please.* Their early vocabulary may also include some multi-word strings, like *love you, do it,* or *go away.* This is in sharp contrast to the children who use what Nelson calls a **referential style**—whose early vocabulary is made up predominantly of nominals.

**expressive style**
One of two styles of early language proposed by Nelson, characterized by low rates of noun-like terms and high use of personal-social words and phrases.

**referential style**
Second style of early language proposed by Nelson, characterized by emphasis on objects and their naming and description.

**FIGURE 8.2**

Each of the lines in this figure represents the vocabulary growth of one of the 13 children studied by Goldfield and Reznick in their longitudinal study. The six children represented in the figure each showed the most common pattern, with slow initial growth, followed by a fairly rapid spurt after about 30 words had been learned (*Source:* Goldfield & Reznick, 1990, Figure 3, p. 177).

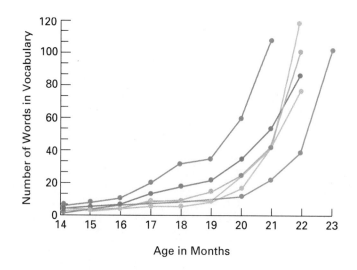

## TABLE 8.2

*Words Learned by Tad from 11 to 21 Months of Age*

| Age | | Nominals ("nouns") | | Predicates ("verbs") | Expressive Words | Indeterminate Words |
|---|---|---|---|---|---|---|
| 11–16 mo. | dog<br>duck<br>daddy<br>mama | teh (teddy bear)<br>dipe (diaper)<br>car<br>owl | keys<br>cheese<br>eye | yuk | | toot toot |
| 18–19 mo. | cow<br>cup<br>spoon<br>apple<br>knee<br>ball<br>jeep | truck<br>juice<br>bowl<br>teeth<br>elbow<br>block | kitty<br>bottle<br>towel<br>cheek<br>map<br>bus | hot<br>happy<br>down<br>up | oops<br>boo<br>hi<br>bye<br>up oh | bath<br>pee pee<br>TV |
| 21 mo. | toe<br>moon<br>bird<br>water | happy sauce<br>bee<br>pole<br>cookie | tree<br>wheel<br>peach | stuck<br>off<br>down<br>out | | back (piggy-back ride) |
| Percentage | | 68 | | 15 | 8 | 8 |

*Source:* After Gentner, 1982, Table 11.1, p. 306.

I'll talk further about such style differences at the end of the chapter. For now I only want to point out that while noun-like terms are the most common early words, they are not the only ones, and some children use them relatively infrequently in the early months.

### The First Sentences

After the first word, the next big step is when the child begins to string words into sentences, initially using only two words, then three and four and more. The first two-word sentences usually appear between 18 and 24 months. In fact you can see two examples in the list of Brenda's 19-month vocabulary shown on the right-hand side of Table 8.1.

But just as the first spoken words are preceded by apparently meaningful gestures, the first two-word sentences have gestural precursors as well. Toddlers often combine a single word with a gesture to create a "two-word meaning" before they actually use two words together in their speech. Elizabeth Bates (Bates et al., 1987) suggests an example: The infant may point to Daddy's shoe and say *Daddy,* as if to convey "Daddy's shoe." Or she may say *Cookie!* while simultaneously reaching out her hand and opening and closing her fingers, as if to say "Give cookie!" In both cases a sentence-like meaning is conveyed by the use of gesture and body language. Linguists call these word-and-gesture combinations **holophrases**, and they are common in children between 12 and 18 months.

Once the actual speaking of two-word sentences begins, the child, of course, continues to use single words and holophrases for some months. But

**holophrases**
The expression of a whole idea in a single word. Characteristic of the child's language from about 12–18 months.

within a year or so, most one-word utterances drop out and the child uses three- and four-word sentences and creates complex combinations of words. To describe this fairly steady (and remarkably rapid) emergence of complex sentences I need to journey into the realm of grammar or syntax.

## The Development of Grammar

In analyzing early grammar development, most linguists follow the lead of Roger Brown (one of the most distinguished students of language development), who divided the process into several steps or phases.

### Stage I Grammar

The first step, which Brown called Stage I grammar, has several distinguishing features: The sentences are *short*—generally two or three words—and they are *simple*. Nouns, verbs, and adjectives are usually included, but virtually all the purely grammatical markers (which linguists call **inflections**) are missing. At the beginning, for example, children learning English do not normally use the *s* for plurals or put the *ed* ending on verbs to make the past tense, nor do they use the *s* of the possessive or auxiliary verbs like *am* or *do*. Because only the really critical words are present in these early sentences, Brown (Brown & Bellugi, 1964; Brown, 1973) describes this as **telegraphic speech**. The child's language sounds rather like what we say when we send a telegram. We keep in all the essential words—usually nouns, verbs, and modifiers—and leave out all the prepositions, auxiliary verbs, and the like.

At this early stage, children's imitation of adults' speech, as well as their spontaneous speech, is telegraphic. If you ask a child of 20- to 24-months to say "I am playing with the dogs," the child is likely to say "play dog," or "I play dog," thus omitting the auxiliary verb (*am*), the verb ending (*ing*), the preposition (*with*), the article (*the*), and the plural ending (*s*).

Interestingly, there is now some dispute among linguists about whether precisely this form of telegraphic speech occurs in children learning all languages. Some research seems to show that what determines the words that children use in their early sentences is the amount of *stress* normally placed on such words when that particular language is spoken. In English (and in many other languages) nouns, verbs, and adjectives are stressed in speech while the inflections are not. But in languages like Turkish, in which inflections are more stressed, children seem to use inflections much earlier (Gleitman & Wanner, 1988). Findings like these certainly raise some interesting questions about the universality of some of the patterns Brown and others have described, such as telegraphic speech. But there is little dispute about the universality of the pattern of initially short and simple sentences.

There is also no dispute about the assertion that even at this early stage children create sentences following rules—not adult rules, to be sure, but rules nonetheless. They focus on certain types of words and put them together in particular orders.

When evidence of this regularity in children's early sentences began to emerge in the early 1960s, a number of linguists, such as Martin Braine,

inflections
The grammatical "markers" such as plurals, possessives, past tenses, and equivalent.

telegraphic speech
A characteristic of early child sentences in which everything but the crucial words is omitted, as if for a telegram.

(1963) tried to write a grammar for this "foreign" language spoken by toddlers. Such efforts have now been largely abandoned, for two reasons. First, although all children studied seem to have some kind of rules for their first sentences, all individual children do not seem to use precisely the same rules (Braine, 1976). Second, it became clear quite quickly that children convey many different *meanings* with exactly the same sentence forms. If we are going to understand this early language, we have to pay attention to semantics as well as to grammar.

For example, young children frequently use a sentence made up of two nouns, such as *Mommy sock* or *sweater chair* (to use some often quoted examples from Lois Bloom's 1973 analysis). We might conclude from this that a "two-noun" form is a basic grammatical characteristic of early child language. But that misses the complexity. For instance, the child in Bloom's study who said *Mommy sock* said it on two different occasions. The first time was when she picked up her mother's sock and the second was when the mother put the child's own sock on the child's foot. In the first case, *Mommy sock* seems to mean Mommy's sock (a possessive relationship). But in the second instance the child seems to convey "Mommy is putting a sock on me," which is an *agent* (Mommy) and *object* (sock) relationship.

Some other different meanings that children convey with their earliest sentences are listed in Table 8.3. Not all children express all of these relationships or meanings in their early word combinations. Nor do all children acquire these several meanings or constructions in a fixed order. But all children appear to express at least several of these patterns in their earliest, simplest sentences (Maratsos, 1983).

### Stage II Grammar

Most linguists mark the beginning of Stage II at the point when the child begins to use any of the grammatical inflections such as plurals, past tenses, auxiliary verbs, prepositions, and the like. You can get a better feeling for the sound of the change from Table 8.4 on the next page, which lists some of the sentences of a little boy named Daniel, recorded by David Ingram (1981).

**TABLE 8.3**

*Some of the Different Meanings Children Appear to Express in Their Stage I Grammar*

| Meaning | Examples |
| --- | --- |
| Agent-action | Sarah eat; Daddy jump |
| Action-object | Eat cookie; read book |
| Possessor-possessed object | Mommy sock; Timothy lunch |
| Action-location | Come here; play outside |
| Located object-location | Sweater chair; juice table |
| Attribute-modified object | Big book; red house |
| Nomination | That cookie; it dog |
| Recurrence | More juice; other book |

*Source:* Maratsos, 1983.

The left-hand column lists some of Daniel's sentences at about 21 months of age, when he was still using the simplest forms; the right hand column lists some of his sentences only 2 1/2 months later (age 23–24 months), when he had just moved into Stage II.

*Adding Inflections.*    You can easily see in Daniel's language that he has not added all the inflections at once. He starts with a few—in his case mostly the *s* for plural—and then adds them a bit at a time. It turns out that within each language community, children seem to add inflections and more complex word orders in fairly predictable sequences. Among children learning English, Roger Brown (1973) has found that the earliest inflection is most often the *ing* added onto a verb, such as in *I playing,* or *doggie running.* Then come prepositions like *on* and *in*; the plural *s* on nouns; irregular past tenses such as *broke* or *ran*; possessives; articles, such as *a* and *the* in English; the *s* that we add to third person verbs, as in *He wants;* regular past tenses like *played* and *wanted;* and the various forms of the auxiliary verb, as in *I am not going.*

**TABLE 8.4**

*Examples of Daniel's Stage I and Stage II Sentences*

| Stage I Sentences (age 21 months) | Stage II Sentences (age 23 months) |
|---|---|
| A bottle | A little boat |
| Broke-it | Cat there |
| Here (the) bottle | Doggies here |
| Hi daddy | Boat here |
| Horse doggie | Give you the book |
| Broke it | It's a boy |
| It a bottle | It's a robot |
| Kitty cat | It's cat |
| Oh a doggie | Little box there |
| Poor Daddy | No book |
| Thank you | Oh cars |
| That hat? | Oh doggie |
| That monkey | Sit down |
| Want a bottle | This a bucket |
| Want bottle | That flowers |
| What that? | There's a boat there |
| | Those little boat |
| | What those? |
| | What's that? |
| | What this? |
| | Where going? |
| | Where the boat? |

*Source:* Reprinted by permission of the publisher from "Early patterns of grammatical development" by D. Ingram, in R. E. Stark (Ed.), *Language behavior in infancy and early childhood.* Tables 6 and 7, pp. 344–345. Copyright 1981 by Elsevier Science Publishing Co., Inc.

*Questions and Negatives.* There are also predictable sequences in the child's developing use of questions and negatives. In each case, the child seems to go through periods when he creates types of sentences that he has not heard adults use, but that are consistent with the particular set of rules he is using. For example, in the development of questions there is a point at which the child gets a *wh* word (who, what, when, where, why) at the front end of a sentence, but doesn't yet have the auxiliary verb put in the right place, such as *Why it is resting now?* Similarly, in the development of negatives, there is a stage in which the *not*, *n't*, or *no* is put in, but the auxiliary verb is omitted, as in *I not crying*, or *there no squirrels*.

*Overregularization.* Another intriguing phenomenon of this second phase of sentence construction that underlines the rule-making and rule-following quality of even the earliest sentences is **overregularization** or overgeneralization. This is what the two little girls were doing in the conversation about the goldfish when they created new regularized forms of superlatives (badder, baddest, worser, and worsest). We can hear the same thing in children's creation of past tenses like *wented, goed,* or *ated.* Stan Kuczaj (1977, 1978) has found that young children initially learn a small number of irregular past tenses and use them correctly for a short time. But then rather suddenly the child seems to discover the rule of adding *ed* and overgeneralizes this rule to all verbs. This type of "error" is particularly common among children between ages 3 and 5.

> **overregularization**
> The tendency on the part of children to make the language regular, such as using past tenses like *beated* or *goed.*

All of the changes I have been describing are delightful to listen to. But the changes are important for theorists, too, who are impressed with the fact that the child creates sentences she could not have heard, but which make excellent sense within the rules of her own grammar.

### Later Grammar Development

Past these early stages, children's language continues to develop in various ways. In particular, more complex and difficult sentence forms are added throughout elementary school, and recurrent overregularization errors are eliminated (Bowerman, 1985). For instance, passive forms like *the food is eaten by the cat,* are not well understood even by 5- and 6-year-olds, and are not used much in spontaneous speech until several years later. "Tag questions" also develop quite late in English speaking children. These are the questions we stick onto the end of a declarative sentence to turn it into a question, such as *You can play the piano, can't you?* or *They are studying math, aren't they?* Getting the right tag onto the sentence is a fairly complex process, and children are simply not skilled at it until age 8 or 9 (Dennis, Sugar, & Whitaker, 1982). Children also learn gradually how to string two sentences or clauses together, or to embed one within another, as in *John is chewing gum and so am I* or *The apple that fell off the tree is red.*

Obviously grammatical development does not end in first grade. Vocabulary continues to increase, and more complex sentence forms are learned later. But the really giant strides occur between 1 and 5 years of age, as the child moves from single words to complex questions, negatives, and commands.

Let me pause for a brief summary of the key points about grammatical development before I move on to a discussion of word meaning.

1. The earliest sentences created by children speaking any language have certain features in common, including shortness, simplicity, and the predominant use of nouns, verbs, and modifiers.
2. From the earliest two-word sentences, children's language is creative. The child is not just copying sentences she has heard; she is creating new ones that "go beyond the data" provided by the language she hears.
3. That creativity seems to be achieved by following some set of rules. The rule system is not the same as for adult language, and not identical from one child to the next, but all children appear to create sentences in a non-random manner.
4. Subsequent changes in children's grammar, while not the same in all languages, are predictable and sequential within any one language. The *rate* of development varies, but the basic outline of the sequence seems to be shared, especially the early steps in the sequence.

These summary statements describe what happens when a child learns a *single* language. But what about children who are exposed to two or more languages from the beginning? How confusing is this for a child? And how can parents ease the process? I've discussed the problems of bilingual children in the box on pages 310–311.

## The Development of Word Meaning

The study of early grammar takes us a long way, but to understand language development, we need to know more than how children learn to string words together to form sentences. We also have to understand how the words in those sentences come to have meaning. Linguists are still searching for good ways to describe (or explain) children's emerging word meaning. So far, several sets of questions have dominated the research.

### What Comes First, the Meaning or the Word?

The most fundamental question is whether the child learns a word to describe a category or class he has *already* created mentally as a result of his manipulations of the world around him, or whether the existence of a word forces the child to create new cognitive categories. This may seem like a highly abstract argument, but it touches on the fundamental issue of the relationship between language and thought. Does the child learn to represent objects to himself *because* he now has language, or does language simply come along at about this point and make the representations easier?

The answer seems to be both (Greenberg & Kuczaj, 1982; Clark, 1983). First of all, I pointed out in chapters 5 and 7 that we now know that quite young babies have at least some kind of ability to represent things to themselves, since they are able to remember and imitate objects and actions over periods of time—long before they have language to assist them. The development of a kind of gestural language before spoken language suggests the same thing. We also know that in the early stages of language development, children seem to apply words (or even to create words) to describe categories or classes they have already created in actions or images. For example, Brenda's word *nene,* which seemed to mean liquid food and the pleasure that goes with it, was probably a word to describe an already existing mental category or scheme.

As further support for the cognitive basis of early language, we know that some grammatical categories, such as prepositions, are not added all at once, but appear *in* the child's language over several years, added only when the child appears to understand the underlying relationship. So, for example, the word *in* is used before the word *between,* and both appear before *in front of* (Johnston, 1985). All of these bits of evidence point to the likelihood that in the early years concepts *precede* language in many instances.

But it seems equally clear that children's concepts and classification systems are affected by the labels attached to objects, too. As the noted Russian psychologist Lev Vygotsky pointed out years ago (1962), there is a point somewhere in the child's second year when she "discovers" that objects have names. In part this discovery itself seems to rest on a new cognitive ability, the ability to categorize things. In one longitudinal study, for example, Alison Gopnik and Andrew Meltzoff (1987) found that the "naming explosion" typically occurs just after, or at the same time as, children first show spontaneous

One of this child's early words was *cookie.* But knowing this doesn't tell us whether the child learned this word early because she already had a concept of cookie, or whether she learned the concept cookie because she knew the word.

## Learning Two Languages: Bilingual Children

There is a whole set of both practical and theoretical questions surrounding the issue of bilingualism:

- Should parents who speak different native languages try to expose their children to both, or will that only confuse the child and make any kind of language learning harder? What's the best way to do this?
- Is it really true that children learn second (or third or fourth) languages more easily than adults do? In theoretical terms, this is a question about the existence of some kind of critical period for language learning.
- If a child arrives at school age without speaking the dominant language of schooling, what is the best way for the child to acquire that second language?

### Learning Two Languages at the Same Time

Parents should have no fears about exposing their child to two or more languages from the very beginning. Such simultaneous exposure does seem to result in slightly slower early steps in word learning and sentence construction, but bilingual children catch up rapidly. Interestingly, among their early vocabularies bilingual children may use two words for the same object, one in each language. Since children learning only one language rarely use two words for the same object, this pattern among bilinguals suggests that they have understood, at some level, that there are two language systems involved (Mikes, 1990). Perhaps because of this greater "metalinguistic" understanding, there is some indication that bilingual children actually have slightly advanced cognitive development compared to monolingual children (Bialystok, 1988; Hakuta & Diaz, 1985).

There are at least two good ways to go about helping a child to learn two languages fluently. The most obvious strategy is to speak both languages to the child from the beginning. If you do this, you can simplify the child's task greatly if you arrange it so that each language comes from a different source. If Mom's native language is English, and Dad's is Italian, have Mom speak only English to the infant or toddler, while Dad speaks only Italian. (The parents will of course speak to each other in whatever language they have in common.) If both parents speak both languages to the child, or mix them up in their own speech, this is a much more difficult situation for the child and language learning will be delayed (McLaughlin, 1984). It will also work if one language is always spoken at home, and the other in a day-care center, or with playmates, or in some other outside situation.

### The Question of Timing

So far I've been talking about exposing the child to both languages very early. But does it work as well if the child learns the second language much later? More generally, is there some age limit, some critical period, beyond which it is no longer possible for a child (or adult) to learn a second language with native-speaker skill?

The conventional wisdom for many years has been that there is such a critical period, with the upper boundary at about age 12 (Lenneberg, 1967; Snow, 1987). That is, linguists and psychologists argued that children younger than age 12 could fairly easily acquire native-like fluency, but adolescents and adults could not. And to speak the second language without an ac-

categorization of mixed sets of objects. Having discovered "categories," the child may now rapidly learn the names for already existing categories. But as Katherine Nelson (1988) argues, if the child assumes that there is a one-to-one

cent was thought to have an even narrower critical period—perhaps the first few years of life. This hypothesis certainly makes sense in terms of the data I described in Chapter 5, showing that babies rapidly lose their ability to make discriminations between sound pairs that do not appear in the language they are hearing. If children older than 1 or 2 can no longer *hear* crucial sound differences in some other language accurately, then surely it would not be possible for older children or adults to learn an unaccented second language.

Reasonable as that seems, it may not be true. Recent research suggests that when the learning conditions are similar, adults actually learn second languages more easily than do children (Snow, 1987). The difficulty for most adults learning a second language is that they are much less likely to be consistently exposed to that language. Children, in contrast, are more likely to be immersed—learning it in school, using the second language in their play with peers.

The one area in which younger learners do seem to be at an advantage is in pronunciation, but a number of studies now show that adults are *able* to learn to speak without accent under sufficiently intense training conditions (Neufeld, 1978). So while it is true that the infant is more sensitive to various sound contrasts, it is not true that the ability to make sound discriminations is totally lost. Those synapses can be recreated with exposure and training at a later time.

## Bilingual Education

Both the questions I have been discussing have some obvious relevance to the issue of bilingual education. In the United States today, there are 2.5 million school-age children for whom English is not the primary language of the home (Hakuta & Garcia, 1989). Many of those children arrive at school with little or no facility in English. Educators have had to grapple with the task of teaching children a second language at the same time that they are trying to teach them subject matter such as reading and mathematics. The problem for the schools has been to figure out the best way to do this. Should the child be immediately immersed in the new language? Should the child learn basic academic skills in his native language and only later learn English as a second language? Or is there some combination of the two that will work?

These are hard questions to answer, in part because there have been so many different variations attempted, with widely varying quality of teaching. Messy as the research is, however, one thread still runs through it: Neither full immersion nor programs teaching English as a second language are as effective as truly bilingual programs in which the child is given at least some of her basic instruction in subject matter in her native language in the first year or two of school, but is also exposed to the second language in the same classroom (Padilla et al., 1991; Willig, 1985). When both languages are maintained for several years before the child is expected to function full-time with English, the results seem to be most positive. Interestingly, in her analysis of this research, Ann Willig has found that the ideal arrangement is very much like what works best at home with toddlers: If some subjects are always taught in one language, and other subjects in the other language, children learn both most easily. But if each sentence is translated, children do not learn the new language as quickly or as well.

correspondence between words and concepts, then not only does there have to be a word for every concept, there also has to be a concept for every word. So the existence of new words helps to create new concepts and new schemes.

Katya Kalugin, an 18-month-old Russian child, is beginning to talk. One of the characteristics of this early age is a kind of "naming explosion" in which children learn a great many nouns in a very short space of time. In this phase children often do just what Katya is doing here—pointing to some object as if to say to the nearby adult, "Tell me what the name of that is." This photo is a video still from the *Childhood* television series (*Source:* ©Thirteen/WNET).

### Extending the Class

But what kinds of concepts does the child start with? It turns out that studying early word usage provides a window to the child's early categories or concepts.

Suppose your 2-year-old, on catching sight of the family tabby, says *See kittie.* No doubt you will be pleased that the child has the right word applied to the animal. But this sentence alone doesn't tell you much about the word meaning the child has developed. What does the word "kittie" mean to the child? Does he think it is a name only for that *particular* fuzzy beast? Or does he think it applies to all furry creatures, all things with four legs, all things with pointed ears, or some other feature? One way to figure out the kind of class or category the child has created is to see what *other* creatures or things a child also calls a kittie. That is, how is the class *extended* in the child's language? If the child has created a *kittie* category that is based on furriness then many dogs and perhaps sheep would also be called kittie. If having a tail is a crucial feature for the child, then some breeds of cat that have no tails might not be called *kittie* by the child. Or, perhaps the child used the word *kittie* only for the family cat. This would imply a very narrow category indeed. The general question for researchers has been whether children tend to use words narrowly or broadly, overextending or underextending them.

Our current information tells us that children *overextend* their early words more often than they *underextend* them, so we're more likely to hear the word *cat* applied to dogs or guinea pigs than we are to hear it used for just one animal, or for a very small set of animals or objects (Clark, 1983). Some examples of the kind of overextensions that children create, collected by Eve Clark (1975), are in Table 8.5.

All children seem to show overextensions like these. But the particular classes the child creates are unique to each child. There doesn't seem to be any tendency for all children to use the word *cat* to apply to all four-footed animals, or to all furry creatures, or whatever. Each child overextends his words using his own distinct "rules," and those rules change as the child's vocabulary grows.

These overextensions *may* tell us something about the way children think, such as that they have broad classes. But before we jump to sweeping conclusions, we have to remember that part of the child's problem is that he simply doesn't know very many words. If he wants to talk about something, point out something, or ask for something, he has to use whatever words he has that are fairly close. Overextensions may thus arise from the child's desire to communicate, and may not tell us that the child fails to make the discriminations involved. The example Clark uses (1977) is of a child who wants to call attention to a horse. She may "know" that the horse is different from a dog, but she doesn't know the word for horse. So she says *doggie,* and the linguist says "Aha! Another overextension of the class." As the child learns the separate labels that are applied to the different subtypes of "fuzzy four-legged creatures" the overextension disappears (Clark, 1987.)

### How Does a Child Know What a Word Refers To?

Another very fundamental question about word meanings that has been the subject of hot debate among linguists in recent years is just how a child figures out which part of some scene a word may refer to. Here's the classic

**TABLE 8.5**

*Some Examples of Overextensions in the Language of Young Children*

| Word | Object or event for which the word was originally used | Other objects or events to which the word was later applied |
|------|--------------------------------------------------------|-------------------------------------------------------------|
| mooi | moon | cakes, round marks on windows, writing on windows and in books, round shapes in books, tooling in leather book covers, round postmarks, letter *O* |
| buti | ball | toy, radish, stone spheres at park entrance |
| baw | ball | (by another child) apples, grapes, eggs, squash, bell clapper, anything round |
| sch | sound of train | all moving machines |
| em | worm | flies, ants, all small insects, heads of timothy grass |
| fafer | sound of trains | steaming coffeepot, anything that hissed or made a noise |
| va | white plush dog | muffler, cat, father's fur coat |

*Source:* Reprinted with permission from Eve V. Clark, "Knowledge, context, and strategy in the acquisition of meaning." In *Georgetown University Round Table 1975: Developmental psycholinguistics: Theory and applications.* Edited by Daniel P. Dato. Copyright 1975 by Georgetown University, Washington, D.C., pp. 83–84.

example. A child sees a brown dog running across the grass with a bone in its mouth. An adult points and says *doggie*. From such an encounter the toddler is somehow supposed to figure out that *doggie* refers to the animal, and not to running, or bone, or dog-plus-bone, or brownness, or ears, or grass, or any other combination of elements in the whole scene.

Many linguists have proposed that a child could only conceivably cope with this monumentally complex task if he operated with some built-in biases or *constraints* (e.g., Markman & Hutchinson, 1984; Waxman & Kosowski, 1990), such as a built-in assumption that words refer to objects *or* events but not both, or an assumption that words refer to whole objects or not to their parts or attributes.

One such bias or constraint that has now been well documented is the tendency of 2- and 3-year-old children to assume that a new object label refers to the "basic" level rather than the subordinate or the superordinate level. The word *dog*, for example, is at the "basic" level, while *collie*, or *Fido* would be subordinate terms and *animal* would be the superordinate term. Faced with a new word for an object, children's first guess is that the term describes the basic level category (Waxman, Shipley, & Shepperson, 1991).

Another built-in assumption or constraint emphasized by many theorists is what Eve Clark (1983, 1987, 1990) has called the *principle of contrast*—if every word has a different meaning, then if a different word is used, it must refer to some different object or a different aspect of an object. For example, in a widely quoted study, Carey and Bartlett (1978) interrupted a play session with 2- and 3-year-old children by pointing to two trays and saying, "Bring me the chromium tray, not the red one, the chromium one." These children already knew the word *red* but did not know the word *chromium*. Nonetheless, most of the children were able to follow the instruction by bringing the non-red tray. Furthermore, a week later about half of them remembered that the word referred to some color and that the color was "not red." Thus they

Suppose Natasha Kalugin wanted to teach one-year-old Vera the word for grass, and pointed in the general direction of the ground, saying "grass" (in Russian, of course). How could Vera know to what the word refers? It might mean the green stuff with little blades; it might mean the ground, or the earthworm, or a bottle cap lying in the grass. The fact that children learn language quite readily, despite the enormity of the task, has pushed many theorists toward notions of built-in constraints. This photo is a video still from the *Childhood* television series (*Source:* ©Thirteen/WNET).

learned the meaning by contrast.

A related principle is that of *mutual exclusivity* (e.g., Markman, 1984; Au & Glusman, 1990). Children seem to begin the language learning process with an assumption that nouns refer to mutually exclusive object categories, and they initially resist using two words for the same object—a bias that interferes with the child's ability to learn superordinate terms such as *animal* or *furniture.*

But by no means do all linguists accept the idea of built-in constraints. Doubters such as Katherine Nelson (1988, 1990) point to a variety of apparently disconfirming facts: Many children's early words seem to cross the boundaries of objects and actions (such as, perhaps, Brenda's word *nene*). Young children also sometimes use more than one word for the same object, such as when children are learning two languages at once. More generally, Nelson points out that most of the research on such constraints or built-in biases has actually been done with children who were past the one-word stage of language. It is possible that such biases, if they exist, emerge as the child is learning language, rather than being built-in. For example, there are grammatical cues that may aid a child in figuring out what aspect of a scene some word may refer to. Verb endings like *ing* or *ed* may provide clues, as would the *s* for plural nouns. Children as young as 2 years seem to be able to use such grammatical cues in assigning meanings to new words (Waxman & Kosowski, 1990). But this does not explain how children acquire their *first* words, before such grammatical markers are understood or used by the child.

Nelson's alternative argument is that in fact the child rarely learns words in a situation in which the adult points and gives some word. Most often, the child tries out some sound or word and the adult guesses what the child may mean. Or the child points and the adult supplies the word. Thus the language the child hears, and the context in which it is spoken, is typically responsive to the child's own actions and emerging categories. The constraints on the process are the child's own conceptual system, and the ability of the adult to interpret the child's meaning rather than some built-in tendencies within the child. I find Nelson's arguments persuasive, but this debate is far from over. Two- and three-year-olds *do* appear to operate with the constraints or biases that various investigators have identified. So even if Nelson is correct, we still have the problem of figuring out how those assumptions or biases develop and whether they are shared by all children learning a variety of languages.

As these few examples illustrate, the study of the development of word meanings has been much more difficult to conceptualize than has been the development of grammar. What linguists are obviously searching for are the rules that govern this process, so that we can understand how and why children use words the way they do. So far, only a few general principles have emerged.

## Using Language: Communication and Self-Direction

In the past decade or so, linguists have also turned their attention to a third aspect of children's language, namely the way children learn to *use* it, either to communicate with others (an aspect of language often called **pragmat-**

**pragmatics**
The rules for the use of language in communicative interaction, such as the rules for taking turns, the style of speech appropriate for varying listeners, and equivalent.

**ics**), or to regulate their own behavior. How early do children know what kind of language to use in specific situations? How early do they learn the "rules" of conversation, such as that you are supposed to take turns?

Two general points are important from this large body of research. First, children seem to learn the pragmatics of language at a remarkably early age. For example, children as young as 18 months show adult-like gaze patterns when they are interacting with a parent: They look at the person who is talking, look away at the beginning of their own speaking turn, and then look at the listener again when they are signaling that they are about to stop talking (Rutter & Durkin, 1987). (Watch yourself the next time you are in a two-person conversation to see these gaze patterns in action.)

Furthermore children as young as 2 years adapt the form of their language to the situation they are in or the person they are talking to. Such a child may say *gimme* to another toddler as they grab the other child's glass but might say *more milk* to an adult (Becker, 1982). Among older children, language is even more clearly adapted to the listener: Four-year-olds use simpler language when they talk to 2-year-olds than when they talk to adults (e.g., Tomasello & Mannle, 1985). First graders explain things more fully to a stranger than to a friend (Sonnenschein, 1986) and are more polite to adults and strangers than to peers. Both of these trends are even clearer among fourth graders.

Partly, of course, all of this tells us something about the child's increasing ability to take another's perspective—a development I talked about in the last chapter. Changing one's language to adapt to another's need demonstrates the ability to comprehend that the other person has different needs or a different view point. But this research also tells us that from the beginning, the child's language is meant to *communicate* and the child will adapt the language form in order to achieve better communication.

Language seems to have another function for the child as well—namely, to help control or monitor her own behavior. Such "private speech," which may consist of more fragmentary sentences, muttering, or instructions to the self, is detectable from the earliest use of words and sentences. Many years ago, Ruth Weir (1962) listened by tape recorder as her 2-year-old son Anthony talked to himself in his crib, saying things like *What color, what color blanket, what color mop, what color glass,* as if he was trying out sentence forms. And when 2- or 3-year-olds play by themselves, they give themselves instructions, or stop themselves with words, or describe what they are doing: *No, not there, I put that there,* or *put it* (Furrow, 1984).

In older children, this self-regulatory use of language is still apparent, particularly when they are working on difficult problems, such as the muttering Flavell heard children doing when they were trying to remember things in his studies of memory strategies I described in Chapter 7. Initially, this self-regulatory language is audible; by age 9 or 10 it has largely gone underground (Bivens & Berk, 1990), with this shift occurring earlier among higher IQ children (Berk, 1986). If we connect this set of findings with the work on information processing I talked about in the last chapter, it begins to sound as if the child uses language audibly to remind himself of some new or complex processing strategy. As the strategy becomes better rehearsed and more flexibly learned, overt language is no longer needed. Such an interpretation is bolstered by the observation that even adults will use audible language in problem solving when they are faced with especially difficult tasks.

Even this brief foray into the research on the child's use of language points out that a full understanding of language development is going to require understanding of both cognitive development and of the child's social skills and understanding. It reminds us once again that the child is not divided up into tidy packages labeled "physical development" or "social development" or "language development," but is a coherent, integrated system.

## Explaining Language Development

If merely describing language development is hard—and it is—explaining it has proven still harder. This may surprise you, since most of us simply take for granted that children just "learn" to talk by listening to the language they hear. It doesn't seem very magical or amazing until you think about it a bit. And then the more you think about it, the more amazing and mysterious it becomes. For one thing, as Steven Pinker (1987) points out, there is a veritable chasm between what the child hears as language input, and the language the child eventually must speak. The input consists of some set of sentences spoken to or in the hearing of the child. Those sentences have intonation, stress, timing; they are spoken in the presence of objects and events; the words are given in particular order. All of these may provide clues for the child. But what the child must acquire from such an input is nothing less than a set of rules for *creating* sentences. And the rules are not directly given in the sentences she hears. How on earth does the child accomplish this feat? We have a number of theories to choose from.

## The Influence of the Environment on Language Development

### Early Theories: Imitation and Reinforcement

The earliest attempts to explain language development were primarily based on learning theory approaches and on the "common sense" idea that learning a language was a fairly straightforward process of imitation or reinforcement.

*Imitation.*   Imitation obviously has to play *some* part, since the child does learn the language he is hearing and doesn't invent his own. Children's babbling does drift toward the set of sounds they are hearing. They do imitate sentences they hear; they do repeat the name of some new object when they hear it (Leonard, et al., 1983); they do learn to speak with the accent of those they are listening to. There is even some evidence from research by Elizabeth Bates (Bates et al., 1982) that those babies who show the most imitation of actions and gestures in the first year of life are also the ones who later learn language more quickly. Thus the *tendency* to imitate may be an important ingredient in the language-learning process.

Still, if you think about all the facts I've given you, you can see that imitation just won't cut it as a sole explanation of language development. In particular, remember that children create types of sentences and forms of words that they have never heard. When a child overregularizes the past tense and invents words like *goed* or *beated* she is not imitating what she hears. Furthermore, when children do imitate adult sentences, they reduce them to a form that is like their own sentences.

*Reinforcement.* A more formal theory of language development based on learning theory was proposed by B. F. Skinner (1957). He argued that adults "shape" the child's first sounds into words, and then the words into sentences, by selectively reinforcing those that are understandable or "correct." When your child says "coo" while reaching for a cookie, and you say "No, say *cookie*" and withhold the cookie until the child says something closer, you are shaping the child's language.

Such an extreme version of a reinforcement theory of language has been largely discredited because of a number of key flaws. First, in the real world parents rarely correct children's grammar. Instead, parents are remarkably forgiving of all sorts of peculiar constructions and meaning, responding instead to the "truth value" of the child's sentences (Brown & Hanlon, 1970; Hirsh-Pasek, Treiman, & Schneiderman, 1984). Second, explicit correction, when it does occur, may actually *slow down* language development rather than speeding it up. Katherine Nelson observed this in her study of early vocabulary growth. Those mothers who engaged in systematic correction of poor pronunciations and rewarded good pronunciation had children who had smaller vocabularies than did children of mothers who corrected less.

Third, children learn many forms of language, such as plurals, with relatively few errors. In effect, there is little to shape or correct. In those cases in which the child does make grammatical mistakes or mispronounces words, the error typically disappears within a short time, even though the parent has reinforced the incorrect version by responding to it (Gleitman & Wanner, 1988).

Fourth, Skinner's theory simply cannot account for the apparent creative and rule governed aspects of children's early language. All in all, the whole process just doesn't sound like shaping.

### Newer Environmental Theories: Talking to the Child and Other Input Theories

Even though neither direct imitation nor shaping seem to account for the development of language, it still seems plausible that the language the child is hearing all around him has *some* effect.

At the simplest possible level, we know that children who hear a lot of language develop vocabulary more rapidly in the early years than do those who are talked to less (e.g., Huttenlocher, Haight, Bryk, Seltzer, & Lyons, 1991)—an example of what Aslin calls *facilitation*. It is probably not quantity alone that is critical here. The fastest language development seems to occur in those infants whose parents use language in either or both of two ways: (1) Their language to the child is *contingent on* or *responsive to* the child's own activities or language efforts—another example of the general principle I talked

When parents spend a lot of time talking to their children, as Mikhail Popov is doing here with his son Stas, they are likely to have children who learn to talk somewhat earlier. This photo is a video still from the *Childhood* television series (*Source:* ©Thirteen/WNET).

about in Chapter 6 (e.g., Clarke-Stewart, 1973; Olson, Bayles, & Bates, 1986). (2) They find opportunities to use play time or reading time to help the child focus on objects and to connect objects and their names. For example, G. J. Whitehurst and his colleagues (Whitehurst et al., 1988) had some parents read picture books to their toddlers and asked them to interact with the child during the reading using a lot of questions that could not be answered just by pointing (such as "What's the name of that?" or "Do you think the kitty will get into trouble?"). Other parents were encouraged to read to the child, but were given no special instructions. After a month, the children in the experimental group had shown a larger gain in vocabulary than had the children in the comparison group.

Research like this tells us that the amount and kind of language interaction a child has with his parents affects his *rate* of language development. But children with less skillful or less talkative parents nonetheless learn language, albeit more slowly. So while such variation in the language environment makes a difference, it doesn't explain the language learning process itself.

*Motherese.* Another aspect of adult talk to young children that may be far more helpful in explaining the child's language development is the fact that such talk is far *simpler* than is adult talk to other adults. Since this distinctively simpler language is most often heard from mothers to their youngsters,

The word linguists often use to describe the particular pattern of speech by adults to young children. The sentences are shorter, simpler, repetitive, and higher pitched.

it has acquired the name of **motherese**, but it is characteristic of virtually all adult talk to infants and young toddlers (Snow & Ferguson, 1977; Schachter & Strage, 1982.) Motherese has several key features:

1. It is spoken in a higher-pitched voice and at a slower pace than is speech to adults, with clear pauses at the end of sentences.
2. The sentences are short and nearly always grammatical.
3. The sentences are grammatically simple, with relatively few modifiers and few clauses. Mothers of 2-year-olds are more likely to say "Mrs. Smith was at the store today" than "I saw your preschool teacher, Mrs. Smith, when I went to the grocery store today."
4. It is highly repetitive. The adult tends to use the same sentences, or minor variations of the same sentences, over and over when talking to a young child (e.g., "Where is the ball? Can you see the ball? Where is the ball? There is the ball!"). The adult also repeats the child's sentences frequently—perhaps 10 percent of the time. Usually these are not perfect repetitions, but expansions or recastings of the child's sentence that turn the child's sentence into a more complete grammatical form. (e.g., if the child said *Mommy coat* the mother might say "Yes, that's mommy's coat.")
5. The vocabulary is concrete, nearly always referring to objects or people that are immediately present. The vocabulary is also limited; adults choose words they think the child will understand.

There is also some newer data indicating that when talking to young children, adults tend to put key words at the ends of phrases or sentences, and to emphasize those words by speaking in a louder and higher voice—a pattern that might focus the child's attention particularly on the ends of sentences (Fernald & Mazzie, 1991).

Presumably parents talk this way to their young children not because they have figured out that this is the right way to teach language, but much more simply because such language is most likely to be understood by their child, and most likely to keep the child's interest. But even though it isn't intended to be helpful for grammatical development, the existence of motherese might nonetheless help to explain language development.

That possibility is strengthened by the finding that babies as young as a few days old can discriminate between motherese and adult-directed speech and that *they prefer to listen to motherese* (Cooper & Aslin, 1990). In particular, it seems to be the higher pitch of motherese that babies prefer to listen to (Fernald & Kuhl, 1987). So the baby is drawn to the parent's voice, and is thus more likely to pay attention to language.

Once the child is paying attention, the very simplicity of the adults' speech may also permit the child to pick out repeating grammatical patterns. Erika Hoff-Ginsberg (1986, 1987), for example, has found that parents who use a lot of repetitions or partial repetitions, or who use a lot of *wh* questions, have children whose grammar develops more rapidly.

Several experimental studies also point to the potential helpfulness of "expansions" and "recastings," in which a child's sentence is repeated back in a grammatically more complete form, thus modeling a more complex grammar. Keith Nelson (e.g., 1977) worked with 2 1/2-year-old children who were not yet spontaneously producing sentences such as negative *wh* sentences (e.g., "Why doesn't it work?") or future tenses of verbs. He then gave the children five 1-hour training sessions over two months. In these sessions each child had either his questions or his verb forms "recast" by the adult—thereby giving the child a consistent model for the more complex forms. Nelson found that the children who heard the expanded questions showed more rapid growth in their spontaneous use of questions; those whose verbs were recast showed improvement in that area. Such results make it plausible that such expansions or corrections are useful for a child's language development.

These newer versions of environmental theories are a great deal more subtle, and undoubtedly more accurate, than simple reinforcement models. But here, too, there are problems. For example, while it is true that children who hear more "recastings" learn grammar sooner, children who rarely hear such forms nonetheless acquire a complex grammar, albeit more slowly. And while something like motherese does seem to occur in the vast majority of cultures and contexts, it does not occur in *all* cultures and contexts. It has been found in tonal languages such as Chinese (Grieser & Kuhl, 1988), but not in one Mayan culture (Pye, 1986), and was considerably reduced among a group of depressed mothers studied in the United States (Bettes, 1988). Children in the latter two groups nonetheless learned language. Thus while motherese may be *helpful,* it cannot be *necessary* for language learning. In Aslin's terms, it serves as facilitation but not induction.

## The Child's Role in Language Development

If such environmental input can't fully explain language development, then we have to turn to the other actor in this drama, the child. Maybe it is what the child *does* with the language he hears that is the critical ingredient. There are two kinds of theories that approach the problem from this end: innateness theories and cognitive theories.

### Innateness Theories

At the extreme end of the continuum of internal or child-related explanations of language development are theorists who take a "nativist" position very similar to the nativist position in perceptual development. Such theorists were particularly struck by two features of language development—the extreme complexity of the task the child must accomplish and the apparent similarities in and stage-like development of the patterns of children's early language. Whenever we see a clear sequence of development that is shared by children in widely differing environments (even in deaf children—a group I have discussed in the box on page 324), it looks very much as if some kind of physiological maturation may lie behind it. The fact that the child seems to accomplish a virtually impossible task within a few short years lends credence to such a view.

Noam Chomsky (1965, 1975, 1986, 1988) has been the theorist most strongly associated with this position. He argues that language is not learned; rather, the child is born with some built-in (albeit largely unconscious) knowledge about the basic principles of language which is reflected in some fashion in basic neurological functioning. This innate knowledge/neurological process allows the child to "decode" the stream of sounds coming from others, turning that stream into a set of rules for a specific language.

The presumed built-in mechanism has gone by various names. David McNeill (1970) called it the **language acquisition device.** Chomsky now refers to it as *universal grammar* (or UG). Whatever it is called, is not thought to be programmed especially for English or Swahili or Arabic. Rather it is programmed for language in some more general sense—just as a computer program is designed to "read" certain kinds of input and analyze that input in specific ways. So, for example, the language acquisition device or UG might be programmed to pay attention to such universal features of language as the distinction between subject and predicate (nouns and verbs). The particular language the child is hearing is passed through this system, and the child emerges with the appropriate set of rules for the language she hears and speaks.

Chomsky's basic idea was initially scoffed at, then embraced, then partially rejected, and has recently become strongly influential again, such as in the theories of built-in constraints on word meanings I talked about earlier in the chapter.

A central weakness of the early versions of innateness theory turned out to be the very observation that initially seemed to lend it the greatest strength—namely, the existence of universal patterns of early language. There are indeed such common patterns—some of which I've talked about in more detail in the box on page 325. But there are also more differences than innateness theorists had initially expected. As researchers such as Dan Slobin and his many colleagues (Slobin, 1985a, 1985b) have looked more systematically at other languages, they have found a lot of surface variation in children's earliest language constructions. Such cross-linguistic studies made it clear that any language acquisition device, if it exists, is probably not tuned to universal *content,* such as the distinction between subject and object (nouns and verbs). Slobin and other theorists in this same group propose instead that what is built-in is a set of universal language-scanning processes—an argument highly reminiscent of information processing models of cognitive development.

Slobin (1985a, 1985b) assumes a basic *language-making capacity* in any child, made up of a set of fundamental information processing strategies he calls *operating principles* or OPs. The essential argument should not be new to you. Just as the newborn infant seems to come programmed with "rules to look by," so Slobin is arguing that infants and children are programmed with "rules to listen by." In support of this contention is all the evidence I described in Chapter 5 showing that very young infants already focus on individual sounds and syllables in the stream of sounds they hear, that they pay attention to sound rhythm, and that they prefer speech of a particular pattern, namely motherese. Slobin also proposes that babies are preprogrammed to pay attention to the beginnings and endings of strings of sounds (especially to endings), and to stressed sounds. These operating principles, combined with the actual features of adults' talk to babies, would help to explain some of the features of children's early grammars. For example, the very rapid learning of verb and noun inflections by Turkish children that I described in the box on page 325 can be explained in terms of an operating principle that says "pay attention to the ends of sound strings." Since all Turkish inflections are *suffixes,* and are entirely regular, the child learns them easily. Children learning languages in which inflections appear as prefixes, or are irregular in sound (as is true for the past tense in English, for example) learn more slow-ly and make more overregularization mistakes.

There are some powerful attractions in these newer approaches. They are consistent with the growing information about apparently built-in percep-tual skills and processing biases, and they begin to merge the study of lan-guage development with the broader study of information processing. They also hold out the promise of being able to account for both the common fea-tures and the variations in early grammatical acquisition. But it is still early in the exploration of this approach, and there are other compelling alterna-tives.

In particular, there are eloquent spokesmen for a theory of language that begins much more explicitly from the cognitive rather than the physio-logical end. One such theorist, Melissa Bowerman, would agree that the child does indeed *construct* language and that the child may indeed start with basic operating principles, but she argues that the process is less automatic, more tied to the broader sweep of cognitive development than Slobin's analysis suggests. In this view, we might think of the child as a "little linguist," apply-ing her emerging cognitive understandings to the problem of language, searching for regularities and patterns.

### Cognitive Processing Explanations

Bowerman's analysis begins with an issue I discussed earlier, namely the question of whether a child first learns meaning or first learns words. And al-though the process clearly works in both directions, Bowerman has been struck by the fact that a large portion of a child's early words seem to symbol-ize categories or relationships the child has already created or understood through his own actions or play. As Bowerman puts it (1985):

> Children possess powerful cognitive skills that enable them to structure and inter-pret their experiences on a nonlinguistic basis, that is, to develop notions of agency, spatial location, causality, possession, and so on. When language starts to come in, it does not introduce new meanings to the child. Rather, it is used to express only those meanings the child has already formulated independently of language. (p. 372)

As further illustration of this link, a number of observers have noted relation-ships between the patterns of children's play and their language. Symbolic play such as drinking from an empty cup, and imitation of sounds and ges-tures, both appear at about the same time as the child's first words. In chil-dren whose language is significantly delayed, both symbolic play and imitation are normally delayed, too (Snyder, 1978; Bates et al., 1987; Ungerer & Sigman, 1984). And at about the point at which two-word sentences ap-pear, we can also see children begin to combine several gestures into a se-quence in their pretend play, such as pouring imaginary liquid, drinking, then wiping the mouth. Those children who are the first to show this se-quencing in their play are also the first to show two- or three-word sentences in their speech (Bates et al., 1987; Shore, 1986; Brownell, 1988).

The child's cognitive process is also involved directly in analyzing the language that she hears. Children not only use rules in their early language,

# Language in the Deaf

Linguists have been interested in the language of deaf children for both practical and theoretical reasons. Can we use any of the information about basic language development to help the deaf child? And can the deaf child help us to understand the process of language development better? In particular, studies of the deaf have been used (1) to explore the role of possibly innate mechanisms, or maturation, in the development of language, and (2) to address the question of the critical period in language development. Many deaf children do not learn any language during their early years. Does this interfere with their ability to learn language later? Does some language *have* to be learned during the first few years for any language to be acquired readily?

## Developmental Patterns of Language Among the Deaf

Some fascinating recent research by Laura Petitto (1991) has begun to answer some of the most basic questions about the earliest language forms in deaf children. She has compared the timing of the development of meaningful gesturing ("signs" in sign language) among deaf children of deaf parents and hearing children of deaf parents—both of which are exposed to sign language from the parents—with the early spoken language of hearing children reared by *hearing* parents. She finds that the timing of either gesture or spoken words is virtually the same in all three groups; the first word/gesture occurs between 9 and 14 months, and the first ten words/gestures are achieved between 13 and 21 months.

Furthermore, in their early use of signs, deaf children seem to go through the same stages as those we hear in the spoken language of hearing children. There is a kind of simple two-word grammar of signs, for example, and the inflections are added later, just as with spoken language. Deaf children using sign language even have difficulty with the signs for "you" and "me," acquiring these pronouns only at about the time we hear them in a speaking child, even though in sign language such pronouns involve straightforward pointing—a gestural skill the child seems to have before age 1 (Bellugi, 1988). All of these findings lend strong support to biological/maturational theories of language learning.

## Critical Period in Language

Studies of deaf children also lend some support to the related biological argument about a possible critical period for language learning. The key finding is that among the deaf, those with deaf parents usually do as well or *better* on measures of written and spoken language than do those with hearing parents (Liben, 1978). One explanation of this consistent observation is that deaf children of deaf parents are learning *a* language at the normal time. Deaf parents use sign language with each other and with their children, so the children learn that language (Schlesinger & Meadow, 1972). But deaf children reared by hearing parents are not exposed to any comprehensible or systematic language in the critical early years (unless, of course, their parents learn sign language) and thus have greater difficulty at later ages when trying to learn written or spoken language.

For theorists attempting to explain language development, these findings surely point toward some kind of biological/maturational substrate for language. At about 8–12 months, children appear to be "ready" to learn some kind of language, to communicate in some sensory modality, whether that be oral or gestural. From the point of view of the parent of a deaf child, the message also seems to be fairly clear: A combination of sign language and spoken language works well for the child and for the relationship between the child and the parent. Not only is the child exposed to a language at the normal time, but the child and parent can communicate with each other—something that is very difficult for the hearing parent who does not sign with a deaf child.

In the early years of research on children's language development, linguists and psychologists were strongly impressed by the apparent similarities in the vocabularies and early sentences children constructed. Then a burst of studies of children learning many different languages—Turkish, Serbo-Croatian, Hungarian, Hebrew, Japanese, a New Guinean language called Kaluli, German, Italian, and others—seemed to point more to differences than to similarities. At this point in our knowledge, what seems clear is that both basic similarities and individual language variations exist and are important in our understanding of how children learn language.

The similarities are still striking. Let me give you some examples:

- The prelinguistic phase seems to be identical in all language communities. All babies coo, then babble; all babies understand language before they can speak it; babies in all cultures begin to use their first words at about 12 months.
- In all language communities studied so far, a one-word phase precedes the two-word phase, with the latter beginning at about 18 months.
- Language learning is affected by the child's own actions. So, for example, in every language studied so far, when children first add verb inflections such as the past tense, they are likely to add them first to verbs that describe actions that bring visible results, such as *drop, fall, break,* or *spill*.
- In all languages studied so far, prepositions describing locations are added in essentially the same order. Words that describe *in, on, under,* and *beside* are learned first. Then the child learns the words for *front* and *back*, but only for objects that have a clear front/back orientation, such as a house or a car.
- Only later does the child use *front*

and *back* to describe opposite sides of objects like blocks or a plate (Slobin, 1985a).
- Children seem to pay more attention to the ends of words than the beginnings, so they learn suffixes before they learn prefixes.

At the same time, both languages and children's early attempts to construct sentences in the language they are hearing differ markedly. Again some examples.

- The specific word order that a child uses in early sentences is not the same for all children in all languages. In some languages a noun/verb sequence is fairly common; in others a verb/noun sequence may be heard.
- Particular inflections are learned in highly varying orders from one language to another. Japanese children, for example, begin very early to use "pragmatic" markers. The word *yo* is used at the end of a sentence when the child is experiencing some resistance from the listener; the word *ne* is used when the child expects approval or agreement. Such pragmatic inflections are rare in the early language of children in other cultures.
- Most strikingly, there are languages in which there seems to be no uninflected "Stage 1" grammar at all. Children learning Turkish, for example, use essentially the full set of noun and verb inflections by age 2 and never go through a stage of using uninflected words. Their language is simple, but it is not telegraphic and it is rarely ungrammatical from the adult's point of view (Aksu-Koc & Slobin, 1985).

Obviously any theory of language acquisition must account for both the common ground and the wide variations from one language to the next.

they seem to *search* for rules. This is one obvious explanation of the overregularizations I talked about earlier, like *wented* and *goed* or *footses*. Since children seem to show the same rule-searching behavior in other areas than language, it is hard to see how this can be a process unique to language learning. If the child is "programmed" to look for rules, then the programming covers all of cognitive development, not just language.

The differences between Slobin's "operating principles" approach and Bowerman's cognitive approach are more a matter of emphasis than of fundamental disagreement. The key assumption is that the child *analyzes* the language he hears, and constructs his own language based on that analysis. The disagreement is over whether the process of analysis is governed by built-in rules or principles, or whether it results from the child's more general construction of the world around him.

### Connectionist Models: A New Approach

Innateness and cognitive-processing theories still dominate theoretical discussions of language acquisition. But there is also a new kid on the block trying to get into the game. I need at least to introduce you to this new approach, known as connectionist theory, although it is not at all clear at this point just what the ramifications of this new view may be.

Theorists in this group take the radical position that language may not be rule-based at all, at least not in the usual sense. Rather, the child may learn such things as the correct way to make past tenses, or the order of words in a sentence, by a much more automatic process of building up a set of probabilities for each option, based on experience.

Using current computer terminology, David Rumelhart and James McClelland—two of the key figures in this new approach—put it this way:

> We suggest . . . that implicit knowledge of language may be stored in connections among simple processing units organized into networks. (1987, p. 195)

There are no "rules" in these networks. Instead there are associations of various strengths resulting from exposure to various forms. For example, associative connections would build up between verbs with similar forms. When a child hears *play* and *played*, not only is this connection strengthened but also the connection between *stay* and *stayed*. In her speech, the child uses whatever version has the strongest built-up connection. One implication of this assumption is that a child might switch from one version to another quite abruptly when the associative strength of version B abruptly becomes greater than the strength for version A. Such an abrupt shift is precisely what we hear when we listen to children learning past tenses, such as when they shift from using correct irregular verb forms like *went* to overregularized forms like *wented* or *goed*.

Rumelhart and McClelland have actually been able to design a computer simulation that shows just such abrupt shifts. It first uses a few irregular past tenses correctly, then begins to "overregularize," and then slowly corrects the overregularizations, one verb form at a time (Rumelhart & McClelland, 1987). If one assumes that such computer simulations mimic actual neuronal functioning, then such a connectionist model could offer a radically different view of how language is learned.

Connectionist models have created a big stir among linguistic theorists. Some have been open to the new ideas and technologies (e.g., Bates & MacWhinney, 1987); many have argued strongly against them, contending that they simply cannot capture the full rule-governed quality of language (e.g., Pinker & Prince, 1988). In particular, critics have pointed out that in the simulations, the computer is not fed the kind of real-life, messy, complex language samples that a child actually has to work with. What the computer gets is a nice, tidy set of verb stems and past tense forms. Early attempts to get a computer to generate rule-like language based on messier, real-life sentence input have apparently not been successful (Bates, 1991). This might mean that we simply need better simulation models, or it might mean that the child's knowledge of the context plays a crucial role. The child knows what Mom was referring to because he and Mom are both looking at the same thing, or the child knows that Mom stopped mid-sentence and went off on a linguistic tangent because his big sister just asked Mom a question. Or of course it could mean that the connectionist models are just plain wrong and that the process really is rule-governed. The one thing we can be sure of at this moment is that connectionist theories will be fully explored over the next years.

 ## A Combined View

Each of the theories I have described has at least some merit, but no one of them really does the whole job. Perhaps if we combined them in some way, we could do better. Stan Kuczaj (1982) has offered one such combination that I find helpful.

He argues that language development is influenced by three things. First, there are innate "organizing predispositions," such as perhaps Slobin's "organizing principles" or even the basic brain architecture which forms the base for neural connections. A second critical influence is the *input,* the set of language experiences actually encountered by the child. In the most extreme cases, we know that a child who hears *no* language or only very limited language will not develop in the same way as does a child who encounters a rich array of sounds and sentences. Indeed, there may be a critical period for language learning, as I suggested in the box on page 324.

Furthermore, the specific form of the input seems to make a difference. Some forms are more helpful to the child than are others, with repetitions, recastings, and expansions high on the list of helpful forms.

Traditional wisdom (before the advent of connectionist models, at least) argues that the third crucial element is what the child *does* with the input. The child begins with the built-in strategies (rules), receives input (hears people talking), processes that sound according to her initial strategies, and then changes the strategies or "rules" (schemes in Piaget's terminology) to fit the new information. The result is a series of rules for understanding and creating language. The strong similarities we see among children in their early language constructions come about both because all children share the same initial processing rules, and because most children are exposed to very similar input from the people around them.

In a sense, all Kuczaj has done is to add together pieces of three different theories. This seems to me to be a step in the right direction, but it is still way too simple. If we know anything about development, it is that separate influences rarely just *add*. They nearly always combine and interact in important ways. What we need to understand now are the ways in which the child's built-in processing rules, his own processing of experience, and the quality of that experience interact to produce language. Linguists and psychologists who have studied language have made progress. We know a lot more now about how *not* to explain language. But we have not yet cracked the code. The fact that children learn complex and varied use of their native tongue within a few years remains both miraculous and largely mysterious.

## Individual Differences in Language Development

All along, I have been talking about the fact that there are wide variations in the speed with which children acquire language skill. I have also mentioned in passing that there may be style differences as well. Let me explore both of these forms of individual variation more fully.

### Power Differences

Anyone who has been around children knows that there are big differences in the timing of children's language development. As just one illustration, look at the differing rates for the three children Roger Brown studied—Eve, Adam, and Sarah—shown in Figure 8.3. The figure shows the **mean length of utterance** (MLU), which is the number of "meaningful units" per sentence for each child, including not only individual words but the various grammatical markers, such as the *s* for plurals or the *ed* for past tense. I have drawn a line at roughly the point at which the child switches from simple sentences to more complex ones. You can see that Eve made this transition at about 21 months, while Adam and Sarah passed over this point about a year later. The possible explanations of such differences should be familiar by now.

*Genetic Explanations.* One obvious possibility is that the rate of language development may be something you inherit—in the same way that intelligence or the rate of physical development may be partially influenced by heredity. Certainly if we assume that part of language is built into the brain, it makes sense to think that some children may inherit a more efficient built-in system than others.

Twin studies and adoption studies designed to test this possibility have yielded the typical mixture of findings. For example, in their extensive study of adopted children, Plomin and DeFries and their colleagues (Hardy-Brown, Plomin & DeFries, 1981; Plomin & DeFries, 1985b) have found that the children's language skill at age 2 was about equally well-predicted by the IQs or language skills of the natural or the adoptive parents. They also found that among the adoptive families, those who talked the most and provided the most toys had children whose language was more advanced. In twin studies, the common finding is that vocabulary size, but *not* grammatical complexity,

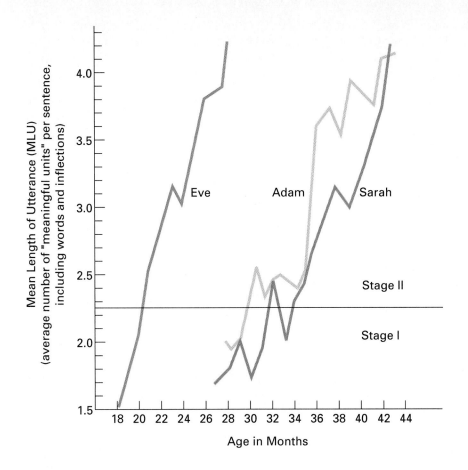

*FIGURE 8.3*

Children go through the various steps and stages of language development at markedly different rates, as you can see clearly here. Eve reached Stage II grammar (noted by the horizontal line across the graph) at about 21 months, while Adam and Sarah were much slower. This does *not* mean, by the way, that Eve has a higher IQ or is "brighter" in some way. Within this range of speed of language development there is essentially no correlation with IQ.

is more similar in identical than in fraternal twins (e.g., Mather & Black, 1984).

What all of this looks like to me is that there are some aspects of language development that are strongly related to the child's overall information processing abilities, such as speed of learning new words and understanding other people's language. Since cognitive abilities have a significant genetic influence, so do these language abilities. But other aspects of language, such as pronunciation and possibly the rate of grammatical development, may be equally influenced by variations in the richness of the child's linguistic environment.

*Environmental Explanations.* I have already talked about some environmental influences. Parents who talk more, who read to the child more and elicit more language from the child, and who respond contingently to the child's language seem to have children who develop language more rapidly. The fact that this same set of relationships is found in families of *adoptive* children is impressive, since we can be fairly sure that what we are seeing here is not just genetic influence in disguise.

Overall, as with IQ, it seems obvious that both the particular genes the child inherits and the environment in which the child is growing up contribute to the rate of language development she will show. I should emphasize once again, though, that although children do differ widely in the timing of their language development, virtually all children progress adequately through the sequence of steps I have been describing. Nearly all children learn to communicate at least adequately; most do so with great skill, regardless of their early rate of progress. One lesson for parents is that you should not panic if your child is still using fairly primitive sentences at 2 1/2 or even 3. Instead of worrying, I would urge you to listen with pleasure to your child's emerging language—to the poetry of it, the wonderfully funny mistakes, the amazingly rapid changes. It is a fascinating process.

### Differences in Style of Language

In talking about the child's earliest words, I pointed out that there seem to be two distinct "types" of early vocabulary, which Katherine Nelson originally called "referential" and "expressive" styles. Later researchers have found further signs of such a difference in grammar, and articulation, as well as differences in the rate or evenness of language development. I have summarized some of the differences in Table 8.6. Elizabeth Bates and her colleagues (Bates et al., 1988; Thal & Bates, 1990) argue that the difference may run fairly deep. Referential-style children are, in some sense, more cognitively oriented children. They are drawn to objects, spend more of their time in solitary play with objects, and interact with other people more often around objects, too. They are much more likely to show a clear spurt in vocabulary development in the early stages, adding a whole lot of object names in a very short space of time. Such children are also advanced in their ability to understand complex adult language.

The expressive-style toddler, on the other hand, is oriented more toward people, toward social interactions. Their early words and sentences include a lot of strings of words that are involved in common interactions with adults. Since many such strings include grammatical inflections, expressive children's early language often sounds more advanced than that of a referential child. But their vocabularies develop more slowly, with no obvious spurt. Interestingly, there are hints in several (but not all) studies that referential children may be more often first-borns or girls, while expressive children are more often later-borns or boys. For example, in the study of vocabulary spurts by Goldfield & Reznick I showed in Figure 8.2, all five of the children whose early vocabulary developed without a clear spurt were later-born.

Just how these differences come about is still being hotly debated. It could be that such children are simply matching the quality of the language they are hearing, a possibility suggested by the ordinal position differences. First-born children may receive much more intensive language input, with much more emphasis on learning names; later-borns may encounter a rather different linguistic environment, with more emphasis on communication. The two styles might also reflect underlying temperamental variations—although the one study I know of that explores this possibility directly has not found such a link (Bates et al., 1988). Whatever the source, the existence of such large differences in the form or style of early language raises serious questions about the assumption that the early stages of language development are the same for all children and about virtually all nativist theories of language development. Unless we assume that there are rather radical varia-

TABLE 8.6

*Some Differences Between Expressive and Referential Children in Early Language*

|  | Expressive | Referential |
|---|---|---|
| Early Words | Low proportion of nouns and adjectives | High proportion of nouns and adjectives |
| Vocabulary Growth | Slow, gradual; rarely any spurts | Rapid, with clear spurts at one-word stage |
| Early Sentences | May have inflections at Stage I, because of high use of "rote strings" (formulas) inserted into sentences (e.g., "What do you want?") | Few rote strings at Stage I grammar, speech is clearly telegraphic at this stage, with no inflections. |
| Articulation | Less clear speech | Clearer speech |
| Demographics | More boys; more later-born children | More girls; more first-borns |

*Source:* After Thal & Bates, 1990.

tions in the input with which the child is working, it is difficult to account for such style differences from a base of common operating principles or other built-in processes. All in all, the literature on style differences in language learning, which seemed like an interesting sidelight when Nelson first described the phenomenon, has turned out to lead to a fascinating set of new questions.

## An Application of the Basic Knowledge: Learning to Read

In Chapter 5, I talked briefly about some of the *perceptual* aspects of learning to read. But of course reading involves language as well. Researchers have found that a child's knowledge of both the sound and the structure of language play very important roles in early reading.

First of all, knowledge of language structure makes a difference. If, as you are reading, you come to a word you don't know, it is a great help to have some idea of the *type* of word that could go there, or even some good guesses about which specific words might be likely. Then it is possible to accept or reject those guesses based on the actual letters on the page. Such knowledge helps children as well. In one study, Dale Willows and Ellen Ryan (1986) found that children with higher levels of "grammatical sensitivity"—children who can fill in a blank in a spoken sentence with a word of the correct grammatical class, for example—were consistently better readers in first, second, and third grade. This is not just a matter of knowing lots of words, although that helps, too. It is more a matter of being aware of or knowing the ways in which sentences are put together.

When the child gets to the point of decoding individual letters, another form of language awareness also seems to be critical, namely awareness of the fact that words are made up of individual sounds. Suppose you say to a child, "Say a word which starts the same as tap." (Maclean, Bryant, & Bradley, 1987). To do this, the child has to understand that the word has a starting sound (*t*) plus other sounds, and then be able to match that starting sound. You can get at this same skill in other ways, too, such as by asking children to recognize or produce rhyming words, or to say the first sound in a syllable. There is now abundant evidence that children who are more skilled at such tasks at age 3, 4, or 5 later learn to read much more easily (e.g., Bryant et al., 1990; Vellutino & Scanlon, 1987). Overall, then, the child's knowledge of language—of grammar, meaning, and sound—has a profound effect on early reading. And the lack of such skills, as I'll discuss much more fully in Chapter 14, may be a major reason for significant reading disabilities.

## S U M M A R Y

1.  Language can be defined as an arbitrary system of symbols that permits us to say and understand an infinite variety of messages. It is rule governed and creative.
2.  Many of the developments during the "prelinguistic" phase (before the first word) are significant precursors to language. The child discriminates language sounds, babbles sounds that more and more closely approximate the sounds he hears, and uses gestures in communicative ways.
3.  At about 1 year of age the earliest words appear. Some of these early words are combined with gestures to convey whole sentences of meaning, a pattern called a holophrase.
4.  By 16–20 months, most children have a vocabulary of 50 or more words; by age 2 the vocabulary may include 200 words. The first two-word sentences normally appear between 18 and 24 months.
5.  The earliest sentences are short and grammatically simple, lacking the various grammatical inflections. Many different meanings, such as location, or possession, or agent-object relationships, can nonetheless be conveyed by the child.
6.  In Stage II, the child begins to add the many grammatical inflections, with children in the same language community typically adding the inflections in a common order.
7.  In later years, children slowly add other elements, such as passive forms and tag questions, and correct earlier "errors."
8.  The development of word meanings (semantic development) follows a less predictable course. Children appear to have many concepts or categories

before they have words for them, but learning new words also creates new categories. When they begin to use words, they also "overextend" their usage.

9. Many linguists believe that in determining word meanings, a child has built-in constraints or biases, such as the assumption that words refer to objects or actions but not both or the principles of contrast or mutual exclusivity.

10. Children appear to have two uses for language: to communicate and to direct their own activity. Communication is the dominant use, and as early as age 2, we can see children adapting their language to the needs of the listener, and learning the various culturally specific customs of language usage.

11. Several theories have been offered to explain language development. Two early environmental explanations, based on imitation or reinforcement, have been largely set aside. More recently, emphasis has been placed on the helpful quality of the simpler form of parent-to-child language called motherese, and on the role of expansions and recastings of children's sentences.

12. Other contending theories today focus more on the role of the child, either positing a set of built-in "operating principles," or emphasizing the child as a "little linguist," analyzing the regularities of language.

13. Combining many of these elements, language development may be seen to be a joint result of the built-in "operating principles," the nature or quality of the input, and the child's processing of that input.

14. Children differ in the rate of development of both vocabulary and grammar. There is some support for a theory of genetic contribution to such differences, but environmental explanations also seem valid.

15. Despite these variations in rate of early development, most children learn to speak skillfully by about age 5 or 6.

16. In the early years of language development, two styles of language can be distinguished, "referential" (focusing on objects and their description) and "expressive" (focusing on words and forms that describe or further social relationships).

17. Research on language can also help to understand the development of reading skill. Some metalinguistic awareness of the grammar, semantics, and segmented sounds of language seem to be critical for reading.


## CRITICAL THINKING QUESTIONS

1. What specific advice could you give to a parent of an infant about how that parent might encourage language development in her or his child?

2. One of the most difficult practical questions in education today has to do with bilingual education. Is it better for a child who comes to school without speaking the dominant cultural language to be taught in her native tongue and learn the dominant language as a foreign language? Is it better for the child simply to be immersed immediately in the dominant language? Or is it better to have some transition period of several years in which the child is exposed to both? There's been a lot of bad re-

search on this question. See if you can design a really good study to test the relative effectiveness of these three strategies. What are the really difficult problems inherent in actually doing such a good study?

3. Why is it useful or important for us to know whether or not a child's early language is a reflection of basic cognitive understandings or whether language develops somewhat separately from cognition?

## KEY TERMS

**babbling**   The vocalizing, often repetitively, of consonant-vowel combinations by an infant, typically beginning at about 6 months of age.

**cooing**   An early stage during the prelinguistic period, from about 1–4 months of age, when vowel sounds are repeated, particularly the *uuu* sound.

**expressive language**   The term used to describe the child's skill in speaking and communicating orally.

**expressive style**   One of two styles of early language proposed by Nelson, characterized by low rates of noun-like terms and high use of personal-social words and phrases.

**holophrases**   The expression of a whole idea in a single word. Characteristic of the child's language from about 12–18 months.

**inflections**   The grammatical "markers" such as plurals, possessives, past tenses, and equivalent.

**language acquisition device**   A hypothesized brain structure that may be "programmed" to make language learning possible.

**mean length of utterance**   Usually abbreviated MLU; the average number of meaningful units in a sentence. Each basic word is one meaningful unit, as is each inflection, such as the *s* for plural or the *ed* for a past tense.

**motherese**   The word linguists often use to describe the

particular pattern of speech by adults to young children. The sentences are shorter, simpler, repetitive, and higher pitched.

**overregularization**   The tendency on the part of children to make the language regular, such as using past tenses like *beated* or *goed.*

**pragmatics**   The rules for the use of language in communicative interaction, such as the rules for taking turns, the style of speech appropriate for varying listeners, and equivalent.

**prelinguistic phase**   The period before the child speaks his first words.

**receptive language**   Term used to describe the child's ability to understand (receive) language, as contrasted to his ability to express language.

**referential style**   Second style of early language proposed by Nelson, characterized by emphasis on objects and their naming and description.

**semantics**   The rules for conveying meaning in language.

**syntax**   The rules for forming sentences; also called grammar.

**telegraphic speech**   A characteristic of early child sentences in which everything but the crucial words is omitted, as if for a telegram.

## SUGGESTED READINGS

Anisfeld, M. (1984). *Language development from birth to three.* Hillsdale, NJ: Lawrence Erlbaum Associates.

   An introductory text covering both language and cognition in the early years. Much more detailed than I have had space for in this chapter and reasonably up to date.

Hakuta, K. (1986). *Mirror of language: The debate on bilingualism.* New York: Basic Books.

   An elegant and readable discussion of many of the issues of bilingualism I've discussed in the box on pages 310–311.

Gleitman, L. R., & Wanner, E. (1988). Current issues in language learning. In M. H. Bornstein & M. E. Lamb (Eds.), *Developmental psychology: An advanced textbook.* (2nd ed.). Hillsdale, NJ: Lawrence Erlbaum Associates.

Not easy, but worth the effort. Gleitman approaches language acquisition from a more-or-less nativist view, which would give you a sense of how such a theorist argues. But this paper also reviews a whole host of other interesting language questions.

Rice, M. L. (1989). Children's language acquisition. *American Psychologist, 44,* 149–156.

A brief, readable review of the current status of our knowledge of language learning.

# PROJECT 11

## Beginning Two-Word Sentences

Some of you have been around young children a lot, and already have some sense for the delightful quality of their early language. But all of you would benefit from some additional listening. I would particularly like you to locate a child who is still in the earliest stages of sentence formation or just beginning to add a few inflections. This is most likely to be a child of 20–24 months, but a child between 24 and 30 months may do fine, too. The one essential ingredient is that the child be speaking at least some two-word sentences. If you are unsure, ask the parent; they can nearly always tell you whether the child has reached this stage or not.

As usual, begin by following whatever procedures your school requires for obtaining appropriate permission for your project. Then arrange to spend enough time with the child at his or her home, in a day-care center, or in any other convenient setting, so that you can collect a list of 50 different *spontaneous* utterances, including both one-word utterances and two- or more-word sentences. By spontaneous I mean those that the child speaks without prompting; try to avoid getting into the situation in which the mother or some other adult actively tries to elicit language from the child, although it is certainly okay if you collect a sample from a time when the child is playing with an adult or doing some activity with a parent or older sibling. The most fruitful time is likely to be when the child is playing with someone, and it is okay to ask the mother to play with the child—but not to play the sort of game in which the object is to get the child to talk. Write down the child's sentences in the order they occur and stop when you have 50. Whenever you can, make notes about the context in which each sentence occurred so that you can judge the meaning more fully.

When you have your list of 50 utterances, take a crack at describing the child's language in any terms emerging from this chapter. For example, is the child using any grammatical inflections? Which ones? Does the pattern conform to what I have described? What about questions or negatives? And what about the different meanings expressed? What is the child's *mean length of utterance* (*MLU*)? To calculate this you will need to count the number of *meaningful units* in each sentence. Each word is a meaningful unit, but so is each grammatical inflection, like the *s* for a plural, the *ed* ending for a past tense, etc. Some specific rules to follow in calculating the MLU:

1.  Do not count such sounds as *uh, um,* or *oh,* but do count *no, yeah,* and *hi.*
2.  All compound words, like *birthday, choo-choo, night-night,* or *pocketbook* should be counted as single words.
3.  Count all irregular past tenses as single words, such as *got, did, went, saw.* But count as two any regular past tense, such as *play-ed,* or any erroneous extension of the past tense, such as *went-ed.*
4.  Count as one all diminutives, such as *doggie* or *mommy.*
5.  Count as one all combinations such as *gonna, wanna,* or *hafta.*
6.  Count as one each auxiliary, such as *is, have, will, can, must,* and as one each inflection, such as the *s* for a plural or a possessive, the *s* for the third person singular verb form, and the *ing* on a verb.

Compare the MLU you obtain with those shown for Adam, Eve, and Sarah in Figure 8.3.

If you are completing this project for a class assignment, turn in your record of the child's sentences along with a page or two of comment.

# PROJECT 12

## Conversation Between Mother and Child

This time I would like you to focus on the social environment—what is said *to* the child as well as the child's response. Again find a child about 2 years old—though it's okay to go up to about 3 1/2. (It can be the same child you listened to in the last project, but you should collect the two sets of observations separately.)

After obtaining permission, arrange to spend some time with the child while the mother is around. If you are working in a nursery school or day-care center, or have access to such a setting, it is all right to study a child and the teacher. But you'll have to get the teacher alone with the single child for a period of time. As with the previous project, the interaction should be as spontaneous as possible. It is okay if the adult and child play together, but not good to have it be a "repeat after me" game or a naming game.

Record the conversation between the mother (or teacher) and the child, making sure that you have the sentences of the two people in the right order. Continue to record the conversation until you have at least 25 sentences for each. You may use a tape recorder if you wish, but you'll find it helpful to write down the sentences as they occur as well.

When you have collected the sentences, see if you can detect any signs of motherese in the adult's language. Did the adult adapt her language to that of the child? Did she repeat the child's utterances with minor modifications? Was there any obvious reinforcement or shaping going on? Did the adult attempt to correct the child's speech, and if so, what was the effect? If you are completing this project for a class assignment, turn in your record of the conversation along with a page or two of analysis and comment.

# THE SOCIAL CHILD

9

# PERSONALITY DEVELOPMENT: ALTERNATIVE VIEWS

I magine yourself sitting in the back of a day-care center, invisible to the eyes of the children but able to watch a group of 2-year-olds. Since you've just read all about cognitive and language development, your attention may be first drawn to the ways the children play with toys and the ways they talk to one another and to the teacher. But it won't be long before it's clear that cognitive and language skills, however fascinating, are only part of the picture. The other part is the child's emerging *social* skills.

How do the children settle differences among themselves? You'll see conflict over toys ("Mine!"), often settled with physical aggression or tears. You'll see the child's relationship with the teachers, more independent than it might have been a year earlier, but often still clinging and needy of attention. You'll see children with one another, perhaps showing signs of helpfulness or altruism as well as aggression, but not much sign of individual friendships. You'll see boys and girls playing together, although probably the girls will be playing more with dolls and boys more with toy cars.

If you watched the same group of children a few years later, many of these patterns would have changed. By age 5 or 6 we see some friendships have formed, but almost entirely between children of the same gender. Clinging and obvious dependence is less in evidence. Disputes are more likely dealt with by yelling and name-calling than by overt aggression.

All of these are developmental changes, analogous to the changes in cognitive structure I talked about in Chapter 7. At the same time, you cannot watch children for very long without seeing the striking variations in their approaches to these social tasks. If you watched your group of children on the first day of kindergarten, you'd probably see one child clinging to his Mom, perhaps weeping and begging her not to leave him alone. Other children say goodbye to Mom, walk right into the room without a backward look, and begin talking to other children immediately. You might see another child standing quietly in the back of the room, and still another child busily exploring the whole room right away, looking at the blocks and story books, trying out several different chairs and desks for size.

Six months later some of these same differences would probably still be visible. The "shy" child who waited at the back of the room is likely to have one or two pals in the class, but not to be the center of the crowd. The child who could hardly bear to let Mom leave may be sitting right up near the teacher. The gregarious, talkative child is probably the one who decides what game they will all play at recess.

**personality**
The collection of individual, relatively enduring patterns of reacting to and interacting with others that distinguishes each child or adult.

Psychologists normally use the word **personality** to describe these differences in the way children and adults go about relating to the people and objects in the world around themselves.

Like the concept of intelligence, the concept of personality is designed to describe *enduring individual differences* in behavior. Whether we are gre-

Six-year-old Chizuka Nakayama, in her first day of school in Japan, already has a recognizable set of temperamental qualities or personality traits, as do all the other children in her class. Where do these differences in temperament or personality come from? This photo is a video still from the *Childhood* television series (*Source:* ©Thirteen/WNET).

garious or shy, whether we plunge into new things or hold back, whether we are independent or dependent, whether we are confident or uncertain—all of these (and many more) are usually thought of as elements of personality.

Underlying the concept of personality is the assumption that these tend to be *persisting* aspects of the individual—that a shy child is likely to become a shy adult, or that a confident 5-year-old will still have some element of confidence 40 years later.

Unlike the concept of intelligence, however, the concept of personality is not reduced to numbers like an IQ score. A few researchers have searched for some measure of the overall *healthiness* of the personality, but for the most part both theorists and researchers have thought of personality in terms of variations on a set of dimensions, such as aggressiveness or dependency, shyness or gregariousness, securely or insecurely attached, and the like. An individual's personality can then be described as a constellation or profile of those key dimensions.

Just as was true for cognition, we need to understand both the common developmental patterns in children's social development and the individual differences in personality. Why do 5-year-olds now show signs of individual friendships? What change makes that possible? Why are same-sex play groups much more obvious at school-age than among preschoolers? And where do the personality differences come from? How does one child come to be shy and another gregarious? How does one child become a bully, another an accepted and popular friend? What are the consequences of those variations over the long term?

In this case, however, it is more difficult to keep these two sets of questions tidily separate, in part because in this area there is not one definitive theory of either personality differences or common developmental patterns. Instead, we have several distinctive theories, each of which casts the questions differently and each of which has led to quite separate bodies of research.

Given that, it makes sense to talk about the theories first, so that you can get some sense of the range of questions that fall under the general label of social and personality development. Then, with the theoretical alternatives as background, I can explore what we know about both basic developmental patterns and individual differences.

## The Major Alternative Views of Personality

Three of the four major theoretical orientations I talked about in Chapter 1 are represented among theories of social and personality development. Biological explanations focus primarily on explaining differences in personality, with a central assumption that such differences are partially or largely inherited. Learning explanations of both the strict behaviorist or social learning subvarieties are designed primarily to explain personality differences, but are also applicable to some developmental questions. Psychoanalytically oriented explanations are designed to describe both developmental change and the origins of individual differences in personality.

## A Biological Approach: Temperament

The most clearly biological approach to social and personality development can be found in various theories of temperament. I have talked about this concept in chapters 1 and 3, so it is not new to you. Most theorists conceive of temperament as a *subset* or portion of personality traits, the individual's "emotional reactivity or behavioral style in interacting with the environment" (Carey, 1981). The term thus describes *how* the child reacts rather than what he can do or why.

The study of temperament has been one of the hottest areas within developmental psychology over the past 10 or 15 years, but we are still in that (exciting) early stage of study in which there is ferment and disagreement. In particular, there is still a lot of dispute about just what aspects of infants' or children's behaviors represent basic temperamental differences. You can get some sense of this dispute by looking at Table 9.1, which lists the proposals of four influential current theorists. The number of dimensions vary and the labels are different, all of which can lead to a good deal of confusion. But if you look closely you can see that there is some common ground. For example, three of the four theories listed in the table focus on some aspect of activity level. Three theories focus on children's responses to novelty, such as approach versus withdrawal; several emphasize the importance of positive or negative mood.

What all these theorists also have in common is a set of basic assumptions, which I can state as a series of propositions—a pattern I will follow with each of the three theoretical approaches I'll talk about in this chapter.

*Proposition 1: Each individual is born with characteristic patterns of responding to the environment and to other people.* In the chapters on perception, cognition, and language, I talked about other kinds of built-in "biases," "schemes," "constraints," or "rules to look by." The idea here is not

**TABLE 9.1**

*Dimensions of Temperament Suggested by Various Theorists*

| Thomas and Chess | Buss and Plomin | Rothbart | Kagan |
|---|---|---|---|
| Basic dimensions:<br>*Activity level*<br>*Rhythmicity*<br>*Approach/withdrawal*<br>*Adaptability to new experience*<br>*Threshold of responsiveness*<br>*Intensity of reaction*<br>*Quality of mood (+ or –)*<br>*Distractibility*<br>*Persistence*<br>Clusters:<br>Easy: (high regularity, positive, highly adaptable, approach)<br>Difficult: (irregular, high intensity, withdrawal, non-adaptable, intense mood)<br>Slow to warm up: (slow adaptability, mildly intense reactions, moderate regularity, mild negative response to new situations) | Basic dimensions:<br>*Activity level:* variations in tempo, in vigor, and in endurance<br>*Emotionality:* variations in the tendency to become distressed or upset easily or intensely (either with fear or anger)<br>*Sociability:* variations in the tendency to seek and be gratified by rewards from social interaction; high level of responsivity toward others | Basic dimensions:<br>*Reactivity:* variations in arousability of motor activity, affect, and such physiological responses as endocrine and autonomic nervous system<br>*Self-regulation:* variations in processes that modulate reactivity, including attention, withdrawal, behavioral inhibition, self-soothing | Basic dimension:<br>*Inhibition:* degree of approach or withdrawal to new situations or objects or unfamiliar persons |

*Sources:* Thomas & Chess, 1977; Buss, 1989; Rothbart, 1989a; Kagan, Reznick, & Snidman, 1990.

so different, except that temperament theorists are saying that we each have *individual* as well as shared "behavioral dispositions" to react to stimuli in particular ways. Most temperament theorists assume that these individual patterns have genetic origins, although some also emphasize variations in prenatal environment.

    *Proposition 2: These behavioral dispositions are rooted in variations in fundamental physiological processes.*   Many (but not all) temperament theorists take the argument a step further and try to trace differences in behavior to underlying differences in the ways a child's brain, nervous system, or hormone system may work (Rothbart, 1989b; Gunnar, 1990). For example, Jerome Kagan has suggested that differences in what he calls behavioral inhibition (and what others might call shyness) are based on differing thresholds for arousal of those parts of the brain, the amygdala and the hypothalamus, that control responses to uncertainty. Arousal of these parts of the brain leads to increases in muscle tension and heart rate. Shy or inhibited children are thought to have a *low* threshold for such a reaction. That is, they more readily become tense and alert in the presence of uncertainty, perhaps even interpreting a wider range of situations as uncertain (Kagan et al., 1990). What we inherit, then, is not "shyness" or some equivalent, but a tendency for the brain to react in particular ways.

*Proposition 3: Temperamental dispositions persist through childhood and into adulthood.* No theorist is proposing that the initial temperamental dispositions remain unchanged by experience. The individual's eventual pattern of behavior (phenotype) is a product of both the original genetic blueprint (genotype) and the subsequent experience. Temperament thus does not inevitably determine personality. Rather, temperamental variations are the building blocks of personality. They create a kind of "bias" in the system toward particular patterns. Given such a bias, there should be at least *some* stability of temperament over time. Such stability ought to show itself in the form of at least modest correlations between measures of a given temperamental dimension from one age to another.

*Proposition 4: Temperamental characteristics affect the way any individual responds to people and things around him, and conversely, affect the way others respond to him.* Highly sociable children seek out contact with others. Children low on the activity dimension are more likely to choose sedentary activities like puzzles or board games than baseball. At the same time, the sociable child, who may smile more than the detached child, elicits different responses from others. Her parents may smile, pick her up, and talk to her more, simply because she has reinforced their behavior by her positive temperament. The temperamentally "difficult" child may elicit higher rates of criticism or punishment, or receive less praise.

Is this little girl's apparent shyness built in genetically in some fashion? Does the brain of a shy or "behaviorally inhibited" child work differently from that of a less inhibited child? Jerome Kagan thinks so, and has some preliminary research to back up his hypothesis.

The concept of *goodness-of-fit,* which I talked about in Chapter 1, is a variation of this same basic proposition. The personality outcome for any given child is going to depend on the fit between her initial temperamental dispositions and the expectations or responses of her family or culture (Lerner et al., 1989).

### The Evidence

All four of these propositions have been at least partially supported by recent research findings.

*Inheritance of Temperament.* The strongest evidence supporting the genetic basis of both infant temperament and later personality is the fact that identical twins are quite a lot more alike in their temperament than are fraternal twins. This is true in studies of adults, even when the identical twins have been reared apart—a set of findings I have explored in the box on page 346—and it is true in studies of children and infants over age 1. One fairly typical set of results, in Table 9.2, comes from several studies by Buss and Plomin of a total of 228 pairs of identical twins and 172 pairs of fraternal twins whose temperament was rated when they were 5 years old. You can see that the correlations between temperament scores of identical twins are consistently high, while those for fraternal twins are essentially zero. However, there are at least two kinds of results that weaken this strong genetic argument. First, studies of twins in the first year of life do *not* show this pattern; identical twin infants are no more alike than are fraternal twin infants (Gunnar, 1990). Second, among adopted children, the correlations between the temperament of the child and that of the natural parent is not a whole lot higher than the correlation with adoptive parents' temperament (Scarr & Kidd, 1983). Most experts have concluded that there is good evidence for at least some genetic component in our usual measures of temperament; most also agree that this genetic influence gets *stronger* with age.

*Physiological Connections.* Exploration of links between measures of temperament and measures of specific physiological functions is very new, but the early results are promising. For example, Kagan and his colleagues

**TABLE 9.2**

*Similarity of Identical and Fraternal Twins on Buss & Plomin's Temperament Dimensions*

| Temperament Scale | Twin Correlations | |
|---|---|---|
| | Identical | Fraternal |
| Emotionality | .63 | .12 |
| Activity | .62 | −.13 |
| Sociability | .53 | −.03 |

*Source:* Buss & Plomin, 1984, Table 9.2, p. 122.

The

Inheritance of

Personality

Patterns:

Evidence from

Adults

In the past decade there has been a whole series of methodologically careful new studies of adult twins that have repeatedly demonstrated that identical twins are more like one another than are fraternal twins on a whole host of measures of personality.

For example, Robert Plomin and his colleagues (Plomin et al., 1988) have taken advantage of the existence of an amazingly extensive and up-to-date twin registry in Sweden that includes 25,000 pairs of twins born between 1886 and 1958. From this set, they were able to identify 99 pairs of identical twins and 229 pairs of fraternal twins reared apart and could then compare these with similar groups of twins reared together. On measures of emotionality and activity, identical twins were more similar than fraternal twins, whether they had been reared together or not. The results were less clear for sociability.

A smaller but much more famous study in the United States is the Minnesota Twin Study (e.g., Tellegen et al., 1988; Bouchard, 1984)—a study that has been the subject of a great many popular articles in magazines like *Time* or *Fortune*. These researchers have been particularly interested in identical twins reared apart, frequently arranging for them to meet one another for the first time. On standard personality tests they find a familiar pattern: Identical twins are simply much more like one another than are fraternal twins, even when the identical twins did not grow up together. This is true on measures such as positive and negative emotionality (which may be similar to Buss and Plomin's dimension of emotionality), but also on less obvious measures, such as a sense of "social potency" or a sense of well-being. Even a measure of traditionalism—an affinity for traditional values and a strong allegiance to established authority—shows slightly higher correlations among identical than among fraternal twins.

What has intrigued the popular press much more, though, are the less precise but far more striking descriptions of the similarities in clothing preferences, interests, posture and body language, speed and tempo of talking, favorite jokes, and hobbies in pairs of identical twins reared apart.

> One male pair who had never previously met arrived in England sporting identical beards, haircuts, wire-rimmed glasses and shirts. . . . One pair had practically the same items in their toilet cases, including the same brand of cologne and a Swedish brand of toothpaste. . . . [One pair] had the same fears and phobias. Both were afraid of water and had adopted the same coping strategy: backing into the ocean up to their knees. (Holden, 1987, p. 18)

It is difficult to imagine what sort of genetic process could account for similar preferences in hairstyles or for a particular brand of toothpaste. But we can't merely dismiss the results because they are hard to explain. At the very least, these findings certainly point to strong genetic components in many of the elements of personal style and emotional responsiveness that temperament researchers are trying to identify and track in children.

(1990) have reported correlations in the range of .60 between a measure of behavioral inhibition in children ages 2 to 5 and a series of physiological measures, such as muscle tension, heart rate, dilation of the pupil of the eye, and the chemical composition of both urine and saliva.

*Consistency of Temperament over Time.*   The accumulating findings on the consistency of temperament over age are beginning to look a lot like the findings on IQ consistency. There is some consistency within infancy, and there is a fair amount of consistency from age 2 onward, but there is not much consistency between measures of temperament in infancy and those obtained on the same children when they are 4, 5, or 10.

In infancy, "difficultness," sociability, and activity level all seem to be at least moderately stable. Cranky 2-month-olds tend to be cranky at age 9 or 12 months; babies who smile more are friendlier later (e.g., Rothbart, 1986). In later childhood there is consistency across even larger time periods. For example, among the subjects in the sample originally selected by Thomas and Chess and followed into adulthood, correlations between temperament scores obtained four years apart in elementary school averaged about .42 (Hegvik, McDevitt, & Carey, 1981), while the correlation between a rating made in early adolescence and another in early adulthood was a robust .62 (Korn, 1984). However, temperament scores on these same subjects as infants were not predictive of temperament in either elementary school or adulthood.

This discontinuity between infancy and later temperament scores is extremely interesting—and poses some serious theoretical challenges. But there is no lack of potential explanations. Just as tests of infant intelligence may simply be measuring very different aspects of functioning than later IQ tests, so the infant and childhood temperament measures may be simply assessing different things. Emotionality ratings in infancy, for example, are heavily influenced by how much a baby cries. In older children and adults, crying is not so much a part of the rating. Or it could be that in early infancy, temperament measures are strongly affected by the infant's prenatal and birth experience and that this overrides genetic patterning, whereas childhood measures are more pure reflections of genetic differences. A variant of the same possibility is that there is such strong canalization of early infant development that the maturational blueprint largely runs the show in the first two years. Only when the canalization becomes less powerful, at about age 2, do we see more persisting individual differences emerging. It is also possible, of course, that any inborn temperamental differences we see in infancy are shaped and changed by the parents' (and others') responses to the child. The consistency we see later, then, results both from any inborn differences there may be and from the consistency of the environment. However one explains this intriguing discontinuity, the fact remains that temperament in children 2 and older does show at least some consistency over periods of years, even decades.

*Temperament and Environment Interactions.*   The simplest thing I can say about the research on temperament/environment interactions is that the findings are complex. Buss and Plomin (1984) have proposed that in general, children in the middle range on temperament dimensions typically adapt *to* their environment, while those children whose temperament is extreme—like extremely difficult children—force their environment to adapt to them. So, for example, temperamentally difficult children are punished more (Rutter, 1978c) than are more adaptable children (a pattern that may help to contribute to the higher rates of significant emotional problems in such children, which I have explored in the box on page 350). But even this statement is too simple. The parent's own child-rearing skills, the stress she experiences, and the amount of social or emotional support she has all affect her ability to deal with an irritable or difficult child (Crockenberg, 1986). For example, Mavis Hetherington (1989) reports that in divorcing families children with difficult temperaments show more problem behavior in response to the divorce; this is especially true if the mother is also depressed and has inadequate social support. Those difficult children whose divorcing mothers were not depressed did not show heightened levels of problems. Thus the child's temperament clearly seems to have an impact, but the effect is not simple or straightforward.

### Strengths, Weaknesses, and Implications

There are two great strengths in this approach to the origins of personality. First, it is a strong antidote to what had been a dominant environmental assumption about the origins of temperament or personality differences. I'm not sure we're looking yet at a real paradigm shift, but the accumulating evidence does make it very difficult to evade the conclusion that here, as in many other areas, there is a good deal more built in than most developmental psychologists had supposed (or felt comfortable assuming) a decade or two ago. The emerging research on the links between behavioral and physiological differences is another important push in the same direction.

Paradoxically, the second strength I see is that this is not a *purely* biological approach; it is an interactionist approach, very much in keeping with much of the current theorizing about development. What is built in creates a bias, but the outcome depends on the transactions between a given child's initial characteristics and the responses of the environment—a position that has a surprisingly psychoanalytic flavor.

On the other side of the ledger I see a number of problems, several of them resulting from the newness of this field of study. First there are still significant problems in measuring temperament. Most current measures of temperament, especially in infants and young children, rely on parents' reports about their own child's behavior or characteristics. Such measures are at least partially suspect because they may reflect the parent's own perceptual biases or temperament as much as they do the child's actual behavior (e.g., Power, Gershenhorn, & Stafford, 1990). A second problem arises from the continuing disagreement about just what dimensions we ought to be studying—a disagreement vividly clear in Table 9.1. Because different researchers have used such varying definitions and measures, it is often difficult to add up the results of several investigations.

More substantively, there are some tricky theoretical problems to be solved, such as how to explain the lack of consistency in temperament between infancy and early childhood. This particular dilemma highlights the fact that current temperament theories are not fundamentally *developmental* theories. Temperament theories allow for change through the mechanism of interaction with the environment. But they do not tell us whether we might expect systematic age differences in children's responses to new situations or to people; they do not tell us whether the child's emerging cognitive skills have anything to do with changes in the child's temperamental patterns. They do not, in a word, tell us how the *shared* developmental patterns may interact with the inborn individual differences.

None of these problems, except arguably the last, constitutes either a refutation or a basic criticism of any of the basic tenets of this theoretical approach. We can simply no longer ignore the importance of genetic differences and basic biology, not only in shaping shared "biases" in the child's initial system, but in shaping individual differences in response tendencies.

## Learning Approaches to Personality

The emphasis shifts rather dramatically when we look at social learning approaches. Instead of looking at what the child brings to the equation, learning theorists have looked primarily at the reinforcement patterns in the environment as the primary cause of differences in children's patterns of behaviors. Albert Bandura, one of the major figures in this theoretical tradition, puts the basic proposition flatly:

> Except for elementary reflexes, people are not equipped with inborn repertoires of behavior. They must learn them. (Bandura, 1977, p. 16)

Bandura is not rejecting biology. He goes on to say that biological factors such as hormones or inherited propensities (such as temperament, presumably) can affect behavior. However, he and others following this approach clearly come down hard on the side of the environment as the major "cause" of the behavior we observe.

These are not new ideas for you. You have already read about the basic concepts in Chapter 1 and encountered a version of such a theory in Skinner's theory of language acquisition. The question here is how to apply this theory specifically to such "personality" characteristics as dependency, nurturance, aggressiveness, activity level, or gregariousness.

In this case, it is not so simple to provide a set of agreed-upon basic propositions. As you will remember from Chapter 1, there are two distinct schools of thought within the "learning" camp—those we might call radical behaviorists and those usually called social learning theorists. Since the two groups make some different assumptions about personality and its origins, let me subdivide.

### Radical Behaviorists and Personality

Two basic propositions form the underpinnings of the application of strict learning principles to personality development.

*Proposition 1: Behavior is "strengthened" by reinforcement.*  If this rule applies to all behavior, then it should apply to attachment, shyness, sharing, or competitiveness, too. Children who are reinforced for clinging to their parents, for example, should show more clinging than do children who are not reinforced for it. Similarly, a nursery school teacher who pays attention to children only when they get rowdy or aggressive should find that the children get steadily more rowdy and aggressive over the course of weeks or months.

## Temperament and Behavior Problems

One of the consistent findings in the research on temperament is that children with difficult temperament are much more likely to show various kinds of emotional disturbances or behavior problems than are children with less extreme temperaments. Included in the category of behavior problems (which I'll be talking about in more detail in Chapter 14, when I discuss abnormal development) are such patterns as overaggressiveness, anxiety, depression, and hyperactivity.

The typical finding is that children who are rated as having aspects of difficult temperament—nonadaptive, irregular rhythm or pattern, withdrawal, intensity, or negativity of mood—are perhaps twice as likely to show one or another of these behavior problems as are children with less difficult temperaments. This is true both of studies in which the children's temperament is rated at age 3 or 4 and behavior problems are counted at elementary school or high school age (e.g., Chess & Thomas, 1984), and of studies of infant temperament, in which the behavior problems are measured in preschool (e.g., Bates et al., 1985; Bates, 1989). So babies with more difficult temperaments are more likely to become preschoolers who show some behavior problems, and preschoolers whose temperament is rated as difficult are more likely to have behavior problems at age 10 or 15 or even as adults.

Such findings may sound like a simple restatement of consistency of temperament. Hyperactivity or aggressiveness or other behavior problems in 5- or 7-year-olds may be simply further manifestations of the basic temperament. But it is not so simple. The majority of children who are rated as showing "difficult" temperament in infancy or the preschool years do not develop behavior problems at later ages. They are more likely to exhibit such problems, but the relationship is not at all inevitable.

As usual, there is a complex interactive process at work. The key seems to be whether the infant's or child's "difficultness" is acceptable to the parents, or can be managed by the family in some effective way—in Lerner's terms, whether there is a "goodness-of-fit." So, for example, a child with a difficult temperament who is less liked by his mother is far more likely to develop behavior problems than is a child with a difficult temperament whose mother likes him more. Difficult temperament also seems to increase the risk of behavior problems if there are any other stresses in the family system (such as divorce), or other deficits in the child. Among retarded children, for instance, the great majority of those with difficult temperament also show behavior problems (Chess & Korn, 1980).

Thus difficult temperament does not *cause* later behavior problems. Rather, it creates a *vulnerability* in the child. Such children seem to be less able to deal with major life stresses. But in a supportive, accepting, low-stress environment, many such children move through childhood without displaying any significant behavior problems.

The lesson for parents is not always an easy one to carry out. If you are under severe stress, that is precisely the moment when it is hard to provide a maximally supportive, accepting environment for any child, let alone a temperamentally difficult child. But it may help to keep in mind that a child with a difficult temperament is going to need more attention, more help, and more support than will a temperamentally less volatile child under any kind of stress, such as when the family moves, or when the child changes schools or baby sitters, or if the family pet dies.

*Proposition 2: Behavior that is reinforced on a "partial schedule" should be even stronger and more resistant to extinction than behavior that is consistently reinforced.* I talked about this phenomenon in Chapter 1 and have already given you some examples of the application of the principles of partial reinforcement in the box on page 350. Parents are nearly always inconsistent in their rewards to their children, so most children are on partial schedules of some kind. Given the strong persistence of behavior rewarded in this way, if we want to understand how children develop those distinctive and stable patterns of behavior defined as personality, we should look for what is being reinforced by the parents on a partial schedule.

*Some Evidence and Applications.* There is an *immense* collection of studies supporting these basic propositions. For example, when experimenters have systematically rewarded some children for hitting an inflated rubber clown on the nose and then watched the children in a play situation, the children who were rewarded showed more hitting, scratching, and kicking than did children who hadn't been rewarded for punching the clown (Walters & Brown, 1963). And partial reinforcement in the form of inconsistent behavior from parents also has the expected effect. For example, Sears, Maccoby, and Levin (1957) found that parents who allow their children to be quite aggressive (who are thus *permissive* toward it), but occasionally react by punishing quite severely, have children who are more aggressive than are children whose parents are nonpermissive and nonpunitive.

Both of these principles have been used successfully in therapeutic interventions with families of out-of-control children, such as in Gerald Patterson's studies of aggressive or noncompliant children that I described in Chapter 1. If you go back and look at Figure 1.3 (page 14) you'll see that the heart of Patterson's model is a link between "poor parental discipline" and resultant conduct problems in the child. He is arguing here that both normal personality patterns and deviant forms of behavior have their roots in daily social exchanges with family members. For example, imagine a child playing in his very messy room. The mother comes into the room and tells the child to clean up his room. The child whines or yells at her that he doesn't want to do it or won't do it. The mother gives in, leaves the room, and the child stops whining or shouting.

Patterson analyzes this exchange as a pair of negatively reinforced events. The mother's giving in is negatively reinforced by the ending of the child's whining or yelling. This makes it more likely that she will give in the next time. She has *learned* to back down in order to get the child to shut up. The child has been negatively reinforced for yelling or whining, since the unpleasant event for him (being told to clean his room) stopped as soon as he whined. So he has learned to whine or yell. Imagine such exchanges occurring over and over, and you begin to understand how a family can create a *system* in which an imperious, demanding, noncompliant child rules the roost.

As I pointed out in Chapter 1, Patterson's thinking has moved beyond the simple propositions I have outlined here. Like the current temperament theorists, he emphasizes that what happens in a given family for a particular child is a joint product of the child's own temperament or response tendencies, the parent's discipline skills, the parent's personality, and the social context of the parent's life. However, Patterson is still assuming that basic

How do you read this scene? To me it looks as if the child is screaming to be picked up and the Mom is resisting the child's loudest entreaties. Nearly every parent will at some time or another have to deal with such an unhappy, screaming child. And nearly all of us have had children throw major tantrums in public. Learning theorists remind us that if a parent regularly gives in to the child's demands, the child may learn that screaming or throwing a tantrum is a good way to get what he or she wants.

learning principles can both describe and explain the ways in which the child's behavior pattern (his "personality") is formed or changed.

### Social Learning Theorists and Personality

Social learning theorists, like Bandura, do not reject either of the propositions I have listed. But they add two more that fundamentally change the nature of the theory.

*Proposition 3: Children learn new behaviors largely through modeling.* Bandura has argued that the full range of social behaviors, from competitiveness to nurturance, is learned by watching others perform those actions. Thus the child who sees her parents making a donation to the local Cancer Society volunteer or taking a casserole next door to the woman who has just been widowed will learn generosity and thoughtful behavior. The child who sees her parents arguing or hitting each other when they are angry will most likely learn violent ways of solving problems.

Children learn from TV, too, and from their playmates, their teachers, and their brothers and sisters. A boy growing up in an environment where he observes playmates and older boys hanging around street corners, shoplifting, or stealing hubcaps is going to learn all those behaviors. His continuous exposure to such antisocial models makes it that much harder for his parents to reinforce more constructive behavior.

This theory, too, has moved beyond its narrow origins and has acquired strong cognitive overtones. Bandura points out that what an individual learns from watching someone else will depend on what she pays attention to, what she is able to remember (both *cognitive* processes), what she is physically able to copy, and what she is motivated to imitate. Although Bandura has not placed much emphasis on the potential developmental ramifications of these ideas, it seems clear that all of these factors are likely to change with age. Thus what a child models will change with age as well.

*Proposition 4: What children learn from reinforcement and from modeling is not just overt behavior but also ideas, expectations, internal standards, and self-concepts.* The child learns standards for his own behavior and expectancies about what he can and cannot do (which Bandura calls *self-efficacy*) from specific reinforcements and from modeling. Once those standards and expectancies or beliefs are established, they affect the child's behavior in consistent and enduring ways. These beliefs and expectancies form the core of what may be called personality, and they are reflected in behavior.

*Some Evidence and Applications.* The impact of observational learning has been demonstrated in literally hundreds of studies (Bandura, 1973, 1977). One interesting—and very practical—sidelight to the process of modeling has been the repeated finding that when there is a conflict between what a model does and what he or she says, it is the *behavior* that is likely to be imitated. In one study, Joan Grusec and her co-workers (Grusec, Saas-Kortsaak, & Simutis, 1978) found that telling children to be generous did little

Parents are not the only models for social learning.

good, but showing them generosity led them to be generous. So the old adage "Do what I say and not what I do" doesn't seem to work.

In his explorations of the concept of self-efficacy, Bandura has also shown that changing someone's belief about his ability to do something has a greater impact on his behavior than merely reinforcing him for performing that behavior (Bandura, 1982). He has been able to use this principle in therapeutic situations, such as working with people with phobias like fear of snakes.

### Strengths, Weaknesses, and Implications

Several implications of this theoretical approach are worth emphasizing. First of all, unlike temperament theorists, who expect at least a certain amount of consistency of behavior in different situations, learning theorists can handle either consistency or inconsistency in children's behavior. If a child is friendly and smiling both at home and at school, this could be explained by saying that the child was being reinforced for that behavior in both settings rather than by assuming that the child had a "gregarious temperament." However, it is equally possible to explain how a child could be the soul of helpfulness at school but never mind his mother at home, or do whatever his father asks but be disobedient to his mother. In cases like this, learning theorists merely go searching for the differing patterns of reinforcement in

Avery Gholston, 2½ is helping her Dad cook. This kind of helpful behavior is very common in children this age, but the fact that you see it at home is no guarantee that you will also see it in nursery school, or vice versa. Learning theories of personality development can handle such inconsistency across situations better than most other theories simply by arguing that the reinforcement contingencies may be quite different in the two settings. The Gholston family clearly emphasizes and reinforces helpfulness at home. This photo is a video still from the *Childhood* television series (*Source:* ©Thirteen/WNET).

the different settings or the different expectancies the child may have acquired. Such inconsistencies are more difficult to account for within a narrow biological approach.

A related implication is that this view of behavior is highly optimistic about the possibility of change. Children's behavior can change if the reinforcement system (or their beliefs about themselves) changes, so "problem behavior" can be modified, as Patterson has done with families of aggressive children.

The great strength of this view of social behavior is that it gives an accurate picture of the way in which many behaviors are learned. It is perfectly clear that children do learn through modeling; and it is equally clear that children (and adults) will continue to perform behaviors that "pay off" for them.

The addition of the cognitive elements to Bandura's theory adds further strength, since it offers a beginning integration of learning models and cognitive-developmental approaches. If we were to apply Piaget's language to Bandura's theory we could talk about the acquisition of a "self-scheme"—a concept of one's own capacities, qualities, standards, and experiences. New experiences are then assimilated to that scheme. You will recall from Chapter 7 that one of the characteristics of the process of assimilation as Piaget proposed it is that new experiences or information are modified as they are taken in. In the same way, Bandura is saying that once the child's self-concept is established, it affects what behaviors she chooses to perform, how she reacts to new experiences, whether she persists or gives up on some new task, and the like. If a child believes he is unpopular, for example, then he will not be surprised if others do not choose to sit by him in the lunchroom. If someone does sit next to him, he's likely to explain it to himself in such a way that he retains his central belief, such as "there must have been no place else to sit." In this way the underlying scheme isn't modified (accommodated) very much.

Thus the self-concept, once well formed, serves as a central mediating process leading to stable differences in behavior. It *can* be modified (accommodated) if the child accumulates enough experience or evidence that doesn't fit with the existing scheme. If the "unpopular" child noticed that classmates regularly chose to sit next to him at lunch even when there were other seats available, he might eventually change his self-scheme, coming to think of himself as "somewhat popular." But since the child (like the adult) will choose activities or situations that fit his self-concept, such as sitting in the corner where no one is likely to see him, he will be partially protected from such "nonconfirming" experiences.

To be sure, Bandura and Piaget would not agree on how this self-concept or self-scheme develops. Piaget emphasizes internal processes while Bandura emphasizes reinforcement as causal factors. But they agree on the impact that such a scheme will have once it has developed.

At the same time, these theories have significant weaknesses, particularly in the more radical versions. First, from the perspective of many psychologists, there is still too much emphasis placed on what happens *to* the child and not enough on what the child is doing with the information he has. Bandura's theory is much less vulnerable to this charge, but most learning theories of personality are highly mechanistic and focused on external events.

Secondly, like temperament theories, these are not really *developmental* theories. They can say how a child might acquire a particular behavior pattern or belief, but they do not take into account the underlying developmental changes that are occurring. Given Bandura's emphasis on the cognitive aspects of the modeling process, a genuinely developmental social learning theory could be proposed. But no such theory exists now so far as I know. Still, all the theories in this group offer useful descriptions of one source of influence on the child's developing pattern of behavior.

 ## Psychoanalytic Theories

Like many temperament theorists, and like social learning theorists of Bandura's stripe, psychoanalytic theorists emphasize the importance of the interaction between inborn characteristics of the child and environment in shaping differences in personality. But unlike temperament or learning theories, psychoanalytic theories are clearly *developmental* as well, describing systematic changes in children's sense of self, in their needs or drives, and in their relationships with others.

I described a number of the key propositions in Chapter 1, so let me simply summarize here:

*Proposition 1: Behavior is governed by unconscious as well as conscious motives and processes.* Freud emphasized three sets of instinctual drives: the sexual drive (libido); life-preserving drives, including avoidance of hunger and pain; and aggressive drives. Erikson emphasizes a more cognitive process, the drive for identity.

*Proposition 2: Personality structure develops over time, as a result of the interaction between the child's inborn drives/needs and the responses of the key people in the child's world.* Because the child is prevented from achieving instant gratification all the time, he is forced to develop new skills—planning, talking, delaying, and other cognitive techniques that allow gratification of the basic needs in more indirect ways. Thus the ego is created, and it remains the planning, organizing, thinking part of the personality. The superego, in turn, develops because the parents try to restrain certain kinds of gratification; the child eventually incorporates these parental standards into his own personality.

*Proposition 3: Development of personality is fundamentally stage-like, with each stage centered on a particular task or a particular form of basic need.* I'll describe both Freud's and Erikson's stages in some detail in a moment. For now, the key point is only that there *are* stages in these theories.

*Proposition 4: The specific personality a child develops depends on the degree of success the child has in traversing these various stages.* In each stage, the child requires a particular kind of supportive environment for successful resolution of that particular dilemma or for meeting that particular need. A child lacking the needed environment will have a very different personality than one whose environment was partially or wholly adequate.

However, while each stage is important, all the psychoanalytic theorists strongly emphasize the crucial significance of the very earliest stages, and focus especially on the adequacy of the relationship between the baby and the central caregiver, usually the mother. This is not quite like saying that infancy is a sensitive period for personality development. Rather, Freud and later psychoanalytic theorists argue that the earliest relationship establishes a pattern and sets the child on a particular pathway through the remainder of the stages.

### Some Differences Between Freud and Erikson

All four of these general propositions are contained in both Freud's and Erikson's theories, but both the details and the emphases differ in important respects. In Freud's theory, for example, all the cognitive skills develop only because the child needs them to obtain gratification; they have no independent life. In Erikson's theory (and in many other variations of psychoanalytic theory) the ego functions are presumed to develop independently, even though they are used in the service of obtaining basic gratification. Indeed the central proposition in Erikson's theory is that personality development is a process of *identity* development, and his concept of identity clearly has strong cognitive overtones.

Freud also emphasizes basic physical maturation more than does Erikson. In Freud's theory, the stages move from one to the next because of maturation of the nervous system. In each stage, the child is attempting to gratify basic physical ("sexual") needs through stimulation of a particular part of the body—that part of the body that is most sensitive at that time. As neurological development proceeds, maximum body sensitivity shifts from the mouth to the anus to the genitals; this maturational change is what drives the stage changes. Erikson grants such physical changes, but places greater emphasis on shifts in the demands of the social environment. Stage 4 (industry versus inferiority) begins at about age 6 because that is when the child goes off to school; in a culture in which schooling was delayed, the timing of the developmental task might be delayed as well.

Because of such theoretical differences, Erikson and Freud have described the stages of development rather differently. You need to be conversant with both sets of stages, so let me describe each.

### Freud's Psychosexual Stages

Freud proposed five stages, which I've summarized in Table 9.3 (p. 358).

*The Oral Stage: Birth–1 Year.*   The mouth, tongue, and lips are the first center of pleasure for the baby and his earliest attachment is to the one who provides pleasure in the mouth, usually his mother. For normal development the infant requires some optimum amount of oral stimulation—not too much and not too little. If the optimum amount of stimulation is not available, then some libidinal energy may remain attached to (*fixated* on, in Freud's terms) the oral mode of gratification. Such an individual will continue to have a strong preference for oral pleasures in later life. (Some of the proposed characteristics of adults who are fixated at the oral stage are listed in Table 9.3.)

**TABLE 9.3**

*Freud's Stages of Psychosexual Development*

| Stage | Age | Erogenous Zones | Major Developmental Task (potential source of conflict) | Some Adult Characteristics of Children Who Have Been "Fixated" at This Stage |
|---|---|---|---|---|
| Oral | 0–1 | Mouth, lips, tongue | Weaning | Oral behavior, such as smoking and overeating; passivity and gullibility. |
| Anal | 2–3 | Anus | Toilet training | Orderliness, parsimoniousness, obstinacy, or the opposite (extreme untidiness, for example). |
| Phallic | 4–5 | Genitals | Oedipus complex; identification with parent of same sex | Vanity, recklessness, and the opposite. |
| Latency | 6–12 | No specific area; sexual energy quiescent | Development of ego defense mechanisms | None: fixation does not normally occur at this stage. |
| Genital | 13–18 and adulthood | Genitals | Mature sexual intimacy | Adults who have successfully integrated earlier stages should emerge from this stage with a more sincere interest in others, realistic enjoyments, mature sexuality. |

*The Anal Stage: 1–3 Years.*   As the trunk matures and comes under more voluntary control, the baby becomes more and more sensitive in the anal region. At about the same time, her parents begin to place great emphasis on toilet training and show pleasure when she manages to perform in the right place at the right time. These two forces together help to shift the major center of physical/sexual energy from the oral to the anal erogenous zone.

The key to the child's successful completion of this stage is whether the parents allow the child sufficient anal exploration and pleasure. If toilet training becomes a major battleground, then some fixation of energy at this stage may occur—with the possible adult consequences of excessive orderliness, stinginess, or the opposite.

*The Phallic Stage: 3–5 Years.*   At about 3 or 4 years of age the genitals increase in sensitivity, ushering in a new stage. One sign of this new sensitivity is that children of both sexes quite naturally begin to masturbate.

According to Freud, the most important event that occurs during the phallic stage is the **Oedipus conflict.** He described the sequence of events more fully (and more believably!) for boys, so let me trace that pattern for you.

The theory suggests that first the boy becomes "intuitively aware of his mother as a sex object" (Rappoport, 1972, p. 74). Precisely how this occurs is not completely spelled out, but the important point is that the boy at about age 4 begins to have a sort of sexual attachment to his mother and to regard his father as a sexual rival. His father sleeps with his mother, holds her and kisses her, and generally has access to her body in a way that the boy does not. The boy also sees his father as a powerful and threatening figure who has the ultimate power—the power to castrate. The boy is caught between desire for his mother and fear of his father's power.

Most of these feelings and the resultant conflict are unconscious. The boy does not have overt sexual feelings or behavior toward his mother. But unconscious or not, the result of this conflict is anxiety. How can the little boy handle this anxiety? In Freud's view, the boy responds with a defensive process called **identification:** The boy "incorporates" his image of his father and attempts to match his own behavior to that image. By trying to make himself as much like his father as possible, the boy not only reduces the chance of an attack from the father, he also takes on some of the father's power as well. Furthermore, it is the "inner father," with his values and moral judgments, that serves as the core of the child's superego.

A parallel process is supposed to occur in girls. The girl sees her mother as a rival for her father's sexual attentions, and also has some fear of her mother (though less than is true for the boy, since the girl may assume she has already been castrated). In this case, too, identification with the mother is thought to be the "solution" to the girl's anxiety.

*The Latency Stage: 5–12 Years.*   Freud thought that after the phallic stage there is a sort of resting period before the next major change in the child's sexual development. The child has presumably arrived at some preliminary resolution of the Oedipal crisis, so that there is a kind of calm after the storm. One of the obvious characteristics of this stage is that the identification with the same-sex parent that defined the end of the phallic stage is now extended to others of the same sex. So during these years children's peer interactions are almost exclusively with members of the same sex, and children often have "crushes" on same-sex teachers or other adults.

*The Genital Stage: 12–18 and Older.*   The further changes in hormones and the genital organs that take place during puberty reawaken the sexual energy of the child. During this period a more mature form of sexual attachment occurs. From the beginning of this period, the child's sexual objects are people of the opposite sex. Freud placed some emphasis on the fact that not everyone works through this period to a point of mature heterosexual love. Some have not had a satisfactory oral period and thus do not have a foundation of basic love relationships. Some have not resolved the Oedipal crisis with a complete or satisfactory identification with the same-sex parent; this failure may affect their ability to cope with rearoused sexual energies in adolescence.

**Oedipus conflict**
The pattern of events Freud believed occurred between ages 3 and 5 when the child experiences a "sexual" desire for the parent of the opposite sex; the resulting fear of possible reprisal from the parent of the same sex is resolved when the child "identifies" with the parent of the same sex.

**identification**
The process of taking into oneself ("incorporating") the qualities and ideas of another person, which Freud thought was the result of the Oedipal crisis at ages 3–5. The child attempts to make himself like his parent of the same sex.

Mikiko Nouhata is toilet training her two-year-old son, Yojiro. At the moment this photo was taken, Yojiro looks pretty pleased with himself, but this moment was preceded by a long period of coaxing from Mikiko (and from the Grandmother, whom you can see in the background) and some fussing and distress from Yojiro. Freud thought that a child in this stage got pleasure both from the anal sensations and from the control he can exert over himself and his parents. The parents, meanwhile, are trying very hard to exert control over the child. According to psychoanalytic theory, the specific resolution of this conflict will affect a child's future personality. This photo is a video still from the *Childhood* television series (*Source:* © Thirteen/WNET).

What we see as the child's "personality," then, is a complex result of all of these processes, depending on the particular stages at which the child may have become fixated, on the particular form of the child's identification with the parents, and on the defense mechanisms that the child adopts. The same themes occur in Erikson's theory, but the particulars are different.

### Erikson's Psychosocial Stages

**psychosocial stages**
The stages of personality development suggested by Erikson, including trust, autonomy, initiative, industry, identity, intimacy, generativity, and ego integrity.

**psychosexual stages**
The stages of personality development suggested by Freud, including the oral, anal, phallic, latency, and genital stages.

The change in emphasis is noticeable in the name itself; Erikson is talking about **psycho*social* stages** not **psycho*sexual* stages.** Another difference is that Erikson's stages cover the entire life span rather than ending at adolescence, as you can see in Table 9.4.

*Basic Trust Versus Basic Mistrust: Birth–1 Year.*   The first task (or "crisis" as Erikson sometimes says) occurs during the first year of life (Freud's oral period). What is at issue is whether the child will develop a sense of basic trust in the predictability of the world and in his ability to affect the events around him. Erikson believes that the behavior of the major caregiver (usually the mother) is critical to the child's successful or unsuccessful resolution of this crisis. Children who emerge from the first year with a firm sense of trust are those with parents who are loving and who respond predictably and reliably

## TABLE 9.4

*The Eight Stages of Development Proposed by Erik Erikson*

| Approximate Age | Ego Quality to Be Developed | Some Tasks and Activities of the Stage |
|---|---|---|
| 0–1 | Basic trust versus basic mistrust | Trust in mother or central caregiver and in one's own ability to make things happen. A key element in an early secure attachment. |
| 2–3 | Autonomy versus shame, doubt | Walking, grasping, and other physical skills lead to free choice; toilet training occurs; child learns control but may develop shame if not handled properly. |
| 4–5 | Initiative versus guilt | Organize activities around some goal; become more assertive and aggressive. Oedipus-like conflict with parent of same sex may lead to guilt. |
| 6–12 | Industry versus inferiority | Absorb all of the basic culture skills and norms, including school skills and tool use. |
| 13–18 | Identity versus role confusion | Adapt sense of self to physical changes of puberty, make occupational choice, achieve adultlike sexual identity, and search for new values. |
| 19–25 | Intimacy versus isolation | Form one or more intimate relationships that go beyond adolescent love; marry and form family groups. |
| 26–40 | Generativity versus stagnation | Bear and rear children, focus on occupational achievement or creativity, and train the next generation. |
| 41+ | Ego integrity versus despair | Integrate earlier stages and come to terms with basic identity. Accept self. |

to the child. A child who has developed a sense of trust will go on to other relationships carrying this sense with him. Those infants whose early care has been erratic or harsh may develop *mis*trust, and they too carry this sense with them into later relationships.

It is important to point out, though, that while trust is critical, Erikson has never said that the ideal position on any one of the dilemmas he describes is at one extreme pole. In the case of this first stage, there is some risk in being totally trusting. The child also needs to develop some healthy mistrust, such as learning to discriminate between dangerous situations and safe ones.

*Autonomy Versus Shame and Doubt: 2–3 Years.* Erikson sees the child's greater mobility at this age as forming the basis for the sense of independence or autonomy. However, if the child's efforts at independence are not carefully guided by the parents and she experiences repeated failures or

If looks could kill! This child is clearly jealous of his new sibling and may well be harboring all sorts of angry and aggressive thoughts. A younger child would probably act out those thoughts and feelings directly. But a child of this age, probably in the period Erikson calls *initiative versus guilt*, feels guilty about his feelings and inhibits the angry actions.

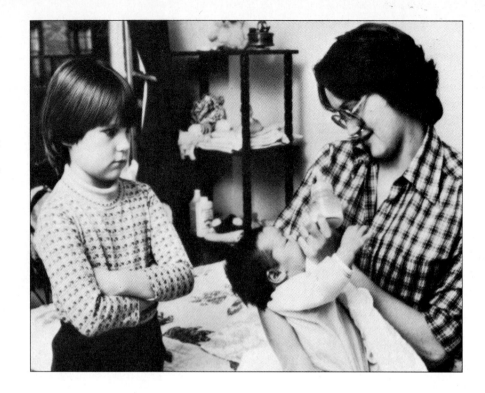

ridicule, then the results of all the new opportunities for exploration may be shame and doubt instead of a basic sense of self-control and self-worth. Once again the ideal is not for the child to have *no* shame or doubt; some doubt is needed for the child to understand what behaviors are acceptable and which are not, which are safe and which are dangerous. But the ideal does lie on the autonomy end of the continuum.

*Initiative Versus Guilt: 4–5 Years.*　This phase, which is roughly equivalent to Freud's phallic stage, is again ushered in by new skills or abilities in the child. The 4-year-old is able to plan a bit and take initiative in reaching particular goals. The child tries out these new cognitive skills and tries to conquer the world around him. He may try to go out into the street on his own. He may take a toy apart, and then find he can't put it back together and throw it—parts and all—at his mother. It is a time of vigor of action and of behaviors that parents may see as aggressive. The risk is that the child may go too far in his forcefulness, or that the parents may restrict and punish too much—either of which can produce guilt. Some guilt is needed, since without it there would be no conscience and no self-control. The ideal interaction between parent and child is certainly not total indulgence. But too much guilt can inhibit the child's creativity and her free interactions with others.

*Industry (Competence) Versus Inferiority: 6–12 Years.* The beginning of schooling is a major force in ushering in this stage. The child is now faced with the need to win approval through specific competence—through learning to read, add and subtract, and perform other school skills. The task of this period is thus simply to develop the repertoire of abilities society demands of the child. The flip side is that the child may be unable to develop the expected skills and will develop instead a basic sense of inferiority. Some failure is necessary so that the child can develop some humility, so as always it is the balance that is at issue. The ideal is for the child to have sufficient success to encourage a sense of competence, but not to have so much emphasis on competence that failure is unacceptable or that the child becomes a kind of "workaholic."

*Identity Versus Role Confusion: 13–18 Years.* The task occurring during puberty is a major one in which the adolescent reexamines his identity and the roles he must occupy. Erikson suggests that two "identities" are involved—a sexual identity and an occupational identity. What should emerge for the adolescent from this period is a reintegrated sense of self, of what one wants to do and be, and of one's appropriate sexual role. The risk is that of confusion, arising from the profusion of roles opening to the child at this age.

*Adult Stages.* As you can see in Table 9.4, Erikson proposed three further stages in adulthood: *intimacy versus isolation, generativity versus stagnation,* and *ego integrity versus despair.* Successful adult development requires the ability to set aside the independent identity enough to commit oneself to a truly intimate relationship; some form of "generativity," which includes bearing and rearing children, creative accomplishments, or leaving one's mark upon the world in some other fashion; and a final reflective integration, resulting in acceptance of who you are and what you have done. Erikson is one of the few theorists who has proposed such a life-span theory, and it has been one of the great attractions of his approach. I am not alone in finding the idea of such continued opportunities for growth in adulthood to be both a provocative and a comforting thought.

### Other Psychoanalytic Views

Before turning to a review of evidence supporting the psychoanalytic view, I want to reemphasize that Erikson is not the only influential modern theorist whose thinking has been strongly affected by Freud or psychoanalysis. Jane Loevinger's theory of ego development has been increasingly influential, particularly among researchers interested in adolescence and adulthood. Among those interested particularly in very early child development, Bowlby's theory of the development of attachment (1969, 1973, 1980) has had a major impact. He offers an interesting blend of psychoanalytic and biological approaches.

Like Freud, Bowlby assumes that the root of human personality lies in the earliest childhood relationships. Significant failure or trauma in those relationships will permanently shape the child's development. Because it is usually the earliest, and is arguably the most central, Bowlby focused his attention on the child's first attachment to the mother. To describe how that attachment comes about, Bowlby introduced several concepts from *ethological theory,* which is the "study of animal and human behavior within an evolutionary context" (Crain, 1980, p. 33). Human evolution, Bowlby suggested, has resulted in the child being born with a repertoire of built-in, instinctive, behaviors that elicit caregiving from others—behaviors like crying, smiling, and making eye contact. Similarly, the mother (or other adult) is equipped with various instinctive responses to the infant, such as responding to a cry, speaking in a higher voice, raising the eyebrows, and opening the eyes wide when talking to an infant. Together these instinctive patterns bring mother and infant together in an intricate chain of stimulus and response that results, within a few months, in the child's forming a specific attachment to that one adult—a process I'll be talking about in some detail in Chapter 11.

Although Bowlby's theory is not a full-fledged stage theory of development in the manner of Freud or Erikson, it is nonetheless based on many of the underlying psychoanalytic assumptions. It has also stimulated and profoundly influenced the large body of current research on attachment.

### The Evidence

Empirical explorations of Freud's or Erikson's theories are relatively rare, largely because both theories are so general that specific tests are very difficult. But let me at least mention three different bodies of work that have some link to psychoanalytic propositions. The first of these is research on the Oedipal period.

A 4-year-old boy, after his mother told him that she loved him, said, "And I love you too, and that's why I can't ever marry someone else" (Watson & Getz, 1990a, p. 29). In their studies of Oedipal behavior, Malcolm Watson and Kenneth Getz (1990a, 1990b) have indeed found that children of about 4 or 5 are likely to make comments like this. More precisely, they have found that 4-year-olds, more than any other age group, show more affectionate behavior toward the opposite-sex parent, and more aggressive or antagonistic behavior toward the same-sex parent, as you can see in Figure 9.1.

This pattern of findings is certainly consistent with Freud's description of the Oedipal period. But Watson and Getz argue that Freud's explanation is incorrect. The phenomenon may arise not from a burgeoning of sexual desires or a fear of retribution, but from the child's emerging understanding of the nature of social roles, particularly the roles of father and mother, husband and wife, and parent and child. The details of their proposal are complex and beyond the point I want to make here. The key for now is that when Watson and Getz measured the child's social understanding separately, they found that the level of the child's understanding was strongly related to the presence of so-called Oedipal behavior. Thus it may be broader cognitive changes, and not any unconscious or defensive processes, that are the source of the pattern.

It may also be possible to test some hypotheses about the Oedipal period by studying children growing up in single-parent families during the crucial years, such as children whose parents divorce when they are under the age of 5. Might such children show larger, or more lasting, effects of divorce than children whose parents divorce when they are older? Given current divorce rates, there are obviously pressing social as well as theoretical reasons for

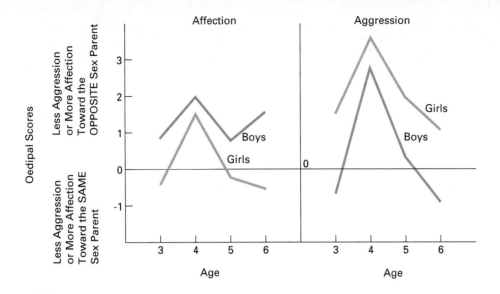

**FIGURE 9.1**

The data in this figure are based on the detailed reports of parents on the affectionate and aggressive behavior of their child toward them. Each parent was asked independently, and each was asked once a day for seven consecutive days. Any score above zero means that the child showed more "Oedipal" behavior—that is, more affection toward the opposite sex parent, and more aggression toward the same-sex parent. There is a clear peak at age 4, just as Freud would have predicted (*Source:* Watson & Getz, 1990b, from Table 3, p. 499).

wanting to understand such effects. I've examined some of the issues and the evidence in the box on pages 366–367.

A third research area that has its roots in psychoanalytic theory is the current work on the security or insecurity of children's early attachments. Both Erikson and Freud argue that the quality of the child's first relationship with the central caregiver will shape her relationships with other children and with other adults at later ages. And of course Bowlby's theory is designed specifically to examine that earliest relationship. I'll be talking a great deal more about early attachments in Chapter 11, but let me give you at least a taste of the research in this area, since it provides a good deal of support for the basic psychoanalytic hypothesis that the quality of the child's earliest relationship affects the whole course of the child's later development. This is particularly clear in the work of Alan Sroufe and his colleagues (e.g., Sroufe, 1983; Erickson, Sroufe, & Egeland, 1985; Sroufe, 1988). In a number of studies, they have first rated children on the security of their attachments to their mothers at about age 1. Later, at preschool or early elementary school age the same children are observed at school or at special summer camps where they must deal with new relationships or strange adults. The consistent finding from studies like this is that securely attached infants are later more capable, more friendly, more open to new relationships, and more skillful with peers.

## The Effects of Divorce: One Test of Psychoanalytic Theory

Current estimates are that nearly 40 percent of white and 75 percent of black children born in the late 1970s will experience their parents' divorce by the time they are 16 (Bumpass, 1984). It is now very nearly the norm for children to spend at least part of their growing- up years in a single-parent household, typically as a result of divorce.

What is the effect on the child of such an experience? Psychoanalytic theory suggests that the impact could be substantial, even devastating. In particular, the damage should be greatest if the divorce occurred before or during the Oedipal period (age 3–5 approximately), since separation from the father during these years would interfere with the identification process. What is more, the detrimental effect should be much greater for boys than for girls. A girl still has her mother to identify with, so at least her sex-role identification is appropriate. But the boy, lacking a father, may never go through the identification process properly and may end up with a very confused sex-role orientation and perhaps a weaker superego.

From the social learning point of view, too, divorce or father absence should have an effect, since it may profoundly alter the specific reinforcement patterns in the family as well as change the child's expectancies. In confirmation of this, Mavis Hetherington and her colleagues (Hetherington, 1979; Hetherington, Cox, & Cox, 1978) have found that mothers become less affectionate and more inconsistent in their discipline in the first few years after a divorce. We might expect, as a result, that the children would become less obedient, less easily managed. Social learning theorists also point to the lack of a male role model for the boy; this should affect the development of sex-role behaviors, particularly if the loss of the father occurs early.

The results of studies of children in divorced families support some, but not all, of these depressing expectations.

First of all, virtually all children show at least short-term distress or disruption following a parental separation. In the first two years or so after a divorce, children typically become more defiant, more negative, often more depressed, angry, or aggressive. On average, their school performance goes down for at least a while, and they may be ill more often. Among adolescents, substance use and abuse also doubles or triples (Doherty & Needle, 1991). As virtually all the research shows, this is a profoundly *disruptive* process for children, no matter what their age (e.g., Emery, 1988; Krantz, 1988; Allison & Furstenberg, 1989). These effects do diminish with time, but for at least a minority of children there are still residues detectable many years later.

For example, in one of the few long-term longitudinal studies, Wallerstein and Kelly (1980; Wallerstein, 1984, 1989) have found that 5 years after the divorce, about one-third of the children they studied showed significant disturbance, including depression. Ten years after the divorce when the children were now mostly in young adulthood, more than 40 percent showed continuing problems. Other researchers have not reported such pessimistic findings, but there is no escaping the fact that divorce has a pervasive effect on a child's development.

Second, most of the research does show that the effect is greater for boys, just as both Freud and the social learning theo-

Some typical findings from a study by Erickson, Sroufe, and Egeland (1985) are in Figure 9.2 on page 368. They observed a group of 4- to 5-year-old children in various preschools, and rated each child on a series of seven-point scales describing such things as "agency" (how confidently and assertively the child approaches tasks and activities), dependency on the teacher, and social skills with other children, and compared these ratings for

rists would expect (e.g., Hetherington, 1989; Kline et al., 1989). Boys whose parents have divorced show more increase in distress and in aggressive or noncompliant behavior, and more school problems than do girls from equivalent families. Interestingly, there are now several studies that show that boys may begin to show such disrupted effects well before the separation or divorce occurs, at the point when family discord begins to be high. So boys may be especially sensitive to discord, whenever it happens (Cherlin et al., 1991).

The findings on the effects of the child's age at the time of divorce are a lot more mixed. Most researchers agree that preschool-age children show more overt distress after a divorce, such as sleeping or eating problems or prolonged crying; adolescents seem more likely to show anger or aggression. But it is not at all clear that either the intensity of the problems or the long-term consequences are greater for children of any particular age. Some researchers do find that preschoolers show the largest negative effects (e.g., Allison & Furstenberg, 1989); others find larger consequences among elementary school-age children or even adolescents (Kline et al., 1989). For example, in her longitudinal study, Wallerstein found that children under age 5 were most visibly upset at the time of divorce, but that they showed the best long-term adjustment. All in all, there does not seem to be anything *uniquely* difficult for a child about having a parental separation during the "Oedipal period."

So much for the bad news. The good news is that we are now beginning to understand some of the factors in both children and families that can reduce or

shorten these effects. Based on all the research, it looks to me as if the *smallest* or *shortest* effects occur for children in the following circumstances:

1. Their families are economically secure after the divorce.
2. Their parents had low levels of open conflict before the divorce and maintain civility afterward. (It is not the conflict between the parents that seems to matter, but the degree of conflict that the child actually sees or hears.)
3. They do not feel caught in the middle between their parents; the parents don't ask the kids to spy on the other parent, for example, or serve as a go-between (e.g., Buchanan, 1991).
4. They see the non-custodial parent (usually the father) regularly and have a positive relationship with him.
5. Their lives are changed or disrupted the least in other ways. A child who can stay in the same house, or the same school, seems to be better off than one who must adjust to multiple changes at once.
6. Their custodial parent (usually the mother) has a relatively stable life, with adequate emotional support from friends and family.

This list of mitigating conditions underlines again that we cannot understand the effects of any family experience without understanding the whole system —the network of relationships, the individual personalities or temperaments, and the emotional and social setting of the family.

securely and insecurely attached children. As you can see in the figure, those children who had been securely attached at one year were significantly more confident and skillful, and less dependent, at age 4 or 5.

In preliminary data on one group of children at ages 10 and 11, Sroufe has found the same pattern, suggesting that the echoes of the earliest attachment relationship can be detected long past early childhood (Sroufe, 1989;

**FIGURE 9.2**

The 96 children in this study had all been rated for the security or insecurity of their attachments when they were a year old. Three to four years later, their behavior was rated while they were playing in preschool. It certainly looks as though repercussions of an early lack of trust or insecure attachment are still visible 3 or 4 years later (*Source:* Erickson, Sroufe, & Egeland, 1985, Table 1, page 154).

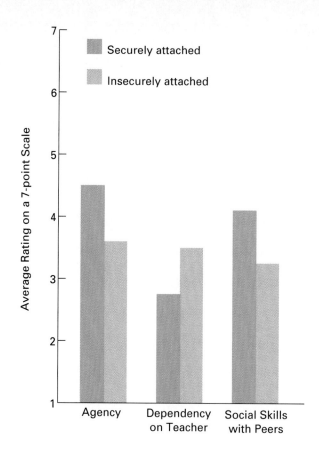

Sroufe & Jacobvitz, 1989). In Sroufe's terms, the relationship formed during the earliest stage of psychosexual development creates a prototype for later relationships.

### Strengths, Weaknesses, and Implications

Psychoanalytic theories like Freud's or Erikson's have several great attractions. First of all, they are *sequential* theories, and there is now increasing evidence (as I've described in earlier chapters) that there are sequences built into many of the child's developing skills. Second, they focus our attention on the importance of the child's relationship with the caregivers. More importantly, both these theories suggest that the child's needs or "tasks" change with age, so that the parents must constantly adapt to the changing child. One of the implications of this is that we should not think of "good parenting" as if it were a global quality. Some of us may be very good at meeting the needs of an infant, but quite awful at dealing with teenagers' identity struggles; others of us may have the opposite pattern. The child's eventual personality, and her overall "health," thus depends on the interaction or transaction that develops in the particular family. This is an extremely attractive element of these theories, since more and more of the research within developmental psychology is moving us toward exactly this conception of the process, as I have already pointed out in talking about both temperament theory and social learning theory.

A third strength is that psychoanalytic theory has offered several concepts, such as defense mechanisms or identification, that have been so widely adopted that they have become a part of everyday language as well as theory.

These strengths have led to a resurgence of influence of both Erikson's theory and the several second-order or third-order psychoanalytic approaches such as Bowlby's.

The great weakness of all the psychoanalytic approaches is fuzziness. As Jack Block puts it (1987):

> For all the richness, insight, and seriousness of psychoanalytic theory regarding the understanding of personality functioning, it has also been imprecise, overly facile with supposed explanations, and seemingly inaccessible scientifically. (p. 2)

Identification may be an intriguing theoretical notion, but how are we to measure it? How do we measure "ego strength" or accurately detect the presence of specific defense mechanisms? Without more precise operational definitions, it is impossible to disconfirm the theory. Those areas in which the general concepts of psychoanalytic theory have been fruitfully applied to our understanding of development have nearly always been areas in which other theorists or researchers have offered more precise definitions or clearer methods for measuring some Freudian or Eriksonian construct, such as Bowlby's concept of security of attachment. Psychoanalytic theory may thus offer a provocative framework for our thinking, but it is not a precise theory of development.

 ## A Tentative Synthesis

I have given you three different views of the origins of those unique, individual patterns of behavior we call personality. Each view can be at least partially supported with research evidence, so it seems impossible to choose one of the three as the "correct" view. But can we combine them in any sensible way? There are those who argue that theories as different as these cannot ever be combined (Reese & Overton, 1970; Overton & Reese, 1973) because they make such different assumptions about the child's role in the whole process. I agree in part. I do not think we can simply add up the different sources of influence and say that personality is merely the sum of inborn temperament, reinforcement patterns, interactions with parents, and some kind of self-scheme.

But more complex combinations may still be fruitful. I have suggested one in Figure 9.3 on the next page. In this model I am suggesting that the child's inborn temperament is a beginning point—an initial bias in the system. Arrow 1 shows a *direct* relationship between that inborn temperament and the eventual personality or behavior we see in a child.

I am suggesting a second direct effect in Arrow 2, between the pattern of the child's environment and his eventual behavior. Whether the parents respond reliably and contingently to the infant will affect his trust, which will show up in a range of behaviors later. Whether the parents reinforce aggressive or friendly behavior will influence the child's future as well.

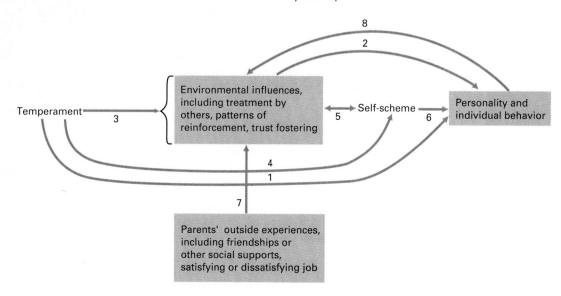

**FIGURE 9.3**

Here is my own proposal for a complex, interactive model describing the formation of individual personality. The effects of inborn temperament and environmental influences do not merely add. Each affects the other, helping to create the child's unique self-scheme, which in turn affects the child's experiences. All of this occurs within the context of the family, which is itself influenced by the parents' own life experiences. What we think of as personality is a complex product of all these forces.

But most of what happens is much more complicated than these direct influences suggest. The way the child is treated is influenced by her temperament (Arrow 3), and both the basic temperament and the family environment affect the child's self-scheme—her expectations for others and herself and her beliefs about her own abilities (arrows 4 and 5). This self-scheme or self-concept, in turn, helps to shape the behavior we see, the "personality" of the child.

Furthermore, this system does not exist in a vacuum. In keeping with Bronfenbrenner's (and others') ecological approach, Arrow 7 suggests that the parents' ability to maintain a loving and supportive relationship with their child is influenced by the parents' own outside experiences—whether they like their job, whether they have enough emotional support to help them weather their own crises (including the crisis of caring for a child).

Several elements in this intricate system are nicely illustrated by a study by Susan Crockenberg (1981). She studied a group of 46 mothers and infants over the first year of the child's life. The child's irritability (an aspect of temperament) was measured when the baby was 5–10 days old, and the security of the child's attachment to the mother was measured when the child was 12 months old. We might expect that irritable babies would be more likely to be insecurely attached, merely because they are more difficult to care for. In fact

**TABLE 9.5**

*Influence of Child's Temperament and Mother's Social Support on Child's Secure or Insecure Attachment*

| Child's Irritability | Mother's Support | Child's Attachment: Secure | Insecure |
|---|---|---|---|
| High | Low | 2 | 9 |
| High | High | 12 | 1 |
| Low | Low | 7 | 2 |
| Low | High | 13 | 2 |

*Source:* Crockenberg, 1981, Table 5, p. 862.

Crockenberg found a small effect of this kind (see Table 9.5). But Crockenberg didn't stop there. She also measured the level of the mother's social support—the degree to which she had family and friends who were sufficiently helpful to assist her in dealing with the strains of a new child or other life changes she might be experiencing. The results of the study show that an insecure attachment in the child was most likely when the mother had *both* an irritable infant *and* low levels of support. If the baby was irritable but the mother had good support, the child's attachment nearly always developed securely. Only when two difficult conditions occurred together did a poor outcome result for the child.

In another study, Crockenberg (1987) found that a higher level of anger and noncompliant behavior was common in toddlers who had been irritable as infants *and* whose mothers were angry and punitive toward them. Furthermore, such angry and punitive behavior in the mother was more likely if the mother had experienced rejection in her own childhood, and if she experienced little support from her partner. We are dealing here with a *system* of effects.

Finally, I have included Arrow 8 in the diagram to underline the *transactional* elements of the system. The child's unique pattern of behaviors and attitudes (personality), after it is formed, affects the environment she will encounter, the experiences she will choose, and the responses of the people around her, which in turn affect her behavior (Scarr & McCartney, 1983).

No doubt even this fairly complex system underestimates the intricacy of the process of personality development in the child.

# S U M M A R Y

1. The word *personality* refers to the unique, individual, relatively enduring pattern of relating to others and responding to the world that is characteristic of each individual. *Personality* is a more inclusive term than *temperament;* the latter refers primarily to inborn style of response to the environment.

2. The origins of personality differences have been described in three distinct theoretical approaches: temperament theories (a primarily biological approach), learning theories, and psychoanalytic theories.

3. Temperament theory proposes that each child is born with innately determined patterns or styles of reacting to people and objects. These patterns shape the child's interactions with the world and affect others' responses to the child.

4. Research supports the proposition that there are reasonably stable differences in temperament among infants and children, at least partially determined by heredity.

5. Traditional learning theorists emphasize the role of basic learning processes, such as reinforcement patterns, in shaping individual behaviors, including patterns of interaction with others.

6. Social learning theories emphasize, in addition, the role of observational learning, and of the child's learned expectancies, standards, and self-efficacy in creating more enduring patterns of response.

7. Psychoanalytic theorists emphasize the importance of unconscious motives and processes as well as the stage-like emergence of personality. In this approach, the relationship of the child with significant adults, particularly in early infancy, is seen as critical.

8. Freud's psychosexual stages are strongly affected by maturation. Particularly significant is the phallic stage, beginning at about age 4, when the Oedipal crisis is met and mastered through the process of identification.

9. Erikson's psycho*social* stages are influenced by both social demands and by the child's physical and intellectual skills. Each of the major stages has a central task or "crisis," each relating to some aspect of the development of identity.

10. Recent research on the Oedipal period, and on the impact of early attachments on later functioning, has provided support for some aspects of the psychoanalytic view.

11. Elements of all three views can be combined into an interactionist view of personality development. Temperament may serve as the base from which personality grows by affecting behavior directly and by affecting the way others respond to the child. Both the temperament and the specific pattern of response from the people in the child's environment affect the child's self-concept or self-scheme, which then helps to create stability in the child's unique pattern of behavior.

## CRITICAL THINKING QUESTIONS

1. Why is the study of children in divorced families a good way to check on the validity of several of Freud's hypotheses about the Oedipal period? What does the evidence from research on divorce tell us about the correctness of those hypotheses?

2. In recent years the concept of "vulnerable" and "invulnerable" children has become prominent in developmental research. How might vulnerability be conceptualized or explained by theorists of each of the several persuasions described in this chapter?

3. If temperament differences are really inborn, then why is there so little correlation between temperament ratings in infancy and those in the same children at age 5 or 6 or older? How much of a problem does this finding pose for temperament theorists?

## KEY TERMS

**identification**   The process of taking into oneself ("incorporating") the qualities and ideas of another person, which Freud thought was the result of the Oedipal crisis at ages 3–5. The child attempts to make himself like his parent of the same sex.

**Oedipus conflict**   The pattern of events Freud believed occurred between ages 3 and 5 when the child experiences a "sexual" desire for the parent of the opposite sex; the resulting fear of possible reprisal from the parent of the same sex is resolved when the child "identifies" with the parent of the same sex.

**personality**   The collection of individual, relatively enduring patterns of reacting to and interacting with others that distinguishes each child or adult.

**psychosexual stages**   The stages of personality development suggested by Freud, including the oral, anal, phallic, latency, and genital stages.

**psychosocial stages**   The stages of personality development suggested by Erikson, including trust, autonomy, initiative, industry, identity, intimacy, generativity, and ego integrity.

## SUGGESTED READINGS

Bates, J. E. (1987). Temperament in infancy. In J. D. Osofsky (Ed.), *Handbook of infant development.* (2nd ed.). New York: Wiley-Interscience.

   A good basic source on this complex topic.

Emery, R. E. (1988). *Marriage, divorce, and children's adjustment.* Newbury Park, CA: Sage.

   Emery not only presents the most current findings on divorce, he also explores in detail the very difficult methodological problems associated with research in this area.

Erikson, E. H. *Identity and the life cycle.* New York: W. W. Norton, 1959 (reissued 1980).

   The middle section of this book, "growth and crises of the healthy personality," is the best description I have found of the psychosocial stages of development.

Patterson, G. R. (1975). *Families.* Champaign, IL: Research Press.

   If you find yourself with a child showing problem behavior, or if you are merely interested in the process of behavior modification, this is a wonderfully interesting and helpful book. It is not recent enough to include many of Patterson's current theoretical concepts, but it is practical and very clear.

Sroufe, L. A. The coherence of individual development. *American Psychologist,* 1979, 34, 834–841.

   A brief, readable paper that reflects much of what I see as the new direction of thinking about personality development.

# 10

# THE CONCEPT OF SELF IN CHILDREN

In the state where I now live, one of the hot political issues has been the idea of "comparable worth" as a basis for determining pay levels for government workers. Those who oppose it say (among other things) that women have not been forced out of higher paying types of jobs. Rather, they say, women *choose* to be secretaries, nurses, or file clerks. As long as there is free choice involved, the argument goes, there is no government responsibility to equalize pay. The counterargument is that no one's choice of occupation is "free." We are all influenced by our images or concepts of ourselves, and by the idea each of us has about the appropriate or suitable jobs for our own gender. A woman *could* choose to become a carpenter or a truck driver, but this decision flies in the face of the sex stereotypes in our culture, and may thus conflict with the woman's own concept of herself.

**self-concept**
The broad idea of "who I am," including the existential self and the categorical self.

I give you this example not to get embroiled in political argument, but to show you that the subject we are about to explore has important practical relevance for each of us. The **self-concept** each of us develops, as I pointed out in the last chapter, serves as a sort of filter for experience, shaping our choices and affecting our responses to others. Our ideas about our own sex roles are a powerful part of that self-concept. In this chapter I want to explore the origins of both the common developmental pathways and the variations in such concepts from one child to the next.

## The Concept of Self: Developmental Patterns

Changes in the child's understanding of "self" within the first year or two of life are a significant part of both psychoanalytic and cognitive-developmental theories, although they use different terminology to describe those changes. Freud emphasized what he called the *symbiotic* relationship between the mother and infant in which the two are joined together as if they are one. He believed that the infant did not understand himself to be separate from the mother. Piaget emphasized that the infant's understanding of the basic concept of object permanence was a necessary precursor for the child's attaining *self-permanence*—a sense of himself as a stable, continuing entity. Both of these aspects of early self-development reappear in current descriptions of the emergence of the sense of self. Michael Lewis, for example (1990; Lewis & Brooks-Gunn, 1979), divides the process into two main steps or tasks.

### The First Step: The "Existential Self"

Lewis argues that the child's first task is to figure out that he is separate from others and that this separate self endures over time and space. He calls this aspect of the self-concept the **existential self**—existential in the sense of "I exist." Agreeing with Freud, Lewis places the earliest glimmers of this understanding in the first two or three months of life. At that time, the baby grasps the basic distinction between self and everything else. In Lewis' view, the roots of this understanding lie in the myriad everyday interactions the baby has with the objects and people in his world. When the child touches the mobile, it moves; when he cries, someone responds; when his mother smiles, he smiles back. By this process the baby separates self from everything else and a sense of *I* begins to emerge.

### The Second Step: The Categorical Self

This is not the end of the story, however. It is not enough merely to understand yourself as an agent in the world or as a person who has experiences. For a full sense of self, the toddler must also understand herself to be an *object* in the world. Just as a ball has properties—roundness, the ability to roll, a certain feel in the hand—so the "self" also has qualities or properties, such as gender, size, a name, or qualities like shyness or boldness, coordination or clumsiness. It is this *self-awareness* that is the hallmark of this second phase of identity development. Lewis refers to this as the **categorical self** because once the child achieves self-awareness the process of defining the self involves placing oneself in a whole series of categories.

*Studying Self-Awareness.* It has not been easy to determine just when a child has developed such self-awareness. The most commonly used procedure involves a mirror. First the baby is placed in front of a mirror, just to see how she behaves. Most infants of about 9–12 months will look at their own images, make faces, or try to interact with the baby in the mirror in some way. After allowing this free exploration for a time, the experimenter, while pretending to wipe the baby's face with a cloth, puts a spot of rouge on the baby's nose, and then again lets the baby look in the mirror. The crucial test of self-recognition, and thus of awareness of the self, is whether the baby reaches for the spot on her *own* nose (not the nose on the face in the mirror).

The results from one of Lewis's studies (Lewis & Brooks, 1978) using this procedure are in Figure 10.1 on the next page. As you can see, none of the 9- to 12-month-old children in this study touched their noses, but by 21 months, three-fourths of the children showed that level of self-recognition. The figure also shows the rate at which children refer to themselves by name when they are shown a picture of themselves, which is another commonly used measure of self-awareness. You can see that this development occurs at almost exactly the same time as self-recognition in a mirror. Both are present by about the middle of the second year of life, a finding confirmed by other investigators (e.g., Bullock & Lütkenhaus, 1990).

We can see signs of this new self-awareness in other behavior as well, such as the 2-year-old's determined rejection of help and insistence on doing things for herself or in the newly proprietary attitude the child takes toward toys

**existential self**
Lewis & Brooks-Gunn's term for the most basic part of the self-scheme or self-concept; the sense of being separate and distinct from others and the awareness of the constancy of the self.

**categorical self**
Aspect of the self-scheme, beginning with self-awareness, in which the child defines herself in terms of a series of categories, such as age, gender, size, or skill.

**FIGURE 10.1**

Two signs of the child's self-awareness are the child's checking his own nose when he sees the rouge spot on his nose in the mirror, and using his own name to respond to a picture of himself. These results from a study by Michael Lewis show that these two behaviors appear at almost exactly the same time (*Source:* Lewis & Brooks, 1978, pp. 214–215).

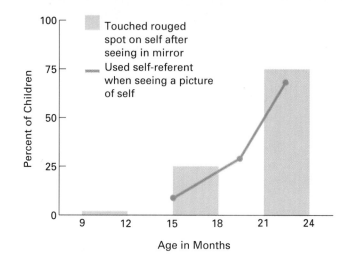

("Mine!"). Looked at this way, much of the legendary "terrible twos" can be understood as an outgrowth of self-awareness. We also see the effects of this new awareness in the emergence of the so-called "self-conscious" emotions, like embarrassment or empathy, which are first seen at about the same time that a child shows self-recognition in the mirror procedure (Lewis et al., 1989).

We also see that the child now begins to *define* herself, to label herself in various ways. Not only does she now know her own name, she also can probably tell you if she is a girl or a boy, and whether she is big or little. By about ages 5 to 7, a child can give you quite a full description of himself on a whole range of dimensions. Still, these early self-concepts remain highly concrete. For example, Susan Harter (1988, 1990; Harter & Pike, 1984) has

When a two-year-old insists on doing things for himself, like tying his own shoes, or grabs a toy saying "MINE!," it may simply mean that the child is trying out the boundaries of his new sense of self, rather than signifying defiance or basic negativity.

found that children between 4 and 7 have clear notions of their own competence on a range of physical, intellectual, and social tasks, such as solving puzzles, being able to count, knowing a lot in school, climbing or skipping or jumping rope, or having lots of friends. But they do not yet have a *global* sense of their own worth.

The self-concept of a preschool child is concrete in another way as well, in that he tends to focus on his own visible characteristics, such as what he looks like, what or who he plays with, where he lives, what he is good or bad at doing, rather than on more enduring, inner qualities. This pattern obviously parallels what we see in cognitive development at the same ages since it is in these same years that children's attention tends to be captured by the external appearance of objects rather than by their enduring properties.

*School Age.*　　Over the elementary school years, the child's self-concept gradually becomes more abstract. One aspect of this shift is that children's self-descriptions begin to be significantly more comparative. For example, they see themselves not just as "smart" or "dumb," but as "smarter than most other kids," or "not as good at baseball as my friends" (Ruble, 1987). The self-concept also becomes more complex, more elaborated, less and less focused on external characteristics and more and more on internal qualities (Harter, 1983, 1985). The child assumes that her own (and other people's) characteristics are relatively stable, and for the first time she develops a global sense of her own self-worth. A number of these themes are illustrated nicely in a study by Montemayor and Eisen (1977) of self-concepts in 9- to 18-year-olds.

These researchers asked each child to give 20 answers to the question "Who am I?" They found that the younger children in this study were still using mostly surface qualities to describe themselves, such as the description by this 9-year-old:

> My name is Bruce C. I have brown eyes. I have brown hair. I have brown eyebrows. I am nine years old. I LOVE! Sports. I have seven people in my family. I have great! eye site. I have lots! of friends. I live on 1923 Pinecrest Dr. I am going on 10 in September. I'm a boy. I have a uncle that is almost 7 feet tall. My school is Pinecrest. My teacher is Mrs. V. I play Hockey! I'm almost the smartest boy in the class. I LOVE! food. I love fresh air. I LOVE school. (Montemayor & Eisen, 1977, pp. 317–318)

In contrast, look at the self-description of this 11-year-old girl in the sixth grade:

> My name is A. I'm a human being. I'm a girl. I'm a truthful person. I'm not very pretty. I do so-so in my studies. I'm a very good cellist. I'm a very good pianist. I'm a little bit tall for my age. I like several boys. I like several girls. I'm old-fashioned. I play tennis. I am a *very* good swimmer. I try to be helpful. I'm always ready to be friends with anybody. Mostly I'm good, but I lose my temper. I'm not well-liked by some girls and boys. I don't know if I'm liked by boys or not. (Montemayor & Eisen, 1977, p. 317–318)

This girl, like the other youngsters of this age in the Montemayor and Eisen study, not only describes her external qualities, she also emphasizes her beliefs, the quality of her relationships, and general personality traits. Thus as the child moves through the concrete operations period, her self-definition becomes more complex, less tied to external features, and more focused on feelings and ideas.

*Adolescence.*  This trend toward greater abstraction in the self-definition continues during adolescence. Compare the answers of this 17-year-old to the "Who am I?" question with the ones you just read:

> I am a human being. I am a girl. I am an individual. I don't know who I am. I am a Pisces. I am a moody person. I am an indecisive person. I am an ambitious person. I am a very curious person. I am not an individual. I am a loner. I am an American (God help me). I am a Democrat. I am a liberal person. I am a radical. I am a conservative. I am a pseudoliberal. I am an atheist. I am not a classifiable person (i.e., I don't want to be.). (Montemayor & Eisen, p. 318)

Obviously this girl's self-concept is even less tied to her physical characteristics or even her abilities than was true of the 11-year-old. She is describing abstract traits or ideology.

You can see the shift I'm describing graphically in Figure 10.2, based on the answers of all 262 subjects in the Montemayor and Eisen study. Each of the subjects' answers to the "Who am I?" question was placed in one or more specific categories, such as references to physical properties ("I am tall," "I have blue eyes") or references to ideology ("I am a Democrat," "I believe in God," etc.). As you can see, appearance was a highly salient dimension in the preteen and early teen years, but became less dominant in late adolescence, at a time when ideology and belief became more salient.

### Identity in Adolescence

This increasing preoccupation with ideology may also be a reflection of the central task of adolescence, as Erikson described it, of *identity versus role confusion.* In Erikson's view, the child's early sense of identity comes partly unglued at puberty with the onset of both rapid body growth and the sexual changes. He refers to this period as one in which the adolescent mind is in a kind of *moratorium* between childhood and adulthood. The old identity will no longer suffice; a new identity must be forged, one that must serve to place the young person among the myriad roles of adult life—occupational roles, sexual roles, and religious roles. Confusion about all these role choices is inevitable. Erikson puts it this way:

> In general it is primarily the inability to settle on an occupational identity which disturbs young people. To keep themselves together they temporarily overidentify, to the point of apparent complete loss of identity, with the heroes of cliques and crowds. . . .They become remarkably clannish, intolerant, and cruel in their exclusion of others who are "different" in skin color or cultural background. . . and often in entirely petty aspects of dress and gesture arbitrarily selected as *the* signs of an in-grouper or out-grouper. It is important to understand. . . such intolerance as the necessary *defense against a sense of identity confusion,* which is unavoidable at [this] time of life. (1980, p. 97–98)

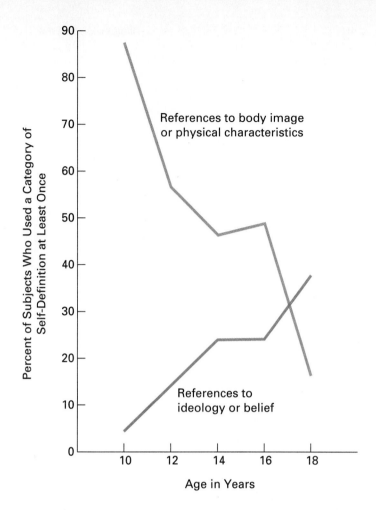

**FIGURE 10.2**

As they get older, children and adolescents define themselves less and less by what they look like and more and more by what they believe or feel (*Source:* Montemayor & Eisen, 1977, from Table 1, p. 316).

The teenage clique or group thus forms a base of security from which the young person can move toward a unique solution of the identity process. Ultimately, each teenager must achieve an integrated view of himself including his own pattern of beliefs, occupational goals, and relationships.

Nearly all the current work on the formation of adolescent identity has been based on James Marcia's descriptions of *identity statuses* (Marcia, 1966, 1980), which are based in turn on Erikson's general conceptions of the adolescent identity process. Following one of Erikson's ideas, Marcia argues that there are two key parts to any adolescent identity formation: a *crisis* and a *commitment.* By a "crisis" Marcia means a period of decision making when old values and old choices are reexamined. This may occur as a sort of upheaval—the classic notion of a crisis—or it may occur gradually. The outcome of the reevaluation is a commitment to some specific role, some particular ideology.

If you put these two elements together, as in Figure 10.3 on the next page, you can see that four different "identity statuses" are possible.

- **Identity achievement:** The person has been through a crisis and reached a commitment.

**identity achievement**
One of four identity statuses proposed by Marcia, involving the successful resolution of an identity "crisis," resulting in a new commitment.

**FIGURE 10.3**

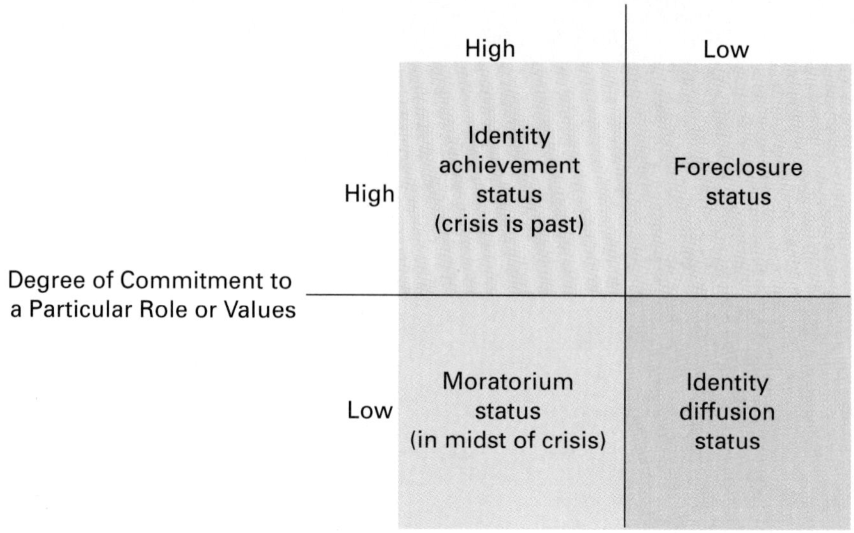

The four identity statuses proposed by Marcia, based on Erikson's theory. For a fully achieved identity, the young person must both have examined his or her values or goals and have reached a firm commitment (*Source:* Marcia, 1980).

Degree of Crisis

|  | High | Low |
|---|---|---|
| **High** | Identity achievement status (crisis is past) | Foreclosure status |
| **Low** | Moratorium status (in midst of crisis) | Identity diffusion status |

Degree of Commitment to a Particular Role or Values

**moratorium**
One of four identity statuses proposed by Marcia, involving an ongoing reexamination but without a new commitment as yet.

**foreclosure**
One of four identity statuses proposed by Marcia, involving an ideological or occupational commitment without having gone through a reevaluation.

**identity diffusion**
One of four identity statuses proposed by Marcia, involving neither a current reevaluation nor a firm personal commitment.

- **Moratorium:** A crisis is in progress, but no commitment has yet been made.
- **Foreclosure:** A commitment has been made without having gone through a crisis. No reassessment of old positions has been made. Instead the young person has simply accepted a commitment defined by parents or some other source.
- **Identity diffusion:** The young person is not in the midst of a crisis (although there may have been one in the past) and no commitment has been made. Diffusion may represent either an early stage in the process (before a crisis) or a failure to reach a commitment after a crisis.

Whether every young person goes through some kind of identity crisis I cannot tell you, since there have been no longitudinal studies covering all the relevant years. But there have been a number of cross-sectional studies, eight of which Alan Waterman (1985) has combined into a single analysis. Figure 10.4 shows the pattern of results for one facet of identity, *vocational identity*.

Several things are interesting about these results. First, notice that the identity achievement status occurs not most typically in high school but at college age. Also note that the moratorium status is relatively uncommon except in the early years of college. So if most young people are going through an identity crisis, that crisis is fairly late and does not last terribly long. Finally, it is interesting that about one-third of young people at every age are in the foreclosure status, which may indicate that many young people simply do not go through a crisis at all, but follow well-defined grooves.

Collectively, these findings suggest that the identity crisis occurs somewhat later than Erikson originally proposed. But this conclusion requires one qualification: It seems likely that young people who go to work immediately after high school will face the need for an occupational identity earlier than is true for those who go to college. Attending college is in some sense a postponement of full adult status. The years in college are a period in which students are actively encouraged to question, doubt, and try out alternatives. Those who go directly into the working world do not have that luxury. In one

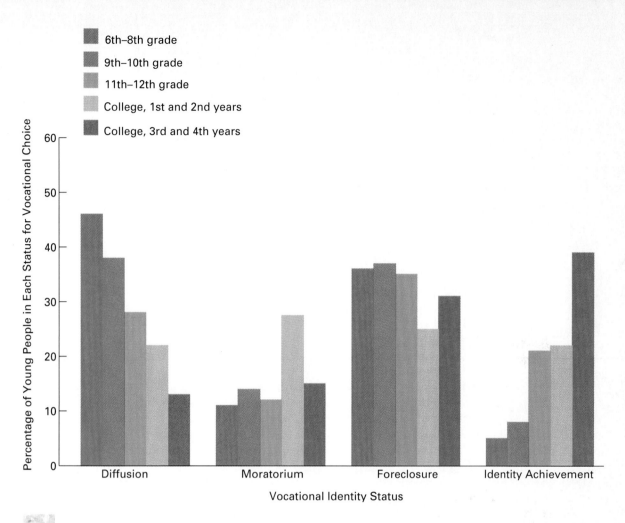

**FIGURE 10.4**

Waterman has combined data from eight different cross-sectional studies of the identity statuses of young people of different ages. As you can see, diffusion and foreclosure are the most common statuses among the younger teenagers, while an achieved identity is the most common status among the college juniors and seniors (*Source:* Waterman, 1985, from Table 2, p. 18).

of the few studies of non-college youth, Gordon Munro and Gerald Adams (1977) found that 45 percent of those who were already working were in the "identity achievement" status for occupational identity, which is higher than the levels shown in Figure 10.4 for college students.

### *Summary of Developmental Changes in Self-Concept*

Let me sum all this up for you. The young child develops first a primitive sense of her own separateness. This is followed quickly by an understanding of her own constancy and of herself as an actor or agent in the world. By 18 to 24 months, most children achieve self-awareness; they grasp the fact that they are also *objects* in the world. At that point, children begin to define themselves in terms of their physical properties (age, size, gender) and their activities and skills. Over the period of concrete and formal operations (from age 6 through adolescence), the content of the child's self-concept becomes more abstract, less and less tied to outward physical qualities, and more based on the assumption of enduring inner qualities. During late adolescence, the whole self-concept also appears to undergo a kind of reorganization, with a new future-oriented, sexual, occupational, and ideological identity created.

## Individual Differences in the Self-Concept

### Self-Esteem

So far, I have talked about the self-concept as if there were no values attached to the categories by which we define ourselves. But that's clearly not the case. There is also an evaluative aspect to the self-concept, an aspect you probably noticed in the answers to the "Who am I?" question that I have already quoted. The 9-year-old clearly makes a lot of positive statements about himself, while the two older subjects offer more mixed evaluations.

By early elementary school age, these evaluative judgments coalesce into a *global* self-evaluation. Children at this age readily answer questions about how well they like themselves as people, or how happy they are, or how well they like the way they are leading their lives. This global evaluation of one's own worth is usually referred to as **self-esteem.**

Susan Harter's extremely interesting research on self-esteem (Harter, 1988, 1990) tells us that this global judgment is not just the sum of a whole series of separate bits of knowledge of how well or poorly we do various tasks or succeed in various relationships. What matters for self-esteem is the degree of *discrepancy* between the value an individual places on some skill or quality and the amount of that skill or quality the individual sees herself as having. Thus children who have high self-esteem are those whose see themselves as meeting their own standards. They are satisfied with themselves. Those with low self-esteem see a discrepancy between what they would like to be (or think they *ought* to be) and what they are. A child who values sports prowess but who isn't big enough or coordinated enough to be good at sports will have lower self-esteem than a child who is equally small or uncoordinated but for whom sports skill is simply not highly valued. Similarly, being good at something (like singing, playing chess, or being able to talk to your mother) won't raise a child's self-esteem unless the child values that particular skill.

*Changes with Age in Self-Esteem.* Because self-esteem involves this aspect of comparison of the self with some standard or some inner value, it is not surprising that for many youngsters it falls rather sharply between the ages of 11 and 13. In those years, children's (and society's) standards are likely to change significantly without an immediate increase in the skills the child needs to meet those new standards. This seems to be a particular problem if the child moves into junior high in the seventh grade and thus experiences both puberty and a change in the social environment at the same time

**self-esteem**
A global judgment of self-worth; how well you like who you perceive yourself to be.

(Simmons & Blyth, 1987). Youngsters who move into a new school environment one year later, in the eighth grade, show a much smaller drop in self-esteem.

Past age 13 or 14, though, both longitudinal and cross-sectional studies show that self-esteem rises steadily and rather substantially through the remainder of the teen years (O'Malley & Bachman, 1983; McCarthy & Hoge, 1982). Eighteen- and twenty-year-olds usually think of themselves more positively than they did when they were 12 or 14. But within this general developmental trend there are, as always, individual variations.

*Individual Differences in Self-Esteem.* We know that among children or teenagers of any given age there are substantial differences in levels of self-esteem. Surprisingly, we know very little about how stable those differences may be over time. It seems reasonable that low or high self-esteem would tend to persist over months or years, and there are a few early studies that show such stability (e.g., Coopersmith, 1967). However, longitudinal studies are scarce, and there are none that have measured global self-esteem in the way that Harter proposes. Harter's own research tells us that the absolute level of self-esteem can and does change when a child's perceived discrepancy goes up, which might happen when there is a change in the importance a child places on some domain, or when her sense of competence in some domain goes down. For example, in her samples of youngsters moving from the sixth to the seventh grade, Harter found that those whose sense of discrepancy increased showed a lowering of self-esteem (Harter, 1990), while those whose sense of discrepancy remained the same did not show a change in self-esteem. So self-esteem is clearly not fixed. But all the theorists in this area, including Harter, assume that the tendency toward low or high self-esteem is a relatively stable personal characteristic, at least after the age of 7 or 8.

Several new studies suggest that it's harder on kids to change schools in sixth or seventh grade, such as by moving to a junior high school like this one, than it is to move only in eighth or ninth grade. Self-esteem drops more in the early-moving group, perhaps because they are having to cope with both moving and puberty at the same time.

We know more about the consequences of low than of high self-esteem at any given age. The most consistent finding is that self-esteem is *strongly* negatively correlated with depression. The lower the self-esteem score, the more depressed the child or teenager describes himself to be (and the higher the risk of suicide as well). The correlations in several of Harter's studies range from −.67 to −.80—remarkably high for research of this type. You can see how striking this relationship is in Figure 10.5, which shows results from studies of three different age groups.

Impressive as these results are, this is still correlational evidence. These findings don't prove that there is a causal connection between low self-esteem and depression. More persuasive is Harter's reported finding from her longitudinal studies that when the self-esteem score rises or falls, the depression score drops or rises accordingly.

*Origins of Differences in Self-Esteem.* Where might these differences come from? First, of course, both parental values and peer values help to shape the importance a child will place on some skill or quality. Peer (and general cultural) standards for appearance, for example, are powerful elements in self-esteem at every age. Similarly, the degree of emphasis parents place on the child performing well on some type of task such as school work, sports, or music is an important element in the child's internal expectations in that area.

At the same time the child's perception of his own competence or acceptability in various domains is shaped both by his own direct experience of

---

*FIGURE 10.5*

What is striking about these findings is not only that the relationship between mood (depression versus cheerfulness) and self-esteem is so strong, but that the relationship is virtually identical in children from grades three through eight (*Source:* Harter, 1988, Figure 9.3, p. 234).

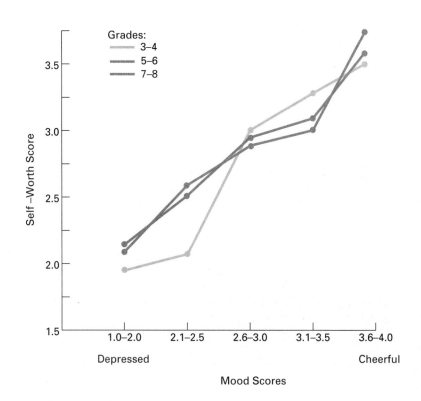

These boys are not just playing baseball; they are also collecting direct information about their own skills (or lack of them)—information that may affect their self-esteem.

success or failure—in schoolwork, in creating relationships with peers, in sports or games—and by the labels that are provided for the child by parents and other adults. Children who are repeatedly told that they are "pretty," "smart," or "a good athlete" are likely to have higher self-esteem than are children who are told that they are "dumb," "clumsy," or a "late bloomer." Similarly, parents' more general beliefs about their child's competence seem to be conveyed as well, perhaps in many subtle ways. For example, Deborah Phillips (1987) has found that among academically bright children, those who underestimate their own abilities are much more likely to think that their parents don't see them as especially bright than is true of children who see their own skills more accurately.

A second major influence on a child's self-esteem is the overall sense of support the child feels from the important people around her, particularly parents and peers. Children who say "yes" when you ask them whether other people generally like them the way they are, or treat them as a person, or feel that they are important, have higher self-esteem scores than do children who report less overall support. You can see the importance of this kind of support, along with the role of perceived discrepancy, in Figure 10.6 on the next page, which is again drawn from Harter's studies. Among third and fourth graders, and among fifth and sixth graders, social support and perceived discrepancy each affect the child's global self-esteem about equally. So a low discrepancy score does not protect the child completely from low self-esteem if she lacks sufficient social support. And a loving and accepting family and peer group does not guarantee high self-esteem either, if the youngster also has a high discrepancy score.

A particularly deadly combination occurs when the child perceives that the parents' support is *contingent* on good performance in some area—getting good grades, making the first-string football team, being popular with other kids. Then if the child does not measure up to the standard he suffers a

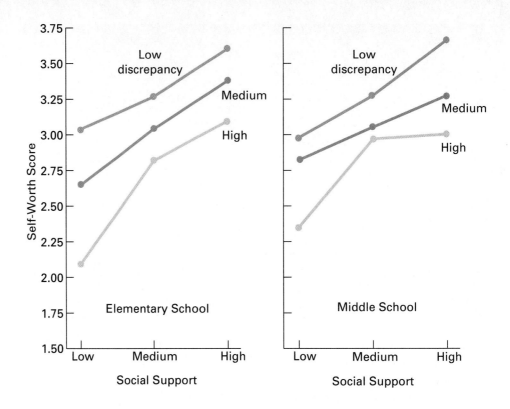

**FIGURE 10.6**

For both the elementary-school and middle-school children in Harter's studies, self-esteem was about equally influenced by the amount of support the child saw herself as receiving from parents and peers, and by the degree of discrepancy between the value the child places on various domains and the skill she sees herself having in each of those domains. Once again, the similarity in the patterns of findings in two different age groups is striking (*Source:* Harter, 1988, Figure 9.2, p. 227).

double whammy, since he experiences both an increased discrepancy between ideal and achievement and a loss of support from the parents.

### Identity Achievement

We could come at the question of individual differences in the self-concept from a different direction by looking at variations in identity achievement. When researchers have done that, they have found that teenagers and young adults who are in the identity achievement or moratorium statuses, compared to those in diffusion or foreclosure, are more independent and autonomous, get better grades in college, are more likely to reason at the level of formal operations, and are more successful in establishing satisfying intimate relationships as young adults (Marcia, 1980). Interestingly, they are also higher in self-esteem, which helps to link the two sets of studies together (e.g., LaVoie, 1976).

## The Self-Concept: A Summing Up

There are obviously many questions still to be answered. But I want to emphasize once again that a child's self-concept, including her level of self-esteem, appears to be a highly significant mediating concept. As Diane Ruble puts it (1987):

> Children, in part, socialize themselves. . . [,] they are motivated to construct rules or theories about themselves and their social environments[,] and . . . such constructions influence their behavior and, in turn, how others respond to them. (p. 244)

Once such a "theory" of the self and a global judgment of one's own self-worth are well established, there are reverberations throughout the child's behavior. Among other things, she systematically chooses experiences and environments that are consistent with her beliefs about herself. The child who believes she can't play baseball behaves differently from the child who believes that she can. The former child is likely to denigrate the importance of sports, or to avoid baseballs, bats, playing fields, and other children who play baseball. If forced to play, she may make self-deprecating remarks like "You know I can't play," or she may play self-defeating games, such as refusing to watch the ball when she swings at it or not running after the ball in right field because she knows she couldn't catch it even if she did get there on time. (If you think all this sounds autobiographical, you're right! Those of you who were bad at baseball, as I believed I was, know that the poorest players are *always* put in right field.)

A child who believes that she can't do long division will behave quite differently in the classroom from the child whose self-concept includes the idea "I am good at math" (or, even more potently, "I am better at math than other kids"). She may not try to work long division problems on the theory that if you don't try, you can't fail. Or she may try much harder, paying the price in anxiety about failure. At a later age, such a child is much less likely to take further math courses, thus reducing her occupational options.

These beliefs are pervasive, many develop early, and although they are somewhat responsive to changing circumstances, they also act as self-fulfilling prophecies. We need to know a good deal more about the origins of the child's self-definitions if we are to understand how to modify the inaccurate elements.

## The Development of Gender and Sex-Role Concepts

The element of the child's self-concept I have mostly left out of the discussion so far is the gender concept and the accompanying concept of sex roles. How do children come to understand that they are a boy or a girl, and when and how do they learn what behaviors are "appropriate" for their gender? I have saved this set of questions for a separate discussion partly because this has been an area of hot debate and extensive research for the past decade (so there is a lot to say), and partly because this set of questions has such central personal relevance for so many of us. Women's and men's roles are changing rapidly in our society. But our stereotypes about men and women, and our own inner sense of what it means to be "male" or "female," have not always kept pace. If we are to understand ourselves, (and rear our children with less confusion, perhaps) we need to know more about the ways in which children learn about gender and sex roles.

### Some Definitions

Before I can delve into these questions, though, I need to define some terms for you. These words and phrases are often used fuzzily or interchangeably, which only confuses things. I will use the following terms and phrases in specific ways. The **gender concept** is the idea that one is a boy or a girl, and that gender is constant over time. *Sex roles* are the set of behaviors, attitudes, rights, duties, and obligations that are part of the "role" of being a boy or a girl, a male or a female. All roles have such collections of duties, rights, and expected behaviors. Teachers are supposed to behave in certain ways, as are employees, or mothers, or baseball managers. These are all roles. Sex roles are somewhat broader than most other roles in our culture, but they are nonetheless roles. A **sex-role concept** is the set of ideas any one of us has about the specific content of a sex role—what males and females do and are supposed to do.

**Sex-role stereotyping** is a process of overextending the sex roles or applying them too rigidly. Any stereotype involves assigning people to rigidly defined categories without taking their individual qualities into account. When we say "men are unemotional" we are displaying a stereotype. The male sex role may include "unemotional" as one of its qualities (men are not "supposed to" cry), but clearly many men show their emotions easily. Stereo-

**gender concept**
The understanding of one's own gender, including the permanence and constancy of gender.

**sex-role concept**
The understanding of what males and females do and are supposed to do.

**sex-role stereotyping**
The process of overextending sex roles or sex-role behavior.

This teacher in a one-room school house in Brazil, like teachers all over the world, is filling the *role* of teacher. Any role is a kind of job description. In filling this particular job, this teacher is meeting not only the overt job description but also the more subtle demands of the role. A sex role is similarly a kind of job description for how to be male or female in a particular society. This photo is a video still from the *Childhood* television series (*Source:* ©Thirteen/ WNET).

types thus go beyond statements of what is "supposed to be" to inaccurately broad statements about "what is."

**Sex typing** and **sex-role behavior** refer to the extent to which a child's behavior (or an adult's) matches the cultural expectation for her or his sex role. A girl may know quite well that she is a girl, and be able to describe the sex roles accurately, but still behave like a tomboy. We would say that her behavior is less "sex typed" than is the behavior of a girl who adopts more traditional play patterns.

If we are going to understand the development of the child's concept of gender, we have to understand all of these elements. How does the child come to know what gender she is? How and when does she develop ideas about sex roles or about sex-role stereotyping? And how well do children match their behavior to the sex roles or the stereotypes?

### Developmental Patterns

*The Development of the Gender Concept.* How soon does a child figure out that she is a girl or he is a boy? It depends on what we mean by "figure out." There seem to be three steps. First, there is **gender identity,** which is simply a child's ability to label his own sex correctly and to identify other people as men or women, boys or girls. Children seem to notice some of the external features that differentiate male from female as early as 15–18 months. And by age 2, if you show them a set of pictures of a same-sex child and several opposite-sex children and say "Which one is you?," most children can correctly pick out the same-sex picture (Thompson, 1975). By 2 1/2 or 3, most children can also label and identify correctly the sex of others as well (point out "Which one is a girl?" or "Which one is a boy?" in a set of pictures). Hair length and clothing seem to be the cues that children are using for these early discriminations.

Accurate labeling, though, does not signify complete understanding. As is true with all the concepts I talked about in Chapter 7, which show increasing subtlety and complexity over the preschool and early school years, the gender concept undergoes further refinements. The second step is **gender stability,** the understanding that you stay the same gender throughout life. Researchers have measured this by asking children such questions as "When you were a little baby, were you a little girl or a little boy?" or "When you grow up will you be a Mommy or a Daddy?" In one representative study, Ronald Slaby and Karin Frey (1975) found that most children understood the stability aspect of gender by about age 4.

Finally, there is the development of true **gender constancy,** which is the recognition that someone stays the same gender even though he may appear to change by wearing different clothes or having different hair length. For example, girls don't change into boys by cutting their hair very short or by wearing boys' clothes. It may seem odd that a child who understands that he will stay the same gender throughout life (gender stability) can nonetheless be confused about the effect of changes in dress or appearance on gender. Yet the sequence of gender stability followed by gender constancy has been observed in numerous studies, including studies of children growing up in other cultures, such as Kenya, Nepal, Belize, and Samoa (Munroe, Shimmin, & Munroe, 1984).

---

**sex typing**
See *sex-role behavior.*

**sex-role behavior**
The performance of behavior that matches the culturally-defined sex role, such as choosing "sex-appropriate" toys, or playing with same-sex children.

**gender identity**
The first step in gender concept development, in which the child labels herself correctly and categorizes others correctly as male or female.

**gender stability**
The second step in gender concept development, in which the child understands that a person's gender continues to be stable throughout the lifetime.

**gender constancy**
The final step in developing a gender concept, in which the child understands that gender doesn't change even though there are external changes like clothing or hair length.

The underlying logic of this sequence may be a bit clearer if I draw a parallel between gender constancy and the concept of conservation I described in Chapter 7. Conservation of mass, number, or weight involves recognition that an object remains the same in some fundamental way even though it changes externally in some fashion. Gender constancy is thus a kind of "conservation of gender," and is not typically understood until about 5 or 6, when the other conservations are first grasped. Dale Marcus and Willis Overton (1978) explored this link in a study in which kindergarten, first, and second grade children were tested for both conservation of quantity and gender constancy. The results, which are in Table 10.1, clearly show that children typically understand both or neither.

In sum, children as young as 2 or 2 1/2 know their own sex and that of people around them, but they do not have a fully developed concept of gender until they are 5 or 6.

*The Development of Sex-Role Concepts and Stereotypes.* Obviously, figuring out your gender and understanding that it stays constant are only part of the story. Learning what goes with, or ought to go with, being a boy or a girl is also a vital part of the child's task.

Researchers have studied this in two ways—by asking children what boys and girls like to do and what they are like (which is an inquiry about stereotypes) and by asking children if it is okay for boys to play with dolls, okay for girls to climb trees, or okay to do equivalent "cross-sex" things (an inquiry about roles).

In our society, adults have clear sex-role stereotypes. We think of men as being competent, skillful, assertive, aggressive, and able to get things done. Adults see women as warm and expressive, tactful, quiet, gentle, aware of others' feelings, and lacking in competence, independence, and logic (Broverman et al., 1972; T. L. Ruble, 1983).

Studies of children show that equivalent stereotyping occurs early. By age 2 children already associate certain tasks and possessions with men and women, such as vacuum cleaners or stoves and food with women and cars and tools with men (Weinraub et al., 1984). By age 3 or 4, children can assign many occupations, toys, and activities to the stereotypic gender. By age 5, chil-

**TABLE 10.1**

*Relationship Between Gender Constancy and Conservation of Quantity in Young Children*

| Pattern of Constancy and Conservation | Child's Grade in School | | |
|---|---|---|---|
| | Kindergarten | First | Second |
| Child has neither gender constancy nor conservation of quantity. | 17 | 4 | 1 |
| Child has conservation but not gender constancy. | 3 | 4 | 4 |
| Child has both. | 4 | 14 | 18 |

*Source:* After Marcus & Overton, 1978, Table 3, p. 440. © The Society for Research in Child Development, Inc.

dren begin to associate certain personality traits with males or females, and these trends are even clearer by the time the children are 8 or 9. The most clearly stereotyped traits are weakness, gentleness, appreciativeness, and soft-heartedness for women, and aggression, strength, cruelty, and coarseness for males. Cross-cultural studies in 24 different countries by John Williams and Deborah Best (1990) show that precisely these same traits are the most clearly stereotyped in virtually all cultures.

A very similar pattern of results is found in studies of children's ideas about what men and women (or boys and girls) *ought* to be like. A study by William Damon (1977) illustrates the point particularly nicely. He told a story to children aged 4 through 9 about a little boy named George who likes to play with dolls. George's parents tell him that only little girls play with dolls; little boys shouldn't. They buy him some other toys, but still George prefers dolls. The children were then asked a batch of questions about this:

Why do people tell George not to play with dolls?
Are they right?
Is there a rule that boys shouldn't play with dolls?
What should George do?
Does George have a right to play with dolls? (p. 242)

Four-year-olds in this study thought it was okay for George to play with dolls. There was no rule against it and he should do it if he wanted to. Six-year-olds, in contrast, thought it was *wrong* for George to play with dolls. By about age 9, children had differentiated between what boys and girls usually do and what is "wrong." One boy said, for example, that breaking windows was wrong and bad, but that playing with dolls was not bad in the same way: "Breaking windows you're not supposed to do. And if you play with dolls, well you can, but boys usually don't."

What seems to be happening is that the 6-year-old, having figured out that she is permanently a girl or he is a boy, is searching for a *rule* about how boys and girls behave (Martin & Halverson, 1981). She picks up information from watching adults, from watching TV, and from listening to the labels that are attached to different activities (e.g., "boys don't cry"). Initially they treat these as absolute, moral rules. Later they understand that these are social conventions, at which point sex-role concepts become more flexible and stereotyping declines somewhat (although it does not in any sense disappear; sex stereotyping is very strong among adults).

One of the interesting sidelights in the research on stereotyping is that the male stereotype and sex-role concept seems to develop a bit earlier and to be stronger than the female stereotype or sex-role concept. More children agree on what men are or should be like than on what women are or should be. This might happen because children have seen women in more different roles (mother and teacher, for example) than they have seen men. Or it could mean that the female role in our society is more flexible than the male role. At any rate, it is clear that the qualities attributed to the male are more highly *valued* than are the female traits (Broverman et al., 1970). We see it as "good" to be independent, assertive, logical, and strong; it is less good to be warm, quiet, tactful, and gentle. Perhaps girls recognize early that the male role is seen more positively and aspire to some of the valued male qualities. That

Does this little boy, like the mythical George in Damon's studies, have a right to play with dolls? Four-year-olds and nine-year-olds are likely to think that he does, but many six-year-olds think it is simply wrong for boys to do girl things, or for girls to do boy things.

would lead to a female role perceived more broadly. Whatever the reason, it is an interesting finding—one with considerable relevance for understanding adult male and female sex roles and stereotyping.

*The Development of Sex-Role Behavior.*   The final element in the equation is the actual behavior children show with their own sex and with the opposite sex.

We have several pieces of information. First of all, if you observe children while they play in a room stocked with a wide range of attractive toys, you'll see that children as young as 2 or 3 show sex stereotyping in their toy choices. Little girls play with dolls or at various housekeeping games, including sewing, stringing beads, or cooking. Boys play with guns, toy trucks, fire engines, and with carpentry tools (Fagot, 1974; O'Brien & Huston, 1985).

Children also begin to show some preference for same-sex playmates very early—as young as 2 1/2 or 3—and are much more sociable with playmates of the same sex at these ages (Maccoby, 1988, 1990; Maccoby & Jacklin, 1987). By school age, peer relationships are almost exclusively same-sex. You can see the early development of this preference in Figure 10.7, which shows the results of a study of preschool play groups by La Freniere, Strayer, and Gauthier (1984). By age 3, about 60 percent of play groups were same-sex groupings and the rate rose from there.

The other intriguing pattern is that children in early elementary school seem to begin to pay more attention to the behavior of same-sex than opposite-sex adults or playmates, and to play more with new toys that are labeled as being appropriate for their own sex (e.g., Ruble, Balaban, & Cooper, 1981; Bradbard et al., 1986). Overall, then, we see many signs that children are both aware of and affected by gender as early as 2 or 2 1/2. But gender becomes a still more potent force in guiding behavior and attitudes at around age 5 or 6.

## Theories of Sex-Role Concepts and Sex-Role Behavior

How can we explain the development of sex-role concepts and sex-role behavior? As you might expect, theorists of virtually every persuasion have tried their hand at explanations.

### Psychoanalytic Explanations

In psychoanalytic theory, particularly Freud's version of it, it is the process of identification that is the major vehicle for the child's acquisition of sex-role concepts and behavior. As you'll remember from Chapter 9, identification is the result of the Oedipus conflict at about ages 3–4. The child "takes in" (incorporates) all the qualities of the same-sex parent as a way of lessen-

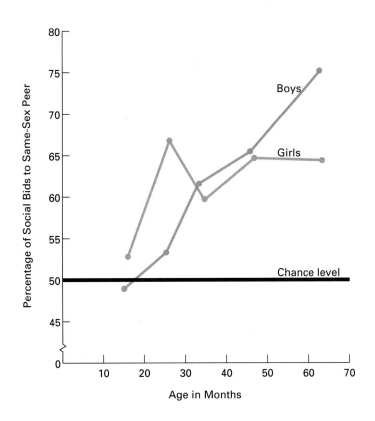

**FIGURE 10.7**

La Freniere and his colleagues counted how often preschool children played with same-sex or opposite-sex playmates. In this study, children as young as 2 1/2 already showed at least some preference for same-sex playmates (*Source:* La Freniere, Strayer, & Gauthier, 1984, figure 1, p. 1961. Copyright by The Society for Research in Child Development, Inc.).

ing his anxiety. If Freud is correct, then we should see children begin to imitate the same-sex parent and other same-sex adults pretty consistently beginning at age 4 or so. But that is not what we see. Most research suggests that children do not show such differential imitation until several years later. Freud's view also doesn't help us explain why children would show sex-typed toy choices or playmate choices as early as 2 or 3, before the Oedipus conflict has occurred. All in all, this theory has not been very helpful in explaining this particular developmental pattern.

### Social-Learning Explanations

Social-learning theorists have fared a good deal better. The major proponent of a social-learning explanation of the development of sex-role behavior has been Walter Mischel (1966, 1970). He has argued that children learn their sex roles by being reinforced directly both for doing sex-appropriate things and for imitating same-sex models, particularly the same-sex parent. Mischel assumes that parents pay more attention to children when they imitate a same-sexed person. In this way, the child learns the appropriate sex role.

There is at least some support for this position. The most consistent finding is that parents do quite specifically encourage sex-typed activities, such as boys playing with blocks or cars and girls playing with dolls, or girls helping with cooking and boys shoveling the snow in the driveway (Lytton & Romney, 1991). One manifestation of this is that parents buy different kinds of toys for boys and girls, beginning in infancy, and use different kinds of toys when they play with boys and girls (Huston, 1983). What is more, there is new evidence that suggests that toddlers whose parents are more consistent in rewarding sex-typed toy choice or play behavior also learn accurate gender labels earlier than do toddlers whose parents are less focused on the gender-appropriateness of the child's play (Fagot & Leinbach, 1989)—a finding clearly consistent with the predictions of social-learning theory.

Interestingly, there is also a fair amount of evidence that differential treatment of sons and daughters is more common among fathers than mothers, and that fathers are particularly likely to be concerned with the appropriate sex-role behavior of their sons (Siegal, 1987). Many fathers seem to be especially uncomfortable with "girlish" behavior in their sons and are much more likely to show disapproval of such behavior in their sons than they are to disapprove of "tomboyish" behavior in their daughters—which may be one reason that the male stereotype develops earlier and is stronger than the female stereotype.

Two other lines of research also lend support to the social-learning position. Anthropologist Beatrice Whiting (Whiting & Edwards, 1988), after examining patterns of gender socialization in 11 different cultures, concludes that "we are the company we keep." In most cultures, girls and boys keep different company, beginning quite early, with girls spending more time with women as well as in child-care responsibilities. To the extent that this is true, it would provide each sex with more same-sex than opposite-sex models, and more opportunity for reinforcement of sex-appropriate behavior such as nurturance directed at younger siblings.

These little boys are already showing strong sex-stereotypes in their choice of toys and play themes (although swords and cowboy hats don't go together in any myth I know of!). We see such sex-stereotyping in toy choices in children as young as 2 or 3. One possible explanation for this very early stereotyping is that parents are more likely to buy trucks and swords for their little boys, dolls and doll clothes for their little girls. But that's not the only possibility.

Finally, Eleanor Maccoby's and Carol Jacklin's studies of children's play groups point to the possibility that reinforcement patterns may play a role in the emergence of same-sex play preferences. Maccoby (1990) points out that beginning as early as age 3 or 4, children increase sharply in their attempts to influence each other's behavior. But boys and girls go about it differently. Girls generally ask questions or make requests; boys are much more likely to make demands or phrase things using imperatives ("Give me that!"). The really intriguing finding is that even at this early age, boys simply don't comply very much with the girls' style of influence attempt. Boys will respond positively to another boy's demand, and girls comply with either boys' or girls' influence attempts. But boys don't do what girls ask. In addition, boys this age play in a more rough and tumble way, which girls seem to find unpleasant. So playing with boys yields little positive reinforcement for girls, and they begin to avoid such interactions and band together. Of course this description does not tell us *why* boys and girls develop such different patterns of peer interaction in the first place. That fascinating question remains for further study.

Collectively, these findings and speculations provide a good deal of support for a social-learning theory of sex-role development. Parents do provide somewhat different environments and reinforcement patterns for their boys and girls. But helpful as it is, this approach still can't account for all of the facts I've given you. First of all, there is less differential reinforcement of boy-behavior versus girl-behavior than you'd expect, and probably not enough to account for the very early and strong discrimination children seem to make on the basis of gender. Even children whose parents seem to treat their young sons and daughters in highly similar ways nonetheless learn gender labels and show same-sex playmate choices.

A second difficulty is the same one that poses problems for psychoanalytic explanations of these phenomena: Most research shows that children consistently imitate same-sex models more than opposite-sex models only after age 5 or 6—although there is still some disagreement on this point (e.g., Bussey & Bandura, 1984). In other words, we don't see clear differential imitation until *after* the child has already developed a strong set of ideas about sex roles. If this is so, then children are not learning their sex role by imitating same-sex adults. What we see instead is that children are differentially *sensitive* to reinforcements from same-sex children and adults. For example, Beverly Fagot (1985) has found that nursery school teachers typically reward *both* boys and girls for more stereotypically *female* or neutral behavior (e.g., cooperativeness, lower levels of activity, quieter play), but boys nonetheless persist in showing stereotypic male behavior. Consistent with Maccoby's and Jacklin's findings on children's play groups, in this study the boys' behavior only changed if other boys showed disapproval or approval. So the boys were more sensitive to reinforcements from other boys; girls were responsive to the teacher's reinforcements and to those from other girls.

Clearly reinforcement patterns and modeling are involved in the process. But there seems to be more going on here than can be accounted for by social-learning theory.

### Cognitive-Developmental Explanations

Lawrence Kohlberg (1966; Kohlberg & Ullian, 1974) offered a third alternative, grounded in Piagetian theory. Kohlberg argued that we have to look at the cognitive part of the child's understanding of gender. Until the child has fully grasped the constancy of gender, we shouldn't see very much sex-typed behavior, and we certainly shouldn't see much imitation of same-sex models. Once the child has understood the gender concept, however, and realizes that he is a boy or she is a girl forever, then in order to maintain cognitive consistency it becomes highly important for the child to learn how to behave in a way that fits the category he or she belongs to. Thus Kohlberg predicted that we should see systematic same-sex imitation only *after* the child has shown full gender constancy.

There have been a handful of studies testing this hypothesis, and although the results are not entirely consistent, the majority have supported it. A study by Diane Ruble is a good example (Ruble, Balaban, & Cooper, 1981). She showed 4- to 6-year-old children a cartoon with a "commercial" in the middle. The commercial showed either two girls playing with a toy or two boys playing with the same toy. After seeing the cartoon, each child was encouraged to play with any of the toys in the room, which included the toy he or she had seen during the commercial.

As you can see in Figure 10.8, children who had already achieved full gender constancy were much more influenced by the gender of the models in the commercial than were children who were at earlier levels of development of the gender concept. Other researchers have found that children who understand gender constancy are more likely to watch same-sex adult models (Slaby & Frey, 1975).

Despite such support for this key prediction, however, Kohlberg's approach still has weaknesses, the most glaring of which is the fact that children show clear signs of sex-typed behavior many years before they have fully grasped gender constancy. Two- and three-year-olds show sex-appropriate toy

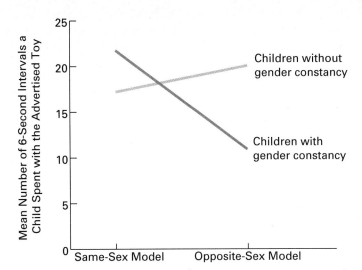

FIGURE 10.8

Results from Ruble's study show that children who had already achieved gender constancy were much more likely to imitate the same-sex model than the opposite-sex model, while this was not true for those who had not achieved gender constancy (*Source:* Ruble, Balaban, & Cooper, 1981, adapted from Figure 1, p. 670. Copyright by the Society for Research in Child Development, Inc.).

and playmate choice at a point when they barely can label their own and others' genders accurately. Furthermore, Kohlberg thought that a child would be differentially sensitive to reinforcements from same-sex adults only after gender constancy was achieved, but Beverly Fagot's study shows that this is present much earlier.

### A New Alternative: Gender Schemas

These various theoretical deficiencies have led a number of psychologists to propose a new alternative, usually called **gender schema** theory, that combines many of the best features of social-learning and cognitive-developmental theories (e.g., Bem, 1981; Martin & Halverson, 1981, 1983; Ruble, 1987). Just as the self-concept can be thought of as a "scheme" or "self-theory," so the child's understanding of gender can be seen in the same way. As Carol Martin and Charles Halverson put it:

> The basic idea [is] that stereotypes are "schemas," or naive theories that are relevant to the self, and function to organize and structure experience by telling the perceiver the kinds of information to look for in the environment and how to interpret such information. (Martin & Halverson, 1983, p. 563)

The gender schema begins to develop as soon as the child notices the differences between male and female, knows his own gender, and can label the two groups with some consistency—all of which happens by age 2 or 3. Perhaps because gender is clearly an either/or category, children seem to understand very early that this is a key distinction, so the category serves as a kind of magnet for new information (Maccoby, 1988). In Piaget's terms, once the child has established even a primitive gender scheme, a great many experiences are assimilated to it. Thus as soon as this schema begins to be formed, children may begin to show preference for same-sex playmates or for gender-stereotyped activities (Martin, Wood, & Little, 1990).

**gender schema**
A fundamental schema created by children beginning at age 18 months or younger by which the child categorizes people, objects, activities, and qualities by gender.

Recent studies by researchers in this group suggest that preschoolers first learn some broad distinctions about what kinds of activities or behavior go with each gender. Then between ages 4 and 6 the child seems to focus on learning a more subtle and complex set of associations for his or her *own* gender—what children of his own gender like and don't like, how they play, how they talk, and what kinds of people they associate with. Then only at about ages 8 to 10 does the child learn the same set of more complex views of the opposite gender (Martin, Wood, & Little, 1990).

The key difference between this theory and Kohlberg's theory is that schema theory does not assume that the child must understand that gender is permanent before any gender schema can be formed. Kohlberg seemed to argue that a gender schema only came into existence when gender constancy was understood. Martin and Halverson and other theorists in this group point out that this schema has precursors at much earlier ages and the early schema is a powerful organizer of both the child's perceptions and behavior. When gender constancy is understood at about 5 or 6, information about gender-appropriate behavior becomes still more salient to the child, and she develops a more elaborated rule or schema of "what people who are like me do." The child of this age treats this "rule" the same way she treats other rules—as absolutes. Later, the child's knowledge of the "gender rule" continues to develop, but her application of it becomes more flexible. (She knows that most boys don't play with dolls, but that they *can* do so if they like, for example.)

Many of us, committed to the philosophical goal of equality for women, have taken the rigidity of children's early sex stereotypes as evidence that we have made little progress toward equality. ("Mommy, you can't be a psychology doctor, you have to be a psychology nurse.") But gender schema theorists emphasize that such rule learning is absolutely normal, and so is the rigid stereotyping that we see in elementary school children's ideas about sex roles. Children are searching for order, for rules that help to make sense of their experiences. And a rule about "what men do" and "what women do" is a helpful schema for children. Like grammatical rules, children first apply this new rule too rigidly, and then later learn the exceptions. But the rule-learning process seems to be a natural one.

Obviously the particular rule about sex roles that a child will develop depends in part on the kinds of models she encounters and the reinforcement pattern she experiences. In our culture, a key source of this rule-generating information is TV and children's books—a subject I have explored in the box on pages 402–403.

## Individual Differences in Sex Roles and Stereotypes

The developmental patterns I have been describing seem to hold for virtually all children. Nonetheless, as usual, we also see quite a lot of variation from child to child in the rigidity of the rule they develop, or in the sex-typing of their behavior.

As a group, boys usually have stronger (more rigid and more traditional) sex-role stereotypes. Among both boys and girls, however, children whose mothers work outside the home have *less* stereotypic views (more flexible rules) (e.g., Powell & Steelman, 1982). This makes perfectly good sense if you think about the origin of the child's sex-role schema. Presumably the child is learning "what women do" partly from observing her mother; if her mother is doing the same sort of work as does her father, her schema is bound to include this greater equality.

### Cross-Sex Children

Another group with less rigid sex stereotypes are children with cross-sex preferences—girls who would rather be boys and boys who would rather be girls (Nash, 1975; Kuhn, Nash, & Brucken, 1978). Having been a tomboy myself, I find such children especially interesting. How does a child come to prefer to be the other sex or to choose cross-sex playmates or toys?

One possibility is that they are directly trained that way. These children may have been specifically reinforced for aspects of the opposite sex's role. Some girls are given trucks and carpentry tools and taught football by their fathers (or mothers). They may come to wish to be boys. We know that tomboy behavior is more accepted and reinforced than is "girlish" behavior in a boy, so it makes sense from a social-learning perspective that there are far more girls who say they would like to be boys than there are boys who say they would rather be girls.

Social-learning theory does not fare so well, though, in explaining the results of research by Carl Roberts and his colleagues (Roberts et al., 1987). They studied a group of boys who showed strong preference for female toys and playmates from their earliest years of life. When Roberts compared these boys to a group of boys with more typical masculine sex-role behaviors, he found little evidence that the more feminine boys had been specifically reinforced for these behaviors, nor that their fathers were providing models for such behavior. What Roberts found instead was that the feminine boys were more feminine in appearance from earliest infancy, that they were more often ill or hospitalized early in life, and that they had relatively less contact with both their mothers and fathers on a daily basis, compared to the more masculine boys. This pattern of findings does not fit nicely with a simple social-learning explanation.

Alternatively, there might be some biological differences. The finding by Roberts et al. that the more behaviorally feminine boys already looked more feminine from earliest infancy is at least consistent with such a possibility, as is their finding that in adulthood, three-fourths of the more feminine boys were homosexual or bisexual in orientation. Further evidence for some biological influence on cross-sex behavior comes from studies of girls who have experienced heightened levels of androgen prenatally. (Recall from Chapter 4 that androgen is largely a "male" hormone.) These "androgenized" girls, in comparison to their normal sisters, are later found to be more interested in rough and tumble play, more often prefer to play with boys, show less interest in dolls or babies, and have fewer fantasies about being a mother (Meyer-Bahlberg, Ehrhardt, & Feldman, 1986).

Findings like these suggest that actual sex-typing of behavior is affected by prenatal hormones. At the same time, it is also clear that a child's basic gender identity—the gender she thinks of herself as being—is strongly influ-

## Sex Stereotyping on TV and in Books

If children are searching for information about what men and women do, as part of the creation of their sex-role "rules" or "schemas," then TV and children's books may have a major impact. From early preschool age, children spend an average of two to four hours a day in the presence of a TV set that is running. (I put it that way because we don't actually know how much of the time children actually *watch* the moving image.) Before they begin school, children have already been exposed to thousands of hours of TV; by the time they are 18 the average child has spent more time in front of a TV set than in a classroom (Calvert & Huston, 1987). So the portrayals of men and women and boys and girls in TV programs are bound to be a very important source of data for the child's emerging sex-role concept.

What researchers have found when they have counted specific behaviors by men and women on TV is that men and women are portrayed in highly stereotypic ways (Huston, 1983; Huston & Alvarez, 1990). Males outnumber females by 2 to 1 or 3 to 1 on virtually every kind of programming except commercials, but in the latter, the "voice-over" is nearly always male. Women are more often shown at home or in romantic situations; men more often appear in work settings, with cars, or playing sports. Men are shown solving problems, being more active, aggressive, and independent. Women are shown as sex objects, or showing emotions, and are more passive and deferent. Females generally play the "handmaiden" roles—they hand the male character his coat, type his reports, and listen to his troubles.

A continuous exposure to these stereotyped males and females does seem to have at least a small effect on child's vision of men and women and their roles. In two longitudinal studies, Morgan (1982, 1987) has found that among elementary and high-school students, those who watched a lot of TV at the beginning of the study reported more traditional sex-role stereotyping a year later. They were more likely, for example, to think that household chores should be done by women than by men. Even more persuasive is an experiment by Emily Davidson (Davidson, Yasuna, & Tower, 1979), who deliberately exposed some 5- and 6-year-olds to highly sex-stereotyped cartoons. Those who had seen such cartoons, compared to control children who had seen neutral cartoons, later gave more stereotyped answers to questions about the qualities of men and women.

enced by the label she is given and the treatment she receives from her parents. Children born with ambiguous genitalia, for example, will grow up to think of themselves as being whichever gender they were reared as, even if that gender does not match their genotype (Money, 1987).

Clearly, the gender a child *thinks* he is affects the gender *schema* he develops. The environment is extremely potent. But at the risk of being unpopular, I want to say that I think we would do well to keep an open mind about the possible biological origins of some sex-role behaviors. The evidence is not all in yet.

### *Androgyny*

**androgyny**
A self-concept including and behavior expressing high levels of both masculine and feminine qualities.

A very different approach to the study of cross-sex sex typing has emerged in the study of **androgyny.** Until perhaps the early 1970s, psychologists had thought of "masculinity" and "femininity" as opposite ends of the same continuum. A person could be one or the other but couldn't be both.

At a more subtle level, Aletha Huston and her colleagues in several studies (e.g., Huston et al., 1984) have found that toy commercials aimed at boys, and those aimed at girls, are simply designed differently. Boys' commercials are fast, sharp, and loud—lots of quick cuts, loud music, and activity. Girls' commercials are gradual, soft, and fuzzy. They have camera fades and dissolves rather than sharp cuts, and use softer background music. Children as young as first grade notice these differences, too. They can watch a commercial of some non-stereotyped toy and tell you whether the *style* of the commercial is suited to a boys' or girls' toy.

Children's textbooks and storybooks show similar stereotyping. In one early analysis, Terry Saario, Carol Jacklin, and Carol Tittle (1973) found that there were very few major female characters in children's books; those there were tended to be weaker, less able to solve problems on their own, and more dependent on male characters. The boys and men in the children's books were shown as strong, dominant, and problem solving. In one older reading book, for example (O'Donnell, 1966), a little girl is shown having fallen off her roller skates. The caption said,

"'She cannot skate,' said Mark. 'I can help her. I want to help her. Look at her, Mother. Just look at her. She is just a girl. She gives up.'"

Blatant examples like this have largely disappeared from children's reading books, partly as a result of the efforts of parent groups. But many such books still contain subtle messages about sex roles and sex-role stereotypes.

Clearly, TV and children's books are having an impact on children's ideas about men and women (just as those same sources influence their aggressive behavior). Current research points to the fact that children of 5 to 8 quite naturally construct rigid rules or schemas about male and female roles as a normal part of their search for regularity in the world around them. But sex-role portrayals on TV seem to foster even more stereotyped (and thus inaccurate) sex-role concepts in children, and reinforce such stereotyped concepts well into elementary and high-school ages. If we showed men and women in more equal roles on TV, we might make it more difficult for the 5- or 6-year-old to develop a simple sex-role schema, but we would be reflecting reality far more.

Since then, Sandra Bem (1974), Janet Spence and Robert Helmreich (1978), and others have argued that it is possible for a person to express *both* masculine and feminine sides of herself, to be both compassionate and independent, both gentle and assertive. In the language I have been using in this chapter, this would mean that a child or adult's self-concept could include elements of both male and female sex roles.

In this new way of looking at sex roles, masculinity and femininity are conceived of as two separate dimensions. Any person can be high or low on either one or both. The terms used to describe the four possible "types" created by this two-dimensional conception are shown in Figure 10.9 on the next page. The two "traditional" sex roles are the masculine and the feminine combinations. But there are two new "types" that become evident when we think about sex roles in this way: Androgynous individuals are those who describe themselves as having both masculine and feminine traits, and undifferentiated individuals are those who describe themselves as lacking both—a group that sounds a lot like those with a "diffuse" identity in Marcia's system.

In our society, "tomboys" like this tree-climbing girl are fairly common and largely accepted. But a boy this age who showed "girlish" behavior would experience much more pressure to change, perhaps especially from Dad.

**FIGURE 10.9**

The current view of masculinity and femininity is that each of us may express some amount of *each* of these qualities, which produces the four possible combinations of sex-role "types" shown here.

Sex
Role
Types

Score on Masculinity Items

|  | High | Low |
|---|---|---|
| High | Androgynous | Feminine |
| Low | Masculine | Undifferentiated |

Score on Femininity Items

This woman aircraft mechanic, doing a job more commonly performed by men, is more likely than is a woman in a more traditional "woman's job" to have had a mother who worked, to have an androgynous self-concept, and high self-esteem.

This categorization system says nothing about the accuracy of the child's or the adult's rule or schema about sex roles. A teenage girl, for example, could have a clear notion of the norms for male or female behavior and still perceive *herself* as having some stereotypically masculine qualities. In some sense then, when we study masculinity/femininity/androgyny we are studying the intersection between the self-scheme and the gender scheme.

Perhaps because young children's ideas about sex roles are still quite rigid (or perhaps because we do not yet have good measures of androgyny for young children) there is little sign of androgyny among children younger than 9 or 10. But variations in androgyny, masculinity, and femininity clearly do exist among adolescents.

Several studies show that roughly 25–35 percent of high-school students can be described as androgynous (Spence & Helmreich, 1978; Lamke, 1982a). More girls seem to show this pattern than do boys, and there are more girls in the "masculine" category than there are boys in the "feminine" group.

Furthermore, for *both* boys and girls, either a masculine or an androgynous sex-role self-concept is associated with higher self-esteem (Lamke, 1982a, 1982b), doubtless because both boys and girls value many of the qualities that are stereotypically masculine, such as independence and competence. Thus a boy can achieve high self-esteem and success with his peers by adopting a traditional masculine sex role. For girls, though, adoption of a traditional feminine sex role without some balancing "male" characteristics seems to carry a risk of lower self-esteem and even poorer relationships with peers (Massad, 1981).

Findings like these suggest the possibility that while the creation of rigid rules or schemas for sex roles is a normal—even essential—process in young children, a blurring of those rules may be an important process in adolescence, particularly for girls, for whom a more androgynous self-concept is associated with positive outcomes.

In all of this, the key point here is not that sex roles or sex-role concepts are bad, but that they develop early in life, are deeply held, and difficult to change. As a result, they affect a great many aspects of child and adult life in powerful ways.

# S U M M A R Y

1. The child's emerging self-concept has several elements, including the awareness of a separate self and the understanding of self-permanence (which may be collectively called the "existential self") and awareness of oneself as an object in the world (sometimes called the "categorical self").

2. The existential self develops in the first year of life; we see real self-awareness and the emergence of the categorical self in the second year.

3. In early childhood, the child begins to place herself in basic categories such as age, size, and gender. These early self-definitions appear to be based primarily on physical attributes and things the child can do.

4. The self-concept becomes gradually more abstract in the elementary and high-school years, including not only actions but also likes and dislikes, beliefs, and more general personality characteristics. Beginning at about age 8 the child also has a global sense of self-worth (self-esteem).

5. At adolescence, there is also a reevaluation of the self, a process Erikson talks of as the "identity crisis." Most adolescents move from a diffuse sense of future occupational or ideological identity, through a period of reevaluation (moratorium), to a commitment to a new self-definition.

6. Self-concepts also include an evaluative dimension. Self-esteem reflects the degree of discrepancy between a child's perception of his own skills in various domains and the importance he places on those domains. Children with high self-esteem show lower levels of depression.

7. There are also individual differences in the speed or completeness of the identity reevaluation at adolescence.

8. Gender identity is part of the self-concept. Children generally acquire gender identity (labeling themselves and others correctly) by about age 2 or 3. They develop gender stability (knowing you stay the same gender throughout life) by about 4, and gender constancy (you don't change gender by changing appearance) by about 5 or 6.

9. Gender constancy is developed at about the same time that most children acquire other "conservation" concepts such as conservation of number or mass.

10. Children's ideas about what males and females do, and what they *ought* to do, are clearly established and maximally stereotyped in early elementary school. Older children are aware of the social conventions, but do not treat them as incontrovertible rules.

11. Sex-typed behavior also appears at age 2 or 3, when children show sex-typed toy preferences and begin to choose same-sex playmates.

12. Theorists of several different traditions have attempted to explain these patterns. Freud's explanation rests on the concept of identification, by which the child comes to imitate the same-sexed parent, thus acquiring appropriate sex-typed behavior. This theory has little support.

13. Social-learning theorists emphasize the role of reinforcement and modeling and argue that children are reinforced for imitating same-sex models. Parents do appear to treat boys and girls in systematically different ways, including punishing boys for girlish behavior, although differential reinforcement appears to be insufficient to account for early sex-typing.

14. Kohlberg proposes a cognitive-developmental model: Children begin to imitate same-sexed models only after they have achieved gender constancy. There is some evidence to support this, but the theory does not explain sex-typed behavior at age 2 or 3.

15. Gender schema theory offers a fourth alternative: Children begin to acquire a rule about what boys do and what girls do as soon as they figure out the difference, and this schema forms the basis of both stereotyping and sex-typed behavior.

16. One important source of information for children's development of a sex-role rule is the portrayal of men and women on TV and in children's books. These portrayals continue to be highly stereotyped.

17. More girls than boys show cross-sex preferences in toy choices and behavior. Both environmental and biological elements may play a part in such cross-sex choices.

18. Young people also differ in the extent to which they see themselves as having feminine and/or masculine qualities or traits. Those who describe themselves with both sets of qualities are called androgynous.

19. Among girls, those who see themselves as more masculine or as androgynous and those who have less stereotypic views of female and male roles are more likely to choose nontraditional occupations in adulthood.

# CRITICAL THINKING QUESTIONS

1. Many parents these days want to raise their children to have egalitarian attitudes about sex roles. If this were one of your goals, given the information provided in this chapter, how would you go about it?

2. Suppose a researcher finds that children who watch a lot of TV have more stereotyped sex-role concepts than do children who watch less TV. Does this prove that watching TV causes such stereotyping? What are the flaws in this type of study? What type of study or experiment would you have to do to avoid those flaws?

3. In research on children's gender concepts, one of the crucial empirical questions has turned out to be how early children begin to show more imitation of same-sex models than of opposite-sex models. Why has this question been so important?

# KEY TERMS

**androgyny**   A self-concept including and behavior expressing high levels of both masculine and feminine qualities.

**categorical self**   Aspect of the self-scheme, beginning with self-awareness, in which the child defines herself in terms of a series of categories, such as age, gender, size, or skill.

**existential self**   Lewis & Brooks-Gunn's term for the most basic part of the self-scheme or self-concept; the sense of being separate and distinct from others and the awareness of the constancy of the self.

**foreclosure**   One of four identity statuses proposed by Marcia, involving an ideological or occupational commitment without having gone through a reevaluation.

**gender concept**   The understanding of one's own gender, including the permanence and constancy of gender.

**gender constancy**   The final step in developing a gender concept, in which the child understands that gender doesn't change even though there are external changes like clothing or hair length.

**gender identity**   The first step in gender concept development, in which the child labels herself correctly and categorizes others correctly as male or female.

**gender schema**   A fundamental schema created by children beginning at age 18 months or younger by which the child categorizes people, objects, activities, and qualities by gender.

**gender stability**   The second step in gender concept development, in which the child understands that a person's gender continues to be stable throughout the lifetime.

**identity achievement**   One of four identity statuses proposed by Marcia, involving the successful resolution of an identity "crisis," resulting in a new commitment.

**identity diffusion**   One of four identity statuses proposed by Marcia, involving neither a current reevaluation nor a firm personal commitment.

**moratorium**   One of four identity statuses proposed by Marcia, involving an ongoing reexamination but without a new commitment.

**self-concept**   The broad idea of "who I am," including the existential self and the categorical self.

**self-esteem**   A global judgment of self-worth; how well you like who you perceive yourself to be.

**sex-role behavior**   The performance of behavior that matches the culturally defined sex role, such as choosing "sex-appropriate" toys, or playing with same-sex children.

**sex-role concept**   The understanding of what males and females do and are "supposed to do."

**sex-role stereotyping**   The process of overextending sex roles or sex-role behavior.

**sex typing**   See *sex-role behavior.*

# SUGGESTED READINGS

Harter, S. (1988). The determinants and mediational role of global self-worth in children. In N. Eisenberg (Ed.), *Contemporary topics in developmental psychology*. New York: Wiley-Interscience.

   I think Harter's work is the best being done today on self-esteem. This paper is a very good introduction to her ideas.

Maccoby, E. E. (1980). *Social development. Psychological growth and the parent-child relationship*. New York: Harcourt Brace Jovanovich.

   This book is no longer new, but it's still an excellent basic text. It includes two chapters that touch on the material I have covered here.

Ruble, D. N. (1988). Sex-role development. In M. H. Bornstein & M. E. Lamb (Eds.), *Developmental psychology: An advanced textbook*. (2nd ed.). Hillsdale, NJ: Lawrence Erlbaum Associates.

   Like many of the chapters in this excellent book, this paper will give you a glimpse of some of the issues and complexities that are part of research on sex roles.

You may want to combine this project with the one I will suggest at the end of Chapter 13, which involves observing aggressive episodes on TV. Recording both aggression or violence and sex-role behaviors will give you a very good sense of the portrayals of "real life" given on TV.

Since I want you to get some practice designing your own project, you can select any one of several approaches:

- Option 1. Watch at least five hours of TV, spread over several time periods, and record the number of male and female characters and describe each as a central character, secondary character, or a minor character.
- Option 2. Watch four to six hours of TV, selecting among several different types of programs, and note the activities of each male and female character in the following categories: aggression, nurturance, problem solving, conformity, and physically exertive behavior.
- Option 3. Watch and analyze the commercials on at least ten programs, making sure that the programs cover the full range of types, from sports to soap operas. You might count the number of male and female participants in the commercials and the nature of their activity in each case, using some of the same categories listed in Option 2.
- Option 4. Watch two hours of Saturday morning cartoons, preferably four separate 30-minute

shows aimed at children from preschool to preteens. Count the number of male and female characters and record the nature of their roles, using some of the same categories as above. Or classify each character as a central character, secondary character, or a minor character.

Whichever one of these projects you choose, you must define your terms carefully and record your data in a manner that makes it understandable. In writing up your report, be sure to state clearly what you did, and what you think your results may mean.

Alternatively (if your instructor prefers) you might write up your report using the standard scientific format, including the following four parts. An *introductory* section should include some of the background literature and describe your hypotheses. A *procedure* section must include details of the programs you observed, how you selected them, what specific behaviors you recorded, how you defined your behavioral categories, and any other details that a reader would need to understand what you actually did. A *results* section should present your findings, using graphs or tables as needed. A *discussion* section compares your results to those of other researchers (as cited in this book or elsewhere) and discusses and explains any puzzling or unexpected findings (if possible). You may also want to suggest additional projects that might help clarify the points of confusion in your own findings.

11

# THE DEVELOPMENT OF SOCIAL RELATIONSHIPS

S everal years ago, at a social gathering, I watched two young friends, Mark and Marcie, with their 4-month-old son Alexander. With very little effort, Alexander managed to attract everyone's attention. He looked around him, occasionally gave brief smiles, kicked his feet, shook a rattle, and cried once in a while. Those simple behaviors were enough to have all the adults in the room hovering over him, trying their best to entice a smile. I was not immune to his charms. I trotted out all my playing-with-baby tricks—raising my eyebrows, smiling broadly, calling his name, tickling him a bit on the cheek or on his feet, and making clucking noises. My reward was one very small smile and a brief gaze.

Mark and Marcie, however, after four months of practice, were a whole lot better than any of the rest of us at soothing and eliciting responses from young Alexander. Either Mom or Dad could get him to smile within just a few seconds; either of them could soothe him quite easily if he cried.

My most immediate reaction to this scene was simple pleasure at seeing loving and attentive parents with their infant. But the psychologist in me was watching too, and I was struck by some other elements in the interaction. First of all, even at four months Alexander was really quite skillful in social exchanges. He couldn't do very many things, but he was very successful at getting attention and care. The second thing, though, is that Alexander and his parents had developed a sort of "dance" that they did much more skillfully with each other than he did with other folks. They had *adapted* to each other.

This brief scene focuses our attention on an aspect of development I have largely neglected so far, namely the child's relationships with others. The self-concept is a critical element in the child's eventual "personality," but the self-concept and the style and pattern of the child's behavior emerge from and are displayed in social exchanges with others. If we are to have the barest grasp of the nature of the child's development, we have to describe and understand the ways in which the child's *social* behavior develops and changes.

 ## Types of Relationships

Willard Hartup, one of the most astute students of social development, suggests that each child needs experience in two rather different kinds of relationships: *vertical* and *horizontal* relationships (1989). A vertical relationship involves an attachment to someone who has greater social power or knowledge, such as with a parent, a teacher, or even with an older sibling. Such relationships are complementary rather than reciprocal, just as the roles of teacher and pupil or boss and employee are complementary rather than re-

Four-month-old Matthew was taped interacting with his mother in a special set-up that allowed separate images of each of the partners to be later combined into this split screen, which shows how they each looked at the same moment. The entire interaction shows very clearly how the "dance" of interaction is well established by this young age. Matthew and his mom are well in tune here, with Matthew leading the way and the mother typically matching her expression and affect to his. This photo is a video still from the *Childhood* television series (*Source:* ©Thirteen/WNET).

ciprocal. The bond may be extremely powerful in both directions, but the actual behaviors the parent and child show toward one another are quite different. Horizontal relationships, in contrast, are reciprocal and egalitarian. The individuals involved, such as same-age peers, have equal social power.

Hartup's point is that these two kinds of relationships serve different functions for the child and both are needed for the child to develop effective social skills. Vertical relationships are necessary to provide the child with protection and security. In these relationships the child creates his basic internal working models and learns many fundamental social skills. But it is in horizontal relationships—in friendships and in peer groups—that the child tries out those basic skills and learns those social skills that can only be learned in a relationship between equals: cooperation, competition, and intimacy.

Clearly, these two kinds of relationships affect one another. But the theory and data tend to be separate, so let me begin by talking about the vertical relationships, in particular the core relationship between child and parent. These days, this relationship is almost universally conceptualized using Bowlby's attachment theory. So let's start there.

## Attachment Theory: Concepts and Terminology

I mentioned Bowlby's theory very briefly in Chapter 9, but I need to elaborate here. You'll recall that his thinking has roots in psychoanalytic thought, particularly in the emphasis on the significance of the earliest relationship between mother and child. But he adds important evolutionary and ethological concepts. In his view, "the propensity to make strong emotional bonds to particular individuals [is] a basic component of human nature, already present in germinal form in the neonate" (1988, p. 3). Such relationships have *survival* value, since they bring nurturance to the infant. They are built and maintained by an interlocking repertoire of instinctive behaviors that create and sustain proximity between parent and child or between other bonded pairs.

In Bowlby's writings, and in the equally influential writings of Mary Ainsworth (1972, 1982, 1989; Ainsworth et al., 1978), the key concepts are that of an **affectional bond,** an **attachment,** and **attachment behaviors.**

Ainsworth defines an affectional bond as "a relatively long-enduring tie in which the partner is important as a unique individual and is interchangeable with none other. In an affectional bond, there is a desire to maintain closeness to the partner" (1989, p. 711). An attachment is a subvariety of emotional bond in which a person's sense of security is bound up in the relationship. When you are attached, you feel (or hope to feel) a special sense of security and comfort in the presence of the other, and you can use the other as a "safe base" from which to explore the rest of the world.

In these terms, the child's relationship with the parent is an attachment, but the parents' relationship with the child is not, since the parent presumably does not feel a greater sense of security in the presence of the infant or use the infant as a safe base. A relationship with a very close friend, or with one's adult partner, however, often is an attachment in the sense Ainsworth and Bowlby mean the term.

Since affectional bonds and attachments are internal states, we cannot see them directly. Instead we deduce their existence by observing attachment behaviors, just as we infer the child's cognitive competence by looking at the way she solves problems. Attachment behaviors are all those behaviors that allow a child or adult to achieve and retain proximity to someone else to whom he is attached. This could include smiling, making eye contact, calling out to the other person across a room, touching, clinging, and crying. (Alexander showed many of these behaviors, didn't he?)

It is important to make clear that there is no one-to-one correspondence between the number of different attachment behaviors a child (or adult) shows on any one occasion and the strength of the underlying attachment. Attachment behaviors are elicited primarily when the individual has need of care, support, or comfort. An infant is in such a needy state a good deal of the time; but an older child will be likely to show attachment behaviors only when he is frightened, tired, or otherwise under stress. It is the *pattern* of these behaviors, not the frequency, that tells us something about the strength or quality of the attachment or the affectional bond.

To understand the early relationship between the parent and the child, we need to look at both sides of the equation—at the development of the parents' bond to the child and of the child's attachment to the parent.

## The Formation of the Parent's Bond to the Child

### *The First Step: The Initial Bond*

If you read the popular press at all, I am sure you have come across articles proclaiming that mothers (or fathers) must have immediate contact with their newborn infant if they are to become properly bonded with the baby. This belief has been based primarily on the work of two pediatricians, Mar-

**affectional bond**
A "relatively long enduring tie in which the partner is important as a unique individual and is interchangeable with none other."

**attachment**
A subvariety of affectional bond in which the central figure is experienced as a safe base from which to explore the world.

**attachment behaviors**
The collection of (probably) instinctive behaviors of one person toward another that brings about or maintains proximity and caregiving, such as the smile of the young infant; behaviors that reflect an attachment.

shall Klaus and John Kennell (1976). They contradicted traditional medical practices and assumptions by hypothesizing that the first few hours after an infant's birth was a "critical period" for the mother's development of a bond to her infant. Mothers who were denied early contact, Klaus and Kennell thought, were likely to form weaker bonds and thus be at higher risk for a range of disorders of parenting.

Klaus and Kennell's theory, and their supporting research, did help lead to real changes in hospital practices, with fathers now routinely present at delivery and mothers and fathers encouraged to hold their newborns immediately. For many reasons this seems like a very good change to me; certainly parents report that they find this first "acquaintance" time to be a joyful occasion, as I pointed out in Chapter 3. But recent research makes it seem more doubtful that such early contact is critical for the formation of a stable long-term affectional bond between mother and child (Myers, 1987). Let me review some of the evidence.

In the short term, we see a few effects of early contact. Some (but not all) researchers have found that mothers who have handled their newborns within the first few hours show more tender fondling, more gazing at the baby in the first few days than do mothers who did not have an opportunity to hold their newborn until later (e.g., Campbell & Taylor, 1980; de Chateau, 1980). There are also some hints that this effect may be greater for those mothers who are least experienced with infants or who have the least support from spouses or families.

Longer-term effects, however, are more difficult to demonstrate. Several studies, including Klaus and Kennell's own early work (e.g., Kennell et al., 1974), show a persisting effect. But many others do not. We see no lasting effects of early contact on such specific behaviors as the amount of smiling toward the child or tender touching. Only on a few global measures of the mother's attitude toward her infant, such as the number of months the mother chooses to stay home with her child before going back to work (assuming she has a choice) or some overall measure of the adequacy of her care, are long-term effects occasionally found.

For example, Susan O'Connor and her colleagues (1980) randomly assigned some poverty-level mothers to a "rooming in" arrangement in which the mother cared for her infant in her own hospital room and thus had extended contact. Other mothers saw their infants only at feeding times. *Neither* group had immediate contact with the infant after birth, so the difference here is in the amount of contact in the first few days, not the timing of the first contact. These two groups were then tracked through the first 18 months of the children's lives. O'Connor's interest has been in a global measure of the mother's behavior that she calls "adequacy of parenting." Inadequate parenting was indicated if the child was physically abused or neglected, if the child was repeatedly hospitalized, or if the parents relinquished custody of the child.

As you can see in Table 11.1 on the next page, very few mothers in either the rooming-in or normal hospital groups showed inadequate parenting, but the rate was significantly higher for the group that had had less contact with the infant in the early days. These findings raise the possibility that among mothers who may be at especially high risk for abuse, extended early contact may help *prevent* later parenting problems. But for the majority of mothers,

**TABLE 11.1**

*Parenting Inadequacy and Abuse*

|  | "Rooming In" Group (143 cases) | Regular Hospital Care Group (158 cases) |
|---|---|---|
| Number of mothers who showed any kind of parenting inadequacy in first 18 months | 2 | 10 |
| Number referred to Children's Protective Service for suspicion of abuse | 1 | 5 |
| Number of children hospitalized for illness or for "failure to thrive" | 1 | 8 |

*Source:* O'Connor et al., 1980, pp. 356–357.

neither early or extended contact appears to be an essential ingredient in the formation of a strong affectional bond between mother and infant.

### The Second Step: The Meshing of Attachment Behaviors

Much more critical for the establishment of the parents' bond to the child is the opportunity for the parent and infant to develop a mutual, interlocking pattern of attachment behaviors. The baby signals her needs by crying or smiling; she responds to being held by soothing or snuggling; she looks at the parents when they look at her. The parents, in their turn, enter into this two-person "dance" with their own (perhaps instinctive) repertoire of caregiving behaviors. They pick the baby up when she cries, wait for and respond to her signals of hunger or other need, smile at the baby when she smiles, and gaze into her eyes when she looks at them. It was this smooth "dance" that I could see between Mark and Marcie and 4-month-old Alexander.

One of the most intriguing things about this process is that we all seem to know how to do this particular dance. In the presence of a young infant most adults will automatically shift into a "baby-play act," which includes smiling, raised eyebrows, very wide open eyes, and a quiet, high-pitched voice. The baby runs through her half of the dance pretty automatically too. But while we can perform all these attachment *behaviors* with many infants, we do not form a bond with every baby we coo at in the grocery store.

For the adult, the critical ingredient for the formation of a bond seems to be the opportunity to develop real mutuality—to practice the dance until the partners follow one another's lead smoothly and pleasurably. This takes time and many rehearsals, and some parents (and infants) become more skillful at it than others, as you can see in Figure 11.1. In general, the smoother and more predictable the process becomes, the more satisfying it seems to be to the parents and the stronger their bond to the infant becomes.

This second step appears to be *far* more important than the initial con-

This Italian mom, filmed as part of the *Childhood* series, shows exactly the same "mock surprise" expression that we see in adults interacting with babies all over the world. Notice the raised eyebrows and open mouth—typical of this expression. Happily (and probably not accidentally) this combination of features is quite likely to elicit a smile from a young baby. (Check yourself next time you are holding or interacting with an infant and see if your expression isn't very like this). This photo is a video still from the *Childhood* television series (*Source:* ©Thirteen/WNET).

tact at birth in establishing a strong parental bond to the child. But this second process, too, can fail. I've explored some of the possible reasons for such a failure in the box on pages 418–419.

### Father-Child Bonds

I have used the word "parents" in the discussion so far, but most of the research I have talked about has involved studies of mothers. Still, many of the same principles seem to hold for fathers as well.

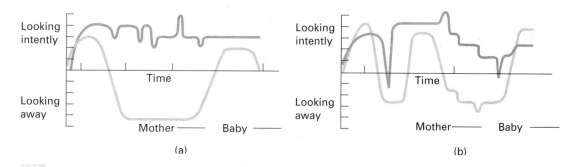

(a)                                        (b)

**FIGURE 11.1**

Barry Brazelton and his colleagues videotaped mothers interacting with their infants, and then went back and rated the intentness of looking-toward or looking-away for each second of interaction by each member of the pair. The pair on the left illustrates a lack of synchrony. When the infant looks away, the mother maintains an intent gaze instead of waiting for the infant to re-engage. In fact the observers noted that this mother trotted out her bag of attention-getting tricks: she talked, touched the child, made faces, nodded her head—all to little avail. The baby only looked at her again after she stopped talking. But the pair on the right are definitely "dancing" together (*Source:* Brazelton, Koslowski, & Main, 1974, pp. 62 & 64).

When

Mutuality

Fails: Child

Abuse and

Other

Consequences

of Failure of

Bonding

The two-part system for fostering a strong bond between the parent and the infant is normally robust and effective. Most parents *do* form such bonds. But the process requires two partners, both of whom must have the necessary signals, skills, and energy to enter into the dance if the bond is to be properly formed. When either partner lacks the skills, the result can be a failure or weakening of the bond, with child abuse or neglect as one possible consequence.

### When the Infant Lacks Skills

For the system to work, the baby has to possess a sufficient repertoire of attachment behaviors to entice and hold the parent's attention and interaction. If some behaviors are missing, real problems can ensue. For example, Selma Fraiberg (1974, 1975) has studied a group of blind babies who smile less than sighted infants and do not show mutual gaze. Most parents of blind infants, after several months of this, begin to think that their infant is rejecting them, or they conclude that the baby is depressed. These parents feel less strongly bonded to their blind infants than to their sighted infants.

Similar problems can arise with parents of premature infants, who may be separated from their parents for the first weeks or months (which *may* interfere with the first bond) and then are likely to be quite unresponsive for the first weeks after they are home from the hospital. Most mothers of premature infants work extra hard in those first months to stimulate their infants. In fact, such mothers show *higher* rates of involvement with and stimulation of their babies in the early months than do mothers of full term babies (Field, 1977;

Barnard, Bee, & Hammond, 1984a). But eventually the mothers withdraw somewhat from the interaction since the babies so seldom respond with real mutuality.

Of course most blind infants, premature infants, or infants who are "different" in some way do not end up being physically abused. Most parents manage to surmount these problems. But the rate of abuse is higher among prematures than term infants, and higher among babies who are sick a lot in the first few months (e.g., Sherrod et al., 1984).

### When the Parent Lacks Skill

The other partner in the dance is obviously the parent, and failure of bonding can just as well come from the parent's end of the system. A parent might lack "attachment skill" because she or he did not form a secure attachment with her or his own parents, and did not learn the needed behaviors in later relationships (Sroufe & Fleeson, 1986). In fact, the majority of abusing parents were *themselves* abused as children, which makes this argument seem plausible. (Although note that the reverse need not be true; adults abused as children do not all abuse their own children. It is possible to break the cycle.) Or the parent could lack skill because he or she approaches the child care task from an essentially *egocentric* stance. For example, Carolyn Newberger and Susan Cook (1983) have found that abusing parents are more likely to describe the task of parenting in terms of their *own* needs that may be met. They may thus be less sensitive or responsive to the child's signals.

The most serious problem on the parent's side of the equation, however, seems to be depression, which disrupts

As is true of mothers, there is no very strong or convincing evidence that early contact between father and newborn is an essential ingredient in fostering the father's bond to the child—a set of findings I described in Chapter 3. And fathers seem to have the same repertoire of attachment behaviors to bring to their interaction with their newborn. For example, Ross Parke found

not only the parent's nurturing behavior, but affects the child's response as well. Babies interacting with depressed mothers, or even with mothers who have been told to look depressed or "blank faced," smile less and are more disorganized and distressed (e.g., Field et al., 1990; Cohn et al., 1990; Gusella et al., 1988). The depressed mothers, for their part, are slower to respond to their infants' signals, and are more negative—even hostile—to their infants (Rutter, 1990). Overall, these relationships appear to lack "synchrony." That is, the mother and infant are not "dancing" well together. Furthermore, these deficiencies in the mother-infant relationship seem to persist, even after the mother is no longer depressed—perhaps indicating that her bond with the infant is less firm. On the infant's side of the equation we also see generalization of the effect of the mother's depression. Tiffany Field and her colleagues (Field et al., 1988) have observed that 3-month-old babies with depressed mothers showed similar distressed or nonsynchronous behaviors when they interacted with a nondepressed adult as they did with their mothers.

Whether any of these conditions will result in abuse seems to depend on a variety of things, including the presence of such complicating conditions as alcoholism in one parent (Famularo et al., 1986), or the presence of other stresses on the family. Single parents, parents with many children, those with small living spaces or uncertain incomes, or those who lack friends or other sources of emotional support are much more likely to abuse their children than are parents with lower levels of stress (Garbarino & Sherman, 1980; Sack, Mason, & Higgins, 1985).

When both the child and the parent lack skills, or are under significant stress, the likelihood that there will be a failure of bonding, and possibly neglect or abuse of the child, is greatly increased.

## What Can Be Done?

Fortunately, it's possible to intervene to help the unattached parent become more attached. Fraiberg (1974) found that she could help the parents of blind babies to "read" the child's hand and body movements instead of waiting for smiles or eye contact. After such training, the parents of the blind babies found their attachment to the infant was strengthened. Benefits of such training are not restricted to more secure attachments, either. Thomas Achenbach and his colleagues (Achenbach et al., 1990) have found that teaching parents to read the baby's signals was also helpful for the long-term development of low birth weight infants. In their longitudinal study, families in the experimental group were seen 11 times with their babies, beginning when the infants were still in the hospital. The mothers were taught to read, and then to respond to, the baby's cues. Seven years later, the children whose families had received such assistance had mental test performances significantly higher than low birth weight children whose families had had no intervention.

Research like this points to the conclusion that any successful intervention program will need to include some intervention in the parent-child relationship itself, not only to teach parents needed child-rearing skills, but to alter the actual patterns of interaction between parent and child so as to help foster a stronger bond of parent to child.

that when fathers are actually holding their newborn infants, they touch, talk to, and cuddle their babies as much as, and in the same ways, that mothers do (Parke & Tinsley, 1981).

Past the early weeks of life, however, we see signs of a kind of "specialization" of parents' behaviors with their infants and toddlers. The "mother role" seems to involve not only routine caregiving, but also more talking, smiling, and quiet interactions. The "father role" involves more playfulness. Fathers do more physical roughhousing with their children and are more likely to play a game of some kind with the child (Parke & Tinsley, 1987). This does not mean that fathers have a weaker affectional bond with the infant; it does mean that the attachment behaviors they show toward the infant are typically somewhat different from those shown by mothers.

Where might such "parenting roles" come from? There are at least a couple of possibilities. One is that the person who is doing the major physical caregiving is quite logically going to end up doing less playing. Since mothers do more caregiving (even in families in which both parents work), the "mother" and "father" roles may be really "caregiver" and "noncaregiver" roles. Another possibility is that these patterns may be part of the sex-role definitions for men and women in our culture. As sex roles change, we may see changes in parenting behaviors too. Of course a third possibility is that these are "natural" or built-in differences in the ways males and females approach infants.

One way to decide among these several alternatives would be to see what happens in families in which the father is the major caregiver or in which both parents work and share caregiving. Unfortunately, the three studies of this kind that I know of have yielded quite contradictory results. Michael Lamb and his colleagues (Lamb et al., 1982) found that in a group of Swedish

At least in American and other Western cultures, the role of father with a young baby seems to involve a lot of play, including roughhousing or physical actions like these. Obviously the baby is enjoying it immensely!

families in which the father had been the major caregiver for one to three months, mothers still talked to and held the infants more, showed more affection, and gave more physical care than did fathers. In contrast, Tiffany Field (Field, 1978) found that in a U.S. sample, primary caregiving fathers showed many signs of a reversal of roles, with more physical care and more holding of their 4-month-olds than was seen among the mothers, although these fathers also showed more physical playing than did mothers, so the reversal was not complete. In still a third study in Australia, Russell (1982) found no differences in play or caregiving behavior between mothers and fathers who shared caregiving.

Probably these findings allow us to reject the hypothesis that distinctively different father and mother roles are somehow instinctive. But we are left with more questions than answers.

 ## The Attachment Process: Child to Parent

For parents, the formation of a strong affectional bond to the child may begin in the first hours or days after the child's birth, but it is greatly strengthened by the increasing skill of the partners in meshing their attachment behaviors. For the infant the sequence is reversed, beginning with attachment behaviors and progressing to the emotional bond and attachment somewhat later. Based on their research, Mary Ainsworth and her colleagues (Ainsworth et al., 1978) suggest that the emergence of a genuine attachment in an infant occurs in several steps, which I've sketched schematically in Figure 11.2 (p. 422).

### Phase 1: Initial Preattachment

During the first two or three months of life, the baby displays a wonderful range of attachment behaviors that Ainsworth describes as "proximity promoting"—they bring people closer. As I pointed out in Chapter 3, the newborn can cry, make eye contact, cling, cuddle, and respond to caregiving efforts by being soothed. But at first, as Ainsworth says, "these attachment behaviors are simply emitted, rather than being directed toward any specific person" (1989, p. 710). At this stage most observers see no sign of an attachment—although there is at least one recent study that may change a few minds on this score. A group of Japanese researchers (Mizukami, Kobayashi, Ishii, & Iwata, 1990) have shown that babies as young as 8-16 weeks of age show a drop in skin temperature (a sign of stress) when their mother leaves the room and an even larger drop if the mother is replaced by a stranger. However, when the mother remained with the baby when the stranger arrived, there was no equivalent sign of stress, suggesting that very young babies may already be using the mother as a "safe base." The conventional wisdom, however, is still that real attachment does not emerge until several months later.

### Phase 2: Attachment in the Making

As the infant begins to discriminate mother and father from other adults, she begins to aim her attachment behaviors somewhat more narrowly. She may smile more to the people who regularly take care of her and may not

## Development of Attachment

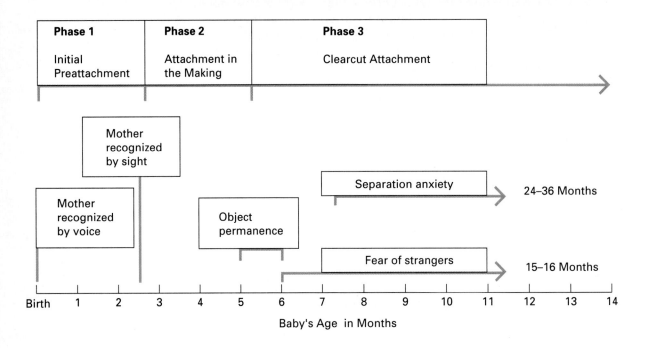

***FIGURE 11.2***

This schematic may help you see how the various threads of development related to the emergence of the child's attachment are woven together.

smile readily to a stranger. Yet despite the change, the infant does not yet have a full-blown attachment. There are still a number of people who are favored with the child's "proximity promoting" behaviors and no one person has become the "safe base." Children in this phase show no visible anxiety about being separated from their parent and no fear of strangers.

### Phase 3: Clear-Cut Attachment

It is only at about 6 months of age that we see signs that the child has formed a genuine attachment, usually toward a single person. At the same time, the dominant mode of the baby's attachment behavior changes: She shifts from using mostly "come here" signals (proximity promoting) to what Ainsworth calls "proximity seeking," which we might think of as "go there" behaviors. Because the 6- to 7-month-old begins to be able to move about the world more freely by creeping and crawling, she can move *toward* the caregiver as well as entice the caregiver to come to her. We also see a child of this age using the "most important person" as a safe base from which to explore the world around her—one of the key signs that an attachment exists.

We do not know just why the first clear attachment appears only at age 6 or 7 months. Babies can discriminate between Mom and other people several months sooner than that and prefer their mother's voice at birth, so why not an earlier attachment? The usual explanation, which I talked about in Chapter 5, is that only at this age has the child achieved object permanence—the awareness that some object or person continues to exist even when they are out of sight. So perhaps only at this age does the child really have some primitive internal representation of the mother (or other adult) to which she can become attached. Most theorists continue to accept this hypothesis, despite the fact that the research evidence is thin. Whatever the explanation, it is clear that a genuine attachment does indeed develop during the second half of the child's first year.

I should note that not all infants have a *single* attachment figure, even at this early point. Some may show strong attachment to both parents, or to a parent and another caregiver, such as a baby-sitter or a grandparent. But even these babies, when under stress, may show a preference for one of their favored persons over the others.

Several related patterns of behavior also emerge once the child has developed a clear attachment: social referencing and separation protest.

*Social Referencing.* By about 10 months, the infant not only uses the preferred person as a safe base, he also uses the mother (or other attachment figure) for clues about new situations—a phenomenon called *social referencing* which I mentioned briefly in Chapter 5. When infants of this age are confronted with a stranger or a new toy, for example, they will first look at their caregiver's face, to check for her expression. If the mother looks pleased or happy, the baby is more likely to show pleasure; if she shows fear, the baby is more likely to be fearful (e.g., Dickstein & Parke, 1988; Hirshberg & Svejda, 1990). There is a practical lesson here for parents whose infants or toddlers show fear or wariness toward strangers: Your child is more likely to accept the stranger if he sees you talking and smiling to the stranger first.

*Separation Protest and Fear of Strangers.* In most children there are two other signs that mark the early months of this first strong attachment: The child begins to show some fear of strangers and she begins to show anxiety and/or clear protest when she is separated from her favored person. Both are rare before 5 or 6 months, rise in frequency until about 12 to 16 months, and then decline.

Such an increase in fear and anxiety has been observed in children from a number of different cultures, and in both home-reared and day-care-reared children in the United States, all of which makes it look as if there are some basic cognitive or other age related developmental timetables underlying this pattern (Kagan, Kearsley, & Zelazo, 1978).

But while the general timing of these two phenomena may be common to virtually all children, the intensity of the fearful reaction is not. Children differ widely in how much fear they show toward strangers or toward novel situations. Some of this difference may reflect basic temperament (Berberian & Snyder, 1982). Heightened fearfulness may also be a response to some upheaval or stress in the child's life, such as a recent move or a parent changing jobs (Thompson & Lamb, 1982). Whatever the origin of such variations in

Not all babies show this much fear of strangers but virtually all babies show at least some wariness, beginning at about 6 or 7 months, and lasting for about a year.

fearfulness, the pattern does eventually disappear in virtually all toddlers, typically by the middle of the second year.

### Attachments to Parents in Preschool and Elementary School Children

By age 2 or 3, most attachment behaviors have become less visible. Children this age are cognitively advanced enough to understand if Mom explains why she is going away and that she will be back, so their anxiety at separation wanes. They can even use a photograph of their mother as a "safe base" for exploration in a strange situation (Passman & Longeway, 1982), which reflects another cognitive advance. Of course attachment behaviors have not completely disappeared. Two-year-olds still want to sit on Mom's or Dad's lap, they are still likely to seek some closeness or proximity when Mom returns from some absence, but in non-fearful or non-stressful situations the child is able to wander further and further from her "safe base" without apparent distress.

This is a considerable advance, but Bowlby points out that the 2- or 3-year-old's cognitive limitations, in particular her difficulty in taking another's perspective, make it impossible for the parent and child to engage in *mutual* planning. Such mutual planning appears only at about age 4, at which point the attachment seems to change in quality. Bowlby describes this new stage or level as a *goal-corrected partnership*. Marvin and Greenberg (1982) describe it this way:

> It now becomes possible for children to realize that they share with their mothers a relationship that is not totally dependent on interaction within physical proximity. That is, mother and child can now share a joint goal or plan whether they are together or apart, and the child thus realizes that the relationship continues even when they are separated. (1982, p. 49)

Just as the first attachment probably requires that the baby understand that his mother will continue to exist when she isn't there, so now the preschooler grasps that the *relationship* continues to exist even when the partners are apart. Children this age are much less distressed at separation, but they get upset if they don't know what's happening or haven't shared in the planning.

Once this understanding has been achieved, visible attachment behaviors go underground even more. Among elementary school children, it is largely only in stressful situations (including fatigue, hunger, family upheaval, problems at school, or the like) that we see overt attachment behaviors.

### Parent-Child Relationships at Adolescence

The parent-child attachment relationship remains in relative equilibrium until adolescence, when the hormonal changes of puberty begin to push the teenager toward a search for a new partner. Most of you can remember quite clearly the changes in your own relationships with your parents when you hit adolescence, so the research findings are not going to surprise you much.

At first there is typically an increase in conflict, an increase that may well be linked to the actual hormonal changes of puberty, rather than to age or to some social force. For example, in a short-term longitudinal study, Laurence Steinberg (1988) followed a group of teenagers over a one-year period, assessing their stages of puberty and the quality of their relationships with their parents at the beginning and end of the year. He found that as the pubertal stages began, family closeness declined and parent-child conflict rose. Other researchers (e.g., Inoff-Germain et al., 1988) have taken this a step further by measuring actual hormone levels and showing links between the rise of the various hormones of puberty and the rise in aloofness toward or conflict with parents. (Remember, though, that these are averages; parent-child conflict is not invariable or inevitable at adolescence. Some families show no such increase.)

At the same time, the overall level of the teenager's autonomy within the family increases steadily throughout the adolescent years, as parents give the youngster more and more room to make independent choices or to participate in family decision making. Steinberg argues that this "distancing" is a normal—even an essential—part of the adolescent development process.

Another trend that is very clear is an increasing amount of time spent with peers. Yet the temporarily heightened family conflict, the "distancing" from the parents, and the increased involvement with the peer group do not seem to signify that the young person's underlying emotional attachment to the parent has disappeared or even greatly weakened. This apparently paradoxical state of affairs is nicely illustrated in a study by Fumiyo Hunter and James Youniss (1982).

Hunter and Youniss had groups of fourth, seventh, and tenth graders and college students answer eight different questions about their relationships with mother, father, and best same-sexed friend. Figure 11.3 on the next page shows the average score, on a four-point scale, for those questions that dealt with the "intimacy" of the relationship—for example, "We talk about problems," or "My mother (father, best friend) knows how I feel." The figure also shows scores for questions about the nurturance of the relation-

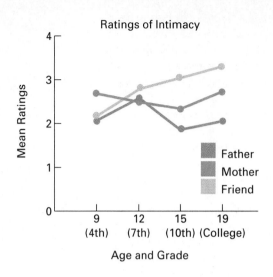
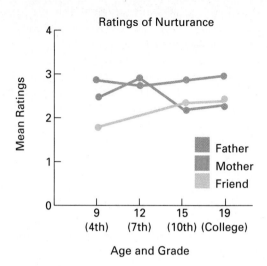

**FIGURE 11.3**

Results from Hunter and Youniss's study show that relationships with friends become increasingly intimate during the adolescent years, while relationships with parents become less so. But young people continue to see their parents as a major source of nurturance throughout these same years, suggesting that the attachment to the parents remains strong, even while peer attachments strengthen. (*Source:* F. T. Hunter & J. Youniss. Changes in functions of three relations during adolescence. *Developmental Psychology*, 1982, *18*, Figures 2 and 3, pp. 809, 810. Copyright 1982 by the American Psychological Association. Reprinted by permission of the publisher and author.)

ship—for example, "My mother (father, best friend) gives me what I need," or "My mother (father, best friend) helps me to solve my problems."

These results show that during adolescence (the seventh- and tenth-graders), intimacy with the mother and father goes down, while intimacy with the friend goes up. But young people across this age range see their parents as consistently high sources of nurturing.

This basic pattern is confirmed in other research. For example, Greenberg reports that a teenager's sense of well-being or happiness is more strongly correlated with the quality of his attachment to the parent than to the quality of his attachments to his peers (Greenberg et al., 1983). So this central relationship with the parent continues to be highly significant in adolescence, even while the teenager is becoming more autonomous.

## Attachments to Fathers and Mothers

I pointed out earlier that both fathers and mothers appear to form strong bonds to their infants, although their behavior with infants varies somewhat. But what about the child's half of this relationship? Are infants and children equally attached to their fathers and mothers?

In general, yes. From the age of 7–8 months, when strong attachments are first seen, infants prefer *either* the father or the mother to a stranger. And when both the father and the mother are available, an infant will smile at or approach either or both, *except* when he is frightened or under stress. When that happens, especially between 8 and 24 months, the child typically turns to the mother rather than the father (Lamb, 1981).

As you might expect, the strength of the child's attachment to the father at this early age seems to be related to the amount of time he has spent with the child. Gail Ross (Ross et al., 1975) found she could predict a baby's attachment to the father by knowing how many diapers the dad changed in a typical week. The more diapers, the stronger the attachment! However, greatly increased time with the father does not seem to be the only element, since Michael Lamb and his Swedish colleagues have found that infants whose father was the major caregiver for at least a month in the first year of the child's life were nonetheless more strongly attached to their mothers than their fathers (Lamb et al., 1983). One resolution of this apparent contradiction is that fathers who invest more time becoming attuned to the infant's signals are likely to have infants who are more strongly attached to them. But for the father to be consistently *preferred* over the mother would probably require essentially full-time paternal care. As this option becomes more common in our society, it will be possible to study such father-child pairs to see if a preference for the father develops.

## Individual Differences in the Quality of Infants' Attachments

Virtually all babies seem to go through the sequence I've described from preattachment to attachment. But the *quality* of the attachment they form to their parents differs. In Bowlby's terminology, infants have different **internal working models of social relationships**—namely, their relationships with parents and key others. This concept introduces a distinctly cognitive flavor to the discussion, much like the concepts of the "self scheme" or the "gender schema" I talked about in the last two chapters. This internal working model of attachment relationships includes such elements as the child's confidence (or lack of it) that the attachment figure will be available or reliable, the child's expectation of rebuff or affection, or the child's sense of assurance that the other is really a safe base for exploration.

The child begins to create this model late in the first year of life. The model then becomes more elaborated and firm through the first four or five years. By age 5, most children have clear internal models of the mother (or other caregiver), a self model, and a model of relationships. Once formed, such models shape and explain experiences and affect memory and attention. We notice and remember experiences that fit our model, and miss or forget experiences that don't match. More importantly, the model affects the child's behavior: The child essentially attempts to recreate, in each new relationship, the pattern with which he is familiar. Alan Sroufe gives a nice example that may make this point clearer:

**internal working models of social relationships** Cognitive construction, for which the earliest relationships may form the template, of the workings of relationships, such as expectations of support or affection, trustworthiness, etc.

What is rejection to one child is benign to another. What is warmth to a second child is confusing or ambiguous to another. For example, a child approaches another and asks to play. Turned down, the child goes off and sulks in a corner. A second child receiving the same negative reaction skips on to another partner and successfully engages him in play. Their experiences of rejection are vastly different. Each receives confirmation of quite different inner working models. (1988, p. 23)

### Secure and Insecure Attachments

secure attachment
Demonstrated by the child's ability to use the parent as a safe base and to be consoled after separation, when fearful, or when otherwise stressed.

insecure attachment
Includes both ambivalent and avoidant patterns of attachment in children; the child does not use the parent as a safe base and is not readily consoled by the parent if upset.

Strange Situation
A series of episodes used by Mary Ainsworth and others in studies of attachment. The child is observed with the mother, with a stranger, left alone, and then reunited with stranger and mother.

Theorists in this tradition share the assumption that the first attachment relationship is the most influential ingredient in the creation of the child's working model. Variations in that first attachment relationship are now almost universally described using Mary Ainsworth's category system (Ainsworth & Wittig, 1969; Ainsworth et al., 1978). She distinguishes between **secure attachment** and two types of **insecure attachment,** which she has assessed using a procedure called the **Strange Situation,** which I described briefly in Chapter 1.

You'll recall that this procedure consists of a series of episodes in a laboratory setting. The child is first with the mother, with the mother and a stranger, alone with the stranger, completely alone for a few minutes, reunited with the mother, left alone, and then reunited first with the stranger, and then the mother. Ainsworth suggested that children's reactions to this situation could be classified into three types: *securely attached, insecure/avoidant,* and *insecure/ambivalent* (also sometimes called resistant). Mary Main (Main & Soloman, 1985) has suggested a fourth group, which she calls insecure/disorganized/disoriented. I have listed some of the characteristics of the different types in Table 11.2.

These attachment types have been observed in studies in many different countries, and in every country secure attachment is the most common pattern (van IJzendoorn & Kroonenberg, 1988), occurring in 60 to 65 percent of all children studied. Where there is variability from one culture to the next it is in the relative incidence of the two types of insecure attachment—differences I have explored in the box on pages 430–431. In every culture, the probability that a child will be insecurely attached is much higher among children reared in poverty level families, in families with a history of abuse, or in families in which the mother is diagnosed as seriously depressed (Spieker & Booth, 1988).

Because all of the current work on the security of attachments has so many theoretical and practical ramifications, I need to take some time to explore some of the issues and implications.

### Is the Security of Attachment Stable Over Time?

One of the key questions is whether security of attachment is stable over time. Does a child who is securely attached to his mother at 12 months show the same secure attachment at 24 or 36 months? Is it still present at school age? This is a particularly important question for those researchers and therapists who are concerned about the possible permanence of effects of early abuse, neglect, or other sources of insecure attachment. Can children recover from such early treatment? Equally, is an initially securely attached child permanently buffered from the effects of later difficult life circumstances?

**TABLE 11.2**

*Behavior of Securely Attached and Insecurely Attached Infants in Ainsworth's Strange Situation at 12 Months of Age*

---

- ***Securely attached.*** Child shows low to moderate levels of proximity seeking to mother; does not avoid or resist contact if mother initiates it. When reunited with mother after absence, child greets her positively and can be soothed if upset. Clearly prefers mother to stranger.

- ***Insecurely attached: detached/avoidant.*** Child avoids contact with mother, especially at reunion after an absence. Does not resist mother's efforts to make contact, but does not seek much contact. Treats stranger and mother about the same throughout.

- ***Insecurely attached: resistant/ambivalent.*** Greatly upset when separated from mother, but mother cannot successfully comfort child when she comes back. Child both seeks and avoids contact, at different times. May show anger toward mother at reunion, and resists both comfort from and contact with stranger.

- ***Insecurely attached: disorganized/disoriented.*** Dazed behavior, confusion, or apprehension. Child may show strong avoidance following strong proximity seeking; may show simultaneously conflicting patterns, such as moving toward mother but keeping gaze averted; may express emotion in a way that seems unrelated to the people present.

---

*Sources:* Ainsworth et al., 1978; Main & Solomon, 1985; Sroufe & Waters, 1977.

As you might imagine, this is not a simple question to answer. The Strange Situation is only a suitable measure of attachment security for a brief period between 12 and perhaps 20 months. At later ages, other measures must be devised, and there is always the question of whether such new measures are really tapping the same underlying quality or process. With this important caveat in mind, however, I can offer some reasonably firm answers.

When the child's family environment or life circumstances are reasonably consistent, the security or insecurity of attachment remains stable. For example, Everett Waters (1978) found that only 2 out of the 50 infants he studied changed in their category of attachment security from 12 to 18 months. And in a stable, middle-class sample, Mary Main and her colleagues (Main, Kaplan, & Cassidy, 1985; Main & Cassidy, 1988) found strong correlations between ratings of security of attachment at 18 months and at 6 years. But when the child's circumstances change in some major way—such as when she starts going to day care or nursery school, or grandma comes to live with the family, or the parents divorce or move—the security of the child's attachment may change as well, either from secure to insecure, or the reverse (e.g., Thompson, Lamb, & Estes, 1982). In poverty level families, in which instability of circumstances is more common, changes in attachment security are also more common (Vaughn et al., 1979).

Findings like this are quite consistent with the notion of attachment as an "internal working model." Bowlby suggests that for the first two or three years, the particular pattern of attachment a child shows is in some sense a

If a secure or an insecure attachment is the product of particular patterns of parent-child interaction, and if cultures differ in such patterns, then it would be reasonable to find varying proportions of secure, avoidant, and resistant attachments among children reared in different cultures.

In fact, researchers have found signs of such cultural variation. The most thorough comparisons have come from two Dutch psychologists, Marinus van IJzendoorn and Pieter Kroonenberg, who have examined the results of 32 different stud-

ies in eight different countries (1988), yielding the results shown in Table 11.3. We need to be cautious about overinterpreting the variations shown in the table since in most cases there are only one or two studies from a given country, normally with quite small samples. The single study from China, for example, included only 36 babies. It is not at all clear that we ought to infer any generalized cultural pattern based on such small numbers of subjects. Still, the findings are thought provoking.

**TABLE 11.3**

*Cross-Cultural Comparisons of Secure and Insecure Attachments*

| Country | Number of Studies | Percentage of Attachment Types | | |
|---------|-------------------|--------|----------|------------|
| | | Secure | Avoidant | Ambivalent |
| West Germany | 3 | 56.6 | 35.3 | 8.1 |
| Great Britain | 1 | 75.0 | 22.2 | 2.8 |
| Netherlands | 4 | 67.3 | 26.3 | 6.4 |
| Sweden | 1 | 74.5 | 21.6 | 3.9 |
| Israel | 2 | 64.4 | 6.8 | 28.8 |
| Japan | 2 | 67.7 | 5.2 | 27.1 |
| China | 1 | 50.0 | 25.0 | 25.0 |
| United States | 18 | 64.8 | 21.1 | 14.1 |
| Overall Average | 32 | 65.0 | 21.3 | 13.7 |

*Source:* Based on Table 1 of van IJzendoorn & Kroonenberg, 1988, pp. 150–151.

property of a *relationship*. For example, recent studies of toddlers' attachments to mothers and fathers show that about 40 percent of the time the child is securely attached to one parent and insecurely attached to the other, with both possible combinations equally represented (Fox, Kimmerly, & Schafer, 1991). By the same argument, in the early years Bowlby would expect that if any given relationship changed markedly, the security of the child's attachment might change as well. But by age 4 or 5, Bowlby argues that the internal working model becomes more general, more a property of the *child*, and thus more resistant to change. At that point, the "child tends to impose it . . . upon new relationships" (Bowlby, 1988, p. 5), including relationships with teachers or peers.

Thus a child may "recover" from an initially insecure attachment or lose a secure one. But consistency over time is more typical, both because chil-

The most striking thing about the data in the table is actually the consistency rather than the difference. In each of the eight countries, a secure attachment was the most common pattern, and in six of the eight, an avoidant pattern was the more common of the two forms of insecure attachment. The only two reliably different patterns have been found in the studies in Israel and Japan, where researchers have observed significantly higher rates of resistant than avoidant attachments. What might be different about these two cultures?

Any explanations I can offer must necessarily be speculative at this point, given the small samples and the lack of detailed exploration of the actual mother-child interaction patterns outside of the Strange Situation. But it is interesting that in both of these cultures it is quite uncommon to find the kind of emotional withdrawal from the baby that seems to be a hallmark of the avoidant type of insecure attachment. The Israeli studies involved kibbutz-reared children, who are cared for primarily in groups by a special child nurse. They see their parents regularly during the day, and for a protracted period in the evening. If the mother were to be depressed, withdrawn, or rejecting the child, that style of interaction would occur in only a portion of the day rather than continuously, a pattern that seems much more likely to lead to an ambivalent than an avoidant attachment.

Japanese culture, too, places great emphasis on continuous mother-infant contact. Mothers are rarely apart from their babies in the early months, which may help prevent the occurrence of an avoidant pattern (Takahashi, 1986). But an ambivalent pattern could develop if the mother herself were somewhat ambivalent about her role as mother, so that she did not always respond quickly or contingently to the child's signals.

Another possibility is that the Strange Situation is simply not an appropriate measure of attachment security in all cultures. For example, since Japanese babies have been separated from their mothers much less frequently than is true for U.S. babies, being left totally alone in the midst of the Strange Situation may be far more stressful for them, which might result in more intense, unconsolable crying and hence a classification of ambivalent attachment.

As more cross-cultural research is done, we may be able to choose better among these (and other) possible explanations. At the moment the most plausible hypothesis is that the same factors in mother-infant interaction contribute to secure and insecure attachments in all cultures, but that cultures differ in the commonness of the significant patterns of interaction.

dren's relationships tend to be reasonably stable for the first few years, and because once the internal model is clearly formed, it tends to perpetuate itself.

### How Is a Secure Attachment Formed?

The common denominators in the backgrounds of securely attached babies seem to be both acceptance of the infant by the parents (e.g., Benn, 1986) and *contingent responsiveness* from the parents to the infant (Sroufe & Fleeson, 1986; Isabella, Belsky, & von Eye, 1989; Pederson et al., 1990). I have mentioned the notion of contingent responsiveness before, but I want to underline yet again that what is involved here is not just that the parents love the baby or take care of the baby well. For contingent responsiveness, the parents need to be sensitive to the child's own cues in their caregiving, as in the pattern shown on the right-hand side of Figure 11.1. The parents of secure babies also seem to be more likely to be emotionally expressive toward their babies—smiling more, using their voices in more expressive ways, and touching the infant more (e.g., Egeland & Farber, 1984).

In contrast, mothers of babies rated as insecure/avoidant are likely to be "psychologically unavailable" to their infants (to use Alan Sroufe's phrase). Mothers may show such a withdrawn or neglecting pattern for a variety of reasons, but as I pointed out in the box on pages 430–431, there is now a good deal of evidence that such a pattern is very common among mothers suffering from significant depression (e.g., Field, 1989).

The third group of infants, those rated as insecure/ambivalent, are likely to have mothers who are inconsistent in their responses to the infant, rejecting the infant's bids for contact some of the time, responding positively at other times. The fourth group, those recently described as insecure/disorganized/disoriented, have not been so well studied, but early signs are that this internal working model is common among children who are maltreated (e.g., Carlson et al., 1989).

Of course the relationship between the parent and the baby might not be the only causal agent involved here. What about infants who begin day care during the first year of life? Might such an experience interfere in some way with the development of a secure attachment to the mother? This is a hotly debated issue among developmental psychologists at the moment. Early research had shown no such increased risk, but Jay Belsky, among others, has recently reopened the debate, based on a number of current studies that appear to show that children who enter alternate care some time in the first year of life may be somewhat more likely to show avoidant attachment (Belsky, 1990). I'll be exploring this question in some detail in Chapter 13, but I wanted to alert you here to the fact that there is still dispute about this important question.

### Security of Attachment Versus Temperament

The findings I have reported so far are consistent with the general theoretical notion that the child's attachment model evolves out of his interactions with his mother or other major caregivers. But another explanation is possible. If you look again at the description of the insecurely attached child—especially the resistant/ambivalent type—you may find that it sounds a lot like Thomas and Chess's descriptions of temperamentally difficult children (Chapter 3). In fact, Chess and Thomas have themselves noted this similarity (1982), and argued that the Strange Situation is really only tapping temperamental differences.

I am not persuaded by this argument for several reasons. First, as Sroufe points out (1985), the fact that a child's attachment classification can change in response to environmental changes would be hard to account for if we were only measuring inborn temperament. Similarly, if it is only temperament, how could we explain the repeated observation that a child can be simultaneously securely attached to one person and insecurely attached to another?

Still, there are potential links. For example, the child's temperament might affect the form of insecure attachment he may develop (Belsky & Rovine, 1987). But even such linkages do not support Thomas and Chess' argument that temperament and attachment security are simply different facets of the same thing. As Bowlby says, "Those who attribute so much to inborn temperament will have to think again" (1988, p. 5).

### Long-Term Effects of Secure/Insecure Attachment

One of the reasons I have spent so much time talking about secure and insecure attachment is that this classification has proven to be extremely helpful in predicting a remarkably wide range of other differences between children, both as toddlers and in later childhood. I talked about some of those differences in Chapter 9 (recall Figure 9.2). In Table 11.4 I have expanded the list. As you can see, those children rated as securely attached to their mothers have also been found to be more sociable, more positive in their behavior toward others, and more emotionally mature in their approach to school and other non-home settings. Most of the information on which I have based the table comes from studies of preschool or early elementary school children. Only one group of researchers, Alan Sroufe and his colleagues, has followed a group of children much past that point, and their sample includes

**TABLE 11.4**

*Some Differences Between Securely and Insecurely Attached Children*

Securely attached infants, at later ages, show a number of characteristics:

- **Sociability.** They get along better with their peers, are more popular, and have more friends. With strange adults they are more sociable and less fearful.
- **Self-Esteem.** They have higher self-esteem.
- **Relationship with siblings.** They have better relationships with siblings, especially if both siblings are securely attached; if both are insecurely attached, the relationship is maximally antagonistic.
- **Dependency.** They show less clinging attention seeking from a teacher and less "negative attention seeking" (getting attention by being bad) in preschool years.
- **Tantrums and aggressive behavior.** They show less aggressive or disruptive behavior.
- **Compliance and good deportment.** They are easier to manage in the classroom, requiring little overt control by the teacher. But they are not overly docile.
- **Empathy.** They show more empathy toward other children and toward adults. They do not show pleasure on seeing others' distress, which is fairly common among avoidant children.
- **Behavior problems.** The results are mixed, but there are a number of studies that show that securely attached infants are less likely to show behavior problems at later ages.
- **Problem solving.** They show longer attention span in free play, more confidence in attempting solutions to tasks with tools, and use the mother or teacher more effectively as a source of assistance.

*Sources:* Cohn, 1990; Frankel & Bates, 1990; Greenberg & Speltz, 1988; Lütkenhaus, Grossman, & Grossman, 1985; Matas, Arend, & Sroufe, 1978; Plunkett, Klein, & Meisels, 1988; Sroufe, 1988, 1989; Teti & Ablard, 1989.

only 32 children so far (Sroufe, 1989). Still, these preliminary results are extremely intriguing because they point to enduring effects of the earliest attachment relationship or of the internal working model based on that relationship.

Sroufe and his coworkers observed their subjects in a specially designed summer camp when the children were 10 or 11. The counselors rated each child on a whole range of characteristics, and observers noted how often children spent time together or with the counselors. The findings are clear: Those with histories of secure attachment were rated as higher in both self-confidence and social competence. They complied more readily with counselor requests, expressed more positive emotions, and had a greater sense of their own ability to accomplish things—a quality described as a sense of "agency." Of the 8 children who had a history of attachment of the avoidant type, 5 showed patterns of either significant social isolation from peers or bizarre behavior; and all 8 of the children with histories of insecure attachment of the resistant or ambivalent type showed some pattern of deviant behavior. Four were markedly passive, 3 were notably hyperactive, and 1 was highly aggressive. Only 2 of the 16 securely attached children showed any of these deviant patterns.

I should emphasize again that these 32 children are the only ones yet studied over this length of time, and it is risky to build too tall a theoretical edifice on such a small empirical foundation. But Sroufe's data fit very well with the results from studies of younger children. Collectively the findings point to potentially long-term consequences of early attachment patterns or internal working models of relationship. But fluidity and change also occur, and we need to know much more about the factors that tend to maintain, or alter, the earliest models.

## Horizontal Relationships: The Child's Relationships with Other Children

Because most theories of social and personality development have strongly emphasized the centrality of parent-child interactions, until recently most psychologists thought of relationships with peers as much less important. But that view is now changing as it becomes clear that peer relationships play a unique and significant role in a child's development. In the first place, lessons about reciprocal relationships can *only* be learned with peers. And relationships with peers also appear to be necessary to aid the child in moving from the dependent relationship with the parents to the ultimate independence of young adulthood.

### Developmental Trends in Peer Relationships

*Infants and Preschoolers.* Children first begin to show some positive interest in other infants as early as 6 months of age. If you place two such babies on the floor facing each other, they will look at each other, touch, pull each other's hair, imitate each other's actions, and smile at one another. By 10 months these behaviors are even more evident. Children this age apparently still prefer to play with objects, but will play with each other if no toys are

*FIGURE 11.4*

O'Brien and Big
sults illustrate
between el
high scho
ideas ab
group
tary
ti

available. By 14 to 18 months, we begin to see two or more children playing together with toys—sometimes cooperating together, sometimes simply playing side by side with different toys. These changes occur earlier in toddlers who have had a lot of contact with other youngsters, such as those in day care or preschool, suggesting that to some extent children *learn* how to play with one another (e.g., Harper & Huie, 1985). By 3 or 4, children show still more organized play with each other, clearly preferring to spend time with peers (especially same-sex peers) rather than alone.

*Elementary Schoolers.*   Even more rigid sex-segregation is clear in children's play groups in elementary schools, and "boundary violations" are highly ritualized, as I am sure you can all remember from your own childhood. Barrie Thorne (1986), who has spent years on playgrounds watching children's play groups and games, describes the wonderful chasing games, which sometimes begin with taunts like "You can't catch me, nyah nyah," or poking, followed by chasing accompanied by screaming by the girls. Then there are "invasions," usually by the boys of the girls' games or the girls' space. Up to about fourth or fifth grade, it is taken as an insult to say about a boy that he "likes" some girl or that a girl likes some boy. By fifth grade that pattern begins to change, although there is still a great deal of teasing about any kind of boy-girl contact.

Over the elementary school years, peers and peer groups become increasingly central in children's daily activities. The vertical relationships with parents or teachers don't disappear; parents and teachers continue to provide a safe base, to answer questions, and to help solve problems. But playing with other kids is what 7-, 8-, 9-, or 10-year-old children prefer. Increasingly over these years, such play occurs in small groups of same-sex pals.

What elementary school-age kids seem to like about these groups is that they *do things* together. If you ask children this age about what makes a

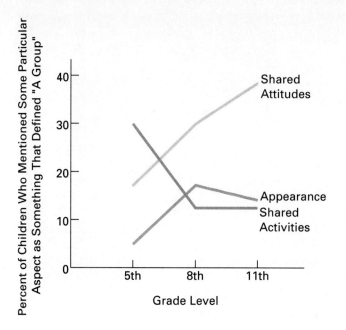

rman's re-
the change
mentary and
ol in children's
out what defines "a
of peers. In elemen-
school, one key func-
n of the peer group is to
provide a chance to do
things together. In adolescence, the peer group is a
vehicle for exploration of attitudes and for separation
from the parents (*Source:*
O'Brien & Bierman, 1988,
Table 1, p. 1363).

group a group, what they mention most often is common activities—riding bikes together, jumping rope together, or whatever. They are much less like-ly to mention common attitudes or values as the basis for a group. You can see this pattern in Figure 11.4, which shows the results of a study by Susan O'Brien and Karen Bierman (1988). They asked fifth-, eighth-, and eleventh-grade subjects to tell them about the different groups of kids that hang around together at their school, and then to say how they could tell that a par-ticular bunch of kids was "a group." For the fifth graders, the single best crite-ria of "a group" was that the kids did things together. For eighth graders, shared attitudes and common appearance became much more important.

I'll be talking much more about the child's *understanding* of social rela-tionships and processes in the next chapter, but let me just point out here that this "concreteness" in the elementary school child's view of peers is en-tirely consistent with what I've already told you about the character of the self-concept in children this same age, and with some of Piaget's ideas about the thinking of a concrete operational child.

*Adolescents.* Many of these patterns change at adolescence. Mixed sex groups begin to appear; conformity to the peer group values and behaviors increases and parents' influence on the child wanes. At the same time, the teenager's view of the importance of groups becomes less concrete and more focused on shared attitudes or the importance of group process. In fact, ado-lescents report that they spend more time *talking* to peers than doing any other thing (Csikszentmihalyi, Larson, & Prescott, 1977).

Most centrally, the *function* of the peer group changes. In elementary school, peer groups are mostly the setting for mutual play, and for all the learning about relationships and the natural world that is part of such play. But the teenager uses the peer group in another way. He is struggling to make a slow transition from the protected life of the family to the independent life of adulthood, and the peer group becomes the *vehicle* for that transition. As Erikson has pointed out, the clannishness and intense conformity to the group is a normal—even an essential—part of the process, necessary for the establishment of an identity.

Such conformity seems to intensify at about age 13 or 14 (at about the same time that we see a drop in self-esteem, as you'll recall from Chapter 10) and then wanes slowly as the teenager begins to arrive at a sense of identity that is more independent of the peer group. For example, Thomas Berndt (1979) finds that among adolescents, the 12- to 14-year-olds are the most likely to say they would be influenced by their peers to do such mildly antisocial activities as soaping someone's windows on Halloween.

Lest you think that all 13- and 14-year-olds run amok with their peers, I should point out two things. First, teenagers report that peer pressure is more likely to be *against* misconduct than toward it (Brown, Clasen, & Eicher, 1986), and second, susceptibility to negative peer pressure is less common among young people who are close to their parents (Steinberg & Silverberg, 1986). Thus while peer influence is particularly strong in these adolescent years, there are important mitigating factors, too.

Over the same years the structure of the peer group also changes. Dunphy's study (1963) of the several steps or stages in the shape and function of the peer group during adolescence is particularly fascinating. He observed the formation, dissolution, and interaction of teenage groups in a high school in Sydney, Australia, between 1958 and 1960. Two types of groups were visible. The first type, which Dunphy called **cliques,** were made up of four to six young people who appeared to be strongly attached to one another. Cliques had strong cohesiveness and high levels of intimate sharing. In the early years of adolescence, these cliques were almost entirely same-sex groups—left over from the preadolescent pattern. Gradually, however, the cliques combined into larger sets he called **crowds,** made up of several cliques and including both genders. Finally, the crowd broke down again into heterosexual cliques, and finally into loose associations of couples. The period of the fully developed crowd (at least in Dunphy's study) occurred at about age 13 to 15—the very years when we see the greatest conformity to peer pressure.

According to Dunphy, the crowd performs the highly important function of helping the teenager make the shift from unisexual to heterosexual social relationships. The 13- or 14-year-old can begin to try out her new heterosexual skills in the somewhat protected environment of the crowd; only after some confidence is developed do we see the beginnings of committed heterosexual pair relationships.

What I have given you so far is only a broad sketch of the changes in peer relationships over the years of childhood and adolescence. Let me fill in the picture by delving into several more specific developmental patterns—in friendships, in such prosocial behavior as helpfulness toward others, and in aggression and dominance.

*Friendship*

Beginning as early as age 2, children not only begin to show interest in peers in general, they also show some signs of individual friendships. These

**cliques**
Groups of 4–6 friends with strong attachment bonds and high levels of group solidarity and loyalty.

**crowds**
Larger and looser groups of friends than cliques, with perhaps 20 members; normally made up of several cliques joined together.

Dunphy's observations of Australian teenagers led him to suggest that there were two "phases" in teen group formation: cliques, which are closely knit groups of four or six friends, and later crowds, which may be looser-knit associations of cliques. Which do you think is shown here? Does Dunphy's description fit with your own memory of the groups you were involved with in high school?

relationships may be an especially important arena for learning about reciprocity and intimacy.

Carollee Howes (1983, 1987) has observed that children as young as 14–24 months old in day-care settings showed preferences for one or more playmates over a full year period. Using a somewhat stricter definition of friendship, Robert Hinde and his coworkers (1985) have found that in a group of 3 1/2-year-olds only about 20 percent showed signs of a stable friendship; by age 4, 50 percent of these same children regularly played more often with one child than with others.

These early friendships do not have all the features we see among older children, but even among preschool friend pairs there is more mutual liking, more reciprocity, more extended interactions, more positive and less negative behavior, and more supportiveness in a novel situation than is true between non-friend pairs. At the same time, the early friendships seem to be less enduring and more based on proximity and shared play interests than is true of friendships in older children (Berndt, 1981).

Individual friendships play a much larger role in the social patterns of elementary school-age children. In one study, John Reisman and Susan Shorr (1978) found that second graders named about four friends each; by seventh grade this had increased to about seven friends each. Many of these friendships are remarkably stable. Thomas Berndt, who has studied children's friendships extensively, finds that between one-half and three-fourths of close friendships in the elementary school years persist as long as a full school year; many last much longer (e.g., Berndt & Hoyle, 1985; Berndt, Hawkins, & Hoyle, 1986), and such stability is as common among first graders as among eighth graders. Individual friendships in the elementary school years are also almost totally sex segregated. John Gottman (1986) reports that perhaps 35 percent of friendships in preschool children in the United States are cross-sex friendships, but by age 7 or 8, such friendships are virtually nonexistent.

Children this age treat their friends quite differently than they treat strangers. They are more *polite* to strangers or non-friends. They are more open with pals, exchanging not only more supportive comments, but also more criticisms.

In the years just before puberty, and during adolescence, friendships continue to be quite stable. They also become increasingly intimate, in the sense that friends more and more share their inner feelings and secrets, and are more knowledgeable about each other's feelings. Loyalty and faithfulness also become more valued characteristics of friendship in adolescence. This trend toward greater intimacy continues throughout the teen years, with intimate sharing reaching a peak in the early twenties, just as Erikson suggests.

### Prosocial Behavior

Another important facet of peer relationships is a set of behaviors psychologists call **prosocial behavior:** "Intentional, voluntary behavior intended to benefit another" (Eisenberg, 1990, p. 240). In everyday language, this is essentially what we mean by **altruism.** This class of behaviors, too, shows a developmental course.

We first see such altruistic behaviors in children of about 2 or 3—at about the same time that they show real interest in play with other children. They will offer to help another child who is hurt, offer a toy, or try to comfort another (Zahn-Waxler & Radke-Yarrow, 1982; Marcus, 1986). As I pointed out in Chapter 7, children this young have only a beginning understanding of the fact that others feel differently from themselves, but they obviously understand enough about the emotions of others to respond in supportive and sympathetic ways when they see other children or adults hurt or sad.

We don't yet have a good enough base of data to be sure about the developmental patterns past these early years. Some kinds of prosocial behaviors seem to increase with age. For example, if you give children an opportunity to donate some treat to another child who is described as in need, older children donate more than younger children do. Helpfulness, too, seems to increase with age up through adolescence. But not all prosocial behaviors show this pattern. Comforting another child, for example, may be more common among preschool and early elementary school children than at older ages (Eisenberg, 1988, 1990). We know more about the changes in the child's *understanding* of such helpful behaviors—a subject I'll be exploring in some detail in the next chapter.

We also know that children vary a lot in the amount of altruistic behavior they show. For those of you interested in knowing more about how helpful

prosocial behavior
See *altruism.*

altruism
Giving or sharing objects, time, or goods with others, with no obvious self-gain.

or altruistic children come to be that way, I've explored some of the research in the box on pages 442–443.

### Negative Interactions: Aggression and Dominance

If you have watched children together, you know that all is not sweetness and light in the land of the young. Children do support and share with their friends, and they do show affectionate and helpful behaviors toward one another, but they also tease, fight, yell, criticize, and argue over objects and territory. Researchers who have studied this "negative" side of children's interactions have looked mostly at **aggression,** which we can define as behavior with the apparent intent to injure some other person or object (Feshbach, 1970).

Every child shows at least some aggression. The basic built-in "signal" for aggression in most instances seems to be frustration. Some early theorists (Dollard et al., 1939) argued that aggression *always* followed frustration and that all aggressions were preceded by frustration. This extreme version of the "frustration-aggression hypothesis" turns out to be wrong but it does seem to be true that the human child is born with a fairly strong natural tendency to behave aggressively after being frustrated.

Over the early years of life, the frequency and form of aggression change, as I've summarized in Table 11.5. When 2- or 3-year-old children are upset or frustrated, they are more likely to throw things or hit each other. As their verbal skills improve, however, there is a shift away from such overt physical aggression toward greater use of verbal aggression, such as taunting or name-calling. Physical aggression continues to decline in elementary school and into adolescence—with one exception. In all-boy pairs or groups, physical aggression seems to remain both relatively high and constant over these years (Cairns et al., 1989).

**aggression**
Usually defined as intentional physical or verbal behaviors directed toward a person or an object with the intent to inflict damage on that person or object.

**TABLE 11.5**

*A Summary of Developmental Changes in the Form and Frequency of Aggression in Children*

|  | 2- to 4-Year-Olds | 4- to 8-Year-Olds |
|---|---|---|
| Frequency of Physical Aggression | At its peak from 2 to 4. | Declines over the period from 4 to 8. |
| Frequency of Verbal Aggression | Relatively rare at 2; increases as the child's verbal skill improves. | A larger percentage of aggresion in this period is verbal rather than physical. |
| Form of Aggression | Primarily "instrumental aggression," which is aimed at obtaining or damaging an object rather than directly hurting someone else. | More "hostile aggression" at these ages, aimed at hurting another person or another person's feelings. |
| Occasion for Aggression | Most often occurs after conflicts with parents. | Most often occurs after conflicts with peers. |

*Sources:* Goodenough, 1931; Hartup, 1974.

A related, but quite separable, aspect of "negative" encounters between children is competition or **dominance.** Whenever there are too few toys for the number of children, not enough time with the teacher to go around, or some other scarcity of desired objects, there will be competition. Sometimes competition results in outright aggression. More often, competition results in the development of a clear **dominance hierarchy,** more popularly known as a "pecking order." Some children seem to be more successful than others at asserting their rights to desired objects, either by threats, by simply taking the object away, by glaring at the other child, or the equivalent.

Clear dominance hierarchies are seen in playgroups of children as young as 2 to 5 years old (e.g., Strayer, 1980). That is, among 10 or 15 children who play together regularly, it is possible to predict who will "win" in any given competition over some desired object or space. Children high in the dominance hierarchy win out over nearly all other children; children at the bottom of the pecking order lose to everyone.

Research on dominance in young children has revealed some extremely interesting patterns. Among 2- to 5-year-olds, a child's place in the group dominance system is *not* related to popularity or to positive interactions to or from the child. But among elementary school children, the dominance and popularity/friendship system may be linked. When Strayer (1980) observed 5- and 6-year-olds in play groups, he found that the dominant children were also the most popular—so long as they were not bullies (Pettit et al., 1990). So among children this age, popularity may reflect both positive actions and perceived dominance.

The overall picture that emerges is that past the age of 4 or 5, *socially competent* children are those who are at the middle to higher end of the dominance hierarchy, who are positive, helpful and supportive of others, and who refrain from overt acts of physical aggression.

## Individual Differences in Peer Relationships

Findings like those on dominance point us to a more general set of questions about variations among children in their social behavior or their social skills. Collectively, children may move toward greater and greater ability to interact effectively with their peers, toward greater altruism, away from overt expression of aggression, and toward greater intimacy in their relationships with peers. But there are clearly enormous differences among children in the degree to which they acquire such skills, in the degree to which they express themselves with overt aggression, and in their popularity (or unpopularity) with peers.

### *Popularity*

Psychologists have used at least three strategies in trying to understand differences in popularity. Those who have taken a longitudinal approach, such as Sroufe, have looked for antecedents of popularity in early attachment relationships. Others have started by first identifying popular and unpopular children and then comparing them in various ways. Still others have contrived to have groups of previously unacquainted children play with one an-

**dominance**
The ability of one person consistently to "win" competitive encounters with other individuals.

**dominance hierarchy**
A set of dominance relationships in a group describing the rank order of "winners" and "losers" in competitive encounters.

From the earliest ages at which we see helpful and kind behavior, there are marked differences among children in the amount of such altruistic behavior they show. Since most of us would like our children to behave in this way toward us, toward their brothers and sisters, and toward other children, it's worthwhile to take a look at what we know about the kind of family environments that seem to foster such positive social interactions.

Research and analyses by Nancy Eisenberg (Eisenberg, 1988; Eisenberg & Miller, 1990), Joan Grusec (e.g., Grusec & Dix, 1986; Mills & Grusec, 1989), and Carolyn Zahn-Waxler (Zahn-Waxler, Radke-Yarrow, & King, 1979; Zahn-Waxler & Radke-Yarrow, 1982) point to several specific child-rearing strategies that seem to make a difference.

### Creating a Loving and Warm Family Climate

It shouldn't surprise you to know that parents who behave in loving, nurturing, and supportive ways toward their children have children who are more helpful, more empathetic, and more thoughtful of others. This effect is much clearer, though, when such warmth is combined with one or more of the following other parental behaviors.

### Explaining Why and Giving Rules

A second significant element in the equation is to be clear to children about what your rules and standards are. A combination of clear rules and loving support is especially effective. This shows up clearly in research by Carolyn Zahn-Waxler and her colleagues. They asked a group of 16 mothers of young children to keep daily diaries of every incident in which someone around the child showed distress, fear, pain, sorrow, or fatigue. For example, John's mother described an incident in which her 2-year-old son was visited by a friend, Jerry:

> Today Jerry was kind of cranky; he just started completely bawling and he couldn't stop. John kept coming over and handing Jerry toys, trying to cheer him up, so to speak. He'd say things like "Here, Jerry," and I said to John: "Jerry's sad; he doesn't feel good; he had a shot today." John would look at me with his eyebrows kind of wrinkled together like he really understood that Jerry was crying because he was unhappy, not that he was just being a crybaby. He went over and rubbed Jerry's arm and said "Nice Jerry" and continued to give him toys. (Zahn-Waxler et al., 1979, p. 321–322)

Zahn-Waxler found that mothers who both explained the consequences of the child's actions (e.g., "If you hit Susan it will hurt her") and who stated the rules clearly, explicitly, and with emotion ("You mustn't hit people!") had children who were much more likely to react to others with helpfulness or sympathy. Research with older children, too, shows that stating the reason for generosity or helpfulness—particularly if the reason focuses on the feelings of other people—increases the likelihood that a child will behave in a kind or helpful manner.

Many of us, as parents, spend a lot of time telling children what *not* to do. The research on altruism in children points to the importance of telling children *why*

other over a period of time, observed the interactions, and then asked the children at the end to choose the children they liked best or least. The picture that emerges from all three types of studies is remarkably consistent. I've listed some of the common themes in Table 11.6 on page 444.

they should not do things, especially in terms of the potential impact on other people. Equally important is stating *positive* rules or guidelines, e.g., "It's always good to be helpful to other people," or "We should share what we have with people who don't have so much."

### Having Children Do Helpful Things

A third thing that fosters helpfulness is giving children a chance to do really helpful things—around the house or in school. Children can help cook (a nurturing activity), take care of pets, make toys to give to hospitalized or poor children, assist in making a casserole to take to the recently widowed neighbor, and teach younger siblings how to play games.

Obviously, not all children do such things spontaneously. They have to be asked, sometimes coerced. If the coercion is too strong, the effect changes: The child may now attribute his "good" behavior to the coercion ("Mother made me do it"), rather than to some inner trait of his own ("I am a helpful/kind person"). When that happens, the coerced altruistic actions do not seem to foster future altruism. So it matters how the "doing of helpful things" is managed.

### Prosocial Attributions

A fourth strategy is to "attribute" your child's helpful or altruistic action to the child's own internal quality: "You're such a helpful child!" or "You certainly do a lot of nice things for other people." This strategy begins to be effective with children at about age 7 or 8, at about the same time that they are beginning to develop generalized notions of their own personality. By explaining your child's actions in terms of some global internal quality of kindness or generosity or thoughtfulness, you may affect the child's self-scheme. Thereafter, the child will try to match his actions to his own self-scheme.

### Modeling Thoughtful and Generous Behavior

A final key—perhaps the most significant—is to demonstrate to your children exactly the generous, thoughtful, and helpful behavior you would like them to show. If there is a conflict between what you say and what you do, children will imitate your actions. So stating the rules or guidelines clearly will do little good if your own behavior does not match what you say.

The importance of demonstrating altruism is very clear in a study by Gil Clary and Jude Miller (1986) of adult volunteers in a telephone crisis counseling agency. Obviously all these volunteers were showing a significant level of altruistic behavior, simply by offering any of their time. But Clary and Miller found that those volunteers who stuck with it, compared to those who dropped out before completing their agreed-upon six months of effort, described their parents as more loving and warm. These "sustained altruists" also said that their parents had both preached the importance of generosity and helpfulness, and had lived up to their own preaching, more than was true for the parents of the volunteers who dropped out. Young people from families like this are more likely to develop "autonomous" altruism—kindness, thoughtfulness, or generosity that comes from a genuine concern, an internal value, rather than from a desire to be liked or approved. So if such autonomous altruism is your goal for your children, you will need to look at your own behavior first.

Some of the items in the table are obviously things that a child can't control, such as physical size or attractiveness. These characteristics do make some difference, but the crucial element in popularity is not what you look like but how you *behave*. Popular children are liked because they behave in positive, supporting, nonpunitive, and nonaggressive ways toward most other children (e.g., Ladd et al., 1988; Black & Hazen, 1990). Of course once a child becomes popular it is far easier to be friendly, positive, and supportive toward those who like you, so there is a feedback loop involved here. But we also know that the same processes operate when children are first becoming acquainted: Those children who are most consistently positive and supportive from the beginning are those who end up being chosen as leaders or as friends (e.g., Dodge, 1983), while those who consistently participate in conflicts are more often rejected (Shantz, 1986).

Rejected children, in particular, are likely to be those who show high levels of aggression toward their peers. Such children seem to have quite different internal working models of relationships and of aggression than do popular children. Kenneth Dodge (Dodge & Frame, 1982; Dodge et al., 1990) has shown that aggressive children are much more likely to see aggression as a useful way to solve problems; more importantly, they "read" attack or antagonism in others' behavior much more readily than is true for less aggressive children. Given an ambiguous event, such as being hit in the back with a kick ball, chronically aggressive boys are much more likely to assume that the ball was thrown on purpose, and they retaliate. Of course such retaliation, in turn, is likely to elicit hostility from others, so their expectation that other people are hostile to them is further confirmed. Other research tells us that such children tend to *over*estimate their own social competence (Patterson et al., 1990), a distortion that may protect them from realizing just how rejected they are by their peers.

This body of research can also be linked to Gerald Patterson's work on aggressive boys. His research supports the conclusion that the child's excess aggressiveness can be traced originally to ineffective parental control. When the child displays this same behavior with peers, he is rejected by those peers

**TABLE 11.6**

*Some Characteristics of Popular and Rejected Children in Elementary School*

**Popular children are more likely to be:**
- Friendly toward others, less punitive, more reinforcing, more supportive.
- Outgoing and gregarious.
- Physically attractive.
- Physically larger or taller or more mature.
- The youngest child in the family.
- Good at specific task skills, such as sports or games.
- More successful in school.

**Rejected children are more likely to be:**
- Physically unattractive.
- Physically or emotionally immature.
- Aggressive or disruptive.
- Less friendly, more likely to be critical than supportive.

*Sources:* Asher, Oden, & Gottman, 1977; Hartup, 1984; Masters & Furman, 1981; Shantz, 1986.

and is then driven more and more toward the only set of peers who will accept him, usually other aggressive or delinquent boys.

In fact, there is now a growing body of research showing that rejection by one's peers in elementary school is one of the very few aspects of childhood functioning that consistently predicts behavior problems or emotional disturbances in adolescence and adulthood (e.g., Kupersmidt & Coie, 1990; Dishion et al., 1991). For example, Leonard Eron, in a 22-year longitudinal study, has found that aggressiveness toward peers (and its accompanying peer rejection) at age 8 was related to various forms of aggressiveness at age 30, including "criminal behavior, number of moving traffic violations, convictions for driving while intoxicated, aggressiveness toward spouses, and how severely the subjects punished their own children" (Eron, 1987, p. 439).

There are obviously several ways we could explain such a link between early unpopularity and later behavior problems. Problems with peers might be merely the most visible reflection of a general maladjustment that later manifests as delinquency or emotional disturbance. It could also mean that a failure to develop friendships itself causes problems that later become more general. Or it could signify a seriously warped internal working model of relationships or all of the above. Whatever the source of the problem, you will be glad to know that it is possible, within limits, to increase a child's acceptance by his peers by teaching him the social skills that seem to be required for friendship, including listening, smiling, and supportiveness (e.g., Bierman, 1986).

### Sex Differences

So far I have mostly steered clear of any discussion of sex differences in social interactions. But since this is an area in which the sex-role stereotypes are very strong, I need to face the question as squarely as I can. Take a look at Table 11.7 on the next page. For each of a series of social behaviors I've listed both the sex-role stereotype and the actually observed differences, so you can see how well they match.

In many areas the match is not good. Contrary to social expectations, girls do not seem to be more dependent, more nurturant, more compliant, or more altruistic. But in two areas there are consistent differences: in the quality of social interactions and in the cluster of behaviors related to aggression or dominance.

I talked a bit about the early differences in boys' and girls' styles of relating to one another in Chapter 10. Throughout childhood and adolescence, these differences become increasingly more pronounced. Maccoby (1990) describes the girls' pattern as an *enabling style*. Enabling includes such behaviors as supporting the partner, expressing agreement, and making suggestions. All these behaviors tend to foster a greater equality and intimacy in the relationship and keep the interaction going. In contrast, boys are more likely to show what Maccoby calls a *constricting* or *restrictive* style. "A restrictive style is one that tends to derail the interaction—to inhibit the partner or cause the partner to withdraw, thus shortening the interaction or bringing it to an end" (p. 517). Contradicting, interrupting, boasting, or other forms of self-display are all aspects of this style.

Maccoby cites several lines of evidence that support this distinction. We know that pairs of boy friends are *more* competitive with each other than are

TABLE 11.7

*Sex-Role Stereotypes and Observed Sex Differences in Social Behavior*

| Behavior and Stereotype | Observed Difference |
|---|---|
| **Aggression/dominance/competitiveness.** Boys expected to show more of all three. | Boys found to show more rough-and-tumble play in the early years and more aggression and competitiveness at virtually all ages. |
| **Risk taking.** Boys expected to show more. | Boys are more willing to try new and daring or faintly dangerous things, such as riding an elephant at the zoo. |
| **Dependency.** Girls expected to show more. | No consistent sex difference has been found in such behaviors as clinging, proximity seeking, or attention seeking in children of any age. |
| **Nurturance/helping/generosity.** Girls expected to show more of all three. | Mixed results. Most studies show no sex difference, but when a difference is found, girls are usually slightly more generous or slightly more likely to help or nurture. |
| **Sociability.** Girls expected to show more. | No clear difference in *amount* of sociability, but clear differences in style of interaction between same-sex pairs. For example, girls' friendships are more intimate. |
| **Compliance.** Girls expected to show more. | Preschool girls comply more readily with adult requests. Among older children there is no consistent finding except that those who exhibit very high levels of noncompliance are more often boys. |
| **Crying.** Girls expected to show more. | No difference. |

*Sources:* Ginsberg & Miller, 1982; Hyde, 1984; Maccoby, 1990; Maccoby & Jacklin, 1974, 1980; Patterson, 1980.

pairs of strangers. We know that aggression between boys does not decline over the years of elementary school, while aggression between girls, and between boys and girls, does drop. We know that friendships between girls are much more intimate, with much more self-disclosure. We know that boy friends are more likely to gather in large groups than as paired pals, and that the boys are less likely to exchange confidences and more likely to engage in some mutual activity, such as sports. We also have a variety of indications that the same differences in style of relationship are evident in adults, with adult women continuing to describe more intimate friendships than do men, and with women continuing to focus their attention in groups or pairs on actions that tend to keep the interaction going. Men are more likely to be task oriented, women to be relationship oriented. These are subtle but profound differences and we still know little about how they arise in earliest childhood and why they diverge so persistently. But this is obviously an important area for future research.

Starting as early as age 3 or 4, girls and boys have quite different styles of interacting with one another. Girls are much more likely to be seen in a pose like this: facing one another, clearly engaging one another in a kind of one-on-one sharing that typifies what Maccoby calls the "enabling" style. If two boys the same age were talking, it's much more likely that they would be sitting side by side, and they'd be more likely to interrupt or contradict one another.

The second major area in which the sex-role stereotype seems to be reasonably accurate is in aggression, assertiveness, and dominance. As expected, boys show more of all three, and this is true beginning as early as toddlerhood and continuing throughout childhood and adulthood.

Where might such differences come from? Eleanor Maccoby and Carol Jacklin (1974), who summarized all the studies done up to 1974, concluded that there is an important biological basis for the aggression differences:

> Let us outline the reasons why biological sex differences appear to be involved in aggression: (1) Males are more aggressive than females in all human societies for which evidence is available. (2) The sex differences are found early in life, at a time when there is no evidence that differential socialization pressures have been brought to bear by adults to "shape" aggression differently for the two sexes. (3) Similar sex differences are found in man and subhuman primates. (4) Aggression is related to levels of sex hormones, and can be changed by experimental administration of these hormones. (Maccoby & Jacklin, 1974, p. 242–243)

Other psychologists (including Maccoby and Jacklin in more recent writings) have emphasized that there are important social influences, at least in our culture, which also may foster higher levels of aggression in boys. For example, in research with Margaret Snow, Maccoby and Jacklin (Snow, Jacklin, & Maccoby, 1983) have found that with children as young as age 1, fathers punish or prohibit behavior in their sons more than in their daughters.

It seems clear that both biological and environmental influences play a role. There probably are hormonal or other biological factors creating higher rates of aggressiveness in boys to begin with. But as I pointed out in Chapter 10, there is also pressure from parents (particularly fathers) for 4- and 5-year-old boys to adopt more "boyish" behaviors and attitudes, which includes playing physical games and being assertive with others. The manner in which

parents respond to the child's aggression also helps to shape it, which shows clearly that aggression is not entirely determined by biology.

We need to know a great deal more about both these pervasive gender differences "if we are to adapt ourselves successfully to the rapid changes in the roles and relationships of the two sexes that are occurring in modern societies" (Maccoby, 1990, p. 519).

S U M M A R Y

1.  Both vertical relationships with adults and horizontal relationships with peers are of central significance in the child's social development. In particular, skills in forming and maintaining reciprocal relationships can only be learned with peers.

2.  An important distinction is between an affectional bond (an enduring tie to a uniquely viewed partner) and an attachment, which also involves the element of security and a safe base.

3.  An attachment is deduced from the existence of attachment behaviors.

4.  The parents' bond to the infant may develop in two phases: (1) An initial strong bond may be formed in the first hours of the child's life and (2) the bond may be strengthened by the repetition of mutually reinforcing and interlocking attachment behaviors.

5.  Immediate contact with the infant after birth does not appear to be necessary for the formation of a strong bond from parent to child.

6.  Fathers as well as mothers form strong bonds to their infants, but fathers show more playful behaviors with their children than do mothers.

7.  Initially the infant shows attachment behaviors toward nearly anyone but no preferential attachment. By 5 to 6 months of age, most infants have formed at least one strong attachment, usually to the major caregiver.

8.  In toddlers and preschoolers, the basic attachment remains but attachment behaviors become less visible except when the child is stressed. By age 4 or 5 the child understands the constancy of the relationship.

9.  The basic attachment to the parents remains strong in adolescence, despite an increase in parent-child conflict, the greater independence of the teenager, and the greater impact of the peer group.

10.  Children typically develop strong attachments to both father and mother.

11.  Children differ in the security of their first attachments, and thus in the internal working model they develop. The secure infant uses the parent as a safe base for exploration and can be readily consoled by the parent.

12.  The security of the initial attachment is reasonably stable, and is fostered by contingent responsiveness and acceptance by the parent.

13.  Securely attached children appear to be more socially skillful, more curious and persistent in approaching new tasks, and more mature.

14.  Children's relationships with peers become more and more central to their social development from age 1 or 2. In elementary school, peer interactions

are focused mostly on common activities; in adolescence, peer groups also become the vehicle for the transition from dependence to independence. The peer group is maximally influential at about age 12 to 14.

15. By age 4 or 5 children have formed individual friendships, and show preferential positive behavior toward friends. Friendship becomes more common, and more stable, in the elementary school years, and more intimate in adolescence.

16. Prosocial behavior, such as helpfulness or generosity, is apparent as early as age 2 or 3 and generally increases throughout childhood.

17. Young children also show such negative social patterns as aggressiveness and dominance. Physical aggression peaks at 3 or 4, and is more and more replaced by verbal aggression among older children. Dominance patterns are also visible in groups of toddlers, as well as older children.

18. Popularity among peers, in elementary school or later, is most consistently based on the amount of positive and supportive social behavior shown by a child toward peers.

19. Rejected children are typically those who show heightened levels of aggression toward peers. Such children have different internal working models than do non-rejected children. They are also at much higher risk for later behavior problems such as delinquency.

20. Two patterns of sex differences in social relationships have been found consistently: (a) boys and girls have quite different styles of interacting with one another, with girls' pairs or groups showing a more "enabling" style, and (b) boys are consistently more aggressive, assertive, and dominant.

## CRITICAL THINKING QUESTIONS

1. Several researchers report that teenager/parent conflict is at its peak in the early stages of puberty. What explanations can you offer for this pattern? Does it fit with your own experience as you recall it?

2. The concept of an "internal working model" has become prominent in current theorizing about many aspects of children's relationships. Why do you think theorists have found this concept to be so useful?

3. Observation tells us that fathers "play" more with their children, while mothers do more routine caregiving. See if you can design an ideal study/experiment to determine whether this is a built-in sex difference, or whether it is a function of who does the major caregiving. Why is the "ideal" study not feasible? What compromises do you have to make to do the study in the real world, and how do those compromises affect the conclusions you can draw?

# KEY TERMS

**affectional bond**   A relatively long-enduring tie in which the partner is important as a unique individual and is interchangeable with none other.

**aggression**   Usually defined as intentional physical or verbal behaviors directed toward a person or an object with the intent to inflict damage on that person or object.

**altruism**   Giving or sharing objects, time, or goods with others, with no obvious self-gain.

**attachment**   A subvariety of affectional bond in which the central figure is experienced as a safe base from which to explore the world.

**attachment behaviors**   The collection of (probably) instinctive behaviors of one person toward another that brings about or maintains proximity and caregiving, such as the smile of the young infant; behaviors that reflect an attachment.

**cliques**   Groups of 4–6 friends with strong attachment bonds and high levels of group solidarity and loyalty.

**crowds**   Larger and looser groups of friends than cliques, with perhaps 20 members; normally made up of several cliques joined together.

**dominance**   The ability of one person consistently to "win" competitive encounters with other individuals.

**dominance hierarchy**   A set of dominance relationships in a group describing the rank order of "winners" and "losers" in competitive encounters.

**insecure attachment**   Includes both ambivalent and avoidant patterns of attachment in children; the child does not use the parent as a safe base and is not readily consoled by the parent if upset.

**internal working models of social relationships**   Cognitive constructions for which the earliest relationships may form the template of the workings of relationships, such as expectations of support or affection, trustworthiness, etc.

**prosocial behavior**   See altruism.

**secure attachment**   Demonstrated by the child's ability to use the parent as a safe base and to be consoled after separation, when fearful or when otherwise stressed.

**Strange Situation**   A series of episodes used by Mary Ainsworth and others in studies of attachment. The child is observed with the mother, with a stranger, left alone, and then reunited with stranger and mother.

# SUGGESTED READINGS

Eisenberg, N., & Mussen, P. H. (1989). *The roots of prosocial behavior in children*. Cambridge: Cambridge University Press.

   A good, current summary of what we know about this aspect of children's social interactions.

Grusec, J. E., & Lytton, H. (1988). *Social development: History, theory, and research*. New York: Springer-Verlag.

   This is the most recent of several good texts on social development. A very good source for further detail on almost any of the topics I've covered in this chapter.

Hartup, W. W. (1989). Social relationships and their developmental significance. *American Psychologist, 44,* 120–126.

   Hartup has always been one of my favorite authors. His style is clear, his ideas interesting. Here he gives a brief review of some of the current work on social interactions.

Lickona, T. (1983). *Raising good children*. Toronto: Bantam Books.

   One of the very best "how to" books for parents I have ever seen, with excellent, concrete advice as well as theory. His emphasis is on many of the issues I raised in the box on rearing altruistic children.

# PROJECT 14

## Observation of Children's Play Groups

Let me give you a tougher assignment than many of the earlier projects, one that will really stretch your skills as an observer and researcher. After obtaining permission in whatever way is required by your instructor, arrange to spend several hours in a day-care center or preschool that includes groups of children of about age 2 to 4. Be sure to do the observation during a time that includes some "free play." If all you observe is snack time, nap, and organized play you will not get a chance to observe the things I want you to look for.

Watch for about 15 minutes without writing anything down. During this time you should pick out about 10 different children who will be the focus of your later observations, 5 boys and 5 girls. Label them in some way that you can use as shorthand, and be sure to indicate whether each is a boy or a girl.

Now begin your real observations. At the beginning of each 3-minute period, for each of your focal 10 children, note (1) how many other children are playing with that child, (2) the gender of all children in the play group, (3) the specific identity of any child in the group you can identify, and (4) the activity the children are engaged in (e.g., doll play, blocks, swings, etc.).

Continue this procedure for each 3-minute period for at least an hour. Inevitably you will have some periods in which one or more of the focal children was not in sight (they are in the bathroom, or elsewhere), and probably there will be some 3-minute periods in which all children are playing together in some activity organized by the teachers. In the former case, merely omit that child from the record for that interval. In the latter (full-group activity), omit that 3-minute period from your record entirely.

I recommend that you make up a data sheet (that might look something like the one that follows) to be used for each 3-minute period. So each time you start a fresh set of observations, you should note them on a separate sheet.

When you are done, you should have 20 data sheets, with up to 20 notations for each of your focal children. For each child first compute the average size of the play group that child was in across 3-minute periods. Second, determine the percentage of periods in which only same-sex playmates were present, only opposite-sex playmates, and mixed-sex groups. Then average these figures across all 10 children: average size of group and percentages of same-sex, opposite-sex, and mixed-sex groups. Also see if you can find any consistent pairs of children who seemed to play together frequently. Were these "friends" usually same-sex pairs?

How do your observations match the patterns of early peer associations I have described in the text? Are there consistent pairings of "friends?" Were some children consistently solitary in their activity, while others were in larger groups? Do children this age mostly choose same-sex pairs? How large are the typical groups? Were boys' groups larger than girls' groups? What kinds of activities were these groups engaged in?

What difficulties did you have in completing the assignment? Was it difficult to determine who was "in" a particular group? This is a difficult kind of observation to do, so don't be discouraged if you found it confusing. You may end up with more respect for the attention to detail required for researchers to do this kind of study well.

*Sample Data Sheet for Project 14*

Number of 3-minute period recorded: _____

Location of children during this period: _____

| Children Observed | # of Playmates | Genders of Each Playmate | Identity of Individual Children | Activity Engaged In |
|---|---|---|---|---|
| #1 | | | | |
| #2 | | | | |
| #3 | | | | |
| #4 | | | | |
| #5 | | | | |
| #6 | | | | |
| # 7 | | | | |
| #8 | | | | |
| #9 | | | | |
| #10 | | | | |

As an alternative to the quite complicated observation I've just suggested, you might also take a more "anthropological" approach to an observation of preschool-age children. Again begin by obtaining permission to observe in some group-care situation involving children somewhere between age 18 months and 4 years. If there are mixed ages, that would be ideal, but it is okay if all the toddlers are the same age.

For this observation you should assume that you are a researcher who has become interested in the earliest forms of altruistic behavior in children, and that there has not yet been any research on this subject. You want to begin simply by observing without any preconceived ideas about how frequently this might occur or under what circumstances.

Observe in the group-care setting for at least two hours, noting down in narrative form any episode that appears to you to fit some general criteria of "altruistic" or "compassionate" behavior. For each episode you will want to record the circumstances involved, the gender of the child, the approximate age of the child, the other children present, and the words used (if any).

After the observation period, look over your notes and try to answer the following questions:

- What definition of altruism guided your observations? Did your definition change as a result of observing the children? Were there several types of "altruistic" actions that you observed that seem to be conceptually distinct?
- What tentative hypotheses about the early development of altruism might you propose for future study, based on the episodes you have observed? Are there hints of sex differences or age differences? Did the specific setting seem to have an effect? Was such behavior more common in pairs of children than in larger groups? Did this behavior occur primarily when one child was hurt or upset, or did it occur in other situations as well?
- How might you test these tentative hypotheses with further research?

12

# THINKING ABOUT RELATIONSHIPS: THE DEVELOPMENT OF SOCIAL COGNITION

**T**hink for a minute about the conversations you have with your friends. Haven't you said things like "I thought Jack was my friend, but now it turns out I can't really trust him," or "I've been trying to figure Jane out. Sometimes she's shy and sometimes she's the life of the party. What do you think is behind that?" or "Lots of people believe that I'm really the confident person I look like on the outside, but you can see how insecure I really am."

All of these statements reflect some aspect of what psychologists have come to call **social cognition**—thinking about people, what they do and should do, and how they feel. If you are anything like I am (and I assume you are) then you, too, spend a great deal of time and energy analyzing other people, trying to understand and predict what your friends, partner, or coworkers will do. In fact, in our everyday life knowledge about people and relationships is probably more important than many of the kinds of knowledge or thinking I talked about in chapters 6 and 7. Where does such knowledge come from? How do children learn about people, about relationships, and about right and wrong?

These questions are not new in this book. I have touched on many facets of social cognition as I have gone along. The infant's emerging ability to recognize individuals and to use facial expressions and other body cues for social referencing is one kind of social cognition, as is the process of learning that other people see the world from different physical and psychological perspectives. One could also argue that the proposed "internal working model" of attachment is a kind of social cognition, as is the child's self-scheme. What I need to do now is to pull these various threads together and describe some of the more general ideas about social cognition that have been emerging in the past few years. In the process, I hope to build a few bridges between the otherwise quite separate discussions of thinking and social relationships.

## Some General Principles and Issues

As you might imagine, researchers and theorists have arrived at the questions and research on social cognition from two different directions—from studies of cognition and studies of social interaction.

### The Cognitive Side of Social Cognition

One way to think about social cognition is simply to conceive of it as the application of general cognitive processes or skills to a different topic, in this case people or relationships. In Chapter 7 I talked about all the ways in which children's thinking changes from infancy through adolescence. We might assume that at any given age a child applies these fundamental ways of thinking to his relationships as well as to objects. In this view, the child's understanding of self and other and of social relationships reflects or is based on her overall level of cognitive development, such as her level of perspective-taking skills (Selman, 1980).

This way of looking at social cognition has a powerful intuitive appeal. After all, it is the same head doing the thinking when a child works on a conservation problem and when she tries to understand people. Furthermore, as you will see very clearly as we go through the evidence, many of the same principles that seem to apply to general cognitive development hold here as well, such as the following:

- *Outer to inner characteristics.* Younger children pay attention to the surface of things, to what they look like; older children look for principles and causes.
- *Observation to inference.* Young children base their conclusions initially only on what they can see or feel; later they make inferences about what ought to be or what might be.
- *Definite to qualified.* Young children's "rules" are very definite and fixed (such as sex-role rules); by adolescence, at the latest, rules have been qualified.
- *Observer's view to general view.* Children also become less "egocentric" with time—less tied to their own individual view, more able to construct a model of some experience or some process that is true for everyone.

All of these dimensions of change describe children's emerging social cognition, just as they describe the development of thinking about objects. But to reduce social cognition merely to such general principles is to ignore some critical differences.

## The Social Side of Social Cognition

The most obvious difference is that people, as objects of thought, are simply not the same as rocks, beakers of water, or balls of clay. Among many other things, people behave *intentionally,* and they can reveal or conceal information about themselves. In fact, learning to "read" other people is one of the key social-cognitive skills, as is grasping the possibility of concealment or misleading cues and taking this into account. Further, unlike relationships with objects, relationships with people are mutual and reciprocal. Other people talk back, respond to your distress, offer things, and get angry.

Children also have to learn special rules that apply to social interactions, such as politeness rules, rules about when you can and cannot speak, or rules about power or dominance hierarchies. Schank and Abelson (1977) have used the word *script* to describe these special social rules, which I think conveys the basic idea nicely. Children presumably learn these scripts from their own experience, developing strong expectations about how people will behave, in what order, and in which settings. Furthermore, these scripts probably change with age not just because children's cognitive skills change, but also simply because the rules (scripts) themselves change as children move from one social setting to another, such as from home to school.

Most of the research on children's emerging social understanding puts the cognitive horse before the social relationship cart, implying that it is the "understanding" part of the system that is paramount. I will inevitably foster this impression further in this chapter, since most of what I will describe will

When Mrs. Nakayama took her daughter Chizuka to school on the very first day, she dressed herself in a traditional kimono and obi as a sign of respect to the teacher and the school. The learning of such politeness rituals or customs, different in each culture, is part of what psychologists call social cognition. This photo is a video still from the *Childhood* television series (*Source:* ©Thirteen/WNET).

be research on the cognitive side. But it is important to keep the social side in mind as well.

## Thinking About Other People: Feelings and Qualities

One of the child's first social needs is to be able to "read" people—to understand what the other person may be feeling or thinking or what they may be like. One way to study the development of such a skill is to look at **empathy**—at the child's ability to match his own feelings with that of another person. Another strategy has been to look at the way children describe others, since that may reveal something about which features of other people the child notices or attends to.

### The Development of Empathy

Empathy involves two aspects, the apprehension of another person's emotional state or condition and then the matching of that emotional state in oneself. The empathizing person feels the same or a congruent feeling as he imagines the other to feel. *Sympathy* involves the same apprehension of the other's emotional state, but it is accompanied not by a matching emotion but by a general feeling of sorrow or concern for the other (Eisenberg et al., 1989). Generally speaking, empathy seems to be the earlier response developmentally, and among older children and adults, sympathy often seems to grow out of an initial empathetic response.

The most thorough analysis of the development of empathy (and sympathy) has been offered by Martin Hoffman (1982, 1984, 1988), who describes

**empathy**
As defined by Hoffman, it is a vicarious affective response that does not necessarily match another's affective state but is more appropriate to the other's situation than to one's own (Hoffman, 1984, p. 285).

four broad steps, which I've summarized in Table 12.1. The first stage, "global empathy," seems to be a kind of automatic empathic distress response. Hoffman says:

> Because infants cannot differentiate themselves from the other, they may at times act as though what happened to the other happened to themselves. An 11-month-old girl, on seeing a child fall and cry, looked as if she was about to cry herself, and then put her thumb in her mouth and buried her head in her mother's lap, which is what she would do if she herself were hurt. (Hoffman, 1988, p. 509–510)

This changes as early as 12 or 18 months, as soon as the child has a clear understanding of the difference between self and other. The toddler still shows a matching emotion, but understands that the distress is the other's and not her own. Nonetheless, her solution to the other's distress is still likely to be egocentric.

Children's empathetic responses become more and more subtle over the preschool and elementary school years, as they become better readers of others' emotions. By middle childhood, many children can even empathize with several contradictory emotions at once, such as when they see another child make a mistake and fall during a game. The observing child may see and empathize with both the hurt and the sense of shame or embarrassment, and be

**TABLE 12.1**

*Stages in the Development of Empathy*

---

- **Stage 1: Global Empathy.** Observed during the first year. If the infant is around someone expressing a strong emotion, he may match that emotion, such as beginning to cry when he hears another infant crying.

- **Stage 2: Egocentric Empathy.** Beginning at about 12 to 18 months, when the child has a fairly clear sense of his separate self, children respond to another's distress with some distress of their own, but may attempt to "cure" the other person's problem by offering what they themselves would find most comforting. They may, for example, show sadness when they see another child hurt, and go to get their *own* mother (or father) to help.

- **Stage 3: Empathy for Another's Feelings.** Beginning as young as 2 or 3, and continuing through elementary school, children note others' feelings, partially match those feelings, and respond to the other's distress in non-egocentric ways. Over these years, children distinguish a wider and wider (and more subtle) range of emotions.

- **Stage 4: Empathy for Another's Life Condition.** In late childhood or adolescence, some children develop a more generalized notion of others' feelings and respond not just to the immediate situation, but to the other individual's general situation or plight. So a young person at this level may become more distressed over another's person's sadness if they know that that sadness is chronic, or if they know that the person's general situation is particularly tragic, than if they see it as a more momentary problem.

---

*Source:* Hoffman, 1982, 1988.

Quite young children—as young as 2 or 3—show this kind of empathic response to other people's distress or delight. As they get older, children empathize with still more subtle emotions, or even with contradictory emotions in others.

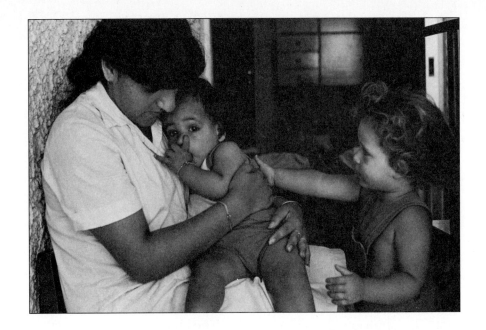

aware that the victim may prefer *not* to be helped. In adolescence a still more abstract level emerges, when the child moves beyond the immediate situation and empathizes (or sympathizes) with another person's general plight.

Notice that these changes reflect several of the general principles I outlined at the beginning of this chapter and they parallel the changes Piaget described. In particular, we see a shift from observation to inference: With increasing age, the child's empathic response is less and less guided by just the immediate, observed emotions seen in others, such as facial expressions or body language, and much more by the child's inferences or deductions about the other person's feelings. But this is not a swift change. For example, research in England by Paul Harris and his associates (Harris, Olthof, & Terwogt, 1981) shows that it isn't really until adolescence that young people are fully aware that other people may hide their emotions or act differently from the way that they feel "inside."

### Describing Other People

We can see the same kind of shift from observation to inference, as well as a clear change in focus from outer to internal characteristics, in studies of children's descriptions of others. There seem to be at least three steps. Up to perhaps ages 6 to 8, when children are asked to describe others, they focus almost exclusively on external features—what the person looks like, where he lives, and what he does. This description by a 7-year-old boy, taken from a study in England by Livesley and Bromley (1973), is typical:

> He is very tall. He has dark brown hair, he goes to our school. I don't think he has any brothers or sisters. He is in our class. Today he has a dark orange [sweater] and gray trousers and brown shoes. (p. 213)

When young children do use internal or evaluative terms to describe people, they are likely to use quite global terms, such as *nice, mean, good,* or *bad*. Furthermore, young children do not seem to see these qualities as lasting or general traits of the individual, applicable in all situations or over time (Rholes & Ruble, 1984). In other words, the young child has not yet developed a concept we might think of as "conservation of personality."

Beginning at about age 7 or 8, though, at just about the same time that children seem to develop a global sense of self-esteem, we see the emergence of similar ideas of global or enduring personality in others. The child begins to focus more on the inner traits or qualities of another person, and to assume that those traits will be visible in many situations (Gnepp & Chilamkurti, 1988). You can see the change in this (widely quoted) description by a nearly-10-year-old:

> He smells very much and is very nasty. He has no sense of humour and is very dull. He is always fighting and he is cruel. He does silly things and is very stupid. He has brown hair and cruel eyes. He is sulky and 11 years old and has lots of sisters. I think he is the most horrible boy in the class. He has a croaky voice and always chews his pencil and picks his teeth and I think he is disgusting. (Livesley & Bromley, 1973, p. 217)

This description still includes many external, physical features, but goes beyond such concrete, surface qualities to the level of personality traits, such as lack of humor or cruelty.

In adolescence, there is another shift. Now young people's descriptions contain more comparisons of one trait with another or one person with another, more recognition of inconsistencies and exceptions, more shadings of gray (Shantz, 1983), as in this description by a 15-year-old:

> Andy is very modest. He is even shyer than I am when near strangers and yet is very talkative with people he knows and likes. He always seems good tempered and I have never seen him in a bad temper. He tends to degrade other people's achievements, and yet never praises his own. He does not seem to voice his opinions to anyone. He easily gets nervous. (Livesley & Bromley, 1973, p. 221)

These changes can be shown less anecdotally with some findings from two studies by Carl Barenboim (1977, 1981). He asked children ranging in age from 6 to 16 to describe three people. Any descriptions that involved comparing a child's behaviors or physical features with another child, or with a norm, he called *behavioral comparisons* (such as "Billy runs a lot faster than Jason" or "She draws the best in our whole class"). Statements that involved some internal personality construct he called *psychological constructs* (such as "Sarah is so kind" or "He's a real stubborn idiot!"), while any that included qualifiers, explanations, exceptions, or mentions of changes in character he called *organizing relationships* (such as "He's only shy around people he doesn't know" or "Usually she's nice to me, but sometimes she can be quite mean"). Figure 12.1 (p. 462) shows the combined findings from the two studies. You can see that behavioral comparisons peaked at around age 8 or 9, that psychological statements peaked at about age 14, and that organizing relationships did not appear until age 10 and were still increasing at age 16.

I am sure that many of you have noticed the strong resemblance between this series of changes and the development of children's self-descriptions that I outlined in Chapter 10. This parallel illustrates yet again that the same underlying cognitive shifts seem to be involved in both understanding of others and understanding of the self.

## Thinking About Relationships

When we shift from the child's understanding of individuals to the study of children's understanding of relationships, I can sing many of the same songs again. Basically the same patterns emerge here no matter what type of relationship we study—the relationship with parents, with other authority figures, with groups, or with friends—but I think the richest vein has been in the research on children's understanding of friendships, so let me take that as illustration.

In the last chapter I described the developmental changes in the actual relationships children have with their friends—what they do together and how enduring and intimate they are. Here I want to talk about how the child *understands* the nature of friendship itself.

Among preschool children, friendships seem to be understood mostly in terms of physical characteristics. If you ask a young child how people make friends, the answer is usually that they "play together," or spend time physically near each other (Selman, 1980; Damon, 1977, 1983). Friendship is understood to involve sharing toys or giving goods to one another.

*FIGURE 12.1*

In two different studies, spanning somewhat overlapping age groups, Carl Barenboim asked children to describe others. You can see that references to psychological constructs rose steadily during the elementary school years and in early adolescence, and seemed to peak at about age 14. References to "organizing relationships" (including exceptions, qualifications, explanations of others' actions, and the like) were uncommon as late as age 10 or 12, but became quite common by early high-school age (*Sources:* Barenboim, 1977, Table 1, p. 1471; Barenboim, 1981, Figure 1, p. 134).

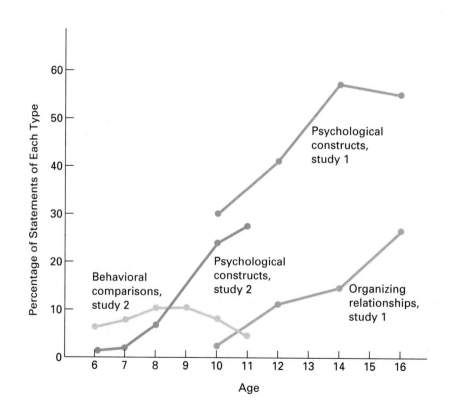

Selman's research and extensive studies by Thomas Berndt (1983, 1986) show that in elementary school this early view of friendship gives way to one in which the key concept seems to be *reciprocal trust*. Friends are now people who help and trust one another. Since this is also the age at which children's understanding of others becomes less external, more psychological, we shouldn't be surprised that friends are now seen as special people, with particular desired qualities other than mere proximity. In particular, generosity and helpfulness become part of the definition of friendship for many children.

At adolescence Berndt finds a further change, as friends come to be seen as people who *understand* one another, who share their innermost thoughts or feelings. Friendships are also seen as more exclusive and long term. Friends should comfort one another, be with one another, and forgive one another. Friendships at this stage are often intense relationships, with many hours spent on the phone or talking in person, sharing every detail, every thought, and every activity (Damon, 1983).

Damon suggests that still another change takes place for some young people in late adolescence or early adulthood, which is parallel to the shift to more qualified statements Barenboim found in his studies of children's descriptions of others. At this point young people understand that even very close friendships cannot fill every need and that friendships are not static: They change, grow, or dissolve, as each member of the pair changes. A really good friendship, then, is one that *adapts* to these changes. At this age, young people say things about friendship like "trust is the ability to let go as well as to hang on" (Selman, 1980, p. 141).

Let me again make these generalizations concrete with some actual research findings, this time from the work of Brian Bigelow and John La Gaipa (1975). They asked children to write an essay about what they expected in their best friends that was different from what they expected from other acquaintances. The answers were scored along many dimensions, three of which I have shown in Figure 12.2 on the next page. You can see that references to "demographic similarity" (e.g., we live in the same neighborhood) peaked in the fourth grade, while mentions of loyalty and commitment peaked in the seventh grade. References to intimacy potential (e.g., "I can tell her things about myself I can't tell anyone else") did not appear at all until the seventh grade, and then increased further in eighth grade.

In an intriguing series of interviews, Robert Selman (1980) has also studied friendships by asking children and adolescents how they settle disagreements or arguments with friends. Table 12.2 (p. 465) lists some of the answers given by children of various ages. You may find, as I do, that these patterns provide some food for thought about your own friendships and ways of resolving conflicts. Can you recognize your own thinking in these comments? The assumptions underlying these definitions, which we might also think of as internal working models of friendship, affect adult relationships as well as childhood or teenage relationships.

## Thinking About What People *Ought* to Do

Social understanding requires not only that the child learn to read others and to understand relationships more deeply, it also requires the child to

**FIGURE 12.2**

Some of the changes in children's ideas about friendship are clear from these findings from Bigelow and La Gaipa's study. The children were asked to write an essay describing what they expected of their friends that they didn't expect from non-friends (*Source:* Bigelow & La Gaipa, 1975, from Table 1, p. 858).

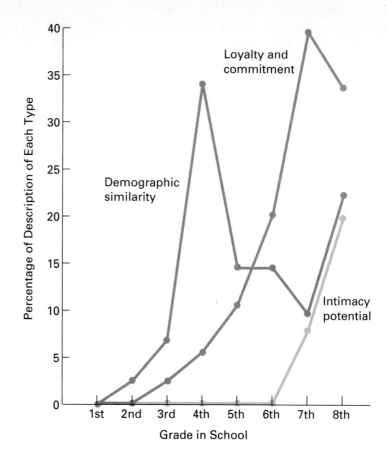

think about or explain other people's *actions*. The facet of this that has most intrigued developmental psychologists is the child's judgment of the "morality" of actions. How does a child decide what is good or bad, right or wrong in other people's behavior and in his own behavior? When you serve on a jury, you are asked to make a judgment of this kind. In everyday life, too, you make such judgments, of your own behavior as well as that of others: Should you give the store clerk back the excess change she handed you? What about someone who lies in a job interview? Does your judgment change if you know that the person desperately needs the job to support his handicapped child?

The two men whose ideas on the development of moral reasoning have been most influential are Piaget (1932) and Lawrence Kohlberg (1964, 1976, 1980, 1981; Colby et al.,1983).

### Piaget's Early Ideas About Moral Judgments

Piaget described several stages of children's reasoning about right and wrong. Up to about age 3 or 4, Piaget thought of the child as *premoral*. Children of this age do not yet understand rules, so they do not make judgments about rule violations. The first stage of actual moral reasoning, according to Piaget, is **heteronomous morality,** also sometimes called **moral realism.** It is characteristic of preschool children (3 to 6 or so). According to Piaget, children of this age are "moral absolutists." They think rules are sacred, absolute,

**heteronomous morality**
Piaget's first proposed stage of moral reasoning, characterized by moral absolutism and belief in immanent justice. Judgments are based on consequences rather than intent.

**moral realism**
Another term for heteronomous morality.

## TABLE 12.2

*Comments by Children of Various Ages About How to Solve Disagreements or Arguments Between Friends*

- "Go away from her and come back later when you're not fighting" (age 5).

- "Punch her out" (age 5).

- "Around our way the guy who started it just says he's sorry" (age 8).

- "Well if you say something and don't really mean it, then you have to mean it when you take it back" (age 8 1/2).

- "Sometimes you got to get away for a while. Calm down a bit so you won't be so angry. Then get back and try to talk it out" (age 14).

- "If you just settle up after a fight that is no good. You gotta really feel that you'd be happy the way things went if you were in your friend's shoes. You can just settle up with someone who is not a friend, but that's not what friendship is really about" (age 15 1/2).

- "Well, you could talk it out, but it usually fades itself out. It usually takes care of itself. You don't have to explain everything. You do certain things and each of you knows what it means. But if not, then talk it out" (age 16).

*Source:* Selman, 1980, pp. 107–113.

fixed, and unchangeable. They believe that actions are either totally right or totally wrong and judge rightness or wrongness largely on the basis of the consequences of the action rather than the intent of the person. By this reasoning, a child who breaks five glasses accidentally is judged as worse than a child who intentionally throws one down and breaks it. They also believe in what is called *immanent justice*—that if you break a rule, punishment (from parents, teachers, or even God) will inevitably follow.

This view gradually changes during the elementary school years to a position Piaget called **autonomous morality** or the **morality of reciprocity.** Children now accept social rules but see them as more arbitrary and changeable. Rules of a game, for example, can be changed if the children playing the game agree on the change. The belief in immanent justice fades too; rule violations are no longer thought to result in inevitable punishment. Most strikingly, the intent of the person performing some action is now taken into account in judging the morality of the action.

There is some support for this element of Piaget's theory (e.g., Ferguson & Rule, 1980, 1982). Children under about age 6 or 7 seem to be more influenced by outcomes than by intentions, although children as young as 3 or 4 are aware of intention or motive, and will take it into account if it is made clear and salient (e.g., Nelson, 1980). Among children older than 9 or 10, however, judgments are much more consistently based on intention. For example, Ferguson and Rule (1982) told children a story about a child who purposely pushes another child off the monkey bars at school, only in some versions the pusher intended only a little damage, while in another version the pusher was really mad and wanted to really hurt the child. Nine- and ten-year-olds thought there was no moral difference between these two since in both cases the intent was to hurt. Younger children thought that intending only a small hurt was not so bad as intending a big hurt.

**autonomous morality**
Piaget's second proposed stage of moral reasoning, developing some time after age 7, characterized by judgment of intent and emphasis on reciprocity.

**morality of reciprocity**
Another term for autonomous morality.

Kohlberg's description of moral development overlaps Piaget's, but extends into adolescence and adulthood. Since virtually all the recent research on moral development has been based on Kohlberg's theory, I need to describe in some detail both the stages he proposes and the procedures he used to measure them.

In order to explore a child's or young person's reasoning about difficult moral issues, such as the value of human life or the reasons for doing "right" things, Kohlberg devised a series of dilemmas. One of the most famous is the dilemma of Heinz:

> In Europe, a woman was near death from a special kind of cancer. There was one drug that the doctors thought might save her. It was a form of radium that a druggist in the same town had recently discovered. The drug was expensive to make, but the druggist was charging ten times what the drug cost him to make. He paid $200 for the radium and charged $2000 for a small dose of the drug. The sick woman's husband, Heinz, went to everyone he knew to borrow the money, but he could only get together about $1000 which is half of what it cost. He told the druggist that his wife was dying, and asked him to sell it cheaper or let him pay later. But the druggist said, "No, I discovered the drug and I'm going to make money from it." So Heinz got desperate and broke into the man's store to steal the drug for his wife. (Kohlberg & Elfenbein, 1975, p. 621)

After hearing this story, the child or young person is asked a series of questions, such as whether Heinz should have stolen the drug. What if Heinz didn't love his wife? Would that change anything? What if the person dying was a stranger? Should Heinz steal the drug anyway?

On the basis of answers to dilemmas like this one, Kohlberg concluded that there were three main levels of moral reasoning, with two substages within each level. I've summarized the stages in Table 12.3, but I need to expand on them here too.

**preconventional morality**
The first level of morality proposed by Kohlberg, in which moral judgments are dominated by consideration of what will be punished and what feels good.

At Level 1, **preconventional morality,** the child's (or teenager's or even adult's) judgments are based on sources of authority who are close by and physically superior to himself—usually the parents. Just as his descriptions of others at this same stage are largely external, so the standards the child uses to judge rightness or wrongness are external rather than internal. In particular, it is the outcomes or consequences of his actions that determine the rightness or wrongness of those actions.

In Stage 1 of this level—the *punishment and obedience orientation*—the child relies on the physical consequences of some action to decide if it is right or wrong. If he is punished, the behavior was wrong; if he is not punished, it was right. He is obedient to adults because they are bigger and stronger.

In Stage 2—*individualism, instrumental purpose, and exchange*—the child begins to do things that are rewarded and avoid things that are punished. (For this reason, the stage is sometimes called a position of "naive hedonism.") If it feels good, or brings pleasant results, it is good. There is some evidence of concern for other people during this phase, but only if that concern can be expressed as something that benefits the child himself as well. So he can enter into agreements like "If you help me, I'll help you."

*TABLE 12.3*

*Kohlberg's Stages of Moral Development*

## Level 1: Preconventional Morality

- ***Stage 1: Punishment and obedience orientation.*** The child decides what is wrong on the basis of what is punished. Obedience is valued for its own sake, but the child obeys because adults have superior power.
- ***Stage 2: Individualism, instrumental purpose, and exchange.*** The child follows rules when it is in his immediate interest. What is good is what brings pleasant results. Right is also what is fair, what is an equal exchange, a deal, an agreement.

## Level 2: Conventional Morality

- ***Stage 3: Mutual interpersonal expectations, relationships, and interpersonal conformity.*** The family or small group to which the child belongs becomes important. Moral actions are those that live up to others' expectations. "Being good" becomes important for its own sake, and the child generally values trust, loyalty, respect, gratitude, and keeping mutual relationships.
- ***Stage 4: Social system and conscience (law and order).*** A shift in focus from the young person's family and close groups to the larger society. Good is fulfilling duties one has agreed to. Laws are to be upheld except in extreme cases. Contributing to society is also seen as good.

## Level 3: Principled or Postconventional Morality

- ***Stage 5: Social contract or utility and individual rights.*** Acting so as to achieve the "greatest good for the greatest number." The child is aware that there are different views and values. Laws and rules should be upheld in order to preserve the social order, but they can be changed. Still, there are some basic nonrelative values, such as the importance of each person's life and liberty, that should be upheld no matter what.
- ***Stage 6: Universal ethical principles.*** The young person develops and follows self-chosen ethical principles in determining what is right. Since laws usually conform to those principles, laws should be obeyed; but when there is a difference between law and conscience, conscience dominates. At this stage, the ethical principles followed are part of an articulated, integrated, carefully thought-out and consistently followed system of values and principles.

*Sources:* After Kohlberg, 1976, and Lickona, 1978.

Some examples would probably help. Here are some responses to variations of the Heinz dilemma, drawn from studies of children and teenagers in a number of different cultures, all of which would be rated as Stage 2 (Snarey, 1985):

> He should steal the food for his wife because if she dies he'll have to pay for the funeral, and that costs a lot (Taiwan).

> [He should steal the drug because] he should protect the life of his wife so he doesn't have to stay alone in life (Puerto Rico).

> *[Suppose it wasn't his wife who was starving but his best friend. Should he steal the food for his friend?]* Yes, because one day when he is hungry his friend would help (Turkey). (p. 221)

**conventional morality**
The second level of
moral judgment pro-
posed by Kohlberg, in
which the person's judg-
ments are dominated by
considerations of group
values and laws.

At the next major level, **conventional morality,** there is a shift from judgments based on external consequences and personal gain to judgments based
on rules or norms of a group to which the child belongs, whether that group
is the family, the peer group, a church, or the nation. What the chosen reference group defines as right or good *is* right or good in the child's view, and
the child internalizes these norms to a considerable extent.

Stage 3 (the first stage of Level 2) is the stage of *mutual interpersonal expectations, relationships, and interpersonal conformity* (sometimes also called the *good
boy/nice girl* stage). Children at this stage believe that good behavior is what
pleases other people. They value trust, loyalty, respect, gratitude, and maintenance of mutual relationships. Andy, a boy Kohlberg interviewed who was at
Stage 3, said:

> I try to do things for my parents, they've always done things for you. I try to do every-
> thing my mother says, I try to please her. Like she wants me to be a doctor and I want
> to, too, and she's helping me get up there. (Kohlberg, 1964, p. 401)

Another mark of Stage 3 is that the child begins to make judgments
based on intentions as well as on outward behavior. If someone "means well"
or "didn't mean to do it," their wrongdoing is seen as less serious than if they
did it "on purpose."

Stage 4 (the second stage of Level 2) shows the child turning to larger
social groups for her norms. Kohlberg labeled this the stage of *social system
and conscience.* It is also sometimes called the *law and order orientation.* People
reasoning at this stage focus on doing their duty, respecting authority, and
following rules and laws. The emphasis is less on what is pleasing to particular
people (as in Stage 3) and more on adhering to a complex set of regulations.
However, the regulations themselves are not questioned.

The transition to Level 3, **principled morality** (also called *post-conventional morality*), is marked by several changes, the most important of which is a
shift in the source of authority. At Level 1 children see authority as totally outside themselves. At Level 2, their judgments or rules of external authority are
internalized, but they are not questioned or analyzed. At Level 3, a new kind
of personal authority emerges in which individual choices are made, with individual judgments based on self-chosen principles.

**principled morality**
The third level of morality proposed by Kohlberg,
in which considerations
of justice, individual
rights, and contracts
dominate moral
judgment.

In Stage 5 at this level—called the *social contract orientation* by Kohlberg—
we see the beginning of such self-chosen principles. Rules, laws, and regulations are not seen as irrelevant; they are important ways of insuring fairness.
But people operating at this level also see times when the rules, laws, and regulations need to be ignored or changed. The American system of government
is based on moral reasoning of this kind, since we have provisions for changing laws and for allowing personal protests against a given law, such as during
the civil rights protests of the 1960s, the Vietnam War protests of the 1960s
and 1970s, or the protests against apartheid in the 1980s.

In his original writing about moral development, Kohlberg also included a sixth stage, the *universal ethical principles orientation.* People who reason in
this way assume personal responsibility for their actions, based upon fundamental and universal principles, such as justice and basic respect for persons.
Kohlberg later waffled a good bit on whether such a stage was the logical and

By this age the majority of teenagers are using Stage 3 moral reasoning (the level of conventional morality). What they think is right or wrong, good or bad, is a function of what they think their family or their peer group thinks is right or wrong. This kind of thinking makes the influence of the peer group even stronger.

necessary end point of the sequence, and on whether people reasoning at such a level actually existed (e.g., Kohlberg, 1978; Kohlberg, Levine, & Hewer, 1983). If they exist at all, it seems likely that such universal ethical principles guide the moral reasoning of only a few very unusual individuals—perhaps those who devote their lives to humanitarian causes, such as Mother Theresa or Gandhi.

In all of this, it is *very* important to understand that what determines the stage or level of a person's moral judgment is not the specific moral choice but the *form of reasoning* used to justify that choice. For example, either the choice that Heinz should steal the drug, or that he should not, could be justified with logic at any given stage. I've already given you some examples of a Stage 2 justification for Heinz's stealing the drug; here's a Stage 5 justification of the same choice, drawn from a study in India:

> [*What if Heinz was stealing to save the life of his pet animal instead of his wife?*] If Heinz saves an animal's life his action will be commendable. The right use of the drug is to administer it to the needy. There is some difference, of course—human life is more evolved and hence of greater importance in the scheme of nature—but an animal's life is not altogether bereft of importance. . . . (from Snarey, 1985, p. 223, drawn originally from Vasudev, 1983, p. 7)

Kohlberg thought that there were at least a few people, perhaps like Mother Theresa, whose moral reasoning was based on universal ethical principles.

If you compare this answer to the ones I quoted before, you can clearly see the difference in the form of reasoning used, even though the action being justified is precisely the same. I could muster equivalent examples of justifications for not stealing the drug at different stages of reasoning (e.g., "It's against the law to steal; it's never justified," or "You should try to persuade the druggist to give you the drug for less, but you shouldn't steal from him. Two wrongs do not make a right").

So far, so good. Assuming that you understand the distinction between the content and the form of reasoning, the description of the stages is fairly straightforward. But Kohlberg was not satisfied merely to describe a sequence. He has argued that this sequence is both universal and hierarchically organized, just as Piaget thought his proposed stages of cognitive development were universal and hierarchical. That is, each stage follows and grows from the preceding one and has some internal consistency. Individuals should not move "down" the sequence, but only "upward" along the stages, if they move at all. Kohlberg did *not* argue that all individuals eventually progress through all six stages, nor even that each stage is tied to specific ages. But he insisted that the order is invariant and universal. Let's take a critical look at these claims.

*Age and Moral Reasoning.* Kohlberg's own findings, confirmed by many other researchers (reviewed by Rest, 1983), show that preconventional reasoning (stages 1 and 2) is dominant in elementary school, and Stage 2 reasoning is still evident among many early adolescents. Conventional reasoning (stages 3 and 4) emerges as important in middle adolescence and remains the most common form of moral reasoning in adulthood. Post-conventional reasoning (stages 5 and 6) is relatively rare, even in adulthood.

Let me give you two examples illustrating these age trends. The first, shown in Figure 12.3, comes from Kohlberg's own longitudinal study of 58 boys, first interviewed when they were 10, and now followed for more than 20 years (Colby et al., 1983). Table 12.4 on the next page shows cross-sectional data from a study by Lawrence Walker and his colleagues (Walker, de Vries, & Trevethan, 1987). They studied ten boys and ten girls at each of four ages, and interviewed the parents of each child as well. Note that Walker scored each response on a nine-point scale rather than just scoring the five main stages. This system, which has become quite common, allows for the fact that many people's reasoning falls between two specific stages.

The results of these two studies are not identical but there is nonetheless remarkable agreement on the order of emergence of the various stages and on the approximate ages at which they predominate. In both studies, Stage 2 reasoning is most dominant at about age 10, and Stage 3 reasoning is most common at about age 16.

*Sequence of Stages.* The evidence also seems fairly strong that the stages follow one another in the sequence Kohlberg proposed. In Kohlberg's own major longitudinal studies of teenagers and young adults in the United States, Israel, and Turkey (Colby et al., 1983; Nisan & Kohlberg, 1982; Snarey et al., 1985), when change in the form of reasoning occurred, it occurred in the hypothesized order. Subjects did not skip stages, and only about 5–7 percent of the time was there any indication of regression (movement down the sequence rather than up it). Similarly, when Walker retested the subjects in his study two years later, he found only 6 percent had moved down, mostly only half a stage, while 22 percent had moved up and none had skipped a stage (Walker, 1989). Such a rate of regression is about what you would expect to find, given the fact that the measurements of stage reasoning are not perfectly reliable.

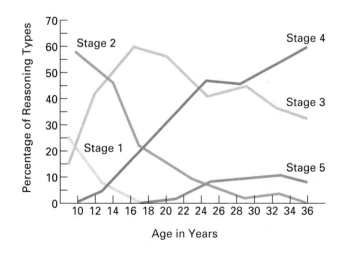

*FIGURE 12.3*

These findings are from Colby and Kohlberg's long-term longitudinal study. As the subjects got older, the stage or level of their answers changed, with conventional reasoning appearing fairly strongly at high-school age (*Source:* Colby et al., 1983, Figure 1, p. 46. © The Society for Research in Child Development).

**TABLE 12.4**

*Children and Their Parents Who Show Moral Reasoning at Each of Kohlberg's Stages*

| Age | Stage | | | | | | | | |
|---|---|---|---|---|---|---|---|---|---|
| | 1 | 1–2 | 2 | 2–3 | 3 | 3–4 | 4 | 4–5 | 5 |
| 6 (1st grade) | 10% | 70% | 15% | 5% | —% | —% | —% | —% | —% |
| 9 (4th grade) | — | 25 | 40 | 35 | — | — | — | — | — |
| 12 (7th grade) | — | — | 15 | 60 | 25 | — | — | — | — |
| 15 (10th grade) | — | — | — | 40 | 55 | 5 | — | — | — |
| Adults (parents with an average age of about 40) | — | — | — | 1 | 15 | 70 | 11 | 3 | — |

*Source:* Walker, de Vries, & Trevethan, 1987, Table 1, p. 849.

Further support for the validity of the proposed sequence comes from studies showing that subjects can understand moral arguments at a lower level, at their own level, or at a stage one step higher than their own, but they do not understand arguments two or more stages above their own (Walker, de Vries, & Bichard, 1984). On the whole, I agree with James Rest (1983) when he says that the evidence is "fairly compelling" that moral judgment changes over time in the sequence Kohlberg describes.

*Universality.*   Perhaps, though, this sequence of stages is only a phenomenon of Western culture. Or has Kohlberg uncovered a genuinely universal process? Thus far, there have been 27 different cultural areas studied, including Western and non-Western cultures and urban and village or tribal societies.

John Snarey, who has reviewed and analyzed these studies (1985), makes several points in support of Kohlberg's position. Snarey notes that in studies of children, as age increases the stage of reasoning consistently moves upward. Furthermore, the few longitudinal studies—which are, of course, the best test of the question of sequence—report "strikingly similar findings" (p. 215), with subjects moving upward in the stage sequence, with only a few reversals. Snarey also notes, however, that cultures differ in the highest level of reasoning observed. In complex urban societies (both Western and non-Western), Stage 5 is typically the highest stage observed, while in less complex, rural, or "folk" societies, Stage 4 is typically the highest. Collectively, this evidence seems to provide quite strong support for the universality of Kohlberg's stage sequence.

*Consistency of Moral Reasoning.*   A final issue touches on a question I raised in Chapter 7 in evaluating Piaget's theory: If these stages are really hierarchical and really represent consistent internal mental structures, then a child or adult should show the same form of reasoning on many different moral problems. And like the findings on consistency in Piaget's stages, the data here are mixed. Some early researchers found a good deal of variation in stage of response from one dilemma to another (e.g., Haan, 1975), but more recent studies, using Kohlberg's revised scoring system, reveal more consistency. For example, in the Walker study I've shown in Table 12.4, the subjects were not only given Kohlberg's hypothetical dilemmas, they were also asked to talk about some real-life dilemma from their own experience. Using the nine-point scale of responses, Walker found that 91 percent of the subjects gave the same or an adjacent level of response to the real-life dilemma as they did to the hypothetical dilemmas. At this point we do not have enough data to be sure, but studies like Walker's point to more consistency than some critics have suggested.

*Moral Development: A Critique.*   Kohlberg's theory about the development of moral reasoning has been one of the most provocative theories in all of developmental psychology. There have been over 1000 studies exploring or testing aspects of the theory, and several competing theories have been proposed. The remarkable thing is how well the theory has stood the test of this barrage of research and commentary. There does appear to be a clear set of stages in the development of moral reasoning, and these stages seem to be universal.

Still, the theory has not emerged unscathed. Some psychologists are less impressed than Snarey with the data on universality (e.g., Shweder, Mahapatra, & Miller, 1987); some are bothered by the relative lack of consistency between moral reasoning and moral behavior (a point I'll take up shortly). Other psychologists place considerable weight on the fact that there is not complete consistency of a child's or adult's response to different moral dilemmas (e.g., Hoffman, 1988). Also troubling is the fact that so few teenagers or adults seem to reason at the post-conventional level (stages 5 or 6). The effective range of variation is primarily between stages 2 to 4, which is not nearly so interesting or impressive as is the full range of stages (e.g., Shweder et al., 1987).

The most vocal critics, however, have been those who have pointed out that Kohlberg is really not talking about all aspects of "moral reasoning." Instead, as Kohlberg himself acknowledged in his later writings (Kohlberg, Levine, & Hewer, 1983), he is talking about the development of reasoning about *justice and fairness.* But what about moral reasoning about doing good, or reasoning based on some other ethic than justice, such as an ethic based on concern for others or for relationships? Let me take a quick look at two such alternative views.

### Eisenberg's Model of Prosocial Reasoning

Most of the moral dilemmas Kohlberg posed for his subjects deal with wrongdoing—with stealing, punishment, and disobeying laws. Few dilemmas tell us anything about the kind of reasoning children use in justifying *prosocial behavior.* I mentioned in Chapter 11 that altruistic behavior is visible in children as young as 2 and 3. But how do children explain and justify such behavior?

Nancy Eisenberg and her colleagues (e.g., Eisenberg, 1986; Eisenberg, Hertz-Lazarowitz, & Fuchs, 1990; Eisenberg et al., 1987) have explored such questions by proposing dilemmas to children in which self-interest is set against the possibility of helping some other person. One story involves a child walking to a friend's birthday party. On the way, he comes upon another child who had fallen and hurt himself. If the birthday-bound child stops to help, he will probably miss the cake and ice cream. What should he do?

On the basis of children's answers to dilemmas like this, Eisenberg proposes a series of five levels of prosocial reasoning, which I've listed in Table 12.5. (I know you are overloaded with lists of stages, but hang in there!) Some sample data from Eisenberg's longitudinal study of a small group of children are in Figure 12.4.

You can see from the figure that hedonistic reasoning—reasoning in which the individual's own needs are put first—declines through the elementary school years, while reasoning that acknowledges the need of the other goes up. Eisenberg also finds in this study that arguments showing the "approval and interpersonal orientation" (which is highly similar to Kohlberg's Stage 3) begin to appear at about age 10 or 11, although they had not become common even at this age.

There are obviously strong parallels between the levels of prosocial reasoning Eisenberg has described and the levels and stages Kohlberg proposed. Children seem to move from a self-centered orientation ("What feels good to me is right") to a stance in which social approval guides both reasoning about

**TABLE 12.5**

*Levels of Prosocial Reasoning Proposed by Eisenberg*

---

- **Level 1: Hedonistic, self-focused orientation.** The child is concerned with self-oriented consequences rather than moral considerations. "I'd help because she'd help me the next time." "I won't help because I'd miss the party." Characteristic of preschoolers and younger elementary school children.
- **Level 2: Needs-oriented orientation.** The child expresses concern for the other person's need rather directly, even if the other's needs conflict with one's own. There is no clear evidence here of sympathy, reflectiveness about the other's role, or internalized values. "She's hurt." "She'd feel better if I helped." This level is seen in some preschoolers, and most elementary school children.
- **Level 3: Approval and interpersonal orientation and/or stereotyped orientation.** You do good things because others will like you if you do, because it is expected of you, or because there is a social rule. "They'd like her if she helped." "It's nice to help." Characteristic of some elementary and some high-school students.
- **Level 4a: Self-reflective empathic orientation:** The young person shows evidence of some sympathetic response ("I'd feel sorry for her") or explicit role taking ("I'm trying to put myself in her shoes"). Not generally seen until high-school age.
- **Level 4b: Transitional level.** Justifications for helping or doing good are based on internalized norms, duties, or responsibilities, but these ideas are not yet strongly stated. "I'd feel good if I helped." Seen in some high-school students and some adults.
- **Level 5: Strongly internalized stage.** Justifications for helping are stated in terms of clear values, such as belief in the dignity or rights of individuals, or maintaining self-respect. "I'd feel a responsibility to help because of my values," or "If everyone helped, society would be a lot better." This level is never observed in elementary school children and only rarely in high-school students.

---

*Source:* Eisenberg, 1986, (pp. 136, 137, 144) and Eisenberg & Mussen, 1989 (Table 8.2, p. 125).

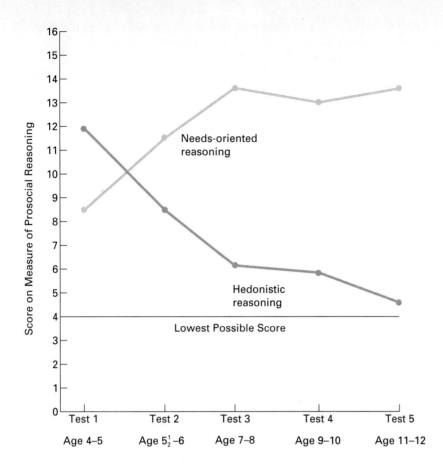

**FIGURE 12.4**

Every two years Eisenberg asked the same group of children what a person should do when confronted with each of a series of dilemmas about doing good (such as helping someone who is hurt). On these measures, the minimum score is 4 and the maximum is 16, so you can see that hedonistic reasoning drops to nearly minimum levels by age 7 or 8, while needs-oriented reasoning (such as "he needs help") rises to high levels at the same age (*Source:* Eisenberg, 1986, Table 7.7, p. 143).

justice and about doing good. What is right is what other people define as right; one should do good things because others will approve of you if you do. Much later, some young people seem to develop internalized, individualized norms to guide both kinds of reasoning.

Despite these obvious parallels, though, researchers have typically found that children's reasoning about prosocial dilemmas such as Eisenberg's, and their reasoning about Kohlberg's justice or fairness dilemmas, are only moderately correlated. The sequences of steps may be similar, but as was true of so many of the developments I talked about in Chapter 7, children seem to move through these sequences at somewhat different speeds. At least among young children, Eisenberg has found that children's prosocial reasoning is a bit ahead of their Kohlbergian reasoning.

Eisenberg's research, as well as the work of others in the same vein, helps to broaden Kohlberg's original conception, without changing the fundamental arguments. In contrast, Carol Gilligan has questioned some of the basic tenets of Kohlberg's model.

### Gilligan's Ethic of Caring

Like Eisenberg, Carol Gilligan (1982a, 1982b, 1987; Gilligan & Wiggins, 1987) begins from a point of dissatisfaction with Kohlberg's focus on a justice and fairness orientation as *the* defining feature of moral reasoning. She argues that such an emphasis on justice is merely one reflection of a more general "male bias" in both research and theory in developmental psychology.

If you think back to what I said in chapters 10 and 11 about the different ways girls and boys relate to one another and the different qualities of their friendships, you'll recall that among boys the key issues seem to be independence, separation, competition, and fairness. In girls' relationships, the key issues seem to be connection, support, and caring. To the extent that theories of human development have focused on the "male" issues—because the theorists are male and see the world through that lens, because we have often studied only males as Kohlberg did, or for whatever reason—we may have neglected an equally important set of developmental questions that may be more central to girls' development.

Gilligan proposes that there are two distinct moral orientations—justice and care. Each has its own central injunction: not to treat others unfairly (justice) and not to turn away from someone in need (caring). Both boys and girls learn both of these injunctions, but Gilligan argues that in general girls are more likely to operate from an orientation of caring or connection, while boys are more likely to operate from an orientation of justice or fairness. Because of these differences, they tend to perceive moral dilemmas quite differently.

Several testable hypotheses can be derived from Gilligan's proposals. First, it is an empirical question whether girls are more likely than boys to use an ethic of caring in defining and deciding moral questions. Second, assuming there is a sex difference in such orientations, then girls' tendency to respond to the Kohlberg dilemmas with a "care" rather than a "justice" approach might lead to a consistent underestimate of the maturity of girls' moral reasoning since their answers would not fit neatly into the Kohlberg scoring scheme.

Gilligan argues that Kohlberg's model focuses too much on an "ethic of justice" and ignores the "ethic of caring" that seems to motivate these young women.

Neither of these hypotheses has been supported by recent research. When researchers have specifically evaluated moral judgments for the presence of care or justice orientations, they have not consistently found that girls are more likely to operate from an orientation of care. Several studies of adults show such a pattern (e.g., Lyons, 1983), but studies of children generally have not.

On the second point there is more data and the findings are quite clear: There are no consistent sex differences in the level of moral reasoning as measured by Kohlberg's scoring system (e.g., Walker, 1984). Further, both boys' and girls' reasoning moves through the stages that Kohlberg described (e.g., Snarey et al., 1985).

In sum, Gilligan seems to be wrong in the specifics of her ideas about sex differences in moral reasoning. Yet her more general conceptualization of sex differences continues to be influential (e.g., Mednick, 1989), perhaps because she has put her finger on a key set of questions, not only about the research agenda psychologists have chosen to address, but about potentially basic differences between boys and girls in their ways of relating and in their ways of thinking about relationships. How deep or widespread such differences may be, and their origins, we do not yet know.

## Social Cognition and Behavior

In Chapter 11 I talked about children's social behavior; in this chapter I have been talking about children's thinking about relationships. What I have not talked much about is the possible connection between the two. Can we predict a child's behavior, such as his moral choices, his generous behavior, or the nature of his relationships, from knowing the stage or level of his social cognition? Yes and no. We cannot predict *precisely* what a child will do in a real-life situation from knowing the form or level of his reasoning, but there are nonetheless some important links between thinking and behavior.

*Empathic Understanding and Behavior.* One possible link that has received a good deal of research attention is the one between empathy and prosocial behavior. The findings are not completely consistent, but in general Eisenberg's research shows that "empathic, other-oriented preschoolers and school-age children are more likely to share or donate valuable objects to others than are children lower in prosocial moral reasoning "(Eisenberg & Mussen, 1989, p. 129). A link between empathy and kind behavior is found particularly clearly among adolescents.

For example, Martin Ford (1982) studied teenagers' empathy and their "social competence." Ford asked ninth and twelfth graders about six hypothetical situations that would demand real social skill, like the following:

> One of your school's best teachers has tragically died in an accident. The students in your grade have gotten together and decided to do something for the teacher's family. The class decides that someone should make a personal visit to the teacher's family. This person would bring flowers and try to tell the family how sorry the students were to lose such a good teacher and a good friend. Who in your grade do you think would be a good person to make the visit to the teacher's family? (Ford, 1982, p. 339)

These situations are hypothetical, but by having students rate *each other*, he could see which teenagers were perceived by their classmates as being particularly skillful or thoughtful in demanding social situations. What he found was that adolescents who were chosen by their peers as being the best in such situations also displayed more empathy and role-taking ability on separate tests.

*Friendship Understanding and Friendship Behavior.*   Similar links appear in studies of relationships. As a general rule, children with more mature reasoning about friendships are less likely to be aggressive with their peers and more likely to show sharing or other helpful behavior toward their friends in actual interactions.

For example, Lawrence Kurdek and Donna Krile (1982) found that among children in the third through the eighth grades, those with higher scores on a measure of understanding of individuals and friendships were more likely to be involved in mutual friendships than were children with lower scores. Similarly, Selman (1980) compared children's scores on a measure of social reasoning with teachers' ratings of the children's social strengths and weaknesses. He found that children with more mature reasoning were more likely to be described by their teachers as showing higher levels of helpful or other prosocial behaviors.

An intriguing exception to this pattern, however, is the finding I reported in the last chapter, that in friendships between boys, competition and not sharing or helpfulness is often the dominant pattern. Furthermore, Berndt finds that among boys, the level of competition or cooperation is unrelated to the boys' overall level of reasoning about friendship or about the justification for helpfulness (Berndt, 1983).

Thus while there is generally a correlation between the maturity of a child's social reasoning and her friend-making skills, more mature reasoning does not invariably increase the level of helpfulness or cooperation in actual friendship pairs.

*Moral Judgment and Behavior.*   Kohlberg's theory has sometimes been criticized on the grounds that children's or adults' moral behavior does not always match their reasoning. But Kohlberg never said that there should be a one-to-one correspondence between the two. Reasoning at Stage 4 (conventional reasoning) does not mean that one will never cheat or always be kind to one's mother. Still, the form of reasoning a young person typically applies to moral problems should have at least *some* connection with real-life choices. Further, Kohlberg argued that the higher the level of reasoning a young person shows, the stronger the link to behavior ought to become. Thus young people reasoning at Stage 4 or Stage 5 should be more likely to follow their own rules or reasoning than should children reasoning at lower levels.

For example, Kohlberg and Candee (1984) studied students involved in the early "Free Speech" movement at Berkeley in the late 1960s (a precursor to the Vietnam War protests). They interviewed and tested the moral judgment levels of a group that had participated at a sit-in in the administration building, plus a group randomly chosen from the campus population. Of those who thought it was morally right to sit in, nearly three-fourths of those reasoning at stages 4 or 5 actually did sit in, compared to only about one-

These boys may be buddies, but chances are their friendship is quite different from the friendships we'd see in girls the same age. Among other things, the level of reasoning about friendship is unrelated to behavior toward friends among boys, while there is a link between the two among girls.

fourth of those reasoning at Stage 3. Thus the higher the stage of reasoning, the more consistent the behavior was with the reasoning.

In other studies, Kohlberg and others approached the question simply by asking whether there is a link between stage of moral reasoning and the probability of making some "moral choice," such as not cheating. Kohlberg (1975), for example, found that only 15 percent of students reasoning at the principled level (Stage 5) cheated when they were given an opportunity, while 55 percent of conventional level and 70 percent of preconventional students cheated.

Similarly, Eisenberg has found that certain types of prosocial reasoning are correlated with a child's altruistic behavior. In a group of 10-year-olds, she found that hedonistic reasoning was negatively correlated with a measure of the child's willingness to donate to UNICEF the nickels they earned for participating in the study (Eisenberg et al., 1987). In addition, there is now strong evidence that delinquents have lower levels of moral reasoning than do non-delinquents (Smetena, 1990), even when the two groups are carefully matched for educational and social class levels. Despite this abundance of evidence for a link between moral reasoning and behavior, no one has found the correspondence to be perfect. After all, in Kohlberg's studies, 15 percent of the principled moral reasoners did cheat, and 25 percent of Stage 4 and Stage 5 reasoners who thought it morally right to participate in a sit-in did not do so. As Kohlberg says, "One can reason in terms of principles and not live up to those principles" (Kohlberg, 1975, p. 672).

What else besides level of reasoning might matter? We don't have all the answers to that question yet, but some influences are clear. First, simple habits are involved. Each of us faces small moral situations every day that we have learned to handle in a completely automatic way. Sometimes these automatic choices may be at a lower level of reasoning than we would use if we sat down and thought about it. (For example, I may make the same donation to a particular charity every year without stopping to consider whether I could now afford more, or whether that charity is really the place where my money could best be used.)

Second, in any given situation, even though you might think it morally right to take some action, you may not see that action as morally *necessary* or obligatory. I might be able to make a good argument for the moral acceptability of a sit-in protest, but still not see it as my *own* duty or responsibility to participate.

Third, the cost to the person of doing something helpful (or refraining from doing something morally "wrong" like cheating) may be an important factor. If helping someone else has little cost in time, money, or effort, then most children and adults will help, regardless of their overall level of reasoning. But when there is some cost—such as was the case for the children in Eisenberg's study who were asked if they wanted to donate some of the nickels they earned to help other children—then we find a more consistent correlation between level of reasoning and behavior. This suggests the more general principle that moral reasoning becomes a factor in moral behavior only when there is something about the situation that heightens the sense of moral conflict, such as when there is a cost involved or when the individual feels personally responsible.

Finally, there are often competing motives or ethics at work as well, such as the pressure of a peer group or motives for self-protection or self-reward. Gerson and Damon (1978) found this very clearly in a study in which they asked groups of four children to divide up ten candy bars. The candy was a reward for work the children had done on a project, and some of the group members had worked harder than others. When asked separately about how the candy bars ought to be divided, children usually argued for various kinds of fair arrangements, such as a model in which the child who worked the hardest should get the most. But when faced with the actual distribution of

Most children and adults will readily show helpful actions such as this one if there is little personal cost attached. But if the cost of helping goes up—such as when you're in a hurry to get somewhere else—then those with higher levels of moral reasoning are more likely to help.

the candy bars, some children gave themselves the most; others went along with a group consensus and divided the candy equally. We might expect that in early adolescence, when the impact of the peer group is particularly strong, this group effect on moral actions would be especially strong too. So kids this age may be most susceptible to group decisions to go joyriding, sneak beer into a party, or soap the teachers' car windows on Halloween (Berndt, 1979).

Thus moral *behavior* results from a complex set of influences, of which the level of moral reasoning is only one element. Our knowledge about these links is improving, but we badly need to know more, both about group pressure and about all the other factors that lead each of us to behave in ways that are less thoughtful, considerate, or fair than we "know how" to do. Kohlberg's own fascination with this set of questions, and with the question of how one raises a person's level of moral reasoning, led him and his colleagues to a series of bold attempts to apply the theory to schooling. I've explored some of this research in the box on pages 482–483.

## Social Cognition and General Cognitive Development

Before I leave this subject, there is one other set of links I need to explore, namely the potential connection between the sequences of development of social cognition, such as Kohlberg's stages of moral reasoning, and the broader sequences of cognitive development I described in Chapter 7. Earlier in this chapter I suggested several key dimensions that seem to characterize both sets of changes, such as a shift in focus from outer to inner characteristics. But I need to look at those possible connections more systematically.

Studies of the relationship between cognitive power (IQ) and social reasoning generally show weak positive relationships (correlations in the range of .20 to .40). That is, children with higher IQs typically show slightly higher social reasoning than do children of the same age with lower IQs (Shantz, 1983).

Surprisingly, there have been relatively few attempts to look at the connections between overall cognitive *structure* and social-cognitive reasoning, so we don't yet know what all the links might be. The most concrete proposal was offered by Kohlberg, who hypothesized that the child first moves to a new level of logical thought, then applies this new kind of logic to relationships as well as objects, and only then applies this thinking to moral problems. More specifically, Kohlberg argued that at least some formal operations and at least some mutual perspective taking in relationships are necessary (but not sufficient) for the emergence of conventional moral reasoning. Full formal operations and still more abstract social understanding may be required for post-conventional reasoning.

The research examining such a sequential development is scant, but supports Kohlberg's hypothesis. Lawrence Walker (1980) found that among a group of fourth to seventh graders he had tested on all three dimensions (concrete and formal operations, social understanding, and moral reasoning), one-half to two-thirds were reasoning at the same level across the differ-

## Moral Education and Moral Development

A lot of what I have been saying in this chapter may seem pretty abstract to you. Kohlberg himself, though, saw many potential practical implications for education. The question that interested him was whether children or young people can be taught higher stages of moral reasoning, and if so, whether such a change in moral reasoning would change their behavior in school.

We know from early research by Elliot Turiel (1966) that at least under some conditions, exposing young people to moral arguments one step above their own level of reasoning can lead to an increase in their level of moral judgment. Young people who attend college also continue to show increases in moral stage scores, while those who quit school after high school typically show no further increase (Rest & Thoma, 1985). Since arguments about moral and philosophical issues in class and over coffee (or a few beers) in the wee small hours of the night are one of the hallmarks of the college experience for many young people, perhaps it is the discussion—the exposure to other people's ideas and other people's logic—that makes a difference.

If that's true, what would happen if high-school students were given systematic opportunities to explore moral dilemmas; would that change them, too? Apparently it can.

One controversial but nonetheless fairly widespread educational application has involved the creation of special discussion classes in which Kohlberg's moral dilemmas (or something similar) are presented and argued. In the process, the teacher attempts to model higher levels of reasoning. Other programs are broader based, involving not just discussion, but also cross-age teaching (to encourage nurturance and caring), empathy training, cooperation games, volunteer service work, and the like. Research shows that on average, such programs seem to shift young people's moral reasoning upward about half a stage (Schaefli, Rest, & Thoma, 1985). The largest effects are generally found in programs focusing exclusively on discussions of moral dilemmas, but broader-based programs work too. Courses lasting longer than 3 or 4 weeks seem to work better than very short programs, and the effects are generally larger with older students—college students and even post-college age adults. Among high-school students, there is some impact but it is not as large.

An even broader-based educational ap-

ent domains, which makes the whole thing look unexpectedly "stage-like." But when a child was ahead in one progression, the sequence was always that the child developed logical thinking first, then more advanced social understanding, and then the parallel moral judgments.

What this research seems to tell us is that there is *some* coherence in a child's or young person's thinking or reasoning about quite different problems. Children who have not yet understood principles of conservation are not likely to understand that another person's behavior may not match his feelings. But once conservation is understood, the child extends this principle to people and to relationships. Similarly, a young person still using concrete operations is unlikely to use post-conventional moral reasoning. But the coherence is not automatic. The basic cognitive understanding makes advances in social and moral reasoning *possible*, but does not guarantee them. Experience in relationships, and with moral dilemmas, is necessary too.

The moral of this (if you will excuse the pun) is that just because a young person or adult shows signs of formal operations does *not* necessarily

plication has been the development of the so-called "just community," in which an entire school is designed as a laboratory for moral education. Kohlberg and his colleagues (Higgins, Power, & Kohlberg, 1984; Kohlberg & Higgins, 1987; Power & Reimer, 1978) have established and studied several such experimental schools. In each, a group of perhaps 60 students formed a separate "school within a school." In the experimental school, all rules were established in weekly community-wide meetings. Each person had one vote, so students and teachers were on an equal footing both in establishing and enforcing the rules. Thus students become *responsible* for the rules and for one another.

Under these conditions, not only did the students' level of Kohlbergian moral reasoning shift upward, so did their reasoning about responsibility and caring. The link between moral reasoning and moral behavior was strengthened as well. In one school, for example, stealing and other petty crimes virtually disappeared after the students had repeatedly discussed the problem and arrived at a just solution. Such an effect makes sense when you think about the factors I listed earlier that seem to affect moral behavior. In these schools, two elements were added that would tend to support more moral behavior: a sense of personal responsibility and a group norm of higher moral reasoning and caring.

Among teenagers, the emotional impact of the group pressure may be especially significant, in addition to whatever effect there may be from exposure to more mature arguments. If you are arguing your position about some moral dilemma, but find yourself in the minority, the "social disequilibrium" you feel may help to make you more open to other arguments and thus change your view. Certainly in experimental schools like those studied by Kohlberg, this added emotional impact is no doubt part of the process (Haan, 1985).

Classes in moral education have not proven to be the "quick fix" that many educators hoped for. The gains in moral reasoning are not huge, and may not be reflected in increases in moral behavior in the school unless there is an effort to alter the overall moral atmosphere of the entire school. But these programs do show that there are provocative and helpful applications of at least some of the abstract developmental theories.

mean that the teenager or young adult will show sensitive, empathetic, and forgiving attitudes toward friends or family. You may find it helpful to bear this in mind in your own relationships.

# S U M M A R Y

1. Many of the principles of developmental change that describe cognitive development more generally also seem to describe the changes in social cognition, including a shift in focus from outer to inner characteristics, from observation to inference, from definite to qualified judgment, and from a particular to a general view.

2. Social cognition differs from other aspects of cognition in that the child must learn that people behave with intention, mask feelings, and operate by special socially defined scripts or rules.

3. Empathy—being able to match or approximate the emotion of another—is seen in young infants, but becomes less egocentric and more subtle through the preschool and elementary school years.

4. Children's descriptions of others shift from a focus on external features, to a focus on personality traits, to a more qualified, comparative description at adolescence, paralleling the shifts in children's self-descriptions.

5. Children's thinking about their relationships, such as friendships, shows strongly parallel shifts, moving from definitions of friendship as people who share physical space or activities, to those emphasizing trust, to those emphasizing intimacy at adolescence.

6. Children's reasoning about what people ought to do, usually called moral reasoning, has been most fully described by Kohlberg.

7. Kohlberg proposed six stages, divided into three levels. The child moves from preconventional morality, dominated by punishment and "what feels good," to conventional morality, dominated by group norms or laws, to post-conventional (principled) morality, dominated by social contracts and basic ethical principles.

8. Cross-sectional and longitudinal research shows that the stages occur in subjects from all countries studied, that the stages occur in the order listed, and that the modal level for young adults in urban cultures is conventional morality.

9. Alternative models of moral reasoning include Eisenberg's stages of prosocial reasoning (reasoning about why to do something good), and Gilligan's concept of an ethic of caring.

10. A child's level of social cognition is at least somewhat predictive of the type of social behavior she will show.

11. Other factors that may influence moral behavior include group pressure, whether the individual sees the moral action as necessary or obligatory, the cost of some moral action, and the presence of other motivations, such as self-interest.

12. Social-cognitive development is also somewhat related to broader sequences of cognitive development. In particular, conventional levels of moral reasoning seem to require (as a necessary, but not sufficient condition) at least beginning formal operations, as well as fairly advanced reasoning about social relationships.

13. The stages of moral reasoning have formed the basis of many programs of "moral education" in schools, designed to raise students' levels of moral reasoning through exposure to discussion of moral dilemmas. Such programs appear to be at least partially successful.

## CRITICAL THINKING QUESTIONS

1. Kohlberg has found that the most typical level of moral reasoning in adulthood is conventional reasoning. What do you think would happen in a society dominated by adults who reasoned at Stage 5 or Stage 6? How might it differ from our present society?

2. If Gilligan were correct about the existence of a basic sex difference in moral orientation, with males more likely operating from an orientation of fairness and justice, while females more often operated from an orientation of care or relationship, what would be the implications for relationships between men and women and for society as a whole?

3. Why might it be important, either practically or theoretically, whether there is any link between children's approach to moral dilemmas and their level of Piagetian cognitive reasoning?

## KEY TERMS

**autonomous morality**   Piaget's second proposed stage of moral reasoning, developing some time after age 7, characterized by judgment of intent and emphasis on reciprocity.

**conventional morality**   The second level of moral judgment proposed by Kohlberg, in which the person's judgments are dominated by considerations of group values and laws.

**empathy**   As defined by Hoffman, it is "a vicarious affective response that does not necessarily match another's affective state but is more appropriate to the other's situation than to one's own" (Hoffman, 1984, p. 285).

**heteronomous morality**   Piaget's first proposed stage of moral reasoning, characterized by moral absolutism and belief in immanent justice. Judgments are based on consequences rather than intent.

**morality of reciprocity**   Another term for autonomous morality.

**moral realism**   Another term for heteronomous morality.

**preconventional morality**   The first level of morality proposed by Kohlberg, in which moral judgments are dominated by consideration of what will be punished and what feels good.

**principled morality**   The third level of morality proposed by Kohlberg, in which considerations of justice, individual rights, and contracts dominate moral judgment.

**social cognition**   Term used to describe a relatively new area of research and theory focused on the child's *understanding* of social relationships.

## SUGGESTED READINGS

Flavell, J. H. (1985). *Cognitive development* (2nd ed.). Englewood Cliffs, NJ: Prentice-Hall.

  I have recommended this excellent text before. In this case, you may want to look at the chapter on social cognition.

Kagan, J., & Lamb, S. (Eds.), (1987). *The emergence of morality in young children.* Chicago: University of Chicago Press.

  Several helpful papers are included in this collection, such as a paper by Gilligan, presenting her general view, and one by Judy Dunn on very early moral understanding.

Riley, S. S. (1984). *How to generate values in young children.* Washington, DC: National Association for the Education of Young Children.

  One of the reviewers of this text recommended Riley's book as "a very practical and useful book filled with lively examples about how children develop integrity, honesty, individuality, self-confidence, and wisdom."

# PROJECT 16

## Understanding Friendship

For this project you will need to locate a child between the ages of about 6 and 12. Arrange with the parents to spend some time with the child, explaining that you want to talk to the child for a school project, and that this is not a "test" of any kind. Try to find a time and a place to be alone with your subject; it will not work as well if siblings or parents are present.

Say to the child something like, "I'd like to talk to you about friends. Let me tell you a story about some children who were friends." Then read the following story:

> Kathy and Becky have been best friends since they were 5 years old. They went to the same kindergarten and have been in the same class ever since. Every Saturday they would try to do something special together, go to the park or the store, or play something special at home. They always had a good time with each other.
>
> One day a new girl, Jeanette, moved into their neighborhood and soon introduced herself to Kathy and Becky. Right away Jeanette and Kathy seemed to hit it off very well. They talked about where Jeanette was from and the things she could be doing in her new town. Becky, on the other hand, didn't seem to like Jeanette very well. She thought Jeanette was a showoff, but was also jealous of all the attention Kathy was giving Jeanette.
>
> When Jeanette left the other two alone, Becky told Kathy how she felt about Jeanette. "What did you think of her, Kathy? I thought she was kind of pushy, butting in on us like that."
>
> "Come on, Becky. She's new in town and just trying to make friends. The least we can do is be nice to her."
>
> "Yeah, but that doesn't mean we have to be friends with her," replied Becky. "Anyway, what would you like to do this Saturday? You know those old puppets of mine, I thought we could fix them up and make our own puppet show."

> "Sure, Becky, that sounds great," said Kathy. "I'll be over after lunch. I better go home now. See you tomorrow."
>
> Later that evening Jeanette called Kathy and surprised her with an invitation to the circus, the last show before it left town. The only problem was that the circus happened to be at the same time that Kathy had promised to go to Becky's. Kathy didn't know what to do, go to the circus and leave her best friend alone, or stick with her best friend and miss a good time. (Selman, 1980, p. 321–322)

After reading the child the story, you need to ask some open-ended questions, and then probe the child's understanding of friendship.

### Open Ended Questions

1. What do you think the problem is in this story?
2. What do you think Kathy will do, choose to be with her old friend Becky or go with the new girl, Jeanette? Why? Which do you think is more important: to be with an old friend or make new friends? Why?
3. Do you have a best friend? What kind of friendship do you have with that person? What makes that person your best friend?

Based on the child's answers, you may then want or need to probe as follows. (You probably will not need to ask *all* these questions; be selective, depending on your child's comments.)

### Probes

1. What kind of friendship do you think Kathy and Becky have? Do you think it is a good or close friendship? What is a really good close friendship? Does it take something special to have a very good friendship? What kinds of things do friends know about each other?

2. What does being friends for a long time, like Kathy and Becky, do for a friendship?
3. What makes close good friendships last?
4. What kinds of things can good friends talk about that other friends sometimes can't? What kinds of problems can they talk over?
5. What makes two friends feel really close to each other?
6. What's the difference between the kind of friendship Becky and Kathy have and Kathy and Jeanette's friendship? Are there different kinds of friendship? What's the difference between "regular" and "best" friendship?
7. Is it better when close friends are like each other or different from each other? Why? In what way

should good friends be the same? In what way should they be different?
8. Which is better to have (be with)—one close friend or a group of regular friends? Why? (Selman, 1980, p. 321–333)

## Scoring

Transcribe your child's answers as close to verbatim as you can. (Tape them if that will help.) Compare your child's answers to the levels of social understanding described in this chapter. At what level does the child appear to be reasoning?

# THE WHOLE CHILD

13

# THE ECOLOGY OF DEVELOPMENT: THE IMPACT OF FAMILIES, SCHOOLS, AND CULTURE

In the midst of a recession, Sam McKenzie's company had to lay off workers, and six months ago Sam lost his job as a machinist. Sam's wife Edith still has her job as a clerk in the local grocery store, but Sam's unemployment compensation is running out. Money is tight. Sam tried hard to persuade himself that these things happen to people, but more and more he blames himself and his lack of education. He also finds it very difficult to have to rely so much on his wife's income, since he thinks it is the man's job to support the family. And he most definitely does not think it is a man's job to get the kids off to school or put the meat loaf in the oven at 5:00. Over the months, he has become increasingly gloomy and irritable. He drinks more, has trouble sleeping, and he and Edith have had a lot more arguments. The kids have also felt the change—not just in the things they can't buy anymore, but in the whole atmosphere at home. Sam hugs them less, snaps at them more, and most of the time is much stricter with them—though there are times, too, when he seems to pay no attention at all. David, who is 13, has started yelling back a lot more than he used to and has been spending more and more time with his school buddies. Nine-year-old Jennifer has reacted differently: She's become much more withdrawn and depressed and no longer spends much time with her friends. Both the kids have had a lot more colds and other sicknesses than usual, too.

What the McKenzie family has experienced is fairly typical of what happens to families when the father loses his job (McLoyd, 1989, 1990). It also illustrates two important points about development—points that I made in a preliminary way in Chapter 1, but that may have gotten a bit lost in all the intervening chapters in which I have explored specific facets of the child's development.

First, to understand the child's development we must go beyond the child himself and whatever intrinsic developmental patterns may exist; we must go beyond the dyad of child and mother, or child and father. We need to look at the whole ecology of development—at the pattern of interaction within the family and at the influences of the larger culture on that family. David and Jennifer McKenzie have been affected by Sam's job loss both directly and indirectly, and some of those effects may be long lasting. For example, Glen Elder's studies (1974, 1981, 1984) show that some children whose families experienced major financial upheavals during the Great Depression in the 1930s continued to show the emotional scars well into adult life.

Second, the McKenzie's story illustrates that there is a *system* of influences at work. Sam's job loss was not just an economic event. It affected Sam's attitudes, his self-esteem, his behavior, and it reverberated through the entire family system, affecting every other person and every relationship.

What I must do in this chapter is explore this larger psychological and ecological system in which the child's development occurs—the family system, with all that it entails, and the larger culture in which the family exists. I introduced some of the current thinking about such family and cultural influences in Chapter 1, but let me both refresh your memory and set the stage by delving a bit more deeply into the theoretical issues.

## Theoretical Approaches

Thirty years ago, most child development texts and books of advice to parents emphasized the role of the parents in "molding" the child, as if the child were some sort of shapeless block of clay (Hartup, 1978). The parents' task was thought to be to *socialize* the child, to shape the child's behavior so that it fit well into the expectations and rules of society. This clay-molding view has now given way to a far more complex view, most commonly called *systems theory.*

### Systems Theory

Systems theorists (e.g., Sameroff, 1983) emphasize that any system—biological, economic, psychological—has certain properties. First and foremost,

Felton Gholston shares child care and household chores with his wife Anita. Here he is helping middle-child Malcolm with his breakfast. Soon the children will be taken to school or day care, and both parents will go to full-time jobs. This family system is quite different from what we see in a Japanese family like the Nouhatas—also filmed as part of the *Childhood* series—in which the mother is a full-time homemaker, and the grandmother lives with the family. This photo is a video still from the *Childhood* television series (*Source:* ©Thirteen/WNET).

a system has "wholeness and order," which is another way of saying that the whole is greater than the sum of its parts. The whole consists both of parts and their *relationship* to one another. The usual analogy is that of a melody, which is far more than a set of individual notes. It is the relationship of those notes to each other that creates the melody.

A second key feature of a system is that it is *adaptive,* in precisely the same way that Piaget talks about the child's cognitive system being adaptive. When there is a change in any part of the system, or some new element is added, the system will "assimilate" if it can, but will "accommodate" if it must. So systems resist change as much as they can by absorbing new data or new parts, but if that doesn't work—as it often doesn't—then the system changes. For example, when a second child is born into a family, the parents may try to keep to their old routines as much as possible but the presence of this new element in the system will inevitably force accommodations as well. And that will be particularly so if the new baby is temperamentally very different from the first child.

Combining these two features of systems, you can see that any change in any one part of a system will affect every other part. Furthermore, there are feedback loops set in motion. In the McKenzie family's experience, for example, Sam's distress led to changes in his behavior toward the children, to which they reacted with changes of their own. Once set in motion, however, the changes in David's and Jennifer's behavior will affect Sam and Edith as well. David has become more defiant, to which Sam responds by becoming even more strict and demanding, which will in turn affect David's behavior still further.

Although virtually all psychologists would now grant the general validity of such a systems approach, figuring out how to conceptualize the various parts of such systems has been no small task. Bronfenbrenner has offered one approach.

### Bronfenbremner's Ecological Approach

Bronfenbrenner (1979), whose work I talked about briefly in Chapter 1, proposed that we think of the ecological system in which the child develops as having a series of layers or concentric circles. Bronfenbrenner's own labels for those layers have not been widely adopted, but the conceptual scheme may still be useful in our exploration of these complexities.

The most central circle, which he calls *microsystems,* includes all those settings in which the child actually lives at least part of the time: the family, the school, the day-care center, and perhaps a child's own job setting. The family microsystem has been the subject of the most intense research scrutiny, but we now also know much more about out-of-home care settings, including day care and schools.

The next layer, which Bronfenbrenner calls *exosystems,* includes a whole range of system elements that the child does not experience directly, but that influence the child because they affect some part of the microsystem. The parent's work and workplace is one such exosystem element, as is the parents' network of friends.

Finally, there is what Bronfenbrenner calls the *macrosystem,* which describes the larger cultural or subcultural setting in which both the micro- and exosystems operate. Ethnic or social class differences in child rearing values or attitudes would be one such influence, as would general economic conditions like the recession that led to Sam McKenzie's layoff. Figure 13.1 shows these three system layers graphically.

You can also see that trying to understand families and larger systems in this way is *immensely* difficult. It is hard to keep all the elements of the system in mind at once, let alone study all the relevant parts simultaneously. Perhaps frustrated by that difficulty, or perhaps because of the long tradition of examining family and cultural effects in more linear ways, psychologists have continued to design research that explores only small pieces of the total system. Thus much of what we know about family and cultural influences on children is piecemeal rather than systemic. But using Bronfenbrenner's conceptualization as a general framework, let us plunge in anyway, beginning with the most studied and most obviously influential microsystem—the family.

**FIGURE 13.1**

This diagram shows my version of Bronfenbrenner's theoretical model. He argues that in order to understand the ecology of the child's development, we have to go beyond the most studied microsystem—the family. We need to look at all other facets of the larger system, including all those elements that influence the child indirectly through their effect on parents or teachers, such as the parents' jobs and the larger culture in which the whole process is embedded.

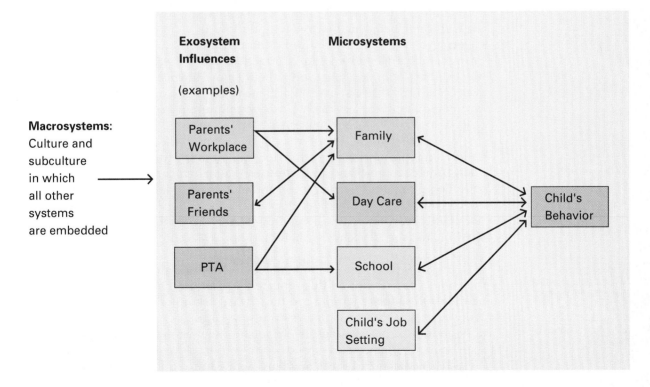

# The Key Microsystem: The Family

With rare exceptions, children grow up in families (even if the "family" consists of only one adult and one child), and each family is a complex system. To understand how that system works, and how it might affect the child, we need to look not only at the actual interactions between the parents and the child, but also at the other factors within the family that will affect those interactions, such as the child's temperament, the parents' personalities, or the family structure.

## Significant Dimensions of Family Interactions

Those researchers who have focused most directly on the patterns of interaction between parents and children have identified several major dimensions on which families differ that seem to be significant for the child: the emotional tone of the family, the responsiveness of the parent to the child, the manner in which control is exercised, and the quality and amount of communication.

*The Emotional Tone of the Family.* The first key element for the child seems to be the relative **warmth versus hostility** of the home. "Warmth" has been difficult to define and measure, but intuitively and theoretically it is clear that it is highly important for the child. A warm parent cares about the child, expresses affection, frequently or regularly puts the child's needs first, shows enthusiasm for the child's activities, and responds sensitively and empathetically to the child's feelings (Maccoby, 1980b). On the other end of the continuum are parents who overtly reject their children—saying and expressing with their behavior that they do not love or want the child. Such differences have an effect. Psychologists have found that children in warm and loving families are more securely attached in the first two years of life, have higher self-esteem, are more empathetic, more altruistic, more responsive to others' hurts or distress, have higher measured IQs in preschool and elementary school, and are less likely to show delinquent behavior in adolescence (e.g., Maccoby, 1980b; Schaefer, 1989; Simons, Robertson, & Downs, 1989).

I suspect that the role of warmth in fostering a secure attachment of the child to the parent is one of the key elements in this picture. You already know from chapters 9 and 11 that securely attached children are more skillful with their peers, more exploratory, and more sure of themselves. Warmth also makes children generally more responsive to guidance, so the parents' affection and warmth increase the potency of the things that parents say to their children and the efficiency of their discipline (Maccoby, 1980b).

*Responsiveness.* A second key element is **responsiveness** by the parent to the child. I've mentioned this repeatedly in earlier chapters, so this is not a new idea. Responsive parents are those who pick up on the child's signals appropriately and then react in sensitive ways to the child's needs. Parents who do more of this have youngsters who learn language somewhat more rapidly, show higher IQs and more speedy cognitive development, are more likely to be securely attached, more compliant with adult requests, and more socially competent (e.g., Bornstein, 1989b; Spangler, 1990).

**warmth versus hostility**
The key dimension of emotional tone used to describe family interactions.

**responsiveness**
An aspect of parent-child interaction. A responsive parent is sensitive to the child's cues and reacts appropriately, following the child's lead.

I am sure it is obvious to all of you that loving a child is a critical ingredient in the child's optimum development. But sometimes it helps to restate the obvious.

*Methods of Control.* It is the nature of children that they will often do things their parents do not want them to do, ask for things they cannot have, or refuse to obey their parents' requests or demands. From early days, parents are inevitably faced with the task of controlling the child's behavior, a process more popularly called *discipline*. Since I have not talked much about this aspect of parent-child interactions, I need to break the subject up into several elements.

One element of control is the *consistency of rules*—simply making it clear to the child what the rules are, what the consequences are of disobeying (or obeying) them, and then enforcing them consistently. Some parents are very clear and consistent; others waffle or are fuzzy about what they expect or will tolerate. Studies of families show that parents who are clear and consistent have children who are much less likely to be defiant or noncompliant—a pattern you'll remember from Gerald Patterson's research on aggressive children. But such clarity does not produce little robots. Children from families with consistent rules are also more competent and sure of themselves (Baumrind, 1967, 1971, 1973), and less aggressive (Patterson, 1980).

A related element is the *level of expectations* the parents have for the child's behavior. Is the child expected to show relatively more mature behavior or does the parent feel it is important not to expect too much too soon?

Studies of such variations show that, within limits, higher expectations seem to be associated with better outcomes. Children whose parents make high demands on them, expecting them to help around the house or to show relatively mature behavior for their age, have higher self-esteem, show more generosity and altruism toward others, and demonstrate lower levels of aggression. Obviously this can be carried much too far. It is totally unrealistic and counterproductive to expect a 2-year-old to set the table every night or to tie his own shoes. But when parents expect the child to be as independent and helpful as is possible for his age, that does seem to foster a sense of competence in the child that carries over into other situations.

Another element of parental control is the degree of **restrictiveness** imposed. This is not the same thing as clear or consistent rule setting. A parent can be relatively low in restrictiveness and still have clear rules. For example, you might have a rule that your 10-year-old can stop off at another child's house after school to play without arranging it ahead of time, but must call you to tell you where he is if he does so. That would be a clear rule, but relatively low restrictiveness. On the other hand, a parent who insists on keeping a child within eyesight at all times or who puts a toddler in a playpen for most of the day rather than risk having the child pull the drawers open or touch the stereo would be considered restrictive.

Restrictive parents also frequently use a distinctive form of language with their children, namely *imperative* sentences, such as "Stop that," "Come here," or "Do what I tell you." They are less likely to explain the rules to the children, but instead use their own power to control the child.

The other end of the continuum is usually listed as *permissive* parenting, which frequently also includes relatively few rules and few imperatives. Sometimes permissive parenting styles emerge from a sense of helplessness about controlling the child at all. In other cases permissiveness reflects a specific

**restrictiveness**
Term used to describe a particular pattern of parental control, involving limitation of the child's movements or options, such as by the use of playpens or harnesses in a young child, or strict rules about play areas or free choices in an older child.

Playpens can be very attractive for parents, since they can help keep a newly-mobile child out of trouble for a while. But because playpens limit the child's independence so much, parents who keep a child this age in one for any length of time each day would be rated as high in restrictiveness.

philosophy of child rearing that emphasizes the child's need for freedom and opportunities to explore.

Highly restrictive parents are likely to have quite obedient, unaggressive children. But such children are also likely to be somewhat timid, and may have difficulty establishing close relationships with peers.

Permissiveness, on the other hand, is also not a wholly positive strategy. Children with highly permissive parents—who may exert far too little control—are likely to show only moderate independence and to be relatively thoughtless of others. On this dimension, as on many others, the "ideal" appears to lie somewhere in the middle.

Overall, it seems clear that children respond very positively to clear rules consistently enforced and realistic demands and expectations, combined with only moderate restrictiveness.

Finally, to understand the process of control we have to understand the role of *punishment*. When a child does something you don't want (like writing on the wall or hitting her brother), or fails to do something you do want (like cleaning his room), most parents respond with some kind of punishment, such as withholding privileges or treats, assigning extra chores, sending a child to his room, "grounding," verbal scolding, or spanking. The most controversial of these is spanking. Because of the importance of the question, I have explored the pros and cons of such physical punishment in the box on page 500. But I want to make a number of other points about punishment strategies in general.

First, as Gerald Patterson (1975) says, "Punishment 'works.' If you use it properly it will produce rapid changes in the behavior of other people" (p. 19). The operative word here, though, is *properly*. The most effective punishments—those that produce long-term changes in the child's behavior without unwanted or negative side effects—are those used *early* in some sequence of misbehavior, with the lowest level of emotion possible, and the mildest level of punishment possible (Patterson, 1975; Holden & West, 1989). Taking a desired toy away when the child *first* uses it to hit the furniture (or a sibling), or consistently removing small privileges when a child misbehaves will "work," especially if the parent is also warm, clear about the rules, and consistent. It is far less effective to wait until the screams have reached a piercing level or until the fourth time a teenager has gone off without telling you where she's going, and then weighing in with yelling, loud comments, and strong punishments.

Second, to a considerable degree, parents get back what they give out in the way of punishment. As I pointed out in Chapter 9, children learn by observation as well as by doing, so they learn the adults' ways of coping with stress and forms of punishment. Yelling at children to stop doing something, for example, may bring a *brief* change in their behavior (which thus reinforces the parent for yelling, by the way). But it also increases the chances that children will yell back on other occasions.

*Communication Patterns.*   Two things about communication within the family seem to make a difference for the child: the amount and richness of language spoken *to* the child, and the amount of conversation and suggestions *from* the child that the parent encourages. Listening is important as well as talking.

# To Spank or Not to Spank

The short, emphatic answer to the question "Should I spank my child?" is NO. I am well aware that this is easier to say than to do (and I admit to having applied a hand to my own children's rear ends on one or two occasions, even knowing that it would do little good and some potential damage). But the information we have about the effects of physical punishment, including spanking, seems to me to be so clear that a firm answer to the question is possible.

In order to make the point clear I need to distinguish between the short term effects of spanking and the longer-term effects. In the short term, spanking a child usually *does* get the child to stop the particular behavior you didn't like, and it seems to have a *temporary* effect of reducing the chance that the child will repeat the bad behavior. Since that's what you wanted, it may seem like a good strategy. But even in the short term there are some negative side effects. The child may have stopped writing on the walls, or throwing water at you, or swearing (or whatever behavior you had forbidden), but after a spanking he is undoubtedly crying, which is unpleasant. It is also a behavior which spanking does not decrease. (It is virtually impossible to get children to stop crying by spanking them!) So you have exchanged one unpleasantness for another, and the second unpleasantness (crying) can't be dealt with by using the same form of punishment.

Another short-term side effect is that when the child stopped doing something unpleasant when you spanked him, *you* were reinforced for spanking. So the more effective the spanking is in reducing the child's unwanted behavior, the more you are being "trained" to use spanking again. A cycle is thus built up.

Whatever apparent benefits come in the short-run from spanking disappear when we take a longer look. Three long-term effects are particularly significant:

1. The child observes you using physical force or violence as a method of solving problems or getting people to do what you want. You thus serve as a model for a behavior you do *not* want your child to use with others. Telling the child that it's okay for parents to behave this way, but not for children, is likely to have little effect, since children will do what you do, not what you say when there is a conflict between the two messages.

2. By repeatedly pairing your presence with the unpleasant or painful event of spanking, you are undermining your own positive value for your child. Over time, this means that you are less able to use *any* kind of reinforcement effectively. Eventually even your praise or affection will be less powerful in influencing your child's behavior. That is a very high price to pay.

3. There is frequently a strong underlying emotional message going with spanking—anger, rejection, irritation, dislike of the child. Even very young children "read" this emotional message quite clearly. Spanking thus helps to create a family climate of rejection instead of warmth, with all the consequences I have described in the main part of this chapter.

I am *not* saying that you should never punish a child. I *am* saying that *physical punishment*, such as spanking, is rarely (if ever) a good way to go about it. Children whose parents use high rates of physical punishment are frequently highly aggressive (Bandura, 1973), or less compliant with adults (Power & Chapieski, 1986). More importantly, their relationships with peers are frequently less good than are those of children whose parents use other forms of control.

But what "other forms of control" will work? If you have been brought up in a family in which spanking was the standard method, you may simply not know other ways. If you find yourself in this position, a parenting class—often offered by community colleges or other community organizations—might be of help.

When I say "listening," I have in mind more than merely saying "uh-huh" periodically when the child talks. I also mean conveying to the child the sense that what he has to say is *worth* listening to, that he has ideas, and that his ideas are important and should be considered in family decisions. In general, children from families with open communication are seen as more emotionally or socially mature (Bell & Bell, 1982; Baumrind, 1971, 1973), although there are some hints from earlier research (e.g., Baldwin, 1948, 1949) that children from highly "democratic" families may be more bossy and aggressive.

More recent work has pointed to the importance of open communication not just for the child, but also for the functioning of the family as a unit. For example, in a study of a national sample of families with adolescents, Howard Barnes and David Olson (1985) measured communication by asking the parents and teenagers to agree or disagree with statements like "It is easy for me to express all my true feelings to my (mother/father/child)." As you can see in Figure 13.2, they found that those families in which parents and child reported good, open communication, compared to those with poorer communication, also described their families as more adaptable in the face of stress or change and said they were more satisfied with their families.

### Patterns of Child Rearing

Each of these dimensions of variation among families has a demonstrable effect on the child, but if we are going to try to use a systems theory approach, it is not enough to look at each dimension independently. We also have to think about how they interact with one another to create *styles* or *patterns* of child rearing.

The most influential proposal about such styles has come from Diana Baumrind (1972), who has looked at combinations of four of the dimensions I've just described: (1) warmth or nurturance, (2) level of expectations, which she describes in terms of "maturity demands," (3) the clarity and consistency of rules, and (4) communication between parent and child. Baumrind saw three specific combinations of these characteristics:

- The **authoritarian parental style** is high in control and maturity demands, but low in nurturance and communication.

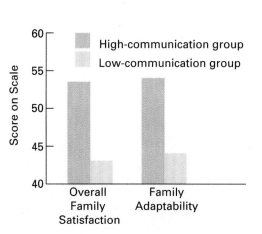

**authoritarian parental style**
One of the three styles described by Baumrind, characterized by high levels of control and maturity demands and low levels of nurturance and communication.

**FIGURE 13.2**

Adolescents and their parents who describe their interactions as involving good, open communication also describe themselves as more satisfied with their overall family life, and see their families as more adaptable than adolescents and parents whose communication is not as good or open (*Source:* Barnes & Olson, 1985, Table 3, p. 445).

- The **permissive parental style** is high in nurturance, but low in maturity demands, control, and communication.
- The **authoritative parental style** is high in all four.

Eleanor Maccoby and John Martin have proposed a variation of Baumrind's category system, shown in Figure 13.3, that I find even more helpful. They emphasize two dimensions, the degree of demand or control on the one hand, and the amount of acceptance/rejection or responsiveness on the other. The intersection of these two dimensions creates four types, three of which correspond fairly closely to Baumrind's authoritarian, authoritative, and permissive types. Maccoby and Martin's fourth type, the neglecting or uninvolved type, was not identified by Baumrind but certainly does occur and seems important to study separately.

*The Authoritarian Type.* Children growing up in authoritarian families—with high levels of demand and control but relatively low levels of warmth or responsiveness—typically are less skilled with peers than are children from other types of families, and they have lower self-esteem. Some of these children appear subdued; others may show high aggressiveness or other indications of being out of control. Which of these two outcomes occurs may depend in part on how skillfully the parents use the various disciplinary techniques. Patterson finds that the "out of control" child is most likely to come from a family in which the parents are authoritarian by inclination, but lack the skills to enforce the limits or rules they set. In a recent study of nearly

**FIGURE 13.3**

Combinations of parent behaviors or attitudes toward children can be classified into types. This particular typology, suggested by Maccoby & Martin, focuses on two dimensions of difference: (a) demanding or controlling vs. undemanding or noncontrolling, and (2) accepting-responsive vs. rejecting-unresponsive. Three of the four types that emerge from this classification are obviously highly similar to the authoritarian/authoritative/permissive types Baumrind suggests [*Source:* Adapted from E. E. Maccoby & J. A. Martin (1983). Socialization in the context of the family: Parent-child interaction. In E. M. Hetherington (Ed.), *Handbook of child psychology*, Figure 2, p. 39. New York: Wiley].

**Degree of Acceptance or Rejection**

|  |  | High Acceptance Responsive; Child-Centered | Low Acceptance(Rejection) Unresponsive; Parent-Centered |
|---|---|---|---|
| **Degree of Demand and Control** | High Demand and Control | authoritative-reciprocal | authoritarian; power-assertive |
|  | Low Demand and Control | indulgent; permissive | negligent; indifferent; uninvolved |

8000 high-school students, Sanford Dornbusch and his coworkers (Dornbusch et al., 1987b) have also found that teenagers from authoritarian families have poorer grades in school than do teenagers from authoritative families.

*The Permissive Type.*    Children growing up with indulgent or permissive parents also show some negative outcomes. Dornbusch finds that they do slightly less well in school in adolescence, are likely to be more aggressive—particularly if the parents are specifically permissive toward aggressiveness—and to be somewhat immature in their behavior with peers and in school. They are less likely to take responsibility and are less independent.

*The Authoritative Type.*    The most consistently positive outcomes have been associated with the authoritative pattern, in which the parents are high in both control and warmth, setting clear limits but also responding to the child's individual needs. Children reared in such families typically show higher self-esteem, are more independent but at the same time are more likely to comply with parental requests, and may show more altruistic behavior as well. They are self-confident and achievement oriented in school and get better grades; they are less likely to show depression or delinquency (Dornbusch et al., 1987b; Steinberg, Elmen, & Mounts, 1989; Crockenberg & Litman, 1990). What is more, recent large scale studies have shown that this link is not an exclusively middle-class or caucasian phenomenon: Authoritarian parenting is correlated with good outcomes among African Americans, Asian Americans and Hispanic Americans as well as among Anglos (Steinberg et al., 1991).

*The Neglecting Type.*    In contrast, the most consistently negative outcomes are associated with the fourth pattern, the neglecting or uninvolved type. You may remember from Chapter 11, in the discussion of secure and insecure attachments, that one of the common family characteristics of children rated as insecure/avoidant is the "psychological unavailability" of the mother. The mother may be depressed or may be overwhelmed by other problems in her life and simply not have made any deep emotional connection with the child. Whatever the reason, such children continue to show disturbances in their relationships with peers and with adults for many years. In less extreme cases the effects are also detectable. Robert Hinde and Joan Stevenson-Hinde (1986), in a short-term longitudinal study, found that children whose mothers were both uninvolved and low in control when the children were 3 1/2 showed a somewhat odd combination of friendliness and high levels of hostility with peers eight months later. And at adolescence, youngsters from neglecting families are more impulsive, antisocial, and much less achievement oriented in school (Block, 1971; Pulkkinen, 1982).

Several conclusions from this research are important. First, it seems clear that children are affected by the family "climate" or style. Although we do not have the sort of longitudinal data needed to be sure, I suspect that these effects persist well into adulthood. Second, many of us are accustomed to thinking about family styles as if permissive and authoritarian patterns were the only options. But Baumrind's work shows clearly that one can be *both* affectionate and firm, and that children respond to this combination in very positive ways.

Finally, even these types do not begin to describe the complexity of the family microsystem. Both the outcomes for the child, and the styles or types themselves, are also affected by the child's own characteristics, by the parents' personalities or daily habits, and by the cast of characters living together in a family unit.

## Other Elements in the Family Microsystem

### The Child's Characteristics.
One of the first things to understand is that the influences in the parent-child system flow both ways. Children influence their parents as well as the other way around. I already talked about one such influence in Chapter 9, namely the child's temperament. Children with "difficult" temperaments seem to elicit more punishment (especially if the family is under some kind of stress), and may also affect a parent's mood. More generally, such children may have much more difficulty adapting to any change in the family system. For example, in her study of divorcing families, Mavis Hetherington (1989) has found that children who had shown difficult temperament in infancy and toddlerhood were far more disrupted by their parents' divorce, especially if the divorce was one in which there were many different stresses. In contrast, temperamentally easy children could handle many more family stresses associated with the divorce before they showed disruptive behavior or poor school performance.

The child's temperament can also affect the parents' relationship with each other. For example, one group of researchers (Stoneman, Brody, & Burke, 1989) has observed that the parental relationship was most negatively affected when the first-born child was a daughter with an "active-emotional" temperament, but the same was not true either for first-born boys, or for any later-born children—yet another illustration of the fact that to understand this system we need to look at it in its entirety. The child's position in the family shows up as an important ingredient in other research as well. Parents generally have higher expectations for maturity in their first-born, and may well be more responsive and more child-centered with the first child. First-borns are also punished more, in part because parents are simply less skilled in using noncoercive forms of control with their first child.

The child's age also makes a difference—a point that may seem obvious, but is well worth reemphasizing. As the child develops, very different demands are made on the parents. As any parent can tell you, caring for an infant is a different task than caring for a 2-year-old or a 12-year-old. The areas in which control will need to be exercised change, the degree of push for independence changes, and the child's intellectual and language abilities change. As an example, you may remember from Chapter 11 the research showing that at the onset of puberty there is a rather sharp change in children's behavior with their parents. They become more distant and provoke more conflict as they insist on more autonomy (e.g., Steinberg, 1987). These changes in the child alter the entire family system.

Other child characteristics that obviously affect the family system, and that I have talked about at various points in earlier chapters, include the child's gender and whether the child has any special needs, such as would be true for a preterm infant or a child with a chronic health problem. The important point is that we should not fall into the trap of thinking that parents have a consistent or permanent style or pattern of child rearing that is the same for all children in a family, or the same for each child over time. There are threads of consistency that run through the variations, I am sure. But each parent-child system is an evolving one, to which both contribute.

*The Parents' Characteristics.* The parents bring their own life histories and their own personalities to this exchange. I could spend a whole chapter talking about the parents' half of this equation, but lacking such space, let me give only two brief illustrations.

First, when either parent is significantly depressed it has a profound effect on the entire family system. Not only is an insecure attachment more likely when the mother is depressed (e.g., Radke-Yarrow et al., 1985; Lyons-Ruth et al., 1990), depressed parents also perceive their children as more difficult and problematic, and are more critical of them—even when objective observers cannot identify any difference in the behavior of such children and the children of non-depressed mothers (Richters & Pellegrini, 1989; Webster-Stratton & Hammond, 1988). Thus the parent's depression changes not only her behavior, but her perception of the child's behavior, both of which alter the family system.

Another characteristic the parent brings with him (or her) that seems to have a very strong effect on the family system, and thus on the child, is the parent's own internal working model of attachment. Mary Main and her colleagues have been able to classify the security or insecurity of the parent's attachment to his or her own parents through the use of an interview (Main, Kaplan, & Cassidy, 1985). They find that those parents who are themselves securely attached are much more likely to have a child who is also securely attached—a finding that has now been replicated by several other investigators (e.g., Crowell & Feldman, 1988).

These characteristics that the parents bring with them to the family interactive system obviously help to shape the style of parenting they show with their children—whether authoritarian, authoritative, or some other. But they do more than that. They affect the parents' perceptions of the child as well as the parents' behavior, and thus affect the system in myriad subtle ways.

*Family Structure.* Another obvious aspect of the family system is the particular configuration of people who live together in a given family unit—an aspect usually called *family structure.*

I suspect that most of us still harbor the illusion that the most common family structure is a father, a mother, and several children—like the family in Figure 13.4 on the next page. And no doubt most of us still think that the majority of children spend all of their childhood and adolescence with the same Mom and Dad. But both of those assumptions are wrong.

Sandra Hofferth (1985) has generated some particularly startling estimates, based on a longitudinal study of over 5000 families who have been followed since 1968. She projects that only 30 percent of white children in the United States born in 1980 will still be living with their two natural parents at age 17. For black children, the figure is only 6 percent. Other estimates, based on cross-sectional comparisons, are somewhat more optimistic (e.g., Bumpass, 1984; Norton & Glick, 1986). But it would appear that at least 60 percent, and

**FIGURE 13.4**

When we think of "the family," no doubt most of us
think of a family like this,
with a father and mother
and several children. But in
fact, in the United States it
now is the exception rather
than the rule for a child to
spend his or her entire
childhood and adolescence
in such a family system.

possibly as many as 70 or 80 percent, of today's children are likely to spend at
least *some* time in a single-parent household, and perhaps 35 percent will
spend at least a part of their childhood living with a stepparent.

Figure 13.5 shows the other types of family structures Hofferth predicts
for the children born in 1980, so you can see the very large variety. Even this,
though, does not convey the enormous variety of family combinations. In one
study Shep Kellam found *86* different family structures in a large sample of
children from a poor, black Chicago neighborhood in 1966 (Kellam, Ensminger, & Turner, 1977). Further complexities are added by the fact that
most families change from one structure to another, sometimes repeatedly.
Divorced mothers, for example, may have live-in relationships with one or
more men before a remarriage or may live for a while with their own parents.
All in all, it is clear that the *majority* of children today experience at least two
different family structures, often many more than that in the course of their
growing up.

Research on the effects of such structures on family interaction patterns,
and on children, has not kept pace with the rate of change in families. In particular, we know relatively little about the many varieties of stepparent families. But let me make a few points.

First, any change in the family structure is accompanied by dislocation
and stress. Whenever a new person is added or subtracted from the family
unit the system faces a major adaptational problem. This seems particularly
troublesome in the case of divorce or separation, when an adult is subtracted
from the family. I described some of the effects of divorce on children in the
box in Chapter 9 (pages 366–367) so you know that there is typically disruption of the child, reflected in poorer school performance and higher rates of
problem behavior in the first few years following the separation. The same
sort of disruption occurs in the parents' behavior too. The adults may show
wide mood swings, experience problems at work, or poor health (Hetherington, 1989). Their parenting style also changes, becoming much less authoritative, almost neglectful.

Interestingly, it appears that many of these negative effects for both the
adult and the children are mitigated when the mother has another adult in

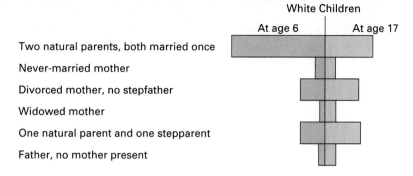

White Children

At age 6 — At age 17

Two natural parents, both married once

Never-married mother

Divorced mother, no stepfather

Widowed mother

One natural parent and one stepparent

Father, no mother present

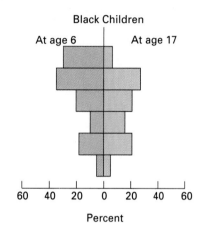

Black Children

At age 6 — At age 17

Two natural parents, both married once

Never-married mother

Divorced mother, no stepfather

Widowed mother

One natural parent and one stepparent

Father, no mother present

60  40  20  0  20  40  60

Percent

**FIGURE 13.5**

These figures represent Sandra Hofferth's estimates of the percentage of children born in 1980 who will be in each of several family types or structures at age 6 and at age 17. Because the patterns are so different for black and for white children, I have separated these out. Hofferth estimates that only about one-fourth of children will spend all of their childhood with both natural parents; an equivalent number will spend at least part of their childhood with a stepparent. At least one change in family structure is now the norm for children in the United States (*Source: Hofferth, 1985, Tables 1 and 2, pages 99–100, 102–103*).

the home—her own mother, a friend, a live-in boyfriend (Dornbusch et al., 1985; Kellam et al., 1977), which suggests that a two-adult system in a family may simply be more stable or easier to manage.

However—and this is an important however—there are various hints that this buffering effect of a second adult in the home does *not* extend to stepparent family structures (mother/stepfather or father/stepmother). For example, Dornbusch finds that stepparent families show higher levels of authoritarian and lower levels of authoritative child-rearing styles (Dornbusch et al., 1987a), and the children have lower school grades and higher rates of delinquency than do children in two-natural-parent families. There is also a curious finding, now replicated several times, that in stepparent families, the closer the parents' relationship is with one another, the *more* problems the children display—which is just the opposite of what is found in non-divorced families (e.g. Hetherington, 1989; Brand et al., 1988). This seems to be especially true in the years immediately following the remarriage and in cases in which the mother and children lived alone for some years.

One can make sense of this finding within a systems perspective by assuming that after the original divorce the children were given more independence and took on various family roles from which they were displaced when the new stepfather appeared on the scene. The closer the relationship of the mother and stepfather, the more displaced the children feel. However we explain it, this finding illustrates how enormously complex the family system is. We simply cannot assume that something like high marital satisfaction is going to have precisely the same effect on every family. The effect will vary as a function of the family's history, the age of the children, the specific style of child rearing, and many other factors.

## A Second Microsystem: Day Care

The increase in women's labor force participation over the past several decades represents a remarkably rapid and massive social change. In 1972, only 24 percent of women in the United States with children under age 1 were in the labor force. By 1988, that figure had more than doubled; the *majority* of such women now work outside the home at least part-time (U.S. Bureau of the Census, 1990). It is thus now typical for infants as well as school-age children to live concurrently in two microsystems. We obviously need to understand the kinds of effects such an experience has on the child. We also need to understand how these two microsystems interact with one another. Does a child in day care have a different kind of family interaction pattern from one who is not?

### Who Is Taking Care of the Children?

It is inaccurate to think of "day care" as a unitary phenomenon. Parents make a wide variety of care arrangements for their children, as you can see from Table 13.1. If we group together all children under 5, the most common pattern is for a child to be cared for in another person's home, sometimes by a relative but more often by another mother who takes in a few children for

**TABLE 13.1**

*Child-Care Arrangements Experienced by Preschool Children in the United States in 1986*

|  | Percentage |
| --- | --- |
| Care in Child's Own Home: | |
| by relative other than | |
| mother or father | 6.7% |
| by nonrelative | 6.1 |
| Care in Another Home | |
| (family day care): | |
| by grandparent | 11.5 |
| by another relative | 6.0 |
| by nonrelative | 23.8 |
| Day-Care Center (including | 14.7 |
| corporate child-care centers): | |
| nursery school/preschool | 6.4 |
| kindergarten/elementary | 1.2 |
| mother cares for child at work | 6.7 |

*Source:* U.S. Bureau of the Census, 1990, Table 616.

Ten or fifteen years ago, it would have been fairly unusual to see children this young in day care. Now it is commonplace in many parts of the world, such as in this center in Japan. This photo is a video still from the *Childhood* television series (*Source:* ©Thirteen/WNET).

care—a pattern usually called *family day care.* Care in the child's own home by someone other than a parent is next most common, with day-care *centers* actually the least common. But this pattern varies somewhat by age. For 3- and 4-year-olds, center care is the most frequent choice, while family day care and at-home care is the dominant pattern for those under 3 (Hofferth & Phillips, 1987).

These three types of care differ from one another in systematic ways. For example, center care typically provides the most cognitive enrichment, while family day-care homes typically provide the least; both center care and family day care give the child an opportunity to play with same-age peers, while at-home care does not (Clarke-Stewart, 1987). Such variations make it very difficult to talk about global effects of day care, since the systems are quite different. Furthermore, the bulk of the research evidence is based on studies of children in center care, and we cannot be sure that these findings will generalize to children in family day care or at-home care by someone other than parents.

Another difficulty in drawing clear conclusions arises from the fact that children enter day care at various ages, and that the stability of their care varies enormously. Some children move often from one arrangement to another; others remain with the same caregiver for many years. Such differences are bound to affect the child's response, and they make the research problem even more complex. Despite these difficulties, the enormous practical relevance of the questions involved here has forced psychologists to try to draw some conclusions—resulting at the moment in a very hot debate. Let me start with the least controversial conclusions.

### Direct Effects of Day Care on the Child

There is widespread agreement on two effects. First, *center* care, but not family day care or care at home, appears to enhance children's intellectual development. This is particularly true for intensive programs (such as the one I talked about in Chapter 6, shown in Figure 6.6), especially ones that begin in the first year of the child's life. It is also particularly true for children from poverty-level families. But some enhancement of cognitive functioning is also found in studies of more typical day-care centers (e.g. Clarke-Stewart, 1984; Caldwell, 1986; Burchinal, Lee, & Ramey, 1989).

Second, some long-term studies show that children who have been in day care, compared to those reared by parents at home, are more aggressive with peers and less compliant with teachers and parents at later ages (e.g., Haskins, 1985; McKinney & Edgerton, 1983). Other researchers have not found such a pattern (e.g., Lamb et al., 1988), while still others have found that children in day care are actually more sociable and skillful with peers at later ages (e.g., Andersson, 1989). Still, the most common finding is of some increase in aggressiveness or noncompliance.

Here is where the agreement ceases and the dispute begins. How should we interpret this effect? Might it reflect the fact that teachers in many day-care centers, in an effort to encourage children to be independent, have also inadvertently reinforced aggressiveness and excessive assertiveness? Maybe. Ramey's program in North Carolina (shown in Figure 6.6) was one in which this increased aggressiveness was found; when the program was later altered to place greater emphasis on the development of positive social skills, the heightened aggressiveness disappeared (Finkelstein, 1982).

Alternatively, some researchers have interpreted the aggressiveness not as a sign of deviance or maladjustment, but rather as a sign that children in day care learn to think for themselves more and are less docile (e.g., Clarke-Stewart, 1990). Still others, such as Jay Belsky—a psychologist who has generally taken the most pessimistic view of all the findings on day care—conclude that these hints of behavioral maladjustment among children in day care are major red flags (Belsky, 1990) and reflect more basic difficulties in the child, such as problems with attachment.

### *The Effects of Day Care on the Child's Attachment to Parents*

The hottest debate concerns just this question of attachment. Specifically, can an infant or toddler develop a secure attachment to her mother or father if she is repeatedly separated from them? We know that the majority of infants develop secure attachments to their fathers even though the father typically goes away every day to work, so it is clear that such regular separations do not *preclude* secure attachment. But does separation from both parents on a daily basis affect the security of the child's attachment?

There is little dispute about the conclusion that children who enter day care at 18 months, 2 years, or later show *no* consistent loss of security of attachment to their parents. The uncertainty has thus been narrowed to the question of the effect of *infant* day care on attachment.

Until about five years ago, most psychologists had concluded that there was no demonstrable effect. But then Belsky, in a series of papers and in testimony before a congressional committee, sounded an alarm (Belsky, 1985, 1987, 1990; Belsky & Rovine, 1988). Combining data from several studies, he concluded that there was a heightened risk of an insecure attachment among infants who enter day care before their first birthday. Controversy erupted.

Belsky's judgment was questioned by some; his conclusions were questioned by many. In the past few years, the hubbub has quieted some, and Belsky's central empirical conclusion has been widely accepted. Summing across many studies, it *is* the case that infants in day care are slightly more likely to be insecurely attached than are those reared at home by parents. In Alison Clarke-Stewart's more recent combined analysis (1990), the actual figures are 36 percent and 29 percent, respectively. This is not a huge difference, but it is statistically significant and fairly consistently found. The present controversy swirls around how to interpret or explain this difference.

Belsky has his supporters. Alan Sroufe, one of the major figures in studies of early attachment, argues that it is entirely sensible that there might be some difference in security as a result of day-care experience (1990). He points out that we know that security of attachment is fostered both by the child's sense of the responsiveness of care and by the opportunity for parent and child to fine-tune their interactive dance. Both of these may be disrupted by placing the child in day care, although clearly in the majority of cases, parents find ways to counteract such disruptions, since the majority of children in day care are nonetheless securely attached.

On the other side of the argument are those, such as Clarke-Stewart, who either don't believe that there is a serious problem to be dealt with, or who argue that there are so many confounding variables that it is impossible to draw any clear conclusion. Here's a sampling of their arguments:

- The percentage of insecurely attached infants noted among those in day care is virtually identical to the worldwide average found by van IJzendoorn and Kroonenberg (1988) in their cross-cultural analysis of attachment studies. Some psychologists argue from this that the level of insecurity observed in U.S. day-care infants simply does not reflect a major problem (e.g., Thompson, 1990; Clarke-Stewart, 1990).
- The Strange Situation may not be an appropriate measure of attachment security for children in day care. To assess security, the child must be at least mildly stressed—otherwise we simply don't see enough attachment behaviors to judge the security of the child's attachment. A child in day care, who is used to repeated separations from Mom, may simply not experience the episodes of the Strange Situation as stressful, and thus may show behavior that looks like avoidance but is really an indication of relative comfort in the situation (e.g., Clarke-Stewart, 1990).
- There is a serious problem of self-selection involved in any comparison of day-care and parent-reared infants. Mothers who work are different in other ways from mothers who do not. More are single mothers, and more prefer to work or find child care onerous. A related problem is that children in the poorest quality day care, or who are moved often from one care arrangement to another, are also likely to come from the least stable families (e.g., Howes & Stewart, 1987; Howes, 1990). It is impossible therefore to attribute the heightened levels of insecure attachment to the day-care experience, rather than to home experiences.

For all these reasons, Alison Clarke-Stewart (1990) concludes that, "At the present time. . . it is not appropriate to interpret the difference, as Belsky appears to, as suggesting that these children are emotionally insecure" (p. 69).

But even if one agrees with Clarke-Stewart that the conclusions are not clear (which I do), what do we say to parents who ask us whether the baby will be okay if Mom goes back to work before the child is a year old? I find myself in agreement here with Alan Sroufe, who argues that precisely *because* we are not sure, the more cautious advice to parents is that one of them should care for the child for the first year. If this is not feasible (and it often is not these days) then there are steps they can take to reduce the risk, including selecting the best possible and most stable care, and ensuring that they have the needed emotional support to sustain a close and loving relationship with the child when they are together.

### The Quality of Care

But just what do we mean by "good day care"? How is a parent to judge? I've summarized some of the key variables in Table 13.2 (p. 514). Not surprisingly, the list bears a strong resemblance to the lists of optimum family care I have given in earlier chapters, although there are other items here that refer specifically to the training of day-care workers and the organization of the day-care home or center. If you are facing this choice for your own children, this list might serve as a starting point in your evaluation of alternatives.

 ## Schools: A Third Microsystem

If the choice of a day-care setting for your child is important, the choice of a school at later ages is no less so. For decades, real estate agents have touted "good" school districts as a reason for settling in one town or one part of a town rather than another. Now we have research to show that the real estate agents were right: Specific characteristics of schools and teachers do affect children's development.

The most common research strategy has been to identify unusually "effective" or "successful" schools—those in which the pupils consistently do better than you would predict knowing the kind of families or neighborhoods the pupils come from (e.g., Rutter, 1983; Good & Weinstein, 1986). In such schools, pupils have higher than expected scores on standardized tests, or better school attendance, or lower rates of disruptive classroom behavior or delinquency, or a higher rate of pupils who go on to college, or higher self-esteem in the pupils. Some schools seem to achieve such good results consistently, year after year, so the effect is not just chance variation. When these successful schools are compared to others in similar neighborhoods that have less impressive track records, certain common themes emerge, which I've summarized in Table 13.3 (p. 515).

What strikes me when I read this list is that effective schools sound a lot like *authoritative* schools, rather than either permissive or authoritarian schools. There are clear goals and rules, good control, good communication, and high nurturance. Not surprisingly, a very similar pattern appears when researchers study effective classrooms: It is the "authoritative" teachers—those with clear goals, clear rules, and effective management strategies, and who are personal and warm with the children—whose pupils do best academically (Linney & Seidman, 1989).

As with any system, however, the quality of the whole is more than the sum of the quality of the individual parts. Each school also has an overall climate or ethos that makes a difference for the youngsters. The most positive school climate occurs when there are widely shared goals, when there is dedication to effective teaching, and when there is concrete assistance provided for such teaching. It is reflected in respect for pupils, for parents, and for the building.

One moral to be drawn from this research is that campaigns to improve schools by changing *what* is taught, such as "back to basics" programs, may be at least partially misdirected. The key seems to be *how* teaching is done and the overall climate of the school.

## Some Exosystem Effects: The Impact of Parents' Work and Social Support on the Family Microsystem

The child herself is directly involved in each of the three microsystems I have talked about—the family, a day-care setting, or the school. When we turn to the next level of analysis, what Bronfenbrenner called the exosystem, the

Benji Gholston's school, like every school, has its own "climate," its own ethos. Research on effective schools shows that the dozens of small ways in which teachers, staff, and students express the school goals and values all affect children in important ways. An "authoritative" school (high in control and in acceptance and responsiveness) not only increases students' academic achievement, it also affects their motivation, their attendance, and their behavior. This photo is a video still from the *Childhood* television series (*Source:* ©Thirteen/WNET).

TABLE 13.2

*Some Characteristics of Day-Care Settings That Affect Outcomes for Children*

---

- **Teacher/child ratio**. In general, the lower the better, although one national study shows that within the range of 5:1 to 10:1 it doesn't matter much. Ratios of 15:1 and higher are much less good.
- **Number of children.** Regardless of how many adults there are with each group of children, the smaller the number of children cared for together—whether in one room in a day-care center or in a home—the better for the child. Thus a group of 30 children cared for by 5 adults is less good than three smaller groups of 10 children cared for by one adult each.
- **Amount of personal contact with adults.** In general, the more time the child spends in one-to-one interaction with an adult, the better, although when the child is cared for by a babysitter at home, it is possible to have too much adult contact. In a day-care home, or center, however, amount of personal contact with an adult is an important feature.
- **Richness of verbal stimulation.** Regardless of the variety of toys available, complex and varied language will stimulate faster language and cognitive development.
- **Space, cleanliness, and colorfulness.** The overall physical organization of the space seems to make a difference. Children show more creative play and exploration in colorful, clean environments that are well adapted to child play. Lots of expensive toys are not critical, but there must be activities that children will find engaging and that provide space to move.
- **Caregiver's knowledge of child development.** Children's development is better in child development centers or homes in which the caregivers have specific training in human development.
- **Marital status of caregivers.** Among family day-care providers, those caregivers who are single and thus responsible for all the care of the home as well as the children spend more time in housekeeping and thus less time with the children than is true of married caregivers.

---

*Source:* Anderson et al., 1981; Clarke-Stewart, 1987; Hunt, 1986; Long, Peters, & Garduque, 1985; Ruopp & Travers, 1982; Smith & Spence, 1981.

child is no longer directly involved, but she may still be strongly affected. The two examples I want to talk about are both aspects of the parents' lives—their jobs and their network of social support.

### The Impact of Parents' Jobs on the Family and the Child

*Mothers' Employment.* Most of the research on mother's employment has focused not on the character of her work or even her satisfaction with it but on the question of whether she works at all. Obviously this question is not entirely separable from all the issues about day care I have already raised, since it is precisely because the mother is working that most children are in alternate care. Since I've already talked about that literature, let me focus here on studies of families with school-age children, in which the impact of the mother's work is not so totally confounded with the effects of the child's alternative care.

The cumulative findings from the hundreds of studies of maternal employment are now fairly clear: For children past infancy and toddlerhood, ma-

*TABLE 13.3*

*Characteristics of Unusually Effective Schools*

- ***Qualities of pupils.*** A *mixture* of backgrounds or abilities seems to be best, although the key appears to be to have a large enough concentration of pupils who come to school with good academic skills. Too great a concentration of children with poor skills makes it more difficult for the rest of the things on this list to occur.
- ***Goals of the school.*** Effective schools have a strong emphasis on academic excellence, with high standards and high expectations. These goals are clearly stated by the administration and shared by the staff.
- ***Organization of classrooms.*** Classes are focused on specific academic learning. Daily activities are structured, with a high percentage of time in actual group instruction. High expectations of performance are conveyed to pupils.
- ***Homework.*** Homework is assigned regularly, graded quickly.
- ***Discipline.*** Most discipline is handled within the classroom, with relatively little fallback to "sending the child to the principal." In really effective schools, not much class time is actually spent in discipline, because these teachers have very good control of the class. They intervene early in potentially difficult situations rather than imposing heavy discipline after the fact.
- ***Praise.*** Pupils receive high doses of praise for good performance or for meeting stated expectations.
- ***Teacher experience.*** Teacher *education* is not related to effectiveness of schools, but teacher *experience* is, presumably because it takes time to learn effective class management and instruction strategies.
- ***Building surroundings.*** Age or general appearance of the school building is not critical, but maintenance of good order, cleanliness, and attractiveness do have an effect.
- ***School leadership.*** Effective schools have strong leaders, and those leaders state their goals clearly and often.
- ***Responsibilities for children.*** In effective schools, children are more likely to be given real responsibilities—in individual classrooms and in the school as a whole.
- ***Size.*** As a general rule, smaller schools are more effective, in part because in such schools children feel more involved and are given more responsibility. This effect is particularly clear in studies of high schools.

*Sources:* Rutter, 1983; Linney & Seidman, 1989.

ternal employment has a generally positive effect, although the results are slightly different for boys and for girls. In the United States, girls whose mothers work are more independent, have more egalitarian sex-role concepts, and admire their mothers more than do girls whose mothers do not work. Boys whose mothers work also have more egalitarian sex-role concepts, but some early studies showed that boys of working mothers had somewhat lower academic achievement than did boys whose mothers stayed home. More recent studies, however, have not replicated this finding *except* in cases in which the mother works more than 40 hours a week (Hoffman, 1989).

Most researchers in this area assume, as I do, that it is not employment per se that produces these effects, but rather that the mother's employment alters the family system in at least two ways. First, having a job—especially a high prestige job or a job she is pleased with—may affect the mother's own view of herself, by increasing her self-esteem or her morale, and thereby changing the way she relates to the rest of the family. For example, a woman who begins working generally acquires more power in the spousal relationship, in part because she now has demonstrable earning power and because she may feel more independent (Blumstein & Schwartz, 1983; Spitze, 1988). Such power or self-esteem also spills over into her interaction with her children, perhaps especially with a daughter.

Second, the mother's employment forces changes in daily routines and in interaction patterns simply because she is not at home for as many hours. Fathers in dual-worker families spend somewhat more time in child-care and household tasks than do fathers with homemaker wives, although it is still true that working mothers do far more of this work than do fathers (e.g., Shelton, 1990). This change in the division of labor may then have an effect on the quality of the parents' interaction with children, as well as altering the role models each parent provides for the child.

These effects of employment on the woman and on her family are not automatic or uniform. The mother's attitude toward her work is an important intervening variable. Numerous studies show that the most negative outcomes are found among children in two subgroups: those with mothers who would prefer to work but are staying at home and those with mothers who dislike their jobs or are unwilling workers (Hoffman, 1984; DeMeis, Hock, & McBride, 1986; Lerner & Galambos, 1986). The most positive outcomes occur when the mother wants to work and works at a job she likes. In such families, the mother's style of child rearing is more likely to be authoritative (Greenberger & Goldberg, 1989).

*Fathers' Employment.* A large chunk of the research on the impact of fathers' work on family life continues to be focused on the reverse effect—what happens when the father does *not* work because of job loss. I have already touched on this set of findings when I talked about the McKenzie family. However, we are also beginning to see research exploring more subtle kinds of connections between the quality of the father's work experience and his family life.

One particularly interesting finding comes from the work of Melvin Kohn and Carmi Schooler (Kohn, 1980; Kohn & Schooler, 1983). They have longitudinal evidence showing that men (or women) whose jobs require higher levels of self-direction and autonomy show increases in intellectual flexibility over time. Routine, highly supervised jobs lead to decreases in intellectual flexibility. Such routine jobs also seem to spill over into family life: Men who work at such jobs place greater emphasis on obedience from their children than is true for more intellectually flexible men. Thus the character of the job the man does affects his way of thinking, particularly his thinking about authority, and he applies that thinking to his interactions with his children.

Other research suggests that some specific jobs seem to have predictably negative spillover into family life. Both police work and military positions, for example, have been found to be linked with higher rates of abuse, family violence, or disruption (Hoffman, 1984). Men with particularly demanding jobs, too, may have less time to spend with their families, which will again alter the interaction patterns.

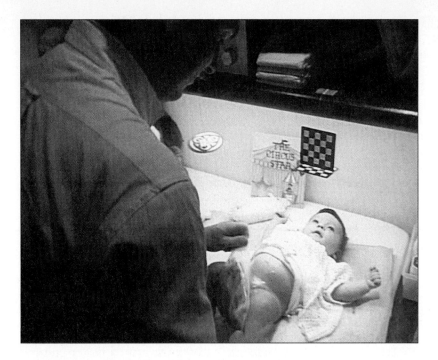

David Kaufman, like Felton Gholston, has done a lot of caregiving for his daughter Michele (whose birth you saw in Chapter 3). Michele may well have a different relationship with her father because he changed so many diapers and spent so much time with her in these early months. But in most families, it is still the mothers who are responsible for managing the household, and they continue to do the majority of housework and child care, whether they work or not. This photo is a video still from the *Childhood* television series (*Source:* ©Thirteen/WNET).

I hope that these few bits illustrate that the kinds of questions psychologists are now asking about parents' employment have become much more subtle and much more oriented to a systems approach. But these questions are also much tougher to answer than the simpler ones we started with.

### Social Support for Parents

A second aspect of the parents' life that affects the family microsystem is the quality of the parents' network of relationships and their satisfaction with the social support they receive from that network. The general point is fairly easy to state: Parents who have access to adequate emotional and physical support—from each other, friends, and family—are able to respond to their children more warmly, more consistently, and with better control (Cochran & Brassard, 1979; Crnic et al., 1983).

The effect of social support on parents is particularly evident when they are experiencing stress of some kind, such as job loss, chronic poverty, teenage childbirth, a temperamentally difficult or handicapped infant, divorce, or even just fatigue. You may recall the discussion in Chapter 9 of a study by Susan Crockenberg (1981) that illustrates the point nicely. She found that temperamentally irritable infants were very likely to end up with an insecure attachment to their mothers only when the mother *lacked* adequate social support. When the mother felt that she had enough support, similarly irritable children were later securely attached, a pattern of results that illustrates the "buffering effect" of social support.

Of course not all "help" from families or friends feels like support. (I'm sure you have all been given unwanted advice from your parents, in-laws, or friends.) The key is not the objective amount of contact or advice received, but the parent's *satisfaction* with the level and quality of the support he or she is experiencing. The moral seems to be that at those times of greatest difficulty or stress—when a new child is born, when a child presents special difficulties, when the family moves or experiences major changes—you most need the emotional and physical support of others. But if you wait until that difficult moment to look around and see who is there to help, you may not find what you need. Social networks must be developed and nurtured over time. But they certainly seem to pay dividends for parents and thus for children.

## Macrosystem Effects: The Impact of the Larger Culture

Families, schools, jobs, social networks—all exist within a larger cultural or subcultural context. By *culture,* I mean "a way of life shared by members of a population" or subpopulation and "the social, technoeconomic, and psychological adaptation worked out in the course of a people's history . . . includ[ing] customs or institutionalized public behaviors, as well as thoughts and emotions that accompany and support those public behaviors" (Ogbu, 1988, p. 11).

By this definition, each of us belongs to several "cultures." We may belong to an ethnic group with a strong cultural tradition. We all belong to a social class group (e.g., working class versus middle class) that defines a cultural niche. We also belong to the larger culture, expressed through such common experiences as television. Each of these cultural experiences will affect the family and thus the child.

### Ethnic Groups

Not all ethnic groups have retained cultural distinctiveness within the American "melting pot." But many groups, particularly those who are physically distinctive, such as African Americans or Asian Americans, have retained or developed characteristic values and family structures that have profound effects on children's development. Again I can give you only examples, but examples should suffice to make the point.

African Americans, in part because of their history of slavery, have developed a distinctly different pattern of family structures than is true for other ethnic groups. A much larger percentage of black children are born to unmarried mothers, divorce is more common, maternal employment is more common, family composition is more fluid, with relatives moving in and out, or friends living with the family for a time—all patterns you can see if you look again at Figure 13.5. Most broadly, African-American households are more likely to involve an *extended family* structure, with three or more genera-

Family systems are strongly influenced by the particular subculture in which they are embedded, including ethnic group cultures. In the United States, an extended family structure, like this one, with three or more generations living together is much more common among blacks than is true in other subgroups.

tions in the same household (Wilson, 1989), very often three generations of women. I mentioned earlier that the presence of the grandmother seems to provide needed social support for the mother in such a family; black children in such three-generation families do better in school and show fewer behavior problems than do black children reared in single-mother households. There is also some evidence that the presence of the grandmother increases the chance that an infant will develop a secure rather than an insecure attachment (Egeland & Sroufe, 1981). Thus the extended family seems to be a successful adaptive strategy for many black families.

African-American families are also characterized by higher rates of authoritarian parenting styles (Dornbusch et al., 1987b). And perhaps as a result, African-American children, on average, achieve less well in school—although there are obviously many other contributing factors to such lower school performance, including family poverty and high stress.

One distinctive feature of Asian-American culture is a set of widely shared values that are reflected in family dynamics and child rearing style. In this subculture, families are generally hierarchically organized with the father as the clear head, with a strong emphasis on the interdependence of family members. One consequence of this is that the child's behavior is seen as a reflection on the family. Asian-American families tend to place strong emphasis on high academic achievement and expect the child to work very hard to reach that goal (Stevenson, 1988; Harrison, et al., 1990). In contrast, in the broader American culture, ability rather than hard work is seen as the key to success—a distinction that leads to very different types of interaction between parents and their children in the two cultural groups. Asian-American mothers spend more time tutoring their children, and have higher standards for the child's achievement. And, indeed, their children do tend to achieve at higher levels in schools (Stevenson, 1988; Slaughter-Defoe et al., 1990).

In both these examples I have only barely skimmed the surface of an increasingly extensive body of research. But I hope this is sufficient to make the general point: Each family (and each school, each day-care center, and microsystem) is embedded within a cultural context that has shaped the internal working models each adult brings to interactions with children. Those differences, in turn, affect the pattern of the child's development.

### Social Class

**social class**
Widely used term to describe broad variations in economic and social positions within society. Four broad groups are most often described: upper class, middle class, working class, and lower class (also called poverty level). For an individual family, the designation is based on the occupations and education of the adults in the household.

Similarly and simultaneously, each family lives within an economic subculture, and these cultural environments—referred to collectively as **social class**—also have profound effects on the functioning of the family microsystem.

Three social classes are usually identified: middle-class, working-class, and poverty-level families. Most of the research contrasts the poverty-level group with everyone else, although there are also differences in values and styles of interaction between working-class and middle-class families (e.g., Luster, Rhoades, & Haas, 1989).

Among many other things, poverty reduces options for parents. They cannot afford prenatal care, so their children are more likely to be born with some sort of disability. When the mother works, she has fewer choices of child care. Such children spend more time in poor quality care, and they shift more from one care arrangement to another. Perhaps because of inadequate access to birth control, poor families are also larger (Broman, Nichols, & Kennedy, 1975), with children more closely spaced, and they live in smaller and less adequate housing. The total environment is more chaotic, more highly stressed, with fewer resources.

Mothers and fathers living in poverty also treat their children quite differently than do mothers and fathers in working-class or middle-class families. They talk to them less, provide fewer age-appropriate toys, spend less time with them in intellectually stimulating activities, are stricter and more physical in their discipline, explaining things less often and less fully (Farran, Haskins & Gallagher, 1980). In the category system shown in Figure 13.3, they are more likely to be authoritarian or neglecting than authoritative (e.g., Dornbusch et al., 1987a).

Some of this pattern of parental behavior is undoubtedly a response to the extraordinary stresses of the poverty environment. Some of the pattern may also be simple imitation of the way these same parents were brought up in their own childhood; some may be a product of ignorance of children's needs. Poor parents with more education, for example, typically talk to their children more and provide more intellectual stimulation than do equally poor parents with lower levels of education. But whatever the cause, children reared in poverty experience not only different physical conditions but quite different interactions with their parents.

Not surprisingly, such children turn out differently, as I have pointed out repeatedly in earlier chapters. Children from poverty environments have higher rates of birth defects and early disabilities, recover less well from early problems, and are more often ill and malnourished throughout their childhood. Typically, they also have lower IQs and move through the sequences of cognitive development described by Piaget more slowly. They do less well in school and are less likely to go on to college (e.g., Patterson et al., 1990).

Such children, in turn, are more likely to be poor as adults, thus continuing the cycle through another generation.

Family poverty thus affects children both directly and indirectly, directly through poorer diet and crowded and chaotic home environments, indirectly through parents' attitudes and child rearing styles. The combined effects, however, are very large indeed.

### A General Cultural Effect: Television

All families, whatever their ethnic or social class group, exist within a larger, shared culture. This culture influences us in a vast number of ways, both obvious and subtle. In modern cultures, one of the most obvious channels of cultural influences is television. And in this case the effect on children is fairly direct.

"By the time American children are 18 years old, they have spent more time watching television than in any other activity except sleep" (Huston et al., 1990). Preschoolers watch TV two to four hours a day (Anderson et al., 1986), and this rate typically rises in the elementary school years and then declines somewhat in adolescence. To be sure, some of the time the child may be playing with toys or talking to Mom while the set is on. Daniel Anderson and his colleagues (1986) find this is especially true of preschool children, who actually watch the TV less than half of the time that the set is on and they are in the room. Still, over the years of childhood, kids spend a *lot* of hours watching the tube.

Just what are children seeing during all of those hours? Preschoolers see more programs designed specifically to be educational or informative, such as *Sesame Street* or *Mr. Rogers' Neighborhood*. As they get older, however, children increasingly watch cartoons, comedies, and adult entertainment programs (Huston et al., 1990). What are the effects of all that exposure?

By the time she is 18, the average child will spend more time watching TV than doing any other single activity except sleeping. It is naive to think that such exposure has no effect on the child, or on the family system.

*Positive, Educational Effects of TV.* Programs specifically designed to be educational, or to teach children positive values, do indeed have demonstrable effects. This is particularly clear among preschoolers, for whom most such programming is designed. Children who watch Sesame Street more regularly, for example, develop larger vocabularies than do children who do not watch or watch less often (Rice et al., 1990), and those who watch programs that emphasize sharing, kindness, and helpfulness, such as *Mr. Rogers' Neighborhood, Sesame Street,* or even *Lassie,* show more kind and helpful behavior (Murray, 1980).

*Effects of TV on Diets.* A less positive effect is on children's diets. The majority of commercials on children's programs are for food, most often cereal (usually sugared cereal), candy, or fast food. Children are affected by these ads, and ask their parents to purchase these advertised foods—a request with which parents often comply (Shonkoff, 1984). No causal link has been established here between ads and poor diet, but we do have some evidence that children's diets contain more highly saturated fat and more sugar than is true for adults' diets. More speculatively, TV viewing by children may also be linked to higher rates of obesity, both because the TV-watching child is less physically active, and because he is often munching on high-sugar or high-fat snacks while watching.

*Television and Aggression.* By far the largest body of research on TV effects has focused on the potential impact of TV on children's aggressiveness, not only because TV programs in the United States are clearly high in aggression, but because any causal relationship between TV violence and children's aggression would be cause for grave concern.

There is no dispute about the high level of violence on TV, nor about the fact that this level has not declined in the past decades despite many public outcries. Nancy Signorielli (1986) estimates that in 1985, situation comedies averaged about two incidents of physical violence per hour, and action/adventure programs averaged eight. The rate is still higher in children's cartoons and would be far higher for all types of programs if verbal aggression were also counted.

It is also important to point out that the "good guys" are just as likely to be violent as the "bad guys," and that violence on most TV programs is rewarded; people who are violent get what they want. In fact, violence is usually portrayed as a successful way of solving problems. Furthermore, the consequences of violence—pain, blood, damage—are seldom shown, so the child is protected from seeing the painful and negative consequences of aggression, and thus receives an unrealistic portrayal of those consequences.

What effect does it have on a child to watch such high rates of violence? Demonstrating a *causal* connection between watching violent TV and behaving violently is rather like demonstrating a causal link between smoking and lung cancer. Unequivocal findings are almost impossible to achieve since the experimental strategy is ruled out: One cannot assign some people randomly to smoke for 30 years, nor assign some children to watch years of violent TV while others watch none.

Several dozen short-term experiments have been done in which some children (or some adults) have been exposed to a few episodes of moderately

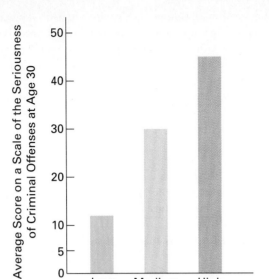

**FIGURE 13.6**

These data from Leonard Eron's 22-year longitudinal study show the relationships between the amount of TV a group of boys watched when they were 8 and the average severity of criminal offenses they had committed by the age of 30. Clearly, those who later showed more criminal behavior had watched more TV as children, but this finding alone does not prove there is a causal link between TV and later violence (*Source:* Eron, 1987, Figure 3, p. 440).

aggressive TV while others watch neutral programs. After this exposure the experimenters then observe the subjects interacting/playing with one another in natural settings and count the number of episodes of aggressive behavior. These studies generally do show that those who watched the aggressive programs show slightly higher rates of actual aggression (e.g., Wood, Wong, & Chachere, 1991). But by and large, as is true of studies of smoking and lung cancer, we must rely on correlational evidence. And as always with correlational evidence, there is a problem of interpretation. For example, children who already behave aggressively may *choose* to watch more TV and more violent TV. And families in which TV is watched a great deal may also be more likely to use patterns of discipline that will foster aggressiveness in the child. One research example will make the point clear.

In his 22-year longitudinal study of aggressiveness from ages 8 to 30, Leonard Eron (1987) has found that the best predictor of a young man's aggressiveness at age 19 was the violence of television programs he watched when he was 8. Twelve years later, when the men were 30, Eron found that the seriousness of criminal behavior was strongly related to the frequency of TV viewing at age 8, as you can see in Figure 13.6.

But Eron also finds that boys who watched a lot of violent television at age 8 were already more highly aggressive with their peers, indicating that aggressive boys choose to watch more violent TV. The advantage of Eron's study is that it is longitudinal, which allows him to sort out some of these alternatives. What he has found is that among the already aggressive 8-year-olds, those who watched the most TV were more delinquent or aggressive as teenagers and as adults (Huesmann, Lagerspetz, & Eron, 1984; Eron, 1987). So the causality runs both ways: "Aggressive children prefer violent television, and the violence on television causes them to be more aggressive" (Eron, 1987, p. 438). Eron goes on to say:

It would, of course, be foolish to maintain that the specific programs these subjects watched at age 8 continued to influence their behavior 22 years later. . . . What was probably important about the programs these children watched were the attitudes and behavioral norms inculcated by continued watching of those and similar programs. In this regard, we can consider continued television violence viewing as rehearsal of aggressive sequences. Thus, one who watches more aggressive sequences on television should have more aggressive strategies more strongly encoded and should respond more aggressively when presented with similar or relevant cues. (1987, p. 440)

Eron's conclusion is buttressed by results from several studies that show that children who watch a lot of violent TV are more likely to see aggression as a good way to solve problems. They are also more fearful and less trusting (Dominck & Greenberg, 1972).

A minority of psychologists is not convinced that the data justify concluding that there is a causal link between violent TV and aggression in children or adults (e.g., Freedman, 1984). But the growing consensus is that such a causal link does indeed exist (e.g., Friedrich-Cofer & Huston, 1986). It is clearly not the only nor even the major cause of aggressiveness among children. But it is significant.

For parents, the clear moral from all the research on TV is that television is an educational medium. Children learn from what they watch—vocabulary words, helpful behaviors, eating habits, and aggressive behaviors and attitudes. The overall content of television—violence and all—may indeed reflect general cultural values. But an individual family can pick and choose among the various cultural messages by controlling what the child watches on TV.

 ## A Reprise: Systems and Interpretations

If you read this chapter one section at a time it is easy to see how each individual factor has an effect on the child's short-term and long-term development. It is much more difficult (for me as well as for you) to get your mind around the idea that all these different elements are part of an intricate system, each part influencing every other part. When a mother returns to work when her baby is 8 months old, the entire system is altered:

- The child is placed in some kind of alternate care.
- The mother has less time with the child.
- The parents' relationship with one another changes, with Dad probably doing more housework and changing more diapers.

And these changes occur within a larger context. It matters whether the mother is working at a job she likes, which is much more likely for an educated middle-class mother than for a poverty-level mother. It matters whether she has adequate social support from family or friends. It matters whether she grew up in a subculture in which women's working was approved or valued, or if her own mother worked. Each of these factors will have an effect on the actual interactions the mother has with her child, and will thus affect the child's developmental pattern.

It is extremely difficult to conceptualize the process in this way, and even harder to design research that allows us to look at all the pieces of the puzzle at the same time. But it is precisely that kind of research we need if we are to be able to understand the full impact of the ecology of the child's development.

# S U M M A R Y

1. To understand children's development we must move beyond examination of the child alone or the mother-child pair. We must examine the total ecological system.

2. A system is understood as being more than the sum of its parts. It is also adaptive to change, and any change in any one part of the system affects every other part.

3. Bronfenbrenner conceives of the child's ecological system as composed of three types of elements: microsystems, such as the family or the school, in which the child is directly involved; exosystems, such as the parent's job, which affect the child indirectly by influencing some aspect of a microsystem; and macrosystems, such as the total culture in which the family exists.

4. Within the family microsystem, several dimensions of parental behavior toward children seem to be particularly significant, including the emotional tone of the family, the method of maintaining control, and the patterns of communication.

5. Families that provide high levels of warmth and affection, compared to those that are more cold or rejecting, have children with more secure attachments and better peer relationships.

6. Families that have clear rules and standards, relatively high levels of expectation or maturity demands, and enforce those rules and expectations consistently, have children with the greatest self-esteem and the greatest competence across a broad range of situations.

7. Children who are talked to frequently, in complex sentences, and who are listened to in turn, not only develop language more rapidly, but also have more positive and less conflicted relationships with their parents.

8. These elements of parental behavior occur in combinations or styles of child rearing. Four such styles, suggested by several theorists, are authoritarian, authoritative, permissive, and neglecting.

9. The authoritative style is high in nurturance, control, communication, and maturity demands; the authoritarian is high in control and maturity demands but low in warmth and communication; the permissive style is high in warmth and low in communication, control, and maturity demands; the neglecting style is low in all dimensions. The authoritative style appears to be the most generally effective for producing confident, competent, independent, and affectionate children. The most negative outcomes are found in neglecting families.

10. The family system is also affected by the child's characteristics, such as temperament, age, gender, and position in the family.

11. Parental characteristics that affect the family system include depression and the parent's own internal working model of attachment.

12. The structure of the family also affects family functioning. The majority of children born today will spend at least a portion of their childhood in one-parent families. Changes in family structure are likely to produce short-term disruption (including often an increase in authoritarian or neglecting child rearing style) before the system adapts to a new form.

13. The majority of infants and preschool children also spend time in a second microsystem, day care. Some children in day care show improvements in cognitive functioning; some also show increases in aggressiveness with peers.

14. Children entering day care in the first year are also at slightly increased risk of an insecure attachment to parents—a finding that has prompted a major debate. The finding is both disturbing and very difficult to interpret.

15. "Effective" schools have many of the same qualities as authoritative parents: They have clear and shared goals, including an emphasis on academic achievement; they have high levels of control without invoking heavy punishment; they are warm; and they have excellent communication, both among staff and between staff and students.

16. A mother's employment affects the family system by changing the mother's self-image, increasing her power, and altering the distribution of labor. The effects on the children are generally positive, especially for girls.

17. Loss of job by a father disrupts the family system, increasing authoritative child rearing, reducing marital satisfaction. Children often show disrupted behavior. The character of a man's job also has an effect on his family interactions.

18. The impact of family change or stress is mitigated by the availability of a sufficient amount of social support from the parents' social network.

19. Ethnic group membership affects a family's structure, values, and specific child rearing practices. African-American families in the United States are more likely to include several generations; Asian-American families place strong emphasis on achievement and hard work.

20. Social class membership also affects family functioning. Poverty-level families have fewer options and experience higher levels of stress without adequate compensating support.

21. The larger culture affects children both directly and indirectly. Television is one obvious direct influence, which can affect specific cognitive gains, diet, and level of aggressiveness.

22. Most research is consistent with the conclusion that there is a causal relationship between viewing TV violence and aggressive behavior.

## CRITICAL THINKING QUESTIONS

1. If you were the parent of an infant under the age of 12 months and you needed to find a day-care setting for your child, what specific things would you be looking for and why?

2. Two examples of the effect of parent characteristics on the family microsystem are given in the text: parental depression and the parents' own internal working models of attachment. What other examples can you think of? How might the family system be affected by each of the characteristics you have listed?

3. One of the arguments made against the conclusion that day care increases the risk of an insecure attachment is that there is "self selection" involved in parents' choice of day care or at-home care. Why is this a problem? What options do researchers have in trying to get around this problem?

## KEY TERMS

authoritarian parental style   One of the three styles described by Baumrind, characterized by high levels of control and maturity demands and low levels of nurturance and communication.

authoritative parental style   One of the three styles described by Baumrind, characterized by high levels of control, nurturance, maturity demands, and communication.

permissive parental style   One of the three styles described by Baumrind, characterized by high levels of nurturance and low levels of control, maturity demands, and communication.

responsiveness   An aspect of parent-child interaction. A responsive parent is sensitive to the child's cues and reacts appropriately, following the child's lead.

restrictiveness   Term used to describe a particular pattern of parental control, involving limitation of the child's movements or options, such as by the use of playpens or harnesses in a young child, or strict rules about play areas or free choices in an older child.

social class   Widely used term to describe broad variations in economic and social positions within society. Four broad groups are most often described: upper class, middle class, working class, and lower class (also called poverty level). For an individual family, the designation is based on the occupations and education of the adults in the household.

warmth versus hostility   The key dimension of emotional tone used to describe family interactions.

## SUGGESTED READINGS

Fox, N., & Fein, G. G. (Eds.), (1990). *Infant day care: The current debate*. Norwood, NJ: Ablex Publishing Corp.

If you want to get the day-care debate from the horses' mouths, this is the source. It includes Belsky's most recent position paper along with a series of commentaries or replies. If nothing else, this book will persuade you that academic arguments are not always dry and dull; there is plenty of heat here!

Pence, A. R. (Ed.), (1988). *Ecological research with children and families. From concepts to methodology*. New York: Teachers College Press.

This volume contains a whole series of papers dealing with various aspects of Bronfenbrenner's ecological approach, both the theory itself and specific studies done to explore parts of the theory.

# PROJECT 17

## Television Aggression

As I suggested earlier, you may want to combine this project with the one at the end of Chapter 10, which involved observing sex-role presentations on TV. If so, you or your instructor may wish to modify the following instructions somewhat. But if you are doing this in isolation, proceed as follows.

Using the definition of violence offered by George Gerbner ("the overt expression of physical force against others or self, or the compelling of action against one's will on pain of being hurt or killed"), select a minimum of four half-hour television programs normally watched by children and count the number of aggressive or violent episodes in each. Extend Gerbner's definition somewhat, however, to count verbal aggression as well as physical aggression.

You may select any four (or more) programs, but I would strongly recommend that you distribute them in the following way:

1. At least one educational television program, such as *Sesame Street* or *Mr. Rogers' Neighborhood.*
2. At least one Saturday morning cartoon. Select at random.
3. At least one early evening adult program that is watched by young children: a family comedy, a western, a crime film, or one of each.

For each program that you watch, record the number of violent episodes, separating the instances of verbal and physical violence.

In thinking or writing about the details of your observations, consider the following questions:

1. What kind of variation in the number of violent episodes is there among the programs that you watched?
2. Are some programs more verbally aggressive and some more physically aggressive?
3. Do the numbers of violent episodes per program correspond to the numbers found by Signorelli?
4. What about the consequences of aggression in the television films? Are those who act violently rewarded or punished? How often do reward and punishment occur?
5. What behaviors other than aggression might a child have learned from watching the programs you viewed? This question is particularly relevant for *Sesame Street* or *Mr. Rogers,* but applies to more traditional entertainment programs as well.
6. In view of the material in this chapter, and your own observations for this project, what rules or limits (if any) would you place on TV viewing for your own child? Why?

# PROJECT 18

## Assessing Information About

## Children from Lay Sources

There is an enormous amount of information about children's development and about the kinds of related social questions I have been dealing with in this chapter in lay sources like magazines and newspapers. For this project you should read and analyze one of the following sets of sources:

- The past year's copies of at least two different women's magazines, e.g., *Ladies' Home Journal, Women's Day, Family Circle.*
- The science section in the Tuesday issue of *The New York Times,* for the past six months.
- The personal health section, or the section on

family and child in the Wednesday issue of *The New York Times* for the past six months.

- Your local newspaper for the same day each week for the past year.
- *Readers' Digest* for the past year.

What articles does your source have on children's development, family functioning, or the impact of society on children? What subjects do they cover? How is scientific evidence reported? Do the articles give you enough information to allow you to judge the quality of the science on which the article is based? If advice is given, does it match advice given in this text? If not, do you have any guesses about why there might be differences?

In writing up your report, be sure to specify what sources you examined, what categories you used in your analysis, and what conclusions you might draw about the quality of information being provided to the lay public about children's development.

# PROJECT 19

## Assessment of Day-care Centers

You will have a far better sense of the variation in quality of day-care centers if you visit some yourself. For this project you should arrange to visit at least three such centers from among those listed in your local phone book. If possible, visit at least one for-profit center and at least one that is run by a charitable organization (e.g., a church-run center) or by an educational institution. Because it would not be reasonable to have every student in your class trying to make private arrangements to visit such centers, your instructor will probably want either to limit the number of students who can select this project or orchestrate the selection and contacting of centers. Be sure to check with your instructor before beginning this project.

### Procedure

You should of course present yourself to the head of each care setting as a student and explain that you are observing as part of a school project. In your own mind, however, you should imagine yourself to be a parent with a young child. You are "shopping" for a care setting for your child.

Arrange to spend at least an hour in each center, sitting as unobtrusively as possible at the side of the room or on the edge of the playground. If you need to walk around so that you can see the full setting, feel free to do so, but don't intrude on the process.

For each center record the following information:

- What is the teacher/child ratio? Does this vary depending on the age of the child?
- How many children are cared for in each group in the center? (Some centers will care for all children as a single "group." Others will have separate rooms for children of different ages. What you want to know is the number of children cared for together.)

In addition, you should rate each center on a series of 5-point scales describing some of the key dimensions listed in Table 13.2, where a score of 1 always means "poor" or "low" and a score of 5 always means "optimum" or "high," as follows:

*Rating*

| | | | | | |
|---|---|---|---|---|---|
| Amount of individual one-on-one contact between adults and children | 1 | 2 | 3 | 4 | 5 |
| Amount of verbal stimulation from adults to children | 1 | 2 | 3 | 4 | 5 |
| Richness and complexity of verbal stimulation from adults to children | 1 | 2 | 3 | 4 | 5 |
| Cleanliness of environment | 1 | 2 | 3 | 4 | 5 |
| Colorfulness of environment | 1 | 2 | 3 | 4 | 5 |
| Adequacy of space | 1 | 2 | 3 | 4 | 5 |
| Summary rating of center | 1 | 2 | 3 | 4 | 5 |

### Analysis

Compare the results for the three centers. If you had a young child, would you be willing to place your child in any of these centers? Be sure to specify why or why not.

Having observed these centers, can you suggest any other criteria that might be helpful for a parent? What sort of research would be needed to determine the importance of any of these features for the child's development?

## PROJECT 20

### Investigation of Day-Care

### Arrangements Available

As any parent can tell you, it is not easy to obtain good information about available day-care options. The purpose of this investigative project is therefore not only to discover as much as possible about the options in your community, but to identify good sources and good strategies for obtaining such information.

### Basic Questions to Answer

- What center care settings are available?
- Who runs the centers? For-profit companies? Churches? Schools? Others?
- How many and what ages of children do these centers accommodate? What are the costs of such center care?

- What is the best way for someone to find out about these care options?
- What family day-care options are available, and how does one locate them? Is there a registry? A licensing process? Are all family day-care providers listed in such registries or licensed?
- Are after-school care settings available as well? Who runs them? How much do they cost?
- Is care available for children in the evenings and at night (as might be needed by a parent who works evenings or night shift)?

### Sources

Much of the information you'll need can be gleaned on the phone or from the phone book. The yellow pages will list day-care centers, usually under "Child care." Data on family day care is much more difficult to come by (both for you and for parents). For information on licensing, especially licensing of home-care or family day-care providers, you will want to talk to local or state government agencies. To locate individual care providers, bulletin boards are often the best data source—those located in places parents are likely to be, such as at colleges or universities, on grocery store bulletin boards, etc. A person or group doing this project will need to sample such sources in some systematic fashion, and then call the providers whose names they find in this way to find out how many children are cared for, what age, for what hours, and what fee is charged.

14

# ATYPICAL DEVELOPMENT

**W**hen Jeffrey was 4, he couldn't walk or talk and spent most of his time in a crib. His parents fed him pureed baby food through a bottle. After six years with a loving foster family, at age 10 Jeffrey is now in a special class in a regular elementary school and is learning to print and read.

Nine-year-old Archie seemed "different from other children even when he started school." Often he was "disoriented" or "distractible." Although he scored in the normal range on an IQ test, he had great difficulty learning to read. Even after several years of special tutoring he could read only by sounding out the words each time; he didn't recognize even familiar words by sight (Cole & Traupmann, 1981).

Janice's parents are worried about her. She's lost weight, even though she's growing fast; she doesn't seem to call up her friends anymore, and is listless and gloomy. This has been going on for about six months now, since about the time she turned 13, and her parents think this is just not normal. They are going to talk to the school counselor about her, and will consider family therapy if it will help.

Vickie is 11. "She absolutely loves to roller-skate, and like any other 11-year-old, she squeals with delight when she's careening down the sidewalk. . . . But Vickie doesn't speak . . . sucks her thumb . . . and has a great deal of trouble making eye contact with others" (*San Francisco Chronicle,* Aug. 21, 1979).

Each of these children is "atypical" in some way. In each, the developmental processes I have been describing in the past 13 chapters haven't quite worked in the normal way. Jeffrey is a Down syndrome child and is mentally retarded. Archie has some kind of learning disability. Janice shows many signs of a clinical depression, while Vickie has a much more serious type of disorder, usually called *autism.*

 ## How Common Are Such Problems?

How common are such problems? Given the critical practical relevance of this question, you'd think that psychologists and epidemiologists would long ago have come to some agreement. But we haven't, in large part because the line between typical and atypical is very much a matter of degree rather than of kind. *Most* children show at least some kinds of "problem behavior" at one time or another. For example, parents report that 10–20 percent of 7-year-olds still wet their beds at least occasionally; 30 percent have nightmares; 20 percent bite their fingernails, and 10 percent swear enough for it to be considered a problem. Another 30 percent or so have temper tantrums (Achenbach & Edelbrock, 1981). Problems like these, especially if they last only a few months, should more properly be considered part of "normal" development. Usually we label a child's development "atypical" or "deviant" only if a problem persists for 6 months or longer, or if the problem is at the extreme end of the continuum for that behavior.

When we count only such extreme or persisting problems, the incidence is much lower—although nonetheless higher than I suspect most of you will have guessed. Table 14.1 gives some current estimates. Some of these numbers are based on extensive data and are widely accepted, such as the 3.5 percent rate of mental retardation. Others are still in some dispute, such as the rate of depression in adolescence. Where the findings are not in agreement, I have given the range of current estimates.

We might also want to combine all these individual rates in some way, to give us some idea of the total percentage of children with one kind of problem or another. Unfortunately this is not a simple matter of addition, since there is a good deal of overlap in the various categories. For example, many children with serious learning disabilities also show an attention deficit disorder or conduct disorders. Still, even if we allow for some overlap, the totals are astonishing: Between 14 and 20 percent of children and teenagers show at least *some* form of significant psychopathology (Brandenburg et al., 1990). If we add in cognitive disorders, the total is at least 20 percent. That is, at least one in five, and maybe as many as one in four children will show at least one form of deviant or abnormal behavior, *at some time in their early years.* The majority of these children will require some type of special help in school, in a

**TABLE 14.1**

*Estimated Incidence of Various Types of Atypical Development*

| Type of Problem | Children 0–18 with That Problem |
|---|---|
| **Psychopathologies:** | |
| Externalizing problems: | |
|    1.   Attention deficit disorder (hyperactivity) | 3 to 5 % |
|    2.   Conduct disorders | 5 to 7 |
|    3.   Arrested by police (delinquency) | 3 |
| Internalizing problems: | |
|    1.   Significant anxiety and fear | 2.5 |
|    2.   Serious or severe depression | |
|        Elementary school-age children | 0.015 |
|        Adolescents | 2 to 10 |
| Psychoses (the most severe pathologies) | 0.08 |
| **Intellectually Atypical Development:** | |
| IQ below 70 (mentally retarded) | 3.5 |
| Speech and language problems, including delayed language, articulation problems, and stuttering | 3.5 |
| Serious learning disability | 4.0 |
| **Physical Problems:** | |
| Autism | 0.04 |
| Significant hearing impairment | 0.5 |
| All other problems, including blindness, cerebral palsy, epilepsy, etc. | 0.2 |

*Sources:* Barkley, 1990; Broman et al., 1987; Brandenberg et al., 1990; Cantwell, 1990; Chalfant, 1989; Kopp & Kaler, 1989; Rutter & Garmezy, 1983; Rutter, 1989; Tuna, 1989.

child guidance clinic, or equivalent. When you think of these figures in terms of the demands this places on the school system and on other social agencies, the prospect is somewhat staggering.

If we are going to meet those needs, we must obviously understand the origins of such atypical patterns. In this chapter I can give you only a glimpse of our current knowledge, but I can at least alert you to the issues and remaining questions about the most common forms of deviance.

## The Psychopathologies of Childhood

### Developmental Psychopathology: A New Approach

developmental psychopathology
A relatively new approach to the study of deviance that emphasizes that normal and abnormal development have common roots, and that pathology can arise from many different pathways or systems.

Our knowledge about the dynamics of deviant development in general, and psychopathology in particular, has been enormously enhanced in the past few years by the emergence of a new theoretical and empirical approach, called **developmental psychopathology,** pioneered by such researchers as Norman Garmezy, Michael Rutter, Dante Cicchetti, Alan Sroufe, and others (e.g., Cicchetti, 1989; Sroufe, 1989; Lewis & Miller, 1990; Rutter & Garmezy, 1983). These theorists have emphasized several key points.

First, normal and abnormal development both emerge from the same basic processes. We cannot understand normal development without studying and understanding abnormal development, and vice versa. The task of a developmental psychopathologist is to uncover the basic processes that underlie both—to see both how they work "correctly" in the case of normal development and to identify the *developmental deviations* and their causes (Sroufe, 1989). Alan Sroufe's studies of the consequences of secure or insecure attachment, which I discussed in chapters 9 and 11, are good examples of research based on such assumptions.

Second, the approach is *developmental.* Theorists in this new tradition are interested in the *pathways* leading to both deviant and normal development, from earliest infancy, through childhood, and into adult life. What are the sequences of experiences that lead to increased risk of depression in adolescence? What is the pathway leading to antisocial behavior or to peer rejection? And what are the factors that may inhibit or exacerbate an early deviation or may turn an initially normal developmental trajectory into a deviant pattern?

One of the potentially exacerbating factors may be the underlying developmental pathway itself. Each age has special tasks, special stresses that interact with the child's ongoing patterns and internal models to produce either normal or deviant behavior. For example, there is growing evidence that rates of depression among young people rise markedly at adolescence. A developmental psychopathologist would ask what is unique about adolescence that would contribute to such heightened depression rates.

He or she would also want to know what special qualities or early experiences a child may bring to the experience of puberty that might increase or decrease the teenager's risk of developing a pathological pattern such as depression. One of the unexpected results of many recent studies of children thought to be "at risk" for particular kinds of problems—such as children reared by depressed parents, children in divorcing families, or abused children—has been the observation that some children seem to be unexpectedly resilient in the face of what appear to be disturbing circumstances. The obverse has also been found repeatedly: Some children seem to be unexpectedly vulnerable, despite what appear to be supportive life circumstances—a phenomenon I mentioned in Chapter 1. Developmental psychopathologists such as Rutter and Garmezy have not only taken the lead in studying such children, they have insisted that these apparent exceptions offer us crucial information about the basic processes of both normal and abnormal development.

Because this is a new way of looking at deviant development, there is not yet an extensive body of research cast in this framework. But this viewpoint can nonetheless help us in examining the origins and manifestations of the array of psychopathologies.

*Types of Problems.* That array has been subdivided in a variety of ways. The cataloging system I find most helpful is to divide the set into two large categories: **externalizing problems** and **internalizing problems.** Externalizing problems, also described as "disturbances of conduct," include attention deficit or hyperactivity, excessive aggressiveness or defiance, and delinquency, in which the deviance is directed outward. Internalizing problems, also called "emotional disturbances," include such patterns as depression, anxiety, or eating disorders, in which the deviance is largely internal to the individual.

**externalizing problems** Category of psychopathologies that includes any deviant behavior primarily directed away from the individual, such as conduct disorders or hyperactivity.

**internalizing problems** A category of psychopathologies in which the deviant behavior is directed inward, including anxiety and depression.

The great majority of children who have been abused, like this child, have long-term emotional or physical problems. But a minority appear to be remarkably resilient—a phenomenon that has greatly interested developmental psychopathologists.

**conduct disorders**
Diagnostic term for individuals showing high levels of aggressive, antisocial, or delinquent behavior.

*Conduct Disorders.*    One obvious type of externalizing problem is, in layman's terms, *delinquency* or *antisocial behavior*. In the most recent revision of the American Psychiatric Association's *Diagnostic and Statistical Manual of Mental Disorders* (called *DSM-III-R*), these patterns are referred to as **conduct disorders.** The category includes such antisocial or aggressive behaviors as argumentativeness, bullying, disobedience, high levels of irritability, and threatening and loud behavior. Children diagnosed as having conduct disorders may also have temper tantrums or may physically or verbally attack others (Achenbach & Edelbrock, 1982). Those labeled as delinquent show any or all of these patterns plus some deliberate violation of the law.

Many antisocial or delinquent behaviors, such as fighting, threatening others, cheating, lying, or stealing, are just as common in 4- and 5-year-olds as they are in adolescence (Achenbach & Edelbrock, 1981). In adolescence, however, these behaviors often become more serious, more lethal, and more consistently displayed. At every age, more boys show this pattern than girls.

Among those who become delinquent, psychologists have found two distinct subgroups. *Socialized-subcultural delinquents* are those who hang around with bad companions, stay out late, have a strong allegiance to their peer group or gang, and may commit various crimes as part of their peer activities. *Unsocialized-psychopathic delinquents* are more often loners and seem to lack conscience or guilt. These are young people who appear to enjoy conflict and who appear to have little trust in anyone.

These two groups of delinquents seem to come from different backgrounds, although there are some common elements. Both seem to have some deficit in *social* cognition; they are less skilled in reading others and in learning the social rules (Schonfeld et al., 1988). Both are likely to have parents (especially fathers) who are also antisocial or criminal. In addition, psychopathic delinquency is characterized by high rates of a variety of different types of criminal acts, often beginning quite early in childhood, and it is found about equally in teenagers from every social class level. Furthermore, while socialized delinquency occurs more frequently in broken homes, this is not true of psychopathic delinquency (Achenbach, 1982).

In contrast, socialized delinquents most often come from poor families living in poor neighborhoods, who provide erratic discipline and little affection to the child (Achenbach, 1982; Moore, Pauker, & Moore, 1984). Families in the same kind of poor neighborhoods whose children do *not* become delinquent are distinguished most by a single ingredient: high levels of maternal love. Young people whose mothers are loving and affectionate toward them are simply far less likely to show delinquency regardless of poverty conditions (Glueck & Glueck, 1972; McCord, McCord, & Zola, 1959).

Conduct disorders and delinquency tend to persist into adulthood, with correlations between aggression in childhood and in early adulthood averaging around .60 or .70—very high correlations for data of this kind (Farrington, 1991). One particularly striking demonstration of continuity of such behavior comes from Leonard Eron's longitudinal study of a group of boys he followed from age 8 to age 30—a study I talked about in both chapters 11 and 13. He found that those who had been most aggressive at age 8 were much more likely to show a variety of antisocial or damaging aggressive behaviors as adults (Eron, 1987) than were the less aggressive 8-year-olds—a finding that has now been replicated in a similar study in England (Farrington, 1991). Consistency over time is particularly likely among boys who showed the earliest and most varied forms of troublemaking (Martin & Hoffman, 1990).

The origins of conduct disorders seem to be strongly environmental. Patterson's research shows that failure in early parental discipline, and/or direct reinforcement for aggressive behavior within the family, are part of the causal chain for many boys (Patterson, Capaldi, & Bank, 1991). But Patterson's work, along with most other current work in this area, shows that a more complex systems model is needed to understand the pathways leading to persistent conduct disorders. To be able to predict which children will develop a conduct disorder we must not only know something about the child's overall environment, we also have to understand the child's temperament, protective factors (like maternal loving affection), and the sustaining conditions, such as lack of social skills or poor peer acceptance (Bates et al., 1991).

Recall from Chapter 11 that children who are rejected by their peers in early elementary school, for whatever reason, are at much higher risk for developing conduct disorders in adolescence or adulthood. And recall that part of the reason for poor peer acceptance seems to lie in a child's social cognition. Rejected children often read social encounters distortedly and quite differently than do socially accepted children. One consequence is that rejected children tend to band together, and such bands or gangs then support one another's antisocial behavior. At each step along this pathway there are diversion possibilities, but the further along one goes, the more persistent the deviant behavior becomes and the less likely it becomes that the individual will be deflected from the deviant pathway by some healing experience.

*Attention Deficit Hyperactivity Disorder.*   A second important category of externalizing psychopathology has been given a rather long-winded name in *DSM-III:* **attention deficit hyperactivity disorder,** often abbreviated as **ADD** or simply as **hyperactivity.** A glance at the diagnostic criteria listed in Table 14.2 on the next page will tell you quickly that the hallmarks of this disorder are physical restlessness and problems with attention—precisely as the label implies (Barkley, 1990).

However, the list in Table 14.2 cannot really convey the quality of behavior of such children. Their interactions with their peers are so distinctively different that strangers need watch videotapes for only a few minutes before they can reliably distinguish between a child diagnosed as hyperactive and a normally behaving child—even when the hyperactive child displays no aggression and the sound is turned off (Henker & Whalen, 1989). The body language is different, the level of activity is different, and the child's social behavior is often inappropriate. About half such children also show conduct disorders, and most do poorly in school, but these seem to be secondary problems, arising from the central hyperactivity and attention deficit.

By definition, this is an early developing disorder. It is also a persistent problem in the majority of children, lasting well into adulthood for at least half of those diagnosed as having this disorder (Henker & Whalen, 1989). But the severity of the long-term problem seems to be strongly influenced by whether or not the child also develops a conduct disorder. It is the combination of hyperactivity and aggressiveness or delinquency that is especially prob-

**attention deficit hyperactivity disorder (ADD)**
The technical term for what is more normally called *hyperactivity,* characterized by short attention span, distractibility, and heightened levels of physical activity.

**hyperactivity**
The common term for *attention deficit hyperactivity disorder.*

**TABLE 14.2**

*Diagnostic Criteria for Attention Deficit Hyperactivity Disorder*

---

The onset of the problem must be before age 7, and the disturbance must last at least 6 months, during which at least 8 of the following are present:

1. Often fidgets with hands or feet or squirms in seat (in adolescents, this may be limited to subjective feelings of restlessness).
2. Has difficulty remaining seated when required to do so.
3. Is easily distracted by extraneous stimuli.
4. Has difficulty awaiting turn in game or group situations.
5. Often blurts out answers to questions before they have been completed.
6. Has difficulty following through on instructions from others (not due to oppositional behavior or failure of comprehension), for example, fails to finish chores.
7. Has difficulty sustaining attention in tasks or play activities.
8. Often shifts from one uncompleted activity to another.
9. Has difficulty playing quietly.
10. Often talks excessively.
11. Often intrudes on or interrupts others, for example, butts into other children's games.
12. Often does not seem to listen to what is being said to him or her.
13. Often loses things necessary for tasks or activities at school or at home (e.g., toys, pencils, books, assignments).
14. Often engages in physically dangerous activities without considering possible consequences (not for purpose of thrill seeking), for example, runs into street without looking.

---

*Source: Diagnostic and statistical manual for mental disorders* (3rd ed., rev.), 1987. Washington, D.C.: American Psychiatric Association, pp. 53–54. Copyright 1987 by the American Psychiatric Association.

lematic (Barkley et al., 1990). You can see one facet of this effect in the results of a recent longitudinal study by Terrie Moffitt (1990) of a group of 434 boys in New Zealand, including all boys born in a particular town over a one-year period. When the boys were 13 they were classed in one of four groups based on the presence or absence of two factors: attention deficit disorder and delinquency. Moffitt then traced backward for each of these groups, looking at scores at earlier ages on measures of antisocial behavior, intelligence, and family adversity. The results for antisocial behavior are in Figure 14.1.

You can see that the boys who, as adolescents, showed *both* hyperactivity and delinquency had been the most antisocial at every earlier age. Hyperactivity that was not accompanied by antisocial behavior at early ages was also not linked to delinquency at 13. Other research tells us that this same group of hyperactive *and* delinquent boys is also the most likely to have continued serious problems in adulthood, including criminal behavior (Weiss & Hechtman, 1986).

Where might hyperactivity come from? Because the pattern begins so early and has such a strong physical component, most clinicians have assumed that this problem has some kind of biological origin. Early research failed to confirm such a biological hypothesis. There was no sign of any overt brain damage and typical neurological tests did not reveal any underlying physical

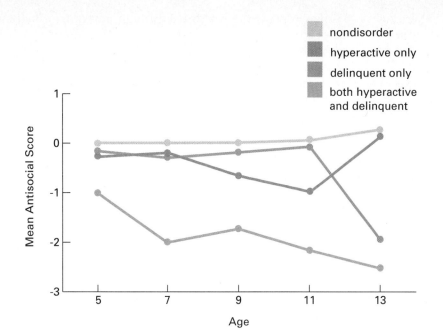

nondisorder

hyperactive only

delinquent only

both hyperactive
and delinquent

FIGURE 14.1

The boys in Moffitt's study
had been studied every two
years from the time they
were 5. When they were 13,
they were assigned to one of
four hyperactivity/delin-
quency categories, and then
Moffitt compared the pathways of these four groups.
Those who were *both* delinquent and hyperactive at 13
had shown markedly higher
rates of antisocial behavior
from the time they were 5,
while those who were only
hyperactive at 13 had been
much less socially deviant at
earlier ages (*Source:* Moffitt,
1990, Figure 1, p. 899).

problem. But the biological hypothesis has gained new support from three
lines of evidence.

First, physicians and psychologists have known for some time that a biological *treatment* is very often effective in reducing or eliminating the deviant
behavior. Many (but not all) hyperactive children treated with a stimulant
medication (most commonly Ritalin) show decreases in demanding, disruptive, and noncompliant behaviors and more attentiveness in the classroom
(Henker & Whalen, 1989).

Second, there is accumulating evidence that a pattern of hyperactivity is
inherited, at least in certain families. About one-fourth of the parents of hyperactive children themselves have a history of hyperactivity (Biederman et
al., 1990). Studies of twins also show a genetic contribution. Among identical
twins, if one is diagnosed as hyperactive the other is highly likely to have the
same diagnosis; among fraternal twins this "concordance rate" is much lower
(Deutsch & Kinsbourne, 1990).

Finally, newer methods of assessing brain function have begun to reveal
differences between the brains of hyperactive and non-hyperactive individuals. In the most widely publicized study, Alan Zametkin and his colleagues
(1990) used Positron-Emission Tomography (PET) scans to examine the glucose (sugar) metabolism in the brains of hyperactive and normal adults. All
the hyperactive adults in this study had reported that they had also been hyperactive as children, and all had at least one offspring with the same diagnosis. Each subject was injected with a concentrated dose of glucose, and then
repeated PET scans showed how the brain metabolized the sugar. Zametkin
found that the hyperactive adults had significantly slower brain metabolism of
the glucose, and this was especially so in the portions of the brain that are
known to be involved in attentiveness and the ability to inhibit inappropriate
responses, such as the prefrontal regions.

Results like this may represent a real breakthrough, not only in helping us to understand the origins of hyperactivity, but conceivably in devising better treatments. At the very least, they greatly strengthen the argument that this disorder has biological origins.

Increased certainty about the origins, however, does not settle all the important questions. From the point of view of developmental psychopathology we also need to understand how such an initially deviant biological pattern affects the child's interactions with parents and peers to produce the common combination of hyperactivity and antisocial behavior. For many hyperactive children, the pathway is doubtless like the one Patterson has described for defiant or aggressive children (Figure 1.3 on p. 14). These kids are just plain hard to raise. Those parents whose child management skills are not up to the task of dealing with the hyperactive toddler's typically higher rates of noncompliance, or those who face major family stresses that prevent them from maintaining good child-care routines, may find that the child's behavior becomes more and more disruptive, which in turn affects the child's emerging social skills adversely. By school age, parent-child conflict is high, as is child-peer conflict. Poor school performance makes it worse by lowering the child's self-esteem. Such children are then on a pathway that is highly likely to lead to continued problems in adolescence and adulthood (Campbell, 1990). In Moffitt's New Zealand study, for example, those boys who eventually showed the combination of hyperactivity and delinquency came from families with much higher levels of stress and fewer resources. The hyperactive boys who did not develop the accompanying antisocial behavior came from families with lower than average levels of stress and more resources.

The more negative and destructive pathway can also sometimes be avoided or ameliorated if the child is given suitable medication early enough in the sequence. The child's behavior then changes, which alters the entire system: Parents become less negative and more effective, and the child learns a different repertoire of social behaviors, a different internal working model.

### *Internalizing Problems: The Example of Depression*

A different set of antecedents and a different pathway are found among children who show internalizing forms of disturbance. The particular form of deviance that has been most often addressed within the framework of developmental psychopathology has been **depression,** so let me use that as an example.

For many years, psychiatrists took the position that significant depression could not occur in children or adolescents. However, there is now abundant evidence that depression is actually quite common in adolescence and occurs at least occasionally among younger children. Both Thomas Achenbach and Michael Rutter, in separate large studies, have found that approximately 10 percent of preadolescent children and 40 percent of adolescents are described by parents or teachers as appearing miserable, unhappy, sad, or depressed (Achenbach & Edelbrock, 1981; Rutter, Tizard, & Whitmore, 1970; 1981). When teenagers themselves are asked about their state of mind the rates of reported depression are lower but still striking: Perhaps one-fifth of them describe moderate to severe levels of depressed mood (Siegel & Griffin, 1984; Gibbs, 1985).

**depression**
A combination of sad mood, sleep and eating disturbances, and difficulty concentrating. When all these symptoms are present it is usually called *clinical depression.*

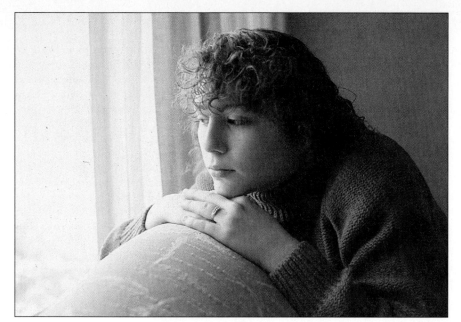

We can't know for sure what has caused this teenager's dejected look, but we do know that depressed moods and significant clinical depressions are considerably more common in the adolescent years than most psychiatrists or psychologists once thought.

When depressive episodes last six months or more and are accompanied by other symptoms such as disturbances of sleeping and eating and difficulty concentrating, they are usually referred to as *clinical depression* or a *depressive disorder.* Recent epidemiological studies indicate that such severe forms of depression are relatively rare in preadolescents but are quite surprisingly common among adolescents. Estimates range widely, as you have already seen in Table 14.1, but at least 2 percent and perhaps as many as 10 percent of teenagers can be diagnosed as clinically depressed (Cantwell, 1990).

Interestingly, among *pre*adolescents, boys are slightly more likely to be described as unhappy or depressed. Among teenagers (as among adults) girls more often report high or chronic levels of depression (e.g., Baron & Perron, 1986). But among both boys and girls, depression is associated with higher rates of suicide or suicide attempts—a phenomenon I've explored in the box on pages 544–545.

The search for the developmental pathways leading to childhood depression begins with the clear finding that children growing up with depressed parents are much more likely than are those growing up with nondepressed parents to develop depression themselves. Of course a genetic factor might be at work here, a possibility supported by at least a few studies of twins and adopted children (Burke & Puig-Antich, 1990). Or we could understand this link between parental and child depression in terms of the changes in the parent-child interaction that are caused by the parent's depression.

I mentioned in Chapter 13 that depressed mothers are much more likely than are non-depressed mothers to have children who are insecurely attached. In particular, their behavior with their child is so nonresponsive that it seems to foster in the child a kind of helpless resignation. Such a sense of helplessness has been found to be strongly related to depression in both adults and adolescents (Dodge, 1990).

## Adolescent Suicide

Suicide is very uncommon in children before adolescence and in children 10 to 14; less than one child in 100,000 commits suicide each year. But among those between 15 and 19, the rate is nine times higher, and this rate has been rising steadily in the United States in past decades (Hawton, 1986).

The likelihood of suicide is about four times as high among adolescent boys as among girls, and nearly twice as high among whites as among nonwhites. Among white teenage boys aged 15 to 19, roughly 15 out of every 100,000 kill themselves each year. In absolute terms, this is less than 1000 deaths per year, far less than the number of deaths by accidents among young people in the same age range. But it does represent an ultimate form of psychopathology.

In contrast, suicide *attempts* are estimated to be three to nine times more common in girls than in boys. Girls, more often than boys, use self-poisoning methods, and these types of suicide attempts are typically less "successful" than are the methods used by males.

It is obviously very difficult to uncover the contributing factors in successful or completed suicides. Researchers and clinicians are forced to rely on second-hand reports by parents or others about the mental state of the suicide before the act. Nonetheless, it does seem clear that some kind of psychopathology is a common ingredient, including but not restricted to depression. Externalizing problems are also common in the histories of completed suicides, as is a family history of psychiatric disorders or suicide or a pattern of drug or alcohol abuse (Hawton, 1986).

But these factors alone are not enough to explain suicidal behavior. David Shaffer and his colleagues, in their recent analysis of the problem of suicide prevention (Shaffer et al., 1988), suggest at least three other elements that seem to be involved. First, there is some triggering stressful event. Studies of suicides suggest that among adolescents, this triggering event is often a disciplinary crisis with the parents or some rejection or humiliation (such as breaking up with a girlfriend or boyfriend or failure in some valued activity). Second,

Of course not all children of depressed parents are themselves depressed. About 60 percent show no abnormality at all. Whether a child moves along a pathway toward depression or not seems to be a function of a whole series of protective or disruptive factors:

- If the parent's depression is short-lived, or is medically treated so that the symptoms are less severe, the child has a much better chance of avoiding depression herself (e.g., Billings & Moos, 1985).
- The more other forms of stress the family experiences in addition to parental depression, such as illness, family arguments, work stress, loss of income, job loss, or marital separation, the more likely the child is to show depressive symptoms.
- The more emotional and logistical support the family receives from others, the less likely the child is to show depressive symptoms (Billings & Moos, 1983).

This set of findings obviously fits nicely into the systems theory framework I described in Chapter 13: The family system can buffer the child from the effects of a parent's depression far more effectively if there are adequate social supports and not too many other stresses.

there is some altered mental state, which might be an attitude of hopelessness or reduced inhibitions from alcohol consumption or rage. Among girls, in particular, a sense of hopelessness seems to be common: a feeling that the world is against them *and they can't do anything about it*. Third, there must be an opportunity—a loaded gun available in the house, a bottle of sleeping pills in the parents' medicine cabinet, or the like.

Attempts to prevent teen suicide have not been notably successful. Despite the fact that most suicides and suicide attempters have displayed significantly deviant behavior for some period of time before the event, most do not find their way to mental health clinics or other professionals, and increasing the availability of such clinics has not proven effective in reducing suicide rates. Reducing access to suicide methods may be more effective, although it is very difficult to accomplish. For example, when the use of natural gas for cooking became prevalent in Great Britain, replacing the high carbon-monoxide-content gas that had been in use be-

fore, suicide rates among all age groups dropped by 25 percent.

Other prevention efforts include programs that provide information to all high-school students about risk factors so that they might recognize a problem in a friend or provide special training in coping skills so that teenagers might be able to find some nonlethal solution to their problems. The few studies that have evaluated such programs do not show that student attitudes had been much changed as a result (Shaffer et al., 1988).

These discouraging results are not likely to change until we know much more about the developmental pathways that lead to this particular form of psychopathology. What makes one teenager particularly vulnerable and another able to resist the temptation? What combination of stressful circumstances is most likely to trigger a suicide attempt, and how do those stressful circumstances interact with the teenager's personal resources? Only when we can answer questions of this kind will we be on the road to understanding teenage suicide.

Having a depressed parent is not at all the only pathway that seems to lead to significant depression in an adolescent. Heightened stresses and life changes in the child's own life—such as parents' divorce, the death of a parent or another loved person, or the father's loss of job (Miller, Birnbaum, & Durbin, 1990)—are other contributing factors. Social isolation from peers in early elementary school has also been linked to internalizing problems at later ages (Hymel et al., 1990). Thus peer *rejection* is associated with externalizing problems and isolation from peers with internalizing problems.

Yet another possible pathway is through lowered self-esteem—a connection you have already encountered in Chapter 10 in Susan Harter's work on self-esteem (Figure 10.6 on p. 388). You will remember that Harter defined self-esteem in terms of the discrepancy between a young person's ideal self or valued goals and her perception of her own qualities and achievements. Harter's studies tell us that a young person who feels she (or he) does not measure up is much more likely to show symptoms of a clinical depression. The fact that depression increases markedly in adolescence makes good sense from this point of view. We know that in adolescence children are much more likely to define themselves and others in *comparative* terms—to judge against some standard or to see themselves as "less than" or "more than" some other person. We also know that at adolescence, appearance becomes highly salient and that a great many teenagers are convinced that they do not live up to the culturally defined appearance standards. Self-esteem thus drops in early adolescence and depression rises.

Harter's work is certainly helpful here, but it does not tell us why some teenagers are likely to see themselves as inadequate, or to respond to such a sense of inadequacy with depression, while others do not. We obviously need to know a good deal more about the pathways that lead a child to be vulnerable to such stresses at puberty or at any other point in life.

### The Role of Short-Term Stress in Psychopathology

I have already mentioned family stress as part of the etiology of several forms of psychopathology, but let me make this connection much more explicit.

James Anthony (1970) has suggested that in any child, a behavior problem emerges only when there is some level of risks or stresses above the threshold that the child can handle. When the level of stress goes down, the child's symptoms often disappear, without any special intervention.

An accumulation of several stresses at the same time seems to have especially consistent negative effects. Michael Rutter (Rutter, Yule, Quinton, Rowlands, Yule, & Berger, 1975), for example, has found that in families in which there was only one stress at a time, such as marital discord, overcrowding, psychiatric disorder in one or both parents, or the death of a family member, the children were no more likely to have behavior problems than were children from families with no stresses. But any *two* stresses occurring together enormously increased the probability that the child would show serious symptoms.

### Vulnerability or Resilience

Yet not all children respond to these stresses in the same way. Some appear to be thrown off their developmental track very easily; others are remarkably resilient in the face of major stress or accumulations of stress. What do we know about these two types of children?

*Vulnerability.* Some kinds of vulnerabilities are inborn: physical abnormalities, prenatal trauma or preterm birth, malnutrition prenatally, or exposure to disease in utero. A tendency toward "difficult" temperament, which also seems to be inborn, is another significant vulnerability, not only because by definition such children have greater difficulty adapting to new experiences, but because their difficult temperament can easily affect the relationships they develop with their parents or other caregivers. Horowitz's model (Figure 1.4 on p. 16), which I have referred to repeatedly, suggests that such initial vulnerabilities greatly increase the likelihood that the child will develop some later problem. Only optimal rearing conditions can protect such children adequately, if then.

Other vulnerabilities emerge during infancy or early childhood. An insecure early attachment, and the internal working model that accompanies it, seems to make a child more vulnerable to stress at later ages, particularly to

Moving is always stressful, and some kids may show some upset at such a time. But the child's distress is much more likely to lead to a behavior problem if he faces several stresses or life changes at the same time. If this family were moving because the parents were also divorcing, for example, the children would be far more likely to show some psychopathology than they would if the move occurred without other upheaval.

stresses that involve losses of or severe strains on key relationships. And any combination of circumstances that results in a high rate of aggressive or disruptive behavior with peers makes a child more vulnerable to a whole variety of stresses in the elementary and high-school years (Masten, 1989).

*Resilience.* Not surprisingly, the picture of the resilient child is essentially the obverse of this. Some aspects of resilience are at least partially inborn, such as high intelligence or an easy temperament. One striking example comes from Emmy Werner's 20-year longitudinal study of all the infants born on the Hawaiian island of Kauai in 1955 (Werner, 1986). She found that among those children reared in poverty environments, the most resilient were likely to have been perceived as "easy" or "good-natured" as babies and were more often first-borns. High intelligence also seems to confer some protection to the child, presumably because such children have a richer or more flexible array of intellectual resources to apply to any problem they encounter.

For example, Ann Masten (1989), in her studies of resilience among school-age children, has found that when children have experienced a year with high levels of life stresses, those with higher IQ are much less likely to respond to that stress by becoming disruptive. Masten speculates that this may be due to the fact that such children, who have a history of successful problem solving, have a stronger sense of self-efficacy, which may help to make them more resistant to frustration.

Early experiences obviously contribute as well: Resilient children are more likely to have formed a secure early attachment with a parent or with some other adult (Rutter, 1971, 1978c). They are also likely to have good peer relationship skills, including low levels of disruptive or aggressive behavior and high levels of supportive and helpful behavior. And like vulnerability, resilience is cumulative.

Overall, it seems very helpful to think of each child as possessing some inborn *vulnerabilities;* some *protective factors,* such as a secure attachment or a middle-class family; and some *resources,* such as higher IQ, an array of friends, or good peer interaction skills. How any given child will react to stressful life circumstances or to normal developmental passages like school entry or adolescence will depend on the relative weight of these three elements.

### Developmental Psychopathology: A Reprise

I think that even this brief foray into research on psychopathology makes clear that a developmental framework is the only one that is going to yield real understanding of the emergence of deviant behavior. Even for a disorder such as hyperactivity, which appears to have major biological causes, the severity and persistence of the disorder can be best understood in terms of the child's cumulative patterns of interaction and the child's own internal models of relationships. Investigations of children's responses to specific risk factors, and of resilience and vulnerability, are one window on the process, since they allow us to look closely at processes that are normally so gradual or subtle that they defy observation (Masten, 1989). Ultimately, studies within this emerging tradition of developmental psychopathology may end up telling us as much about normal development as about the emergence of pathology.

## Intellectually Atypical Development

If you go back and look at Table 14.1 you'll see that the various forms of intellectually atypical development rank right up there with the various psychopathologies in frequency of occurrence among children. Roughly one in ten children shows at least some form of intellectual abnormality.

### Mental Retardation

*Definitions and Labels.* Of all the atypical children listed in Table 14.1, probably those studied most thoroughly are those labeled **mentally retarded.** Not too many decades ago, when mental ability was thought of as a fixed trait, mental subnormality was considered a kind of incurable disease. Labels like "idiot" or "feeble-minded" were used. But this older view has changed a great deal. Not only have the old negative labels been changed, but the basic assumptions about the nature of retardation have changed too.

Mental retardation is now viewed as a *symptom* rather than as a disease. And like any symptom, it can change. A child's life circumstances or health may change, and his or her IQ score may go up or down as a result. Remember from Chapter 6 that *many* children's IQ test scores vary as much as 30 or 40 points over childhood. Of course many children with low IQ scores will continue to function at a low level throughout life. However, it is important for educators and parents to understand that a single low IQ score need not invariably mean that the child will function at that level forever. For many children, improvement is possible.

*The Assessment of Retardation.* A child is normally designated as retarded if he tests below an IQ of 70 *and* has significant problems in **adaptive be-**

**mentally retarded**
Those children who show a pattern of low IQ, poor adaptive behavior, and poor skills in information processing.

**adaptive behavior**
An aspect of a child's functioning often considered in diagnosing mental retardation. Can the child adapt to the tasks of everyday life?

**havior**—such as an inability to dress or eat alone or a problem getting along with others or adjusting to the demands of a regular school classroom. As Thomas Achenbach (1982) says, "Children doing well in school are unlikely to be considered retarded no matter what their IQ scores" (p. 214).

Low IQ scores are customarily divided up into several ranges, with different labels attached to each, as you can see in Table 14.3. I've given both the labels used by psychologists and those that may be more common in the school system. (There are no school system labels for children with IQs below about 35 since schools very rarely deal with children functioning at this level.)

The farther down the IQ scale you go, the fewer children there are. More than 80 percent of all children with IQs below 70 are in the "mild" range; only about 2 percent of the low IQ youngsters (perhaps 3500 children in the United States) are profoundly retarded (Broman et al., 1987).

*Cognitive Functioning in Retarded Children.* In recent years there has been a great deal of fascinating research on thinking and information processing in retarded children, much of it by Ann Brown, Joseph Campione, and their colleagues (Campione, Brown, & Ferrara, 1982; DeLoache & Brown, 1987). As you may recall from Chapter 7, this research has been a significant ingredient in the emerging information processing approach to studying cognitive development in children. Brown and Campione find that retarded children:

1. Think and react more slowly.
2. Require much more complete and repeated instruction to learn new information or a new strategy. In comparison, normal IQ children may discover a strategy for themselves, or profit from incomplete instruction.
3. Do not generalize or transfer something they have learned in one situation to a new problem or task. They thus appear to lack those "executive" functions that enable older, higher IQ children (or adults) to compare a new problem to familiar ones, or to scan through a repertoire of strategies until they find one that works.

*TABLE 14.3*

*IQ Scores and Labels for Children Classed as Retarded*

| Approximate IQ Score Range | Label Used by Psychologists | Label Used in Schools |
| --- | --- | --- |
| 68–83 | Borderline retarded | (No special label) |
| 52–67 | Mildly retarded | Educable mentally retarded (EMR) (also called "mildly mentally handicapped") |
| 36–51 | Moderately retarded | Trainable mentally retarded (or "moderately mentally handicapped") |
| 19–35 | Severely retarded | (No special label) |
| Below 19 | Profoundly retarded | (No special label) |

On simple tasks, retarded children learn in ways and at rates that are similar to younger normal IQ children. The more significant deficit lies in higher-order processing. These children *can* learn, but they do so more slowly and require far more exhaustive and task-specific instruction.

*Causes of Retardation.*    About 15 to 25 percent of mentally retarded children have some identifiable physical problem (Broman et al., 1987). **Chromosomal anomalies** such as Down syndrome or the Fragile X syndrome, are one major culprit. As Scarr and Kidd (1983) put it, "Having too much or too little [genetic material] will affect intelligence, always for the worse" (p. 380). A child may also inherit a specific disease or **inborn errors of metabolism,** which can cause retardation if not treated. The best known such inherited metabolism error is phenylketonuria (PKU), described in Chapter 2.

Still a third physical cause of retardation is **brain damage,** which can result from a large number of causes, including prenatal maternal diseases like syphilis or cytomegalovirus, malnutrition, or alcoholism. Brain damage may also occur during delivery or by some accident after birth (e.g., auto accidents or falling out of a treehouse onto your head).

The remaining three-fourths of retarded children show no signs of any brain damage or other physical disorder. In almost all cases, such children come from families in which the parents have low IQs, there is serious family

**chromosomal anomalies**
Any chromosomal pattern in which the individual has too many or too few chromosomes. Almost always associated with mental retardation.

**inborn errors of metabolism**
Any one of several inherited disorders (including PKU) resulting in an inability to digest or metabolize particular enzymes. Some such disorders are associated with retardation if not treated.

**brain damage**
Some injury to the brain, either during prenatal development or later, that results in improper functioning of the brain.

About 15 percent of mentally retarded children have clear physical abnormalities, such as Down syndrome.

disorganization, mental illness in the parents, or emotional or cognitive deprivation in the home. Often both genetic and environmental influences operate simultaneously.

As I pointed out in Chapter 6, psychologists generally agree that at least half of the variation in IQ scores is attributable to genetic differences. So it is reasonable to assume that many children who score below 70 on an IQ test simply have a less advantageous genetic endowment.

Heredity, however, is clearly not the only ingredient in this soup. When children from families like the ones I have just described are placed from early infancy in special enrichment programs, such as the Ramey program I talked about in Chapter 6, their IQs can be significantly increased. We also know that many children with some kind of physical disorder at birth, such as low birth weight or cytomegalovirus, turn out to have normal IQs when they are reared in enriched or supportive environments (Haskins, 1986).

Large scale studies have now shown quite conclusively that these several causes of retardation are not distributed evenly across the range of low IQ scores. The lower the IQ, the higher the likelihood that there is some clear physical problem. This is especially clear from the results of the Collaborative Perinatal Project, which involved nearly 40,000 children studied from before birth to age 7—the same study from which I drew the findings showed in Figure 6.3 on p. 226. In this sample, 71.7 percent of white and 53.9 percent of black children with IQs below 50 had some kind of major disorder of the central nervous system. In contrast, among those with IQs between 50 and 70, only 13.9 percent of whites and 6.3 percent of blacks had any identifiable physical abnormality (Broman et al., 1987). You can see this difference even more vividly in another set of data from the same study. In a fair number of cases the sample happened to include several children from the same family. So Broman and her colleagues were able to look at the IQs of the *siblings* of the retarded children. The results for white children are in Figure 14.2.

The siblings of those with IQs below 50 had normal IQs; none was retarded. But the siblings of the mildly retarded were themselves fairly likely to be mildly retarded as well, a pattern that suggests quite different causes in the two groups. Among black children, whose family circumstances are more like-

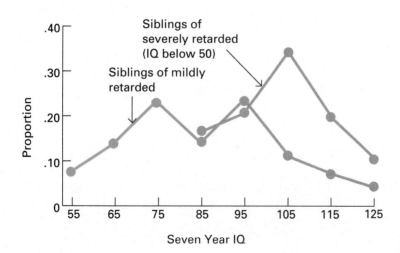

*FIGURE 14.2*

Findings like these suggest that there are really two different kinds of retarded individuals: those whose retardation is caused by physical abnormalities, who usually have IQs below 50, and those whose retardation arises from cultural-familial origins, usually with IQs from 50 to 70. Siblings of the latter group are *also* more likely to be retarded (*Source:* Broman et al., 1987, Figure 10-1, p. 269).

ly to be impoverished, the results are less clear. Siblings in both groups are about equally likely to be retarded themselves. But the findings as a whole strongly support the conclusion that there are really two distinct types of retardation, each with its own set of causes.

One implication of this conclusion is that interventions like Ramey's are more likely to be effective in preventing or ameliorating milder retardation with familial-cultural causes. This is not to say that we should ignore environmental enrichment or specific early training for children with physically caused retardation. Greater breadth of experience would enrich their lives and might help to bring their level of functioning closer to the top end of their "reaction range." But even massive early interventions are not likely to make most brain damaged or genetically anomalous children intellectually normal (Spiker, 1990).

### Learning Disorders

*Definitions and Labels.*   Some children with normal IQs and essentially good adaptive functioning nonetheless have difficulty learning to read, write, or do arithmetic. By most estimates, roughly 4 percent of children in the United States have serious problems of this type, while another 14 to 15 percent have more moderate difficulties. These figures should be taken with a good deal of caution, since there is still a great deal of confusion and dispute about just how learning disorders ought to be defined or what they should be called.

Schools most often describe such children as having a **learning disability,** or **specific learning disability,** often abbreviated **LD** or **SLD.** But you will also hear the term **dyslexia** (literally, "nonreading"). Each of these labels was originally intended to be applied only if a child's problem is confined to a fairly narrow range of tasks, but all three are used more broadly and fuzzily than that, often describing almost any kind of problem with reading, writing, or arithmetic.

The labeling problem has been seriously confounded by the fact that school districts receive federal funds to pay for special education for children identified as learning disabled, but do *not* receive such funds for education of children labeled as "slow learners." Thus there is a strong financial incentive to label almost any kind of delayed or slow learning a "learning disability."

Further, even setting aside this political consideration, the designation of a learning disability is basically a *residual* diagnosis. It is the label we apply to a child who does not learn some school task, who is *not* generally retarded, and does *not* show emotional disturbance or a hearing or vision problem. Thus we can say what learning disability is *not*; what we cannot say is what it *is*.

The identification problem is complicated still further by the fact that among children identified as LD, the specific form of the problem varies widely. Some display difficulties in reading only, some have trouble with reading and spelling (such as the boy whose writing sample is shown in Figure 14.3), and others have more difficulty with arithmetic. Given such variability, we shouldn't be surprised that the search for causes has been fraught with difficulties. As Sylvia Farnham-Diggory says (1986), "We are trying to find out what's wrong with children whom we won't be able to accurately identify until after we know what's wrong with them" (p. 153).

**learning disability (LD)**
See *specific learning disability*.

**specific learning disability (SLD)**
Term commonly used to describe a disorder in understanding or processing language or symbols.

**dyslexia**
A form of specific learning disability in which the individual has difficulty with reading.

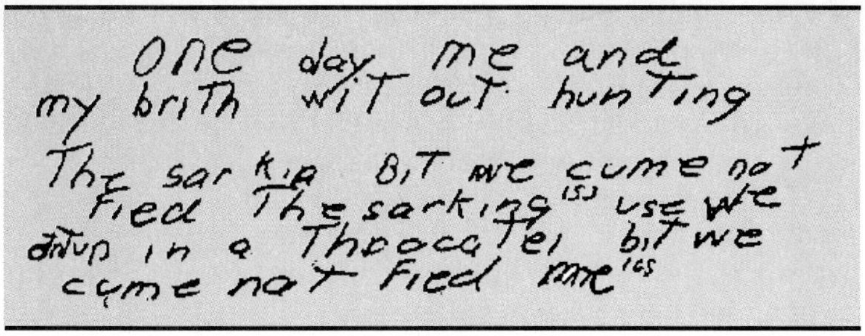
One day me and
my brith wiT out hunting
The sar kin BiT we cume not
Fied The sarking 153 use we
drup in a Throcatel biT we
cume not Fied me 165

*FIGURE 14.3*

This is part of a story written by 13-year-old Luke, who has a significant and persisting learning disability. The little numbers next to some of the words are Luke's notes on how many words he has written—a relevant issue since he was supposed to write a 200-word story (*Source:* Farnham-Diggory, 1978, p. 61).

*Possible Causes.* The most commonly offered explanation of specific learning disability—particularly by educators and parents—is that the child suffers from some kind of "minimal brain damage." Such children rarely show any outward signs of major brain damage, but perhaps there is some lesser damage, undetected by normal neurological tests, which nonetheless shows itself when the child is faced with a complex task like learning to read (Hynd & Semrud-Clikeman, 1989). This hypothesis avoids the stigma of mental retardation, and makes it clear that no one is at fault for the child's problem. But you should understand that this is a *hypothesis* and not a fact. Most children with specific learning disabilities do *not* show any signs of brain damage on standard tests.

A weaker version of this hypothesis, not unlike current ideas about the origin of hyperactivity, is that learning disabled children suffer not from brain *damage* but from brain *dysfunction;* that is, their brains simply do not work in quite the same way as do normal children's. One theory has been that the right and left hemispheres of LD children's brains do not participate in various kinds of cognitive processing in the same way as is true for normal learning children. Another theory has been that parts of the LD child's brain may simply mature more slowly, thus giving a kind of unevenness of skill (Brumback & Staton, 1983). But the evidence for both of these theories is weak, at best (Obrzut, Hynd, & Boliek, 1986).

Another possibility, as you may recall from the discussion of reading in Chapter 8, is that reading disability reflects a more general problem with language. There is now abundant evidence that children with reading problems are likely to have one or both of two kinds of language problems: (1) a relative lack of awareness of the individual sounds in words, and (2) relative lack of knowledge of the semantic and grammatical structure of language (e.g., Vellutino & Scanlon, 1987; Pennington et al., 1990; Scarborough, 1990). Further, researchers have shown that providing training in hearing individual sounds improves the reading skills of poor readers. Of course findings like these do not tell us why a child might have such language deficits in the first place; it is still possible that the source of the problem does indeed lie in the brain. But this research does tell us what type of intervention may be most successful.

I want to emphasize that the continuing confusion and disagreement about identification and explanation of learning disability occurs despite thousands of research studies and a great deal of theorizing by thoughtful and capable people. Not surprisingly, the uncertainty at the theoretical level is reflected in confusion at the practical level. Children are labeled "learning disabled" and assigned to special classes, but whether the child will be helped by a particular type of intervention program will depend on whether that specific program is (1) any good and (2) happens to match his or her type of disability. Remediation does seem to be possible, but it is *not* simple, and a program that works well for one child may not work at all for another. Of course this is not good news for parents whose child may be having difficulty with some aspect of schooling, whose only recourse is trial and error and eternal vigilance. But it reflects the disordered state of our knowledge.

### Giftedness

For parents whose children lie at the other end of the intellectual continuum, the academically or artistically gifted, the problem is almost as tough. Finding good programs for such children is a continuing dilemma. Let me give you an extreme example, a child named Michael described by Halbert Robinson (1981):

> When Michael was 2 years and 3 months old, the family visited our laboratory. At that time, they described a youngster who had begun speaking at age 5 months and by 6 months had exhibited a vocabulary of more than 50 words. He started to read English when he was 13 months old. In our laboratory he spoke five languages and could read in three of them. He understood addition, subtraction, multiplication, division, and square root, and he was fascinated by a broad range of scientific constructs. He loved to make puns, frequently bilingual ones. (p. 63)

Michael's IQ on the Stanford Binet was in excess of 180 at age 2; two years later, when Michael was 4 1/2, he performed on the test like a 12-year-old, and was listed as having an IQ beyond 220.

#### Definitions and Labels.
We can certainly all agree that Michael is astonishingly gifted. The term *gifted,* though, is used in almost as many ways as is the phrase *learning disabled* (Sternberg & Davidson, 1986). **Giftedness** includes those with exceptional specific talents, such as musical or artistic skills, or specific mathematical or spatial ability, as well as those with very high IQs. This broadening of the definition of giftedness has gained support in recent years, so that now I think there is agreement that giftedness is not a single thing. There are many kinds of exceptional ability, each of which may reflect unusual speed or efficiency with one or another type of cognitive function.

Within school systems, however, by far the most common definition of giftedness is based on IQ test scores. Robinson suggested that it may be useful to divide the group of high IQ children into two sets, the "garden variety gifted," with high IQs (perhaps 130 to 150) but without extraordinary ability in any one area, and the "highly gifted" (like Michael) with extremely high IQ scores and/or remarkable skill in one or more areas. These two groups of children may have quite different experiences at home and in school.

**giftedness**
Normally defined in terms of very high IQ (above 140 or 150), but may also be defined in terms of remarkable skill in one or more specific areas, such as mathematics or memory.

*Cognitive and Social Functioning in Gifted Children.*　Just as retarded children show slower and less efficient information processing, the gifted show extremely rapid and flexible strategies. They learn quickly and transfer that learning broadly (Sternberg & Davidson, 1985). Further, they seem to have unusually good *metacognitive* skills: They know what they know and what they don't know, and they make good use of cognitive plans (Jackson & Butterfield, 1986).

Whether such advanced intellectual abilities transfer to *social* situations is not so well established. Many parents are concerned about placing their gifted child in a higher grade because of fears that the child will not be able to cope socially; others have assumed that rapid development in one area should be linked to rapid development in all areas.

One famous and remarkable early study of gifted children, by Lewis Terman, pointed to the latter conclusion. Terman selected about 1500 children with high IQs from the California school system in the 1920s. These children—now adults in their 60s, 70s, and even 80s—have been followed regularly throughout their lives (Terman, 1925; Terman & Oden, 1947, 1959; Sears & Barbee, 1977; Sears, 1977). Terman found that the gifted children he studied were better off than their less gifted classmates in many ways other than school performance. They were healthier and interested in many more things such as hobbies and games. Both the boys and the girls in this study went on to complete many more years of education than was typical of children of their era and had successful careers as adults.

More recent research has painted a less uniformly rosy picture. On the plus side are studies that show that the self-esteem of gifted children is as high or higher than that of less bright children. There is also no sign that gifted children have higher rates of depression or other psychopathology. Furthermore, good social development seems to be just as likely for gifted children who have been accelerated through school as for those who have been kept with their age mates but provided with "enrichment" programs (Janos & Robinson, 1985; Robinson & Janos, 1986).

Such optimism about the social robustness of gifted children may have to be tempered somewhat, however, in the case of the highly gifted subgroup, such as those with IQs above 180. These children are *so* different from their peers that they are likely to be seen as strange or disturbing. And these highly gifted children do show higher rates of emotional problems than do non-gifted children (Janos & Robinson, 1985). Also on the negative side of the ledger is the fact that many gifted children are so bored by school that they drop out. One observer (Fetterman, 1990) estimates that as many as *30 percent* of all school dropouts would test as gifted. Given the fact that there is little sign of social maladjustment associated with grade-skipping, it seems to make very good sense to encourage accelerated schooling, if only to help ward off terminal boredom for the gifted child.

*Causes of Giftedness.*　In most cases, giftedness seems to result from some combination of "good genes" and an enriched or supportive environment. There is little doubt that heredity plays a very significant causal role. Much of the evidence I reviewed in Chapter 6 supports such a conclusion. However, even if such good genes are equally distributed across social class groups, environmental enrichment is not, and a bright child in a middle-class family is more likely to receive that extra boost of stimulation that turns "bright" into "gifted." We know, for example, that children who test at a gifted level are much more likely to come from middle-class families. Terman found this, and so have more recent researchers (Freeman, 1981; Robinson, 1981). Some of this difference may well be genetic variance in disguise, since very bright parents not only pass on more advantageous genes, they are also likely to be well educated and financially well-off. But studies like the French adoption study I reported in Chapter 6 (Table 6.3 on p. 226) show clearly that family enrichment has an independent effect.

What we do not know is whether there is any specific kind of stimulation or enrichment that is likely to foster giftedness. There is little evidence from the research on the families of gifted children to show that these mothers and fathers are "pushing" their children. In fact, the parents nearly always express surprise at their children's remarkable achievements (Robinson, 1981). What seems most likely is that a generally supportive and enriched environment helps to move each child toward the upper end of his or her intellectual reaction range, whatever that range may be.

 ## Physically Atypical Development

The last group of children I want to talk about, albeit briefly, are those with some clear physical problem, such as blindness, deafness, or autism. Many of these children experience very substantial difficulties in everyday living; most require special schooling or special facilities in school; many require continued assistance throughout life. Still, with improved instruction, intervention, and mechanical assistance, many children with significant physical handicaps are leading full and satisfying lives.

### Autism

**autism**
A severe form of disorder including emotional unresponsiveness and social cognition deficiencies. Present from birth, it appears to have a physical origin.

For many decades **autism** was listed in the catalog of psychopathologies, but virtually all current researchers and theorists now agree that autism is a "neurodevelopmental disorder."

Given the symptoms of autism, it is perhaps not so surprising that earlier psychologists thought that the source of the problem lay in the child's social relationships (Howlin & Yule, 1990): Autistic children show severe impairments both in their ability to relate socially and in their ability to communicate. They are generally unresponsive to the people around them, do not cuddle or respond to affection as do normal infants, do not make eye contact in a normal way, and show significant retardation of language. Some do not develop language at all; others develop vocabularies and may even use two-word sentences, but they may develop their own words for common objects. They also typically show resistance to new events or to any changes in their environment, and often show ritualistic or repetitive behavior, such as twirling or finger movements.

We are still a long way from understanding the specific cause of this pattern of deviance, but all the evidence I know of points to one clear conclusion: Children are *born* with this disorder. It is not caused by poor parenting.

Understandably, parents rearing autistic children may *become* less responsive or affectionate with the child, but there is no indication that parents are causing this problem by inadequate child rearing.

Where we have made real progress is in understanding the nature of the deficit itself. There is now growing evidence, particularly from the work of a group of British researchers such as Alan Leslie (e.g., Leslie & Frith, 1988) and Simon Baron-Cohen (1989, 1991), that autistic children largely lack the capacity for perspective taking or for social cognition in general. As infants they are unskilled at discriminating others' emotions. As toddlers they show little pretend play, lack skill in the pragmatics of language, and do not adapt their language to the listener's needs. They do very poorly at all the tasks that tap the emerging "theory of mind" at age 4 or 5, including tests of the understanding of appearance/reality distinction and of false belief.

You can readily see that a deficit of this kind would lead not only to strange social relationships, but to odd language behavior as well. From the earliest months, a normal child's language has a social and communicative intent. However, this communicative process requires that the child have at least some rudimentary ability to take another's perspective or an awareness that there *is* another there with whom to communicate. Autistic children seem to lack some of this ability or awareness.

Whether this lack arises from some flawed genetic information, or from some damage prenatally, we do not know. Perhaps it is both. Genetic disorders are implicated from the finding that as many as 10 percent of autistic children are now diagnosed with the Fragile X chromosomal anomaly (Rutter & Garmezy, 1983), and from the fact that siblings of autistic children are 50 times as likely to show this disorder as is true in the general population. Those siblings who do not show the full syndrome frequently show lesser problems, such as learning disabilities or lower IQ (Howlin & Yule, 1990). Prenatal damage is suggested by the common pattern of epileptic seizures among autistic children. Whatever the specific origin, the evidence jointly points to the conclusion that autism reflects different brain functions of some kind.

### Blindness and Hearing Impairments

*The Deaf Child.*   Most children with hearing loss can function adequately with the assistance of a hearing aid. In fact, many physicians are now fitting **hearing-impaired** children with hearing aids during infancy rather than waiting until the child is of preschool age. The situation is quite different, though, for the profoundly deaf—the child whose hearing loss is so severe that even with mechanical assistance his comprehension of sound, especially language, is significantly reduced. I raised some of the issues connected with the early rearing of deaf children in the box on pages 324–325 in Chapter 8, and you may want to go back and reread that section at this stage. The basic point is that if the emphasis is placed exclusively on *oral* language, the deaf child has much more difficulty developing either speech or reading than if the child is taught sign language, lip reading, and oral language at the same time (e.g., Greenberg, Calderon, & Kusche, 1984; Moores, 1985). Even with such good early training, however, most deaf children require special schooling.

**hearing-impaired**
The phrase currently used in place of "hard of hearing" to describe children or adults with significant hearing loss.

This autistic child, who makes little eye contact and shows few signs of friendliness or involvement with others, is being treated in an operant conditioning program. When he shows desired behavior, he is quickly reinforced with some food he likes. Such programs have been moderately successful in improving the social behavior of autistic children, which helps make their behavior more acceptable but does not make much of a dent in the basic cognitive deficit.

*The Blind Child.*　If I had asked you, before you read this chapter, to tell me which would be worse, to have been blind or deaf from birth, most of you would have said it would be far worse to be blind. Yet from the point of view of the child's ability to function in most normal settings, blindness is a smaller handicap. The blind child can learn to read (with Braille), can talk with others, can listen to a teacher, and so on. Because of this greater academic potential, and because of the enormous role of language in forming and maintaining social relationships, there are more options open to the blind adult than to most deaf adults.

Still, there are obviously important limitations for the blind and important potential pitfalls. One of these lies in the earliest relationship with the parent, which is discussed in the box on page 560. Later relationships may be impaired for the same reasons.

*Interventions with the Blind and the Deaf.*　The long-term consequences of either deafness or blindness seem to depend in part on how early intervention is begun. Early intervention that involves the family seems especially helpful, which is precisely what we should expect from the perspective of developmental psychopathology. If family interventions such as Fraiberg's can help families to form secure attachments and to establish more optimum patterns of interaction, then some of the second- and third-order effects of the child's physical problem may be avoided.

## Sex Differences in Atypical Development

One of the most fascinating facts about atypical development is that virtually all forms of disorder are more common in boys than in girls. I've put some of the comparisons in Table 14.4, but even this list does not convey the extent of the difference. With very few exceptions, studies of the impact of environmental stresses show that boys are more adversely affected. This is true in studies of divorce, parental discord, parental mental illness, parental

Terry Berrigan, like his children (and his wife), is deaf. Yet his children are learning a language at the appropriate time: sign language. Research on the deaf suggests that deaf children of deaf parents actually do better academically and linguistically than do deaf children of hearing parents, in large part because they have learned language at the normal time. This photo is a video still from the *Childhood* television series (*Source:* ©Thirteen/WNET).

job loss, and many others. In these situations boys are more likely to show disturbed behavior or a decline in school performance, or some other indication of a problem (Zaslow & Hayes, 1986).

How are we to explain differences like this? One possibility is that the double X chromosome gives the girl protection from some forms of inherited disorder or anomaly. Girls are obviously less likely to inherit any recessive disease that is carried on the sex chromosomes. We also have some hints that

**TABLE 14.4**

*Sex Differences in the Incidence of Atypical Development*

| Type of Problem | Approximate Ratio of Males to Females |
|---|---|
| **Psychopathologies:** | |
| Attention deficit hyperactivity disorder | 2:1 |
| Conduct disorders including delinquency | 5:1 |
| Anxiety and depression: preadolescence | 1:1 |
| Anxiety and depression: adolescence | 1:2 |
| Estimated number of all children with all diagnoses seen in psychiatric clinics | 2:1 |
| **Intellectual atypical development:** | |
| Mental retardation | 3:2 |
| Learning disabilities | 3:2 |
| **Physical problems:** | |
| Blindness or significant visual problems | 1:1 |
| Hearing impairment | 5:4 |
| Autism | 3:1 |

*Sources:* Achenbach, 1982; Anthony, 1970; Eme, 1979; Rutter & Garmezy, 1983; Rutter, 1989.

## Basic Attachments Between Blind Babies and Their Mothers

In Chapter 11, I mentioned Selma Fraiberg's work with blind infants as part of the discussion of the parent's attachment to the child. Because Fraiberg's work is so fascinating, I want to expand on that brief discussion here.

Fraiberg (1974, 1975, 1977) found that blind babies begin to smile at about the same age as sighted babies (about 4 weeks) but that they smile less often. At about 2 months, when the sighted baby begins to smile regularly at the sight of the parent's face, the blind baby's smiles become less and less frequent. The blind infant's smile is also less intense, more fleeting.

The other thing blind babies don't do is enter into mutual gaze. They don't look right at their parents, and everything we know about parents' responses to their babies underlines the importance of mutual gaze for the parents' feeling of attachment to the baby. When the blind baby does not look, the parents often report feeling "rejected."

Generally, the facial expressions of the blind infant are muted and sober. Many observers, including parents, conclude that the baby is depressed or indifferent.

Fraiberg found that most of the mothers of the blind babies in her studies gradually withdrew from their infants. They provided the needed physical care, but they stopped playing with the baby, and gave up trying to elicit smiles or other social interactions. They often said they didn't "love" this baby.

Fortunately, it's possible to solve this particular problem. Fraiberg found that these mothers could be helped to form a strong bond with their infant if they could be shown how to "read" the baby's other signals. The blind child's face may be sober and relatively expressionless, but her hands and body move a lot and express a great deal. When the child *stops* moving when you come into the room, this means she is listening to your footsteps. Or she may move her hands when she hears your voice rather than smiling as a sighted child would do.

When parents of blind children learn to respond to these alternative "attachment behaviors" in their babies, then the mutuality of the relationship can be reestablished. And when this happens, and the parents are able to provide more varied stimulation, blind children develop more normal behavior in other ways. In particular, they don't show the "blindisms" so often observed in blind youngsters, such as rocking, sucking, head banging, and other repetitive actions.

there may be a gene on the X chromosome that affects the individual's ability to respond effectively to stress. Since girls have two X chromosomes they are less likely to suffer from any disorder in that gene. If this explanation is valid, then the appropriate conclusion is not that *all* boys are more vulnerable, but that *more* boys than girls have some minor neurological dysfunction or high vulnerability to stressors of various kinds.

Two other physiological factors may also be important, each potentially explaining one or two of the differences listed in Table 14.4. Hormonal differences are one obvious alternative. Since it is possible to construct an argument for the role of male hormones in aggressive behavior (see Chapter 11), it is not a very great leap to the hypothesis that the higher incidence of conduct disorders among boys may also be related in some way to hormone variations. Another possibility is that since girls of any age are more physically mature than are boys of the same age, they may have more resources with which to meet various problems.

Experiences after birth may also contribute to the differing rates of deviance. One hypothesis is that adults are simply more tolerant of disruptive or difficult behavior in boys than in girls. By this argument, both boys and girls initially respond similarly to stressful situations, but boys learn early that various forms of acting-out, tantrums, or defiance are tolerated or not punished severely. Girls learn to inhibit these responses—perhaps even to internalize them—because adults respond quite differently to them. There is not much research that tests such a hypothesis, but there are at least fragments of support (e.g., Eme, 1979).

Whatever the explanation—and none of the existing explanations seems very satisfactory to me—it is nonetheless extremely interesting that girls do seem to be less vulnerable, less likely to show virtually any type of atypical development.

## The Impact of an Atypical Child on the Family

Throughout this chapter I have touched on the impact of the child's problem on the family. In some instances of course, deficiencies or inadequacies in the family are part of the *cause* of the child's atypical development. But whether the original cause lies in the family or not, once a child does show some form of deviant development the family is inevitably affected, often adversely.

*Grief.*   One of the first reactions is often a form of grief, almost as if the child had died. This reaction makes sense if you think about the fact that the *fantasy* "perfect child" did die or was never born. The parents grieve for the "child that never will be," which is expressed poignantly here by one parent:

> I wept for the perfect baby I had lost, for the sunsets he would never see, for the 4-year-old who would never be able to play outside unsupervised. (Featherstone, 1980, p. 26)

As with other forms of grief, denial, depression, and anger are all natural elements. For many parents, there is also some guilt (e.g., "If only I hadn't had those drinks at that party while I was pregnant").

In some cases this process may result in an emotional rejection of the infant, aggravated by the difficulty that many atypical infants have in entering fully into the mutually adaptive parent-child process. Such rejection seems to be particularly common when the marital relationship is conflicted, or when the family lacks adequate social support (Howard, 1978)—a pattern that makes good sense if we think of the family unit as a system rather than merely as a set of dyadic interactions.

*Adaptation by the Family.*   Once the initial shock and grief is dealt with as well as it can be, the family must work toward an ongoing adaptive system with the atypical child. There are often massive financial burdens, problems of finding appropriate schooling, and endless daily adjustments to the child's special needs.

I look at the people down the street. Their kids are 15 and 18 and now they can just get in the car and take off when they want to . . . and then I think, "When will that happen for us? We'll always have to be thinking of Christopher. . . . We'll never have that freedom." (Featherstone, 1980, p. 17)

The system that evolves most often leaves the mother primarily in charge of the atypical child; with physically handicapped children especially, fathers seem quite often to withdraw from interaction with or care of the disabled child (Bristol, Gallagher, & Schopler, 1988). This is not a general withdrawal of the father from the family system, since such fathers continue to be involved with their other children. Not surprisingly, mothers left with this responsibility are likely to respond with depression, although depression is also common among fathers. Parents of atypical children are also more likely to have low self-esteem and have lower feelings of personal competence (Howard, 1978). Where the marital relationship was poor before the birth of the child, the presence of the handicapped child in the family system seems to increase the likelihood of further discord. However, there is no consistent indication that having an atypical child results in an average increase in marital disharmony or risk of divorce (Howard, 1978; Longo & Bond, 1984).

The fact that many (even most) parents manage to adapt effectively to the presence of an atypical child is testimony to the devotion and immense effort expended. But there is no evading the fact that rearing such a child is very hard work, and that it strains the family system in ways that rearing a normal child does not.

 ## A Final Point

As a final point, I think it is crucial to state clearly what has been implicit throughout this chapter: Children whose development is atypical in some respect are much more *like* normally developing children in other respects than they are unlike them. Blind, deaf, and retarded children all form attachments in much the same way that physically and mentally normal children do (e.g., Lederberg & Mobly, 1990). Children with conduct disorders go through the same sequences of cognitive development that more adjusted children show. It is very easy, when dealing with an atypical child, to be overwhelmed by the sense of differentness. But as Sroufe and Rutter and the other developmental psychopathologists are beginning to say so persuasively, the same basic processes are involved.

# S U M M A R Y

1. Approximately 20 percent of all children in the United States will need some form of special assistance because of atypical development at some time in childhood or adolescence.

2. Studies of psychopathology are more and more being cast in a *developmental* framework, with emphasis on the complex pathways that lead to deviance or normality. Such a framework also emphasizes the importance of the child's own resilience or vulnerability to stresses.

3. Psychopathologies can be divided into two groups: externalizing and internalizing.

4. One type of externalizing problem is conduct disorders, including excess aggressiveness and delinquency. Such disorders are more common among children from poverty-level families, particularly those with erratic discipline or lack of love. A subset of delinquents, however, called *unsocialized* or *psychopathic* delinquents, come from all social classes and are marked by early onset and broad range of delinquent activities.

5. Attention deficit hyperactivity disorder is another type of externalizing problem, beginning in early childhood and typically persisting. The problems encountered by such children are much more acute if they also display conduct disorders.

6. Hyperactivity appears to have an initial biological cause, but deviant patterns are aggravated or ameliorated by subsequent experience.

7. Depression is one form of internalizing problem. It becomes much more common in adolescence, as does suicide. Depressed youngsters are more likely to have a family history of parental depression or to have developed low self-esteem.

8. Family stress, or stress experienced directly by the child, especially multiple simultaneous stresses, exacerbate any existing or underlying tendency toward pathology.

9. Children with inborn vulnerabilities (difficult temperament or physical problems), few protective factors, and few resources are more likely to respond to stressful circumstances with pathology.

10. Children with mental retardation, normally defined as IQ below 70 combined with significant problems of adaptation, show slower development and more immature or less efficient forms of information processing strategies.

11.  Two groups of retarded can be identified: those with clear physical abnormalities, overrepresented among the severely retarded, and those without physical abnormalities but with low IQ parents and/or deprived environments, who are overrepresented among the mildly retarded.

12.  Children with serious specific learning disabilities make up roughly 4 percent of the school population. Such problems *may* be caused by undetected minimal brain damage, uneven or slow brain development, or other kinds of physical dysfunction. Or, they may reflect broader language or cognitive deficits, or both.

13.  *Gifted* is a term applied to children with very high IQs, or to those with unusual creativity or special skill. Their information processing is unusually flexible and generalized. Socially they appear to be generally well adjusted, except for the small group of unusually highly gifted students.

14.  Physical problems uncomplicated by retardation represent much smaller percentages of children. Included are autism, blindness, and deafness.

15.  Boys show almost all forms of atypical development more often than girls do. This may reflect genetic differences, hormone differences, or differences in cultural expectations.

16.  Families with atypical children experience chronically heightened stress and demands for adaptation. This is frequently accompanied by depression or other disturbance in the parents.

# CRITICAL THINKING QUESTIONS

1.  What kind of impact is an atypical child likely to have on the family system? Are there any general effects, regardless of the nature of the child's "atypicalness"? Or does the impact depend entirely on the child's specific problem? What else might affect the response of the family system to the child's abnormality? How could you study this?

2.  Suppose you had a daughter who had been tested as having an IQ above 150. Your school offers you a choice of either a special enrichment program in which the normal curriculum is supplemented with additional classes or acceleration to a higher grade. Given the information in this chapter, which would you choose and why?

3.  A decade or so ago there was a lot of interest in the possibility that we might be able to screen infants or toddlers for existing or *potential* problems, so that intervention could begin very early. In practical terms, such screening has turned out to be extremely difficult, but there are also moral and ethical questions involved. What do you think those questions might be? And why has accurate screening been so difficult to devise?

## KEY TERMS

**adaptive behavior** An aspect of a child's functioning often considered in diagnosing mental retardation. Can the child adapt to the tasks of everyday life?

**attention deficit hyperactivity disorder (ADD)** The technical term for what is more normally called *hyperactivity,* characterized by short attention span, distractibility, and heightened levels of physical activity.

**autism** A severe form of disorder including emotional unresponsiveness and significant social cognition deficiencies. Present from birth, it appears to have a physical origin.

**brain damage** Some injury to the brain, either during prenatal development or later, that results in improper functioning of the brain.

**chromosomal anomalies** Any chromosomal pattern in which the individual has too many or too few chromosomes. Almost always associated with mental retardation.

**conduct disorders** Diagnostic term for individuals showing high levels of aggressive, antisocial, or delinquent behavior.

**depression** A combination of sad mood, sleep and eating disturbances, and difficulty concentrating. When all these symptoms are present it is usually called *clinical depression.*

**developmental psychopathology** A relatively new approach to the study of deviance that emphasizes that normal and abnormal development have common roots and that pathology can arise from many different pathways or systems.

**dyslexia** A form of specific learning disability in which the individual has difficulty with reading.

**externalizing problems** Category of psychopathologies that includes any deviant behavior primarily directed away from the individual, such as conduct disorders or hyperactivity.

**giftedness** Normally defined in terms of very high IQ (above 140 or 150), but may also be defined in terms of remarkable skill in one or more specific areas, such as mathematics or memory.

**hearing-impaired** The phrase currently used in place of "hard of hearing" to describe children or adults with significant hearing loss.

**hyperactivity** The common term for *attention deficit hyperactivity disorder.*

**inborn errors of metabolism** Any one of several inherited disorders (including PKU) resulting in an inability to digest or metabolize particular enzymes. Some such disorders are associated with retardation if not treated.

**internalizing problems** A category of psychopathologies in which the deviant behavior is directed inward, including anxiety and depression.

**learning disability (LD)** See *specific learning disability.*

**mentally retarded** Those children who show a pattern of low IQ, poor adaptive behavior, and poor skills in information processing.

**specific learning disability (SLD)** Term commonly used to describe a disorder in understanding or processing language or symbols.

## SUGGESTED READINGS

Edgerton, R. B. (1979) *Mental retardation.* Cambridge, Mass: Harvard University Press.

  Not absolutely current, but this is an excellent, brief, readable introduction to the whole topic.

Lewis, M., & Miller, S. M. (Eds.) (1990). *Handbook of developmental psychopathology.* New York: Plenum.

This book was very definitely written for fellow professionals, so it is often very dense and technical. But if you are interested in any aspect of psychopathology, this is absolutely the most current and valuable source.

Vellutino, F. R. (1987). Dyslexia. *Scientific American, 256*, 34–41.

> Vellutino is one of the most articulate spokesmen for the view that learning disabilities are fundamentally problems of language, not problems of perception as had been assumed for many years. In this brief paper he lays out his case.

Any of the following three books on teenage suicide might also be helpful:

Griffin, M., & Felsenthal, C. (1983). *A cry for help.* New York: Doubleday.

Klagsbrun, F. (1984). *Too young to die: Youth and suicide.* Pocket Books.

Peck, M. L. (1985). *Youth Suicide.* New York: Springer.

# PROJECT 21

## Investigating Programs for the

## Gifted and Retarded

School systems vary widely in the kind of programs they have available for gifted and retarded students. If your school is located in an area with several different school systems within reasonable proximity, it would be interesting to compare at least two districts.

### Basic Questions to Ask

- How are students identified as "gifted" or "retarded" in a given school district? Is the placement based on IQ test scores alone? If so, what is the cut-off? And why is a student tested in the first place? Teacher reference? Parent request?

- Once selected, what programs are available for each group? Special classes? Enrichment programs offered within regular classes? Part-day programs?
- Is there a district policy regarding grade-skipping for gifted children? Are gifted children allowed or encouraged to take classes at local colleges or universities?
- Are there special programs for children with unusual talents, such as musical or mathematical or artistic talent?
- Once a child is selected into a special program, is there any procedure for that child to leave the program at a later date? For example, can a child identified as retarded later be retested and be placed full-time in a regular classroom?

Most of what you will need to find out will have to come from officials in the school district offices. Written policies may exist; if not, you will need to arrange to interview either the district superintendent, a suitable sub-official, or a public information officer. Information may also be available through parent organizations, such as those devoted to promoting the welfare of retarded children.

15

# PUTTING IT ALL TOGETHER: THE DEVELOPING CHILD

I remember the sense of unfairness I had in a world history class in high school when, after I had carefully learned all the kings of England in order, and all the kings of France in order, I was asked to say who had been king of France at the same time as Henry VIII had ruled England. I hadn't the foggiest idea; we had never studied it that way.

You may have something of the same feeling about the developing child. For example, you know a good deal about the sequence of development of language and about the sequential changes in cognitive functioning and in attachments, but you probably have not hooked these different developmental sequences to one another very well. If I asked you now what was happening at the same time that the child first used two-word sentences, you would probably have a difficult time answering. So what I want to do in this brief chapter is to put the child back together a bit by looking at the things that are happening simultaneously.

I also want to take another look at some of the key questions I raised in Chapter 1, in light of all the information you have read since then: What are the major influences on development? Does the timing of experience matter? What is the nature of developmental change? Are there stages or sequences? And how best can we understand individual differences in development?

## Ages and Stages

Several concepts are helpful in looking at simultaneous developments at each of several ages or stages.

### Transitions and Consolidations

My reading of the process of development is that it is made up of a series of alternating periods of rapid growth (accompanied by disruption or disequilibrium) and periods of relative calm or consolidation. Change is obviously going on all the time, from conception throughout childhood (and adulthood). However, I am persuaded that there are particular times when the changes pile up or when one central change affects the whole system. This might be a major physiological development like puberty, a change from one status to another or one role to another like the shift from preschooler to school child, or a highly significant cognitive change, such as the beginning of symbol usage at about 18 months. These "pileups" of change often seem to result in the child's coming "unglued" for a while. The old patterns of relationships, thinking, and talking don't work very well any more and it takes a while to work out new patterns.

Erikson frequently uses the word *dilemma* to label these periods. Klaus Riegel (1975) once suggested the phrase *developmental leaps,* which conveys nicely the sense of excitement and blooming opportunity that often accompany these pivotal periods. I'm going to use the more pedestrian term *transition* to describe the times of change or upheaval, and the term *consolidation* to describe the in-between times, when change is more gradual.

### Systems

Putting all the parts and pieces together also requires thinking in systems theory terms—a set of ideas I discussed most fully in Chapter 13. Not only must we think of the family as a system embedded within the larger social system; we must also think of the child as a system. A change in any one part influences all the others. So a rapid increase of skill in one area, like language, demands adaptation in all parts of the developing system. Because the child can now talk, her social interactions change, her thinking changes, no doubt even her nervous system changes, as new synapses are created and redundant ones are pruned. Similarly, the child's early attachment may affect her cognitive development by altering the way she approaches new situations; the hormonal changes of puberty affect parent-child relations. With these thoughts in mind, let us look at several age periods.

### From Birth to 18 Months

Figure 15.1 on the next page shows the various changes during the first 18 months of life. The rows of the figure roughly correspond to the chapters of this book; what we need to do now is read up and down the figure rather than just across the rows. You will see in the figure that I have subdivided this period into three sections, the first from birth to about age 2 months, the second from 2 to about 8 months, and the final one from 8 to 18 months.

*From Birth to 2 Months.*   The overriding impression one gets of the newborn infant—despite the child's remarkable skills and capacities—is that the neonate is very much on automatic pilot. There seem to be built-in rules or schemas that govern the way the infant looks, listens, explores the world, and relates to others. One of the really remarkable things about these rules, as I pointed out in Chapters 3 and 5, is how well designed they are to lead both the child and the caregivers into the "dance" of interaction and attachment. Think of an infant being breast-fed. The baby has the needed rooting, sucking, and swallowing reflexes to take in the milk; in this position, the mother's face is at just about the optimum distance from the baby's eyes for the infant's best focusing. The mother's facial features, particularly her eyes and mouth, are just the sort of visual stimuli that the baby is most likely to look at. The baby is particularly sensitive to the range of sounds of the human voice, particularly the upper register, so the higher-pitched, lilting voice most mothers use is easily heard by the infant. During breast-feeding the release of a hormone called *cortisol* in the mother also has the effect of relaxing her and making her more alert to the baby's signals. Both the adult and the infant are thus primed to interact with each other.

*From 2 Months to 8 Months.*   Sometime around 6 to 8 weeks, however, there are several changes in the system. Both because of the child's early explorations and because of simple physical maturation, the child's actions and perceptual examinations of the world seem to switch into a different

FIGURE 15.1

This brief summary chart shows some of the simultaneous developments during infancy as well as some of the possible transitions or sub-periods. For each transition point, I have outlined the one development or set of developments that seems to me to be pivotal.

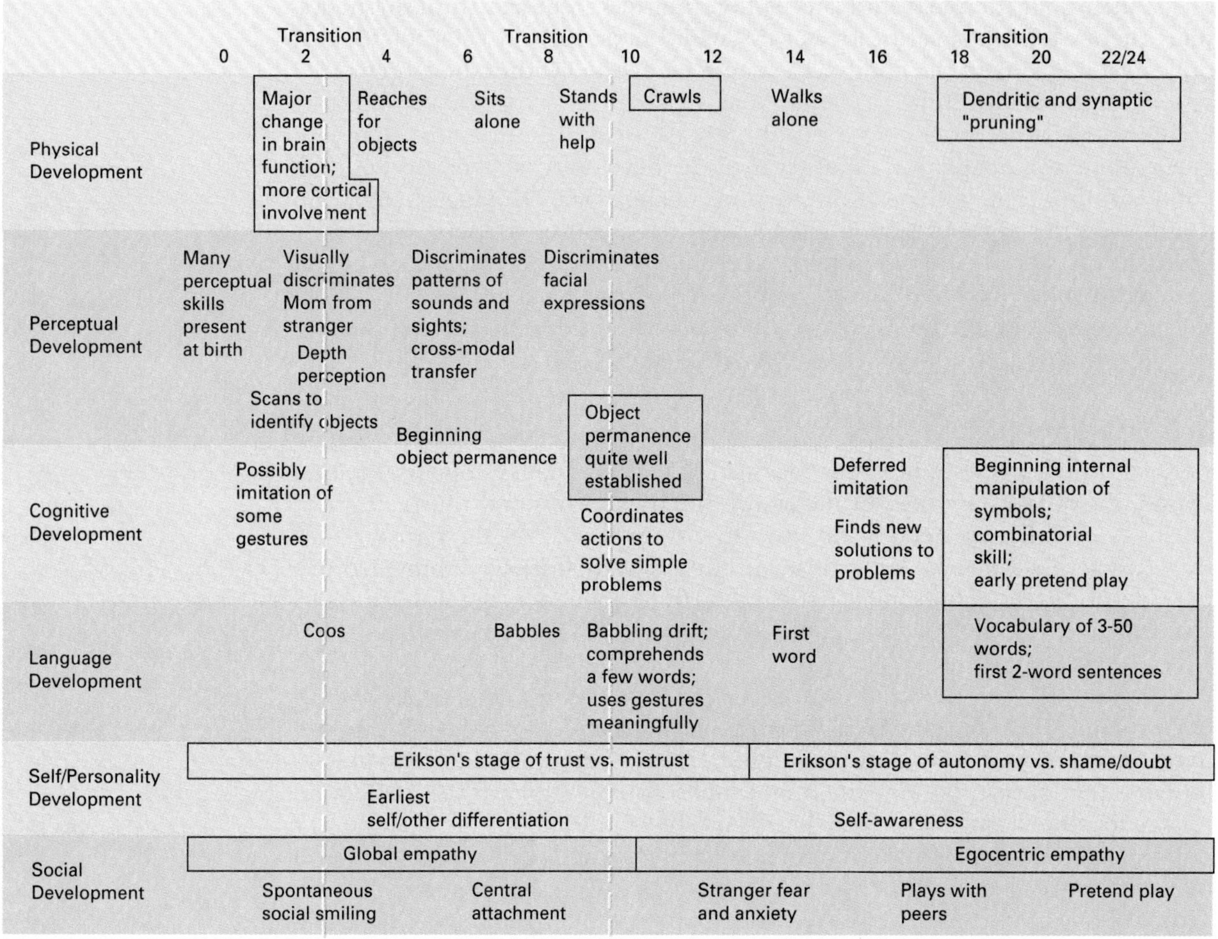

| | Transition 0 2 4 | | Transition 6 8 10 12 | | 14 16 | Transition 18 20 22/24 |
|---|---|---|---|---|---|---|
| **Physical Development** | Major change in brain function; more cortical involvement | Reaches for objects | Sits alone — Stands with help — Crawls | | Walks alone | Dendritic and synaptic "pruning" |
| **Perceptual Development** | Many perceptual skills present at birth | Visually discriminates Mom from stranger; Depth perception; Scans to identify objects | Discriminates patterns of sounds and sights; cross-modal transfer | Discriminates facial expressions | | |
| **Cognitive Development** | | Possibly imitation of some gestures | Beginning object permanence | Object permanence quite well established; Coordinates actions to solve simple problems | Deferred imitation; Finds new solutions to problems | Beginning internal manipulation of symbols; combinatorial skill; early pretend play |
| **Language Development** | | Coos | Babbles | Babbling drift; comprehends a few words; uses gestures meaningfully | First word | Vocabulary of 3-50 words; first 2-word sentences |
| **Self/Personality Development** | Erikson's stage of trust vs. mistrust | Earliest self/other differentiation | | | Erikson's stage of autonomy vs. shame/doubt; Self-awareness | |
| **Social Development** | Global empathy | Spontaneous social smiling | Central attachment | | Egocentric empathy; Stranger fear and anxiety | Plays with peers — Pretend play |

gear—one controlled much more by the cortex and less by the primitive portions of the brain. The child now looks at objects differently, apparently trying to identify what an object is rather than merely where it is. At this age she also begins to reliably discriminate one face from another, smiles more, sleeps through the night, and generally becomes a more responsive creature.

Because of these changes in the baby, and also because it takes most mothers six to eight weeks to recover physically from the delivery (and for the mother and father jointly to begin to adjust to the immense change in their routine), there are big changes in mother-infant interaction patterns as well at this time. The need for routine caretaking continues, of course (ah, the joys of diapers!), but as the child stays awake for longer periods, smiles, and makes eye contact more, exchanges between parent and child become more playful and more smoothly paced.

Once this transition has occurred there seems to be a brief period of consolidation lasting perhaps six months. Of course change continues during this consolidation period. There are gradual neurological changes, with the motor and perceptual areas of the cortex continuing to develop. The child's perceptual skills also show rapid change in these months, with depth perception, clear cross-modal transfer, and identification of patterns of sounds and sights all emerging. The child is also exploring the world around him in an active way, which seems essential for the development of the object concept and other changes in cognitive skill.

*From 8 to 18 Months.*    This brief consolidation comes to an end somewhere between 7 and 9 months, when a series of changes creates a new disequilibrium, a new transition. First, the baby forms a strong central attachment, followed a few months later by separation anxiety and fear of strangers. Second, the infant begins to move around independently (albeit very slowly and haltingly at first). Third, communication between infant and parents changes substantially, as the baby begins to use meaningful gestures, to engage in imitative gestural games, and to comprehend individual words. Fourth, object permanence is grasped at a new level; the baby now understands that objects and people can continue to exist even when they are out of sight. At the very least, these changes profoundly alter the parent-child interactive system, requiring the establishment of a new equilibrium, a new consolidation.

This new system seems to endure with only minor adjustments until 18 or 20 months of age, at which point the child's language and cognitive development appear to take another major leap forward—a set of changes I'll describe shortly.

So far, all I have done is to talk about simultaneous developments in various sub-periods. That's helpful for grasping the totality of development, but doesn't help much with understanding the system of interactions or the causal connections between the various changes. So let me speculate a bit about some possible causal links.

Of the two transitions I've described, the one at 2 months seems easiest to explain. The key causal event seems to be a set of changes in the nervous system, although we are obviously a long way from describing those changes in detail or connecting such neurological changes to observed changes in the baby's behavior.

The transition at roughly 8 months is more difficult. In particular, we do not know whether the confluence of these several changes is merely accidental—a series of separate lines of development that happen to come together at roughly this age—or whether there are one or two key underlying changes that are causally involved in all. We know that dendritic and synaptic development and myelinization of nerves are all still occurring rapidly at these ages and are obviously implicated in many of the changes we see at this transition, but neurological changes are continuous. So far as we know there is no special set of neurological changes that occurs at about 8 months that would account for something like the shift in pre-language skills.

Another candidate for a key change is the development of object permanence, which may rest on basic neurological change but which is also a prod-

The set of cognitive and social changes we see in babies of about 8–10 months—about the age of this charmer—seems to result in a whole new level of interaction with Dads and Moms. (Anyone who thinks there is little joy in parenthood should look at this picture.)

uct of 8 months of assimilation of and accommodation to basic experience. Once achieved, however, such an understanding may have a variety of repercussions, including stimulating the development of a basic attachment. Although as I have pointed out several times, the research examining such a link directly has not provided strong support for this hypothesis.

We might also turn this hypothesis on its head and argue that the attachment may cause or affect the child's cognitive development. For example, there is a growing body of evidence showing that securely attached toddlers explore more freely, persist longer in their play, and develop the object concept more rapidly (e.g., Bates et al, 1982). Such a connection might exist because the securely attached child is simply more comfortable exploring the world around him from the safe base of his secure person. He thus has a richer and more varied set of experiences, which may stimulate more rapid cognitive development. Alternatively, it may be that the sort of parent-child interaction that fosters a secure attachment is *also* optimal for fostering language and cognitive skill. In particular, *contingent responsiveness* from the parent seems to be a positive ingredient in the emergence not only of a secure attachment but of more rapid cognitive growth.

These speculations about causal links between parallel changes may give you some sense of the issues with which physiologists and psychologists are now grappling. But don't let them obscure the basic point: Whatever causes this set of changes, once they have occurred the system is now remarkably different than it was even a few months before. The baby has now become a far more active participant within her environment and in her interactions with the people around her. Inevitably, this enriches and widens the range of her experience and demands new types of behaviors from her caregivers.

## The Preschool Years: From 18 Months to 6 Years

The consolidation in the system that emerges at about 8 to 10 months typically lasts until roughly 18 or 24 months, when again there is an upheaval.

*The Transition.* The most striking thing about the transition at 18–24 months is the beginning of the use of symbols in language and in thinking. This fundamental shift is reflected in many different aspects of the child's life. We see it in language, in the child's approach to cognitive tasks, and in play, where the child now pretends, having an object *stand for* something else.

At this same age, as I pointed out briefly in Chapter 8, the child also shows a rapid and broad emergence of *combinatorial skills* (Brownell, 1986; Brownell & Carriger, 1990): At about the time that the child first strings two words together into a sentence we also first see strings of two pretend actions in the child's play, and the first turn-taking and cooperation in his interactions with other children. Interestingly, studies of mentally retarded children tell us that it is *mental age* and not chronological age that is the critical predictor of these changes (Siebert, Hogan, & Mundy, 1986). When the child reaches the mental age of about 20 months all of these combinatorial skills emerge in rapid order.

If you go back and look at Figure 15.1, you'll see that there is also a highly significant neurological change at about this same time: the "pruning" of dendrites and synapses, which seems to streamline the wiring in some fashion. But what comes first here? Is the cognitive achievement of symbols the key event, with the neurological pruning resulting from that change? Or is the achievement of the understanding of symbols based on the neurological changes? Or, most likely, are the two changes interacting with each other? Whatever the cause, it is clear once again that the system and all its facets change radically as a result.

*From 2 to 6: Consolidation and Further Transitions.* Until recently, conventional wisdom had it that once a child had passed through the transition at 18 or 24 months, the remaining years from 2 to 6 were in the form of a long, gradual consolidation. However, as you can see in Figure 15.2 on p. 577, it now begins to look as if there may well be another inflection point and another transition between about ages 4 and 5.

In the period between 2 and 4, all the toddler's new skills make the child more independent, as does the child's growing mobility. The 18-month-old walks well; by 2 he can run. As any parent can tell you, children in this period vigorously push the limits of this newfound independence. Collectively, these new skills also influence the form of the child's attachment behavior. When language is rudimentary and the child's locomotion is poor, then clinging, touching, holding, and crying are just about the only stress-re-

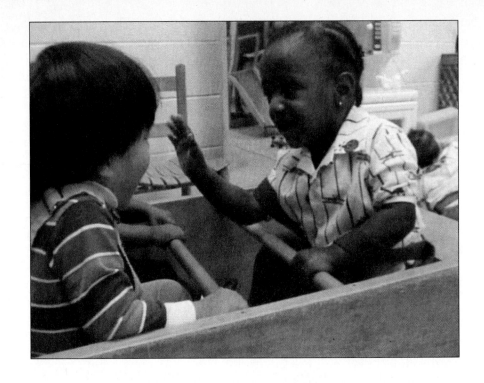

The kind of cooperative play Avery Gholston is showing here with a day-care playmate does not occur much before 24 months of age but becomes common thereafter. This photo is a video still from the *Childhood* television series (*Source:* ©Thirteen/WNET).

lated attachment behaviors available to the child. As language becomes more skillful, however, she is able to stay in touch with adults and peers in new ways—even symbolically, by thinking about her mother or father. The attachment may be no less strong, but it can be maintained at greater physical distance.

At about age 4, however, there are several cognitive changes that seem to produce another shift. At this point the child seems to develop a different understanding of his own and others' minds, so that he realizes (in some preliminary, primitive way) that we are all representing reality in our own way, that we each understand things in our own fashion. This affects his ability to understand others, which in turn affects all his social relationships. The child's internal working model of attachment also seems to undergo a change. Now the child seems to represent to himself not just a particular person (such as Mom) but relationships in a more general way. Whether there is a common denominator in these several skills is not so clear yet. However, there is at least a growing awareness among psychologists that there may be some very interesting things going on cognitively at about this age.

As in the case of the period of infancy, though, it would be a mistake to argue that the changes in cognition, language, and motor skill are the only causal agents in the pattern of development in the preschool years. The cognitive changes are clearly affected by the child's play, particularly play with peers.

FIGURE 15.2

A brief summary of parallel developments during the preschool years.

| | Age in Years | | | | |
|---|---|---|---|---|---|
| | 2 | 3 | 4 | 5 | 6 |
| Physical Development | Runs easily; climbs stairs one step at a time | Rides trike; uses scissors; draws | Climbs stairs one foot per step; kicks and throws large ball | Hops and skips; some ball games with more skill | Jumps rope; skips |
| Cognitive Development | Symbols; 2- and 3-step play sequences | Classification mostly by function | Beginning systematic classification by shape or size or color | Conservation of number and quantity | |
| | | Beginning ability to take others' physical perspective | Theory of mind | No spontaneous use of rehearsal in memory tasks | |
| | | Transductive reasoning | | | |
| Language Development | 2-word sentences | 3- and 4-word sentences with grammatical markers | Continued improvement of inflections, past tense, plurals, passive sentences, and tag questions | | |
| Self/Personality Development | Self-definition based on comparisons of size, age, gender; gender identity | Gender stability | | Categorical self based on physical properties or skills | |
| | | | | Gender constancy | |
| | Erikson's stage of autonomy vs. shame /doubt | Erikson's stage of initiative vs. guilt | | | |
| | Attachments to parents shown less frequently, mostly under stress | | | | |
| Social Development | Cooperative play Multi-step turn-taking sequences in play with peers | Empathy for another's feelings | | | |
| | | Some altruism; same-sex peer choice | Beginning signs of individual friendships | Sociodramatic play | Roles in play |

Two and 3-year-olds, left alone, play with toys and may show some pretend play. But when children play together, they expand one another's experience with objects, suggesting new ways of pretending to one another. Since this play with objects seems to be a key part of the child's growing cognitive skill, we can see that time spent in play with other youngsters is much more than social. Conflict and disagreement are also key parts of children's play, affecting not only the child's emerging social skills, but stimulating cognitive development as well (Bearison, Magzamen, & Filardo, 1986). When two children disagree about how to explain something, or insist on their own different views, such experience enhances the child's awareness that there *are* other perspectives, other ways of thinking or playing.

Of course play with other children is also a part of the child's developing concept of sex roles. Noticing whether other people are boys or girls and what toys boys and girls play with are the first steps in the long chain of sex-role learning.

One way to think about this whole set of years is that the child is making a slow but immensely important shift from dependent baby to independent child. This shift is made possible by physical change, by language, by many and varied play encounters with other children, and by new abilities to control impulses. At the same time (and from some of the same causes) the child's thinking is *decentering*, becoming less egocentric and less tied to the outside appearances of things. Pretend play is probably a key ingredient in these changes, as is the emerging theory of mind.

All of these changes, of course, alter the family system in profound ways. Certainly the fact that the child now uses and understands language helps enormously in the parent-child communication. But the simultaneous shift from dependent infant to independent preschooler is not so easy. The 2-year-old has figured out that he is a distinct person and different from Mom; he is trying out his limits. But all these newfound skills and new independence are not accompanied by impulse control. Two-year-olds are pretty good at doing; they are lousy at *not* doing. They see something, they go after it; when they want something, they want it NOW! If frustrated, they wail, scream, or shout (isn't language wonderful?). A large part of the conflict parents experience with children at this age comes about because the parent *must* limit the child, not only for the child's own survival, but to help teach the child impulse control (Escalona, 1981).

Once this 2-year-old transition has been weathered, the years from 3 to 6 are often relatively smooth within the family, although the arrival of a new baby or the child's transition to day care or preschool may be occasions for additional family adjustments.

### The Elementary School Years: From 6 to 12

*The Transition.* For most children the next major transition occurs somewhere between 5 and 7 (White, 1965; Kegan, 1985). One of the most noticeable aspects of this transition is the much discussed cognitive shift from "preoperational" to "concrete operational" thinking (to use Piaget's labels). As I pointed out in Chapter 7, it is not so clear that what is going on here is a rapid, pervasive, structural change to a whole new way of thinking. Children don't make this shift all at once in every area of their thinking or relationships. Expertise, or the lack of it, makes a major difference. But there appears to be at least some agreement that there are nonetheless important changes normally taking place at about this age in the types of information processing strategies children use and in the abstractness of the concepts they grasp.

At the same time, most children start school. It may not be accidental that these two things occur together. Schooling begins at about ages 5–7 in virtually every culture, perhaps reflecting some recognition that children of that age are cognitively and socially "ready" for the demands of formal schooling.

Like the earlier transitions, this one is often marked by increases in problem behavior, difficulties adjusting to school, or other symptoms. But it is also frequently a time of excitement and even joy for children.

*The Consolidation.* Figure 15.3 on p. 580 shows the parallel lines of development during the elementary school years. Freud called this the *latency pe-*

*riod* as if it were a period of waiting, with nothing very important happening internally. In one sense he was right; it appears to be a relatively calm period. But there is a great deal of both internal and external change, nonetheless.

The cognitive changes are pervasive. One facet of this is that the child now looks beyond the surface of things to search for underlying rules. We see this in the development of conservation, in gender constancy, and in children's relationships with one another. Another facet is the child's growing ability to take others' perspectives. She understands that others think and feel differently than she does. This is reflected in children's peer interactions as well as their thinking. It is in elementary school that we see the beginnings of reciprocal friendships, for example.

Just what role physical change plays in this collection of developments I do not know. Clearly there *are* physical changes going on. Girls, in particular, are going through the first steps of puberty during elementary school. However, we don't know whether the rate of physical development in these years is connected in any way to the rate of the child's progress through the sequence of cognitive or social understandings. There has been no research that I know of that hooks the first row in Figure 15.3 with any of the other rows, except that bigger, more coordinated, early developing children are likely to have slightly faster cognitive development and be somewhat more popular with peers. Obviously this is an area in which we need far more knowledge.

### Adolescence: From 12 to 20

*The Transition.* In some ways the early years of adolescence have a lot in common with the early years of toddlerhood. Two-year-olds are famous for their negativism and for their constant push for more independence; at the same time, they are struggling to learn a vast array of new skills. Teenagers show many of these same qualities, albeit at more abstract levels. Many of them go through a period of negativism, particularly with parents, right at the beginning of the pubertal changes. And many of the conflicts with parents center around issues of independence—they want to come and go when they please, listen to the music they prefer at maximum volume, and wear the clothing and hair styles that are currently "in."

While this push for independence is going on, they are also facing a whole new set of demands and skills to be learned—new social skills and new levels of cognitive complexity found in formal operations tasks. The sharp increases in the rate of depression and the drop in self-esteem we see at the beginning of adolescence seem to be linked to this surplus of new demands and changes. A number of investigators have found that those adolescents who have the greatest number of simultaneous changes at the beginning of puberty—changing to junior-high school, moving to a new town or new house, perhaps a parental separation or divorce—also show the greatest loss in self-esteem, the largest rise in problem behavior, and the biggest drop in grade point average (e.g., Eccles & Midgley, 1990; Simmons, Burgeson, & Reef, 1988). Young adolescents who can cope with these changes one at a time, such as when the youngster remains in the same school through eighth grade before shifting to junior- or senior-high school, show fewer symptoms of stress.

Still, although the facets of this transition are certainly broad and easy to see (summarized in Figure 15.4 on p. 582), it is difficult to pin down the caus-

FIGURE 15.3

A summary of parallel changes during the elementary school years. The keys to the transition at age 5 or 6 seem to be both the many cognitive changes and the beginning of school, which brings with it new social demands as well as new intellectual challenges.

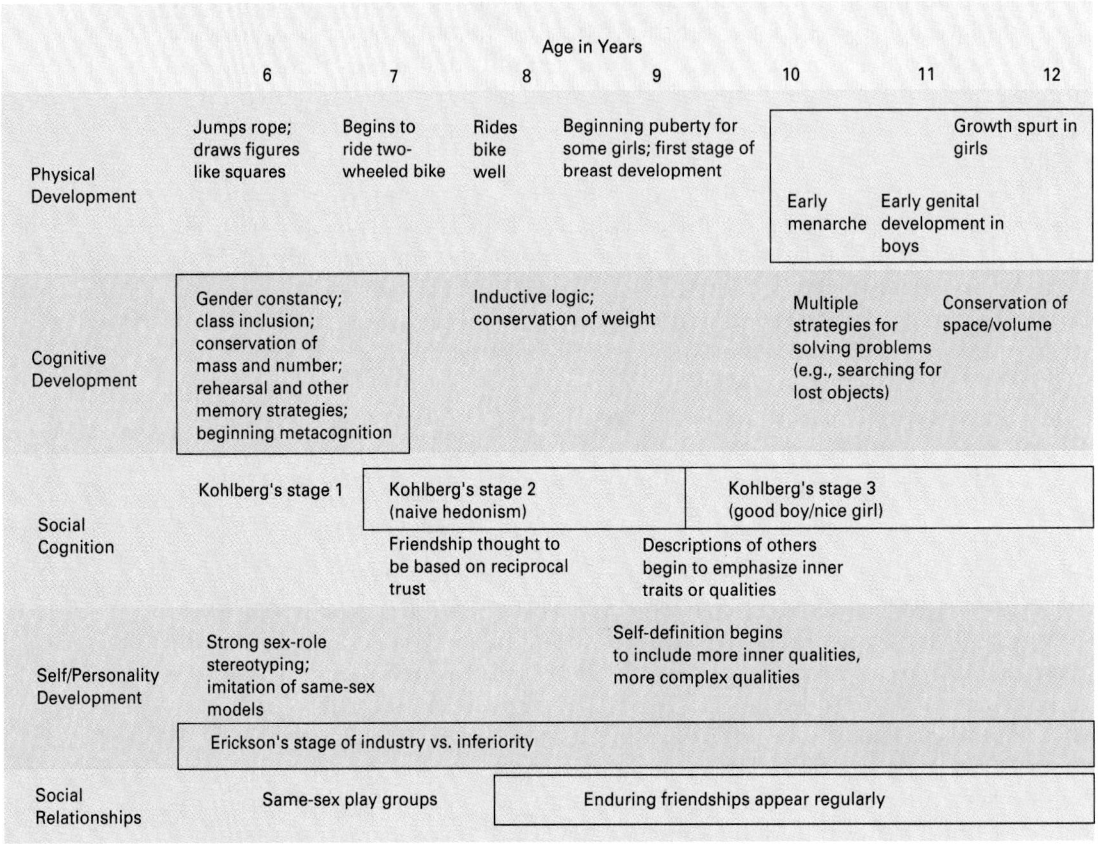

| | Age in Years | | | | | | |
|---|---|---|---|---|---|---|---|
| | 6 | 7 | 8 | 9 | 10 | 11 | 12 |
| Physical Development | Jumps rope; draws figures like squares | Begins to ride two-wheeled bike | Rides bike well | Beginning puberty for some girls; first stage of breast development | Early menarche / Early genital development in boys | Growth spurt in girls | |
| Cognitive Development | | Gender constancy; class inclusion; conservation of mass and number; rehearsal and other memory strategies; beginning metacognition | Inductive logic; conservation of weight | | Multiple strategies for solving problems (e.g., searching for lost objects) | Conservation of space/volume | |
| Social Cognition | Kohlberg's stage 1 | Kohlberg's stage 2 (naive hedonism) | Friendship thought to be based on reciprocal trust | Kohlberg's stage 3 (good boy/nice girl) / Descriptions of others begin to emphasize inner traits or qualities | | | |
| Self/Personality Development | Strong sex-role stereotyping; imitation of same-sex models | | | Self-definition begins to include more inner qualities, more complex qualities | | | |
| | Erickson's stage of industry vs. inferiority | | | | | | |
| Social Relationships | Same-sex play groups | | Enduring friendships appear regularly | | | | |

es and connections among the several different manifestations of change. I have already talked about some of the possible connections. It seems likely that the changes in the child's thinking from concrete operations to at least beginning formal operations helps to cause other developments. One of the characteristics of formal operations thinking is the ability to imagine possibilities that you have never experienced and to manipulate ideas in your head. These new skills seem to help foster the broad questioning of old ways, old values, and old patterns that are part of adolescence for many teenagers. In support of such a link, recall the research I mentioned in Chapter 12 that shows that beginning formal operations thinking seems to be a necessary precursor to the emergence of more advanced forms of social cognition and moral judgment.

Other researchers have also found some links between early formal reasoning and the process of identity formation (Leadbeater & Dionne, 1981; Rowe & Marcia, 1980). Using Marcia's identity status categories, these investigators have shown that teenagers and young adults who have achieved a clear

One of the consequences of the child's new gender constancy is a *strong* preference for playmates of the same sex—a pattern we can see very clearly in this group of Ghanian girls, filmed as part of the *Childhood* series. This photo is a video still from the *Childhood* television series (*Source:* ©Thirteen/WNET).

identity are also much more likely to be reasoning at the level of formal operations than are those who are still in the diffusion or moratorium status. Thus formal operations thinking may *enable* the young person to rethink many aspects of his life, but it does not guarantee that he will do so.

The most speculative links at present are those between the physical changes of puberty and the social/cognitive/personal changes at adolescence. One possibility, of course, is that there is a direct, causal connection between hormonal and other physical changes and the emergence of new cognitive skills or social behaviors. As J. M. Tanner says:

> There is clearly no reason to suppose that the link between maturation of [brain] structure and appearance of [cognitive] function suddenly ceases at age 6 or 10 or 13. On the contrary, there is every reason to believe that the higher intellectual abilities also appear only when maturation of certain structures is complete. (Tanner, 1970, p. 123)

There is a growing body of research exploring such potential links. Steinberg's research, which I talked about in Chapter 11, shows one possible connection. Recall that he has found that the rise in parent-teenager conflict at adolescence seems to be predicted not by age but by pubertal status. Steinberg's basic hypothesis has been at least somewhat strengthened by the results of research in which actual hormone levels have been measured. For example, a number of researchers have found that in girls, the rise in estradiol at the beginning of puberty is associated with increases in verbal aggression and a loss of impulse control, while in boys, several studies show that increases in testosterone are correlated with increases in irritability and impatience (Paikoff & Brooks-Gunn, 1990). But a number of other investigations of such hormone/behavior links have not yielded such tidy results. At the very least it is already clear that the links between pubertal hormones and

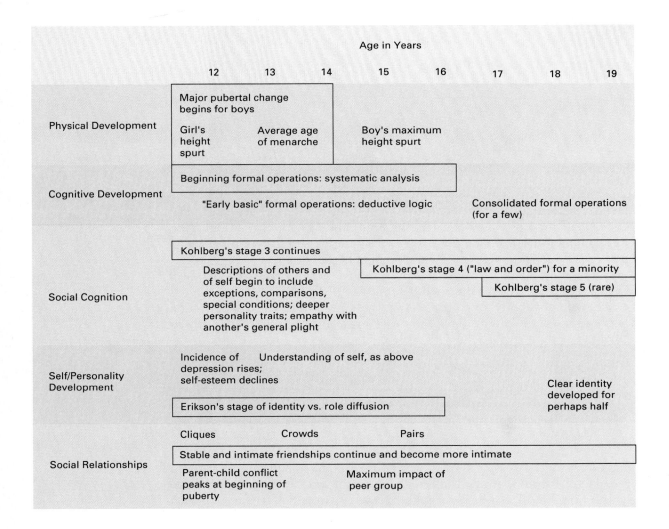

**FIGURE 15.4**

A brief summary of parallel developments during adolescence. The transition at roughly age 12 seems to be most centrally triggered by puberty and by the change in roles that puberty brings. Major cognitive and social-cognitive changes, however, are also prominent.

changes in adolescent behavior are considerably more complicated than we had first imagined.

One of the complications is that pubertal changes also have highly significant indirect effects as well. When the child's body grows and becomes more like that of an adult, the parents and others begin to treat the child differently and the child begins to see himself as grown-up. Both of these changes may help to trigger some of the searching self-examinations that are part of this period of life.

For the family, these combined changes require some major adaptations. The teenager is demanding new levels of authority and power, while simultaneously asking for nurturance and guidance. The presence of a sexually charged pubescent young person in the house may also reawaken unresolved adolescent issues in the parents, just when they are themselves facing a sense of physical decline in their 40s or 50s. Then, too, teenagers stay up late, which severely restricts private time for parents. Perhaps, then, it is not surprising that many parents (particularly fathers) report that marital satisfaction is at its lowest ebb during their children's adolescence (Rollins & Galligan, 1978). Despite these strains, though, it is impressive that most families manage to move through this adjustment time rather well, and a new equilibrium is formed in the late teen years.

*The Consolidation.* Beyond the early year or two of puberty there is a long period of consolidation, with more gradual change occurring throughout the high-school years. This is not an entirely smooth process of course; you will remember from Chapter 10 that a clear identity is often not achieved until college age, if then. The formation of emotionally intimate sexual or pre-sexual partnerships is also a relatively late development during the teenage years. So as with all of the other periods labeled "consolidations," change is continuous. But once the major disequilibrium of puberty is weathered, the period of adolescence is not nearly as full of "storm and stress" as popular literature might have us believe.

## Returning to Some Basic Questions

With this brief overview in mind, let me now go back to some of the questions I raised in Chapter 1 and see if the answers can be made any clearer.

### What Are the Major Influences on Development?

In Chapter 1 and throughout the book I have contrasted nature and nurture, nativism and empiricism, as basic explanations of developmental patterns. In every instance I have also said that the real answer lies in the interaction between the two. It is this interactive message that I want you to take with you. I can perhaps make the point clearest by going back to Aslin's five models of environmental/internal influences on development I showed in Figure 1.2 on p. 10. You'll recall that he is proposing one purely physical model (which he calls *maturation*) in which some particular development would occur regardless of environmental input and one purely environmental pattern (which he calls *induction*) in which some development is entirely a function of experience. In fact, however, probably neither the pure maturational nor the pure induction model actually occur at all. It seems that *all* of development is a product of various forms of interaction between internal and external influences.

Even in those areas of development that appear to be the most clearly biologically determined or influenced—such as physical development or early perceptual development—normal development can occur *only* if the child is growing in an environment that falls within the range of adequate or sufficient environments. The fact that the vast majority of environments fall within that range in no way reduces the importance of the environment.

Similarly, even those aspects of development that seem most obviously to be a product of environment, such as the quality of the child's first attachment, rest on a physiological substrate and perhaps on instinctive patterns of attachment behaviors. The fact that all intact children possess that substrate and those instincts makes them no less essential for development.

At the same time, it is not enough merely to say that all development is a product of interaction of nature and nurture. Aslin's second, third, and fourth models illustrate three of the many forms the interaction may take. We also know that the form of the interaction varies not only as a function of the aspect of development we are talking about but also of the child's age. It may help to think of different facets of development along a continuum, with those most fully internally programmed on one end and those most externally influenced on the other.

Physical development defines one end of this continuum, since it is very strongly shaped by internal forces. *Given the minimum necessary environment,* maturational timetables are extremely powerful and robust, particularly during infancy and adolescence.

Next along the continuum is probably language (although some experts will argue with this conclusion, given the possible dependency of language development upon prior cognitive developments). Language seems to emerge with only minimal environmental support—though here, too, the environment must fall within some acceptable range. At the very least, the child

In the United States, at least, one of the major family adjustments required when children reach adolescence centers around the use of the family car. How much should a 16-year-old be trusted? What rules should be in force? This mark of independence is similar to what happens at age 6 or 7 when the child is allowed to go off on her bicycle.

must hear language spoken (or see it signed). At the same time, specific features of the linguistic environment seem to matter a bit more than is true for physical development. The amount parents talk to the child affects vocabulary growth, for example, and parents who respond contingently to their children's vocalizations seem to be able to speed up the process, both examples of what Aslin calls *facilitation*.

Cognitive development falls somewhere in the middle of the continuum. Clearly there are powerful internal forces at work. John Flavell puts it this way:

> There is an impetus to childhood cognitive growth that is not ultimately explainable by this environmental push or that experiential shove (1985, p. 283). . . . What [research] has mainly shown us, in my opinion, is how well guaranteed or "canalized" . . . many of our fundamental cognitive acquisitions are. Alternatively put, they show how many environmental inputs and experiences seem developmentally helpful or sufficient and how few seem developmentally necessary. (1985, p. 286)

Whether the impressive regularity of the sequences of cognitive development arises from built-in processes like assimilation and accommodation, or whether there are physiological changes in information processing capacity, or some combination of the two, we don't yet know. But it is clear that this engine is moving along a shared track. At the same time, we know that the specific qualities of the environment affect both cognitive power and structure. Children with varied and age-appropriate toys, with encouragement for exploration and achievement, and with parents who are responsive to the child's overtures show faster cognitive development and higher eventual IQ scores—not just facilitation in Aslin's models, but actual attunement.

Social and emotional development lie at the end of the continuum where the impact of the environment seems to be the greatest, although even here there are obviously genetic factors at work. Temperament may well be inborn, and attachment behaviors may be instinctive; both of these inborn factors certainly shape the child's earliest encounters with others. But the balance of nature/nurture seems to lean more toward nurture in this area. In particular, the security of the child's attachment and the quality of the child's relationships with others outside of the family seem to be powerfully affected by the specific quality of the interactions within the family. The overall stress on or support for the family also makes a difference in the emergence of various behavior disorders, as well as on the child's everyday encounters with significant others.

Even this fairly complex analysis, however, only begins to scratch the surface. For one thing, many of the statements I have just made need to be modified in terms of *when* a particular environmental event takes place.

### Does Timing Matter?

You've encountered many variations of the timing hypothesis through the chapters of this book but the most pervasive question has been whether the early years of life are a critical or sensitive period, establishing many of the trajectories of the child's later development. A. D. B. Clarke (1968; Clarke & Clarke, 1976) poses the question with an analogy: When we con-

The fact that virtually all babies have some chance to crawl or to practice the component motions does not mean that such experience is unimportant. Without normal experience babies do *not* crawl. It is clear that most (if not all) so-called maturational sequences require particular kinds of environmental inputs if they are to occur at all.

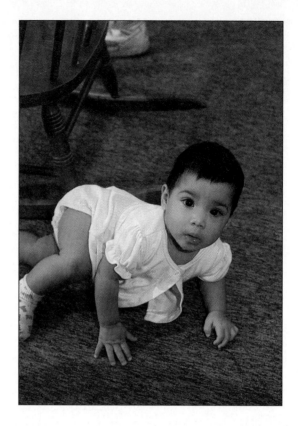

struct a house, does the shape of the foundation determine the final structure completely, does it partially influence the final structure, or can many final structures be built on the original foundation? What if there are flaws or weaknesses in the original foundation? Are these flaws permanent or can they be corrected later, after the house is completed?

You have read findings that support both views. Those who emphasize canalization, such as Sandra Scarr, point to the fact that virtually all children successfully complete the sensorimotor period; a large percentage of low birth weight or other initially vulnerable babies nonetheless catch up to their normal-birth peers by the time they are 2 or 3; even mild and moderately retarded children achieve some form of what Piaget called *concrete operations.*

On the other side of the argument are the obvious cases in which an early experience has been highly formative. Some prenatal influences are permanent; some effects of early cognitive impoverishment, malnutrition, or abuse may also be long-lasting.

Thus the early years of life seem both to be a sensitive period for some kinds of development and a period of highly canalized development. There are at least two different resolutions of this apparent paradox. First, if we think of canalization not just as a product of powerful built-in programming, but as the result of such programming *occurring in a sufficiently supportive environment,* much of the apparent dispute disappears (Scarr-Salapatek, 1976; Turkheimer & Gottesman, 1991). It is only when a child's particular environment falls outside of the range of sufficiently supportive environments that we see a so-called "environmental effect," such as a child reared

Environment can also have a genuinely accelerating or augmenting effect—what Aslin calls attunement. This child, and others who grow up in such rich environments, is likely to have a higher IQ and better school performance than is a child growing up in poverty.

in an extremely impoverished orphanage setting or a child who is regularly physically abused. In these conditions environmental effects can be strongly negative and long-lasting, and the earlier such a deviation occurs, the more pervasive the effects seem to be. In this way of looking at critical periods versus cana-lization, infancy may be less *frequently* pivotal in the pattern of the child's development than are more minor deviations in toddlerhood or the preschool years. But when the deviations in infancy are extreme enough to deflect the infant from the normal developmental path—such as in the case of severe abuse or malnutrition—the effect is larger than at any other age.

Robert Cairns (1991) offers a second resolution to the apparent dispute between infancy as a critical period and infancy as highly canalized. He points out that in any given period, some facets of development may be highly cana-lized while other facets may be strongly responsive to environmental variation. In infancy, for example, physical, perceptual, and perhaps linguistic development may be strongly canalized, but the development of attachments and of internal working models of attachment are clearly affected by the specific experiences the child has within the family. Indeed I would argue that all internal working models—of attachment, gender identity, self-concept, and peer relations—are likely to be more powerfully affected by early than by later experiences, simply because the model, once formed, affects and filters all later experience.

A particularly nice example of this kind of early effect comes from one of Alan Sroufe's studies of the later consequences of early attachment quality. He and his colleagues (Sroufe, Egeland, & Kreutzer, 1990) compared two groups of elementary-school children. One group had had a good adaptation in infancy, with a secure attachment, but for various reasons had not functioned well in the preschool years. The second group had shown poor adaptation at both ages. When these two groups of children were assessed at elementary-school age, Sroufe found that those who had had a good early start "rebounded" better. They had better emotional health and peer competence at school age than did those who had had a poor adaptation in infancy, even though both groups had functioned poorly as preschoolers. The infancy experience is not totally formative; the child's current circumstances also have a major impact. But at least in this domain, early experience leaves a lingering trace.

Timing and internal models interact in yet another way when we look at the effect of earliness or lateness of some experience such as puberty. What matters in this case seems not to be the actual timing, but the child's interpretation of that timing, the child's internal model.

Still a third way to think about timing is to emphasize the importance of specific psychological tasks at different ages. Erikson's theory, for example, emphasizes each of a series of psychological dilemmas. Any experience that affects the way a child resolves a particular task will be formative at that time; at an earlier or later time the same experience may have much less effect. Alan Sroufe and Michael Rutter (1984) have offered a broader list of age-graded tasks, given in Table 15.1. In this way of looking at things, the child is seen as *focusing* on different aspects of the environment at different times. Thus during the period from 1 to 2 1/2, when the child is focused on mastery of the object world, the quality and range of inanimate experiences the child has access to may be of special importance—a hypothesis which matches the facts I gave you in Chapter 6 about the impact of the early environment on children's IQs and cognitive development.

Overall, I do not think that any specific age is critical for all aspects of development; I do think that for any aspect of development, some ages are more central than others and that during those times patterns are set which affect later experience. As Alan Sroufe says, "Development is hierarchical; it is not a blackboard to be erased and written upon again. Even when children change rather markedly, the shadows of the earlier adaptation remain" (1983, p. 73–74).

## What Is the Nature of Developmental Change?

My bias has no doubt been apparent all through the book, so you can predict my conclusion that developmental change is more qualitative than quantitative. Certainly the child acquires more vocabulary words, more information processing strategies. But these are used in different ways by older children than by younger ones. Further, it seems clear that these qualitative changes occur in sequences. Such sequences are apparent in physical development, cognitive development, and social and moral development.

*Stages.* Whether it is meaningful to speak of stages, however, is still an open question. Some examples of hierarchically organized stages have certainly been found; Kohlberg's stages of moral reasoning is the most obvious example. And there are certainly examples of apparently stage-like changes across domains, such as what happens at about 18–24 months when the child seems to discover the ability to combine symbols and we see new behavior in language, thinking, and play with other children. Nonetheless, the majority of the evidence has not supported the notion of pervasive changes in structure. More commonly, each new skill and each new understanding seems to be acquired in a fairly narrow area first and only later generalized more fully. In fact one of the things that differentiates the gifted or higher IQ child from the lower IQ or retarded child is how quickly and broadly the child generalizes some new concept or strategy to new instances.

Despite this non-stage-like quality of most developmental change, it is still true that if you compare the patterns of relationship, thinking, and problem solving of two children of widely differing ages—say a 5-year-old and an 11-year-old—they will differ in almost every respect. So there is certainly orderliness in the sequences and some links between them but probably not major stages quite like those Piaget proposed.

*Continuities.* In the midst of all of this change, all these sequences, and all the new forms of relating and thinking, there is also continuity. Each child carries forward some core of individuality. The notion of temperament certainly implies such a core, as does the concept of an internal working model. Alan Sroufe once again offers an elegant way of thinking about this central core. Continuity in development, he says, "takes the form of coherence across

*TABLE 15.1*

*Tasks or Issues in Each of Several Age Periods*

| Age in Years | Issues or Tasks |
| --- | --- |
| 0–1 | Biological regulation; harmonious dyadic interaction; formation of an effective attachment relationship. |
| 1–2 1/2 | Exploration, experimentation, and mastery of the object world (caregiver as secure base); individuation and autonomy; responding to external control of impulses. |
| 3–5 | Flexible self-control; self-reliance; initiative; identification and gender concept; establishing effective peer contacts (empathy). |
| 6–12 | Social understanding (equity, fairness); gender constancy; same-sex chumships; sense of "industry" (competence); school adjustment. |
| 13+ | "Formal operations" (flexible perspective taking; "as if" thinking); loyal friendships (same sex); beginning heterosexual relationships; emancipation; identity. |

*Source:* Sroufe & Rutter, 1984, adapted from Sroufe, 1979.

transformations" (1983, p. 51). Thus the specific behavior that we see in the child may change; the clinging toddler may not be a clinging 9-year-old. However, the underlying attachment model or the temperament that led to the clinging will still be at least partially present, manifesting in new ways. In particular, it has become increasingly clear that some *maladaptations* persist over time, as seen in the consistency of high levels of aggression or tantrum behavior and in the persistence of some of the maladaptive social interactions that flow from insecure attachments. Our task as psychologists is to understand both coherence or consistency and the underlying patterns of development or transformation.

 ## Individual Differences

The whole issue of individual continuities emphasizes the fact that development is individual as well as collective. I have talked about individual differences in virtually every chapter, so you know that both inborn differences and emergent or environmentally produced differences are present among children in every aspect of development. All of this is familiar stuff by now and bears little repeating. But there are two dimensions of individual differences I want to touch on one more time: sex differences and vulnerability or resilience.

### Sex Differences in Development

Although I have talked about sex differences repeatedly, I suspect it will be helpful for you to see all the findings pulled together into a single summary, as in Table 15.2 on p. 592. And at the risk of repeating myself, I want to make a couple of points about these various findings.

First, even where the differences are very clear, such as with aggressiveness, the actual magnitude of the difference is normally quite small, and the two distributions (male and female) overlap almost completely. That is, *within* each sex there is almost a full range of performance or behavior on each of the dimensions listed in the table. It is only when we look at average scores for the two sexes that we see a difference. There are a few exceptions to this statement, perhaps most notably the markedly higher rate of abnormality and deviance among boys and boys' greater skill at spatial visualization.

Second, both biological and environmental causes seem to be at work in producing the differences we do see. The difference in aggressiveness seems to have biological roots, but parental treatment may well magnify the biological difference. Similarly, differences in early language skill may be partly a result of differing maturational rates. I know that it is not particularly popular today to look for any kind of biological causes of sex differences. But the evidence seems inescapable.

A third point is not visible in the summary in Table 15.2, but is nonetheless critical. Psychologists are beginning to discover that apparently similar experiences may have quite different effects on boys than on girls. For example, Simpson and Stevenson-Hinde (1985) have found that shyness is associated with *negative* family interactions in boys but with *positive* family interactions in girls. As Michael Rutter puts it, "It is not only that parents may treat boys and girls somewhat differently, which they do. . . , but also that the patterns of effects differ between the sexes" (1987, p. 1262). This conclusion has now led nearly all researchers to analyze their results separately for boys and girls, but we are a long way from understanding the pattern of findings that has emerged. Thus while the more obvious and expected forms of sex differences appear only weakly if at all, there may be more subtle forms of sex differences that we are only beginning to understand.

## Vulnerability or Resilience

I want to try to tie together many of the threads I have been weaving in this chapter by returning to a dimension of individual differences I talked about at some length in Chapter 14: vulnerability or resilience. I think it is useful to define these concepts somewhat differently than usual, in terms of the *range of environments which will be sufficiently supportive for optimal development.* By this definition, a vulnerable infant is one with a narrow range of potentially supportive environments. For such a child, only the most stimulating, the most responsive, and the most adaptive environment will do. When the child's environment falls outside of that range, the probability of a poor outcome is greatly increased. A resilient child, in contrast, is one for whom any of a very wide range of environments will support optimum development. A resilient child may thus be more strongly canalized, and a vulnerable child may be less so.

Any given child may also be relatively more vulnerable or resilient in some areas of development than others. So a child might be vulnerable intellectually but quite resilient emotionally or personally.

Some kinds of vulnerabilities are inborn, such as genetic abnormalities, prenatal trauma or stress, preterm birth, or malnutrition. Any such child will thrive only in a highly supportive environment. You've encountered this pattern again and again through the chapters of this book.

- Low birth weight infants typically have normal IQs if they are reared in middle-class homes, but have a high risk of serious retardation if they are reared in poverty (Werner, 1986).
- Prenatally malnourished infants, or those with other complications during pregnancy or delivery, look normal if reared in highly stimulating special preschools, but have significantly lower IQs if reared at home by low education mothers (Zeskind & Ramey, 1981; Breitmayer & Ramey, 1986).
- Temperamentally irritable babies are more likely to become insecurely attached if their mothers have insufficient emotional and social support (Crockenberg, 1981).
- Children born with cytomegalovirus are much more likely to have learning problems in school if they are reared in poverty-level environments than if they are reared in middle-class families (Hanshaw et al., 1976).

So far that's fairly straightforward. But let me propose a further, more speculative, theoretical step: I think that vulnerability in this sense does not remain constant throughout life. A more general proposition, which I suggest as a working hypothesis, is that each time the child's environment falls outside of the range of acceptably supporting environments *for that child* (that is, each time there is a mismatch between the child's needs and what is avail-

*TABLE 15.2*

*Summary of Sex Differences in Development in Childhood and Adolescence*

**Physical development:**
- **Rate of maturation**    Girls are on a faster developmental timetable; this is particularly apparent prenatally and at adolescence.
- **Quality of maturation**    Girls' physical growth is more regular and predictable with fewer uneven spurts.
- **Strength and speed**    Little difference until puberty, when boys become both stronger and faster, developing larger percentage of muscle and smaller percentage of fat.
- **Heart and circulation**    At puberty boys develop larger heart and lungs and a greater capacity for carrying oxygen in the blood.

**Perceptual development:**
- **Perceptual acuity**    No sex differences.
- **Discrimination ability**    No sex differences.
- **Perceptual style**    No sex differences in reflection/impulsivity.

**Cognitive development:**
- **Cognitive structure**    No sex difference until adolescence, when boys show somewhat higher incidence of formal operations thinking.
- **IQ**    No sex difference on total IQ.
- **Verbal skills**    Girls are slightly faster in some aspects of early language; girls have better articulation and fewer reading problems; at adolescence, girls are slightly better at verbal reasoning.
- **Mathematics skills**    Before adolescence, girls are slightly better at arithmetic computation; at adolescence, boys are slightly but consistently better at tasks requiring mathematical reasoning.
- **Spatial ability**    Boys are better at almost any task requiring spatial visualization. This becomes a larger and more consistent difference at adolescence.

**Social development:**
- **Aggression/dominance/competitiveness**    Boys are more aggressive, more competitive, and more dominant on virtually all measures, beginning in toddlerhood and continuing through adolescence (and into adult life).
- **Nurturance/helping/generosity**    Few differences, but when a difference is found, girls are slightly more nurturing and helpful.
- **Interactive style**    Subtle but significant differences in style of interaction. Girls' friendships are more intimate and girl-girl interactions are more supportive, while boy-boy interactions are more competitive.
- **Compliance**    Girls appear to be somewhat more compliant to adult requests in early childhood. At later ages, boys are more likely to show high levels of *noncompliance.*
- **Identity formation**    No clear differences.

**Other differences:**
- **Vulnerability**    Boys are more likely to show virtually all forms of physical, emotional, and cognitive vulnerability to stress, and higher levels of deviant development, except that at adolescence, girls show higher rates of depression.

I have used this photo at the end of every edition of this book because it speaks to me so eloquently of the quality of joy, of discovery, that is so much a part of development.

able), the child becomes *more vulnerable*, while each period during which the child's needs are met makes the child more resilient. For example, I would predict that a temperamentally difficult child whose family environment was nonetheless sufficient to foster a secure attachment will become more resilient and more able to handle the next set of tasks, while a temperamentally easy child who nonetheless developed an insecure attachment would become more vulnerable to later stress or environmental insufficiency.

Furthermore, the qualities of the environment that are critical for a child's optimum development no doubt change as the child passes from one age to another. Responsive and warm interactions with parents seem particularly central in the period from perhaps 6 to 18 months. Richness of cognitive stimulation seems particularly central between perhaps 1 year and 4 years, while opportunity for practicing social skills with peers may be especially central at a later age. Thus as the tasks change with age, the optimum environment will change also. Among other things, this means that the same family may be very good with a child of one age and not so good with a child of another age.

Most generally, this model leads to the conclusion that even the most "vulnerable" child can show improvement if her environment improves markedly. Because some congenitally vulnerable children do not encounter sufficiently supportive environments, their vulnerability will continue to increase. In this way, early problems will often persist. But at the same time, improvement is possible, even likely. *Most* children manage to survive and thrive, despite stresses and vulnerabilities. As Emmy Werner puts it, "We could not help being deeply impressed by the resilience of most children and youth and their capacity for positive change and personal growth" (1986, p. 5).

 ## A Final Point: The Joy of Development

On a similarly optimistic note, I want to end both this chapter and the book by reminding you of something I said at the very beginning. In the midst of all the "crises," "transitions," and "vulnerabilities," there is a special *joyous* quality to development. When a child masters a new skill, she is not just pleased, she is delighted and will repeat that new skill at length, quite obviously getting vast satisfaction from it. A 5-year-old I know learned to draw stars and drew them on everything in sight, including paper, walls, clothes, and napkins. It was so much *fun* to draw stars. A 10-year-old who learns to do cartwheels will delightedly display this new talent to anyone who will watch and will practice endlessly.

The same joyous quality can be part of the family's development as well. Confronting and moving successfully through one of the periodic (and inevitable) upheavals in family life can be immensely pleasing. Watching your child progress, liking your child, enjoying walking or talking together are all deeply satisfying parts of rearing children. When parents cry at their son's or daughter's high-school graduation or wedding, it is not merely sentiment. It is an expression of that sense of love, pride, and wonderment that you have gotten this far.

©Thirteen/WNET

# S U M M A R Y

1. The child's development may be thought of as a series of alternating periods of transition and consolidation. The transitions occur when there are individual major changes, or pileups of smaller change.
2. To understand development we must understand the system, not just the individual parts. A change in any part of the system affects all the other facets.
3. Within infancy, there appear to be at least two transition periods, one at about 2 months, and the other at roughly 8 months.
4. The two-month transition seems particularly influenced by neurological change; the one at 8 months has many threads and we do not yet know the causal links between them.
5. The transition at 18 months is marked by the remarkable emergence of symbolic activity, evidenced in language, thinking, and play. A general combinatorial ability (stringing several concepts or actions together) also appears at about this time.
6. These cognitive accomplishments combine with major new motor skills to allow the child significantly greater independence, which in turn fosters further cognitive growth.
7. The transition at age 5 to 7 is marked both by the beginning emergence of still more powerful cognitive skills and by the beginning of school. A general "decentering" is manifested in children's relationships with their peers as well as in their thinking.
8. The transition at adolescence is triggered primarily by the physical changes of puberty but is accompanied by still further cognitive changes, major alterations in patterns of peer interaction, increases in family disruption, and increases in depression.
9. A shift toward formal operations at adolescence may be one contributor to a rise in self-questioning; pubertal changes may have both direct and indirect effects on the other developments of this period.
10. All facets of development are the product of some combination or interaction of internal and external influences.
11. Nonetheless, the various facets of development can be arrayed along a continuum from those most affected by internal influences to those most affected by external influences, in the following order: physical development, language, cognition, and social/personality development.
12. Paradoxically, development in the early years of life appears to be both highly canalized and (at extremes of environment) highly sensitive to environmental variation.
13. The early years of life may also be especially important for all children because internal working models are established in that period.

14.     Each age period can also be thought of as having a set of central tasks; experiences that are especially important for the successful completion of those tasks will thus be "critical" for that age.

15.     Development seems clearly to be made up of a large number of widely shared (if not universal) sequences. But whether there are broad, structurally different stages is less clear.

16.     Individual differences are also pervasive, resulting not only from varying heredity and differing prenatal experience, but also from differing training and experience after birth. Sex differences, however, are less substantial than popular ideas might lead us to think, although boys and girls may nonetheless respond quite differently to similar experiences.

17.     The dimension of vulnerability/resilience is another way to think about individual differences. The dimension may be defined in terms of the range of environments which will support optimal development for a particular child. A large range implies resilience; a narrow range defines vulnerability.

18.     Vulnerability may be increased or decreased over time, depending on the adequacy or inadequacy of environments at each of a series of points in development. Children may thus recover from, or surmount, even very poor starts.

19.     For both the child and the parent, development is full of joy as well as travail.


# CRITICAL THINKING QUESTIONS

1.      Imagine that you are a parent with a new infant. You and your partner have decided that you want eventually to have two children and you are beginning to think about just how close together you might want the two children to be. What have you learned in this course that might enter into your decision?

2.      The majority of women now return to (or begin) work outside the home sometime during their children's early years. What effect do you think the *timing* of such maternal employment might have on the child and on the family? What time (or times) would be likely to be least disruptive, given what you know about each of the ages/stages of development?

3.      In most cultures of the world, children start formal schooling at about age 6 or 7, which is about the same time that we normally see a set of cognitive changes in the child. But what is causing what here? Does schooling cause the cognitive changes, or do children start school at that age because people in many cultures have recognized that they are now "ready" for more complex thought? How might you go about trying to sort out these alternative explanations?

# SUGGESTED READINGS

Many of the books I have suggested in earlier chapters are relevant here as well, including both the Rosenblith and Sims-Knight (1989) and Osofsky (1987) books on infancy, and Flavell's book on cognitive development (1985), which includes an elegant discussion of many of the basic issues I have been talking about in this chapter. Let me also suggest several other books that give the flavor of particular ages.

Adelson, J. (Ed.) (1980). *Handbook of adolescent psychology.* New York: Wiley-Interscience.

Like the following Collins book, this is a collection of papers covering virtually every facet of a particular age period. Since most of these papers were written in the late 1970s, they do not include the more current work. But this is still the broadest and most detailed single source I know of on adolescence.

Collins, W. A. (Ed.) (1984). *Development during middle childhood. The years from six to twelve.* Washington, D.C.: National Academy Press.

This collection of papers touches on all facets of school-age children: biology, cognition, self-understanding, family and peer relationships, school, and atypical development. An excellent source of information about this often neglected period.

Dunn, J. (1988). *The beginnings of social understanding.* Cambridge, MA: Harvard University Press.

In the first brief chapter of this book, Dunn talks very clearly about all the changes in social relationships and in thinking about relationships that can be seen in children between ages 2 and 4.

# GLOSSARY

**accommodation**   That part of the adaptation process by which a person modifies existing schemes to fit new experiences or creates new schemes when old ones no longer handle the data.

**achievement test**   A test usually given in schools, designed to assess a child's learning of specific material taught in school, such as spelling or arithmetic computation.

**acuity**   Sharpness of perceptual ability—how well or clearly one can see, hear, or use other senses.

**adaptive behavior**   An aspect of a child's functioning often considered in diagnosing mental retardation. Can the child adapt to the tasks of everyday life?

**affectional bond**   A relatively long-enduring tie in which the partner is important as a unique individual and is interchangeable with none other.

**aggression**   Usually defined as intentional physical or verbal behaviors directed toward a person or an object with the intent to inflict damage on that person or object.

**altruism**   Giving or sharing objects, time, or goods with others, with no obvious self-gain.

**amniocentesis**   A medical test for genetic abnormalities in the embryo or fetus that may be done at about 15 weeks of gestation.

**androgyny**   A self-concept including and behavior expressing high levels of both masculine and feminine qualities.

**anoxia**   A shortage of oxygen. If it is prolonged, it can result in brain damage. This is one of the potential risks at birth.

**Apgar score**   An assessment of the newborn completed by the physician or midwife at one minute and again at five minutes after birth, assessing five characteristics: heart rate, respiratory rate, muscle tone, response to stimulation, and color.

**assimilation**   That part of the adaptation process that involves the "taking in" of new experiences or information into existing schemes. Experience is not taken in "as is," however, but is modified (or interpreted) somewhat so as to fit the pre-existing schemes.

**attachment**   A subvariety of affectional bond in which the central figure is experienced as a safe base from which to explore the world.

**attachment behaviors**   The collection of (probably) instinctive behaviors of one person toward another that brings about or maintains proximity and caregiving, such as the smile of the young infant; behaviors that reflect an attachment.

**attention deficit hyperactivity disorder (ADD)**   The technical term for what is more normally called *hyperactivity,* characterized by short attention span, distractibility, and heightened levels of physical activity.

**authoritarian parental style**   One of the three styles described by Baumrind, characterized by high levels of control and maturity demands and low levels of nurturance and communication.

**authoritative parental style**   One of the three styles described by Baumrind, characterized by high levels of control, nurturance, maturity demands, and communication.

**autism**   A severe form of disorder including emotional unresponsiveness and social cognition deficiencies. Present from birth, it appears to have a physical origin.

**autonomous morality**   Piaget's second proposed stage of moral reasoning, developing some time after age 7, characterized by judgment of intent and emphasis on reciprocity.

**autosomes**   The 22 pairs of chromosomes in which both members of the pair are the same shape and carry parallel information.

**axon**   The long appendage-like part of a neuron; the terminal fibers of the axon serve as transmitters in the synaptic connection with the dendrites of other neurons.

**babbling**   The vocalizing, often repetitively, of consonant-vowel combinations by an infant, typically beginning at about 6 months of age.

**Bayley Scales of Infant Development**   The best known and most widely used test of infant "intelligence."

**behavior genetics**   The study of the genetic basis of behavior, such as intelligence or personality.

**blastocyst**   The name used for the small mass of cells, about two weeks after conception, that implants itself into the wall of the uterus.

**brain damage**   Some injury to the brain, either during prenatal development or later, that results in improper functioning of the brain.

**canalization**   Term used to describe the degree to which development may be shaped by underlying maturational forces (as opposed to environment) during some period in the lifespan.

**categorical self**   Aspect of the self-scheme, beginning with self-awareness, in which the child defines herself in terms of a series of categories, such as age, gender, size, or skill.

**cephalocaudal**   From the head downward. Describes one recurrent pattern of physical development in infancy.

**cesarean section (C-section)**   Delivery of the child through an incision in the mother's abdomen.

**chorionic villus sampling (CVS)**   A technique for prenatal genetic diagnosis involving taking a sample of cells from the placenta. Can be performed earlier in the pregnancy than amniocentesis.

**chromosomal anomalies**   Any chromosomal pattern in which the individual has too many or too few chromosomes. Almost always associated with mental retardation.

**chromosomes**   Structures in the cells in the body that contain genetic information. Each chromosome is made up of many genes.

**class inclusion**   The relationship between classes of objects, such that a subordinate class is included in a superordinate class, as bananas are part of the class "fruit."

**classical conditioning**   One of three major types of learning. An automatic unconditioned response such as an emotion or a reflex comes to be triggered by a new cue, called the conditioned stimulus (CS), after the CS has been paired several times with the original unconditioned stimulus.

**cliques**   Groups of 6-8 friends with strong attachment bonds and high levels of group solidarity and loyalty.

**cohort**   A group of persons of approximately the same age who have shared similar major life experiences, such as cultural training, economic conditions, or type of education.

**color constancy**   The ability to see the color of an object as remaining the same despite changes in illumination or shadow. One of the basic perceptual constancies that make up "object constancy."

**competence**   The behavior of a person as it would be under ideal or perfect circumstances. It is not possible to measure competence directly.

**componential intelligence**   One of three types of intelligence in Sternberg's triarchic theory of intelligence; that type of intelligence typically measured on IQ tests, including analytic thinking, remembering facts, and organizing information.

**conceptual tempo**   A dimension of individual differences in perceptual/conceptual style suggested by Kagan, describing the general pace with which objects (or people) are examined or explored.

**concrete operational stage**   The stage of development proposed by Piaget between ages 6 and 12, in which mental operations such as subtraction, reversibility, and multiple classification are acquired.

**conditioned stimuli**   In classical conditioning, the stimuli that, after being paired a number of times with an unconditioned stimulus, come to trigger the unconditioned response.

**conduct disorders**   Diagnostic term for individuals showing high levels of aggressive, antisocial, or delinquent behavior.

**confluence model**   Zajonc's term for his explanation of family size and ordinal position effects on IQ. Assumes that a child's IQ is partially determined by the average intellectual level of the family members with whom the child has contact.

**conservation**   The concept that objects remain the same in fundamental ways, such as weight or number, even when there are external changes in shape or arrangement. Typically understood by children after age 5.

**contextual intelligence**   One of three types of intelligence in Sternberg's triarchic theory of intelligence; often also called "street smarts," this type of intelligence includes skills in adapting to an environment, and in adapting an environment to one's own needs.

**control group**   The group of subjects in an experiment that receives either no special treatment or some neutral treatment.

**conventional morality**   The second level of moral judgment proposed by Kohlberg, in which the person's judgments are dominated by considerations of group values and laws.

**cooing**   An early stage during the prelinguistic period, from about 1-4 months of age, when vowel sounds are repeated, particularly the *uuu* sound

**correlation**   A statistic used to describe the degree or strength of a relationship between two variables. It can range from +1.00 to -1.00. The closer it is to 1.00 the stronger the relationship being described.

**cortex**   The convoluted gray portion of the brain which governs most complex thought, language, and memory, among other functions.

**critical period**   A period of time during development when the organism is especially responsive to and learns from a specific type of stimulation. The same stimulation at other points in development has little or no effect.

**cross-modal transfer**   The ability to coordinate information from two senses, such as matching the shape of the mouth with the sound being spoken, or to transfer information gained through one sense to another sense at a later time, such as identifying visually something you had previously explored only tactually.

**cross-sectional studies**   Studies in which different groups of individuals of different ages are all studied at the same time.

**crossing over**   The process that occurs during meiosis in which genetic material from pairs of chromosomes may be exchanged.

**crowds**   Larger and looser groups of friends than cliques, with perhaps 20 members; normally made up of several cliques joined together.

**cumulative deficit**   Any difference between groups in IQ (or achievement test) scores that becomes larger over time.

**deductive logic**   Reasoning from the general to the particular, from a rule to an expected instance, or from a theory to a hypothesis. Characteristic of formal operational thought.

**dendrites**   The branch-like parts of a neuron that serve as the receptors in synaptic connections with the axons of other neurons.

**deoxyribonucleic acid**   Called DNA for short, this is the chemical of which genes are composed.

**dependent variable**   The variable in an experiment which is expected to show the impact of manipulations of the independent variable.

**depression**   A combination of sad mood, sleep and eating disturbances, and difficulty concentrating. When all these symptoms are present it is usually called *clinical depression.*

**developmental psychopathology**   A relatively new approach to the study of deviance that emphasizes that normal and abnormal development have common roots, and that pathology can arise from many different pathways or systems.

**dilation**   The first stage of childbirth when the cervix opens sufficiently to allow the infant's head to pass into the birth canal.

**dominance**   The ability of one person consistently to "win" competitive encounters with other individuals.

**dominance hierarchy**   A set of dominance relationships in a group describing the rank order of "winners" and "losers" in competitive encounters.

**Down syndrome**   A genetic anomaly in which every cell contains three copies of chromosome 21 rather than two. Children born with this genetic pattern are usually mentally retarded and have characteristic physical features.

**dyslexia**   A form of specific learning disability in which the individual has difficulty with reading.

**ectomorphic**   Body type defined by bone length; an ectomorphic individual is tall and slender, usually with stooped shoulders.

**effacement**   The flattening of the cervix which, along with dilation, allows the delivery of the infant.

**ego**   In Freudian theory, that portion of the personality that organizes, plans, and keeps the person in touch with reality. Language and thought are both ego functions.

**egocentrism**   A cognitive state in which the individual (typically a child) sees the world only from his own perspective, without awareness that there are other perspectives.

**embryo**   The name given to the organism during the period of prenatal development from about two to eight weeks after conception, beginning with implantation of the blastocyst into the uterine wall.

**empathy**   As defined by Hoffman, it is "a vicarious affective response that does not necessarily match another's affective state but is more appropriate to the other's situation than to one's own" (Hoffman, 1984, p. 285).

**empiricism**   Opposite of *nativism*. The theoretical point of view that all perceptual skill arises from experience.

**endocrine glands**   These glands, including the adrenals, the thyroid, the pituitary, the testes, and the ovaries, secrete hormones governing overall physical growth and sexual maturing.

**endomorphic**   Body type defined by amount of body fat; an endomorphic individual is soft and round in shape.

**equilibration**   The third part of the adaptation process, as proposed by Piaget, involving a periodic restructuring of schemes into new structures.

**estrogen**   The female sex hormone secreted by the ovaries.

**executive processes**   Proposed subset of information processes involving organizing and planning strategies. Similar in meaning to metacognition.

**existential self**   Lewis & Brooks-Gunn's term for the most basic part of the self-scheme or self-concept; the sense of being separate and distinct from others and the awareness of the constancy of the self.

**experiential intelligence**   One of three types of intelligence described by Sternberg in his triarchic theory of intelligence; includes creativity, insight, seeing new relationships among experiences.

**experiment**   A research strategy in which subjects are assigned randomly to groups which are then provided with experiences that vary along some key dimension.

**experimental group**   The group (or groups) of subjects in an experiment that is given some special treatment intended to produce some specific consequence.

**expressive language**   The term used to describe the child's skill in speaking and communicating orally.

**expressive style**   One of two styles of early language proposed by Nelson, characterized by low rates of noun-like terms and high use of personal-social words and phrases.

**externalizing problems**   Category of psychopathologies that includes any deviant behavior primarily directed away from the individual, such as conduct disorders or hyperactivity.

**extinction**   A decrease in the strength of some response after nonreinforcement.

**fallopian tube**   The tube down which the ovum travels to the uterus and in which conception usually occurs.

**fetal alcohol syndrome (FAS)**   A pattern of physical and mental abnormalities, including mental retardation and minor physical anomalies, found often in children born to alcoholic mothers.

**fetus**   The name given to the developing organism from about eight weeks after conception until birth.

**fontanels**   The "soft spots" in the skull present at birth. These disappear when the several bones of the skull grow together.

**foreclosure**   One of four identity statuses proposed by Marcia, involving an ideological or occupational commitment without having gone through a reevaluation.

**formal operational stage**   Piaget's name for the fourth and final major stage of cognitive development, occurring during adolescence, when the child becomes able to manipulate and organize ideas as well as objects.

**gametes**   Sperm and ova. These cells, unlike all other cells of the body, contain only 23 chromosomes rather than 23 pairs.

**gender concept**   The understanding of one's own gender, including the permanence and constancy of gender.

**gender constancy**   The final step in developing a gender concept, in which the child understands that gender doesn't change even though there are external changes like clothing or hair length.

**gender identity**   The first step in gender concept development, in which the child labels herself correctly and categorizes others correctly as male or female.

**gender schema**   A fundamental schema created by children beginning at age 18 months or younger by which the child categorizes people, objects, activities, and qualities by gender.

**gender stability**   The second step in gender concept development, in which the child understands that a person's gender continues to be stable throughout the lifetime.

**genes**   Uniquely coded segments of DNA in chromosomes that affect one or more specific body processes or developments.

**genotype**   The pattern of characteristics and developmental sequences mapped in the genes of any specific individual. Will be modified by individual experience into the phenotype.

**giftedness**   Normally defined in terms of very high IQ (above 140 or 150), but may also be defined in terms of remarkable skill in one or more specific areas, such as mathematics or memory.

**glial cells**   One of two major classes of cells making up the nervous system, glial cells provide the firmness and structure, the "glue" to hold the system together.

**gonadotropic hormone**   Hormones produced in the pituitary gland which stimulate the sex organs to develop.

**goodness-of-fit**   A hypothesis about the interaction of nature and nurture suggesting that negative outcomes occur when the child's characteristics do not fit with the demands of a particular family or school environment.

**habituation**   An automatic decrease in the intensity of a response to a repeated stimulus, which enables the child or adult to ignore the familiar and focus attention on the novel.

**hearing-impaired**   The phrase currently used in place of "hard of hearing" to describe children or adults with significant hearing loss.

**heteronomous morality**   Piaget's first proposed stage of moral reasoning, characterized by moral absolutism and belief in immanent justice. Judgments are based on consequences rather than intent.

**holophrases**   The expression of a whole idea in a single word. Characteristic of the child's language from about 12-18 months.

**hyperactivity**   The common term for *attention deficit hyperactivity disorder.*

**id**   In Freudian theory, the first, primitive portion of the personality; the storehouse of basic energy, continually pushing for immediate gratification.

**identification**   The process of taking into oneself ("incorporating") the qualities and ideas of another person, which Freud thought was the result of the Oedipal crisis at ages 3-5. The child attempts to make himself like his parent of the same sex.

**identity achievement**   One of four identity statuses proposed by Marcia, involving the successful resolution of an identity "crisis," resulting in a new commitment.

**identity diffusion**   One of four identity statuses proposed by Marcia, involving neither a current reevaluation nor a firm personal commitment.

**impulsivity**   One end of the continuum of conceptual tempo described by Kagan. Impulsive individuals examine objects or arrays quickly, with rapid scans, and may make more errors if fine discriminations are required.

**inborn errors of metabolism**   Any one of several inherited disorders (including PKU) resulting in an inability to digest or metabolize particular enzymes. Some such disorders are associated with retardation if not treated.

**independent variable**   A condition or event that an experimenter varies in some systematic way in order to observe the impact of that variation on the subjects' behavior.

**inductive logic**   Reasoning from the particular to the general, from experience to broad rules. Characteristic of concrete operational thinking.

**inflections**   The grammatical "markers" such as plurals, possessives, past tenses, and equivalent.

**information processing**   A way of looking at cognition and cognitive development that emphasizes both fundamental processes built into the "hardware" and the "software" of thinking, such as memory strategies, problem solving strategies, and planning.

**insecure attachment**  Includes both ambivalent and avoidant patterns of attachment in children; the child does not use the parent as a safe base and is not readily consoled by the parent if upset.

**Intelligence quotient (IQ)**  Originally defined in terms of a child's mental age and chronological age, IQs are now computed by comparing a child's performance with that of other children of the same chronological age.

**internal working model of social relationships**  Cognitive construction, for which the earliest relationships may form the template, of the workings of relationships, such as expectations of support or affection, trustworthiness, etc.

**internalizing problems**  A category of psychopathologies in which the deviant behavior is directed inward, including anxiety and depression.

**intrinsic reinforcements**  Those inner sources of pleasure, pride, or satisfaction that serve to increase the likelihood that an individual will repeat the behavior that led to the feeling.

**language acquisition device**  A hypothesized brain structure that may be "programmed" to make language learning possible.

**learning disability (LD)**  See *specific learning disability.*

**libido**  The term used by Freud to describe the pool of sexual energy in each individual.

**longitudinal study**  A research design in which the same subjects are observed or assessed repeatedly over a period of months or years.

**low birth weight (LBW)**  The phrase now used (in place of the word *premature*) to describe infants whose weight is below the optimum range at birth. Includes infants born too early (preterm or short gestation infants) and those who are "small-for-date."

**maturation**  The sequential unfolding of physical characteristics, governed by instructions contained in the genetic code and shared by all members of the species.

**mean length of utterance**  Usually abbreviated MLU; the average number of meaningful units in a sentence. Each basic word is one meaningful unit, as is each inflection, such as the *s* for plural or the *ed* for a past tense.

**medulla**  A portion of the brain that lies immediately above the spinal cord; largely developed at birth.

**meiosis**  The process of cell division that produces gametes in which only one member of each chromosome pair is passed on to the new cell.

**menarche**  Onset of menstruation in girls.

**mentally retarded**  Those children who show a pattern of low IQ, poor adaptive behavior, and poor skills in information processing.

**mesomorphic**  Body type characterized by amount of muscle mass; a mesomorphic male is square-chested, broad-shouldered, and muscular.

**metacognition**  General and rather loosely used term describing an individual's knowledge of his own thinking processes. Knowing what you know and how you go about learning or remembering.

**metamemory**  A subcategory of metacognition; knowledge about your own memory processes.

**midbrain**  A section of the brain lying above the medulla and below the cortex that regulates attention, sleeping, waking, and other "automatic" functions. Largely developed at birth.

**mitosis**  The process of cell division common for all cells other than gametes, in which both new cells contain 23 pairs of chromosomes.

**morality of reciprocity**  Another term for autonomous morality.

**moral realism**  Another term for heteronomous morality.

**moratorium**  One of four identity statuses proposed by Marcia, involving an ongoing reexamination but without a new commitment.

**motherese**  The word linguists often use to describe the particular pattern of speech by adults to young children. The sentences are shorter, simpler, repetitive, and higher pitched.

**motor development**  Growth and change in ability to do physical activities, such as walking, running, or riding a bike.

**myelin**  Material making up a sheath that develops around most axons. This sheath is not completely developed at birth.

**myelinization**  The process by which myelin is added.

**nativism**  See *empiricism.* The view that perceptual skills are inborn and do not require experience to develop.

**nature/nurture controversy**  A common label for the classic dispute about the relative roles of heredity versus environment.

**negative reinforcement**  The strengthening of a behavior that occurs because of the removal or cessation of an unpleasant stimulus.

**neurons**  The second major class of cells in the nervous system, neurons are responsible for transmission and reception of nerve impulses.

**object constancy**  The general phrase describing the ability to see objects as remaining the same despite changes in retinal image.

**object identity**  Part of the object concept. The recognition that objects remain the same from one encounter to the next.

**object permanence**  Part of the object concept. The recognition that an object continues to exist even when it is temporarily out of sight.

**observational learning (modeling)**  Learning of motor skills, attitudes, or other behaviors through observing someone else perform them.

**Oedipus conflict**  The pattern of events Freud believed occurred between ages 3 and 5 when the child experiences a "sexual" desire for the parent of the opposite sex; the resulting fear of possible reprisal from the parent of the same sex is resolved when the child "identifies" with the parent of the same sex.

**operant conditioning**  One of the three major types of learning in which the probability of a person performing some behavior is affected by positive or negative reinforcements.

**operations**  Term used by Piaget for complex, internal, abstract, reversible schemes, first seen at about age 6.

**ossification**  The process of hardening by which soft tissue becomes bone.

**overregularization**  The tendency on the part of children to make the language regular, such as using past tenses like *beated* or *goed.*

**ovum**  The gamete produced by a women, which, if fertilized by a sperm from the male, forms the basis for the developing organism.

**partial reinforcement**  Reinforcement of behavior on some schedule less frequent than every occasion.

**perceptual constancies**  A collection of constancies, including shape, size, and color constancy.

**performance**  The behavior shown by a person under actual circumstances. Even when we are interested in competence, all we can ever measure is performance.

**permissive parental style**  One of the three styles described by Baumrind, characterized by high levels of nurturance and low levels of control, maturity demands, and communication.

**personality** The collection of individual, relatively enduring, patterns of reacting to and interacting with others that distinguishes each child or adult.

**phenotype** The expression of a particular set of genetic information in a specific environment; the observable result of the joint operation of genetic and environmental influences.

**pituitary gland** One of the endocrine glands that plays a central role in controlling the rate of physical maturation and sexual maturing.

**placenta** An organ that develops during gestation between the fetus and the wall of the uterus. The placenta filters nutrients from the mother's blood, acting as liver, lungs, and kidneys for the fetus.

**positive reinforcement** Strengthening of a behavior by the presentation of some pleasurable or positive stimulus.

**postpartum depression** A severe form of the common experience of postpartum blues. Affecting perhaps 20 percent of women, this form of clinical depression typically lasts six to eight weeks.

**power** That aspect of intellectual skill that has to do with how well or how quickly a child can perform cognitive tasks. A dimension of individual difference in intellectual skill.

**pragmatics** The rules for the use of language in communicative interaction, such as the rules for taking turns, the style of speech appropriate for varying listeners, and equivalent.

**preconventional morality** The first level of morality proposed by Kohlberg, in which moral judgments are dominated by consideration of what will be punished and what feels good.

**prelinguistic phase** The period before the child speaks his first words.

**preoperational stage** Piaget's term for the second major stage of cognitive development, from age 2 to 6, marked at the beginning by the ability to use symbols and by the development of basic classification and logical abilities.

**preterm** Descriptive phrase now widely used to label infants born before 37 weeks gestational age.

**principled morality** The third level of morality proposed by Kohlberg, in which considerations of justice, individual rights, and contracts dominate moral judgment.

**prosocial behavior** See *altruism.*

**proximodistal** From the center outward. With cephalocaudal, describes the pattern of physical changes in infancy.

**psychosexual stages** The stages of personality development suggested by Freud, including the oral, anal, phallic, latency, and genital stages.

**psychosocial stages** The stages of personality development suggested by Erikson, including trust, autonomy, initiative, industry, identity, intimacy, generativity, and ego integrity.

**puberty** The collection of hormonal and physical changes at adolescence that brings about sexual maturity.

**punishment** Unpleasant consequences, administered after some undesired behavior by a child or adult, with the intent of extinguishing the behavior.

**rapid eye movement (REM) sleep** One of the characteristics of sleep during dreaming, which occurs during the sleep of newborns, too.

**receptive language** Term used to describe the child's ability to understand (receive) language, as contrasted to his ability to express language.

**referential style** Second style of early language proposed by Nelson, characterized by emphasis on objects and their naming and description.

**reflection** The other end of the "tempo" dimension of perceptual style. Reflective individuals examine objects or arrays very carefully and slowly. When fine discriminations are required, they normally perform better than impulsive individuals.

**reflexes** Automatic body reactions to specific stimulation, such as the knee jerk or the Moro reflex. Many reflexes remain among adults, but the newborn also has some "primitive" reflexes that disappear as the cortex is fully developed.

**responsiveness** An aspect of parent-child interaction. A responsive parent is sensitive to the child's cues and reacts appropriately, following the child's lead.

**restrictiveness** Term used to describe a particular pattern of parental control, involving limitation of the child's movements or options, such as by the use of playpens or harnesses in a young child, or strict rules about play areas or free choices in an older child.

**rubella** A form of measles that, if contracted during the first three months of a pregnancy, may have severe effects on the developing baby.

**saccadic movements** The rapid adjustments of the aim of the eye toward some object, such as when you scan an object to identify it or to learn its properties, or to locate some new object in your visual field.

**scheme** Piaget's word for the basic actions of knowing, including both physical actions (sensorimotor schemes, such as looking or reaching) and mental actions, such as classifying, comparing, or reversing. An experience is assimilated to a scheme, and the scheme is modified or created through accommodation.

**secular trends** Patterns of change over several cohorts in such things as the timing of menarche or height or weight.

**secure attachment** Demonstrated by the child's ability to use the parent as a safe base and to be consoled after separation, when fearful, or when otherwise stressed.

**self-concept** The broad idea of "who I am," including the existential self and the categorical self.

**self-esteem** A global judgment of self-worth; how well you like who you perceive yourself to be.

**semantics** The rules for conveying meaning in language.

**sensitive period** Similar to a critical period except broader and less specific. A time in development when a particular type of stimulation is particularly important or effective.

**sensorimotor stage** Piaget's term for the first major stage of cognitive development, from birth to about 18 months, when the child moves from reflexive to voluntary action.

**sequential designs** A family of research designs which involve multiple cross-sectional, or multiple longitudinal, studies, or a combination of the two.

**sex chromosomes** The X and Y chromosomes, which determine the sex of the child. In humans, XX is the female pattern, XY the male pattern.

**sex-role behavior** The performance of behavior that matches the culturally-defined sex role, such as choosing "sex-appropriate" toys, or playing with same-sex children.

**sex-role concept** The understanding of what males and females do and are "supposed to do."

**sex-role stereotyping** The process of overextending sex roles or sex-role behavior.

**sex typing** See *sex-role behavior.*

**shape constancy** The ability to see an object's shape as remaining the same despite changes in the shape of the retinal image. A basic perceptual constancy.

**size constancy** The ability to see an object's size as remaining the same despite changes in size of the retinal image. A key element in this constancy is the ability to judge depth.

**small-for-date** A term used to describe an infant who weighs less than is normal for the number of weeks of gestation completed.

**social class** Widely used term to describe broad variations in economic and social positions within society. Four broad groups are most often described: upper class, middle class, working class, and lower class (also called poverty level). For an individual family, the designation is based on the occupations and education of the adults in the household.

**social cognition**   Term used to describe a relatively new area of research and theory focused on the child's *understanding* of social relationships.

**specific learning disability (SLD)**   Term commonly used to describe a disorder in understanding or processing language or symbols.

**Stanford-Binet**   The best-known American intelligence test. It was written by Louis Terman and his associates based upon the first tests by Binet and Simon.

**states of consciousness**   Five main sleep/awake states have been identified in infants, from deep sleep to active awake states.

**Strange Situation**   A series of episodes used by Mary Ainsworth and others in studies of attachment. The child is observed with the mother, with a stranger, left alone, and then reunited with stranger and mother.

**structures**   Aspects of intellectual skill that change with age and are shared by all children. Focus on *how* the child arrives at a particular answer, rather than on the correctness of the answer.

**superego**   In Freudian theory, the "conscience" part of personality, which develops as a result of the identification process. The superego contains the parental and societal values and attitudes incorporated by the child.

**synapse**   The point of communication between the axon of one neuron and the dendrites of another, where nerve impulses are passed from one neuron to another, or from a neuron to some other type of cell, such as a muscle cell.

**syntax**   The rules for forming sentences; also called grammar.

**telegraphic speech**   A characteristic of early child sentences in which everything but the crucial words is omitted, as if for a telegram.

**teratogen**   Any outside agent, such as a disease or a chemical, whose presence significantly increases the risk of deviations or abnormalities in prenatal development.

**theory of mind**   Phrase used to describe one aspect of the thinking of 4- and 5-year-olds when they show signs of understanding not only that other people think differently, but something about the way others' minds work.

**tracking**   Also called smooth pursuit. The smooth movements of the eye used to follow the track of some moving object.

**transductive reasoning**   Reasoning from the specific to the specific; assuming that when two things happen together, one is the cause of the other.

**triarchic theory of intelligence**   A theory proposed by Sternberg, proposing the existence of three types of intelligence, the componential, the contextual, and the experiential.

**unconditioned response**   In classical conditioning this is the basic unlearned response that is triggered by the unconditioned stimulus.

**unconditioned stimulus**   In classical conditioning this is the cue or signal that automatically triggers (without learning) the unconditioned response.

**uterus**   The female organ in which the blastocyst implants itself and within which the embryo/fetus develops. (Commonly referred to as the womb.)

**very low birth weight**   The phrase now commonly used to describe infants who weigh 1500 grams (3 1/3 lbs) or less at birth.

**warmth versus hostility**   The key dimension of emotional tone used to describe family interactions.

**WISC-R**   The Wechsler Intelligence Scale for Children, Revised. Another well-known American IQ test which includes both verbal and performance (nonverbal) subtests.

**zygote**   Term used to describe the developing organism from conception until implantation is complete.

# REFERENCES

Abel, E. L. (1984). *Fetal alcohol syndrome and fetal alcohol effects*. New York: Plenum.

Abrams, B., Newman, V., Key, T., & Parker, J. (1989). Maternal weight gain and preterm delivery. *Obstetrics and Gynecology, 74,* 577–1989.

Achenbach, T. M. (1982). *Developmental psychopathology* (2nd ed.). New York: Wiley.

Achenbach, T. M., & Edelbrock, C. S. (1981). Behavioral problems and competencies reported by parents of normal and disturbed children aged 4 through 16. *Monographs of the Society for Research in Child Development, 46* (1, Whole No. 188).

Achenbach, T. M., & Edelbrock, C. S. (1982). *Manual for the child behavior checklist and child behavior profile*. Burlington, VT: Child Psychiatry, University of Vermont.

Achenbach, T. M., Phares, V., Howell, C. T., Rauh, V. A., & Nurcombe, B. (1990). Seven-year outcome of the Vermont intervention program for low-birthweight infants. *Child Development, 61,* 1672–1681.

Adler, A. (1948). *Studies in analytical psychology*. New York: Norton.

Ainsworth, M. D. S. (1972). Attachment and dependency: A comparison. In J. L. Gewirtz (Ed.), *Attachment and dependency* (pp. 97–138). Washington, DC: V. H. Winston.

Ainsworth, M. D. S. (1982). Attachment: Retrospect and prospect. In C. M. Parkes & J. Stevenson-Hinde (Eds.), *The place of attachment in human behavior* (pp. 3–30). New York: Basic Books.

Ainsworth, M. D. S. (1989). Attachments beyond infancy. *American Psychologist, 44,* 709–716.

Ainsworth, M. D. S., & Wittig, B. A. (1969). Attachment and exploratory behavior of one-year-olds in a strange situation. In B. M. Foss (Ed.), *Determinants of infant behavior* (Vol. 4). London: Methuen.

Ainsworth, M. D. S., Bell, S. M., & Stayton, D. J. (1972). Individual differences in strange situation behavior of one-year-olds. In H. R. Schaffer (Ed.), *The origins of human social relations* (pp. 17–51). London: Academic Press.

Ainsworth, M. D. S., Blehar, M., Waters, E., & Wall, S. (1978). *Patterns of attachment*. Hillsdale, NJ: Erlbaum.

Aksu-Koc, A. A., & Slobin, D. I. (1985). The acquisition of Turkish. In D. I. Slobin (Ed.), *The crosslinguistic study of language acquisition: Vol. 1 The data* (pp. 839–878). Hillsdale, NJ: Erlbaum.

Allison, P. D., & Furstenberg, F. F., Jr. (1989). How marital dissolution affects children: Variations by age and sex. *Developmental Psychology, 25,* 540–549.

American Psychiatric Association (1987). *Diagnostic and statistical manual of mental disorders* (3rd ed. rev.). Washington, DC: Author.

Anderson, C. W., Nagle, R. J., Roberts, W. A., & Smith, J. W. (1981). Attachment to substitute caregivers as a function of center quality and caregiver involvement. *Child Development, 52,* 53–61.

Anderson, D. R., Lorch, E. P., Field, D. E., Collins, P. A., & Nathan, J. G. (1986). Television viewing at home: Age trends in visual attention and time with TV. *Child Development, 57,* 1024–1033.

Andersson, B. (1989). Effects of public day-care: A longitudinal study. *Child Development, 60,* 857–886.

Anisfeld, M. (1984). *Language development from birth to three*. Hillsdale, NJ: Erlbaum.

Anisfeld, M. (1991). Neonatal imitation. *Developmental Review, 11,* 60–97.

Anthony, E. J. (1970). The behavior disorders of childhood. In P. H. Mussen (Ed.), *Carmichael's manual of child psychology* (Vol. 2, 3rd ed.) (pp. 667–764). New York: Wiley.

Apgar, V. A. (1953). A proposal for a new method of evaluation of the newborn infant. *Anesthesia and Analgesia, 32,* 260–267.

Archer, J. (1981). Sex differences in maturation. In K. J. Connolly & H. F. R. Prechtl (Eds.), *Maturation and development: Biological and psychological perspectives*. Clinics in Developmental Medicine No. 77/78 (pp. 19–31). London: William Heinemann.

Asher, S. R., Oden, S. L., & Gottman, J. M. (1977). Children's friendships in school settings. In L. G. Katz (Ed.), *Current topics in early childhood education* (Vol. 1) (pp. 33–62). Norwood, NJ: Ablex.

Aslin, R. N. (1977). Development of binocular fixation in human infants. *Journal of Experimental Child Psychology, 23,* 133–150.

Aslin, R. N. (1981a). Experiential influences and sensitive periods in perceptual development: A unified model. In R. N. Aslin, J. R. Alberts, & M. R. Petersen (Eds.), *Development of perception. Psychobiological perspectives: Vol. 2. The visual system*. New York: Academic Press.

Aslin, R. N. (1981b). Development of smooth pursuit in human infants. In D. F. Fisher, R. A. Monty, & J. W. Senders (Eds.), *Eye movements: Cognition and visual perception* (pp. 31–51). Hillsdale, NJ: Erlbaum.

Aslin, R. N. (1987a). Motor aspects of visual development in infancy. In P. Salapatek & L. Cohen (Eds.), *Handbook of infant perception: Vol. 1. From sensation to perception* (pp. 43–113). Orlando, FL: Academic Press.

Aslin, R. N. (1987b). Visual and auditory development in infancy. In J. D. Osofsky (Ed.), *Handbook of infant development* (2nd ed.) (pp. 5–97). New York: Wiley-Interscience.

Aslin, R. N., & Smith, L. B. (1988). Perceptual development. *Annual Review of Psychology, 39,* 435–473.

Astbury, J., Orgill, A. A., Bajuk, B., & Yu, V. Y. H. (1990). Neurodevelopmental outcome, growth and health of extremely low-birthweight survivors: How soon can we tell? *Developmental Medicine and Child Neurology, 32,* 582–589.

Astington, J. W., Harris, P. L., & Olson, D. (Eds.) (1988). *Developing theories of mind*. New York: Cambridge University Press.

Attie, I., & Brooks-Gunn, J. (1989). Development of eating problems in adolescent girls: A longitudinal study. *Developmental Psychology, 25,* 70–79.

Attie, I., Brooks-Gunn, J., & Petersen, A. (1990). A developmental perspective on eating disorders and eating problems. In M. Lewis & S. M. Miller (Eds.), *Handbook of developmental psychopathology* (pp. 409–420). New York: Plenum.

Au, T. K., & Glusman, M. (1990). The principle of mutual exclusivity in word learning: To honor or not to honor? *Child Development, 61,* 1474–1490.

Baer, D. M. (1970). An age-irrelevant concept of development. *Merrill-Palmer Quarterly, 16,* 238–245.

Baird, P. A., Sadovnick, A. D., & Yee, I. M. L. (1991). Maternal age and birth defects: A population study. *The Lancet, 337,* 527–530.

Bakeman, R., & Gottman, J. M. (1987). Applying observational methods: A systematic view. In J. D. Osofsky (Ed.),

*Handbook of infant development* (2nd ed.) (pp. 818–854). New York: Wiley-Interscience.

Baldwin, A. L. (1948). Socialization and the parent-child relationship. *Child Development, 19,* 127–136.

Baldwin, A. L. (1949). The effect of home environment on nursery school behavior. *Child Development, 20,* 49–62.

Bamford, F. N., Bannister, R. P., Benjamin, C. M., Hillier, V. F., Ward, B. S., & Moore, W. M. O. (1990). Sleep in the first year of life. *Developmental Medicine and Child Neurology, 32,* 718–724.

Bandura, A. (1973). *Aggression: A social learning analysis.* Englewood Cliffs, NJ: Prentice-Hall.

Bandura, A. (1977). *Social learning theory.* Englewood Cliffs, NJ: Prentice-Hall.

Bandura, A. (1982). The self and mechanisms of agency. In J. Suls (Ed.), *Psychological perspectives on the self* (Vol. 1, pp. 3–40). Hillsdale, NJ: Erlbaum.

Bandura, A. (1986). *Social foundations of thought and action: A social cognitive theory.* Englewood Cliffs, NJ: Prentice-Hall.

Barenboim, C. (1977). Developmental changes in the interpersonal cognitive system from middle childhood to adolescence. *Child Development, 48,* 1467–1474.

Barenboim, C. (1981). The development of person perception in childhood and adolescence: From behavioral comparisons to psychological constructs to psychological comparisons. *Child Development, 52,* 129–144.

Barkley, R. A. (1990). Attention deficit disorders: History, definition, and diagnosis. In M. Lewis & S. M. Miller (Eds.), *Handbook of developmental psychopathology* (pp. 65–76). New York: Plenum.

Barkley, R. A., Fischer, M., Edelbrock, C. S., & Smallish, L. (1990). The adolescent outcome of hyperactive children diagnosed by research criteria: I. An 8-year prospective follow-up study. *Journal of the American Academy of Child and Adolescent Psychiatry, 29,* 546–557.

Barnard, K. E., & Bee, H. L. (1983). The impact of temporally patterned stimulation on the development of preterm infants. *Child Development, 54,* 1156–1167.

Barnard, K. E., & Eyres, S. J. (1979). *Child health assessment. Part 2: The first year of life* (DHEW Publication No. HRA 79–25). Washington, DC: U.S. Government Printing Office.

Barnard, K. E., Bee, H. L., & Hammond, M. A. (1984). Developmental changes in maternal interactions with term and preterm infants. *Infant Behavior and Development, 7,* 101–113.

Barnard, K. E., Hammond, M. A., Booth, C. L., Bee, H. L., Mitchell, S. K., &

Spieker, S. J. (1989). Measurement and meaning of parent-child interaction. In J. J. Morrison, C. Lord, & D. P. Keating (Eds.), *Applied developmental psychology* (Vol. 3) (pp. 40–81). San Diego: Academic Press.

Barnes, H. L., & Olson, D. H. (1985). Parent-adolescent communication and the circumplex model. *Child Development, 56,* 438–447.

Baron, P., & Perron, L. M. (1986). Sex differences in the Beck depression inventory scores of adolescents. *Journal of Youth and Adolescence, 15,* 165–171.

Baron-Cohen, S. (1989). Perceptual role taking and protodeclarative pointing in autism. *British Journal of Developmental Psychology, 7,* 113–127.

Baron-Cohen, S. (1991). Do people with autism understand what causes emotion? *Child Development, 62,* 385–395.

Barr, H. M., Streissguth, A. P., Darby, B. L., & Sampson, P. D. (1990). Prenatal exposure to alcohol, caffeine, tobacco, and aspirin: Effects on fine and gross motor performance in 4-year-old children. *Developmental Psychology, 26,* 339–348.

Barrett, D. E., Radke-Yarrow, M., & Klein, R. E. (1982). Chronic malnutrition and child behavior: Effects of early caloric supplementation on social and emotional functioning at school age. *Developmental Psychology, 18,* 541–556.

Bates, E. (1991). Connectionism and the study of change. Paper presented at the biennial meetings of the Society for Research in Child Development, Seattle.

Bates, E., & MacWhinney, B. (1987). Competition, variation, and language learning. In B. MacWhinney (Ed.), *Mechanisms of language acquisition* (pp. 157–194). Hillsdale, NJ: Erlbaum.

Bates, E., Bretherton, I., & Snyder, L. (1988). *From first words to grammar. Individual differences and dissociable mechanisms.* Cambridge: Cambridge University Press.

Bates, E., Bretherton, I., Beeghly-Smith, M., & McNew, S. (1982). Social bases of language development: A reassessment. In H. W. Reese & L. P. Lipsitt (Eds.), *Advances in child development and behavior* (Vol. 16) (pp. 8–68). New York: Academic Press.

Bates, E., Camaioni, L., & Volterra, V. (1975). The acquisition of performatives prior to speech. *Merrill-Palmer Quarterly, 21,* 205–226.

Bates, E., O'Connell, B., & Shore, C. (1987). Language and communication in infancy. In J. D. Osofsky (Ed.), *Handbook of infant development* (2nd ed.) (pp. 149–203). New York: Wiley-Interscience.

Bates, J. E. (1987). Temperament in infancy. In J. D. Osofsky (Ed.), *Handbook of infant development* (2nd ed.) (pp. 1101–1149). New York: Wiley-Interscience.

Bates, J. E. (1989a). Applications of temperament concepts. In G. A. Kohnstamm, J. E. Bates, & M. K. Rothbart (Eds.), *Temperament in childhood* (pp. 321–356). Chichester, England: Wiley.

Bates, J. E. (1989b). Concepts and measures of temperament. In G. A. Kohnstamm, J. E. Bates, & M. K. Rothbart (Eds.), *Temperament in childhood* (pp. 3–26). Chichester, England: Wiley.

Bates, J. E., Bales, K., Bennett, D. S., Ridge, B., & Brown, M. M. (1991). Origins of externalizing behavior problems at eight years of age. In D. J. Pepler & K. H. Rubin (Eds.), *The development and treatment of childhood aggression* (pp. 93–120). Hillsdale, NJ: Erlbaum.

Bates, J. E., Maslin, C. A., & Frankel, K. A. (1985). Attachment security, mother-child interaction, and temperament as predictors of behavior problem ratings at age three years. In I. Bretherton & E. Waters (Eds.), *Growing points of attachment theory and research. Monographs of the Society for Research in Child Development, 50,* (1–2, Serial No. 209) (pp. 167–193).

Baumrind, D. (1967). Child care practices anteceding three patterns of preschool behavior. *Genetic Psychology Monographs, 75,* 43–88.

Baumrind, D. (1971). Current patterns of parental authority. *Developmental Psychology Monograph, 4* (1, Part 2).

Baumrind, D. (1972). Socialization and instrumental competence in young children. In W. W. Hartup (Ed.), *The young child: Reviews of research* (Vol. 2, pp. 202–224). Washington, DC: National Association for the Education of Young Children.

Baumrind, D. (1973). The development of instrumental competence through socialization. In A. D. Pick (Ed.), *Minnesota Symposium on Child Psychology* (Vol 7, pp. 3–46). Minneapolis: University of Minnesota Press.

Bayley, N. (1969). *Bayley scales of infant development.* New York: Psychological Corporation.

Bearison, D. J., Magzamen, S., & Filardo, E. K. (1986). Socio-cognitive conflict and cognitive growth in young children. *Merrill-Palmer Quarterly, 32,* 51–72.

Becker, J. A. (1982). Children's strategic use of requests to mark and manipulate social status. In S. A. Kuczaj, II (Ed.), *Language development: Vol. 2. Language, thought, and culture* (pp. 1–36).

Hillsdale, NJ: Erlbaum.

Bee, H. L., Barnard, K. E., Eyres, S. J., Gray, C. A., Hammond, M. A., Spietz, A. L., Snyder, C., & Clark, B. (1982). Prediction of IQ and language skill from perinatal status, child performance, family characteristics, and mother-infant interaction. *Child Development, 53,* 1135–1156.

Bell, L. G., & Bell, D. C. (1982). Family climate and the role of the female adolescent: Determinants of adolescent functioning. *Family Relations, 31,* 519–527.

Bellinger, D. (1987, April). *Social class differences in the effects of in utero exposure to lead.* Paper presented at the biennial meetings of the Society for Research in Child Development, Baltimore.

Bellugi, U. (1988). The acquisition of a spatial language. In F. S. Kessel (Ed.), *The development of language and language researchers: Essays in honor of Roger Brown* (pp. 153–186). Hillsdale, NJ: Erlbaum.

Belsky, J. (1985). Prepared statement on the effects of day care. In Select Committee on Children, Youth, and Families, House of Representatives, 98th Congress, Second Session, I*mproving child care services: What can be done?* Washington, DC: U.S. Government Printing Office.

Belsky, J. (1987, April). *Science, social policy and day care: A personal odyssey.* Paper presented at the biennial meetings of the Society for Research in Child Development, Baltimore.

Belsky, J. (1990). The "Effects" of infant day care reconsidered. In N. Fox & G. G. Fein (Eds.), *Infant day care: The current debate* (pp. 3–40). Norwood, NJ: Ablex.

Belsky, J., & Rovine, M. (1987). Temperament and attachment security in the strange situation: An empirical rapprochement. *Child Development, 58,* 787–795.

Belsky, J., & Rovine, M. (1988). Nonmaternal care in the first year of life and the security of infant-parent attachment. *Child Development, 59,* 157–167.

Belsky, J., Lang, M. E., & Rovine, M. (1985). Stability and change in marriage across the transition to parenthood: A second study. *Journal of Marriage and the Family, 47,* 855–865.

Bem, S. L. (1974). The measurement of psychological androgyny. *Journal of Consulting and Clinical Psychology, 42,* 155–162.

Bem, S. L. (1981). Gender schema theory: A cognitive account of sex-typing. *Psychological Review, 88,* 354–364.

Benn, R. K. (1986). Factors promoting secure attachment relationships between employed mothers and their sons. *Child Development, 57,* 1224–1231.

Berberian, K. E., & Snyder, S. S. (1982). The relationship of temperament and stranger reaction for younger and older infants. *Merrill-Palmer Quarterly, 28,* 79–94.

Berch, D. B., & Bender, B. G. (1987, December). Margins of sexuality. *Psychology Today, 21,* 54–57.

Berg, J. M. (1974). Aetiological aspects of mental subnormality. In A. M. Clarke & A. D. B. Clarke (Eds.), *Mental deficiency: The changing outlook* (3rd ed.) (pp. 82–117). New York: Free Press.

Berg, W. K., & Berg, K. M. (1987). Psychophysiological development in infancy: State, startle, and attention. In J. D. Osofsky (Ed.), *Handbook of infant development* (2nd ed.) (pp. 238–317). New York: Wiley-Interscience.

Berk, L. E. (1986, May). Private speech: Learning out loud. *Psychology Today, 20,* 34–39, 42.

Berkowitz, G. S., Fiarman, G. S., Mojica, M. A., Bauman, J., & de Regt, R. H. (1989). Effect of physician characteristics on the cesarean birth rate. *American Journal of Obstetrics and Gynecology, 161,* 146–149.

Berkowitz, G. S., Skovron, M. L., Lapinski, R. H., & Berkowitz, R. L. (1990). Delayed childbearing and the outcome of pregnancy. *New England Journal of Medicine, 322,* 659–664.

Berndt, T. J. (1979). Developmental changes in conformity to peers and parents. *Developmental Psychology, 15,* 608–616.

Berndt, T. J. (1981). Age changes and changes over time in prosocial intentions and behavior between friends. *Developmental Psychology, 17,* 408–416.

Berndt, T. J. (1983). Social cognition, social behavior, and children's friendships. In E. T. Higgins, D. N. Ruble, & W. W. Hartup (Eds.), *Social cognition and social development. A sociocultural perspective* (pp. 158–192). Cambridge, England: Cambridge University Press.

Berndt, T. J. (1986). Children's comments about their friendships. In M. Perlmutter (Ed.), Cognitive perspectives on children's social and behavioral development. *Minnesota Symposia on Child Psychology* (Vol. 18, pp. 189–212). Hillsdale, NJ: Erlbaum.

Berndt, T. J., & Hoyle, S. G. (1985). Stability and change in childhood and adolescent friendships. *Developmental Psychology, 21,* 1007–1015.

Berndt, T. J., Hawkins, J. A., & Hoyle, S. G. (1986). Changes in friendship during a school year: Effects on children's and adolescents' impressions of friendship and sharing with friends. *Child Development, 57,* 1284–1297.

Bertenthal, B. I., & Campos, J. J. (1987). New directions in the study of early experience. *Child Development, 58,* 560–567.

Bettes, B. A. (1988). Maternal depression and motherese: Temporal and intonational features. *Child Development, 59,* 1089–1096.

Bialystok, E. (1988). Levels of bilingualism and levels of linguistic awareness. *Developmental Psychology, 24,* 560–567.

Biederman, J., Faraone, S., Keenan, K., Knee, D., & Tsuang, M. (1990). Family-genetic and psychosocial risk factors in DSM-III attention deficit disorder. *Journal of the American Academy of Child and Adolescent Psychiatry, 29,* 526–533.

Bierman, K. L. (1986). Process of change during social skills training with preadolescents and its relation to treatment outcome. *Child Development, 57,* 230–240.

Bigelow, B. J., & La Gaipa, J. J. (1975). Children's written descriptions of friendships: A multidimensional analysis. *Developmental Psychology, 11,* 857–858.

Bijstra, J., van Geert, P., & Jackson, S. (1989). Conservation and the appearance-reality distinction: What do children really know and what do they answer? *British Journal of Developmental Psychology, 7,* 43–53.

Billings, A. G., & Moos, R. H. (1983). Comparisons of children of depressed and nondepressed parents: A social-environmental perspective. *Journal of Abnormal Child Psychology, 11,* 463–486.

Billings, A. G., & Moos, R. H. (1985). Children of parents with unipolar depression: A controlled 1-year follow-up. *Journal of Abnormal Child Psychology, 14,* 149–166.

Binet, A., & Simon, T. (1905). Methodes nouvelles pour le diagnostic du niveau intellectuel des anormaux. *L'Anee Psychologique, 11,* 191–244.

Bivens, J. A., & Berk, L. E. (1990). A longitudinal study of the development of elementary school children's private speech. *Merrill-Palmer Quarterly, 36,* 443–463.

Bjorklund, D. F., & Arce, S. (1987, April). *Acquiring a mnemonic: Age and category knowledge effects.* Paper presented at the biennial meetings of the Society for Research in Child Development, Baltimore.

Bjorklund, D. F., & Muir, J. E. (1988). Remembering on their own: Children's development of free recall memory. In R. Vasta (Ed.), *Annals of child development* (Vol. 5, pp. 79–124). Greenwich, CT: JAI Press.

Black, B., & Hazen, N. L. (1990). Social

status and patterns of communication in acquainted and unacquainted preschool children. *Developmental Psychology, 26,* 379–387.

Blackman, J. A. (1990). Update on AIDS, CMV, and herpes in young children: Health, developmental, and educational issues. In M. Wolraich & D. K. Routh (Eds.), *Advances in developmental and behavioral pediatrics* (Vol. 9, pp. 33–58). London: Jessica Kingsley Publishers.

Blanche, S., Rouzioux, C., & Moscatto, M. L. (1989). A prospective study of infants born to women seropositive for human immunodeficiency virus Type 1. *New England Journal of Medicine, 320,* 1643–1648.

Block, J. (1971). *Lives through time.* Berkeley, CA: Bancroft.

Block, J. (1987, April). *Longitudinal antecedents of ego-control and ego-resiliency in late adolescence.* Paper presented at the biennial meetings of the Society for Research in Child Development, Baltimore.

Bloom, L. (1973). *One word at a time.* The Hague: Mouton.

Blumstein, P., & Schwartz, P. (1983). *American couples.* New York: William Morrow.

Bohannon, J. N., III, Warren-Leubecker, A., & Hepler, N. (1984). Word order awareness and early reading. *Child Development, 55,* 1541–1548.

Bornstein, M. H. (1987). Sensitive periods in development: Definition, existence, utility, and meaning. In M. H. Bornstein (Ed.), *Sensitive periods in development: Interdisciplinary perspectives* (pp. 3–18). Hillsdale, NJ: Erlbaum.

Bornstein, M. H. (1988). Perceptual development across the life cycle. In M. H. Bornstein & M. E. Lamb (Eds.), *Developmental psychology: An advanced textbook* (2nd ed.) (pp. 151–204). Hillsdale, NJ: Erlbaum.

Bornstein, M. H. (1989a). Stability in early mental development: From attention and information processing in infancy to language and cognition in childhood. In M. H. Bornstein & N. A. Krasnegor (Eds.), *Stability and continuity in mental development* (pp. 147–170). Hillsdale, NJ: Erlbaum.

Bornstein, M. H. (Ed). (1989b). Maternal responsiveness: Characteristics and consequences. *New Directions for Child Development, 43.*

Boston Women's Health Collective. (1984). *The new our bodies, ourselves: A book by and for women* (2nd ed.). New York: Simon & Schuster.

Bouchard, C., Tremblay, A., Déspres, J., Nadeau, A., Lupien, P. J., Thériault, Dussault, J., Moorjani, S., Pinault, S., & Fournier, G. (1990). The response to

long-term overfeeding in identical twins. *The New England Journal of Medicine, 322,* 1477–1482.

Bouchard, T. J., Jr., & McGue, M. (1981). Familial studies of intelligence: A review. *Science, 212,* 1055–1059.

Bouchard, T. J., Jr. (1984). Twins reared apart and together: What they tell us about human diversity. In S. Fox (Ed.), *The chemical and biological bases of individuality.* New York: Plenum Press.

Boukydis, C. F. Z., & Burgess, R. L. (1982). Adult physiological response to infant cries: Effects of temperament, parental status, and gender. *Child Development, 53,* 1291–1298.

Bower, T. G. R. (1966). The visual world of infants. *Scientific American, 215,* 80–92.

Bower, T. G. R. (1975). Infant perception of the third dimension and object concept development. In L. B. Cohen & P. Salapatek (Eds.), *Infant perception: From sensation to cognition* (pp. 33–50). New York: Academic Press.

Bower, T. G. R. (1977a). *The perceptual world of the child.* Cambridge, MA: Harvard University Press.

Bower, T. G. R. (1977b). Blind babies see with their ears. *New Scientist, 73,* 256–257.

Bowerman, M. (1985). Beyond communicative adequacy: From piecemeal knowledge to an integrated system in the child's acquisition of language. In K. E. Nelson (Ed.), *Children's language* (Vol. 5) (pp. 369–398). Hillsdale, NJ: Erlbaum.

Bowerman, M. (1987). Commentary: Mechanisms of language acquisition. In B. MacWhinney (Ed.), *Mechanisms of language acquisition* (pp. 443–466). Hillsdale, NJ: Erlbaum.

Bowlby, J. (1969). Attachment and loss: Vol. 1. *Attachment.* New York: Basic Books.

Bowlby, J. (1973). *Attachment and loss: Vol. 2. Separation, anxiety, and anger.* New York: Basic Books.

Bowlby, J. (1980). *Attachment and loss: Vol. 3. Loss, sadness, and depression.* New York: Basic Books.

Bowlby, J. (1988). Developmental psychiatry comes of age. *The American Journal of Psychiatry, 145,* 1–10.

Brackbill, Y. (1979). Obstetrical medication and infant behavior. In J. D. Osofsky (Ed.), *Handbook of infant development* (pp. 76–125). New York: Wiley.

Brackbill, Y., & Nevill, D. D. (1981). Parental expectations of achievement as affected by children's height. *Merrill-Palmer Quarterly, 27,* 429–441.

Brackbill, Y., McManus, K., & Woodward, L. (1985). *Medication in maternity.* Ann Arbor: University of Michigan Press.

Bradbard, M. R., Martin, C. L., Endsley, R.

C., & Halverson, C. F. (1986). Influence of sex stereotypes on children's exploration and memory: A competence versus performance distinction. *Developmental Psychology, 22,* 481–486.

Bradley, R. H. (1989). The use of the HOME inventory in longitudinal studies of child development. In M. H. Bornstein & N. A. Krasnegor (Eds.), *Stability and continuity in mental development* (pp. 191–216). Hillsdale, NJ: Erlbaum.

Bradley, R. H., & Caldwell, B. M. (1984). 174 children: A study of the relationship between home environment and cognitive development during the first 5 years. In A. W. Gottfried (Ed.), *Home environment and early cognitive development: Longitudinal research* (pp. 5–56). New York: Academic Press.

Bradley, R. H., Caldwell, B. M., Rock, S. L., Barnard, K. E., Gray, C., Hammond, M. A., Mitchell, S., Siegel, L., Ramey, C. D., Gottfried, A. W., & Johnson, D. L. (1989). Home environment and cognitive development in the first 3 years of life: A collaborative study involving six sites and three ethnic groups in North America. *Developmental Psychology, 25,* 217–235.

Bradley, R. J., & Caldwell, B. M. (1976). The relation of infants' home environment to mental test performance at fifty-four months: A follow-up study. *Child Development, 47,* 1172–1174.

Braine, M. D. S. (1963). The ontogeny of English phrase structure: The first phase. *Language, 39,* 1–13.

Braine, M. D. S. (1976). Children's first word combinations. *Monographs of the Society for Research in Child Development, 41* (Whole No. 164).

Brand, E., Clingempeel, W. E., & Bowen-Woodward, K. (1988). Family relationships and children's psychological adjustment in stepmother and stepfather families: Findings and conclusions from the Philadelphia Stepfamily Research Project. In E. M. Hetherington & J. D. Arasteh (Eds.), *Impact of divorce, single parenting, stepparenting on children* (pp. 299–324). Hillsdale, NJ: Erlbaum.

Brandenburg, N. A., Friedman, R. M., & Silver, S. E. (1990). The epidemiology of childhood psychiatric disorders: Prevalence findings from recent studies. *Journal of the American Academy of Child and Adolescent Psychiatry, 29,* 76–83.

Brazelton, T. B. (1983). *Infants and mothers. Differences in development,* (rev. ed.). New York: Delte/Seymour Lawrence.

Brazelton, T. B., Koslowski, B., & Main, M. (1974). The origins of reciprocity: The early mother-infant interaction. In M. Lewis and L. A. Rosenblum (Eds.),

*The effect of the infant on its caregiver* (pp. 49–76). New York: Wiley.

Breitmayer, B. J., & Ramey, C. T. (1986). Biological nonoptimality and quality of postnatal environment as codeterminants of intellectual development. *Child Development, 57,* 1151–1165.

Breland, H. M. (1974). Birth order, family configuration, and verbal achievement. *Child Development, 45,* 1011–1019.

Bristol, M. M., Gallagher, J. J., & Schopler, E. (1988). Mothers and fathers of young developmentally disabled and nondisabled boys: Adaptation and spousal support. *Developmental Psychology, 24,* 441–451.

Brody, E. B., & Brody, N. (1976). *Intelligence: Nature, determinants and consequences.* New York: Academic Press.

Broman, S. H., Nichols, P. L., & Kennedy, W. A. (1975). *Preschool IQ: Prenatal and early developmental correlates.* Hillsdale, NJ: Erlbaum.

Broman, S., Nichols, P. L., Shaughnessy, P., & Kennedy, W. (1987). *Retardation in young children.* Hillsdale, NJ: Erlbaum.

Bromwich, R. M. (1976). Focus on maternal behavior in infant intervention. *American Journal of Orthopsychiatry, 46,* 439–446.

Bronfenbrenner, U. (1975). Nature with nurture: A reinterpretation of the evidence. In A. Montague (Ed.), *Race and IQ.* New York: Oxford University Press.

Bronfenbrenner, U. (1979). *The ecology of human development.* Cambridge, MA: Harvard University Press.

Bronfenbrenner, U., Alvarez, W. F., & Henderson, C. R., Jr. (1984). Working and watching: Maternal employment status and parents' perceptions of their three-year-old children. *Child Development, 55,* 1362–1378.

Bronson, G. W. (1974). The postnatal growth of visual capacity. *Child Development, 45,* 873–890.

Bronson, G. W. (1991). Infant differences in rate of visual encoding. *Child Development, 62,* 44–45.

Brooks-Gunn, J. (1987). Pubertal processes and girls' psychological adaptation. In R. M. Lerner & T. T. Foch (Eds.), *Biological-psychosocial interactions in early adolescence* (pp. 123–154). Hillsdale, NJ: Erlbaum.

Brooks-Gunn, J., & Furstenberg, F. F., Jr. (1989). Adolescent sexual behavior. *American Psychologist, 44,* 249–257.

Brooks-Gunn, J., & Warren, M. P. (1985). The effects of delayed menarche in different contexts: Dance and nondance students. *Journal of Youth and Adolescence, 13,* 285–300.

Broverman, I. K., Broverman, D., Clarkson, F. E., Rosenkrantz, P. S., & Vogel, S. R. (1970). Sex-role stereotypes and clinical judgments of mental health. *Journal of Consulting and Clinical Psychology, 34,* 1–7.

Broverman, I. K., Vogel, S. R., Broverman, D. M., Clarkson, F. E., & Rosenkrantz, P. S. (1972). Sex role stereotypes: A current appraisal. *Journal of Social Issues, 28* (2), 59–79.

Brown, B. B., Clasen, D. R., & Eicher, S. A. (1986). Perceptions of peer pressure, peer conformity dispositions, and self-reported behavior among adolescents. *Developmental Psychology, 22,* 521–530.

Brown, R. (1965). *Social psychology.* New York: Free Press.

Brown, R. (1973). *A first language: The early stages.* Cambridge, MA: Harvard University Press.

Brown, R., & Bellugi, U. (1964). Three processes in the acquisition of syntax. *Harvard Educational Review, 334,* 133–151.

Brown, R., & Hanlon, C. (1970). Derivational complexity and order of acquisition. In J. R. Hayes (Ed.), *Cognition and the development of language* (pp. 155–207). New York: Wiley.

Brownell, C. A. (1986). Convergent developments: Cognitive-developmental correlates of growth in infant/toddler peer skills. *Child Development, 57,* 275–286.

Brownell, C. A. (1988). Combinatorial skills: Converging developments over the second year. *Child Development, 59,* 675–685.

Brownell, C. A. (1990). Peer social skills in toddlers: Competencies and constraints illustrated by same-age and mixed-age interaction. *Child Development, 61,* 836–848.

Brownell, C. A., & Carriger, M. S. (1990). Changes in cooperation and self-other differentiation during the second year. *Child Development, 61,* 1164–1174.

Brumback, R. A., & Staton, R. D. (1983). Learning disability in childhood depression. *American Journal of Orthopsychiatry, 53,* 269–281.

Bryant, P. E., MacLean, M., Bradley, L. L., & Crossland, J. (1990). Rhyme and alliteration, phoneme detection, and learning to read. *Developmental Psychology, 26,* 429–438.

Buchanan, C. M. (1991). V*ariation in adjustment to divorce: The role of feeling caught in the middle between parents.* Paper presented at the biennial meetings of the Society for Research in Child Development, Seattle.

Buehler, J. W., Kaunitz, A. M., Hogue, C. J. R., Hughes, J. M., Smith, J. C., & Rochat, R. W. (1986). Maternal mortality in women aged 35 years or older: United States. *Journal of the American Medical Association, 255,* 53–57.

Bullock, M., & Gelman, R. (1979).

Preschool children's assumptions about cause and effect: Temporal ordering. *Child Development, 50,* 89–96.

Bullock, M., & Lütkenhaus, P. (1990). Who am I? Self-understanding in toddlers. *Merrill-Palmer Quarterly, 36,* 217–238.

Bumpass, L. (1984). Children and marital disruption: A replication and update. *Demography, 41,* 71–82.

Burchinal, M., Lee, M., & Ramey, C. (1989). Type of day-care and preschool intellectual development in disadvantaged children. *Child Development, 60,* 128–137.

Burke, P., & Puig-Antich, J. (1990). Psychobiology of childhood depression. In M. Lewis & S. M. Miller (Eds.), *Handbook of developmental psychopathology* (pp. 327–340). New York: Plenum.

Buss, A. (1989). Temperaments as personality traits. In G. A. Kohnstamm, J. E. Bates, & M. K. Rothbart (Eds.), *Temperament in childhood* (pp. 49–58). Chichester, England: Wiley.

Buss, A. H., & Plomin, R. (1984). *Temperament: Early developing personality traits.* Hillsdale, NJ: Erlbaum.

Buss, A. H., & Plomin, R. (1986). The EAS approach to temperament. In R. Plomin & J. Dunn (Eds.), *The study of temperament: Changes, continuities and challenges* (pp. 67–80). Hillsdale, NJ: Erlbaum.

Bussen, K., & Bandura, A. (1984). Influence of gender constancy and social power on sex-linked modeling. *Journal of Personality and Social Psychology, 47,* 1292–1302.

Butterfield, E. C., Siladi, D., & Belmont, J. M. (1980). Validating theories of intelligence. In H. W. Reese & L. P. Lipsitt (Eds.), *Advances in child development and behavior* (Vol. 15, pp. 96–152). New York: Academic Press.

Cairns, R. B. (1991). Multiple metaphors for a singular idea. *Developmental Psychology, 27,* 23–26.

Cairns, R. B., Cairns, B. D., Necherman, H. J., Ferguson, L. L., & Gariepy, J. (1989). Growth and aggression. 1. Childhood to early adolescence. *Developmental Psychology, 25,* 320–330.

Caldwell, B. M. (1986). Day care and early environmental adequacy. In W. Fowler (Ed.), *Early experience and the development of competence, New Directions for Child Development, 32,* 11–30.

Caldwell, B. M., & Bradley, R. H. (1978). *Manual for the home observation of the environment.* Unpublished manuscript. Little Rock, AR: University of Arkansas.

Calvert, S. L., & Huston, A. C. (1987). Television and children's gender schemata. *New Directions for Child*

*Development, 38,* 75–88.

Campbell, S. B. (1990). The socialization and social development of hyperactive children. In M. Lewis & S. M. Miller (Eds.), *Handbook of developmental psychopathology* (pp. 77–92). New York: Plenum

Campbell, S. B., & Taylor, P. M. (1980). Bonding and attachment: Theoretical issues. In P. M. Taylor (Ed.), *Parent-infant relationships* (pp. 3–24). New York: Grune & Stratton.

Campione, J. C., Brown, A. L., & Ferrara, R. A. (1982). Mental retardation and intelligence. In J. R. Sternberg (Ed.), *Handbook of human intelligence* (pp. 392–492). Cambridge, England: Cambridge University Press.

Campione, J. C., Brown, A. L., Ferrara, R. A., Jones, R. S., & Steinberg, E. (1985). Breakdowns in flexible use of information: Intelligence-related differences in transfer following equivalent learning performance. *Intelligence, 9,* 297–315.

Campione, J. C., & Brown, A. L. (1984). Learning ability and transfer propensity as sources of individual differences in intelligence. In P. H. Brooks, C. McCauley, & R. Sperber (Eds.), *Learning and cognition in the mentally retarded.* Hillsdale, NJ: Erlbaum.

Campos, J. J., Langer, A., & Krowitz, A. (1970). Cardiac responses on the visual cliff in prelocomotor human infants. *Science, 170,* 196–197.

Cantwell, D. P. (1990). Depression across the early life span. In M. Lewis & S. M. Miller (Eds.), *Handbook of developmental psychopathology* (pp. 293–310). New York: Plenum.

Capron, C., & Duyme, M. (1989). Assessment of effects of socio-economic status on IQ in a full cross-fostering study. *Nature, 340,* 552–554.

Capute, A. J., Palmer, F. B., Shapiro, B. K., Wachtel, R. C., Ross, A., & Accardo, P. J. (1984). Primitive reflex profile: A quantification of primitive reflexes in infancy. *Developmental Medicine & Child Neurology, 26,* 375–383.

Capute, A. J., Palmer, F. B., Shapiro, B. K., Wachtel, R. C., Schmidt, S., & Ross, A. (1986). Clinical linguistic and auditory milestone scale: Prediction of cognition in infancy. *Developmental Medicine & Child Neurology, 28,* 762–771.

Carey, S., & Bartlett, E. (1978). Acquiring a single new word. *Papers and Reports on Child Language Development, 15,* 17–29.

Carey, W. B. (1981). The importance of temperament-environment interaction for child health and development. In M. Lewis & L. A. Rosenblum (Eds.), *The uncommon child* (pp. 31–56). New York: Plenum.

Carlson, V., Cicchetti, D., Barnett, D., & Braunwald, K. (1989). Disorganized/disoriented attachment relationships in maltreated infants. *Developmental Psychology, 25,* 525–531.

Caron, A. J., & Caron, R. F. (1981). Processing of relational information as an index of infant risk. In S. Friedman & M. Sigman (Eds.), *Preterm birth and psychological development* (pp. 219–240). New York: Academic Press.

Carter, C. S. (1988). Patterns of infant feeding, the mother-infant interaction and stress management. In T. M. Field, P. M. McCabe, & N. Schneiderman (Eds.), *Stress and coping across development* (pp. 27–46). Hillsdale, NJ: Erlbaum.

Carver, R. P. (1990). Intelligence and reading ability in grades 2–12. *Intelligence, 14,* 449–455.

Case, R. (1985). *Intellectual development. Birth to adulthood.* Orlando, FL: Academic Press.

Case, R. (1986). The new stage theories in intellectual development: Why we need them; What they assert. In M. Perlmutter (Ed.), *Perspectives on intellectual development. The Minnesota Symposia on Child Psychology* (Vol. 19, pp. 57–96). Hillsdale, NJ: Erlbaum.

Case, R., Hayward, S., Lewis, M., & Hurst, P. (1988). Toward a neo-Piagetian theory of cognitive and emotional development. *Developmental Review, 8,* 1–51.

Casey, M. B. (1986). Individual differences in selective attention among prereaders: A key to mirror-image confusions. *Developmental Psychology, 22,* 58–66.

Cernoch, J. M., & Porter, R. H. (1985). Recognition of maternal axillary odors by infants. *Child Development, 56,* 1593–1598.

Chalfant, J. C. (1989). Learning disabilities: Policy issues and promising approaches. *American Psychologist, 44,* 392–398.

Cherlin, A. J., Chase-Lansdale, P. L., Furstenberg, F. E., Kiernan, K. E., & Robins, P. K. (1991). *The effects of divorce on children's emotional adjustment: Two prospective studies.* Paper presented at biennial meetings of Society for Research in Child Development, Seattle.

Chess, S., & Korn, S. J. (1980). Temperament and behavior disorder in mentally retarded children. *Journal of Special Education, 23,* 122–130.

Chess, S., & Thomas, A. (1982). Infant bonding: Mystique and reality. *American Journal of Orthopsychiatry, 52,* 213–222.

Chess, S., & Thomas, A. (1984). *Origins and evolution of behavior disorders: Infancy to early adult life.* New York: Brunner/Mazel.

Chi, M. T. (1978). Knowledge structure and memory development. In R. S. Siegler (Ed.), *Children's thinking: What develops?* (pp. 73–96). Hillsdale, NJ: Erlbaum.

Chi, M. T. H., & Ceci, S. J. (1987). Content knowledge: Its role, representation, and restructuring in memory development. In H. W. Reese (Ed.), *Advances in child development and behavior* (Vol. 20, pp. 91–142). Orlando, FL: Academic Press.

Chi, M. T. H., Hutchinson, J. E., & Robin, A. F. (1989). How inferences about novel domain-related concepts can be constrained by structured knowledge. *Merrill-Palmer Quarterly, 35,* 27–62.

Chomsky, N. (1965). *Aspects of a theory of syntax.* Cambridge, MA: M.I.T. Press.

Chomsky, N. (1975). *Reflections on language.* New York: Pantheon Books.

Chomsky, N. (1986). *Knowledge of language: Its nature, origin, and use.* New York: Praeger.

Chomsky, N. (1988). *Language and problems of knowledge.* Cambridge: M.I.T.

Christophersen, E. R. (1989). Injury control. *American Psychologist, 44,* 237–241.

Chumlea, W. C. (1982). Physical growth in adolescence. In B. B. Wolman (Ed.), *Handbook of developmental psychology* (pp. 471–485). Englewood Cliffs, NJ: Prentice-Hall.

Cicchetti, D. (1989). Developmental psychopathology: Past, present, and future. In D. Cicchetti (Ed.), *The emergence of a discipline: Rochester symposium on developmental psychopathology* (Vol. 1, pp. 1–12). Hillsdale, NJ: Erlbaum.

Cicchetti, D., & Beeghly, M. (1990). *Children with Down syndrome: A developmental perspective* (p. ix), New York: Cambridge University Press.

Clapp, J. F., III (1989). The effects of maternal exercise on early pregnancy outcome. *American Journal of Obstetrics and Gynecology, 161,* 1453–1457.

Clark, E. V. (1975). Knowledge, context, and strategy in the acquisition of meaning. In D. P. Date (Ed.), *Georgetown University round table on language and linguistics.* Washington DC: Georgetown University Press.

Clark, E. V. (1977). Strategies and the mapping problem in first language acquisition. In J. Macnamara (Ed.), *Language learning and thought* (pp. 147–168). New York: Academic Press, 1977.

Clark, E. V. (1983). Meanings and concepts. In J. H. Flavell & E. M. Markman (Eds.), *Handbook of child psychology: Cognitive development* (Vol. 3, pp. 787–840). New York: Wiley.

Clark, E. V. (1987). The principle of contrast: A constraint on language acquisition. In B. MacWhinney (Ed.), *Mechanisms of language acquisition* (pp. 1–34). Hillsdale, NJ: Erlbaum.

Clark, E. V. (1990). On the pragmatics of contrast. *Journal of Child Language, 41,* 417–431.

Clarke, A. D. B. (1968). Learning and human development—the 42nd Maudsley lecture. *British Journal of Psychiatry, 114,* 161–177.

Clarke, A. M., & Clarke, A. D. B. (1976). *Early experience: Myth and evidence.* New York: Free Press.

Clarke-Stewart, A. (1973). Interactions between mothers and their young children: Characteristics and consequences. *Monographs of the Society for Research in Child Development, 38* (Serial No. 153).

Clarke-Stewart, A. (1984). Day care: A new context for research and development. In M. Perlmutter (Ed.), *Minnesota Symposia on Child Psychology* (Vol. 17, pp. 61–100). Hillsdale, NJ: Erlbaum.

Clarke-Stewart, A. (1987). The social ecology of early childhood. In N. Eisenberg (Ed.), *Contemporary topics in developmental psychology* (pp. 292–318). New York: Wiley-Interscience.

Clarke-Stewart, A. (1990). "The 'effects' of infant day care reconsidered" reconsidered: Risks for parents, children, and researchers. In N. Fox & G. G. Fein (Eds.), *Infant day care: The current debate* (pp. 61–86). Norwood, NJ: Ablex.

Clary, E. G., & Miller, J. (1986). Socialization and situational influences on sustained altruism. *Child Development, 57,* 1358–1369.

Cochran, M. M., & Brassard, J. A. (1979). Child development and personal social networks. *Child Development, 50,* 601–616.

Cohn, D. A. (1990). Child-mother attachment of six-year-olds and social competence at school. *Child Development, 61,* 151–162.

Cohn, J. F., Campbell, S. B., Matias, R., & Hopkins, J. (1990). Face-to-face interactions of postpartum depressed and nondepressed mother-infant pairs at 2 months. *Developmental Psychology, 26,* 15–23.

Colby, A., Kohlberg, L., Gibbs, J., & Lieberman, M. (1983). A longitudinal study of moral judgment. *Monographs of the Society for Research in Child Development, 48* (1–2, Serial No. 200).

Cole, M., & Traupmann, K. (1981). Comparative cognitive research: Learning from a learning disabled child. In W. A. Collins (Ed.), *Aspects of the development of competence: The Minnesota Symposia on Child Psychology* (Vol. 14, pp. 125–154). Hillsdale, NJ: Erlbaum.

Collins, W. A. (Ed.) (1984). *Development during middle childhood: The years from six to twelve.* Washington, DC: National Academy Press.

Colombo, J. (1982). The critical period concept: Research, methodology, and theoretical issues. *Psychological Bulletin, 91,* 260–275.

Colombo, J., & Mitchell, D. W. (1990). Individual differences in early visual attention: Fixation time and information processing. In J. Colombo & J. Fagen (Eds.), *Individual differences in infancy: Reliability, stability, prediction* (pp. 193–228). Hillsdale, NJ: Erlbaum.

Connolly, K., & Dalgleish, M. (1989). The emergence of a tool-using skill in infancy. *Developmental Psychology, 25,* 894–912.

Cook, M., & Birch, R. (1984). Infant perception of the shapes of tilted plane forms. *Infant Behavior and Development, 7,* 389–402.

Cooper, R. P., & Aslin, R. N. (1990). Preference for infant-directed speech in the first month after birth. *Child Development, 61,* 1584–1595.

Coopersmith, S. (1967). *The antecedents of self-esteem.* San Francisco: Freeman.

Crain, W. C. (1980). *Theories of development.* Englewood Cliffs, NJ: Prentice-Hall.

Crisafi, M. A., & Brown, A. L. (1986). Analogical transfer in very young children: Combining two separately learned solutions to reach a goal. *Child Development, 57,* 953–968.

Crnic, K. A., Greenberg, M. T., Ragozin, A. S., Robinson, N. M., & Basham, R. B. (1983). Effects of stress and social support on mothers and premature and full-term infants. *Child Development, 54,* 209–217.

Crockenberg, S. (1987). Predictors and correlates of anger toward and punitive control of toddlers by adolescent mothers. *Child Development, 58,* 964–975.

Crockenberg, S. B. (1981). Infant irritability, mother responsiveness, and social support influences on the security of infant-mother attachment. *Child Development, 52,* 857–865.

Crockenberg, S. B. (1986). Are temperamental differences in babies associated with predictable differences in care-giving? *New Directions for Child Development, 31,* 53–74.

Crockenberg, S., & Litman, C. (1990). Autonomy as competence in 2–year-olds: Maternal correlates of child defiance, compliance, and self-assertion. *Developmental Psychology, 26,* 961–971.

Crook, C. (1987). Taste and olfaction. In P. Salapatek & L. Cohen (Eds.), *Handbook of infant perception: Vol. 1. From sensation to perception* (pp. 237–264). Orlando, FL: Academic Press.

Crowell, J. A., & Feldman, S. S. (1988). Mothers' internal models of relationships and children's behavioral and developmental status: A study of mother-child interaction. *Child Development, 50,* 1273–1285.

Csikszentmihalyi, M., Larson, R., & Prescott, S. (1977). The ecology of adolescent activity and experience. *Journal of Youth and Adolescence, 6,* 281–294.

Cutrona, C. E., & Troutman, B. R. (1986). Social support, infant temperament, and parenting self-efficacy: A mediational model of postpartum depression. *Child Development, 57,* 1507–1518.

Damon, W. (1977). *The social world of the child.* San Francisco: Jossey-Bass.

Damon, W. (1983). The nature of social-cognitive change in the developing child. In W. F. Overton (Ed.), *The relationship between social and cognitive development* (pp. 103–142). Hillsdale, NJ: Erlbaum.

Dannemiller, J. L. (1989). A test of color constancy in 9- and 20-week-old human infants following simulated illuminant changes. *Developmental Psychology, 25,* 171–184.

Danner, F. W., & Day, M. C. (1977). Eliciting formal operations. *Child Development, 48,* 1600–1606.

Davidson, E. S., Yasuna, A., & Tower, A. (1979). The effect of television cartoons on sex-role stereotyping in young girls. *Child Development, 50,* 597–600.

DeCasper, A. J., & Fifer, W. P. (1980). Of human bonding: Newborns prefer their mothers' voices. *Science, 208,* 1174–1176.

DeCasper, A. J., & Sigafoos, A. D. (1983). The intrauterine heartbeat: A potent reinforcer for newborns. *Infant Behavior and Development, 6,* 19–25.

DeCasper, A. J., & Spence, M. J. (1986). Prenatal maternal speech influences newborns' perception of speech sounds. *Infant Behavior and Development, 9,* 133–150.

de Chateau, P. (1980). Effects of hospital practices on synchrony in the development of the infant-parent relationship. In P. M. Taylor (Ed.), *Parent-infant relationships* (pp. 137–168). New York: Grune & Stratton.

DeLoache, J. S. (1989). The development of representation in young children. In H. W. Reese (Ed.), *Advances in child development and behavior* (Vol. 22, pp. 2–37). San Diego, CA: Academic Press.

DeLoache, J. S., & Brown, A. L. (1987). Differences in the memory-based searching of delayed and normally developing young children. *Intelligence, 11,* 277–289.

DeLoache, J. S., Cassidy, D. J., & Brown,

A. L. (1985). Precursors of mnemonic strategies in very young children's memory. *Child Development, 56,* 125–137.

DeMeis, D. K., Hock, E., & McBride, S. L. (1986). The balance of employment and motherhood: Longitudinal study of mothers' feelings about separation from their first-born infants. *Developmental Psychology, 22,* 627–632.

Dempster, F. N. (1981). Memory span: Sources of individual and developmental differences. *Psychological Bulletin, 89,* 63–100.

Dennis, M., Sugar, J., & Whitaker, H. A. (1982). The acquisition of tag questions. *Child Development, 53,* 1254–1257.

Dennis, W. (1960). Causes of retardation among institutional children: Iran. *Journal of Genetic Psychology, 96,* 47–59.

de Regt, R. H., Minkoff, H. L., Feldman, J., & Schwarz, R. H. (1986). Relation of private or clinic care to the cesarean birth rate. *New England Journal of Medicine, 315,* 619–624.

Deutsch, C. K., & Kinsbourne, M. (1990). Genetics and biochemistry in attention deficit disorder. In M. Lewis & S. M. Miller (Eds.), *Handbook of developmental psychopathology* (pp. 93–108). New York: Plenum.

Diagram Group, The. (1977). *Child's body.* New York: Paddington.

Dickerson, J. W. T. (1981). Nutrition, brain growth and development. In K. J. Connolly & H. F. R. Prechtl (Eds.), *Maturation and development: Biological and psychological perspectives.* Clinics in Developmental Medicine No. 77/78 (pp. 110–130). London: Heinemann.

Dickstein, S., & Park, R. D. (1988). Social referencing in infancy: A glance at fathers and marriage. *Child Development, 59,* 506–511.

Dietrich, K. N., Krafft, K. M., Bornschein, R. L., Hammond, P. B., Berger, O., Succop, P. A., & Bier, M. (in press). Effects of low-level fetal lead exposure on neurobehavioral development in early infancy. *Pediatrics.*

Dietz, W. H., & Gortmaker, S. L. (1985). Do we fatten our children at the television set? Obesity and television viewing in children and adolescents. *Pediatrics, 75,* 807–812.

Dishion, T. J. (1990). The family ecology of boys' peer relations in middle childhood. *Child Development, 61,* 874–892.

Dishion, T. J., Patterson, G. R., Stoolmiller, M., & Skinner, M. L. (1991). Family, school, and behavioral antecedents to early adolescent involvement with antisocial peers. *Developmental Psychology, 27,* 172–180.

DiVitto, B., & Goldberg, S. (1979). The effects of newborn medical status on early parent-infant interaction. In T. Field, A.

Sostek, S. Goldberg, & H. H. Shuman (Eds.), *Infants born at risk.* New York: Spectrum.

Dodge, K. A. (1983). Behavioral antecedents of peer social status. *Child Development, 54,* 1386–1399.

Dodge, K. A. (1990). Developmental psychopathology in children of depressed mothers. *Developmental Psychology, 26,* 3–6.

Dodge, K. A., & Frame, C. L. (1982). Social cognitive biases and deficits in aggressive boys. *Child Development, 53,* 620–635.

Dodge, K. A., Coie, J. D., Pettit, G. S., & Price, J. M. (1990). Peer status and aggression in boys groups: Developmental and contextual analysis. *Child Development, 61,* 1289–1309.

Doherty, W. J., & Needle, R. N. (1991). Psychological adjustment and substance use among adolescents before and after a parental divorce. *Child Development, 62,* 328–337.

Dollard, J., Doob, L. W., Miller, N. E., Mowrer, O. H., & Sears, R. R. (1939). *Frustration and aggression.* New Haven, CT: Yale University Press.

Dominick, J. R., & Greenberg, B. S. (1972). Attitudes toward violence: The interaction of television exposure, family attitudes, and social class. In G. A. Comstock & E. A. Rubenstein (Eds.), *Television and social behavior* (Vol. 3, pp. 314–335). Washington, DC: U.S. Government Printing Office.

Dornbusch, S. M., Carlsmith, J. M., Bushwall, S. J., Ritter, P. L., Leiderman, H., Hastdorf, A. H., & Goss, R. T. (1985). Single parents, extended households, and the control of adolescents. *Child Development, 56,* 326–341.

Dornbusch, S. M., Gross, R. T., Duncan, P. D., & Ritter, P. L. (1987a). Stanford studies of adolescence using the National Health Examination Survey. In R. M. Lerner & T. T. Foch (Eds.), *Biological-psychosocial interactions in early adolescence* (pp. 189–206). Hillsdale, NJ: Erlbaum.

Dornbusch, S. M., Ritter, P. L., Liederman, P. H., Roberts, D. F., & Fraleigh, M. J. (1987b). The relation of parenting style to adolescent school performance. *Child Development, 58,* 1244–1257.

Downey, G., & Coyne, J. C. (1990). Children of depressed parents: An integrative review. *Psychological Bulletin, 108,* 50–76.

Dreyer, P. H. (1982). Sexuality during adolescence. In B. B. Wolman (Ed.). *Handbook of developmental psychology* (pp. 559–601). Englewood Cliffs, NJ: Prentice-Hall.

Duke, P. M., Carlsmith, J. M., Jennings,

D., Martin, J. A., Dornbusch, S. M., Gross, R. T., & Siegel-Gorelick, B. (1982). Educational correlates of early and late sexual maturation in adolescence. *Journal of Pediatrics, 100,* 633–637.

Dunn, J. (1985). Pretend play in the family. In A. W. Gottfried & C. C. Brown (Eds.), *Play interactions: The contribution of play material and parental involvement to children's play development.* Lexington, MA: Lexington Press.

Dunphy, D. C. (1963). The social structure of urban adolescent peer groups. *Sociometry, 26,* 230–246.

Dunst, C. J., Brooks, P. H., & Doxsey, P. A. (1982). Characteristics of hiding places and the transition to stage IV performance in object permanence tasks. *Developmental Psychology, 18,* 671–681.

Eaton, W. O., & Enns, L. R. (1986). Sex differences in human motor activity level. *Psychological Bulletin, 100,* 19–28.

Eccles, J. S., & Hoffman, L. W. (1984). Sex roles, socialization, and occupational behavior. In H. W. Stevenson & A. E. Siegel (Eds.), *Child development research and social policy* (Vol. 1, pp. 367–420). Chicago: University of Chicago Press.

Eccles, J. S., & Midgley, C. (1990). Changes in academic motivation and self-perception during early adolescence. In R. Montemayor, G. R. Adams, T. P. Gullotta (Eds.), *From childhood to adolescence: A transitional period?* (pp. 134–155). Newbury Park, CA: Sage.

Edgerton, R. B. (1979). *Mental retardation.* Cambridge, MA: Harvard University Press.

Egeland, B., & Farber, E. A. (1984). Infant-mother attachment: Factors related to its development and changes over time. *Child Development, 55,* 753–771.

Egeland, B., & Sroufe, L. A. (1981). Attachment and early maltreatment. *Child Development, 52,* 44–52.

Ehrenhaft, P. M., Wagner, J. L., & Herdman, R. C. (1989). Changing prognosis for very low birth weight infants. *Obstetrics and Gynecology, 74,* 528–535.

Eichorn, D. H., Hunt, J. V., & Honzik, M. P. (1982). Experience, personality, and IQ: Adolescence to middle age. In D. H. Eichorn, J. A. Clausen, N. Haan, M. P. Honzik, & P. H. Mussen (Eds.), *Present and past in middle life* (pp. 89–116). New York: Academic Press.

Eisenberg, N. (1986). *Altruistic emotion, cognition, and behavior.* Hillsdale, NJ: Erlbaum.

Eisenberg, N. (1988). The development of prosocial and aggressive behavior. In M. H. Bornstein & M. E. Lamb (Eds.),

*Developmental psychology: An advanced textbook* (2nd ed.) (pp. 461–496). Hillsdale, NJ: Erlbaum.

Eisenberg, N. (1990). Prosocial development in early and mid-adolescence. In R. Montemayor, G. R. Adams, & T. P. Gullotta (Eds.), *From childhood to adolescence: A transitional period?* (pp. 240–268). Newbury Park, CA: Sage.

Eisenberg, N., & Miller, P. (1990). The development of prosocial behavior versus nonprosocial behavior in children. In M. Lewis & S. M. Miller (Eds.), *Handbook of developmental psychopathology* (pp. 181–190). New York: Plenum.

Eisenberg, N., & Miller, P. A. (1987). The relation of empathy to prosocial and related behaviors. *Psychological Bulletin, 101,* 91–119.

Eisenberg, N., & Mussen, P. H. (1989). *The roots of prosocial behavior in children.* Cambridge: Cambridge University Press.

Eisenberg, N., Fabes, R. A., Schaller, M., & Miller, P. A. (1989). Sympathy and personal distress: Development, gender differences, and interrelations of indexes. *New Directions for Child Development, 44,* 107–126.

Eisenberg, N., Hertz-Lazarowitz, R., & Fuchs, I. (1990). Prosocial moral judgment in Israeli kibbutz and city children: A longitudinal study. *Merrill-Palmer Quarterly, 36,* 273–285.

Eisenberg, N., Shell, R., Pasternack, J., Lennon, R., Beller, R., & Mathy, R. M. (1987). Prosocial development in middle childhood: A longitudinal study. *Developmental Psychology, 23,* 712–718.

Eisenberg-Berg, N., & Hand, M. (1979). The relationship of preschoolers' reasoning about prosocial moral conflicts to prosocial behavior. *Child Development, 50,* 356–363.

Elardo, R., Bradley, R., & Caldwell, B. (1975). The relation of infants' home environments to mental test performance from six to thirty-six months: A longitudinal analysis. *Child Development, 46,* 71–76.

Elder, G. H., Jr. (1974). *Children of the Great Depression.* Chicago: University of Chicago Press.

Elder, G. H., Jr. (1981). Scarcity and prosperity in postwar childbearing: Explorations from a life course perspective. *Journal of Family History, 5,* 410–431.

Elder, G. H., Jr. (1984). Families, kin, and the life course: A sociological perspective. In R. D. Parke (Ed.), *Review of child development research: Vol. 7. The family* (pp. 80–136). Chicago: University of Chicago Press.

Elliott, R. (1988). Tests, abilities, race, and conflict. *Intelligence, 12,* 333–350.

Eme, R. F. (1979). Sex differences in childhood psychopathology: A review. *Psychological Bulletin, 86,* 374–395.

Emery, R. E. (1988). *Marriage, divorce, and children's adjustment.* Newbury Park, CA: Sage.

Emmerich, W., & Shepard, K. (1982). Development of sex-differentiated preferences during later childhood and adolescence. *Child Development, 18,* 406–417.

Entwisle, D. R., & Alexander, K. L. (1990). Beginning school math competence: Minority and majority comparisons. *Child Development, 61,* 454–471.

Entwisle, D. R., & Doering, S. G. (1981). *The first birth.* Baltimore: Johns Hopkins University Press.

Erickson, M. F., Sroufe, L. A., & Egeland, B. (1985). The relationship between quality of attachment and behavior problems in preschool in a high-risk sample. In I. Bretherton & E. Waters (Eds.), Growing points of attachment theory and research. *Monographs of the Society for Research in Child Development, 50* (Whole No. 209) (pp. 147–166).

Ericsson, K. A., & Crutcher, R. J. (1990). The nature of exceptional performance. In P. B. Baltes, D. L. Featherman, & R. M. Lerner (Eds.), *Life-span development and behavior* (Vol. 10, pp. 188–218). Hillsdale, NJ: Erlbaum.

Erikson, E. H. (1950/1963). *Childhood and society.* New York: Norton.

Erikson, E. H. (1964). *Insight and responsibility.* New York: Norton.

Erikson, E. H. (1974). *Dimensions of a new identity: The 1973 Jefferson lectures in the humanities.* New York: Norton.

Erikson, E. H. (1980). *Identity and the life cycle.* New York: Norton. (Original work published 1959)

Eron, L. D. (1987). The development of aggressive behavior from the perspective of a developing behaviorism. *American Psychologist, 42,* 435–442.

Escalona, K. S. (1981). The reciprocal role of social and emotional developmental advances and cognitive development during the second and third years of life. In E. K. Shapiro & E. Weber (Eds.), *Cognitive and affective growth: Developmental interaction* (pp. 87–108). Hillsdale, NJ: Erlbaum.

European Collaborative Study (1991). Children born to women with HIV-1 infection: Natural history and risk of transmission. *The Lancet, 337,* 253–260.

Fagan, J. F. (1984). The intelligent infant: Theoretical implications. *Intelligence, 8,* 1–9.

Fagan, J. F., & Shepherd, P. A. (1986). *The Fagan Test of Infant Intelligence: Training manual.* Cleveland, OH: Infantest Corporation.

Fagard, J., & Jacquet, A. (1989). Onset of bimanual coordination and symmetry versus asymmetry of movement. *Infant Behavior and Development, 12,* 229–235.

Fagot, B. I. (1974). Sex differences in toddlers' behavior and parental reaction. *Developmental Psychology, 10,* 544–558.

Fagot, B. I. (1985). Beyond the reinforcement principle: Another step toward understanding sex role development. *Developmental Psychology, 21,* 1097–1104.

Fagot, B. I., & Leinbach, M. D. (1989). The young child's gender schema: Environmental input, internal organization. *Child Development, 60,* 663–672.

Famularo, R., Stone, K., Barnum, R., & Whatron, R. (1986). Alcoholism and severe child maltreatment. *American Journal of Orthopsychiatry, 56,* 481–485.

Fantz, R. L. (1956). A method for studying early visual development. *Perceptual and Motor Skills, 6,* 13–15.

Farber, S. L. (1981). *Identical twins reared apart: A reanalysis.* New York: Basic Books.

Farnham-Diggory, S. (1986). Time, now, for a little serious complexity. In S. J. Ceci (Ed.), *Handbook of cognitive, social, and neuropsychological aspects of learning disability* (Vol. 1). Hillsdale, NJ: Erlbaum.

Farran, D. C., Haskins, R., & Gallagher, J. J. (1980). Poverty and mental retardation: A search for explanations. *New Directions for Exceptional Children, 1,* 47–66.

Farrington, D. P. (1991). Childhood aggression and adult violence: Early precursors and later-life outcomes. In D. J. Pepler & K. H. Rubin (Eds.), *The development and treatment of childhood aggression* (pp. 5–29). Hillsdale, NJ: Erlbaum.

Faust, M. S. (1983). Alternative constructions of adolescent growth. In J. Brooks-Gunn & A. C. Petersen (Eds.), *Girls at puberty. Biological and psychosocial perspectives* (pp. 105–126). New York: Plenum Press.

Featherstone, H. (1980). *A difference in the family.* New York: Basic Books.

Feingold, A. (1988). Cognitive gender differences are disappearing. *American Psychologist, 43,* 95–103.

Feldman, S. S. (1987). Predicting strain in mothers and fathers of 6-month-old infants: A short-term longitudinal study. In P. W. Berman & F. A. Pedersen (Eds.), *Men's transitions to parenthood* (pp. 13–36). Hillsdale, NJ: Erlbaum.

Ferguson, T. J., & Rule, B. G. (1980). Effects of inferential set, consequence severity, and basis for responsibility on children's evaluation of aggressive acts. *Developmental Psychology, 16,* 141–146.

Ferguson, T. J., & Rule, B. G. (1982).

Influence of inferential set, outcome intent, and outcome severity on children's moral judgments. *Developmental Psychology, 18,* 843–851.

Fernald, A., & Kuhl, P. (1987). Acoustic determinants of infant preference for motherese speech. *Infant Behavior and Development, 10,* 279–293.

Fernald, A., & Mazzie, C. (1991). Prosody and focus in speech to infants and adults. *Developmental Psychology, 27,* 209–221.

Feshbach, S. (1970). Aggression. In P. H. Mussen (Ed.), *Carmichael's manual of child psychology* (Vol. 2, 3rd ed.) (pp. 159–260). New York: Wiley.

Fetterman, D. (1990, June). Wasted genius. *Stanford,* 30–33.

Field, T. M. (1977). Effects of early separation, interactive deficits, and experimental manipulations on infant-mother face-to-face interaction. *Child Development, 48,* 763–771.

Field, T. (1989). Maternal depression effects on infant interaction and attachment behavior. In D. Cicchetti (Ed.), *The emergence of a discipline; Vol. 1 Rochester symposium on developmental psychopathology* (pp. 139–164). Hillsdale, NJ: Erlbaum.

Field, T. M. (1978). Interaction behaviors of primary versus secondary caretaker fathers. *Developmental Psychology, 14,* 183–185.

Field, T. M., De Stefano, L., & Koewler, J. H., III. (1982). Fantasy play of toddlers and preschoolers. *Developmental Psychology, 18,* 503–508.

Field, T. M., Sandberg, D., Garcia, R., Vega-Lahr, N., Goldstein, S., & Guy, L. (1985). Pregnancy problems, postpartum depression, and early mother-infant interactions. *Developmental Psychology, 21,* 1152–1156.

Field, T. M., Woodson, R., Greenberg, R., & Cohen, D. (1982). Discrimination and imitation of facial expressions by neonates. *Science, 218,* 179–181.

Field, T., Healy, B., Goldstein, S., & Guthertz, M. (1990). Behavior-state matching and synchrony in mother-infant interactions of nondepressed versus depressed dyads. *Developmental Psychology, 26,* 7–14.

Field, T., Healy, B., Goldstein, S., Perry, S., Bendell, D., Schanberg, S., Zimmerman, E. A., & Duhn, C. (1988). Infants of depressed mothers show "depressed" behavior even with nondepressed adults. *Child Development, 59,* 1569–1579.

Finkelstein, N. W. (1982). Aggression: Is it stimulated by day care? *Young Children, 37,* 3–9.

Fischer, K. W. (1980). A theory of cognitive development: The control and construction of hierarchies of skills. *Psychological Review, 87,* 477–531.

Fischer, K. W., & Canfield, R. L. (1986). The ambiguity of stage and structure in behavior: Person and environment in the development of psychological structures. In I. Levin (Ed.), *Stage and structure: Reopening the debate* (pp. 246–267). Norwood, NJ: Ablex.

Fischer, K. W., & Pipp, S. L. (1984). Processes of cognitive development: Optimal level and skill acquisition. In R. J. Sternberg (Ed.), *Mechanisms of cognitive development* (pp. 45–80). New York: W. H. Freeman.

Fitzgerald, L. F., & Betz, N. E. (1983). Issues in the vocational psychology of women. In W. B. Walsh & S. H. Osipow (Eds.), *Handbook of vocational psychology* (Vol. 1, pp. 83–160). Hillsdale, NJ: Erlbaum.

Flavell, J. H. (1982a). On cognitive development. *Child Development, 53,* 1–10.

Flavell, J. H. (1982b). Structures, stages, and sequences in cognitive development. In W. A. Collins (Ed.), *The Concept of Development: The Minnesota Symposia on Child Psychology* (Vol. 15, pp. 1–28). Hillsdale, NJ: Erlbaum.

Flavell, J. H. (1985). *Cognitive development* (2nd ed.). Englewood Cliffs, NJ: Prentice-Hall.

Flavell, J. H. (1986). The development of children's knowledge about the appearance-reality distinction. *American Psychologist, 41,* 481–425.

Flavell, J. H., Everett, B. A., Croft, K., & Flavell, E. R. (1981). Young children's knowledge about visual perception: Further evidence for the level 1-level 2 distinction. *Developmental Psychology, 17,* 99–103.

Flavell, J. H., Green, F. L., & Flavell, E. R. (1989). Young children's ability to differentiate appearance-reality and level 2 perspectives in the tactile modality. *Child Development, 60,* 201–213.

Flavell, J. H., Green, F. L., & Flavell, E. R. (1990). Developmental changes in young children's knowledge about the mind. *Cognitive Development, 5,* 1–27.

Flavell, J. H., Green, F. L., Wahl, K. E., & Flavell, E. R. (1987). The effects of question clarification and memory aids on young children's performance on appearance-reality tasks. *Cognitive Development, 2,* 127–144.

Fleming, A. S., Ruble, D. L., Flett, G. L., & Shaul, D. L. (1988). Postpartum adjustment in first-time mothers: Relations between mood, maternal attitudes, and mother-infant interactions. *Developmental Psychology, 24,* 781.

Ford, M. E. (1982). Social cognition and social competence in adolescence. *Developmental Psychology, 18,* 323–340.

Fox, N. A., Kimmerly, N. L., & Schafer, W. D. (1991). Attachment to mother/attachment to father: A meta-analysis. *Child Development, 62,* 210–225.

Fox, N., & Fein, G. G. (Eds.) (1990). *Infant day care: The current debate.* Norwood, NJ: Ablex.

Fraiberg, S. (1974). Blind infants and their mothers: An examination of the sign system. In M. Lewis & L. A. Rosenblum (Eds.), *The effect of the infant on its caregiver* (pp. 215–232). New York: Wiley.

Fraiberg, S. (1975). The development of human attachments in infants blind from birth. *Merrill-Palmer Quarterly, 21,* 315–334.

Fraiberg, S. (1977). *Insights from the blind.* New York: New American Library.

Francis, P. L., Self, P. A., & Horowitz, F. D. (1987). The behavioral assessment of the neonate: An overview. In J. D. Osofsky (Ed.), *Handbook of infant development* (2nd ed.) (pp. 723–779). New York: Wiley-Interscience.

Frankel, K. A., & Bates, J. E. (1990). Mother-toddler problem solving: Antecedents in attachment, home behavior, and temperament. *Child Development, 61,* 810–819.

Freedman, D. G. (1979). Ethnic differences in babies. *Human Nature, 2,* 36–43.

Freedman, J. L. (1984). Effect of television violence on aggressiveness. *Psychological Bulletin, 96,* 227–246.

Freeman, J. (1981). The intellectually gifted. *New directions for exceptional children, 7,* 75–86.

Freud, S. (1905). Three contributions to the theory of sex. *The basic writings of Sigmund Freud* (A. A. Brill, trans.). New York: Random House.

Freud, S. (1965). *A general introduction of psychoanalysis* (J. Riviere, Trans.). New York: Washington Square Press. (Original work published in 1920)

Friedrich-Cofer, L., & Huston, A. C. (1986). Television violence and aggression: The debate continues. *Psychological Bulletin, 100,* 364–371.

Furrow, D. (1984). Social and private speech at two years. *Child Development, 55,* 355–362.

Gallagher, J. J., & Ramey, C. T. (1987). *The malleability of children.* Baltimore: Paul H. Brookes Publishing Co.

Ganchrow, J. R., Steiner, J. E., & Daher, M. (1983). Neonatal facial expressions in response to different qualities and intensities of gustatory stimuli. *Infant Behavior and Development, 6,* 189–200.

Garbarino, J., & Sherman, D. (1980). High-risk neighborhoods and high-risk families: The human ecology of child maltreatment. *Child Development, 51,* 188–198.

Garber, H. L. (1988). *The Milwaukee Project. Preventing mental retardation in children at risk.* Washington, DC: American Association on Mental Retardation.

Gardner, H. (1983). *Frames of mind: The theory of multiple intelligence.* New York: Basic Books.

Garmezy, N., & Rutter, M. (Eds.) (1983). *Stress, coping, and development in children.* New York: McGraw-Hill.

Garn, S. M. (1980). Continuities and change in maturational timing. In O. G. Brim, Jr., & J. Kagan (Eds.), *Constancy and change in human development* (pp. 113–162). Cambridge, MA: Harvard University Press.

Gelman, R. (1972). Logical capacity of very young children: Number invariance rules. *Child Development, 43,* 75–90.

Gelman, R., & Baillargeon, R. (1983). A review of some Piagetian concepts. In J. H. Flavell & E. M. Markman (Eds.), *Handbook of child psychology: Cognitive development* (Vol. 3, pp. 167–230). New York: Wiley.

Gentner, D. (1982). Why nouns are learned before verbs: Linguistic relativity versus natural partitioning. In S. A. Kuczaj II (Ed.), *Language development: Vol. 2. Language, thought, and culture* (pp. 301–334). Hillsdale, NJ: Erlbaum.

Gerson, R. P., & Damon, W. (1978). Moral understanding and children's conduct. *New Directions for Child Development, 2,* 41–60.

Gesell, A. (1925). *The mental growth of the preschool child.* New York: Macmillan.

Gewirtz, J. L., & Boyd, E. F. (1977). Does maternal responding imply reduced infant crying? A critique of the 1972 Bell and Ainsworth report. *Child Development, 48,* 1200–1207.

Gibbs, J. T. (1985). Psychosocial factors associated with depression in urban adolescent females: Implications for assessment. *Journal of Youth and Adolescence, 14,* 47–60.

Gibson, E. J. (1969). *Principles of perceptual learning and development.* New York: Appleton-Century-Crofts.

Gibson, E. J., & Spelke, E. S. (1983). The development of perception. In J. H. Flavell & E. M. Markman (Eds.), *Handbook of child psychology: Vol 3. Cognitive development* (pp. 1–76). New York: Wiley.

Gibson, E. J., & Walk, R. D. (1960). The "visual cliff." *Scientific American, 202,* 80–92.

Gilligan, C. (1982a). New maps of development: New visions of maturity. *American Journal of Orthopsychiatry, 52,* 199–212.

Gilligan, C. (1982b). *In a different voice: Psychological theory and women's development.* Cambridge, MA: Harvard University Press.

Gilligan, C. (1987). Adolescent development reconsidered. New *Directions for Child Development, 37,* 63–92.

Gilligan, C., & Wiggins, G. (1987). The origins of morality in early childhood relationships. In J. Kagan & S. Lamb (Eds.), *The emergence of morality in young children* (pp. 277–307). Chicago: The University of Chicago Press.

Ginsburg, H. J., & Miller, S. M. (1982). Sex differences in children's risk-taking behavior. Child Development, 53, 426–428.

Ginsburg, H. P. (1981). *Piaget and education: The contributions and limits of genetic epistemology.* In I. E. Sigel, D. M. Brodzinsky, & R. M. Golinkoff (Eds.), New directions in Piagetian theory and practice (pp. 315–332). Hillsdale, NJ: Erlbaum.

Ginsburg, H. P., & Opper, S. (1969). *Piaget's theory of intellectual development.* Englewood Cliffs, NJ: Prentice-Hall.

Gleitman, L. R., & Wanner, E. (1988). Current issues in language learning. In M. H. Bornstein & M. E. Lamb (Eds.), *Developmental psychology: An advanced textbook* (2nd ed.) (pp. 297–358). Hillsdale, NJ: Erlbaum.

Glueck, S., & Glueck, E. (1972). *Identification of pre-delinquents: Validation studies and some suggested uses of Glueck Table.* New York: Intercontinental Medical Book Corp.

Gnepp, J., & Chilamkurti, C. (1988). Children's use of personality attributions to predict other people's emotional and behavioral reactions. *Child Development, 50,* 743–754.

Golden, M., & Birns, B. (1983). Social class and infant intelligence. In M. Lewis (Ed.), *Origins of intelligence. Infancy and early childhood* (2nd ed.) (pp. 347–398). New York: Plenum.

Goldfield, B. A., & Reznick, J. S. (1990). Early lexical acquisition: Rate, content, and the vocabulary spurt. *Journal of Child Language, 17,* 171–183.

Goldfield, E. C. (1989). Transition from rocking to crawling: Postural constraints on infant movement. *Developmental Psychology, 25,* 913–919.

Goldman-Rakic, P. S. (1987). Development of cortical circuitry and cognitive function. *Child Development, 58,* 601–622.

Good, T. L., & Weinstein, R. S. (1986). Schools make a difference. Evidence, criticisms, and new directions. *American Psychologist, 41,* 1090–1097.

Goodenough, F. L. (1931). *Anger in young children.* Minneapolis: University of Minnesota Press.

Goodsitt, J. V., Morse, P. A., Ver Hoeve, J. N., & Cowan, N. (1984). Infant speech recognition in multisyllabic contexts. *Child Development, 55,* 903–910.

Gopnik, A., & Astington, J. W. (1988). Children's understanding of representational change and its relation to the understanding of false belief and the appearance-reality distinction. *Child Development, 59,* 26–37.

Gopnik, A., & Meltzoff, A. (1987). The development of categorization in the second year and its relation to other cognitive and linguistic developments. *Child Development, 58,* 1523–1531.

Gopnik, A., & Slaughter, V. (1991). Young children's understanding of changes in their mental states. *Child Development, 62,* 83–97.

Gottfredson, L. (1981). Circumscription and compromise: A developmental theory of occupational aspirations. *Journal of Counseling Psychology Monograph, 28,* 545–579.

Gottlieb, G. (1976). Conceptions of prenatal development: Behavioral embryology. *Psychological Review, 83,* 215–234.

Gottman, J. M. (1986). The world of coordinated play: Same- and cross-sex friendship in young children. In J. M. Gottman & J. G. Parker (Eds.), *Conversations of friends. Speculations on affective development* (pp. 139–191). Cambridge, England: Cambridge University Press.

Granrud, C. E. (1986). Binocular vision and spatial perception in 4- and 5-month-old infants. *Journal of Experimental Psychology: Human Perception & Performance, 12,* 36–49.

Gratch, G. (1979). The development of thought and language in infancy. In J. D. Osofsky (Ed.), *Handbook of infant development* (pp. 439–461). New York: Wiley.

Greenberg, J., & Kuczaj, S. A., II. (1982). Towards a theory of substantive word-meaning acquisition. In S. A. Kuczaj II (Ed.), *Language development: Vol. l. Syntax and semantics* (pp. 275–312). Hillsdale, NJ: Erlbaum.

Greenberg, M. T., & Speltz, M. L. (1988). Attachment and the ontogeny of conduct problems. In J. Belsky & T. Nezworski (Eds.), *Clinical implications of attachment* (pp. 177–218). Hillsdale, NJ: Erlbaum.

Greenberg, M. T., Calderon, R., & Kusche, C. (1984). Early intervention using simultaneous communication with deaf infants: The effect on communication development. *Child Development, 55,* 607–616.

Greenberg, M. T., Siegel, J. M., & Leitch, C. J. (1983). The nature and importance of attachment relationships to parents and peers during adolescence. *Journal of Youth and Adolescence, 12,* 373–386.

Greenberg, M., & Morris, N. (1974). Engrossment: The newborn's impact upon the father. *American Journal of Orthopsychiatry, 44,* 520–531.

Greenberger, E., & Goldberg, W. A. (1989). Work, parenting, and the socialization of children. *Developmental Psychology, 25,* 22–35.

Greenough, W. T. (1991). Experience as a component of normal development: Evolutionary considerations. *Developmental Psychology, 27,* 14–17.

Greenough, W. T., Black, J. E., & Wallace, C. S. (1987). Experience and brain development. *Child Development, 58,* 539–559.

Grieser, D. L., & Kuhl, P. K. (1988). Maternal speech to infants in a tonal language: Support for universal prosodic features of motherese. *Developmental Psychology, 24,* 14–20.

Griffin, M., & Felsenthal, C. (1983). *A cry for help.* New York: Doubleday.

Grinker, J. A. (1981). Behavioral and metabolic factors in childhood obesity. In M. Lewis & L. A. Rosenblum (Eds.), *The uncommon child* (pp. 115–150). New York: Plenum.

Grusec, J. E., & Dix, T. (1986). The socialization of prosocial behavior: Theory and reality. In C. Zahn-Waxler, E. M. Cummings, & R. Iannotti (Eds.), *Altruism and aggression. Biological and social origins* (pp. 218–237). Cambridge, England: Cambridge University Press.

Grusec, J. E., & Lytton, H. (1988). *Social development. History, theory, and research.* New York: Springer-Verlag.

Grusec, J. E., Saas-Kortsaak, P., & Simutis, Z. M. (1978). The role of example and moral exhortation in the training of altruism. *Child Development, 49,* 920–923.

Gunnar, M. R. (1990). The psychobiology of infant temperament. In J. Colombo & J. Fagen (Eds.), *Individual differences in infancy: Reliability, stability, prediction* (pp. 387–410). Hillsdale, NJ: Erlbaum.

Guralnick, M. J., & Paul-Brown, D. (1984). Communicative adjustments during behavior-request episodes among children at different developmental levels. *Child Development, 55,* 911–919.

Gusella, J. L., Muir, D., & Tronick, E. Z. (1988). The effect of manipulating maternal behavior during an interaction on three-and six-month-olds' affect and attention. *Child Development, 59,* 1111–1124.

Guttentag, R. E., Ornstein, P. A., & Siemens, L. (1987). Children's spontaneous rehearsal: Transitions in strategy acquisition. *Cognitive Development, 2,* 307–326.

Gzesh, S. M., & Surber, C. F. (1985). Visual perspective-taking skills in children. *Child Development, 56,* 1204–1213.

Haan, N. (1975). Hypothetical and actual moral reasoning in a situation of civil disobedience. *Journal of Personality and Social Psychology, 32,* 636–642.

Haan, N. (1985). Processes of moral development: Cognitive or social disequilibrium? *Developmental Psychology, 21,* 996–1006.

Haith, M. M. (1980). *Rules that babies look by.* Hillsdale, NJ: Erlbaum.

Haith, M. M. (1990). Progress in the understanding of sensory and perceptual processes in early infancy. *Merrill-Palmer Quarterly, 36,* 1–26.

Haith, M. M., Bergman, T., & Moore, M. J. (1977). Eye contact and face scanning in early infancy. *Science, 198,* 853–855.

Hakuta, K. (1986). *Mirror on language: The debate on bilingualism.* New York: Basic Books.

Hakuta, K., & Diaz, R. M. (1985). The relationship between degree of bilingualism and cognitive ability: A critical discussion and some new longitudinal data. In K. E. Nelson (Ed.), *Children's language* (Vol. 5, pp. 319–344). Hillsdale, NJ: Erlbaum.

Hakuta, K., & Garcia, E. E. (1989). Bilingualism and education. *American Psychologist, 44,* 374–379.

Halpern, D. F. (1986). *Sex differences in cognitive abilities.* Hillsdale, NJ: Erlbaum.

Hanshaw, J. B. (1981). Cytomegalovirus infections. *Pediatrics in Review, 2,* 245–251.

Hanshaw, J. B., Scheiner, A. P., Moxley, A. W., Gaev, L., Abel, V., & Scheiner, B. (1976). School failure and deafness after "silent" congenital cytomegalovirus infection. *New England Journal of Medicine, 295,* 468–470.

Hardy-Brown, K., Plomin, R., & DeFries, J. C. (1981). Genetic and environmental influences on the rate of communicative development in the first year of life. *Developmental Psychology, 17,* 704–717.

Harper, L. V., & Huie, K. S. (1985). The effects of prior group experience, age, and familiarity on the quality and organization of preschoolers' social relationships. *Child Development, 56,* 704–717.

Harris, P. L., Olthof, T., & Terwogt, M. M. (1981). Children's knowledge of emotion. *Journal of Child Psychology and Psychiatry, 22,* 247–261.

Harrison, A. O., Wilson, M. N., Pine, C. J., Chan, S. Q., & Buriel, R. (1990). Family ecologies of ethnic minority children. *Child Development, 61,* 347–362.

Harter, S. (1983). Developmental perspectives on the self-system. In E. M. Hetherington (Ed.), *Handbook of child psychology: Socialization, personality, and social development* (Vol. 4) (pp. 275–386). New York: Wiley.

Harter, S. (1985). Competence as a dimension of self-evaluation: Toward a comprehensive model of self-worth. In R. L. Leahy (Ed.), *The development of the self* (pp. 55–122). Orlando, FL: Academic Press.

Harter, S. (1988). The determinations and mediational role of global self-worth in children. In N. Eisenberg (Ed.), *Contemporary topics in developmental psychology* (pp. 219–242). New York: Wiley-Interscience.

Harter, S. (1990). Processes underlying adolescent self-concept formation. In R. Montemayor, G. R. Adams, & T. P. Gullotta (Eds.), *From childhood to adolescence: A transitional period?* (pp. 205–239). Newbury Park, CA: Sage.

Harter, S., & Pike, R. (1984). The Pictorial Perceived Competence Scale for Young Children. *Child Development, 55,* 1969–1982.

Hartup, W. W. (1974). Aggression in childhood: Developmental perspectives. *American Psychologist, 29,* 336–341.

Hartup, W. W. (1978). Perspectives on child and family interaction: Past, present, and future. In R. M. Lerner & G. B. Spanier (Eds.), *Child influences on marital and family interaction* (pp. 23–46). New York: Academic Press.

Hartup, W. W. (1984). The peer context in middle childhood. In W. A. Collins (Ed.), *Development during middle childhood. The years from six to twelve* (pp. 240–282). Washington, DC: National Academy Press.

Hartup, W. W. (1989). Social relationships and their developmental significance. *American Psychologist, 44,* 120–126.

Harvard Education Letter (1986, January). Girls' math achievement: What we do and don't know. (Vol. II, No. 1–5)

Harvard Education Letter (1987, March). Adolescent health: Squander now, pay later. (Vol. III, No. 2, 4).

Haskins, R. (1985). Public school aggression among children with varying daycare experience. *Child Development, 56,* 689–703.

Haskins, R. (1986). Social and cultural factors in risk assessment and mild mental retardation. In D. C. Farran & J. D. McKinney (Eds.), *Risk in intellectual and psychosocial development* (pp. 29–60). Orlando, FL: Academic Press.

Haskins, R. (1989). Beyond metaphor: The efficacy of early childhood education. *American Psychologist, 44,* 274–282.

Haskins, R., & McKinney, J. D. (1976).

Relative effects of response tempo and accuracy on problem solving and academic achievement. *Child Development, 47,* 690–696.

Hawton, K. (1986). *Suicide and attempted suicide among children and adolescents.* Beverly Hills, CA: Sage.

Hayes, C. D. (1987). *Risking the future, Volume 1: Adolescent sexuality, pregnancy, and childbearing.* Washington, DC: National Academy Press.

Hegvik, R. L., McDevitt, S. C., & Carey, W. B. (1981, August). *Longitudinal stability of temperament characteristics in the elementary school period.* Paper presented at the meeting of the International Society for the Study of Behavioral Development, Toronto.

Henker, B., & Whalen, C. K. (1989). Hyperactivity and attention deficits. *American Psychologist, 44,* 216–223.

Henley, E. D., & Altman, J. (1978). The young adult. In D. W. Smith, E. L. Bierman, & N. M. Robinson (Eds.), *The biologic ages of man* (pp. 187–208). Philadelphia: W. B. Saunders.

Henneborn, W. J., & Cogan, R. (1975). The effect of husband participation on reported pain and the probability of medication during labour and birth. *Journal of Psychosomatic Research, 19,* 215–222.

Hess, E. H. (1972). "Imprinting" in a natural laboratory. *Scientific American, 227,* 24–31.

Hetherington, E. M. (1979). Divorce: A child's perspective. *American Psychologist, 34,* 851–858.

Hetherington, E. M. (1989). Coping with family transitions: Winners, losers, and survivors. *Child Development, 60,* 1–14.

Hetherington, E. M., Cox, M., & Cox, R. (1978). The aftermath of divorce. In M. H. Stevens, Jr. & M. Mathews (Eds.), *Mother/child, father/child relationships* (pp. 149–176). Washington, DC: National Association for the Education of Young Children.

Higgins, A., Power, C., & Kohlberg, L. (1984). The relationship of moral atmosphere to judgments of responsibility. In W. M. Kurtines & J. L. Gewirtz (Eds.), *Morality, moral behavior, and moral development* (pp. 74–108). New York: Wiley-Interscience.

Higgins, A. T., & Turnure, J. E. (1984). Distractibility and concentration of attention in children's development. *Child Development, 55,* 1799–1810.

Hinde, R. A., & Stevenson-Hinde, J. (1986). Relating childhood relationships to individual characteristics. In W. W. Hartup & Z. Rubin (Eds.), *Relationships and development* (pp. 27–50). Hillsdale, NJ: Erlbaum.

Hinde, R. A., Titmus, G., Easton, D., &

Tamplin, A. (1985). Incidence of "friendship" and behavior toward strong associates versus nonassociates in preschoolers. *Child Development, 56,* 234–245.

Hines, M. (1982). Prenatal gonadal hormones and sex differences in human behavior. *Psychological Bulletin, 92,* 56–80.

Hirsh-Pasek, K., Trieman, R., & Schneiderman, M. (1984). Brown and Hanlon revisited: Mothers' sensitivity to ungrammatical forms. *Journal of Child Language, 11,* 81–88.

Hirshberg, L. M., & Svejda, M. (1990). When infants look to their parents: I. Infants' social referencing of mothers compared to fathers. *Child Development, 61,* 1175–1186.

Hoff-Ginsberg, E. (1986). Function and structure in maternal speech: Their relation to the child's development of syntax. *Developmental Psychology, 22,* 155–163.

Hoff-Ginsberg, E. (1987, April). *Why some properties of maternal speech benefit language growth (and others do not).* Paper presented at the biennial meetings of the Society for Research in Child Development, Baltimore.

Hofferth, S. L. (1985). Updating children's life course. *Journal of Marriage and the Family, 47,* 93–115.

Hofferth, S. L. (1987a). Teenage pregnancy and its resolution. In S. L. Hofferth & C. D. Hayes (Eds.), *Risking the future. Adolescent sexuality, pregnancy, and childbearing. Working papers* (pp. 78–92). Washington, DC: National Academy Press.

Hofferth, S. L. (1987b). Social and economic consequences of teenage childbearing. In S. L. Hofferth & C. D. Hayes (Eds.), *Risking the future. Adolescent sexuality, pregnancy, and childbearing. Working papers* (pp. 123–144). Washington, DC: National Academy Press.

Hofferth, S. L., & Phillips, D. A. (1987c). Child care in the United States, 1970 to 1995. *Journal of Marriage and the Family, 49,* 559–571.

Hoffman, L. W. (1989). Effects of maternal employment in the two-parent family. *American Psychologist, 44,* 283–292.

Hoffman, M. L. (1982). Development of prosocial motivation: Empathy and guilt. In N. Eisenberg (Ed.), *The development of prosocial behavior* (pp. 281–314). New York: Academic Press.

Hoffman, M. L. (1984). Empathy, its limitations, and its role in a comprehensive moral theory. In W. M. Kurtines & J. L. Gewirtz (Eds.), *Morality, moral behavior, and moral development* (pp. 283–302). New York: Wiley.

Hoffman, M. L. (1988). Moral develop-

ment. In M. H. Bornstein & M. E. Lamb (Eds.), *Developmental psychology: An advanced textbook* (2nd ed.) (pp. 497–548). Hillsdale, NJ: Erlbaum.

Holden, C. (September, 1987). Genes and behavior: A twin legacy. *Psychology Today,* 18.

Holden, G. W., & West, M. J. (1989). Proximate regulation by mothers: A demonstration of how differing styles affect young children's behavior. *Child Development, 60,* 64–69.

Holloway, S. D., & Hess, R. D. (1985). Mothers' and teachers' attributions about children's mathematics performance. In I. E. Sigel (Ed.), *Parental belief systems. The psychological consequences for children* (pp. 177–200). Hillsdale, NJ: Erlbaum.

Honzik, M. P. (1986). The role of the family in the development of mental abilities: A 50-year study. In N. Datan, A. L. Greene, & H. W. Reese (Eds.), *Life-span developmental psychology. Intergenerational relations* (pp. 185–210). Hillsdale, NJ: Erlbaum.

Hopkins, J., Marcus, M., & Campbell, S. B. (1984). Postpartum depression: A critical review. *Psychological Bulletin, 95,* 498–515.

Horn, J. M. (1983). The Texas adoption project: Adopted children and their intellectual resemblance to biological and adoptive parents. *Child Development, 54,* 268–275.

Horowitz, F. D. (1982). The first two years of life: factors related to thriving. In S. G. Moore & C. R. Cooper (Eds.), *The young child. Reviews of research* (Vol. 3, pp. 15–34). Washington, DC: National Association for the Education of Young Children.

Horowitz, F. D. (1987). *Exploring developmental theories: Toward a structural/behavioral model of development.* Hillsdale, NJ: Erlbaum.

Horowitz, F. D. (1990). Developmental models of individual differences. In J. Colombo & J. Fagen (Eds.), *Individual differences in infancy: Reliability, stability, prediction* (pp. 3–18). Hillsdale, NJ: Erlbaum.

Howard, J. (1978). The influence of children's developmental dysfunctions on marital quality and family interaction. In R. M. Lerner & G. B. Spanier (Eds.), *Child influences on marital and family interaction. A life-span perspective* (pp. 275–298). New York: Academic Press.

Howat, P. M., & Saxton, A. M. (1988). The incidence of bulimic behavior in a secondary and university school population. *Journal of Youth and Adolescence, 17,* 221–231.

Howes, C. (1983). Patterns of friendship. *Child Development, 54,* 1041–1053.

Howes, C. (1987). Social competence with peers in young children: Developmental sequences. *Developmental Review, 7,* 252–272.

Howes, C. (1990). Can the age of entry into child care and the quality of child care predict adjustment in kindergarten? *Developmental Psychology, 26,* 292–303.

Howes, C., & Stewart, P. (1987). Child's play with adults, toys, and peers: An examination of family and child-care influences. *Developmental Psychology, 23,* 423–430.

Howlin, P., & Yule, W. (1990). Taxonomy of major disorders in childhood. In M. Lewis & S. M. Miller (Eds.), *Handbook of developmental psychopathology* (pp. 371–384). New York: Plenum.

Hoy, E. A., Bill, J. M., & Sykes, D. H. (1988). Very low birthweight: A long-term developmental impairment? *International Journal of Behavioral Development, 11,* 37–67.

Hubbard, F. O. A., & van IJzendoorn, M. H. (1987). Maternal unresponsiveness and infant crying. A critical replication of the Bell & Ainsworth study. In L. W. C. Tavecchio & M. H. van IJzendoorn (Eds.), *Attachment in social networks* (pp. 339–378). Amsterdam: Elsevier Science Publishers B. V. (North-Holland).

Hubel, D. H., & Weisel, T. N. (1963). Receptive fields of cells in striate cortex of very young, visually inexperienced kittens. *Journal of Neurophysiology, 26,* 994–1002.

Huesmann, L. R., Lagerspetz, K., & Eron, L. D. (1984). Intervening variables in the television violence-aggression relation: Evidence from two countries. *Developmental Psychology, 20,* 746–775.

Humphreys, L. G., Davey, T. C., & Park, R. K. (1985). Longitudinal correlation analysis of standing height and intelligence. *Child Development, 56,* 1465–1478.

Hunt, J. McV. (1986). The effect of variations in quality and type of early child care on development. *New Directions for Child Development, 32,* 31–48.

Hunter, F. T., & Youniss, J. (1982). Changes in functions of three relations during adolescence. *Developmental Psychology, 18,* 806–811.

Hunter, J. (1986). Cognitive ability, cognitive aptitudes, job knowledge, and job performance. *Journal of Vocational Behavior, 29,* 349–362.

Huntington, L., Hans, S. L., & Zeskind, P. S. (1990). The relations among cry characteristics, demographic variables, and developmental test scores in infants prenatally exposed to methadone. *Infant Behavior and Development, 13,* 533–538.

Huston, A. C. (1983). Sex-typing. In E. M. Hetherington (Ed.), *Handbook of child psychology: Socialization, personality, and social development* (Vol. 4, pp. 387–463). New York: Wiley.

Huston, A. C., & Alvarez, M. M. (1990). The socialization context of gender role development in early adolescence. In R. Montemayor, G. R. Adams, & T. P. Gullotta (Eds.), *From childhood to adolescence: A transitional period?* (pp. 156–181). Newbury Park, CA: Sage.

Huston, A. C., Greer, D., Wright, J. C., Welch, R., & Ross, R. (1984). Children's comprehension of televised formal features with masculine and feminine connotations. *Developmental Psychology, 20,* 707–716.

Huston, A. C., Wright, J. C., Rice, M. L., Kerkman, D., & St. Peters, M. (1990). Development of television viewing patterns in early childhood: A longitudinal investigation. *Developmental Psychology, 26,* 409–420.

Hutt, S. J., Lenard, H. G., & Prechtl, H. F. R. (1969). Psychophysiological studies in newborn infants. In L. P. Lipsitt & H. W. Reese (Eds.), *Advances in child development and behavior* (Vol. 4, pp. 128–173). New York: Academic Press.

Huttenlocher, J., Haight, W., Bryk, A., Seltzer, M., & Lyons, T. (1991). Early vocabulary growth: Relation to language input and gender. *Developmental Psychology, 27,* 236–248.

Hyde, J. S. (1984). How large are gender differences in aggression? A developmental meta-analysis. *Developmental Psychology, 20,* 722–736.

Hyde, J. S., & Linn, M. C. (1988). Gender differences in verbal ability: A meta-analysis. *Psychological Bulletin, 104,* 53–69.

Hyde, J. S., Fennema, E., & Lamon, S. J. (1990). Gender differences in mathematics performance: A meta-analysis. *Psychological Bulletin, 107,* 139–155.

Hymel, S., Rubin, K. H., Rowden, L., & LeMare, L. (1990). Children's peer relationships: Longitudinal prediction of internalizing and externalizing problems from middle to late childhood. *Child Development, 61,* 2004–2021.

Hynd, G. W., & Semrud-Clikeman, M. (1989). Dyslexia and brain morphology. *Psychological Bulletin, 106,* 447–482.

Ingram, D. (1981). Early patterns of grammatical development. In R. E. Stark (Ed.), *Language behavior in infancy and early childhood* (pp. 327–358). New York: Elsevier/North-Holland.

Inhelder, B., & Piaget, J. (1958). *The growth of logical thinking from childhood to adolescence.* New York: Basic Books.

Inoff-Germain, G., Arnold, G. S., Nottelmann, E. D., Susman, E. J., Cutler, G. B., Jr., & Chrousos, G. P. (1988). Relations between hormone levels and observational measures of aggressive behavior of young adolescents in family interactions. *Developmental Psychology, 24,* 129–139.

Isabella, R. A., & Belsky, J. (1991). Interactional synchrony and the origins of infant-mother attachment: A replication study. *Child Development, 62,* 373–384.

Isabella, R. A., Belsky, J., & von Eye, A. (1989). Origins of infant-mother attachment: An examination of interactional synchrony during the infant's first year. *Developmental Psychology, 25,* 12–21.

Istvan, J. (1986). Stress, anxiety, and birth outcomes. A critical review of the evidence. *Psychological Bulletin, 100,* 331–348.

Jacklin, C. N. (1989). Female and male: Issues of gender. *American Psychologist, 44,* 127–133.

Jackson, E., Campos, J. J., & Fischer, K. W. (1978). The question of decalage between object permanence and person permanence. *Developmental Psychology, 14,* 1–10.

Jackson, N. E., & Butterfield, E. C. (1986). A conception of giftedness designed to promote research. In R. J. Sternberg & J. E. Davidson (Eds.), *Conceptions of giftedness* (pp. 151–181). Cambridge, England: Cambridge University Press.

Jacobson, J. L., Jacobson, S. W., Fein, G. G., Schwartz, P. M., & Dowler, J. K. (1984). Prenatal exposure to an environmental toxin: A test of the multiple effects model. *Developmental Psychology, 20,* 523–532.

Jacobson, S. W., Fein, G. G., Jacobson, J. L., Schwartz, P. M., & Dowler, J. K. (1984). Neonatal correlates of prenatal exposure to smoking, caffeine, and alcohol. *Infant Behavior and Development, 7,* 253–265.

Janos, P. M., & Robinson, N. M. (1985). Psychosocial development in intellectually gifted children. In F. D. Horowitz & M. O'Brien (Eds.), *The gifted and talented. Developmental perspectives* (pp. 149–196). Washington, DC: American Psychological Association.

Jensen, A. R. (1980). *Bias in mental testing.* New York: The Free Press.

Johnson, C., Lewis, C., Love, S., Lewis, L., & Stuckey, M. (1984). Incidence and correlates of bulimic behavior in a female high school population. *Journal of Youth and Adolescence, 13,* 15–26.

Johnson, E. S., & Meade, A. C. (1987). Developmental patterns of spatial ability: An early sex difference. *Child Development, 58,* 725–740.

Johnston, J. R. (1985). Cognitive prerequisites: The evidence from children learning English. In D. I. Slobin (Ed.), *The crosslinguistic study of language acquisition: Vol. 2. Theoretical issues* (pp. 961–1004). Hillsdale, NJ: Erlbaum.

Jones, K. L., Smith, D. W., Ulleland, C. N., & Streissguth, A. (1973). Pattern of malformation in offspring of chronic alcoholic mothers. *Lancet, 1,* 1267–1271.

Jung, C. G. (1916). *Analytical psychology.* New York: Moffat, Yard.

Jung, C. G. (1939). *The integration of personality.* New York: Holt, Rinehart and Winston.

Kagan, J. (1965). Reflection-impulsivity and reading ability in primary grade children. *Child Development, 36,* 609–628.

Kagan, J. (1971). *Change and continuity in infancy.* New York: Wiley.

Kagan, J., & Lamb, S. (Eds.) (1987). *The emergence of morality in young children.* Chicago: University of Chicago Press.

Kagan, J., & Moss, H. A. (1962). *Birth to maturity.* New York: Wiley.

Kagan, J., Kearsley, R., & Zelazo, P. (1978). *Infancy: Its place in human development.* Cambridge, MA: Harvard University Press.

Kagan, J., Lapidus, D. R., & Moore, N. (1978). Infant antecedents of cognitive functioning: A longitudinal study. *Child Development, 49,* 1005–1023.

Kagan, J., Reznick, J. S., & Snidman, N. (1990). The temperamental qualities of inhibition and lack of inhibition. In M. Lewis & S. M. Miller (Eds.), *Handbook of developmental psychopathology* (pp. 219–226). New York: Plenum Press.

Kagan, J., Rosman, B. L., Day, D., Albert, J., & Phillips, W. (1964). Information processing in the child: Significance of analytic and reflective attitudes. *Psychological Monographs, 78* (Serial No. 578).

Kail, R. (1991a). Developmental change in speed of processing during childhood and adolescence. *Psychological Bulletin, 109,* 490–501.

Kail, R. (1991b). Processing time declines exponentially during childhood and adolescence. *Developmental Psychology, 27,* 259–266.

Kamin, L. J. (1974). *The science and politics of IQ.* Hillsdale, NJ: Erlbaum.

Kandel, E. R. (1985). Nerve cells and behavior. In E. R. Kandel & J. H. Schwartz (Eds.), *Principles of neural science,* (2nd ed.) (pp. 13–24). New York: Elsevier.

Kataria, S., Frutiger, A. D., Lanford, B., & Swanson, M. S. (1988). Anterior fontanel closure in healthy term infants. *Infant Behavior and Development, 11,* 229–233.

Kaye, Katherine, Elkind, L., Goldberg, D., & Tytun, A. (1989). Birth outcomes for infants of drug abusing mothers. *New York State Journal of Medicine, 89,* 256–261.

Kaye, Kenneth. (1982). *The mental and social life of babies. How parents create persons.* Chicago: University of Chicago Press.

Keating, D. P. (1980). Thinking processes in adolescence. In J. Adelson (Ed.), *Handbook of adolescent psychology* (pp. 211–246). New York: Wiley.

Keating, D. P., & Clark, L. V. (1980). Development of physical and social reasoning in adolescence. *Developmental Psychology, 16,* 23–30.

Keating, D. P., List, J. A., & Merriman, W. E. (1985). Cognitive processing and cognitive ability: Multivariate validity investigation. *Intelligence, 9,* 149–170.

Keeney, T. J., Cannizzo, S. R., & Flavell, J. H. (1967). Spontaneous and induced verbal rehearsal in a recall task. *Child Development, 38,* 935–966.

Kegan, R. (1985). The loss of Pete's dragon: Developments of the self in the years five to seven. In R. L. Leahy (Ed.), *The development of the self* (pp. 179–204). Orlando, FL: Academic Press.

Keith, L. G., MacGregor, S., Friedell, S., Rosner, M., Chasnoff, I. J., & Sciarra, J. J. (1989). Substance abuse in pregnant women: Recent experience at the perinatal center for chemical dependence of Northwestern Memorial Hospital. *Obstetrics and Gynecology, 73,* 715–720.

Kellam, S. G., Ensminger, M. E., & Turner, R. J. (1977). Family structure and the mental health of children: Concurrent and longitudinal community-wide studies. *Archives of General Psychiatry, 34,* 1012–1022.

Kempe, R. S., & Kempe, H. (1978). *Child abuse.* Cambridge, MA: Harvard University Press.

Kennell, J. H., Jerauld, R., Wolfe, H., Chesler, C., Kreger, N.C., McAlpine, W., Steffa, M., & Klaus, M. H. (1974). Maternal behavior one year after early and extended post-partum contact. *Developmental Medicine and Child Neurology, 16,* 172–179.

Kessner, D. M. (1973). *Infant death: an analysis by maternal risk and health care.* Washington, DC: National Academy of Sciences.

Kestenbaum, R., Farber, E. A., & Sroufe, L. A. (1989). Individual differences in empathy among preschoolers: Relation to attachment history. *New Directions for Child Development, 44,* 51–64.

Kilpatrick, S. J., & Laros, R. K. (1989). Characteristics of normal labor. *Obstetrics and Gynecology, 74,* 85–87.

Kitchen, W. H., Ford, G. W., Rickards, A. L., Lissenden, J. V., & Ryan, M. M. (1987). Children of birth weight < 1000 g: Changing outcome between ages 2 and 5 years. *Journal of Pediatrics, 110,* 283–288.

Kitzinger, S., & Davis, J. A. (Eds.) (1978). *The place of birth.* Oxford: Oxford University Press.

Klagsbrun, F. (1984). *Too young to die: Youth & suicide.* New York: Pocket Books.

Klaus, H. M., & Kennell, J. H. (1976). *Maternal-infant bonding.* St. Louis, MO: Mosby.

Kline, M., Tschann, J. M., Johnston, J. R., & Wallerstein, J. S. (1989). Children's adjustment in joint and sole physical custody families. *Developmental Psychology, 25,* 430–438.

Kohlberg, L. (1964). Development of moral character and moral ideology. In M. L. Hoffman & L. W. Hoffman (Eds.), *Review of child development research* (Vol. 1, pp. 283–332). New York: Russell Sage Foundation.

Kohlberg, L. (1966). A cognitive-developmental analysis of children's sex-role concepts and attitudes. In E. E. Maccoby (Ed.), *The development of sex differences* (pp. 82–172). Stanford, CA: Stanford University Press.

Kohlberg, L. (1975). The cognitive-developmental approach to moral education. *Phi Delta Kappan,* June, 670–677.

Kohlberg, L. (1976). Moral stages and moralization: The cognitive-developmental approach. In T. Lickona (Ed.), *Moral development and behavior: Theory, research, and social issues* (pp. 31–53). New York: Holt, Rinehart and Winston.

Kohlberg, L. (1978). Revisions in the theory and practice of moral development. *New Directions for Child Development, 2,* 83–88.

Kohlberg, L. (1980). *The meaning and measurement of moral development.* Worcester, MA: Clark University Press.

Kohlberg, L. (1981). *Essays on moral development. Vol. 1. The philosophy of moral development.* New York: Harper & Row.

Kohlberg, L. (1984). *Essays on moral development: Vol. 2. The psychology of moral development.* San Francisco: Harper & Row.

Kohlberg, L., & Candee, D. (1984). The relationship of moral judgment to moral action. In W. M. Kurtines & J. L. Gewirtz (Eds.), *Morality, moral behavior, and moral development* (pp. 52–73). New York: Wiley.

Kohlberg, L., & Elfenbein, D. (1975). The development of moral judgments concerning capital punishment. *American Journal of Orthopsychiatry, 54,* 614–640.

Kohlberg, L., & Higgins, A. (1987). School democracy and social interaction. In W. M. Kurtines & J. L. Gewirtz

(Eds.), *Moral development through social interaction* (pp. 102–130). New York: Wiley-Interscience.

Kohlberg, L., & Ullian, D. Z. (1974). Stages in the development of psychosexual concepts and attitudes. In R. C. Friedman, R. M. Richart, & R. L. Vande Wiele (Eds.), *Sex differences in behavior* (pp. 209–222). New York: Wiley.

Kohlberg, L., Levine, C., & Hewer, A. (1983). Moral stages: A current formulation and a response to critics. *Contributions to human development 10.* Basel, Switzerland: S. Karger.

Kohn, M. L. (1980). Job complexity and adult personality. In N. J. Smelser & E. H. Erikson (Eds.), *Themes of work and love in adulthood* (pp. 193–212). Cambridge, MA: Harvard University Press.

Kohn, M. L., & Schooler, C. (1983). *Work and personality: An inquiry into the impact of social stratification.* Norwood, NJ: Ablex Press.

Kopp, C. B. (1983). Risk factors in development. In M. M. Haith & J. J. Campos (Eds.), *Handbook of child psychology: Infancy and developmental psychobiology* (Vol. 2) (pp. 1081–1188). New York: Wiley.

Kopp, C. B. (1990). Risks in infancy: appraising the research. *Merrill Palmer Quarterly, 36,* 117–140.

Kopp, C. B., & Kaler, S. R. (1989). Risk in infancy: Origins and implications. *American Psychologist, 44,* 224–230.

Kopp, C. B., & Parmelee, A. H. (1979). Prenatal and perinatal influences on infant behavior. In J. D. Osofsky (Ed.), *Handbook of infant development* (pp. 29–75). New York: Wiley.

Korn, S. J. (1978, September). Temperament, vulnerability, and behavior. Paper presented at the Louisville Temperament Conference, Louisville.

Korn, S. J. (1984). Continuities and discontinuities in difficult/easy temperament: Infancy to young adulthood. *Merrill-Palmer Quarterly, 30,* 189–199.

Korner, A. F. (1987). Preventive intervention with high-risk newborns: Theoretical, conceptual, and methodological perspectives. In J. D. Osofsky (Ed.), *Handbook of infant development* (2nd ed.) (pp. 1006–1036). New York: Wiley-Interscience.

Korner, A. F., Hutchinson, C. A., Koperski, J. A., Kraemer, H. C., & Schneider, P. A. (1981). Stability of individual differences of neonatal motor and crying patterns. *Child Development, 52,* 83–90.

Krantz, S. E. (1988). Divorce and children. In S. M. Dornbusch & M. H. Strober (Eds.), *Feminism, children, and the new families* (pp. 249–273). New York: The Guilford Press.

Kreitler, S., & Kreitler, H. (1989). Horizontal decalage: A problem and its solution. *Cognitive Development, 4,* 89–119.

Kuczaj, S. A., II. (1977). The acquisition of regular and irregular past tense forms. *Journal of Verbal Learning and Verbal Behavior, 49,* 319–326.

Kuczaj, S. A., II. (1978). Children's judgments of grammatical and ungrammatical irregular past tense verbs. *Child Development, 49,* 319–326.

Kuczaj, S. A., II. (1982). On the nature of syntactic development. In S. A. Kuczaj II (Ed.), *Language development: Vol. 1. Syntax and semantics* (pp. 37–72). Hillsdale, NJ: Erlbaum.

Kuhl, P. K. (1983). Perception of auditory equivalence classes for speech in early infancy. *Infant Behavior and Development, 6,* 263–285.

Kuhl, P. K., & Meltzoff, A. N. (1984). The intermodal representation of speech in infants. *Infant Behavior and Development, 7,* 361–381.

Kuhn, D. (1988). Cognitive development. In M. H. Bornstein & M. E. Lamb (Eds.), *Developmental psychology: An advanced textbook* (2nd ed.) (pp. 205–260). Hillsdale, NJ: Erlbaum.

Kuhn, D., Nash, S. C., & Brucken, L. (1978). Sex role concepts of two-and three-year-olds. *Child Development, 49,* 445–451.

Kunkel, M. A., et al. (1986). Analysis of deletions in DNA from patients with Becker and Duchenne muscular dystrophy. *Nature, 322,* 73–77.

Kupersmidt, J. B., & Coie, J. D. (1990). Preadolescent peer status, aggression, and school adjustment as predictors of externalizing problems in adolescence. *Child Development, 61,* 1350–1362.

Kurdek, L. A., & Krile, D. (1982). A developmental analysis of the relation between peer acceptance and both interpersonal understanding and perceived social self-competence. *Child Development, 53,* 1485–1491.

La Freniere, P., Strayer, F. F., & Gauthier, R. (1984). The emergence of same-sex affiliative preferences among preschool peers: A developmental/ethological perspective. *Child Development, 55,* 1958–1965.

Ladd, G. W., Price, J. M., & Hart, C. H. (1988). Predicting preschoolers' peer status from their playground behaviors. *Child Development, 59,* 986–992.

Lamb, M. E. (1981). The development of father-infant relationships. In M. E. Lamb (Ed.), *The role of the father in child development* (2nd ed.) (pp. 459–488). New York: Wiley.

Lamb, M. E., Frodi, A. M., Hwang, C., Frodi, M., & Steinberg, J. (1982).

Mother- and father-infant interaction involving play and holding in traditional and nontraditional Swedish families. *Developmental Psychology, 18,* 215–221.

Lamb, M. E., Frodi, M., Hwang, C., & Frodi, A. M. (1983). Effects of paternal involvement on infant preferences for mothers and fathers. *Child Development, 54,* 450–458.

Lamb, M. E., Hwang, C., Bookstein, F. L., Broberg, A., Hult, G., & Frodi, M. (1988). Determinants of social competence in Swedish preschoolers. *Developmental Psychology, 24,* 58–70.

Lamke, L. K. (1982a). Adjustment and sex-role orientation. *Journal of Youth and Adolescence, 11,* 247–259.

Lamke, L. K. (1982b). The impact of sex-role orientation on self-esteem in early adolescence. *Child Development, 53,* 1530–1535.

Landry, S. H., Loveland, K., Hughes, S., Hall, S., & McEvoy, R. (1987, April). *Speech acts and the pragmatic deficits of autism.* Paper presented at the biennial meetings of the Society for Research in Child Development, Baltimore.

Langlois, J. H., Ritter, J. M., Roggman, L. A., & Vaughn, L. S. (1991). Facial diversity and infant preferences for attractive faces. *Developmental Psychology, 27,* 79–84.

Langlois, J. H., Roggman, L. A., & Rieser-Danner, L. A. (1990). Infants' differential social responses to attractive and unattractive faces. *Developmental Psychology, 26,* 153–159.

Langlois, J. H., Roggman, L. A., Casey, R. J., Ritter, J. M., Rieser-Danner, L. A., & Jenkins, V. Y. (1987). Infant preferences for attractive faces: Rudiments of a stereotype? *Developmental Psychology, 23,* 263–369.

Lauerman, J. (1990). The time machine. *Harvard Magazine, 92* (3), 43–46.

LaVoie, J. C. (1976). Ego identity formation in middle adolescence. *Journal of Youth and Adolescence, 5,* 371–385.

Lazar, I., & Darlington, R. (1982). Lasting effects of early education: A report from the consortium for longitudinal studies. *Monographs of the Society for Research in Child Development, 47,* (Serial No. 195).

Leach, P. (1983). *Babyhood,* (2nd ed., rev.). New York: Knopf.

Leadbeater, B. J., & Dionne, J. (1981). The adolescent's use of formal operational thinking in solving problems related to identity resolution. *Adolescence, 16,* 111–121.

Leaf, D. A. (1982). Exercise and pregnancy compatible. *The Physician and Sports Medicine, 9,* 22, 24.

Lederberg, A. R., & Mobley, C. E. (1990). The effect of hearing impairment on the quality of attachment and mother-toddler interaction. *Child Development, 61,* 1596–1604.

Lee, V. E., Brooks-Gunn, J., Schnur, E., & Liaw, F. (1990). Are Head Start effects sustained? A longitudinal follow-up comparison of disadvantaged children attending Head Start, no preschool, and other preschool programs. *Child Development, 61,* 495–507.

Lenneberg, E. H. (1967). *Biological foundations of language.* New York: Wiley.

Leon, G. R., Perry, C. L., Mangelsdorf, C., & Tell, G. (1989). Adolescent nutritional and psychological patterns and risk for the development of an eating disorder. *Journal of Youth and Adolescence, 18,* 273–282.

Leonard, L. B., Chapman, K., Rowan, L. E., & Weiss, A. L. (1983). Three hypotheses concerning young children's imitations of lexical items. *Developmental Psychology, 19,* 591–601.

Lerner, J. V., & Galambos, N. L. (1986). Child development and family change: The influences of maternal employment in infants and toddlers. In L. P. Lipsitt & C. Rovee-Collier (Eds.), *Advances in infancy research* (Vol. 4, pp. 40–86). Norwood, NJ: Ablex.

Lerner, J. V., & Lerner, R. M. (1983). Temperament and adaptation across life: Theoretical and empirical issues. In P. B. Baltes & O. G. Brim, Jr. (Eds.), *Life-span development and behavior* (Vol. 5, pp. 198–233). New York: Academic Press.

Lerner, J. V., Nitz, K., Talwar, R., & Lerner, R. M. (1989). On the functional significance of temperamental individuality: A developmental contextual view of the concept of goodness of fit. In G. A. Kohnstamm, J. E. Bates, & M. K. Rothbart (Eds.), *Temperament in childhood* (pp. 509–522). Chichester, England: Wiley.

Lerner, R. M. (1985). Adolescent maturational changes and psychosocial development: A dynamic interactional perspective. *Journal of Youth and Adolescence, 14,* 355–372.

Lerner, R. M. (1986). *Concepts and theories of human development* (2nd ed.). New York: Random House.

Lerner, R. M. (1987). A life-span perspective for early adolescence. In R. M. Lerner & T. T. Foch (Eds.), *Biological-psychosocial interactions in early adolescence* (pp. 9–34). Hillsdale, NJ: Erlbaum.

Leslie, A. M., & Frith, U. (1988). Autistic children's understanding of seeing, knowing and believing. *British Journal of Developmental Psychology, 6,* 315–324.

Lester, B. M. (1987). Prediction of developmental outcome from acoustic cry analysis in term and preterm infants. *Pediatrics, 80,* 529–534.

Lester, B. M., & Dreher, M. (1989). Effects of marijuana use during pregnancy on newborn cry. *Child Development, 60,* 765–771.

Levano, K. J., Cunningham, G., Nelson, S., Roark, M., Williams, M. L., Guzick, D., Dowling, S., Rosenfeld, C. R., & Buckley, A. (1986). A prospective comparison of selective and universal electronic fetal monitoring in 34,995 pregnancies. *New England Journal of Medicine, 315,* 615–619.

Lewin, R. (1975, September). Starved brains. *Psychology Today,* pp. 29–33.

Lewis, C. C. (1981). How adolescents approach decisions: Changes over grades seven to twelve and policy implications. *Child Development, 52,* 538–544.

Lewis, M. (1990). Social knowledge and social development. *Merrill-Palmer Quarterly, 36,* 93–116.

Lewis, M., & Brooks, J. (1978). Self-knowledge and emotional development. In M. Lewis & L. A. Rosenblum (Eds.), *The development of affect* (pp. 205–226). New York: Plenum.

Lewis, M., & Brooks-Gunn, J. (1979). *Social cognition and the acquisition of self.* New York: Plenum.

Lewis, M., & Miller, S. M. (Eds.) (1990). *Handbook of developmental psychopathology.* New York: Plenum.

Lewis, M., Sullivan, M. W., Stanger, C., & Weiss, M. (1989). Self development and self-conscious emotions. *Child Development, 60,* 146–156.

Liben, L. S. (1978). The development of deaf children: An overview of issues. In L. S. Liben (Ed.), *Deaf children: Developmental perspectives* (pp. 3–20). New York: Academic Press.

Lickona, T. (1978). Moral development and moral education. In J. M. Gallagher & J. A. Easley, Jr. (Eds.), *Knowledge and development* (Vol. 2, pp. 21–74). New York: Plenum.

Lickona, T. (1983). *Raising good children.* Toronto: Bantam Books.

Linn, M. C., & Petersen, A. C. (1985). Emergence and characterization of sex differences in spatial ability: A meta-analysis. *Child Development, 56,* 1479–1498.

Linney, J. A., & Seidman, E. (1989). The future of schooling. *American Psychologist, 44,* 336–340.

Lipsitt, L. P. (1982). Infant learning. In T. M. Field, A. Houston, H. C. Quay, L. Troll, & G. E. Finley (Eds.), *Review of human development* (pp. 62–78). New York: Wiley.

Lipsitt, L. P. (1990). Learning and memory in infants. *Merrill-Palmer Quarterly, 36,* 53–66.

Livesley, W. J., & Bromley, D. B. (1973). *Person perception in childhood and adolescence.* London: Wiley.

Lo, Y-M. D., Patel, P., Wainscoat, J. S., Sampietro, M., Gillmer, M. D. G., & Fleming, K. A. (December 9, 1989). Prenatal sex determination by DNA amplification from maternal peripheral blood. *The Lancet,* 1363–1365.

Long, F., Peters, D. L., & Garduque, L. (1985). Continuity between home and day care: A model for defining relevant dimensions of child care. In I. E. Sigel (Ed.), *Advances in applied developmental psychology* (Vol. 1, pp. 131–170). Norwood, NJ: Ablex.

Longo, D. C., & Bond, L. (1984). Families of the handicapped child: Research and practice. *Family Relations, 33,* 57–65.

Lozoff, B. (1989). Nutrition and behavior. *American Psychologist, 44,* 231–236.

Luster, T., Rhoades, K., & Haas, B. (1989). The relation between parental values and parenting behavior: A test of the Kohn hypothesis. *Journal of Marriage and the Family, 51,* 139–147.

Lütkenhaus, P., Grossmann, K. E., & Grossmann, K. (1985). Infant-mother attachment at twelve months and style of interaction with a stranger at the age of three years. *Child Development, 56,* 1538–1542.

Lyons, N. P. (1983). Two perspectives: On self, relationships, and morality. *Harvard Educational Review, 53,* 125–145.

Lyons-Ruth, K., Connell, D. B., Grunebaum, H. U., & Botein, S. (1990). Infants at social risk: Maternal depression and family support services as mediators of infant development and security of attachment. *Child Development, 61,* 85–98.

Lytton, H. (1977). Do parents create, or respond to, differences in twins? *Developmental Psychology, 12,* 456–459.

Lytton, H., & Romney, D. M. (1991). Parents' differential socialization of boys and girls: A meta-analysis. *Psychological Bulletin, 109,* 267–296.

Maccoby, E. E. (1980a). Commentary on G. R. Patterson, "Mothers: The unacknowledged victims." *Monographs of the Society for Research in Child Development, 45* (Serial No. 186).

Maccoby, E. E. (1980b). *Social development. Psychological growth and the parent-child relationships.* New York: Harcourt Brace Jovanovich.

Maccoby, E. E. (1984). Socialization and developmental change. *Child Development, 55,* 317–328.

Maccoby, E. E. (1988). Gender as a social category. *Developmental Psychology, 24,* 755–765.

Maccoby, E. E. (1990). Gender and relationships. A developmental account.

*American Psychologist, 45,* 513–520.

Maccoby, E. E., & Jacklin, C. N. (1974). *The psychology of sex differences.* Stanford, CA: Stanford University Press.

Maccoby, E. E., & Jacklin, C. N. (1980). Sex differences in aggression: A rejoinder and reprise. *Child Development, 51,* 964–980.

Maccoby, E. E., & Jacklin, C. N. (1987). Gender segregation in childhood. In H. W. Reese (Ed.), *Advances in child development and behavior* (Vol. 20, pp. 239–288). Orlando, FL: Academic Press.

Maccoby, E. E., & Martin, J. A. (1983). Socialization in the context of the family: Parent-child interaction. In E. M. Hetherington (Ed.), *Handbook of child psychology: Socialization, personality, and social development* (Vol. 4, pp. 1–102). New York: Wiley.

Macfarlane, A. (1977). *The psychology of childbirth.* Cambridge, MA: Harvard University Press.

Maccoby, E. E., Doering, C. H., Jacklin, C. N., & Kraemer, H. (1979). Concentrations of sex hormones in umbilical-cord blood: Their relation to sex and birth order of infants. *Child Development, 50,* 632–642.

Maclean, M., Bryant, P., & Bradley, L. (1987). Rhymes, nursery rhymes, and reading in early childhood. *Merrill-Palmer Quarterly, 33,* 255–282.

MacWhinney, B. (1987). The competition model. In B. MacWhinney (Ed.), *Mechanisms of language acquisition* (pp. 249–308). Hillsdale, NJ: Erlbaum.

Magenis, R. E. (1977). Parental origin of the extra chromosome in Down's syndrome. *Human Genetics, 37,* 7–16.

Magnusson, D., Stattin, H., & Allen, V. L. (1986). Differential maturation among girls and its relation to social adjustment: A longitudinal perspective. In P. B. Baltes, D. L. Featherman, & R. M. Lerner (Eds.), *Life-span development and behavior* (Vol. 7, pp. 136–173). Hillsdale, NJ: Erlbaum.

Main, M., & Cassidy, J. (1988). Categories of response to reunion with the parent at age 6: Predictable from infant attachment classifications and stable over a 1-month period. *Developmental Psychology, 24,* 415–426.

Main, M., & Solomon, J. (1985). Discovery of an insecure disorganized/disoriented attachment pattern: Procedures, findings and implications for the classification of behavior. In M. Yogman & T. B. Brazelton (Eds.), *Affective development in infancy* (pp. 95–124). Norwood, NJ: Ablex.

Main, M., Kaplan, N., & Cassidy, J. (1985). Security in infancy, childhood, and adulthood: A move to the level of representation. In I. Bretherton & E. Waters

(Eds.), Growing points of attachment theory and research. *Monographs of the Society for Research in Child Development, 50* (Serial No. 209, pp. 66–104).

Malina, R. M. (1982). Motor development in the early years. In S. G. Moore & C. R. Cooper (Eds.), *The young child. Reviews of research* (Vol. 3, pp. 211–232). Washington, DC: National Association for the Education of Young Children.

Malina, R. M. (1990). Physical growth and performance during the transition years (9–16). In R. Montemayor, G. R. Adams, & T. P. Gullotta (Eds.), *From childhood to adolescence: A transitional period?* (pp. 41–62). Newbury Park, CA: Sage.

Mangelsdorf, S., Gunnar, M., Kestenbaum, R., Lang, S., & Andreas, D. (1990). Infant proneness-to-distress temperament, maternal personality, and mother-infant attachment: Associates and goodness of fit. *Child Development, 61,* 820–831.

Marano, H. (1979). Breast-feeding. New evidence: It's far more than nutrition. *Medical World News, 20,* 62–78.

Maratsos, M. (1983). Some current issues in the study of the acquisition of grammar. In J. H. Flavell & E. M. Markman (Eds.), *Handbook of child psychology: Cognitive development* (Vol. 3, pp. 707–786). New York: Wiley.

Marcia, J. E. (1966). Development and validation of ego identity status. *Journal of Personality and Social Psychology, 3,* 551–558.

Marcia, J. E. (1980). Identity in adolescence. In J. Adelson (Ed.), *Handbook of adolescent psychology,* (pp. 159–187). New York: Wiley.

Marcus, D. E., & Overton, W. F. (1978). The development of cognitive gender constancy and sex role preferences. *Child Development, 49,* 434–444.

Marcus, R. F. (1986). Naturalistic observation of cooperation, helping, and sharing and their association with empathy and affect. In C. Zahn-Waxler, E. M. Cummings, & R. Iannotti (Eds.), *Altruism and aggression. Biological and social origins* (pp. 256–279). Cambridge, England: Cambridge University Press.

Marini, Z., & Case, R. (1989). Parallels in the development of preschoolers' knowledge about their physical and social worlds. *Merrill-Palmer Quarterly, 35,* 63–87.

Markovitz, H., Schleifer, M., & Fortier, L. (1989). Development of elementary deductive reasoning in young children. *Developmental Psychology, 25,* 787–793.

Martin, B., & Hoffman, J. A. (1990). Conduct disorders. In M. Lewis & S. M. Miller (Eds.), *Handbook of developmental psychopathology* (pp. 109–118). New York: Plenum.

Martin, C. L., & Halverson, C. F., Jr. (1981). A schematic processing model of sex typing and stereotyping in children. *Child Development, 52,* 1119–1134.

Martin, C. L., & Halverson, C. F., Jr. (1983). The effects of sex-typing schemas on young children's memory. *Child Development, 54,* 563–574.

Martin, C. L., & Little, J. K. (1990). The relation of gender understanding to children's sex-typed preferences and gender stereotypes. *Child Development, 61,* 1427–1439.

Martin, C. L., Wood, C. H., & Little, J. K. (1990). The development of gender stereotype components. *Child Development, 61,* 1891–1904.

Martorano, S. C. (1977). A developmental analysis of performance on Piaget's formal operations tasks. *Developmental Psychology, 13,* 666–672.

Marvin, R. S., & Greenberg, M. T. (1982). Preschoolers' changing conceptions of their mothers: A social-cognitive study of mother-child attachment. *New Directions for Child Development, 18,* 47–60.

Massad, C. M. (1981). Sex role identity and adjustment during adolescence. *Child Development, 52,* 1290–1298.

Masten, A. S. (1989). Resilience in development: Implications of the study of successful adaptation for developmental psychopathology. In D. Cicchetti (Ed.), *The emergence of a discipline: Vol. 1. Rochester Symposium on Developmental Psychopathology* (pp. 261–294). Hillsdale, NJ: Erlbaum.

Masters, J. C., & Furman, W. (1981). Popularity, individual friendship selection, and specific peer interaction among children. *Developmental Psychology, 17,* 344–350.

Matas, L., Arend, R. A., & Sroufe, L. A. (1978). Continuity of adaptation in the second year: The relationship between quality of attachment and latter competence. *Child Development, 49,* 547–556.

Mather, P. L., & Black, K. N. (1984). Heredity and environmental influences on preschool twins' language skills. *Developmental Psychology, 20,* 303–308.

Mathew, A., & Cook, M. (1990). The control of reaching movements by young infants. *Child Development, 61,* 1238–1257.

Maurer, D., & Maurer, C. (1988). *The world of the newborn.* New York: Basic Books.

Mayer, J. (1975). Obesity during childhood. In M. Winick (Ed.), *Childhood obesity* (pp. 73–80). New York: Wiley.

McCabe, A. E., Siegel, L. S., Spence, I., & Wilkinson, A. (1982). Class-inclusion reasoning: Patterns of performance from three to eight years. *Child Development, 53,* 779–785.

McCall, R. B. (1981). Nature-nurture and the two realms of development: A proposed integration with respect to mental development. *Child Development, 52,* 1–12.

McCall, R. B. (1984). Developmental changes in mental performance: The effect of the birth of a sibling. *Child Development, 55,* 1317–1321.

McCall, R. B., Appelbaum, M. I., & Hogarty, P. S. (1973). Developmental changes in mental performance. *Monographs of the Society for Research in Child Development, 38* (Serial No. 150).

McCarthy, J. D., & Hoge, D. R. (1982). Analysis of age effects in longitudinal studies of adolescent self-esteem. *Developmental Psychology, 18,* 372–379.

McCord, W., McCord, J., & Zola, I. K. (1959). *Origins of crime.* New York: Columbia University Press.

McCormick, M. C., Gortmaker, S. L., & Sobol, A. M. (1990). Very low birth weight children: Behavior problems and school difficulty in a national sample. *Journal of Pediatrics, 117,* 687–693.

McFalls, J. A., Jr. (1990). The risks of reproductive impairment in the later years of childbearing. *Annual Review of Sociology, 16,* 491–519.

McHale, S. M., & Lerner, R. M. (1990). Stages of human development. In R. M. Thomas (Ed.), *The encyclopedia of human development and education* (pp. 163–166). Oxford: Pergamon Press.

McIntosh, K. (1984). Viral infections of the fetus and newborn. In M. E. Avery & H. W. Taeusch, Jr. (Eds.), *Schaffer's diseases of the newborn* (5th ed.) (pp. 754–768). Philadelphia: W. B. Saunders.

McKey, R. H., Condelli, L., Granson, H., Barrett, B., McConkey, C., & Plantz, M. (1985, June). *The impact of Head Start on children, families and communities* (final report of the Head Start Evaluation, Synthesis and Utilization Project). Washington, DC: CSR.

McKinney, J. D., & Edgerton, M. (1983, April). Classroom adaptive behavior. Paper presented at the biennial meetings of the Society for Research in Child Development, Detroit.

McLaughlin, B. (1984). *Second-language acquisition in childhood: Vol. 1. Preschool children* (2nd ed.). Hillsdale, NJ: Erlbaum.

McLoyd, V. C. (1989). Socialization and development in a changing economy: The effects of parental job and income loss on children. *American Psychologist, 44,* 393–302.

McLoyd, V. C. (1990). The impact of economic hardship on black families and children: Psychological distress, parenting, and socioemotional development. *Child Development, 61,* 311–346.

McNeill, D. (1970). *The acquisition of language: The study of developmental psycholinguistics.* New York: Harper & Row.

Mednick, M. T. (1989). On the politics of psychological constructs. *American Psychologist, 44,* 1118–1123.

Meltzoff, A. N. (1988). Infant imitation and memory: Nine-month-olds in immediate and deferred tasks. *Child Development, 59,* 217–225.

Meltzoff, A. N., & Borton, R. W. (1979). Intermodal matching by human neonates. *Nature, 282,* 403–404.

Meltzoff, A. N., & Moore, M. K. (1983). Newborn infants imitate adult facial gestures. *Child Development, 54,* 702–709.

Mervis, C. B., & Mervis, C. A. (1982). Leopards are kitty-cats: Object labeling by mothers for their thirteen-month-olds. *Child Development, 53,* 267–273.

Meyer-Bahlburg, H. F. L., Ehrhardt, A. A., & Feldman, J. F. (1986). Long-term implications of the prenatal endocrine milieu for sex-dimorphic behavior. In L. Erlenmeyer-Kimling & N. E. Miller (Eds.), *Life-span research on the prediction of psychopathology* (pp. 17–30). Hillsdale, NJ: Erlbaum.

Mikes, M. (1990). Some issues of lexical development in early bi- and trilinguals. In G. Conti-Ramsden & C. E. Snow (Eds.), *Children's language* (Vol. 7, pp. 103–120). Hillsdale, NJ: Erlbaum.

Mikkelsen, M., & Stone, J. (1970). Genetic counseling in Down's syndrome. *Human Heredity, 20,* 457–464.

Miller, G. A. (1956). The magical number seven, plus or minus two: Some limits on our capacity for processing information. *Psychological Review, 63,* 81–96.

Miller, S. M., Birnbaum, A., & Durbin, D. (1990). Etiologic perspectives on depression in childhood. In M. Lewis & S. M. Miller (Eds.), *Handbook of developmental psychopathology* (pp. 311–340). New York: Plenum.

Mills, R. S. L., & Grusec, J. E. (1989). Cognitive, affective, and behavioral consequences of praising altruism. *Merrill-Palmer Quarterly, 35,* 299–326.

Mischel, W. (1966). A social learning view of sex differences in behavior. In E. E. Maccoby (Ed.), *The development of sex differences* (pp. 56–81). Stanford, CA: Stanford University Press.

Mischel, W. (1970). Sex typing and socialization. In P. H. Mussen (Ed.), *Carmichael's manual of child psychology* (Vol. 2, pp. 3–72). New York: Wiley.

Mitchell, P. R., & Kent, R. D. (1990). Phonetic variation in multisyllable babbling. *Journal of Child Language, 17,* 247–265.

Mizukami, K., Kobayashi, N., Ishii, T., & Iwata, H. (1990). First selective attach-ment begins in early infancy: A study using telethermography. *Infant Behavior and Development, 13,* 257–271.

Moffitt, T. E. (1990). Juvenile delinquency and attention deficit disorder: Boys' developmental trajectories from age 3 to age 15. *Child Development, 61,* 893–910.

Money, J. (1987). Sin, sickness, or status? Homosexual gender identity and psychoneuroendocrinology. *American Psychologist, 42,* 384–399.

Montemayor, R., & Eisen, M. (1977). The development of self-conceptions from childhood to adolescence. *Developmental Psychology, 13,* 314–319.

Montpetit, R. R., Montoye, H. J., & Laeding, L. (1967). Grip strength of school children, Saginaw, Michigan— 1964. *Research Quarterly, 38,* 231–240.

Moon, C., & Fifer, W. P. (1990). Syllables as signals for 2-day-old infants. *Infant Behavior and Development, 13,* 377–390.

Moore, E. G. J. (1986). Family socialization and the IQ test performance of traditionally and transracially adopted black children. *Developmental Psychology, 22,* 317–326.

Moore, K. A., Hofferth, S. L., Wertheimer, R. F., Waite, L. J., & Caldwell, S. B. (1981). Teenage childbearing: Consequences for women, families, and government welfare expenditures. In K. G. Scott, T. Field, & E. Robertson (Eds.), *Teenage parents and their offspring* (pp. 35–54). New York: Grune & Stratton.

Moore, K. L. (1988). *The developing human. Clinically oriented embryology* (4th ed.). Philadelphia: W. B. Saunders.

Moore, R., Pauker, J. D., & Moore, T. E. (1984). Delinquent recidivists: Vulnerable children. *Journal of Youth and Adolescence, 13,* 451–457.

Moores, D. F. (1985). Early intervention programs for hearing impaired children: A longitudinal assessment. In K. E. Nelson (Ed.), *Children's language* (Vol. 5, pp. 159–196). Hillsdale, NJ: Erlbaum.

Morgan, M. (1982). Television and adolescents' sex role stereotypes: A longitudinal study. *Journal of Personality and Social Psychology, 43,* 947–955.

Morgan, M. (1987). Television, sex-role attitudes, and sex-role behavior. *Journal of Early Adolescence, 7,* 269–282.

Morrison, D. M. (1985). Adolescent contraceptive behavior: A review. *Psychological Bulletin, 98,* 538–568.

Morrongiello, B. A. (1988a). Infants' localization of sounds along the horizontal axis: Estimates of minimum audible angle. *Developmental Psychology, 24,* 8–13.

Morrongiello, B. A. (1988b). The development of auditory pattern perception skills. In C. Rovee-Collier & L. P. Lipsitt

(Eds.), *Advances in infancy research* (Vol. 5, pp. 137–173). Norwood, NJ: Ablex.

Morrongiello, B. A., Fenwick, K. D., & Chance, G. (1990). Sound localization acuity in very young infants: An observer-based testing procedure. *Developmental Psychology, 26,* 75–84.

Morse, P. A., & Cowan, N. (1982). Infant auditory and speech perception. In T. M. Field, A. Houston, H. C. Quay, L. Troll, & G. E. Finley (Eds.), *Review of human development* (pp. 32–61). New York: Wiley.

Moses, L. J., & Flavell, J. H. (1990). Inferring false beliefs from actions and reactions. *Child Development, 61,* 929–945.

Mosher, F. A., & Hornsby, J. R. (1966). On asking questions. In J. S. Bruner, R. R. Olver, & P. M. Greenfield (Eds.), *Studies in cognitive growth* (pp. 68–85). New York: Wiley.

Munro, G., & Adams, G. R. (1977). Ego-identity formation in college students and working youth. *Developmental Psychology, 13,* 523–524.

Munroe, R. H., Shimmin, H. S., & Munroe, R. L. (1984). Gender understanding and sex role preference in four cultures. *Developmental Psychology, 20,* 673–682.

Murray, A. D., Dolby, R. M., Nation, R. L., & Thomas, D. B. (1981). Effects of epidural anesthesia on newborns and their mothers. *Child Development, 52,* 71–82.

Murray, J. L., & Bernfield, M. (1988). The differential effect of prenatal care on the incidence of low birth weight among blacks and whites in a prepaid health care plan. *New England Journal of Medicine, 319,* 1385–1391.

Murray, J. P. (1980). *Television & youth. 25 years of research and controversy.* Stanford, CA: The Boys Town Center for the Study of Youth Development.

Myers, B. J. (1987). Mother-infant bonding as a critical period. In M. H. Bornstein (Ed.), *Sensitive periods in development: Interdisciplinary perspectives* (pp. 223–246). Hillsdale, NJ: Erlbaum.

Naeye, R. L., & Peters, E. C. (1984). Mental development of children whose mothers smoked during pregnancy. *Obstetrics & Gynecology, 64,* 601–607.

Nash, S. C. (1975). The relationship among sex-role stereotyping, sex-role preference, and the sex difference in spatial visualization. *Sex Roles, 1,* 15–32.

National Center for Health Statistics (1984, September). Advance report on final natality statistics, 1982. *Monthly Vital Statistics Report, 33* (No. 6), Supplement.

National Center for Health Statistics (1989). *Health, United States, 1988.* Washington, DC: U.S. Government Printing Office.

Neerhof, M. G., MacGregor, S. N., Retzky, S. S., & Sullivan, T. P. (1989). Cocaine abuse during pregnancy: Peripartum prevalence and perinatal outcome. *American Journal of Obstetrics and Gynecology, 161,* 633–638.

Neimark, E. D. (1982). Adolescent thought: Transition to formal operations. In B. B. Wolman (Ed.), *Handbook of developmental psychology* (pp. 486–502). Englewood Cliffs, NJ: Prentice-Hall.

Nelson, C. A. (1987). The recognition of facial expression in the first two years of life: Mechanisms of development. *Child Development, 58,* 889–909.

Nelson, C. A. (1989). Past, current, and future trends in infant face perception research. *Canadian Journal of Psychology, 43,* 183–198.

Nelson, Katherine. (1973). Structure and strategy in learning to talk. *Monographs of the Society for Research in Child Development, 38* (Serial No. 149).

Nelson, Katherine. (1988). Constraints on word learning. *Cognitive Development, 3,* 221–246.

Nelson, Katherine. (1990). Comment on Behrend's "Constraints and development." *Cognitive Development, 5,* 331–339.

Nelson, Keith. (1977). Facilitating children's syntax acquisition. *Developmental Psychology, 13,* 101–107.

Nelson, S. A. (1980). Factors influencing young children's use of motives and outcomes as moral criteria. *Child Development, 51,* 823–829.

Neufeld, G. (1978). On the acquisition of prosodic and articulatory features in adult second language learning. *Canadian Modern Language Review, 34.*

Newberger, C. M., & Cook, S. J. (1983). Parental awareness and child abuse: A cognitive-developmental analysis of urban and rural samples. *American Journal of Orthopsychiatry, 53,* 512–524.

Newcombe, N. S., & Baenninger, M. (1989). Biological change and cognitive ability in adolescence. In G. R. Adams, R. Montemayor, & T. P. Gullotta (Eds.), *Biology of adolescent behavior and development* (pp. 168–194). Newbury Park, CA: Sage.

Nilsson, L. A. (1977). *A child is born.* New York: Delacorte Press, Seymour Lawrence.

Nisan, M., & Kohlberg, L. (1982). Universality and variation in moral judgment: A longitudinal and cross-sectional study in Turkey. *Child Development, 53,* 865–876.

Norton, A. J., & Glick, P. C. (1986). One parent families: A social and economic profile. *Family Relations, 35,* 9–18.

Nottelmann, E. D., Susman, E. J., Blue, J. H., Inoff-Germain, G., Dorn, L. D., Loriaux, D. L., Cutler, G. B., Jr., & Chrousos, G. P. (1987). Gonadal and adrenal hormone correlates of adjustment in early adolescence. In R. M. Lerner & T. T. Foch (Eds.), *Biological-psychosocial interactions in early adolescence* (pp. 303–324). Hillsdale, NJ: Erlbaum.

Novick, L. F., Berns, D., Stricof, R., Stevens, R., Pass, K., Wetheres, J. (1989). HIV seroprevalence in newborns in New York State. *Journal of the American Medical Association, 261,* 1745–1750.

Nowakowski, R. S. (1987). Basic concepts of CNS development. *Child Development, 58,* 568–595.

O'Brien, M., & Huston, A. C. (1985). Development of sex-typed play behavior in toddlers. *Developmental Psychology, 21,* 866–871.

O'Brien, S. F., & Bierman, K. L. (1988). Conceptions and perceived influence of peer groups: Interviews with preadolescents and adolescents. *Child Development, 59,* 1360–1365.

Obrzut, J. E., Hynd, G. W., & Boliek, C. A. (1986). Lateral asymmetries in learning-disabled children: A review. In S. J. Ceci (Ed.), *Handbook of cognitive, social, and neuropsychological aspects of learning disabilities* (Vol. 1, pp. 441–474). Hillsdale, NJ: Erlbaum.

O'Connor, S., Vietze, P. M., Sandler, H. M., Sherrod, K. B., & Altemeier, W. A. (1980). Quality of parenting and the mother-infant relationships following rooming-in. In P. M. Taylor (Ed.), *Parent-infant relationships* (pp. 349–368). New York: Grune & Stratton.

O'Donnell, M. (1966). *Around the corner.* New York: Harper & Row.

Ogbu, J. U. (1988). Cultural diversity and human development. *New Directions for Child Development, 42,* 11–28.

Oller, D. K. (1981). Infant vocalizations: Exploration and reflectivity. In R. E. Stark (Ed.), *Language behavior in infancy and early childhood* (pp. 85–104). New York: Elsevier/North-Holland.

Olshan, A. F., Baird, P. A., & Teschke, K. (1989). Paternal occupational exposures and the risk of Down syndrome. *American Journal of Human Genetics, 44,* 646–651.

Olson, S. L., Bayles, K., & Bates, J. E. (1986). Mother-child interaction and children's speech progress: A longitudinal study of the first two years. *Merrill-Palmer Quarterly, 32,* 1–20.

O'Malley, P. M., & Bachman, J. G. (1983). Self-esteem: Change and stability between ages 13 and 23. *Developmental*

Psychology, 19, 257–268.

Osofsky, J. D. (Ed.) (1987). *Handbook of infant development.* New York: Wiley-Interscience.

Overton, W. F., & Reese, H. W. (1973). Models of development: Methodological implications. In J. R. Nesselroade & H. W. Reese (Eds.), *Lifespan developmental psychology. Methodological issues* (pp. 65–86). New York: Academic Press.

Overton, W. F., Ward, S. L., Noveck, I. A., Black, J., & O'Brien, D. P. (1987). Form and content in the development of deductive reasoning. *Developmental Psychology, 23*, 22–30.

Padilla, A. M., Lindholm, K. J., Chen, A., Duran, R., Hakuta, K., Lambert, W., & Tucker, G. R. (1991). The English-only movement: Myths, reality, and implications for psychology. *American Psychologist, 46*, 120–130.

Page, D. C., Mosher, R., Simpson, E. M., Fisher, E. M. C., Mardon, G., Pollack, J., McGillivray, B., de la Chapelle, A., & Brown, L. G. (1987). The sex-determining region of the human Y chromosome encodes a finger protein. *Cell, 51*, 1091–1104.

Paikoff, R. L., & Brooks-Gunn, J. (1990). Physiological processes: What role do they play during the transition to adolescence? In R. Montemayor, G. R. Adams, & T. P. Gullotta (Eds.), *From childhood to adolescence. A transitional period?* (pp. 63–81). Newbury Park, CA: Sage.

Palkovitz, R. (1985). Fathers' birth attendance, early contact, and extended contact with their newborns: A critical review. *Child Development, 56*, 392–406.

Parke, R. D., & Tinsley, B. J. (1987). Family interaction in infancy. In J. D. Osofsky (Ed.), *Handbook of infant development* (2nd ed.) (pp. 579–641). New York: Wiley.

Parke, R. D., & Tinsley, B. R. (1981). The father's role in infancy: Determinants of involvement in caregiving and play. In M. E. Lamb (Ed.), *The role of the father in child development* (2nd ed.) (pp. 429–458). New York: Wiley.

Parke, R. D., & Tinsley, B. R. (1984). Fatherhood: Historical and contemporary perspectives. In K. A. McCluskey & H. W. Reese (Eds.), *Life-span developmental psychology. Historical and generational effects* (pp. 203–248). Orlando, FL: Academic Press.

Parmelee, A. H., Jr. (1986). Children's illnesses: Their beneficial effects on behavioral development. *Child Development, 57*, 1–10.

Parmelee, A. H., Jr., & Sigman, M. D. (1983). Perinatal brain development

and behavior. In M. M. Haith & J. J. Campos (Eds.), *Handbook of child psychology: Infancy and developmental psychobiology* (Vol. 2) (pp. 95–156). New York: Wiley.

Parmelee, A. H., Jr., Wenner, W. H., & Schulz, H. R. (1964). Infant sleep patterns from birth to 16 weeks of age. *Journal of Pediatrics, 65*, 576–582.

Parsons, J. E., Adler, T. F., & Daczala, C. M. (1982). Socialization of achievement attitudes and beliefs: parental influences. *Child Development, 53*, 310–321.

Passman, R. H., & Longway, K. P. (1982). The role of vision in maternal attachment: Giving 2-year-olds a photograph of their mother during separation. *Developmental Psychology, 18*, 530–533.

Patterson, C. J., Kupersmidt, J. B., & Griesler, P. C. (1990). Children's perceptions of self and of relationships with others as a function of sociometric status. *Child Development, 61*, 1335–1349.

Patterson, C. J., Kupersmidt, J. B., & Vaden, N. A. (1990). Income level, gender, ethnicity, and household composition as predictors of children's school-based competence. *Child Development, 61*, 484–494.

Patterson, G. R. (1975). *Families. Applications of social learning to family life.* Champaign, IL: Research Press.

Patterson, G. R. (1980). Mothers: The unacknowledged victims: *Monographs of the Society for Research in Child Development, 45* (Serial No. 186).

Patterson, G. R., Capaldi, D., & Bank, L. (1991). An early starter model for predicting delinquency. In D. J. Pepler & K. H. Rubin (Eds.), *The development and treatment of childhood aggression* (pp. 139–168). Hillsdale, NJ: Erlbaum.

Patterson, G. R., DeBarsyshe, B. D., & Ramsey, E. (1989). A developmental perspective on antisocial behavior. *American Psychologist, 44*, 329–335.

Peck, M. L. (1985). *Youth suicide.* New York: Springer.

Pederson, D. R., Moran, G., Sitko, C., Campbell, K., Ghesquire, K., & Acton, H. (1990). Maternal sensitivity and the security of infant-mother attachment: A Q-sort study. *Child Development, 61*, 1974–1983.

Pence, A. R. (Ed.) (1988). *Ecological research with children and families. From concepts to methodology.* New York: Teachers College Press.

Pennington, B. F., Bender, B., Puck, M., Salbenblatt, J., & Robinson, A. (1982). Learning disabilities in children with sex chromosome anomalies. *Child Development, 53*, 1182–1192.

Pennington, B. F., Van Orden, G. C., Smith, S. D., Green, P. A., & Haith, M. M. (1990). Phonological processing

skills and deficits in adult dyslexics. *Child Development, 61*, 1753–1778.

Perry, D. G., & Bussey, K. (1979). The social learning theory of sex differences: Imitations alive and well. *Journal of Personality and Social Psychology, 37*, 1699–1712.

Petersen, A. C. (1987). The nature of biological-psychosocial interactions: The sample case of early adolescence. In R. M. Lerner & T. T. Foch (Eds.), *Biological-psychosocial interactions in early adolescence* (pp. 35–62). Hillsdale, NJ: Erlbaum.

Petersen, A. C., & Taylor, B. (1980). The biological approach to adolescence. In J. Adelson (Ed.), *Handbook of adolescent psychology* (pp. 117–158). New York: Wiley.

Peterson, G. H., Mehl, L. E., & Leiderman, P. H. (1979). The role of some birth-related variables in father attachment. *American Journal of Orthopsychiatry, 49*, 330–338.

Pettit, G. S., Bakshi, A., Dodge, K. A., & Coie, J. D. (1990). The emergence of social dominance in young boys' play groups: Developmental differences and behavioral correlates. *Developmental Psychology, 26*, 1017–1025.

Phillips, D. A. (1987, April). *Parents as socializers of children's perceived academic competence.* Paper presented at the biennial meetings of the Society for Research in Child Development, Baltimore.

Piaget, J. (1932). *The moral judgment of the child.* New York: Macmillan.

Piaget, J. (1952). *The origins of intelligence in children.* New York: International Universities Press.

Piaget, J. (1954). *The construction of reality in the child.* New York: Basic Books.

Piaget, J. (1962). *Play, dreams and imitation in childhood.* New York: Norton.

Piaget, J. (1970). Piaget's theory. In P. H. Mussen (Ed.), *Carmichael's manual of child psychology* (3rd ed.) (Vol. 1, pp. 703–732). New York: Wiley.

Piaget, J. (1977). *The development of thought. Equilibration of cognitive structures.* New York: The Viking Press.

Piaget, J., & Inhelder, B. (1959). *La génese des structures logiques e'le'mentaires: classifications et se'riations.* Neuchâtel: Delachaux et Niestlé.

Piaget, J., & Inhelder, B. (1969). *The psychology of the child.* New York: Basic Books.

Pick, H. L., Jr. (1986). Reflections on the data and theory of cross-modal infancy research. In L. P. Lipsitt & C. Rovee-Collier (Eds.). *Advances in infancy research* (Vol. 4 , pp. 230–239). Norwood, NJ: Ablex.

Pinker, S. (1987). The bootstrapping

MacWhinney (Ed.), *Mechanisms of language acquisition* (pp. 399–442). Hillsdale, NJ: Erlbaum.

Pinker, S., & Prince, A. (1988). On language and connectionism: Analysis of a parallel distributed processing model of language acquisition. *Cognition, 28,* 73–193.

Plomin, R. (1989). Environment and genes: Determinants of behavior. *American Psychologist, 44,* 105–111.

Plomin, R., & DeFries, J. C. (1983). The Colorado adoption project. *Child Development, 54,* 276–289.

Plomin, R., & DeFries, J. C. (1985a). A parent-offspring adoption study of cognitive abilities in early childhood. *Intelligence, 9,* 341–356.

Plomin, R., & DeFries, J. C. (1985b). *Origins of individual differences in infancy. The Colorado Adoption Project.* Orlando, FL: Academic Press.

Plomin, R., Loehlin, J. C., & DeFries, J. C. (1985). Genetic and environmental components of "environmental" influences. *Developmental Psychology, 21,* 391–402.

Plomin, R., Pedersen, N. L., McClearn, G. E., Nesselroade, J. R., & Bergeman, C. S. (1988). EAS temperaments during the last half of the life span: Twins reared apart and twins reared together. *Psychology and Aging, 3,* 43–50.

Plomin, R., & Rende, R. (1991). Human behavior genetics. *Annual Review of Psychology, 42,* 161–190.

Plunkett, J. W., Klein, T., & Meisels, S. J. (1988). The relationship of preterm infant-mother attachment to stranger sociability at 3 years. *Infant Behavior and Development, 11,* 83–96.

Porter, R. H., Balogh, R. D., & Makin, J. W. (1988). Olfactory influences on mother-infant interactions. In C. Rovee-Collier & L. P. Lipsitt (Eds.), *Advances in infancy research* (Vol. 5, pp. 39–69). Norwood, NJ: Ablex.

Poulson, C. L., Nunes, L. R. D., & Warren, S. F. (1989). Imitation in infancy: A critical review. In H. W. Reese (Ed.), *Advances in child development and behavior* (Vol. 22, pp. 272–298). San Diego, CA: Academic Press.

Powell, B., & Steelman, L. C. (1982). Testing an undertested comparison: Maternal effects on sons' and daughters' attitudes toward women in the labor force. *Journal of Marriage and the Family, 44,* 349–355.

Power, C., & Peckham, C. (1990). Childhood morbidity and adulthood ill health. *Journal of Epidemiology and Community Health, 44,* 69–74.

Power, C., & Reimer, J. (1978). Moral atmosphere: An educational bridge between moral judgment and action. *New Directions for Child Development, 2,* 105–116.

Power, T. G., & Chapieski, M. L. (1986). Child rearing and impulse control in toddlers: A naturalistic investigation. *Developmental Psychology, 22,* 271–275.

Power, T. G., Gershenhorn, S., & Stafford, D. (1990). Maternal perception of infant difficultness: The influence of maternal attitudes and attributions. *Infant Behavior and Development, 13,* 421–437.

Prechtl, H. F. R., & Beintema, D. J. (1964). The neurological examination of the full-term newborn infant. *Clinics in Developmental Medicine, 12.* London: Hinemann.

Pulkkinen, L. (1982). Self-control and continuity in childhood delayed adolescence. In P. Baltes & O. Brim (Eds.), *Life span development and behavior* (Vol. 4, pp. 64–107). New York: Academic Press.

Pye, C. (1986). Quiché Mayan speech to children. *Journal of Child Language, 13,* 85–100.

Pyle, R., Mitchell, J., Eckert, E., Halverson, P., Neuman, P., & Goff, G. (1983). The incidence of bulimia in freshman college students. *International Journal of Eating Disorders, 2,* 75–85.

Radke-Yarrow, M., Cummings, E. M., Kuczynski, L., & Chapman, M. (1985). Patterns of attachment in two- and three-year-olds in normal families and familes with parental depression. *Child Development, 56,* 884–893.

Ramey, C. T., & Campbell, F. A. (1987). The Carolina Abecedarian Project. An educational experiment concerning human malleability. In J. J. Gallagher & C. T. Ramey (Eds.), *The malleability of children* (pp. 127–140). Baltimore: Paul H. Brookes.

Ramey, C. T., & Haskins, R. (1981a). The modification of intelligence through early experience. *Intelligence, 5,* 5–19.

Ramey, C. T., & Haskins, R. (1981b). Early education, intellectual development, and school performance; A reply to Arthur Jensen and J. McVicker Hunt. *Intelligence, 5,* 41–48.

Ramey, C. T., Lee, M. W., & Burchinal, M. R. (1989). Developmental plasticity and predictability: Consequences of ecological change. In M. H. Bornstein & N. A. Krasnegor (Eds.), *Stability and continuity in mental development* (pp. 217–234). Hillsdale, NJ: Erlbaum.

Ramey, C. T., Yeates, K. W., & Short, E. J. (1984). The plasticity of intellectual development: Insights from inventive intervention. *Child Development, 55,* 1913–1925.

Rappoport, L. (1972). *Personality development: The chronology of experience.* Glenview, IL: Scott, Foresman.

Razel, M. (1985). A reanalysis of the evidence for the genetic nature of early motor development. In I. E. Sigel (Ed.), *Advances in applied developmental psychology* (Vol. 1, pp. 171–212). Norwood, NJ: Ablex.

Reese, H. W., & Overton, W. F. (1978). Models of development and theories of development. In L. R. Goulet & P. B. Baltes (Eds.), *Life-span developmental psychology* (pp. 116–149). New York: Academic Press.

Reisman, J. E. (1987). Touch, motion, and proprioception. In P. Salapatek & L. Cohen (Eds.), *Handbook of infant perception: Vol. 1. From sensation to perception* (pp. 265–304). Orlando, FL: Academic Press.

Reisman, J. M., & Shorr, S. I. (1978). Friendship claims and expectations among children and adults. *Child Development, 49,* 913–916.

Resnick, M. B., Carter, R. L., Ariet, M., Bucciarelli, R. L., Evans, J. H., Furlough, R. R., Ausbon, W. W., & Curran, J. S. (1989). Effect of birth weight, race, and sex on survival of low-birth-weight infants in neonatal intensive care. *American Journal of Obstetrics and Gynecology, 161,* 184–187.

Rest, J. R. (1983). Morality. In J. H. Flavell & E. M. Markman (Eds.), *Handbook of child psychology: Cognitive development* (Vol. 3, pp. 556–629). New York: Wiley.

Rest, J. R., & Thoma, S. J. (1985). Relation of moral judgment development to formal education. *Developmental Psychology, 21,* 709–714.

Rholes, W. S., & Ruble, D. N. (1984). Children's understanding of dispositional characteristics of others. *Child Development, 55,* 550–560.

Ricciuti, H. N. (1981). Developmental consequences of malnutrition in early childhood. In M. A. Lewis & L. A. Rosenblum (Eds.), *The uncommon child* (pp. 151–172). New York: Plenum.

Rice, M. L. (1989). Children's language acquisition. *American Psychologist, 44,* 149–156.

Rice, M. L., Huston, A. C., Truglio, R., & Wright, J. (1990). Words from "Sesame Street": Learning vocabulary while viewing. *Developmental Psychology, 26,* 421–428.

Richardson, K., & Sheldon, S. (Eds.) (1988). *Cognitive development to adolescence.* Hillsdale, NJ: Erlbaum.

Richters, J., & Pellegrini, D. (1989). Depressed mothers' judgments about

Depressed mothers' judgments about their children: An examination of the depression-distortion hypothesis. *Child Development, 60,* 1068–1075.

Riegel, K. F. (1975). Adult life crises. A dialectic interpretation of development. In N. Datan & L. H. Ginsberg (Eds.), *Lifespan developmental psychology. Normative life crises* (pp. 99–128). New York: Academic Press.

Rierdan, J., Koff, E., & Stubbs, M. L. (1989). Timing of menarche, preparation, and initial menstrual experience: Replication and further analysis in a prospective study. *Journal of Youth and Adolescence, 18,* 413–426.

Riley, S. S. (1984). *How to generate values in young children.* Washington, DC: National Association for the Education of Young Children.

Roberts, C. W., Green, R., Williams, K., & Goodman, M. (1987). Boyhood gender identity development: A statistical contrast of two family groups. *Developmental Psychology, 23,* 544–557.

Robertson, E. G. (1981). Adolescence, physiological maturity, and obstetric outcomes. In K. G. Scott, T. Field, & E. Robertson (Eds.), *Teenage parents and their offspring.* New York: Grune & Stratton.

Robinson, H. B. (1981). The uncommonly bright child. In M. Lewis & L. A. Rosenblum (Eds.), *The uncommon child* (pp. 57–82). New York: Plenum.

Robinson, N. M., & Janos, P. M. (1986). Psychological adjustment in a college-level program of marked academic acceleration. *Journal of Youth and Adolescence, 15,* 51–60.

Roche, A. F. (1979). Secular trends in human growth, maturation, and development. *Monographs of the Society for Research in Child Development, 44,* (3–4, Serial No. 179).

Roche, A. F. (1981). The adipocyte-number hypothesis. *Child Development, 52,* 31–43.

Rogers, J. L. (1984). Confluence effects: Not here, not now! *Developmental Psychology, 20,* 321–331.

Rollins, B. C., & Feldman, H. (1970). Marital satisfaction over the family life cycle. *Journal of Marriage and the Family, 32,* 20–28.

Rollins, B. C., & Galligan, R. (1978). The developing child and marital satisfaction of parents. In R. M. Lerner & G. M. Spanier (Eds.), *Child influences on marital and family interaction. A life-span perspective* (pp. 71–106). New York: Academic Press.

Rooks, J. P., Weatherby, N. L., Ernst, E. K. M., Stapleton, S., Rosen, D., & Rosenfield, A. (1989). Outcomes of care in birth centers. The national birth center study. *The New England Journal of Medicine, 321,* 1804–1811.

Roosa, M. W. (1984). Maternal age, social class, and the obstetric performance of teenagers. *Journal of Youth and Adolescence, 13,* 365–374.

Roosa, M. W. (1988). The effect of age in the transition to parenthood: Are delayed childbearers a unique group? *Family Relations, 37,* 322–327.

Rose, S. A., & Ruff, H. A. (1987). Cross-modal abilities in human infants. In J. D. Osofsky (Ed.), *Handbook of infant development* (2nd ed.) (pp. 318–362). New York: Wiley-Interscience.

Rosenblith, J. F., & Sims-Knight, J. E. (1989). *In the beginning. Development in the first two years of life.* Newbury Park, CA: Sage.

Ross, G., Kagan, J., Zelazo, P., & Kotelchuck, M. (1975). Separation protest in infants in home and laboratory. *Developmental Psychology, 11,* 256–257.

Rothbart, M. K. (1986). Longitudinal observation of infant temperament. *Developmental Psychology, 22,* 356–365.

Rothbart, M. K. (1989a). Temperament in childhood: A framework. In G. A. Kohnstamm, J. E. Bates, & M. K. Rothbart (Eds.), *Temperament in childhood* (pp. 59–75). Chichester, England: Wiley.

Rothbart, M. K. (1989b). Biological processes in temperament. In G. A. Kohnstamm, J. E. Bates, & M. K. Rothbart (Eds.), *Temperament in childhood* (pp. 77–110). Chichester, England: Wiley.

Rothbart, M. K., & Derryberry, D. (1981). Development of individual differences in temperament. In M. E. Lamb and A. L. Brown (Eds.), *Advances in developmental psychology* (Vol. 1, pp. 37–86) Hillsdale, NJ: Erlbaum.

Rovee-Collier, C. (1986). The rise and fall of infant classical conditioning research: Its promise for the study of early development. In L. P. Lipsitt & C. Rovee-Collier (Eds.), *Advances in infancy research* (Vol. 4, pp. 139–162). Norwood, NJ: Ablex.

Rovet, J., & Netley, C. (1983). The triple X chromosome syndrome in childhood: Recent empirical findings. *Child Development, 54,* 831–845.

Rowe, I., & Marcia, J. E. (1980). Ego identity status, formal operations, and moral development. *Journal of Youth and Adolescence, 9,* 87–99.

Rubin, K. H., Fein, G. G., & Vandenberg, B. (1983). Play. In E. M. Hetherington (Ed.), *Handbook of child psychology: Socialization, personality, and social development* (Vol. 4, pp. 693–774). New York: Wiley.

Ruble, D. N. (1987). The acquisition of self-knowledge: A self-socialization perspective. In N. Eisenberg (Ed.), *Contemporary topics in developmental psychology* (pp. 243–270). New York: Wiley-Interscience.

Ruble, D. N. (1988). Sex-role development. In M. H. Bornstein & M. E. Lamb (Eds.), *Developmental psychology: An advanced textbook* (2nd ed.) (pp. 411–460). Hillsdale, NJ: Erlbaum.

Ruble, D. N., Balaban, T., & Cooper, J. (1981). Gender constancy and the effects of sex-typed televised toy commercials. *Child Development, 52,* 667–673.

Ruble, T. L. (1983). Sex stereotypes: Issues of change in the 1970's. *Sex Roles, 9,* 397–402.

Ruff, H. A. (1990). Individual differences in sustained attention during infancy. In J. Colombo & J. Fagen (Eds.), *Individual differences in infancy: Reliability, stability, prediction* (pp. 247–270). Hillsdale, NJ: Erlbaum.

Rumelhart, D. E., & McClelland, J. L. (1987). Learning the past tenses of English verbs: Implicit rules or parallel distributed processing. In B. MacWhinney (Ed.), *Mechanisms of language acquisition* (pp. 195–248). Hillsdale, NJ: Erlbaum.

Ruopp, R., & Travers, J. (1982). Janus faces day care: Perspectives on quality and cost. In E. F. Zigler & E. W. Gordon (Eds.), *Day care: Scientific and social policy issues* (pp. 72–101). Boston: Auburn House.

Russell, G. (1982). Shared-caregiving families: An Australian study. In M. E. Lamb (Ed.), *Nontraditional families* (pp. 139–172). Hillsdale, NJ: Erlbaum.

Rutter, D. R., & Durkin, K. (1987). Turn-taking in mother-infant interaction: An examination of vocalizations and gaze. *Developmental Psychology, 23,* 54–61.

Rutter, M. (1971). Parent-child separation: Psychological effects on the children. *Journal of Child Psychology and Psychiatry, 12,* 233–260.

Rutter, M. (1978). Family, area and school influences in the genesis of conduct disorders. In L. Hersov, M. Berber, & D. Schaffer (Eds.), *Aggression and antisocial behavior in childhood and adolescence* (pp. 95–114). Oxford: Pergamon.

Rutter, M. (1983). School effects on pupil progress: Research findings and policy implications. *Child Development, 54,* 1–29.

Rutter, M. (1987). Continuities and discontinuities from infancy. In J. D. Osofsky (Ed.), *Handbook of infant development* (2nd ed.) (pp. 1256–1296). New York: Wiley-Interscience.

Rutter, M. (1989). Isle of Wight revisited: Twenty-five years of child psychiatric epidemiology. *Journal of the American*

*Academy of Child and Adolescent Psychiatry, 28,* 633–653.

Rutter, M. (1990). Commentary: Some focus and process considerations regarding effects of parental depression on children. *Developmental Psychology, 26,* 60–67.

Rutter, M., & Garmezy, N. (1983). Developmental psychopathology. In E. M. Hetherington (Ed.), *Handbook of child psychology: Socialization, personality, and social development* (Vol. 4, pp. 775–912). New York: Wiley.

Rutter, M., Tizard, J., & Whitmore, K. (1970/1981). *Education, health and behaviour.* Huntington, NY: Krieger. (Original work published 1970)

Rutter, M., Yule, B., Quinton, D., Rowlands, O., Yule, W., & Berger, M. (1975). Attainment and adjustment in two geographical areas, III: Some factors accounting for area differences. *British Journal of Psychiatry, 126,* 520–533.

Ryan, A. S., & Martinez, G. A. (1989). Breast-feeding and the working mother: A profile. *Pediatrics, 83,* 524–531.

Ryder, R. W., et al. (1989). Perinatal transmission of the human immunodeficiency virus type 1 to infants of seropositive women in Zaire. *New England Journal of Medicine, 320,* 1637–1642.

Saario, T. N., Jacklin, C. N., & Tittle, C. K. (1973). Sex role stereo-typing in the public schools. *Harvard Educational Review, 43,* 386–416.

Sack, W. H., Mason, R., & Higgins, J. E. (1985). The single parent family and abusive child punishment. *American Journal of Orthopsychiatry, 55,* 252–259.

Sady, S. P., & Carpenter, M. W. (1989). Aerobic exercise during pregnancy. Special considerations. *Sports Medicine, 7,* 357–375.

Salk, L. (1960). The effects of the normal heartbeat sound on the behavior of the newborn infant; implications for mental health. *World Mental Health, 12,* 168–175.

Sameroff, A. J. (1982). Development and the dialectic: The need for a systems approach. In W. A. Collins (Ed.), *The Minnesota Symposia on Child Psychology, Vol. 15.* Hillsdale, NJ: Erlbaum.

Sameroff, A. J. (1983) Developmental systems: Contexts and evolution. In W. Kessen (Ed.), *Handbook of child psychology: History, theory, and methods* (Vol. 1, pp. 237–294). New York: Wiley.

Sameroff, A. J., & Cavanaugh, P. J. (1979). Learning in infancy: A developmental perspective. In J. D. Osofsky (Ed.), *Handbook of infant development.* (pp. 344–392). New York: Wiley.

*San Francisco Chronicle* (August 21, 1979).

Sanders, B., Soares, M. P., & D'Aquila, J. M. (1982). The sex difference on one test of spatial visualization: A nontrivial difference. *Child Development, 53,* 1106–1110.

Sattler, J. M. (1988). *Assessment of children.* San Diego: Jerome M. Sattler.

Saunders, W. L., & Shepardson, D. (1987). A comparison of concrete and formal science instruction upon science achievement and reasoning ability of sixth grade students. *Journal of Research in Science Teaching, 24,* 39–51.

Savage-Rumbaugh, E. S. (1990). Language acquisition in a nonhuman species: Implications for the innateness debate. *Developmental Psychobiology, 23,* 599–620.

Scafidi, F. A., Field, T. M., Schanberg, S. M., Bauer, C. R., Tucci, K., Roberts, J., Morrow, C., & Kuhn, C. M. (1990). Massage stimulates growth in preterm infants: A replication. *Infant Behavior and Development, 13,* 167–188.

Scarborough, H. S. (1990). Very early language deficits in dyslexic children. *Child Development, 61,* 1728–1743.

Scarr, S., & Kidd, K. K. (1983). Developmental behavior genetics. In M. M. Haith & J. J. Campos (Eds.), *Handbook of child psychology: Infancy and developmental psychobiology* (Vol. 2, pp. 345–434). New York: Wiley.

Scarr, S., & McCartney, K. (1983). How people make their own environments: A theory of genotype-environment effects. *Child Development, 54* 424–435.

Scarr, S., & Weinberg, R. A. (1983). The Minnesota adoption studies: Genetic differences and malleability. *Child Development, 54,* 260–267.

Scarr-Salapatek, S. (1976). An evolutionary perspective on infant intelligence: species patterns and individual variations. In M. Lewis (Ed.), *Origins of intelligence* (pp. 165–198). New York: Plenum.

Schachter, F. F., & Strage, A. A. (1982). Adults' talk and children's language development. In S. G. Moore & C. R. Cooper (Eds.), *The young child. Reviews of Research* (Vol. 3, pp. 79–96). Washington, DC: National Association for the Education of Young Children.

Schaefer, E. S. (1989). Dimensions of mother-infant interaction: Measurement, stability, and predictive validity. *Infant Behavior and Development, 12,* 379–393.

Schaefli, A., Rest, J. R., & Thoma, S. J. (1985). Does moral education improve moral judgment? A meta-analysis of intervention studies using the Defining Issues Test. *Review of Educational Research, 55,* 319–352.

Schank, R. C., & Abelson, R. (1977). *Scripts, plans, goals, and understanding.*

*Scripts, plans, goals, and understanding.* Hillsdale, NJ: Erlbaum.

Schlesinger, H. S., & Meadow, K. P. (1972). *Sound and sign.* Berkeley, CA: University of California Press.

Schneider, W., & Pressley, M. (1989). *Memory development between 2 and 20.* New York: Springer-Verlag.

Schonfeld, I. S., Shaffer, D., O'Connor, P., & Portny, S. (1988). Conduct disorder and cognitive functioning: Testing three causal hypotheses. *Child Development, 59,* 993–1007.

Schramm, W. F., Barnes, D. E., & Bakewell, J. M. (1987). Neonatal mortality in Missouri home births, 1978–84. *American Journal of Public Health, 77,* 930–935.

Scollon, R. (1976). *Conversations with a one-year-old.* Honolulu: University of Hawaii Press.

Sears, P. S., & Barbee, A. H. (1977). Career and life satisfactions among Terman's gifted women. In J. C. Stanley, W. C. George, & C. H. Solano (Eds.), *The gifted and the creative* (pp. 28–66). Baltimore: Johns Hopkins University Press.

Sears, R. R. Sources of life satisfactions of the Terman gifted men. (1977). *American Psychologist, 32,* 119–128.

Sears, R. R., Maccoby, E. E., & Levin, H. (1977). *Patterns of child rearing.* Stanford, CA: Stanford University Press. (Original work published in 1957)

Seidman, D. S., Ever-Hadani, P., & Gale, R. (1989). The effect of maternal weight gain in pregnancy on birth weight. *Obstetrics and Gynecology, 74,* 240–246.

Seitz, V. (1988). Methodology. In M. H. Bornstein & M. E. Lamb (Eds.), *Developmental psychology: An advanced textbook* (2nd ed.) (pp. 51–84). Hillsdale, NJ: Erlbaum.

Selman, R. L. (1980). *The growth of interpersonal understanding.* New York: Academic Press.

Sepkoski, C. (1987). *A longitudinal study of the effects of obstetric medication.* Paper presented at the biennial meetings of the Society for Research in Child Development, Baltimore.

Shaffer, D., Garland, A., Gould, M., Fisher, P., & Trautman, P. (1988). Preventing teenage suicide: A critical review. *Journal of the American Academy of Child and Adolescent Psychiatry, 27,* 675–687.

Shantz, C. U. (1983). Social cognition. In J. H. Flavell & E. M. Markman (Eds.), *Handbook of child psychology: Vol. III Cognitive development* (pp. 495–555). New York: Wiley.

Shantz, D. W. (1986). Conflict, aggression, and peer status: An observational study. *Child Development, 57,* 1322–1332.

Sheldon, W. H. (1940). The varieties of human physique. New York: Harper & Row.

Shelton, B. A. (1990). The distribution of household tasks. Does wife's employment status make a difference? *Journal of Family Issues, 11,* 115–135.

Sherrod, K. B., O'Connor, S., Vietze, P. M., & Altemeier, W. A., III. (1984). Child health and maltreatment. *Child Development, 55,* 1174–1183.

Shiono, P. H., Klebanoff, M. A., & Rhoads, G. G. (1986). Smoking and drinking during pregnancy. Their effects on preterm birth. *Journal of the American Medical Association, 225,* 82–84.

Shonkoff, J. P. (1984). The biological substrate and physical health in middle childhood. In W. A. Collins (Ed.),. *Development during middle childhood. The years from six to twelve* (pp. 24–69). Washington, DC: National Academy Press.

Shore, C. (1986). Combinatorial play, conceptual development, and early multiword speech. *Developmental Psychology, 22,* 184–190.

Shweder, R. A., Mahapatra, M., & Miller, J. G. (1987). Culture and moral development. In J. Kagan & S. Lamb (Eds.), *The emergence of morality in young children* (pp. 1–82). Chicago: The University of Chicago Press.

Siegal, M. (1987). Are sons and daughters treated more differently by fathers than by mothers? *Developmental Review, 7,* 183–209.

Siegel, L. J., & Griffin, N. J. (1984). Correlates of depressive symptoms in adolescents. *Journal of Youth and Adolescence, 13,* 475–487.

Siegler, R. S. (1976). Three aspects of cognitive development. *Cognitive Psychology, 8,* 431–520.

Siegler, R. S. (1978). The origins of scientific reasoning. In R. S. Siegler (Ed.), *Children's thinking: What develops?* (pp. 109–150). Hillsdale, NJ: Erlbaum.

Siegler, R. S. (1981). Developmental sequences within and between concepts. *Monographs of the Society for Research in Child Development, 46,* (2, Serial No. 189).

Siegler, R. S., & Richards, D. D. (1982). The development of intelligence. In R. J. Sternberg (Ed.), *Handbook of human intelligence* (pp. 897–974). Cambridge: Cambridge University Press.

Sigman, M., Neumann, C., Carter, E., Cattle, D. J., D'Souza, S., & Bwibo, N. (1988). Home interactions and the development of Embu toddlers in Kenya. *Child Development, 59,* 1251–1261.

Signorielli, N. (1986). Selective television viewing: A limited possibility. *Journal of Communication, 36* (No. 3), 64–81.

Simmons, R. G., & Blyth, D. A. (1987). *Moving into adolescence: The impact of pubertal change and school context.* New York: Aldine de Gruyter.

Simmons, R. G., Blyth, D. A., & McKinney, K. L. (1983). The social and psychological effects of puberty on white females. In J. Brooks-Gunn & A. C. Petersen (Eds.), *Girls at puberty. Biological and psychosocial perspectives* (pp. 229–272). New York: Plenum.

Simmons, R. G., Burgeson, R., & Reef, M. J. (1988). Cumulative change at entry to adolescence. In M. R. Gunnar & W. A. Collins (Eds.), *Development During the Transition to Adolescence. Minnesota Symposia on Child Psychology* (Vol. 21, pp. 123–150). Hillsdale, NJ: Erlbaum.

Simons, R. L., Robertson, J. F., & Downs, W. R. (1989). The nature of the association between parental rejection and delinquent behavior. *Journal of Youth and Adolescence, 18,* 297–309.

Skinner, B. F. (1957). *Verbal behavior.* New York: Prentice-Hall.

Skodak, M., & Skeels, H. M. (1945). A follow-up study of children in adoptive homes. *Journal of Genetic Psychology, 66,* 21–58.

Slaby, R. G., & Frey, K. S. (1975). Development of gender constancy and selective attention to same-sex models. *Child Development, 46,* 849–856.

Slater, A. M., & Bremner, J. G. (Eds.) (1989). *Infant development.* Hillsdale, NJ: Erlbaum.

Slaughter-Defoe, D. T., Nakagawa, K., Takanishi, R., & Johnson, D. J. (1990). Toward cultural/ecological perspectives on schooling and achievement in African- and Asian-American children. *Child Development, 61,* 363–383.

Slobin, D. I. (1985a). Introduction: Why study acquisition crosslinguistically? In D. I. Slobin (Ed.), *The crosslinguistic study of language acquisition: Vol. 1. The data* (pp. 3–24). Hillsdale, NJ: Erlbaum.

Slobin, D. I. (1985b). Crosslinguistic evidence for the language-making capacity. In D. I. Slobin (Ed.), *The crosslinguistic study of language acquisition: Vol. 2. Theoretical issues* (pp. 1157–1256). Hillsdale, NJ: Erlbaum.

Smetena, J. G. (1988). Adolescents' and parents' conceptions of parental authority. *Child Development, 59,* 321–334.

Smetena, J. G. (1990). Morality and conduct disorders. In M. Lewis & S. M. Miller (Eds.), *Handbook of developmental psychopathology* (pp. 157–180). New York: Plenum.

Smith, A. N., & Spence, C. M. (1981). National day care study: optimizing the day care environment. *American Journal of Orthopsychiatry, 50,* 718–721.

Smith, D. W. (1978). Prenatal life. In D. W. Smith, E. L. Bierman, & N. M. Robinson (Eds.), *The biologic ages of man* (2nd. ed.) (pp. 42–62). Philadelphia: W. B. Saunders.

Smith, D. W., & Stenchever, M. A. (1978). Prenatal life and the pregnant woman. In D. W. Smith, E. L. Bierman, & N. M. Robinson (Eds.), *The biologic ages of man* (2nd ed.) (pp. 42–77). Philadelphia: W. B. Saunders.

Smoll, F. L., & Schutz, R. W. (1990). Quantifying gender differences in physical performance: A developmental perspective. *Developmental Psychology, 26,* 360–369.

Snarey, J. R. (1985). Cross-cultural universality of social-moral development: A critical review of Kohlbergian research. *Psychological Bulletin, 97,* 202–232.

Snarey, J. R., Reimer, J., & Kohlberg, L. (1985). Development of social-moral reasoning among kibbutz adolescents: A longitudinal cross-sectional study. *Developmental Psychology, 21,* 3–17.

Snow, C. E. (1987). Relevance of the notion of a critical period to language acquisition. In M. H. Bornstein (Ed.), *Sensitive periods in development. Interdisciplinary perspectives* (pp. 183–210). Hillsdale, NJ: Erlbaum.

Snow, C. E., & Ferguson, C. A. (Eds.). (1977). *Talking to children.* Cambridge: Cambridge University Press.

Snow, M. E., Jacklin, C. N., & Maccoby, E. E. (1983). Sex-of-child differences in father-child interaction at one year of age. *Child Development, 54,* 227–232.

Snyder, L. (1978). Communicative and cognitive abilities and disabilities in the sensorimotor period. *Merrill-Palmer Quarterly, 24,* 161–180.

Sonnenschein, S. (1986). Development of referential communication skills: How familiarity with a listener affects a speaker's production of redundant messages. *Developmental Psychology, 22,* 549–552.

Sontag, L. W., Baker, C. T., & Nelson, V. L. (1958). Mental growth and personality development: A longitudinal study. *Monographs of the Society for Research in Child Development, 23* (Serial No. 68).

Sosa, R., Kennell, J. H., Klaus, M. H., Robertson, S., & Urrutia, J. (1980). The effect of a supportive companion on perinatal problems, length of labor and mother-infant interaction. *New England Journal of Medicine, 303,* 597–600.

Sostek, A. M., Katz, K. S., Valvano, J., & Smith, Y. (1987). *Development and kindergarten readiness in children born prematurely with IVH.* Paper presented at the biennial meetings of the Society for Research in Child Development, Baltimore.

Spangler, G. (1990). Mother, child, and situational correlates of toddler social competence. *Infant Behavior and Development, 13,* 405–419.

Spelke, E. S. (1979). Exploring audible and visible events in infancy. In A. D. Pick (Ed.), *Perception and its development: A tribute to Eleanor J. Gibson* (pp. 221–236). Hillsdale, NJ: Erlbaum.

Spelke, E. S. (1982). Perceptual knowledge of objects in infancy. In J. Mehler, E. C. T. Walker, & M. Garrett (Eds.), *Perspectives on mental representation* (pp. 409–430). Hillsdale, NJ: Erlbaum.

Spelke, E. S. (1985). Perception of unity, persistence, and identity: Thoughts on infants' conceptions of objects. In J. Mehler & R. Fox (Eds.), *Neonate cognition* (pp. 89–113). Hillsdale, NJ: Erlbaum.

Spelke, E. S., & Owsley, C. J. (1979). Intermodal exploration and knowledge in infancy. *Infant Behavior and Development, 2,* 13–27.

Spelke, E. S., von Hofsten, C., & Kestenbaum, R. (1989). Object perception in infancy: Interaction of spatial and kinetic information for object boundaries. *Developmental Psychology, 25,* 185–196.

Spence, J. T., & Helmreich, R. L. (1978). *Masculinity and femininity.* Austin, TX: University of Texas Press.

Spieker, S. J., & Booth, C. L. (1988). Maternal antecedents of attachment quality. In J. Belsky &. T. Nezworski (Eds.), *Clinical implications of attachment* (pp. 95–135). Hillsdale, NJ: Erlbaum.

Spiker, D. (1990). Early intervention from a developmental perspective. In D. Cicchetti & M. Beeghly (Eds.), *Children with Down syndrome. A developmental perspective* (pp. 424–448). Cambridge: Cambridge University Press.

Spitze, G. (1988). Women's employment and family relations: A review. *Journal of Marriage and the Family, 50,* 595–618.

Sroufe, L. A. (1983). Infant-caregiver attachment and patterns of adaptation in preschool: The roots of maladaption and competence. In M. Perlmutter (Ed.), *Minnesota Symposium on Child Psychology* (Vol. 16, pp. 41–84). Hillsdale, NJ: Erlbaum.

Sroufe, L. A. (1985). Attachment classification from the perspective of infant-caregiver relationships and infant temperament. *Child Development, 56,* 1–14.

Sroufe, L. A. (1988). The role of infant-caregiver attachment in development. In J. Belsky & T. Nezworski (Ed.), *Clinical implications of attachment* (18–40). Hillsdale, NJ: Erlbaum.

Sroufe, L. A. (1989). Pathways to adaptation and maladaption: Psychopathology as developmental deviation. In D. Cicchetti, (Ed.), *The Emergence of a Discipline: Rochester Symposium on Developmental Psychopathology.* (Vol. 1, pp. 13–40). Hillsdale, NJ: Erlbaum.

Sroufe, L. A. (1990). A developmental perspective on day care. In N. Fox & G. G. Fein (Eds.), *Infant day care: The current debate* (pp. 51–60). Norwood, NJ: Ablex.

Sroufe, L. A., & Fleeson, J. (1986). Attachment and the construction of relationships. In W. W. Hartup & Z. Rubin (Eds.), *Relationships and development* (pp. 51–72). Hillsdale, NJ: Erlbaum.

Sroufe, L. A., & Jacobvitz, D. (1989). Diverging pathways, developmental transformations, multiple etiologies and the problem of continuity in development. *Human Development, 32,* 196–203.

Sroufe, L. A., & Rutter, M. (1984). The domain of developmental psychopathology. *Child Development, 55,* 17–29.

Sroufe, L. A., & Waters, E. (1977). Attachment as an organizational construct. *Child Development, 48,* 1184–1199.

Sroufe, L. A., Egeland, B., & Kreutzer, T. (1990). The fate of early experience following developmental change: Longitudinal approaches to individual adaptation in childhood. *Child Development, 61,* 1363–1373.

Starfield, B., & Pless, I. B. (1980). Physical health. In O. G. Brim, Jr., & J. Kagan, *Constancy and change in human development* (pp. 272–324). Cambridge, MA: Harvard University Press.

Stark, E. (1986, October). *Young, innocent and pregnant.* Psychology Today, pp. 28–35.

Stattin, H., & Klackenberg-Larsson, I. (1991). The short- and long-term implications for parent-child relations of parents' prenatal preferences for their child's gender. *Developmental Psychology, 27,* 141–147.

Stein, Z., Susser, M., Saenger, G., & Morolla, F. (1975). *Famine and human development: The dutch hunger winter of 1944–1945.* New York: Oxford University Press.

Steinberg, L. (1987). Impact of puberty on family relations: Effects of pubertal status and pubertal timing. *Developmental Psychology, 23,* 451–460.

Steinberg, L. (1988). Reciprocal relation between parent-child distance and pubertal maturation. *Developmental Psychology, 24,* 122–128.

Steinberg, L. D., & Silverberg, S. (1986). The vicissitudes of autonomy in early adolescence. *Child Development, 57,* 841–851.

Steinberg, L., Elmen, J. D., & Mounts, N. S. (1989). Authoritative parenting, psychosocial maturity, and academic success among adolescents. *Child Development, 60,* 1424–1436.

Steinberg, L., Mounts, N. S., Lamborn, S. D., & Dornbusch, S. D. (1991). Authoritative parenting and adolescent adjustment across varied ecological niches. *Journal of Research on Adolescence, 1,* 19–36.

Steiner, J. E. (1979). Human facial expressions in response to taste and smell stimulation. In H. W. Reese & L. P. Lipsitt (Eds.), *Advances in child development and behavior* (Vol. 13, pp. 257–296). New York: Academic Press.

Sternberg, R. J. (1985). *Beyond IQ: A triarchic theory of human intelligence.* New York: Cambridge University Press.

Sternberg, R. J. (1986). *Intelligence applied.* New York: Harcourt Brace Jovanovich.

Sternberg, R. J., & Davidson, J. E. (1985). Cognitive development in the gifted and talented. In F. D. Horowitz & M. O'Brien (Eds.), *The gifted and talented. Developmental perspectives* (pp. 37–74). Washington, DC: American Psychological Association.

Sternberg, R. J., & Davidson, J. E. (Eds.) (1986). *Conceptions of giftedness.* Cambridge, England: Cambridge University Press.

Sternberg, R. J., & Suben, J. G. (1986). The socialization of intelligence. In M. Perlmutter (Ed.), *Perspectives on Intellectual Development. The Minnesota Symposia on Child Psychology* (Vol. 19, pp. 201–236). Hillsdale, NJ: Erlbaum.

Stevenson, H. W. (1988). Culture and schooling: Influences on cognitive development. In E. M. Hetherington, R. M. Lerner, & M. Perlmutter (Eds.), *Child development in life span perspective* (pp. 241–258). Hillsdale, NJ: Erlbaum.

Stevenson, H. W., & Lee, S. (1990). Contexts of achievement: A study of American, Chinese, and Japanese children. *Monographs of the Society for Research in Child Development, 55,* (1–2, Serial No. 221).

Stevenson, H. W., Lee, S., Chen, C., Lummis, M., Stigler, J., Fan, L., & Ge, F. (1990). Mathematics achievement of children in China and the United States. *Child Development, 61,* 1053–1066.

Stewart, R. B., Cluff, L. E., & Philp, R. (1977). *Drug monitoring: A requirement for responsible drug use.* Baltimore: Williams & Wilkins.

Stigler, J W., Lee, S., & Stevenson, H. W. (1987). Mathematics classrooms in Japan, Taiwan, and the United States. *Child Development, 58,* 1272–1285.

Stoneman, Z., Brody, G. H., & Burke, M. (1989). Sibling temperaments and maternal and paternal perceptions of marital, family, and personal functioning. *Journal of Marriage and the Family, 51,* 99–113.

Storfer, M. D. (1990). *Intelligence and giftedness.* San Francisco: Jossey-Bass.

Strayer, F. F. (1980). Social ecology of the preschool peer group. In A. Collins (Ed.), *Minnesota Symposia on Child Psychology* (Vol. 13, pp. 165–196). Hillsdale, NJ: Erlbaum.

Streissguth, A. P., Aase, J. M., Clarren, S. K., Randels, S. P., LaDue, R. A., & Smith, D. F. (1991b). Fetal alcohol syndrome in adolescents and adults. *Journal of the American Medical Association, 265,* 1961–1967.

Streissguth, A. P., Barr, H. M., & Sampson, P. D. (1990). Moderate prenatal alcohol exposure: Effects on child IQ and learning problems at age 7 1/2 years. *Alcoholism: Clinical and Experimental Research, 14,* 662–669.

Streissguth, A. P., Barr, H. M., Martin, D. C., & Herman, C. S. (1980). Effects of maternal alcohol, nicotine, and caffeine use during pregnancy on infant mental and motor development at eight months. *Alcoholism: Clinical and Experimental Research, 4,* 152–164.

Streissguth, A. P., Barr, H. M., Sampson, P. D., Darby, B. L., & Martin, D. C. (1989). IQ at age 4 in relation to maternal alcohol use and smoking during pregnancy. *Developmental Psychology, 25,* 3–11.

Streissguth, A. P., Carmichael-Olson, H., Sampson, P. D., & Barr, H. M. (1991a). *Alcohol vs. tobacco as prenatal correlates of child behavior: Follow-up to 11 years.* Paper presented at the biennial meetings of the Society for Research in Child Development, Seattle.

Streissguth, A. P., Landesman-Dwyer, S., Martin, J. C., & Smith, D. W. (1980). Teratogenic effects of alcohol in humans and laboratory animals. *Science, 209,* 353–361.

Streissguth, A. P., Martin, D. C., Barr, H. M., Sandman, B. M., Kirchner, G. L., & Darby, B. L. (1984). Intrauterine alcohol and nicotine exposure: Attention and reaction time in 4-year-old children. *Developmental Psychology, 20,* 533–541.

Streissguth, A. P., Martin, D. C., Martin, J. C., & Barr, H. M. (1981). The Seattle longitudinal prospective study on alcohol and pregnancy. *Neurobehavioral Toxicology and Teratology, 3,* 223–233.

Striegel-Moore, R. H., Silberstein, L. R., & Rodin, J. (1986). Toward an understanding of risk factors for bulimia. *American Psychologist, 41,* 246–263.

Strobino, D. M. (1987). The health and medical consequences of adolescent sexuality and pregnancy: A review of the literature. In S. L. Hofferth & C. D. Hayes (Eds.), *Risking the future. Adolescent sexuality, pregnancy, and childbearing. Working papers* (pp. 93–122). Washington, DC: National Academy Press.

Stunkard, A. J., Harris, J. R., Pedersen, N. L., & McClearn, G. E. (1990). The body-mass index of twins who have been reared apart. *New England Journal of Medicine, 322,* 1483–1487.

Sue, S., & Okazaki, S. (1990). Asian-American educational achievements: A phenomenon in search of an explanation. *American Psychologist, 45,* 913–920.

Taffel, S. M., Placek, P. J., & Liss, T. (1987). Trends in the United States cesarean section rate and reasons for the 1980-85 rise. *American Journal of Public Health, 77,* 955–959.

Takahashi, K. (1986). Examining the strange-situation procedure with Japanese mothers and 12–month-old infants. *Developmental Psychology, 22,* 265–270.

Tamis-LeMonda, C., & Bornstein, M. H. (1987). Is there a "sensitive period" in human mental development? In M. H. Bornstein (Ed.), *Sensitive periods in development: Interdisciplinary perspectives* (pp. 163–182). Hillsdale, NJ: Erlbaum.

Tanner, J. M. (1962). *Growth at adolescence* (2nd ed.). Oxford: Blackwell Scientific Publications.

Tanner, J. M. (1970). Physical growth. In P. H. Mussen (Ed.), *Carmichael's manual of child psychology* (Vol. 1, 3rd ed.) New York: Wiley.

Tanner, J. M. (1975). Growth and endocrinology of the adolescent. In L. J. Gardner (Ed.), *Endocrine and genetic diseases of childhood and adolescence* (2nd ed.) (pp. 14–63). Philadelphia: W. B. Saunders.

Tanner, J. M. (1978). *Fetus into man. Physical growth from conception to maturity.* Cambridge, MA: Harvard University Press.

Tanner, J. M., Hughes, P. C. R., & Whitehouse, R. H. (1981). Radiographically determined widths of bone, muscle and fat in the upper arm and calf from 3-18 years. *Annals of Human Biology, 8,* 495–517.

Taylor, M., & Hort, B. (1990). Can children be trained in making the distinction between appearance and reality? *Cognitive Development, 5,* 89–99.

Tellegen, A., Lykken, D. T., Bouchard, T. J., Wilcox, K. J., Segal, N. L., & Rich, S. (1988). Personality similarity in twins reared apart and together. *Journal of Personality and Social Psychology, 54,* 1031–1039.

Teller, D. Y., & Bornstein, M. H. (1987). Infant color vision and color perception. In P. Salapatek & L. Cohen (Eds.), *Handbook of infant perception: Vol. 1. From sensation to perception* (pp. 185–236). Orlando, FL: Academic Press.

Templin, M. C. (1957). Certain language skills in children: Their development and interrelationships. *University of Minnesota Institute of Child Welfare Monograph, 26.*

Terman, L. (1916). *The measurement of intelligence.* Boston: Houghton Mifflin.

Terman, L. (1925). Mental and physical traits of a thousand gifted children. *Genetic studies of genius* (Vol. 1). Stanford, CA: Stanford University Press.

Terman, L., & Merrill, M. A. (1937). *Measuring intelligence: A guide to the administration of the new revised Stanford-Binet tests.* Boston: Houghton Mifflin.

Terman, L., & Oden, M. (1947). *Genetic studies of genius (Vol. 4) The gifted child grows up.* Stanford, CA: Stanford University Press.

Terman, L., & Oden, M. (1959). *Genetic studies of genius (Vol. 5) The gifted group at mid-life.* Stanford, CA: Stanford University Press.

Teti, D. M., & Ablard, K. E. (1989). Security of attachment and infant-sibling relationships: A laboratory study. *Child Development, 60,* 1519–1528.

Tew, M. (1985). Place of birth and perinatal mortality. *Journal of the Royal College of General Practitioners, 35,* 390–394.

Thal, D., & Bates, E. (1990). Continuity and variation in early language development. In J. Colombo & J. Fagen (Eds.), *Individual differences in infancy: Reliability, stability, prediction* (pp. 359–385). Hillsdale, NJ: Erlbaum.

Thelen, E. (1981). Rhythmical behavior in infancy: An ethological perspective. *Developmental Psychology, 17,* 237–257.

Thelen, E. (1984). Learning to walk: Ecological demands and phylogenetic constraints. In L. P. Lipsitt & C. Rovee-Collier (Eds.), *Advances in infancy research* (Vol. 3, pp. 213–260). Norwood, NJ: Ablex.

Thelen, E. (1987). The role of motor development in developmental psychology: A view of the past and an agenda for the future. In N. Eisenberg (Ed.), *Contemporary topics in developmental psychology* (pp. 3–33). New York: Wiley-Interscience.

Thelen, E. (1989). The (re)discovery of motor development: Learning new things from an old field. *Developmental Psychology, 25,* 946–949.

Thelen, E., Kelso, J. A. S., & Fogel, A. (1987). Self-organizing systems and infant motor development. *Developmental Review, 7,* 39–65.

Thomas, A., & Chess, S. (1977).

Thomas, A., & Chess, S. (1977). *Temperament and development*. New York: Brunner/Mazel.

Thomas, A., Chess, S., Sillen, J., & Mendez, O. (1974). Cross-cultural study of behavior in children with special vulnerabilities to stress. In D. F. Ricks, A. Thomas, & M. Roff (Eds.), *Life history research in psychopathology* (pp. 53–67). Minneapolis: University of Minnesota Press.

Thomas, R. M. (Ed.) (1990a). *The encyclopedia of human development and education. Theory, research, and studies*. Oxford: Pergamon Press.

Thomas, R. M. (1990b). Body image and body language. In R. M. Thomas (Ed.), *The encyclopedia of human development and education. Theory, research, and studies* (pp. 377–378). Oxford: Pergamon Press.

Thomas, R. M. (1990c). Basic concepts and applications of Piagetian cognitive development theory. In R. M. Thomas (Ed.), *The encyclopedia of human development and education. Theory, research, and studies* (pp. 53–55). Oxford: Pergamon Press.

Thompson, R. A. (1990). The effects of infant day care through the prism of attachment theory: A critical appraisal. In N. Fox & G. G. Fein (Eds.), *Infant day care: The current debate* (pp. 41–50). Norwood, NJ: Ablex.

Thompson, R. A., & Lamb, M. E. (1982a). Stranger sociality and its relationship to temperament and social experience during the second year. *Infant Behavior and Development, 5*, 277–287.

Thompson, R. A., Lamb, M. E., & Estes, D. (1982b). Stability of infant-mother attachment and its relationship to changing life circumstances in an unselected middle-class sample. *Child Development, 53*, 144–148.

Thompson, S. K. (1975). Gender labels and early sex role development. *Child Development, 46*, 339–347.

Thorne, B. (1986). Girls and boys together. . . but mostly apart: Gender arrangements in elementary schools. In W. W. Hartup & Z. Rubin (Eds.), *Relationships and development* (pp. 167–184). Hillsdale, NJ: Erlbaum.

Tobin-Richards, M. H., Boxer, A. M., & Petersen, A. C. (1983). The psychological significance of pubertal change: Sex differences in perceptions of self during early adolescence. In J. Brooks-Gunn and A. C. Petersen (Eds.), *Girls at puberty. Biological and psychosocial perspectives* (pp. 127–154). New York: Plenum.

Tomasello, M., & Mannle, S. (1985). Pragmatics of sibling speech to one-year-olds. *Child Development, 56*, 911–917.

Tomlinson-Keasey, C., Eisert, D. C., Kahle, L. R., Hardy-Brown, K., & Keasey, B. (1978). The structure of concrete operational thought. *Child Development, 50*, 1153–1163.

Trehub, S. E., & Rabinovitch, M. S. (1972). Auditory-linguistic sensitivity in early infancy. *Developmental Psychology, 6*, 74–77.

Trehub, S. E., Bull, D., & Thorpe, L. A. (1984). Infants' perception of melodies: The role of melodic contour. *Child Development, 55*, 821–830.

Trehub, S. E., Thorpe, L. A., & Morrongiello, B. A. (1985). Infants' perception of melodies: Changes in a single tone. *Infant Behavior and Development, 8*, 213–223.

Tuna, J. M. (1989). Mental health services for children: The state of the art. *American Psychologist, 44*, 188–199.

Turiel, E. (1966). An experimental test of the sequentiality of developmental stages in the child's moral judgment. *Journal of Personality and Social Psychology, 3*, 611–618.

Turkheimer, E., & Gottesman, I. I. (1991). Individual differences and the canalization of human behavior. *Developmental Psychology, 27*, 18–22.

U.S. Bureau of the Census (1990). *Statistical abstract of the United States 1990* (110th ed.). Washington, DC: U.S. Government Printing Office.

Ungerer, J. A., & Sigman, M. (1984). The relation of play and sensorimotor behavior to language in the second year. *Child Development, 55*, 1448–1455.

Uzgiris, I. C. (1973). Patterns of cognitive development in infancy. *Merrill-Palmer Quarterly, 19*, 21–40.

van IJzendoorn, M. H., & Kroonenberg, P. M. (1988). Cross-cultural patterns of attachment: A meta-analysis of the Strange Situation. *Child Development, 59*, 147–156.

Vandenberg, B. (1984). Developmental features of exploration. *Developmental Psychology, 20*, 3–8.

Vaughn, B. E., Egeland, B., Sroufe, L. A., & Waters, E. (1979). Individual differences in infant-mother attachment at twelve and eighteen months: Stability and change in families under stress. *Child Development, 50*, 971–975.

Vaughn, B. E., Lefever, G. B., Siefer, R., & Barglow, P. (1989). Attachment behavior, attachment security, and temperament during infancy. *Child Development, 60*, 728–737.

Vellutino, F. R. (1987). Dyslexia. *Scientific American, 256*, 34–41.

Vellutino, F. R., & Scanlon, D. M. (1987). Phonological coding, phonological

awareness, and reading ability: Evidence from a longitudinal and experimental study. *Merrill-Palmer Quarterly, 33*, 321–364.

Vernon, P. A. (Ed.) (1987). *Speed of information-processing and intelligence*. Norwood, NJ: Ablex.

Vihko, R., & Apter, D. (1980). The role of androgens in adolescent cycles. *Journal of Steroid Biochemistry, 12*, 369–373.

Vorhees, C. F., & Mollnow, E. (1987). Behavioral teratogenesis: Long-term influences on behavior from early exposure to environmental agents. In J. D. Osofsky (Ed.), *Handbook of infant development* (2nd ed.) (pp. 913–971). New York: Wiley-Interscience.

Vygotsky, L. S. (1962). *Thought and language*. New York: Wiley.

Waber, D. P. (1977). Sex differences in mental abilities, hemispheric lateralization, and rate of physical growth at adolescence. *Developmental Psychology, 13*, 29–38.

Waddington, C. H. (1957). *The strategy of the genes*. London: Allen & Son.

Wahlström, J. (1990). Gene map of mental retardation. *Journal of Mental Deficiency Research, 34*, 11–27.

Wald, N. J., Cuckle, H. S., Densem, J. W., Nanchahal, K., Royston, P, Chard, T., Haddow, J. E., Knight, G. J., Palomaki, G. E., & Canick, J. A. (1988). *British Medical Journal, 297*, 883–887.

Walker, L. J. (1980). Cognitive and perspective-taking prerequisites for moral development. *Child Development, 51*, 131–139.

Walker, L. J. (1984). Sex differences in the development of moral reasoning: A critical review. *Child Development, 55*, 677–691.

Walker, L. J. (1989). A longitudinal study of moral reasoning. *Child Development, 60*, 157–160.

Walker, L. J., de Vries, B., & Bichard, S. L. (1984). The hierarchical nature of stages of moral development. *Developmental Psychology, 20*, 960–966.

Walker, L. J., de Vries, B., & Trevethan, S. D. (1987). Moral stages and moral orientations in real-life and hypothetical dilemmas. *Child Development, 58*, 842–858.

Wallerstein, J. (1989, January 22). Children after divorce. Wounds that don't heal. *The New York Times Magazine*, pp.19–21, 41–44.

Wallerstein, J. S. (1984). Children of divorce: preliminary report of a ten-year follow-up of young children. *American Journal of Orthopsychiatry, 54*, 444–458.

Wallerstein, J. S., & Kelly, J. B. (1980). *Surviving the breakup. How children and parents cope with divorce*. New York: Basic

Books.

Walters, R. H., & Brown, M. (1963). Studies of reinforcement of aggression. III. Transfer of responses to an interpersonal situation. *Child Development, 34,* 563–571.

Ward, S. L., & Overton, W. F. (1990). Semantic familiarity, relevance, and the development of deductive reasoning. *Developmental Psychology, 26,* 488–493.

Waterman, A. S. (1985). Identity in the context of adolescent psychology. *New Directions for Child Development, 30,* 5–24.

Waters, E. (1978). The reliability and stability of individual differences in infant-mother attachment. *Child Development, 59,* 483–494.

Watson, J. D., & Crick, F. H. C. (1953). Molecular structure of nucleic acid. A structure for deoxyribose nucleic acid. *Nature, 171,* 737–738.

Watson, M. W., & Getz, K. (1990a). Developmental shifts in Oedipal behaviors related to family role understanding. *New Directions for Child Development, 48,* 5–28.

Watson, M. W., & Getz, K. (1990b). The relationship between Oedipal behaviors and children's family role concepts. *Merrill-Palmer Quarterly, 36,* 487–506.

Waxman, S. R., & Kosowski, T. D. (1990). Nouns mark category relations: Toddlers' and preschoolers' word-learning biases. *Child Development, 61,* 1461–1473.

Waxman, S. R., Shipley, E. F., & Sheperson, B. (1991). Establishing new subcategories: The role of category labels and existing knowledge. *Child Development, 62,* 127–138.

Waxman, S., & Gelman, R. (1986). Preschoolers' use of superordinate relations in classification and language. *Cognitive Development, 1,* 139–156.

Webster-Stratton, C., & Hammond, M. (1988). Maternal depression and its relationship to life stress, perceptions of child behavior problems, parenting behaviors and child conduct problems. *Journal of Abnormal Child Psychology, 16,* 299–315.

Wechsler, D. (1974). *Manual for the Wechsler Intelligence Scale for Children—Revised.* New York: Psychological Corp.

Wegman, M. E. (1990). Annual summary of vital statistics—1989. *Pediatrics, 86,* 845–847.

Weinberg, R. A. (1989). Intelligence and IQ: Landmark issues and great debates. *American Psychologist, 44,* 98–104.

Weinraub, M., Clemens, L. P., Sockloff, A., Ethridge, T., Gracely, E., & Myers, B. (1984). The development of sex role stereotypes in the third year: Relationships to gender labeling, gender identity, sex-typed toy preference,

and family characteristics. *Child Development, 55,* 1493–1503.

Weir, R. (1962). *Language in the crib.* The Hague: Mouton.

Weiss, G., & Hechtman, L. (1986). *Hyperactive children grown up.* New York: Guilford Press.

Wellman, H. M. (1982). The foundations of knowledge: concept development in the young child. In S. G. Moore & C. C. Cooper (Eds.), *The young child. Reviews of research* (Vol. 3, pp. 115–134). Washington, DC. National Association for the Education of Young Children.

Wen, S. W., Goldenberg, R. L., Cutter, G. R., Hoffman, H. J., Cliver, S. P., Davis, R. O., & DuBard, M. D. (1990). Smoking, maternal age, fetal growth, and gestational age at delivery. *American Journal of Obstetrics and Gynecology, 162,* 53–58.

Werker, J. F., & Tees, R. C. (1984). Cross-language speech perception: Evidence for perceptual reorganization during the first year of life. *Infant Behavior and Development, 7,* 49–63.

Werler, M. M., Pober, B. R., & Holmes, L. B. (1985). Smoking and pregnancy. *Teratology, 32,* 473–481.

Werner, E. E. (1979). *Cross cultural child development: A view from planet earth.* Monterey, CA: Brooks/Cole.

Werner, E. E. (1986). A longitudinal study of perinatal risk. In D. C. Farran & J. D. McKinney (Eds.), *Risk in intellectual and psychosocial development* (pp. 3–28). Orlando, FL: Academic Press.

Werner, E. E., Bierman, J. M., & French, F. E. (1971). *The children of Kauai.* Honolulu: University of Hawaii Press.

Werner, H. (1948). *Comparative psychology of mental development.* Chicago: Follett.

Werner, L. A., & Gillenwater, J. M. (1990). Pure-tone sensitivity of 2- to 5-week old infants. *Infant Behavior and Development, 13,* 355–375.

White, S. (1965). Evidence for a hierarchical arrangement of learning processes. In L. P. Lipsitt & C. C. Spiker (Eds.), *Advances in child development and behavior* (Vol. 2, pp. 187–220).

Whitehurst, G. J., Falco, F. L., Lonigan, C. J., Fischel, J. E., DeBaryshe, B. D., Valdez-Menchaca, M. C., & Caulfield, M. (1988). Accelerating language development through picture book reading. *Developmental Psychology, 24,* 552–559.

Whiting, B. B., & Edwards, C. P. (1988). *Children of different worlds: The formation of social behavior.* Cambridge, MA: Harvard University Press.

Wiesenfeld, A. R., Malatesta, C. Z., & DeLoach, L. L. (1981). Differential parental response to familiar and unfamiliar infant distress signals. *Infant Behavior and Development, 4,* 281–296.

Wilcox, A. J., Weinberg, C. R., O'Connor, J. F., Baird, D. D., Schlaatterer, J. P., Canfield, R. E., Armstrong, E. G., & Nisula, B. C. (1988). Incidence of early loss of pregnancy. *New England Journal of Medicine, 319,* 189–194.

Willerman, L. (1987). *Where are the shared environmental influences on intelligence and personality?* Paper presented at the biennial meetings of the Society for Research in Child Development, Baltimore.

Williams, J. E., & Best, D. L. (1990). *Measuring sex stereotypes. A multination study.* Newbury Park, CA: Sage.

Willig, A. (1985). Meta-analysis of studies on bilingual education. *Review of Educational Research, 55,*

Willows, D. M., & Ryan, E. B. (1986). The development of grammatical sensitivity and its relationship to early reading achievement. *Reading Research Quarterly, 21,* 253–266.

Wilson, M. N. (1989). Child development in the context of the black extended family. *American Psychologist, 44,* 380–385.

Winick, M. (1980). *Nutrition in health and disease.* New York: Wiley.

Winick, M., Meyer, K. K., & Harris, R. C. (1975). Malnutrition and environmental enrichment by early adoption. *Science, 190,* 1173–1175.

Wood, W., Wong, F. Y., & Chachere (1991). Effects of media violence on viewers' aggression in unconstrained social interaction. *Psychological Bulletin, 109,* 371–383.

Yeates, K. O., MacPhee, D., Campbell, F. A., & Ramey, C. T. (1983). Maternal IQ and home environment as determinants of early childhood intellectual competence: A developmental analysis. *Developmental Psychology, 19,* 731–739.

Yonas, A., & Owsley, C. (1987). Development of visual space perception. In P. Salapatek & L. Cohen (Eds.), *Handbook of infant perception: Vol. 2 From perception to cognition* (pp. 80–122). Orlando, FL: Academic Press.

Zahn-Waxler, C., & Radke-Yarrow, M. (1982). The development of altruism: Alternative research strategies. In N. Eisenberg (Ed.), *The development of prosocial behavior* (pp. 109–138). New York: Academic Press.

Zahn-Waxler, C., Radke-Yarrow, M., & King, R. A. (1979). Child-rearing and children's prosocial initiations toward victims of distress. *Child Development, 50,* 319–330.

Zajonc, R. B. (1983). Validating the confluence model. *Psychological Bulletin, 93,* 457–480.

Zajonc, R. B., & Marcus, G. B. (1975). Birth order and intellectual development. *Psychological Review, 82,* 74–88.

Zametkin, A. J., Nordahl, T. E., Gross, M., King, A. C., Semple, W. E., Rumsey, J., Hamburger, S., & Cohen, R. M. (1990). Cerebral glucose metabolism in adults with hyperactivity of childhood onset. *The New England Journal of Medicine, 323,* 1361–1366.

Zaslow, M. J., & Hayes, C. D. (1986). Sex differences in children's responses to psychosocial stress: Toward a cross-context analysis. In M. E. Lamb, A. L. Brown, & B. Rogoff (Eds.), *Advances in developmental psychology* (Vol. 4) (pp. 285–238). Hillsdale, NJ: Erlbaum.

Zeskind, P. S., & Lester, B. M. (1978). Acoustic features and auditory perceptions of the cries of newborns with prenatal and peri-natal complications. *Child Development, 49,* 580–589.

Zeskind, P. S., & Ramey, C. T. (1981). Preventing intellectual and interactional sequelae of fetal malnutrition: A longitudinal, transactional, and synergistic approach to development. *Child Development, 52,* 213–218.

Zigler, E., & Hodapp, R. M. (1991). Behavioral functioning in individuals with mental retardation. *Annual Review of Psychology, 42,* 29–50.

# PICTURE CREDITS

# AUTHOR INDEX

Pulkkinen, L., 503
Pye, C., 321
Pyle, R., 160

Quinton, D., 546

Rabinovitch, M. S., 182
Radke-Yarrow, M., 162, 439, 442, 505
Ramey, C. T., 80, *81*, 103, 232, *234*, 235, 242, 510, 591
Rappoport, L., 359
Razel, M., 163
Reed, E. W., 61
Reef, M. J., 579
Reese, H. W., *176*, 369
Reimer, J., 483
Reisman, J. E., 176
Reisman, J. M., 438
Rende, 225
Resnick, M. B., 101
Rest, J. R., 470, 472, 482
Reznick, J. S., *302*, 302, 330, *343*
Rhoads, G. G., 71
Rhoades, K., 520
Rholes, W. S., 461
Ricciuti, H. N., 159
Rice, M. L., 334, 522
Richards, D. D., 209
Richardson, K., 287
Richters, J., 505
Riegel, K. F., 570
Rierdan, J., 153
Riesser-Danner, L. A., 180
Riley, S. S., 485
Roberts, C. W., 401
Robertson, E. G., 78
Robertson, J. F., 496
Robin, A. F., 273
Robinson, H. B., 554, 556
Robinson, N. M., 555
Roche, A. F., 159, 160
Rodin, J., 161
Rogers, J. L., 230
Roggman, L. A., 180
Rollins, B. C., 103, 583
Romney, D. M., 396
Rooks, J. P., 97
Roosa, M. W., 77, 103
Rose, S. A., 185
Rosenblith, J. F., 55, 96, 122, 597
Rosman, B. L., *195*
Ross, G., 427
Rothbart, M. K., 116, *343*, 343, 347
Rovee-Collier, C., 109
Rovet, J., 63
Rovine, M., 103, 433, 510
Rowe, I., 580
Rowlands, O., 546
Rubin, K. H., 256, 257
Ruble, D. N., 379, 389, 395, 398, *399*, 399, 408, 461
Ruble, T. L., 392
Ruff, H. A., 185, 194, 195, *196*, 196
Rule, B. G., 465
Rumelhart, D., 326
Ruopp, R., *514*

Russell, G., 421
Rutter, D. R., 15
Rutter, M., 118, 316, 347, 419, 512, *515*, *535*, 536, 537, 542, 546, 547, 557, *559*, 588, *589*, 590–591
Ryan, A. S., 116
Ryan, E. B., 331
Ryder, R. W., 69

Saario, Terry, 403
Saas-Kortsaak, P., 353
Sack, W. H., 419
Sadovnic, A. D., 77
Sady, S. P., 75
Sameroff, A. J., 13, 109, 492
Sampson, P. D., 72–73, 162
Sanders, B., 237
Sattler, J. M., 215
Saunders, W. B., *152*
Saunders, W. L., 265
Savage-Rumbaugh, S., 297
Saxon, A. M., 160
Scafidi, F. A., 102
Scanlon, D. M., 332, 553
Scarborough, H. S., 553
Scarr, S., 49, 63–64, 224, 236, 345, 371, 550, 586
Scarr-Salapatek, S., 8, 586
Schachter, F. F., 320
Schaefer, E. S., 496
Schaefli, A., 482
Schafer, W. D., 430
Schank, R. C., 457
Schleifer, M., 267
Schlesinger, H. S., 324
Schneider, W., 276, 281, 287
Schneiderman, M., 318
Schonfeld, I. S., 538
Schooler, C., 516
Schopler, E., 562
Schramm, W. F., 97
Schulz, H. R., *113*
Schutz, R. W., 135, 144
Schwartz, P., 516
Scollon, R., 300, *301*
Sears, P. S., 555
Sears, R. R., 351
Seidman, D. S., 74
Seidman, E., 512, *515*
Seitz, V., 40
Self, P. A., *103*
Selman, R. L., 457, 462, 463, 465, 478
Seltzer, M., 318
Semrud-Clikeman, G. W., 553
Sepkoski, C., 96
Shaffer, D., 544, 545
Shantz, C. U., 461, 481
Shantz, D. W., *444*, 444
Sheldon, S., 287
Sheldon, W. H., 130
Shelton, B. A., 516
Shepherd, P. A., 219
Shepardson, D., 265
Shepperson, B., 314
Sherman, D., 419
Sherrod, K. B., 418

Shimmin, H. S., 391
Shiono, P. H., 71
Shipley, E. F., 314
Shonkoff, J. P., 139, 522
Shore, C., 323
Shorr, S. I., 438
Short, E. J., 232
Shweder, R. A., 473
Siebert, J. M., 575
Siegal, M., 396
Siegel, L. J., 542
Siegler, R. S., 209, 276, 279, 280, *281*, 281
Sigafoos, A. D., 109
Sigel, I. E., 287
Sigman, M., 227, 323
Sigman, M. D., 57
Signorielli, N., 522, 528
Siladi, D., 208, 209
Silberstein, L. R., 161
Silverberg, S., 437
Simmons, R. G., 153, 385, 579
Simon, T., 210, 242
Simons, R. L., 496
Simpson, A. E., 590
Sims-Knight, J. E., 55, 96, 122, 597
Simutis, Z. M., 353
Skeels, H. M., 224
Skinner, B. F., 22, 318
Skinner, M. L., 13
Skodak, M., 224
Slaby, R. G., 391, 398
Slater, A. M., 122
Slaughter, V., 261
Slaughter-Defoe, D. T., 519
Slobin, D. E., 7, 322, 323, 325, 326, 327
Smetna, J. G., 479
Smith, A. N., *514*
Smith, D. W., *54*, 55, 155
Smoll, F. L., 135, 144
Snarey, J. R., 471, 472, 477
Snidman, N., 343
Snow, C. E., 320
Snow, M. E., 310, 311
Snyder, S. S., 299, 301, 323, 423
Soares, M. P., 237
Sobol, A. M., 102
Solomon, J., 428, *429*
Sonnenschein, S., 316
Sontag, L. W., *220*
Sosa, R., 98
Sostek, A. M., 102
Spangler, G., 496
Spelke, E. S., 184, 186, 190, 198, 200
Speltz, M. L., *433*
Spence, C. M., *514*
Spence, J. T., 403, 405
Spence, M. J., 184
Spieker, S. J., 428
Spiker, D., 552
Spitze, G., 516
Sroufe, L. A., 365, 366, 367, *368*, 368, 373, 418, 427, *429*, 431, 432, *433*, 433, 434, 511, 512, 519, 536, 588, *589*, 589, 590
Stafford, D., 348
Starfield, B., 156
Stark, E., 306

# SUBJECT INDEX

Note: Italicized page numbers indicate material in tables and figures.

Abortion, prenatal testing and, 66–67
Accidents, 157–158
Accommodation, 27, 247–249
Achievement tests, 213–214
Acquired immune deficiency syndrome (AIDS),
  transmission to infants, 68–69
Activity level, temperament and, 344–345
Acuity
  auditory, 174–175
  defined, 172
  visual, 172–174
Adaptive behavior, 548
Adolescence. *See also* Puberty
  androgyny in, 404–406
  cognitive development in, *582*
  commitment in, 380–383
  conduct disorders in, 539–546, *540*
  depression and anxiety in, 542–546, 579
  description of others in, 461–462
  developmental stages of, 579–583
  eating disorders in, 160–161
  effect of rate of physical change on behavior in, 147
  empathy in, 458–460
  family communication patterns in, 501, *501*
  formal operational thought in, 580
  friendship in, 436–439, 445
  growth spurt in, 132, *133*, 135
  health or illness in, 156–158
  hormone changes between birth and, 139
  hormones in, 138–140
  identity in, 380–383, 580–583
  intimacy in, 425–426, 436–437
  language, 584
  moral development in, 466–477
  moral judgment in, 478–481
  muscle changes in, 134–135
  parent-child relationships at, 425–426
  peer relationships in, 436–439
  physical development in, 132–133, 140–144, *141, 582*
  pregnancy in, 77–78, 147
  prenatal hormones and, 139
  psychosexual stages of, *358,* 359
  psychosocial stages of, *361,* 363
  self-definition in, 380–383
  self-esteem in, 384–385
  sexual development in, 138–144, *141*
  sexuality in, 140–143, 146–147
  shape of body in, 132–133
  suicide and, 543, 544–545
Adoption

IQ studies and, 224
  language development and, 328–331
Adrenal gland, *138,* 139
Adult stages, 363
Affectional bond, 414
Age
  of child, and family functioning, 505–508
  language development and, 310–311
  mental versus chronological, 210–211, 571–583
  moral reasoning and, 470–471
  of mother at pregnancy, 76–78
  perceptual development and, 172–201
Aggression, 350, 440, 478, 538–542
  biological basis for, 447–448
  as conduct disorder, 538–539
  day care and, 510
  hyperactivity and, 542
  individual differences in, 590–591
  negative interaction and, 440–441
  popularity and, 444–445
  reinforcement and, 351, 355
  violence on television and, 522–524
Alcohol
  prenatal development and, 71–72
  suicide and, 544
Altruism, 439–440, 442–443
Amniocentesis, 66
Analgesics, 95–96
Anal stage, 358
Androgen, 401
Androgyny, 402–406
Anesthesia, 95–96
Anorexia nervosa, 158, 160–161
Anoxia, 100
Antisocial behavior, 13, 538–539, 540
Anxiety, 537
  pregnancy and, 79
Apgar score, 102–103, *103*
Asian-Americans, IQ of, 235–237
Aslin's concept of maintenance, 235
Assimilation, 27, 247–248
Attachment, 414–453, 588
  of blind infants to mothers, 560
  of child to parent, 421–427, 496, 510–512, 560, 573–576
  day care and, 423, 429
  defined, 414
  individual differences in quality of, 427–434
  of parent to child, 414–421
  social development and, 414–441
  theory, 413–414
Attachment behaviors
  depression and, 413
  described, 414
  in infancy, 573–575

meshing of, 416–417
  in preschool period, 424–425
Attention-deficit hyperactivity disorder, 539–542, *540*
Attunement, 10
Atypical development, 533–567
  adaptation by the family and, 561–562
  emotionally, 536–548
  impact of, on family, 561–562
  mentally, 548–552
  physically, 556–558
  sex differences in, 558–561, *559*
  various types, *535*
Auditory development
  acts of infants and children in, 181–187
  acuity in, 174–175
  deafness, 324–325, 557
  detecting locations in, 175
  discriminating individual voices in, 183–184
  speech sound patterns and, 181–182, 184
Australia, 421
Authoritarian parental style, 501–503
Authoritative parental style, 502–503, 506
Authority
  in conventional morality, 468–470
  in preconventional morality, 466–467
Autism, 556–557
Autonomous morality, 465
Autonomy, 361–362
Autosomes, 50
Axon, 56

Babbling, 298
Babinsky reflex, 105–106
Ballet dancers, 153–154, *154*
Basic trust, 360–361
Bayley Scales of Infant Development, 213
Behavior
  adaptive, 548–549
  antisocial, 538–542
  attachment, 413, 414, 416–417, 424–425, 538–540, *540,* 573–575
  effect of television violence on, 521–524
  expectations and, 129–131
  moral judgment and, 478–481
  in occupation, 400–406
  physical development and, 144–147
  physiology and, 343–344
  prosocial, 439–440, 442–443, 473–475
  social cognition and, 473–481
Behavior genetics, 18
Behaviorism, personality development and, 349–356
Behavior problems, 538–548
  adaptation by the family and, 561–562
  anxiety, 79

**645**

attention-deficit hyperactivity disorder, 539–542
conduct disorders, 538–539
depression, 418–419, 430, 432, 579
role of short-term stress in, 546
temperament and, 345, 347, 350
Bilingualism, 308, 310–311
Biological approach to personality development, 342–349
basic propositions in, 342–345
evidence to support, 345–348
strengths, weaknesses, and implications of, 348–349
Biological theories of development, 18
maturation and, 18
personality development, 342–345
Birth, 90–103. *See also* Infants; Newborn; Prenatal development
cesarean-section delivery in, 99–100
choices, 93–95
conditions during, 92–99
first greeting in, 92–93
hormone changes between adolescence and, 138–140
normal process of, 90–92
problems at, 99–102
Birth centers, 96–97
Birth order, 504–505
IQ and, 229–230
Bisexuality, 60
Blacks, IQ tests and, 229, 235–236
Blastocyst, 54–55
Blindness, 557–558
attachment and, 560
in infant, *185*, 186–187, 418–419, 557–558, 560
intervention for, 558
Body type, 129–130
Bone, changes in, 133
Books, sex-role stereotyping in, 402–403
Brain
fetal, 56–57
malnutrition and development of, 159, 162
stages of development of, 135–138, 571–572
thyroid hormone and, *138*
Brain damage
hyperactivity and, 540–541
learning disability and, 553–554
mental retardation and, 550
Breast-feeding, 116–117, 415, 571
Bronfenbrenner's ecological approach, 494–495
Bulimia, 158, 160–161

Canalization, 8–9
Caring, ethic of, 475–477
Categorical self, 377–380
Cephalocaudal pattern of development, 133
Cesarean-section delivery, 99–100
Child abuse, 416
as failure of attachment, 418–419, 432
Child development
basic theories of, 17–27

changes in body fat in, 135
changes in body shape in, 132–133
changes in bones in, 133–134
depression and, 542
differences in rate, 147–154
focus in study of, 5–7
health or illness in, 156–158
height and weight changes in, 131–132
hormone changes in, 138–140
individual differences in, 147–156
major influences on, 7–17
motor development in, 145–146, *145–146*, 150–151
muscle changes in, 134–135
nature of developmental change and, 17
nervous system changes in, 135–138
perception and, 171–204
prenatal hormones and, 139
research on, 28–36
Chorionic villus sampling, 66
Chromosomes, 48–55
anomalies in, 61–65, 550, 557–560
mental retardation and, 61–64, 550, 557
Classical conditioning, 20–21, 108
of newborn infant, 108
Classification skills
in concrete operational stage, 264–266
in development of word meaning, 312–313
in preoperational stage, 255–259, 262–263
Class inclusion
in concrete operational stage, 265
in preoperational stage, 258–259, 263, 266
Clique, 437
Clustering strategies, 278
Cocaine, prenatal development and, 73
Cognitive development, 208–242, 583–590. *See also* IQ (intelligence quotient)
in adolescence, 579–583
Bandura's ideas concerning, 23
from birth to 18 months, 250–254
criticisms of Piaget's theory, 273–276
day care and, 232–233
from 8 to 18 months, 574
in the elementary-school years, 578–579
enrichment in family and, 509–510
individual differences in, 590–594
influence of environment on, 225–235
influence of heredity on, 222–225, 234–235
information-processing approach, 276–284
IQ tests and, 210–238
language development and, 323, 326–327
nature of developmental change and, 589–590
overview of stages, 272
as part of developmental system, 571
Piaget's basic ideas concerning, 26–27, 246–255, 258–259
in the preschool years, 575–578

racial differences in, 217, 235–237
rate of physical development and, 147–152
in retarded children, 549–550
sex differences in, 237–239
sex-role development and, 398–399
social cognition versus, 456–457
Sternberg's triarchic theory of intelligence and, 220–222, *221*
synthesis of approaches to, 284–285
three views of intelligence and, 208–210
timing and, 585–588
Cognitive processing, language development and, 323, 325
Cohort, 32
Colic, 114
College students
identity achievement by, 382–383
moral education of, 482
Color constancy, 188–189
Commitment, in adolescence, 381–383
Communication
within the family, 499–501
using language in, 315–317
Competence, 213, 363
Competition, 446–447
Componential intelligence, 220
Computer, human mind as, 276–284
Conception, 46–54
genetics of, 48–53
process of, 46–54
Concrete operational stage, 249, 264–268, 586
overview of child in, 267–268
Piaget's view of, 264–265
post-Piagetian work on, 265–266
Conditioned stimuli, 20
Conduct disorders, 538–539
origins of, 539
Conflict, adolescent, 425–426
Confluence model, 229
Connectionist models, 326–327
Conscience, 25
Conservation
in concrete operational stage, 265, 266
gender constancy and, 391, *392*
in preoperational stage, 258, *260*, 262
Constraint seeking, 265
Contextual intelligence, 222
Contingent responsiveness, 431, 574
Control, methods of, in family, 497–499, 501–504
Control group, 34
Conventional morality, *467*, 468
Cooing, 298
Cooperation, 477–481
Correlation, 33
Cortex, 136
Cortisol, 571
Crime, 538, 540
Critical period, 11
Crossing over, 49
Cross-modal transfer, 184–187, 253
Cross-sectional study, 31–32
Cross-sex children, 401–402
Crowd, 437

Crying, 113–115
Culture, and development, 518–524
    ethnic groups and, 518–520
    as macrosystem, 518–525
    social class and, 520–521
    television and, 521–524
Cumulative deficit, 225
Cystic fibrosis, 64–65, *65*
Cytomegalovirus (CMV), 69

Day care, 508–512, *508*
    arrangements, 508–509, *508*
    attachment behavior and, 510–512
    child's attachment to parents and,
        510–512
    cognitive development and, 232–233
    direct effects, 509–510
    IQ and, 233–234, *234*
    as a microsystem, 508–512
    quality of care in, 512
    relationships with peers and, 434–435
Deafness, 324–325
    interventions for, 558
    language and, 324
Deductive logic
    in concrete operational stage, 265
    in formal operational stage, 269–270
Defense mechanisms, 25, 369
Delinquent behaviors, 538–539
Dendrites, 56, 74–75
    and diet, 159
    pruning of synapses and, 136–137, *137*
Deoxyribonucleic acid (DNA), 49, 54
Dependent variable, 34
Depression, 537, 542, 579
    in adolescence, 542–546
    attachment behavior and, 418–419,
        428–432
    genetic factors in, 543
    helplessness and, 543
    of parent, and child abuse, 418–419
    postpartum, 103–105
Depth perception, 177–178
    visual cliff and, 177
Description, of other people, 460–462
Developmental psychopathology, 536
Diet, 586
    eating disorders and, 160–161
    malnutrition and, 73, 160–161
    physical development and, 159–162
    during pregnancy, 73–74
Diethylstilbestrol (DES), 70
Difficult child, 117, 298
    temperament and, 342–349
Dilation, 90
Disability. *See also* Atypical development
    learning, 552–554
    physical, 556–558
Discrimination, in visual perception,
    176–178
Diseases, 156–158
    breast-feeding and, 116–117
    genetic basis of, 61–65, 66
    of mother, and prenatal development,
        11, 52, 65–69
    placenta and, 68

Discipline, 538–539. *See also* Methods of
    control
Divorce, 15
    effect on attachment behavior, 429
    influence on family functioning,
        506–508
    Oedipal period and, 364–365, 366–367
    social support and, 517–518
    temperament of child and, 348,
        579–580
Dolls, 256–257
Dominance, 441
Dominance hierarchy, 441
Dominant gene, 50
Doubt, 361–362
Down syndrome, 61–63
    age of mother and, 76–77
    prenatal detection of, 67
Drugs
    during childbirth, 95–96
    hyperactivity and, 541
    impact of, on fetus, 69–73, 96
    suicide and, 544
*DSM-III-R (Diagnostic and Statistical Manual
    of Mental Disorders)*, 538–539
Dyslexia, 552

Early words, in language development,
    312–313
Easy child, 117
    vulnerability and, 591, 593–594
Eating, 115
Eating disorders, 158, 160–161, 537
Ecological perspective, 13
*Ecology of Human Development, The,*
    (Bronfenbrenner), 13
Ectodermal cells, 55
Ectomorphic body type, 130
Education, moral, 482–483. *See also*
    Schooling
Effacement, 90
Ego, 25
Egocentrism, 457
    in preoperational stage, 255
    sociodramatic play and, 255
Eisenberg, N., model of prosocial
    reasoning, 473–475
    Kohlberg's stages compared with, 474–
        475
Elaboration, 278
Elementary-school children
    attachment to parents, 424–425
    developmental stages of, 578–579
    peer relationships of, 435–437
    self-definition by, 379–380, *381*
    self-esteem of, 384, 387
    sex-role behavior of, 394–400
    sex-role stereotyping by, 392–394,
        400–406, *402–403*
Embedded Figures Test, 55–56
Embryo, development of, 55–56. *See also*
    Fetus
Emotion, in family, 496
Empathy, 458–462, 477–478
    development of, 458–460, *459*
    sympathy and, 458

Empiricism, 170, 197–200
Employment. *See also* Occupation
    of father, 516–517
    IQ test scores and, 215–218
    of mother, 511–512, 514–516
Endocrine glands, 138
Endodermal cells, 55
Endomorphic body type, 130
Environment
    changes in vulnerability and, 593–594
    giftedness and, 554–556
    heredity versus, 7–16, 234–235
    HOME Inventory and, 227–229
    IQ and, 225–235
    language development and, 317–321,
        329–330
    mental retardation and, 62, 550–551
    personality development and, 342–343
    prenatal development and, 65–76
    social class and, 520–521
    temperament and, 347–348
Epigenetic landscape (Waddington), 9
Equilibration, 27, 247, 249
Erikson, Erik, 380–382
    basic ideas of, 360–363
    differences between Freud and, 357
    impact of divorce and, 366–367
    psychosocial stages of development,
        360–363, *361*
    strengths and weaknesses of theories of,
        368–369
Erogenous zone, *358*
Estradiol, 139
Estrogen, 139
Ethics, 468
Ethnic groups, 518–520
Executive processes, 281
Exercise
    by children and adolescents, 158
    obesity and, 160–161
    during pregnancy, 75
Existential self, 377
Expectations
    child behavior and, 129–130
    IQ test scores and, 216–217
    level of, in family, 497–498
    of parents, and mathematical
        achievement, 239
    reinforcement and, 353
Experience
    growth as determinant of, 129
    information processing and, 276
    learning theory and, 19–24, *29*
Experiential intelligence, 220
Experiment, 34–36
Experimental group, 34
Expertise, cognitive development and,
    273–274
Expressive language, 299
Expressive style, 302
Externalizing problems, 537
Extinction, 21

Facial expression, infants and, 413
Facilitation, 10
Fallopian tube, 46–47

*Families* (Patterson), 24
Family, 496–508. *See also* Fathers; Mothers;
    Parents
  and altruism, 442–443
  conduct disorders and, 538–539
  emotional tone of, 496
  environment, 225–230
  giftedness and, 554–556
  impact of atypical child on, 561–562
  impact of parents' work on, 513–517
  impact of social support, 513–514,
    517–518
  IQ and, 226–230
  mental retardation and, 550–552
  as microsystem, 504–508
  stepparent, 506
Fat, changes in body, 135
Fathers. *See also* Mothers; Parents
  attachment of child to, 417–421
  attachment to infant, 426–427
  employment of, 516–517
  presence in delivery room, 98
Fear, of strangers, 423–424
Fetal alcohol syndrome (FAS), 71–72
Fetus. *See also* Birth
  abortion of, 66–67
  alcohol and, 71–72
  amniocentesis, 66–67
  development of, 55
  diet of mother and, 73–76
  drugs and, 69–73
  environment and, 61–76
  prenatal hormones and, 59–60, 139,
    401, 403
Fontanels, 133
Foreclosure, 382, *382*
Formal operational stage, 249, 268–272,
    580
  current work on, 269–272
  expertise and, 273–274
  Piaget's view of, 268–269
Fragile X syndrome, 64
France, 210
Fraternal twins, 52
  temperament and, 345, *345*
Freud, Sigmund, 25, 356–359
  basic ideas of, 25, 356–359
  differences between Erikson and, 357
  impact of divorce and, 366–367
  psychosexual stages of development,
    357–359, *358*
  strengths and weaknesses of theories of,
    368–369
Friendship, 437–439. *See also* Intimacy
  in adolescence, 425–426, 436–437, 439,
    463
  in childhood, 434–435
  developing understanding of, 462–463
  elementary school, 435–436, 441–445
  of preschool children, 434–435
  social reasoning and, 478
  understanding and behavior, 478

Games, in preschool play, 257
Gametes, 48
Gender

atypical development and, 590–591
differences in infant, 118–119
eating disorders and, 160–161
effects of parents' divorce and, 366–367
ethic of caring and, 476–477
genetic basis of, 50–52
hormones in adolescence and, 139–140
individual differences in development,
    590–591
IQ and, 237–239
Oedipus conflict and, 359, 366–367
perceptual skills and, 196
personality and rate of physical develop-
    ment based on, 152–154
physical growth and, 154–155
prenatal development and, 81–82
prenatal sexual differentiation, 59–60
sexual development based on, 141–143
Gender concept, 389–390, 396–399
  development of, 391–392
Gender constancy, 391–392, *392*
Gender identity, 391
  of cross-sex children, 401, 403–404
Gender schemas, 399, 427
Gender stability, 391
Generativity, 363
Generosity, 352–354, 442–443
Genes, 49–53
  differences in prenatal development
    and, 49–50
  sexual differentiation and, 50–52, 59–60
Genetic counseling, 66–67
Genetic errors, 61–65
  sex chromosome anomalies, 63–64
  single-gene defects, 64–65
Genital herpes, 68
Genital stage, *358*, 359–360
Genotype, 52
Gestural language, 299
Gibson, E., 198–200
Giftedness, 554–556
  causes of, 555–556
  cognitive and social functioning, 555
  definitions and, 554
  depression and, 555
Gilligan, C., ethic of caring, 475–477
  Kohlberg's stages compared with,
    476–477
Glial cells, 56, 136
Goal-corrected partnership, 424
Gonadotropic hormones, 139
Goodness-of-fit, 15–16, 345
Grammar. *See also* Syntax
  development of, 304–308
  later development of, 307
  reading and, 331–332
  Stage I, 304–305, *305*, 325
  Stage II, 305–307
Grasp reflex, 105–106
Grief, 561
Growth, 8. *See also* Physical development
Guilt, 362

Habituation, 110, 171
Head Start, 231–232
Health, patterns of, 156–158

Hearing. *See* Auditory development
Hearing-impaired children, 557–558, *559*
Height and weight changes, 131–132, *132,
    143*
Helpfulness, 439, 442–443
Heredity
  giftedness and, 555–556
  influence on IQ, 222–225
  interaction with environment, 234–235
  language development and, 328–329
  mental retardation and, 61–64, 548–550
  physical development and, 159
  temperament and, 345, 346
  versus environment, 7–16
Herpes simplex, 69
Heteronomous morality, 464
Heterosexuality, 60
Holophrases, 303–304
Home delivery, 97–98
HOME Inventory (Home Observation for
    Measurement of the Environment),
    227–229
Homosexuality, 60
Horizontal relationships, 434–441
Hormones
  in adolescence, 139–140, *140*
  between birth and adolescence, 139
  cross-sex preferences and, 401, 403–404
  number of earlier pregnancies and, 78
  in prenatal development, 59–60, 139, 401
Horowitz's model, 15–16, 235
Hostility, warmth versus, 496
Huntington's disease, 64
Hyperactivity, 539
  biological basis for, 540–542
  positive-emission tomography (PET)
    and, 541
  treatment for, 541
Hypothalamus gland, 139
Hypothesis scanning, 265

Id, 25
Identical twins, 52
  temperament and, 345, *345*
Identification, 359, 368–369
  aggression and, 440
  in sex-role development, 398–399
  in visual perception, 178–179
Identities
  in concrete operational stage, 264
  in preoperational stage, 255, 258,
    261–262
  in psychosocial stages, 363
Identity achievement, 363, 388
  in adolescence, 380–383
  formal operational stage and, 580
  gender, 389–391
  individual differences in, 384–388
  origins of, 381–383
Identity crisis, in adolescence, 380–383
Identity diffusion, 382, *382*
Identity formation, 580–581
Identity status, 381–383, *382*
Ideological identity, in adolescence,
    380–382
Illness

patterns of, 156–158
pregnancy and, 11
Imitation
of facial expressions, 413
in language development, 317–318, 322–323
Piaget and, 253
Imprinting, 11
Impulsivity, 194–196
Inborn error of metabolism, 550
Independence, 579
in adolescence, 579–583
in preschool period, 575–576
Independent variable, 34
Induction, 10, 583
Inductive logic
in concrete operational stage, 265
in formal operations, 269
Infants. *See also* Birth; Newborn; Prenatal development
abused, 418–419
attachment of parents to, 414–421
attachment to parents, 93, 98–99, 421–428
auditory development and, 174–175
autism and, 556–557, *559*
birth and, 90–105
blind, *185,* 186–187, 418–419, 560
breast-feeding versus bottle-feeding, 116–117, 415, 571
combining information from several senses by, 184–187
daily life of, 112–115
day care and, 80, *81,* 232–233, 423, 434–435, 508–512
development of self-concept and, 376–379
developmental stages of, 571–575, *572*
effects on parents, 117–118
environmental effects on IQ, 227–229
first sentences of, 303–304
first words of, 300–303
gender differences and, 118–119
hearing-impaired, 557
HOME Inventory and, 227–229
imprinting and, 11
individual differences among, 115–119
IQ tests for, 211–213, 232
low-birth-weight, 15, 70–71, 100–102
patterns of physical development, 131–139, 158
peer relationships of, 434–435
perception of, 172–200
poverty and, 15
prelinguistic phase of, 298–299
preoperational stage and, 249, 254–255
psychosexual stages of, 357–358
psychosocial stages of, 360–362
quality of attachments and, 427–434
reflexes and, 105–106
sensitive period of, 11
sensorimotor stage of, 250–254
smell and, 175–176
taste and, 175–176
touch and, 105–107, 176
toys and, 144–146

visual development and, 106–107, 172–174
walking skills, 144–145
Inferiority, 363
Inflections, 304, 306
Information processing, 208–210, 275–284, *278*
approach, 209–210
changes in processing strategy, 281–282
developmental approaches to, 276–277
individual differences in, 282–283
other links of, 283
speed of, 282–283
Initiative, 362
Innateness theories, of language development, 321–323
Insecure attachment, 428, 510–512
day care and, 510–512
long-term effects of, 433–434
in other cultures, 430–431
stability over time, 428–431
temperament and, 364–368, 432–433
Intellectual power, 208–209
measurement of, 210–214
Intelligence. *See* Cognitive development; IQ (intelligence quotient)
Interaction effect, 81
Internalizing problems, 537
Internal models of experience, 12
Internal models of relationships, 427, 463
Internal representations, 249, 253–254
Interviews, 30–31
Intimacy, 476, 583–584. *See also* Friendship
in adolescence, 425–426, 436–437, 439
in elementary-school friendships, 435–436
Intonation pattern, 298–299
Intrinsic reinforcements, 23–24
IQ (intelligence quotient). *See also* Cognitive development
adoption and, 224
birth order and, 229–230
birth weight and, 15
calculation of, 210–211
day care and, 233–234, *234*
environment and, 225–235
family chaos and, 33
giftedness and, 212, 554–556
HOME Inventory and, 227–229
influence of heredity on, 222–225
mental retardation and, 61–63, 80–81, 284, 548–551
physical development and, 151–152
punishment and, 225–230
race differences in, 235–237
sex differences in, 237–239
social class and, 225–226
social reasoning and, 481, 483
IQ tests, 210–214, 239–240
achievement tests versus, 213–214
blacks and, 216–217, 235–237
factors influencing scores, 222
first, 210–211
limitations of traditional, 219–220
memory tasks and, 276
modern, 211–213

Piaget and, 209
predictions made by, 214–218
in the schools, 216–217
stability of scores on, 218–220
Sternberg's triarchic theory of intelligence versus, 220–222
Iranian children and practice, 162
Israel, 471

Jobs, IQ test scores and success in, 215–218

Klinefelter's syndrome, 63
Knowledge, formal operations and, 268–272
Kohlberg, L.
Eisenberg's model compared with, 474–475
Gilligan's theory and, 476–477
stages of moral development, 466–473, 589

Language
blindness and, 558, 560
deafness and, 324, 558
reading difficulty and, 552
Language acquisition device, 322
Language development, 296–336
auditory development and, 182–184
bilingualism and, 308, 310–311
child's role in, 321–323, 326–327
combined view of, 327–328
communication and self-direction in, 315–317
connectionist models of, 326–327
cross-cultural comparisons of, 325
deafness and, 321, 324
definition of language, 296–298
differences in style of, 330–331
early steps in, 298–304
from 18 months to 6 years, 575–578
explaining, 317
grammar in, 304–308
individual differences in, 328–331
influence of environment on, 317–321
learning to read and, 331–332
major influences on, 584–585
in preschool period, 575–578
word meaning in, 308–315
Latency stage, 359
Lead, 76, 80
Learning disabilities, 552–554
Learning theories of development, 19–24, 27
applications of, 24
behaviorism and, 349, 351–352
classical conditioning, 19–21, 108
and habituation, 107–112
language development and, 317–318
operant conditioning, 21, 108–109
personality development and, 349–356
schematic, 109–110
social-learning theory, 22, 29, 352–354, 366–367, 396–398, 401
Libido, 25
Listening, 181–183. *See also* Auditory development

Locomotor patterns, 144, 575–576
Locus of gene, 49–50
Logic
  in concrete operational stage, 265–266
  in formal operational stage, 269
Longitudinal study, 32–33
Low-birth-weight infants, 15, 80, 100–102

Maintenance, 10
Malnutrition
  physical development and, 158–162
  prenatal development, 73, 80–81
Manipulative skills, 144
Marriage, divorce and, 350, 366–367, 429,
    506–508
Masturbation, 358
Mathematics
  race and ability in, 236–237
  sex and ability in, 238–239, *238*
Maturation, 8–9, 18, 158, 583
Mean length of utterance (MLU), 328
Medulla, 135
Meiosis, 48–49
Memory, strategies for using, 277–279, *278*
Menarche, 141–142, 153
Mental age, 210–211, 575
Mental retardation, 548–552
  adaptation by the family and, 561–562
  assessment of, 548–549
  causes of, 550–552
  cognitive functioning in, 549–550
  in fetal alcohol syndrome, 71
  genetic basis of, 61–65, 550–552
  IQ tests and, 233–234, 283
  labels and, 548, *549*
  problem solving and, 283
Mesodermal cells, 55
Mesomorphic body type, 130, 153
Metacognition, 281
Metamemory, 281
Methods of control, 497–499
Mexican-Americans, IQ and, 229
Midbrain, 135
Miscarriage, 47
Mitosis, 48
Modeling, 17, 352–356. *See also*
    Observational learning
  aggression and, 352–356
  altruism and, 443
Moral development
  Kohlberg's stages of, 466–473
  moral education and, 482–483
  Piaget's theories of, 464–465
Morality of reciprocity, 465
Moral judgment, 464–465, 478–481
  Piaget's early ideas about, 461–465
Moral realism, 464
Moratorium, 380–382, *382*
Moro reflex, 105–106, *106*, 110
Mother-child interaction, 511
  in breast-feeding, 116–117
  low birth weight and, 101
  trust in, 360
Motherese, 319–321
Mothers. *See also* Family; Fathers; Parents;
    Pregnancy; Prenatal development

attachment of child to, 414–416
attachment to infant, 416
childbirth and, 90–102
depression of, 103–105, 432
employment of, 511–512, 514–516
talking to children by, 318–321
Motion, sense of, 176
Motor development, 144–146, *145–146,*
    150–151
Motor skills, of newborn infants, 107–110,
    150
Multiple sclerosis, 138
Muscles, changes in, 134–135
Muscular dystrophy, 52, *65,* 66
Muttering, 316
Mutuality, 416
  child abuse as failure of, 418–419
Myelin, 137
Myelinization, 137–138, 573

Narrative report, 28
Nativism, 170
  language development and, 321–327
  versus empiricism, 197–198
Nature/nurture controversy, 7–16,
    197–198
Negative interactions, 440–441
  aggression, 440
  competition and dominance, 441
  sex differences in, 445–448
Negative reinforcement, 21
Neglecting parental style, 503, 506
Neo-Piagetians, 274–275
Nervous system
  changes in, with growth, 135–138,
    573–574, 575
  development of, 135–138
  fetal, 56–57
Neurons, 56, 136
Newborn. *See also* Birth; Infants; Prenatal
    development
  attachment of parents to, 414–421
  attachment to parents, 421–427
  birth, 90–103
  breast-feeding versus bottle-feeding,
    116–117
  daily life of, 112–115
  developmental stages of, 571–572, *572*
  operant conditioning of, 108–109
  reflexes and skills of, 105
Nonlocomotor patterns, 144
Nurture. *See* Nature/nurture controversy

Obesity, 158, 160–161
Object concept, 189–193
Object constancy, 188
Object identity, 190
Object perception, 189–190
Object permanence, 190–192
Observation, in research, 28–30
Observational learning (modeling),
    22–23. *See also* Modeling
Occupation
  chromosomal anomalies associated
    with, 61
  IQ test scores and, 215–218

Oedipal period, 364–369
Oedipus conflict, 359
Operant conditioning, 21, 109
  of newborn infant, 172
Operational thinking, 578
Operations, 249
Oral stage, 357
Organizing relationships, 461, *462*
Organizing strategies, 278–279
Orphans, 586–587
Ossification, 133
Ovaries, *138,* 139
Overextension, in language, 313, *313*
Overregularization, 307
Ovum, 46–47
  twins and, 52

Parents. *See also* Family; Fathers; Mothers
  altruistic behavior and, 442–443
  attachment of, to child, 414–421
  attachment of child to, 421–427
  authoritarian parental style, 501,
    502–503
  authoritative parental style, 502, 503,
    506
  characteristics of child and, 504–505
  child abuse by, *416,* 418–419
  communication patterns and, 499, 501
  first greeting of newborn and, 92–93
  impact of atypical child on, 561–562
  influence on self-esteem and identity,
    384–386
  methods of control used by, 497–499
  neglecting parental style, 502, 503, 506
  permissive parental style, 502, 503
  quality of attachments and, 427–434
  sex-role behavior and, 395–400
  social support for, 517–518
  structure of family and, 505–508
  warmth versus hostility of, 496
  work roles of, 514–517
Partial reinforcement, 22
Peers, 441–448
  adolescent relationships with, 436–437
  day care and relationships with,
    434–436
  early interaction with, 434–436
  elementary-school interactions with,
    435, 436
  infant and preschool relationships with,
    434–435
  moral judgment and, 478–481
  sex-role behavior and, 396–398
Perception, 172
  individual differences in, 193–196
  of newborn infant, 170–204, 571–575
  in prelinguistic phase, 298
Perceptual constancies, 187
Perceptual development, 170–204
  basic sensory skills, 172–176
  combining information from several
    senses in, 184–187
  differentiation and, 199
  explanations of, 196–200
  hearing, 175
  individual differences in, 193–196

Reaction range, 234
Reading
  basic steps in, 331–332
  effect of language skills in, 331–332
  learning disability involving, 553–554
  unlearning shape constancy in, 189
Reasoning
  moral, 470–471
  in preoperational stage, 259, 263,
    269–272
  social, 477–481
Receptive language, 299
Recessive gene, 50, 64
Reciprocal trust, 463
Recognition memory, 285
Referential style, 302
Reflection, 194
Reflexes, 105–106
Rehearsal, 278
Reinforcement
  intrinsic, 23
  in language development, 317–318
  negative, 21
  partial, 22, 351–352
  personality development and, 349–352,
    355
  positive, 21
  vicarious, 22
Repetition, in motherese, 320–321
Resilience, 15, 546–548
  individual differences in, 591–594
Responses, of others, and child growth,
  129–130
Responsiveness, 496
Restrictiveness, 498
Reversibility, 265
Role confusion, 363
Rubella (German measles), 68
Rules
  clarity and consistency of, 442–443, 497
  in gender identity, 399–400
  Saccadic movements, 173

Schemas, 109
  in gender identity, 399–400
Schematic learning, of newborn infants,
  109
Schemes, 247
Scholastic Aptitude Tests (SATs), 214
Schools, 512–513. See also Preschools
  authoritative, 512
  beginning of, 578–579
  for blindness, 558
  for deafness, 557
  IQ and, 230–231
  as a microsystem, 512–513
Secondary sex characteristics, 140–144
Secular trends, 159
Secure attachment, 428
  day care and, 510–512
  formation of, 431–432
  long-term effects of, 433–434
  in other cultures, 430–431
  stability over time, 428–431
  temperament and, 172, 364–368,
    432–433
Sedatives, 95

Seeing. See Visual development
Self-awareness, 377–379
Self-concept, 376–389
  defined, 376
  developmental patterns and, 376–384
  effect of growth on, 130–131
  gender concept in, 389–395, 399–400
  individual differences in, 384–388
  personality development and, 353–356
  sex-role behavior in, 391, 394
  sex-role concept in, 390, 392–394
  sex-role stereotyping in, 390, 392–394
  social development and, 412
  summary of, 389
  vocational identity and, 382–383
Self-definition, in adolescence, 380
Self-efficacy, 353–354
  vocational identity and, 382–383
Self-esteem, 384–389
  androgyny and, 404–406
  authoritarian parental style and,
    501–502
  changes with age in, 384–385
  individual differences in, 385–388
  origins of, 386–388
  popularity and, 441, 444–445
  vocational identity and, 382–383
Self-permanence, 376
Self-regulation, in language use, 316–317
Self-scheme, 355, 427
Semantics
  defined, 296
  development of, 308–309, 311–315
  early stages in, 298–304
Sensation, defined, 172
Sensitive period, 11
Sensorimotor stage, 249–254
  current work on, 253–254
  overview of, 254
  Piaget's views of, 250–252, 250–251
  play in, 256
  substages of, 250–251
Sentences
  first, 303–304, 306
  syntax of early, 304–308, 305, 306
Separation protest, 423–424
Sequential designs, 32–33
Sex chromosomes, 50
Sex differences
  in atypical development, 558–561
  developmental change and, 590–591
  in infants, 118–119
  in IQ, 237–239, 238
  physical development and, 154, 156
  popularity and, 445–448, 446
  in prenatal development, 81–82
Sex-linked inheritance patterns, 52
Sex-role behavior, 391
  androgyny and, 404–406
  cross-sex children and, 401, 403–404
  development of, 394–395
  theories of development of, 395–400
Sex-role concept, 390
  androgyny and, 404–406
  cross-sex children and, 401, 403–404
  development of, 392–394
  theories of development of, 395–400

vocational identity and, 382–383
Sex roles, defined, 390–391
Sex-role stereotyping, 390
  development of, 392–394
  individual differences in, 400–406
  social interactions and, 445–448, 446
  in television and books, 402–403
  vocational identity and, 382–383
Sex typing, 391
Sexual identity, in adolescence, 380–383
Sexuality
  adolescent, 146–147
  development of sexual maturity,
    140–144
  Freud's psychosexual stages and, 25–26
  prenatal hormones and, 59–60, 139,
    401, 403
Shame, 361–362
Shape, changes in body, 132
Shape constancy, 188–189
Shyness, individual differences in, 590
Siblings, 52
Sickle-cell anemia, 65, 66–67
Sign language, deafness and, 324–325
Size constancy, 188
Sleeping, 112–113, 113
Slow-to-warm-up child, 118
Small-for-date infants, 100
Smell, 175–176
Smiling, 560
  temperament and, 347
Smoking, prenatal development and,
  70–71
Sociability, temperament and, 347–348
Social class. See also Poverty
  conduct disorders and, 538–539
  differences in infant according to, 119
  impact of larger culture and, 520–521
  impact on secure and insecure attach-
    ments, 428
  IQ and, 232, 236–237
  perceptual skills and, 196
  physical development and, 155
  prenatal development and, 82
  vulnerability of children and, 118
Social cognition, 455–487, 576–577
  behavior and, 477–481
  cognitive side of, 456–457
  defined, 456
  and delinquent behavior, 538
  describing people in, 460–462
  development of empathy in, 458–460
  general cognitive development and,
    481–483
  general principles and issues, 456–458
  social side of, 457–458
  theories of, 463–477
  thinking about relationships in, 462–463
Social development, 412–453
  in adolescence, 579–583
  attachment and, 412–434
  from birth to 18 months, 571–575
  in the elementary-school years, 578–579
  giftedness and, 555
  individual differences in, 590–594
  major influences on, 585
  nature of developmental change and,